T0320495

Handbook of Research on Advanced Concepts in Real–Time Image and Video Processing

Md. Imtiyaz Anwar
National Institute of Technology, Jalandhar, India

Arun Khosla
National Institute of Technology, Jalandhar, India

Rajiv Kapoor
Delhi Technological University, India

A volume in the Advances in Multimedia and
Interactive Technologies (AMIT) Book Series

Published in the United States of America by
    IGI Global
    Information Science Reference (an imprint of IGI Global)
    701 E. Chocolate Avenue
    Hershey PA, USA 17033
    Tel: 717-533-8845
    Fax: 717-533-8661
    E-mail: cust@igi-global.com
    Web site: http://www.igi-global.com

Library of Congress Cataloging-in-Publication Data

Names: Anwar, Md. Imtiyaz, 1982- editor. | Khosla, Arun, 1967- editor. |
    Kapoor, Rajiv, editor.
Title: Handbook of research on advanced concepts in real-time image and video
    processing / Md. Imtiyaz Anwar, Arun Khosla, and Rajiv Kapoor, editors.
Other titles: Advanced concepts in real-time image and video processing
Description: Hershey, PA : Information Science Reference, [2018] | Series:
    Information science reference
Identifiers: LCCN 2017012029| ISBN 9781522528487 (hardcover) | ISBN
    9781522528494 (ebook)
Subjects: LCSH: Video recording. | Image processing--Digital techniques. |
    Real-time data processing. | Digital video--Editing.
Classification: LCC TR850 .A26 2018 | DDC 777--dc23 LC record available at https://lccn.loc.gov/2017012029

This book is published in the IGI Global book series Advances in Multimedia and Interactive Technologies (AMIT) (ISSN: 2327-929X; eISSN: 2327-9303)

British Cataloguing in Publication Data
A Cataloguing in Publication record for this book is available from the British Library.

For electronic access to this publication, please contact: eresources@igi-global.com.

Advances in Multimedia and Interactive Technologies (AMIT) Book Series

Joel J.P.C. Rodrigues

National Institute of Telecommunications (Inatel), Brazil & Instituto de Telecomunicações, University of Beira Interior, Portugal

ISSN:2327-929X
EISSN:2327-9303

MISSION

Traditional forms of media communications are continuously being challenged. The emergence of user-friendly web-based applications such as social media and Web 2.0 has expanded into everyday society, providing an interactive structure to media content such as images, audio, video, and text.

The **Advances in Multimedia and Interactive Technologies (AMIT) Book Series** investigates the relationship between multimedia technology and the usability of web applications. This series aims to highlight evolving research on interactive communication systems, tools, applications, and techniques to provide researchers, practitioners, and students of information technology, communication science, media studies, and many more with a comprehensive examination of these multimedia technology trends.

COVERAGE

- Digital Games
- Social Networking
- Multimedia Services
- Multimedia technology
- Audio Signals
- Gaming Media
- Web technologies
- Digital Communications
- Multimedia Streaming
- Digital Watermarking

IGI Global is currently accepting manuscripts for publication within this series. To submit a proposal for a volume in this series, please contact our Acquisition Editors at Acquisitions@igi-global.com or visit: http://www.igi-global.com/publish/.

Titles in this Series

For a list of additional titles in this series, please visit: www.igi-global.com/book-series

Transforming Gaming and Computer Simulation Technologies across Industries
Brock Dubbels (McMaster University, Canada)
Information Science Reference • copyright 2017 • 297pp • H/C (ISBN: 9781522518174) • US $210.00 (our price)

Feature Detectors and Motion Detection in Video Processing
Nilanjan Dey (Techno India College of Technology, Kolkata, India) Amira Ashour (Tanta University, Egypt) and
Prasenjit Kr. Patra (Bengal College of Engineering and Technology, India)
Information Science Reference • copyright 2017 • 328pp • H/C (ISBN: 9781522510253) • US $200.00 (our price)

Mobile Application Development, Usability, and Security
Sougata Mukherjea (IBM, India)
Information Science Reference • copyright 2017 • 320pp • H/C (ISBN: 9781522509455) • US $180.00 (our price)

Applied Video Processing in Surveillance and Monitoring Systems
Nilanjan Dey (Techno India College of Technology, Kolkata, India) Amira Ashour (Tanta University, Egypt) and
Suvojit Acharjee (National Institute of Technology Agartala, India)
Information Science Reference • copyright 2017 • 321pp • H/C (ISBN: 9781522510222) • US $215.00 (our price)

Intelligent Analysis of Multimedia Information
Siddhartha Bhattacharyya (RCC Institute of Information Technology, India) Hrishikesh Bhaumik (RCC Institute
of Information Technology, India) Sourav De (The University of Burdwan, India) and Goran Klepac (University
College for Applied Computer Engineering Algebra, Croatia & Raiffeisenbank Austria, Croatia)
Information Science Reference • copyright 2017 • 520pp • H/C (ISBN: 9781522504986) • US $220.00 (our price)

Emerging Technologies and Applications for Cloud-Based Gaming
P. Venkata Krishna (VIT University, India)
Information Science Reference • copyright 2017 • 314pp • H/C (ISBN: 9781522505464) • US $195.00 (our price)

Digital Tools for Computer Music Production and Distribution
Dionysios Politis (Aristotle University of Thessaloniki, Greece) Miltiadis Tsalighopoulos (Aristotle University of
Thessaloniki, Greece) and Ioannis Iglezakis (Aristotle University of Thessaloniki, Greece)
Information Science Reference • copyright 2016 • 291pp • H/C (ISBN: 9781522502647) • US $180.00 (our price)

Contemporary Research on Intertextuality in Video Games
Christophe Duret (Université de Sherbrooke, Canada) and Christian-Marie Pons (Université de Sherbrooke, Canada)
Information Science Reference • copyright 2016 • 363pp • H/C (ISBN: 9781522504771) • US $185.00 (our price)

701 East Chocolate Avenue, Hershey, PA 17033, USA
Tel: 717-533-8845 x100 • Fax: 717-533-8661
E-Mail: cust@igi-global.com • www.igi-global.com

List of Contributors

Table of Contents

Detailed Table of Contents

Chapter 1

    T. J. Narendra Rao, National Institute of Technology Karnataka, India
    G N Girish, National Institute of Technology Karnataka, India
    Mohit P. Tahiliani, National Institute of Technology Karnataka, India
    Jeny Rajan, National Institute of Technology Karnataka, India

Automatic visual surveillance systems serve as in-place threat detection devices being able to detect and recognize anomalous activities which otherwise would lead to potentially harmful situations, and alert the concerned authorities to take appropriate counter actions. However, development of an efficient visual surveillance system is quite challenging. Designing an unusual activity detection mechanism which is accurate and real-time is the primary challenge. Review of literature carried out led to the inference that there are some attributes which are essential for a successful unusual event detection mechanism for surveillance application. The desired approach must detect genuine anomalies in real-world scenarios with acceptable accuracy, should adapt to changing environments and, should require less computational time and memory. In this chapter, an attempt has been made to provide an insight into some of the prominent approaches employed by researchers to solve these issues with a hope that it will benefit researchers towards developing a better surveillance system.

Chapter 2

    Kratika Arora, Sant Longowal Institute of Engineering and Technology, India
    Ashwani Kumar Aggarwal, Sant Longowal Institute of Engineering and Technology, India

With an ever-increasing use and demand for digital imagery in the areas of medicine, sciences, and engineering, image retrieval is an active research area in image processing and pattern recognition. Content-based image retrieval (CBIR) is a method of finding images from a huge image database according to persons' interests. Content-based here means that the search involves analysis of the actual content present in the image. As the database of images is growing day by day, researchers/scholars are searching for better techniques for retrieval of images with good efficiency.This chapter first gives an overview of the various image retrieval systems. Then, the applications of CBIR in various fields and existing CBIR systems are described. The various image content descriptors and extraction methods are also explained. The main motive of the chapter is to study and compare the features that are used in Content Based Image Retrieval system and conclude on the system that retrieves images from a huge database with good precision and recall.

Chapter 3

Shaifali Madan Arora, MSIT, India
Kavita Khanna, NCU, India

Recent years have witnessed a great technological evolution in video display and capturing technologies leading to the development of new standards of video coding including MPEG-X, H.26X and HEVC. The cost of computations, storage and high bandwidth requirements makes a video data expensive in terms of transmission and storage. This makes video compression absolutely necessary prior to its transmission in order to accommodate for different transmission media's capabilities. Digital video compression technologies therefore have become an important part of the way we create, present, communicate and use visual information. The main aim behind a video compression system is to eliminate the redundancies from a raw video signal. The tradeoff involved in the process of video compression is between the speed, quality and resource utilization. The current chapter explores the techniques, challenges, issues and problems in video compression in detail along with the major advancements in the field.

Chapter 4

Poonam Fauzdar, GLA University, India
Sarvesh Kumar, GLA University, India

In this paper we applianced an approach for segmenting brain tumour regions in a computed tomography images by proposing a multi-level fuzzy technique with quantization and minimum computed Euclidean distance applied to morphologically divided skull part. Since the edges identified with closed contours and further improved by adding minimum Euclidean distance, that is why the numerous results that are analyzed are very assuring and algorithm poses following advantages like less cost, global analysis of image, reduced time, more specificity and positive predictive value.

Chapter 5

Satbir Singh, Delhi Technological University, India
Rajiv Kapoor, Delhi Technological University, India
Arun Khosla, Dr. B.R. Ambedkar NITJ, India

This chapter emphasizes on the approach to include information from different type of sensors into the visible domain real time tracking. Since any individual sensor is not able to retrieve the complete information, so it is better to use information from distinct category of sensors. The chapter firstly enlightens the significance of introducing the cross-domain treatment into video based tracking. Following this, some previous work in the literature related to this idea is briefed. The chapter introduces the categorization of the cross-domain activity usage for real time object tracking and then each category is separately discussed in detail. The advantages as well as the limitations of each type of supplemented cross domain activity will be discussed. Finally, the recommendation and concluding remarks from the authors in lieu of future development of this cutting-edge field will be presented.

    Ramesh Kumar Meena, NIT Jalandhar, India
    Sarwan Kumar Pahuja, NIT Jalandhar, India
    Abdullah Bin Queyam, NIT Jalandhar, India
    Amit Sengupta, IIT Delhi, India

Presently, non-invasive techniques are in vogue and preferred standard clinical approach because of its limitless advantages in monitoring real time phenomenon occurring within our human body without much interference. Many techniques such as ultrasound, magnetocardiography, CT scan, MRI etc., are used for real time monitoring but are generally not recommended for continuous monitoring. The limitations created by above used techniques are overcome by a proposed technique called non-invasive bio-impedance technique such as Electrical Impedance Technique (EIT). EIT imaging technique is based on internal electrical conductivity distribution of the body. The reconstruction of cross sectional image of resistivity required sufficient data collection by finite element method using MATLAB software. The EIT technique offers some benefits over other imaging modalities. It is economical, non-invasive, user friendly and emits no radiation thus appears to be one of the best fit technology for mass health care to be used by the basic health worker at a community level.

    Amruta Laxman Deshmukh, SGGS, India
    Satbir Singh, Delhi Technological University, India
    Balwinder Singh, Centre for Development of Advanced Computing (C-DAC), India

There are many reasons for invisibility of objects on road in daylight, majority of them are Fog (condensed water droplets in atmosphere), smog (soot particles in air). This reduced visibility is one of the prime factors responsible for accident of vehicles and disadvantage in surveillance system. This chapter takes account of a method that comprises of a complete embedded system for the process of restoring the captured foggy images. Use of a novel 'Mean Channel Prior' algorithm for defogging is presented. Further detailed step by step explanation is given for hardware implementation of MATLAB code. Hardware consists of raspberry pi which is an ARM7 Quad Core processor based mini computer model. System serves as portable, low cost and low power processing unit with provision of interfacing a camera and a display screen.

    Rakesh Asery, Dr B. R. Ambedkar National Institute of Technology Jalandhar, India
    Ramesh Kumar Sunkaria, Dr. B. R. Ambedkar National Institute of Technology Jalandhar,
        India
    Puneeta Marwaha, Dr. B. R. Ambedkar National Institute of Technology Jalandhar, India
    Lakhan Dev Sharma, Dr. B. R. Ambedkar National Institute of Technology Jalandhar, India

In this chapter authors introduces content-based image retrieval systems and compares them over a common database. For this, four different content-based local binary descriptors are described with and without Gabor transform in brief. Further Nth derivative descriptor is calculated using (N-1)th derivative, based on rotational and multiscale feature extraction. At last the distance based query image matching is used to find the similarity with database. The performance in terms of average precision, average retrieval rate, different orders of derivatives in the form of average retrieval rate, and length of feature vector v/s performance in terms of time have been calculated. For this work a comparative experiment has been conducted using the Ponce Group images on seven classes (each class have 100 images). In addition, the performance of the all descriptors have been analyzed by combining these with the Gabor transform.

      Mokhtar Taffar, University of Jijel, Algeria
      Serge Miguet, LIRIS, Université de Lyon 2, UMR CNRS 5205, France

In this chapter, we tackle in the same process the problems of face detection and gender classification, where the faces present a wide range of the intra-class appearance are taken from arbitrary viewpoints. We try to develop complete probabilistic model to represent and learn appearance of facial objects in both shape and geometry with respect to a landmark in the image, and then to be able to predict presence and position of the appearance of the studied object class in new scene. After have predicted the facial appearance and the geometry of invariants, geometric hierarchical clustering combines different prediction of positions of face invariant. Then, the algorithm of cluster selection with a best appearance localizes faces in the image. Using a probabilistic classification, each facial feature retained in the detection step will be weighted by a probability to be male or female. This set of features contributes to determine the gender associated to a detected face. This model has a good performance in presence of viewpoint changes and a large appearance variability of faces.

      Tawanda Mushiri, University of Johannesburg, South Africa
      Charles Mbohwa, University of Johannesburg, South Africa
      Simbarashe Sarupinda, CUT, Zimbabwe

Developing nations have implemented toll gates in their countries major trunk highways as a move towards the improvement in fiscal levels. However, several problems have arisen in the toll collection system that has been implemented. The system exists as an incomplete system in comparison to internationally acclaimed systems and methods. This chapter therefore seeks to introduce an automated toll collection system which has enhanced security features and intelligent vehicle classification methods. Utilising machine intelligence and computer vision methods in the system, the researchers intend to develop the automated and intelligent toll collection system for developing nation's tollgates. The mechatronic system will combat security loopholes and enhance the efficiency of the toll collection process.

      Alka Srivastava, Sant Longowal Institute of Engineering and Technology Punjab, India
      Ashwani Kumar Aggarwal, Sant Longowal Institute of Engineering and Technology Punjab,
         India

Nowadays, there are a lot of medical images and their numbers are increasing day by day. These medical images are stored in the large database. To minimize the redundancy and optimize the storage capacity of images, medical image fusion is used. The main aim of medical image fusion is to combine complementary information from multiple imaging modalities (e.g. CT, MRI, PET, etc.) of the same scene. After performing medical image fusion, the resultant image is more informative and suitable for patient diagnosis. There are some fusion techniques which are described in this chapter to obtain fused image. This chapter presents two approaches to image fusion, namely spatial domain Fusion technique and transforms domain Fusion technique. This chapter describes Techniques such as Principal Component Analysis which is spatial domain technique and Discrete Wavelet Transform and Stationary Wavelet Transform which are Transform domain techniques. Performance metrics are implemented to evaluate the performance of image fusion algorithm.

Chapter 12

S. Vasavi, V. R. Siddhartha Engineering College, India
Reshma Shaik, V. R. Siddhartha Engineering College, India
Sahithi Yarlagadda, V. R. Siddhartha Engineering College, India

Object recognition and classification (human beings, animals, buildings, vehicles) has become important in a surveillance video situated at prominent areas such as airports, banks, military installations etc., Outdoor environments are more challenging for moving object classification because of incomplete appearance details of moving objects due to occlusions and large distance between the camera and moving objects. As such, there is a need to monitor and classify the moving objects by considering the challenges of video in the real time. Training the classifiers using feature based is easier and faster than pixel-based approaches in object classification. Extraction of a set of features from the object of interest is most important for classification. Textural features, color features and structural features can be chosen for classifying the object. But in real time video, object poses are not always the same. Zernike moments have been shown to be rotation invariant and noise robust due to Orthogonality property.

Chapter 13

Uday Pratap Singh, Madhav Institute of Technology and Science, India
Sanjeev Jain, Madhav Institute of Technology and Science, India

Efficient and effective object recognition from a multimedia data are very complex. Automatic object segmentation is usually very hard for natural images; interactive schemes with a few simple markers provide feasible solutions. In this chapter, we propose topological model based region merging. In this work, we will focus on topological models like, Relative Neighbourhood Graph (RNG) and Gabriel graph (GG), etc. From the Initial segmented image, we constructed a neighbourhood graph represented different regions as the node of graph and weight of the edges are the value of dissimilarity measures function for their colour histogram vectors. A method of similarity based region merging mechanism (supervised and unsupervised) is proposed to guide the merging process with the help of markers. The region merging process is adaptive to the image content and it does not need to set the similarity threshold in advance. To the validation of proposed method extensive experiments are performed and the result shows that the proposed method extracts the object contour from the complex background.

Images have always been considered an effective medium for presenting visual data in numerous applications ranging from industry to academia. Consequently, managing and indexing of images become essential in order to retrieve relevant images effectively and efficiently. Therefore, the proposed chapter aims to elaborate one of the advanced concepts of image processing, i.e., Content Based Image Retrieval (CBIR) and image feature extraction using advanced methods known as radial moments. In this chapter, various radial moments are discussed with their properties. Besides, performance measures and various similarity measures are elaborated in depth. The performance of radial moments is evaluated through an extensive set of experiments on benchmark databases such as Kimia-99, MPEG-7, COIL-100, etc.

Chapter 15

Implementing high-performance, low-cost hardware accelerators for the computationally intensive image and video processing algorithms has attracted a lot of attention in the last 20 years. Most of the recent research efforts were trying to figure out new design automation methods to fill the gap between the ability of realizing efficient accelerators in hardware and the tight performance requirements of the complex image processing algorithms. High-Level synthesis (HLS) is a new method to automate the design process by transforming high-level algorithmic description into digital hardware while satisfying the design constraints. This chapter focuses on evaluating the suitability of using HLS as a new tool to accelerate the most demanding image and video processing algorithms in hardware. It discusses the gained benefits and current limitations, the recent academic and commercial tools, the compiler's optimization techniques and four case studies.

Chapter 16

Computer vision is one of the most active research fields in technology today. Giving machines the ability to see and comprehend the world at the speed of sight creates endless applications and opportunities. Feature detection and description algorithms are considered as the retina for machine vision. However, most of these algorithms are typically computationally intensive, which prevents them from achieving real-time performance. As such, embedded vision accelerators (FPGA, ASIC, etc.) can be targeted due to their inherent parallelizability. This chapter provides a comprehensive study on some of the recent feature detection and description algorithms and their hardware solutions. Specifically, it begins with a synopsis on basic concepts followed by a comparative study, from which the maximally stable extremal regions (MSER) and the scale invariant feature transform (SIFT) algorithms are selected for further analysis due to their robust performance. The chapter then reports some of their recent algorithmic derivatives and highlights their recent hardware designs and architectures.

Chapter 17

Pooja Sharma, DAV University, India

In the proposed chapter, a novel, effective, and efficient approach to face recognition is presented. It is a fusion of both global and local features of images, which significantly achieves higher recognition. Initially, the global features of images are determined using polar cosine transforms (PCTs), which exhibit very less computation complexity as compared to other global feature extractors. For local features, the rotation invariant local ternary patterns are used rather than using the existing ones, which help improving the recognition rate and are in alignment with the rotation invariant property of PCTs. The fusion of both acquired global and local features is performed by mapping their features into a common domain. Finally, the proposed hybrid approach provides a robust feature set for face recognition. The experiments are performed on benchmark face databases, representing various expressions of facial images. The results of extensive set of experiments reveal the supremacy of the proposed method over other approaches in terms of efficiency and recognition results.

Preface

In this modern era, images and videos are dominant tools for real world applications. It is quite easy, effective and meaningful to communicate through images or in the form of frames of a video. Image and video processing refers to the processing of information through a picture or group of pictures for a variety of tasks such as image enhancement, object tracking, disease diagnosis through biomedical imaging, security and many more. *Handbook of Research on Advanced Concepts in Real-Time Image and Video Processing* aims to serve the researchers/professionals associated with the design, realization and deployment of image and video processing systems meant for real-time applications. Academicians, researchers, graduate students and technology developers will find this text to be useful through exposure to pertinent topics in real time imaging and in furthering their own research efforts in this important domain. This book focuses on applications in the domain of medical imaging, video surveillance, biometrics, face recognition, image compression, retrieval and much more along with the realization of such applications. The book will serve as a very useful reference to students/researchers who have keen interest in the design of real-world image and video applications.

This book is organized into 17 chapters. A brief description of each of the chapters follows:

In order to detect the person with abnormal harmful activity through visual inspection, a video surveillance system with an efficient algorithm is required. Chapter 1 provides the prominent approaches used for an efficient visual surveillance system that is capable of detecting genuine anomalies in real-world scenarios with adequate accuracy.

Chapter 2 deals with image retrieval techniques based on certain image features such as color, shape and texture. It also discusses the applications for different image retrieval techniques. The various image content descriptors and extraction methods are also explained and compared with a huge database with good precision and recall.

Transmission of video data is expensive with respect to the number of computations, requirement of storage space and bandwidth. Therefore, video compression techniques have become a fundamental part of the way the visual information is created, presented and communicated. In this regard, the authors of Chapter 3 have explored the techniques, challenges and issues in video compression in detail along with the major advancements in the field.

Chapter 4 is based on segmentation of computed tomography brain images. In this chapter authors have proposed a multi-level fuzzy technique with quantization and minimization of computed Euclidean distance applied to morphologically divided skull part. It also shows the merits and demerits of this kind of segmentation that helps in real-time diagnosis of patient's condition.

For many situations, one kind of sensor is not able to capture all the information and hence the information is required to be captured through various type of sensors. In Chapter 5, the authors have highlighted the approach of visible domain real-time tracking with the help of different types of sensors by following cross-domain treatment.

Apart from other applications of image processing, medical imaging is one of the most important field of research. Non-invasive techniques are the standard clinical approach for long time monitoring in contrast to CT scan or MRI. In Chapter 6, the authors have discussed about Electrical Impedance Technique (EIT), a non-invasive method to reconstruct across sectional images along with its benefits over other imaging modalities.

The next chapter deals with the hardware realization of antifogging system that takes into account the poor visibility during bad weather specially in the presence of fog. Attenuation and scattering is the prime factor for the degradation in visibility and responsible for road accidents in the presence of fog. Chapter 7 takes account of a mean channel prior method that includes a complete embedded system for the process of restoring the captured foggy images and the method is implemented on a portable hardware that consists of an ARM7 Quad Core processor.

Chapter 8 is a survey on image retrieval techniques including a comparative study over a common database. The authors described different content based local binary descriptor with and without Gabor transform in brief. The derivative descriptor is calculated using feature extraction. The performance of image retrieval methods has been compared in terms of average precision, average retrieval rate etc. on different set of images.

In Chapter 9, the authors have presented the problems in face detection and gender classification and proposed a probabilistic model to present and learn the appearance of face in terms of shape and geometry. The probabilistic approach for gender classification has a good performance in presence of viewpoint changes and a large appearance variability of faces.

Chapter 10 presents the idea of automatic toll collection systems at toll gates via number plate detection of a vehicle. The proposed toll collection system has high security features and intelligent vehicle classification methods. Combining machine intelligence and computer vision, the proposed system is expected to minimize the security loopholes.

A comparative analysis of medical image fusion in both spatial as well as transform domain has been presented in Chapter 11. The primary aim of medical image fusion is to combine complementary information from multiple imaging modalities (e.g. CT, MRI, PET, etc.) of the same scene so as to extract more information from the fused image.

Object recognition and classification of human being, vehicle or animals has become important for surveillance system at prominent areas as well as sensitive zones such as airports, railway stations, banks, hospitals or defense area. Data collected from surveillance cameras in outdoor environments for moving object recognition need to be monitored either manually or using intelligent systems. For real time implementation, it is more challenging task. Chapter 12 deals with the issues of object appearance like occlusion using invariant feature extraction.

Chapter 13 is based on object extraction using region merging based topological model as automatic object segmentation is usually very hard. The segmentation process followed by color histogram vectors are used to construct neighborhood graph for different regions. A similarity based adaptive region merging mechanism is proposed in this chapter to extract the object contour from the complex background.

Managing and indexing of images become essential in order to retrieve relevant images effectively and efficiently to present visual data in numerous applications ranging from industry to academia. In this regard, Chapter 14 proposed Content Based Image Retrieval (CBIR) and image feature extraction using advanced methods known as radial moments for image retrieval. The chapter discussed important radial moments with their properties and measures performances through an extensive set of experiments on benchmark databases.

From the last two decades, high performance low-cost hardware accelerators for real-time implementation of image and video processing algorithms has attracted a lot of attention. Chapter 15 focused on a new method known as High Level Synthesis (HLS) for transforming high-level algorithmic description into digital hardware while satisfying the design constraints.

In the modern era, computer vision is one of the most active research field in image processing domain. The visual ability of machine can create the endless applications for real world where feature detection and description algorithms are considered as the retinal part for machine vision. Such algorithms can be embedded in to hardware vision accelerators (FPGA, ASIC, etc.). Chapter 16 provides a study about recent feature detection and description algorithms and their hardware solutions.

Finally, Chapter 17 includes a novel, effective, and efficient approach for face biometrics using face recognition. The proposed face recognition system used fusion of both global and local features of images, which significantly achieves higher recognition at very less computational complexity. Polar Cosine Transforms (PCTs) are used to determine the global features of images and the experiments are performed on benchmark face databases that represents various expressions of facial images.

Our aim is to provide text materials to researchers and students for the improvement of their thinking ability towards the real-world applications through image and video processing. The efforts will minimize the daily life problems, even where a man's eyes can't reach.

In brief, we are happy with the end product that has been possible through the contributions of various authors, efforts of reviewers and the background support from the IGI Global team. We are very hopeful that this book will guide the readers to visualize a scene beyond their vision.

Md. Imtiyaz Anwar
NIT Jalandhar, India

Arun Khosla
NIT Jalandhar, India

Rajiv Kapoor
DTU, India

Chapter 1
Anomalous Event Detection Methodologies for Surveillance Application:
An Insight

T. J. Narendra Rao
National Institute of Technology Karnataka, India

Mohit P. Tahiliani
National Institute of Technology Karnataka, India

G N Girish
National Institute of Technology Karnataka, India

Jeny Rajan
National Institute of Technology Karnataka, India

ABSTRACT

Automatic visual surveillance systems serve as in-place threat detection devices being able to detect and recognize anomalous activities which otherwise would lead to potentially harmful situations, and alert the concerned authorities to take appropriate counter actions. However, development of an efficient visual surveillance system is quite challenging. Designing an unusual activity detection mechanism which is accurate and real-time is the primary challenge. Review of literature carried out led to the inference that there are some attributes which are essential for a successful unusual event detection mechanism for surveillance application. The desired approach must detect genuine anomalies in real-world scenarios with acceptable accuracy, should adapt to changing environments and, should require less computational time and memory. In this chapter, an attempt has been made to provide an insight into some of the prominent approaches employed by researchers to solve these issues with a hope that it will benefit researchers towards developing a better surveillance system.

DOI: 10.4018/978-1-5225-2848-7.ch001

INTRODUCTION

In recent days, due to growing terrorism and hence rising concern about global security, it has become crucial to have in-place efficient threat detection systems. These systems must be able to detect and recognize potentially harmful situations and alert the authorities to take appropriate action(s). This process of active surveillance has been promisingly achieved by means of intelligent video analysis through automatic threat detection systems. Visual Sensor Networks (VSNs) are the most sought-after solution for this purpose. The security personnel can rely on this kind of systems to have better situational awareness, enabling them to respond to critical situations more efficiently.

A VSN consists of a group of nodes called camera nodes (or smart camera devices or sensors) each equipped with a low power embedded processor, energy source and an image sensor. It also consists of a transceiver for communication with other nodes and with the central base station or the sink where the data is collected and further processed for end-user consumption (Marcus & Marques, 2012) as shown in Figure 1. VSNs support a great number of vision-based applications such as in surveillance, environment monitoring, smart meeting rooms, smart homes, tele-presence systems, etc. (Soro & Heinzelman, 2009). In this chapter, the focus revolves around the all-important surveillance application of VSNs.

BACKGROUND

Visual Sensor Networks for Surveillance Application

Of late, VSNs consisting of surveillance cameras are in wide use due to their highly effective monitoring ability which is beyond human capacity. Considerable numbers of surveillance cameras have been deployed in public places with a purpose of crime detection, reduction and crisis management (Gong,

Figure 1. Representative image of a homogeneous Visual Sensor Network

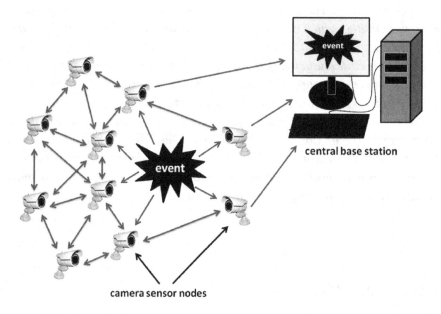

Loy, & Xiang, 2011). With conventional visual surveillance systems, human operators were employed to monitor activities, detect any unusual incidents such as the behaviors in Figure 2(a, b, c) and to bring it to the notice of the concerned authorities. Unfortunately, many possible threats may get miss-detected in such a manual system due to exhaustive number of video sequences to watch (Figure 2(d)), boredom and tiredness because of prolonged monitoring, lack of prior knowledge about anomalies etc. As a result, surveillance footages are not being useful for crime prevention, instead they often end up as passive records or as evidence for post-event investigations. Miss-detections of anomalies can prove disastrous in critical contexts such as at borders, airports etc. For example, the perpetrators of the bombing at the Luton train station in London in 2005 and during the marathon at Boston in 2013 were captured on CCTV prior to the incidents. The Nissan Pathfinder vehicle used in the attempted attack on Times Square, New York in 2010 was also captured on CCTV as well. However, these images were unfortunately used only for post-event investigations (Mould, Regens, Jensen et al., 2014).

So, technology providers and end-users have recognized the inadequacy of manual surveillance process alone in meeting the needs of screening and timely detection of interesting events from an exhaustively enormous amount of video data that is generated. To fulfill such a need, video content analysis paradigm is shifting from a fully human operator model to a machine-assisted and automated model. Such systems perform the task of detecting the unusual or actual crime events when they occur and trigger an alert. Some of the applications of an automated surveillance system involving unusual event detection include (Gong et al., 2011),

Figure 2. Representative images of (a) the act of abandoning an object, (b) the act of violence, (c) the act of running suspiciously in a mall, (d) a human operator monitoring a large number of video screens. (The bounding box is used to indicate the anomaly)
Source: (a, b) Image reprinted from the open source CAVIAR (Caviar: context aware vision using image-based active recognition, 2011) and BEHAVE (Fisher, 2011) datasets respectively, (c) Image reprinted with permission from the first author of (Adam, Rivlin, Shimshoni, & Reinitz, 2008).

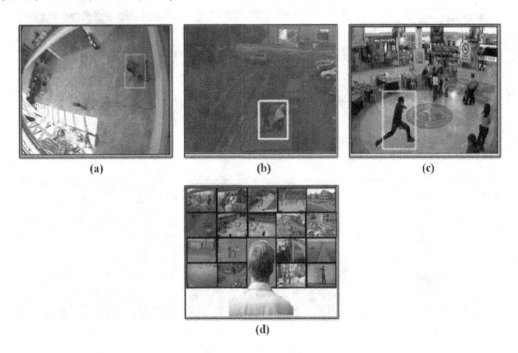

(a)   (b)   (c)

(d)

- **Intruder Detection:** Fence trespassing detection when an intruder is caught crossing the prohibited perimeter in sensitive and restricted areas (Figure 3(a, b)).
- **Unattended Object Detection:** To trigger an alarm when an object is placed in a controlled area for extended time period (Figure 3(c)).
- **Loitering Detection:** To detect persons who stay in an area for a protracted time without any apparent lawful purpose (Figure 3(d, e)).
- **Tailgating Detection:** To detect the illegal follow-through behavior at access control points, e.g., doorways, where multiple persons enter while only one of them is authorized.
- **Crowd Management:** To avoid overcrowding situations at transportation hubs and shopping malls etc. (Figure 3(f)), where the statistics on the crowd volume are collected by dedicated software.

However, development of such surveillance systems which serve their true purpose faces certain challenges. Developing an efficient anomalous event detection algorithm is the foremost challenge which is the focus of this chapter.

An insight into some of the prominent research works of the past decade has been provided. Also, some of the prime properties/features which have a major impact on the performance of any anomalous event detection approach have been identified from the literature and discussed in detail with reference to associated works.

Figure 3. Representative images of the different applications of an automated surveillance system. (a, b) intruder detection, (c) unattended object detection, (d, e) loitering detection, (f) crowd management
Source: (a) Image reprinted with permission from IPS Intelligent Video Analytics, (b, c) Image reprinted from open source ViSOR (Vezzani & Cucchiara, 2010) and PETS ((CVPR), 2009) datasets respectively, (d) image reprinted with permission from IPS Intelligent Video Analytics, (e) image reprinted with permission from the first author of (Adam et al., 2008), (f) image reprinted from the open source UCF Crowd Counting dataset (Idrees, Saleemi, Seibert, & Shah, 2007).

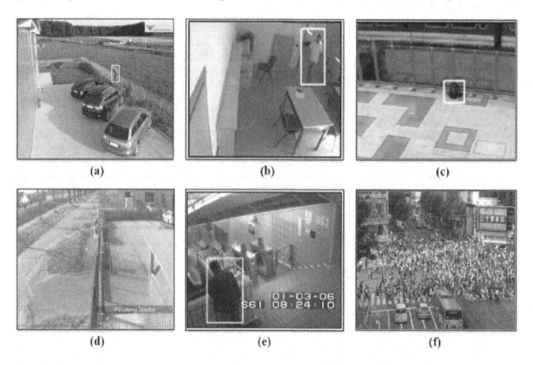

(a)   (b)   (c)

(d)   (e)   (f)

The rest of this chapter describes the different unusual event detection approaches from the literature, the parameters to be considered in the design of an ideal surveillance system followed by conclusion of the chapter.

THE ANOMALOUS EVENT DETECTION METHODOLOGIES

In surveillance applications, the primary objective of an automated VSN is the detection of suspicious events in a scene which are basically anomalous or unusual. Anomaly by definition is anything that departs from the normal. From the technical perspective, they are patterns deviating spatio-temporally from the frequently observed patterns. Also, they are events that occur occasionally i.e., those which have low probability of occurrence. But the unusual events cannot be generalized, because, a particular activity would be an anomaly in a particular context while in another it might be a normal activity. Since unusual events cannot be defined explicitly, the surveillance systems need to consider the implicit assumption that the events that occur occasionally are potentially suspicious (Roshtkhari & Levine, 2013). They are rare, difficult to describe, hard to predict and can be subtle. However, with a large number of observations, it is relatively simple to verify if they are actually unusual (Zhong, Shi, & Visontai, 2004). These facts form the basis for the anomalous event detection methodologies.

These approaches are generally derived from human action recognition category of approaches which are extended towards learning and differentiating the usual and unusual actions. In the literature, the approaches for unusual behaviour detection have been broadly classified into rule based methods and statistical methods (Boiman & Irani, 2007). In the former methods, the normal/abnormal behaviors are predefined by a set of rules for detection in the form of a training set. As a result, the rules have to be defined for a new or changing context every time. In the latter case, they do not assume any rules. Instead, they try to automatically learn the notion of normal behaviour from the given data and thus detect the abnormal ones. Hence, statistical methods are considered to be more promising.

Object tracking has been the basis in many of the works of anomaly detection. Here, a trajectory is obtained by tracking the path of a moving object (Figure 4(a, b)) and an anomaly will be identified through the deviation from the learnt trajectories. Such approaches have the drawbacks that they are not suitable for detecting abnormal patterns in a crowded or complex scene and that composition of the blob is to be known for human behavior analysis (Roshtkhari & Levine, 2013).

On the other hand, non-tracking approaches also exist which rely on extracting and analyzing local low-level visual features, such as motion and texture to detect local spatio-temporal anomalies in videos (Figure 4(c)). The main limitation of these methods is that only local temporal changes are captured which cannot be used for behavioral understanding due to the absence of contextual information. The recent drift in anomaly detection is to use spatio-temporal video volumes along with the consideration of contextual information i.e., the compositional relationship between the volumes for the purpose of anomaly detection (Figure 4(d)).

A systematic literature review was carried out and 14 prominent algorithms designed to detect unusual or anomalous events in surveillance video have been chosen for discussion. A comprehensive insight into each chosen anomaly detection algorithm is provided. The discussion includes the overview, benefits and/or limitations of the methods.

Figure 4. Representative images of (a, b) object tracking. Non-tracking methods based on (c) spatio-temporal feature points selection and (d) spatio-temporal volume construction
Source: (a, b, c) Modified images from the open source ViSOR (Vezzani & Cucchiara, 2010), CAVIAR (Caviar: context aware vision using image-based active recognition, 2011) and KTH (Laptev & Caputo, 2011) datasets respectively, (d) from (Rao, Girish & Rajan, 2016)

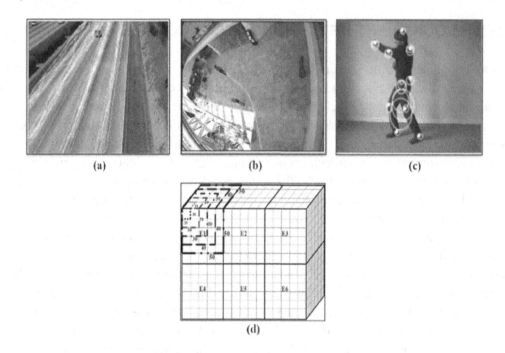

Trajectory Based Approaches for Anomaly Detection

Trajectory Snippet Histograms Method

Iscen et al. (Iscen, Armagan & Duygulu, 2014) researched with an aim to discover the common characteristics shared among unusual events. A novel descriptor named trajectory snippet histograms was also proposed to encode the rapid motions in videos and to differentiate usual from unusual videos.

The authors believed that unusual events shared irregular and fast movements in common, resulting from being scared or surprised, or from sudden actions like falling etc. In order to find the trajectories, the feature points were densely sampled and their optical flow is computed. The extracted trajectories are used to encode the motion in the snippets (short time intervals). For a snippet, three trajectory snippet histograms were computed using the length of the trajectory and the variances along X and Y dimensions are computed. They are combined together to form the descriptor. The histograms were used to differentiate unusual videos from usual ones. A snippet codebook is formed using the features extracted from the snippet for the whole video clip. For each snippet of the training set, n-nearest neighbors were identified using the snippet histograms as the feature vector. After checking the number of neighbors, the snippet with more number of neighbors were eliminated and remaining ones were used to construct initial models. SVM classifier was trained on these models. For detection of unusual patches, the trained SVM models were run on test models to extract the histogram snippet trajectories. The models were ranked based on the top ten summed up SVM detection scores (for appearance consistency) and based on ratio of retrieved features from the unusual videos to the ones from the usual videos (for purity scores) for each model. These two were combined and ranked again for each model. The top ranked models were inferred as unusual event patches.

Kullback-Liebler (KL) Divergence Method

Based on the assumption that activities of interest in surveillance application occur rarely when compared to regular behaviors, Xu et al. (Xu, Denman, Fookes, & Sridharan, 2015) proposed a novel approach for rare event detection using Kullback-Liebler function based on the concept of weakly supervised learning, which means having binary labels at the clip level.

The authors consider two modes of feature representation – a discrete optical flow and trajectory representations. The video is divided into uniform clips and the trajectories represented by a sequence of locations in time are extracted using MPEG motion vectors, particle video or the KLT tracker. Low Fourier coefficients are used to describe the extracted trajectories. A codebook is formed out of the Fourier coefficients of the trajectories by using k-means algorithm. Since in real world scenarios the clips labeled '1' (having the event of interest) is much smaller than the clips labeled '0' (not having the event of interest), the authors have applied the KL divergence to effectively and efficiently separate the video clips into these two classes. The detection of rare events is based on partitioning of the video clips generated by the probability distribution of codewords, into two classes - those containing the codewords specified for the event of interest are labeled '1' and others are labeled '0'.

Benefits:

- The KL divergence method supports real-time detection of rare events.

Probability Based Trajectory Analysis method

Anomaly detection in crowded scenes is always a challenging task due to variation of the definitions of anomalous and usual events, poor resolution of the scene, ambiguity in appearance, and severe inter-object occlusions. In 2015, Zhou et al. (S. Zhou, Shen, Zeng, & Zhang, 2015) proposed a novel trajectory based statistical framework to detect abnormal behaviors in crowded contexts.

The trajectories of the pedestrians in a crowded scene were captured by using the KLT feature tracker. Based on the destination of the people in the crowd, the crowd can be subdivided into smaller groups whose members move coherently. Hence, the captured motion trajectories of a pedestrian group were merged based on this assumption to create a representative trajectory which describes the potential motion pattern of the group. The clustering was done by applying the hierarchical k-means clustering. The representative trajectories belonging to a training video are used to model normal crowd behavior in that context. This modeling of both structured and unstructured crowd scenes is done by using the Multi-Observation Hidden Markov Model (MOHMM). The trajectory set of the video clips of normal crowded scene are used for training the MOHMM. Anomalies were detected by identifying the trajectories of clips with low likelihoods. The authors assumed that the new normal event trajectory observations evolve from the training representative trajectories. Hence an abnormal behavior trajectory will have very low probability as given by the learned MOHMM of being evolved from training trajectory model.

Benefits:

- The use of trajectory capture concept helps preserve important global motion information of the crowd.
- The false alarm rate of detecting unusual events could be decreased due to the stability of distribution of trajectories.
- Limitations:
- The method cannot localize the abnormal events within the video clip inferred to be anomalous.

Context-Incoherent Patterns Analysis for Anomaly Detection

In large areas and complex monitoring scenes, there is a need for multiple cameras for monitoring, most of which are separated and non-overlapped. Hence, a novel global abnormal event detection algorithm was proposed by Guo et al. (Guo et al., 2015) in 2015 for multiple disjoint synchronous camera network. Global unusual events here are the context-incoherent patterns which span across multiple disjoint camera fields of view.

The local activities occurring in each camera view is to be captured in order to understand the corresponding global event happening across multiple disjoint cameras. Hence, for modeling the background in each camera the authors make use of Gaussian Mixture Model (GMM). When any object enters into the field of view, the corresponding foreground pixels are detected and a color histogram based mean-shift tracking algorithm is employed to capture the spatio-temporal trajectory of the object. The entry and exit points (termed as nodes) of each of the trajectories within a camera view are then determined using k-means algorithm. The trajectories are grouped into clusters by the use of trajectory clustering algorithm in order to find the links (temporal dependencies) between the different entry and exit nodes. The links between the nodes spanning across different cameras are learnt by employing Modified Dynamic Time Warping (MDTW) analysis. These temporal dependencies within and across the cameras are modeled using Probabilistic Graphical Model (PGM). The model or the structure of the links obtained is further optimized using Monte Carlo (MC) algorithm which performs the task of adding a link, deleting a link and swapping two links. The parameters of the optimized Probabilistic Graphical Model are learnt in a Bayesian learning setting. If the log likelihood of a global event is less than the predetermined threshold, it is inferred to be anomalous.

Benefits:

- The use of the combination of MDTW and MC enables accurate capturing of the dependency structures.

Limitations:

- The method is less robust in the case of networks having long temporal dependencies.

Non-Tracking Approaches for Anomaly Detection

Inference by Composition Method

A method named Inference by Composition (IBC) was proposed by Boiman and Irani (Boiman & Irani, 2007) for detecting the irregularities in visual data.

This involves the use of the spatio-temporal patches extracted from previous visual examples (database) to compose the new observed visual data which can be an image or a video sequence (query). The regions in the query which can be constructed using large contiguous chunks of data extracted from the database are considered to be very likely or normal, whereas the regions which cannot be composed or which can be composed using only small fragments from the database are regarded to be unlikely or suspicious. To account for local non-rigid deformations in the chunks of data, the large chunks are broken down to ensembles of many small patches at different scales with their relative geometric positions considered. Now, during the inference process a search is made for ensemble of patches in the database which have similar configuration (both in descriptors and relative arrangement) as in the ensemble of patches considered from the query.

Benefits:

- The method can also be used to detect saliency in images and video sequences without any prior information.
- It is general enough to address a wide range of problems such as attention in images/videos, recognition of suspicious behaviour, recognition of unusual objects, automatic visual inspection etc. in computer vision in a single unified framework.

Limitations:

- It cannot handle extreme occlusions.
- The time and memory complexity is linear in the size of the database.

Local Optical Flow Method

Adam et al. (Adam et al., 2008) presented a novel algorithm for detection of certain types of unusual events from videos of real world scenarios.

Multiple, local, low-level feature monitors which extract specific low-level measurements/observations are utilized to monitor the scene and to detect unusual events. The observations extracted are actually the optical flow direction at the monitor's location. The extracted observations are stored in the cyclic buffer of the monitor. Each time a new observation is stored, the oldest observation is removed from the buffer. Given a new observation, each monitor computes the likelihood of this observation when compared to the likelihood of the observations currently stored in buffer. If the likelihood result falls below a threshold, then the monitor outputs an alert. The algorithm uses an integration rule to integrate the decisions from all the monitors to decide whether to produce an unusual event alert to the user or not. Additionally, the authors have identified certain algorithm-independent requirements which are to be satisfied by a video analysis or unusual event detection mechanism for its successful deployment in large-scale surveillance projects. In short, the requirements need an algorithm to be computationally simple, to be automatically working after only a minimal setup, to be working well in cluttered and crowded environments, the algorithm should be capable of adapting to changing environments and should be such that the field technician can know the suitability of the algorithm (predictable performance).

Benefits:

- The authors claim that the unusual event detection algorithm satisfies all of the above requirements.

Limitation:

- The method cannot detect events as unusual events which are composed of unusual sequences of short-term normal actions.

Mixture of Dynamic Textures Method

The Mixture of Dynamic Textures (MDT) method proposed by Mahadevan et al. (Mahadevan, Li, Bhalodia, & Vasconcelos, 2010) uses joint modeling of the appearance and dynamics of the scene along with the ability to detect temporal and spatial unusualness to determine anomalies in a crowded scene.

The authors attempted to develop a model which relies on joint modeling of dynamics and appearance suitable for crowded scenes which are composed of highly dynamic backgrounds. Because crowded scenes are typically composed of distinct sub-entities accurate detection requires the ability to model multiple components of different appearance and dynamics. The authors used the Mixtures of Dynamic Textures model in their work to design a framework for spatial and temporal anomaly detection. For temporal abnormality detection, spatio-temporal patches are extracted from the cells formed and the MDT is learnt during training. The patches with low probability are considered to be anomalies. For spatial abnormality detection, a spatial abnormality map is created using the centre-surround saliency technique to identify dynamic textures that are unusual by comparison to neighboring image patches. The spatial abnormality map is finalized by estimating the likelihood of each patch with respect to the adjacent blocks using a single MDT for entire patch collection. The final spatiotemporal abnormality map is obtained by the summation of temporal and spatial abnormality maps which is thresholded to identify low probability textures within the video.

Limitations:

- The method is computationally intensive.

Bag of LBPs Method

It is challenging to model and detect events in densely crowded environments due to the variety of events and the noise in the scenes. Xu et al. (Xu, Denman, Fookes, & Sridharan, 2011) proposed an approach for anomalous event detection in such crowded scenes using dynamic textures.

Local Binary Patterns (LBP) from Three Orthogonal Planes (LBP-TOP) descriptors was used to describe these textures. This algorithm involved three parts: feature extraction using LBP-TOP, model training and detection. In the first part, LBPs are defined using the spatial texture which is the joint distribution of the intensities from an m x n neighborhood. LBP is extended to volume LBP (VLBP) by combining temporal information with the spatial textures to model dynamic textures. To reduce the total number of patterns, LBPs are calculated only from three orthogonal planes (XY, XT and YT). LBP-TOP based dynamic textures are modeled using Latent Dirichlet Allocation (LDA) as bag of LBPs. During training phase, LBP-TOP features are extracted from the Spatio-temporal patches of sub-regions formed in the Region of Interest (ROI) in the scene. The LDA models are trained using the outputs of the LBP-TOP descriptors. In the detection process, for each patch, LBP-TOP features are extracted. The LDA model that corresponds to the patch is used to calculate the log likelihood of the patch. If the likelihood value is less than a threshold, then an alarm is generated at the location of the patch.

Benefits:

- The method is an unsupervised approach and does not involve object tracking and background subtraction.

Limitations:

- The method does not consider the spatio-temporal order of the LBP-TOP patterns in a spatio-temporal patch.

Dynamic Sparse Coding Method

An unsupervised framework of dynamic sparse coding and online re-constructability has been presented by Zhao et al. (Zhao, Fei-Fei, & Xing, 2011) to detect unusual events in videos.

In this approach, given a video sequence, the sliding window employed scans it along the spatial and temporal axes and divides the video into a set of events, each represented by group of spatio-temporal cuboids. Thus, the task of unusual event detection is formulated as finding the unusual group of cuboids present in the same sliding window. Initially a dictionary is learnt from video using sparse coding and later updated as more data becomes available in an online manner. As per the basic idea, the knowledge of usual events is represented using learnt dictionary. According to the authors, the input signal to sparse coding in case of unusual event detection is a group of weight vectors with both spatial and temporal location information representing an event. The relationship between these vectors represented by the arrangement of the cuboids is also considered. Given the learnt dictionary of usual events, a re-construction weight vector is learnt for query event and then a normality measure is computed from the re-construction weight vector. During the detection of unusual events, an event is unusual if it is either not re-constructible from the dictionary of usual events with small error or if constructible it may involve a combination of a large number of bases from the usual event dictionary.

Benefits:

- It is a fully unsupervised approach.
- It is capable of automatic construction of the normal event dictionary from the initial portion of the video sequence itself and updating itself using each newly observed event.

Spatio-Temporal Compositions Method

In 2013, Roshtkhari and Levine (Roshtkhari & Levine, 2013) proposed an approach for detecting anomalous events in videos using spatio-temporal compositions.

The Spatio-Temporal Compositions (STC) method is based on spatio-temporal video volume formation through dense sampling at various spatial and temporal scales and considering local and global volume composition. A codebook is constructed by grouping redundant and similar volumes, and each video volume is assigned a codeword based on similarity. Then, the relative compositions /arrangements of the volumes inside each ensemble (group of volumes) are modeled probabilistically. Finally, an inference mechanism is developed to make decision about whether any region in the newly observed sample is anomalous. A similarity map is constructed for all frames by calculating its similarity to all previous observations. If the similarity of a region is less than a threshold it contains unusual behavior(s).

Benefits:

- Contextual information regarding the volumes is considered.
- Method is capable of online unsupervised learning of valid behaviors.
- Real-time video analysis for unusual event detection is possible.
- Only a small training set of only few frames (few seconds) of normal events from the video itself is sufficient to initiate the online learning process.
- The algorithm has low computational complexity and less memory requirement for the database.
- The algorithm is capable of handling significant illumination variations and is robust to spatial and temporal scale changes.

Dominant and Anomalous Behavior Detection Method

The same authors presented a novel approach (Javan Roshtkhari & Levine, 2013) for video parsing and simultaneous online learning of dominant and anomalous behaviors in surveillance videos.

This method is similar to the above approach but with certain deviations. Here, Spatio-temporal volumes (STVs) were represented by the histogram of the spatio-temporal gradient of the video in polar coordinates. Similar volumes were grouped into clusters in an online manner using an online single-pass fuzzy clustering approach. Each STV was assigned to all the codewords with a similarity measure. The spatio-temporal arrangements of the volumes in the clusters were analyzed to obtain the contextual information. This was modeled using the probabilistic framework by estimating the probability density/distribution function (pdf) of the volume arrangement in each ensemble (a large contextual region) using histograms. Now, the ensembles were classified into two sets of spatially oriented and temporally oriented ensembles to individually characterize the different activities in the video. In order to construct a behavioral model for the video as well as identify the dominant behavior in the video, the ensembles were clustered by using their histograms as a feature vector. A symmetric Kullback-Leibler (KL) divergence function was used to measure the difference between the pdfs. The two codebooks resulted were used in computing the descriptors that best described a new observation in the query and was compared with two similarity thresholds to decide whether it was normal or abnormal.

Benefits:

- The method is real-time.
- It requires less number of initialization frames.
- It can learn dominant and anomalous behaviors automatically.
- It requires significantly less computational time.
- It is robust to illumination variations.

Limitations:

- The method does not consider trajectories and hence cannot learn long term actions.

Smart Camera Network for Anomaly Detection

Huang and Lee (Huang & Lee, 2014) developed a low-cost distributed smart-camera system to detect abnormal events by analysing the sequential behaviour of a crowd of people and by applying collaborative strategy.

In the first phase, the method captured some frames in a particular interval and Histogram of Oriented Gradients (HOG) was analyzed to determine the presence of any person in a frame. Then, a Region of Interest (ROI) was drawn around the detected person. The height of the ROI was the feature extracted to represent the person and a feature vector was formed from the changes in the ROI for the individual, for event recognition. The system then has to convert the height of each ROI to its original size in order to construct the complete feature vector for each person. For a crowd of people, the combined feature vector must have a smaller dimension in order to save computational energy. For this purpose the authors used an indirect encoding scheme where each feature vector was reduced to include three new features - the maximal change of the ROI height, the number of image frames within which the maximal change happens, and the frequency of the considerable ROI change. A SVM classifier was trained on a powerful workstation and dispatched to all the smart cameras. Then, the recognition phase operated on each camera and the identified behavior sequences were shared with the nearest cameras to ensure completeness of each feature vector. The transmission happened only if an unusual event was detected, to reduce transmission load on the system.

Benefits:

- The methods used a simple and efficient strategy to organize the behavior sequence, a new indirect encoding scheme to represent a crowd with relatively few features.
- The cameras worked collaboratively to detect abnormal events by collective decision.
- The transmission occurs only upon unusual event detection thereby reducing the transmission load.

Hierarchical Feature Representation and Gaussian Process Regression Method

A method for detecting both local and global anomalies using hierarchical spatio-temporal interest point (STIP) feature representation and Gaussian process regression has been proposed by Cheng et al. (Cheng, Chen, & Fang, 2015) in 2015.

The authors used two level hierarchical representations for the events and their interactions. Under low-level representation, the STIP features of an event are extracted using a detector which consists of a 2-D Gaussian filter for spatial direction and 1-D Gabor filter for temporal domain and are defined using a suitable descriptor. These descriptors of the normal events are quantized into a visual vocabulary using k-means algorithm based on Euclidean distance. The local anomaly detection is by measuring the k-nearest neighbors (k-NN) distance of a test cuboid against the visual vocabulary. The possible interactions in the video are acquired by extracting the ensembles of the nearby STIP features. In order to find the frequent geometric relations of the nearby STIP features from training videos, the ensembles are clustered using a bottom-up greedy clustering approach, into a high-level codebook of interaction templates. Each template in the codebook is formulated into a k-NN regression problem and a model is constructed using Gaussian Process Regression (GPR) for learning and inferring. The likelihood based on semantic and structural similarities of a test ensemble with respect to the GPR models of normal events is calculated using global negative log likelihood (GNLL) for global anomaly detection.

Benefits:

- The GPR method can detect both local and global anomalies through hierarchical event representation.
- Clustering method used to extract templates of inter-event interactions from training videos is said to be efficient.
- The method is adaptive and can learn new interactions while individually locate anomalous events.
- The use of STIPs instead of spatio-temporal patches reduces the space and time complexity of event modeling.
- The method is robust to noise.

Contextual Information Based Approach for Anomaly Detection

The STC method (Roshtkhari & Levine, 2013) has to deal with a very large number of overlapping volumes due to dense sampling around every pixel. This greatly increases the complexity of the code-book construction process to group these volumes and their assignment to the volumes. Also, a single experimental threshold is used for inference. In 2016, Rao et al. (Rao et al., 2017) proposed a modified approach for anomaly detection. An attempt was made to develop an adaptive inference mechanism applicable to a wide range of activities in variety of contexts so as to meet the needs of an actual surveillance application, while further simplifying the method of STC.

The proposed anomalous event detection algorithm works at two stages – the initialization and the anomalous events detection. Under initialization, the method is trained with a short video sequence of few seconds composed of the normal behaviors observed in the context of deployment. This initialization will enable the algorithm to learn and model the usual activity pattern in the context. The training sequence is divided into spatio-temporal blocks (ensembles). Each of the ensembles is then sampled to construct spatio-temporal volumes at different spatial and temporal scales and a temporal gradient is defined for each of them. A codebook is formed out of these volumes by grouping similar ones in order to reduce the memory needed to store the volumes and also to aid in the probabilistic modeling process. To understand and obtain the contextual information, each of the ensembles is probabilistically modeled. The probability of the topology of the volumes is determined through a non-parametric approach.

The anomaly detection is reduced to the problem of detecting the events in the query that are not similar enough to the usual events of the training sequence. The query video sequence considered is sampled similar to training video to construct ensembles and volumes. If there exists a nonzero gradient descriptor, only then the codeword assignment and further processing is carried out. Else, it is ignored in order to avoid the unnecessary wastage of processing power. The probability calculation is similar to that of training and the posterior probabilities of all the ensembles of the query sequence are obtained. At this point, the proposed method is modified to achieve the unsupervised learning of new normal events. The decision making regarding the presence of anomaly is done depending on the context by the three adaptive inference mechanisms proposed based on the normally encountered contexts under surveillance. First one for crowded/non-crowded real-world contexts, where the posterior probability of an ensemble less than a threshold is inferred to have anomalous events in it. Second, for non-crowded contexts consisting of a definite activity pattern where, pattern of the query ensemble posterior probabilities which does not match with that of the training are anomalous. Third, for contexts involving object detection where, if similarity between the training and any query is found to be less than threshold then the query is considered to have unusual event and the ensemble of this query with minimum probability contains the anomalous object.

Benefits:

- The method avoids the employment of background subtraction, object tracking, or other processes such as foreground segmentation.
- The initialization is very fast due to the use of very short training sequence.
- The event-driven query processing eliminates computational energy wastage.
- The adaptive inference mechanisms increase the robustness of the method to changing contexts.
- The event-driven high resolution localization enhances the visibility of the anomalous activity(s).
- The anomalous event detection is in real-time.
- The algorithm has reduced computational complexity and less memory requirement than that of STC.
- Contextual information around an event is considered which is essential for correctly understanding the normalcy of an activity.
- The method is capable of unsupervised learning of valid behaviors making it adaptive to changing environments.

DISCUSSION ON THE REQUIREMENTS OF AN EFFICIENT SURVEILLANCE SYSTEM AS ABSTRACTED FROM THE LITERATURE

The study of the above described approaches leads to an inference that an efficient anomalous event detection algorithm must meet with certain requirements. They are discussed in the following subsections along with how they are achieved in the corresponding papers.

Detection of Events in Real-World Contexts

As the first requirement, the technique must be able to accurately identify the genuine suspicious events, in any real-world context such as in crowded and/or occluded environments and/or under varying illumination conditions, instead of working merely in controlled environments. The involved activities can be combinations of simple/complex, periodic/non-periodic and/or single/multiple activities. Hence it becomes necessary to evaluate the performance of the developed algorithms under real-world situations. This foremost requirement has been achieved to different extents in the works considered as shown by the experimental details summarized from the corresponding papers.

Real-life video datasets such as the Subway Surveillance dataset (Adam et al., 2008), Anomalous Walking Patterns dataset (Boiman & Irani, 2007), UT-Interaction dataset (Ryoo & Aggarwal, 2012), UCSD Pedestrian dataset (Ped.1 and Ped. 2) (Mahadevan et al., 2010), PETS dataset (PETS2001, PETS2006) ((CVPR), 2009), QMUL Junction dataset (Loy, Xiang, & Gong, 2009), MIT Traffic dataset (Wang, Ma, & Grimson, 2009), Spatio-Temporal Anomaly Detection dataset (Zaharescu & Wildes, 2010), MSR II Action dataset (Yuan, Liu, & Wu, 2011), KTH dataset (Laptev & Caputo, 2011), Weizmann dataset (Gorelick, Blank, Shechtman, Irani, & Basri, 2011), Unusual Crowd Activity dataset (Unusual crowd activity dataset, University of Minnesota), saliency detection video (Boiman & Irani, 2007) and other videos captured in realistic environments such as in malls, mail rooms etc. were used for performance analysis in the papers. Figure 5 shows some sample snapshots from the videos in the above datasets.

In Trajectory Snippet Histograms method two videos sets of domain specific videos (S1) and random action videos (S2) of YouTube videos was used for experimentation. For the test of classification of unusual from usual videos, the authors claim that it gave 76.25% accurate result for S1 given 1 sec snippet and codebook of size 100. For S2, it gave accuracy of 75% for snippets of sizes 0.5 sec and 1 sec and with codebook of 100 and 150 words respectively. When compared with other descriptors, the method was found to be competitive or better.

The KL divergence method was tested on the real world MIT Traffic database. The events of interest to be detected include taking left, right turns at the intersection and two kinds of jay walking amidst the occlusion caused by pedestrians, vehicles etc. Experiments were conducted on varying combinations of classifiers, feature descriptors and parameters. The performance evaluation was based on the mean of the area under the curve (AUC) of the ROC curves plotted for the testing video clips considered. The method produced highest mean for the left, right turn and first form of jay walking events and second best mean for the other jay walking event, when compared to the mean produced by other state-of-the-art learning models.

Figure 5. Sample frames from the different datasets used for experiments in the different works. (a, b) Subway Surveillance dataset. (c) Anomalous Walking Patterns dataset. (d) UT-Interaction dataset. (e, f) UCSD Pedestrian dataset (Ped.1 and Ped. 2). (g, h, i, j) PETS dataset (PETS2001, PETS2006), (k) QMUL Junction dataset. (l) MIT Traffic dataset. (m, n, o, p) Spatio-Temporal Anomaly Detection dataset (Train, Boat-River, Boat-Sea and Belleview video sequences). (q) MSR II Action dataset. (r) KTH dataset. (s) Weizmann dataset. (t) Unusual Crowd Activity dataset. (u) saliency detection video. (v, w) videos captured in malls. (x) mail room video

In (Zhou et al., 2015) the Unusual Crowd Activity dataset was used for testing. The initial part of the eleven video sequences of three different scenarios consists of a normal behavior and ends with abnormal behaviors. The performance analysis was performed against three other baseline approaches and the authors claim that the ROC curve plotted showed higher detection rate for the method.

In (Guo et al., 2015) two datasets namely the synthetic dataset and the real videos captured from their institute was used. The synthetic dataset is a 17-node network with 10,000 global trajectories with random start time. The combination of MDTW and MC, when compared to alternative dependency learning methods accurately captured the dependency structures. The second dataset contains synchronized videos from three disjointed and uncalibrated cameras installed at building roof. The authors claim that the method produces higher detection rate when evaluated against two other relevant methods.

The IBC approach has been tested by the authors and proved to be effective, for various applications such as in the detection of unusual things in a new observed image e.g., unexpected poses were detected as unfamiliar image configurations i.e., unusual events, detection of saliency in images or videos using saliency detection video, detection of suspicious behaviors given a few examples of valid behaviors, in automatic visual inspection in quality assurance.

The Subway Surveillance dataset consists of videos from two cameras at the entrance and exit of a subway train station. Adam et al. used this dataset to show that their Local Optical Flow method achieved 81% and 100% detection rate (DR) respectively for the two videos with a very few false alarms (FA). Also, the video of a dining hall site was used where 91% was the detection rate (DR) with no false alarms (FA). They also experimented on a video of a bus terminal, a video of the exit-lane of an industrial facility, three mall videos (Adam et al., 2008) and achieved appreciable results.

Mahadevan et al. developed the UCSD Pedestrian dataset to evaluate the performance of their MDT method. It contains video sequences from two pedestrian walkways where abnormal events such as the presence of non-pedestrians on a walkway (bicyclists, skaters, small carts, etc.) occur. The authors claim that MDT produced lower equal error rate (EER) and higher detection rate at equal error when compared to other relevant methods. The same dataset was used for testing of Bag of LBPs method which showed better results than MDT. The Subway Surveillance dataset was used to show that the Dynamic Sparse Coding method showed slightly higher detection rate than that of state-of-the-art methods. You Tube videos were also used to prove effectiveness of the method.

The developers of STC method used the Anomalous Walking Patterns dataset and the Spatio-Temporal Anomaly Detection dataset (which contains real-world videos like the Train, the Belleview and the Boat-Sea video sequences with more complicated dynamic backgrounds along with varying illumination conditions with simplistic motions such as movements observed in the scene as unusual events) along with the UCSD Pedestrian dataset and Subway Surveillance dataset for performance analysis. The authors compared the results with other anomaly detection approaches, mainly the IBC, MDT, Local Optical Flow. Parameters such as frame level anomaly detection, pixel level localization ability and continuous learning ability under variable and difficult illumination conditions were used and analyzed through the ROC and PR curves, and EER values. Overall, the STC proved to be superior in terms of anomaly detection and real-time performance.

The Spatio-Temporal Anomaly Detection dataset and UCSD Pedestrian dataset were used for testing the method in (Roshtkhari & Levine, 2013). The ROC curves were plotted for two alternate pixel-level anomaly detection methods and two pixel-level background models, for the first dataset. The method showed comparable or superior results. The ROC curves for MDT and Local Optical Flow for UCSD Pedestrian dataset showed that the method gave better performance. The EER calculated for both frame level and pixel level detection for different methods indicated that this method gave superior results and outperformed all other real-time algorithms.

To test the smart camera network in (Huang & Lee, 2014), the authors used the target events like earthquake, gun shooting and fighting. The authors say that, the recognition accuracy of the classifier decreased with the increase in non-relevant behaviors. When the classifier was trained to recognize multiple events, it gave similar but less precise result compared to that of single event recognition. To evaluate the collective decision method, the authors impaired the behaviour of each person up to 20% to represent incomplete data. The result showed that an increase in the number of cameras led to better performance.

The real-world datasets such as UCSD Pedestrian dataset, Subway Surveillance dataset, and QMUL Junction dataset were used for performance evaluation of Gaussian Process Regression method (Cheng et al., 2015). The performance was evaluated in terms of the EER and AUC of the ROC curves. Overall, the method achieved 80% detection rate for the three challenging datasets. The authors claim that the method outperformed the other state-of-the-art methods.

Rao et al. (Rao et al., 2017) used seven different standard datasets namely, the Subway Surveillance dataset, Anomalous Walking Patterns dataset, the UT-Interaction dataset, the MSR Action Dataset II, KTH dataset, the Weizmann dataset and the Spatio-temporal Anomaly Detection dataset (Train, Boat-river and Canoe video sequences) with simple and complex activities, in both non-crowded and crowded environments and under varied illumination conditions for performance analysis of their method (Rao et al., 2017). Overall results show that the method exhibited promising results, with an anomalous event detection rate of 91.35% across all datasets, with only six false alarms. The method produced appreciable results for the standard datasets with a reduced computational complexity in comparison to STC (Roshtkhari & Levine, 2013) and other state-of-the-art methods. Figure 6 shows sample detections of anomalous events in experimented datasets, by this method.

Comparative Analysis and Discussion

A comparative analysis of the performance of some of above works which have used one or more common datasets and evaluation parameters for performance assessment in the corresponding references has been presented here. Since detection accuracy is the primary concern for any approach, from Table 1, STC seems to perform better on UCSD dataset and Dynamic Sparse Coding as well as STC perform equally better on Subway Surveillance dataset. Table 2 shows the Equal Error Rate (EER) percentage produced by the methods against the UCSD dataset. Apart from a strong detection rate, an anomaly detection approach is also expected to have a low EER value i.e., having low percentage of false positives and miss-detections. Correspondingly, from Table 2, STC tops over other methods with least EER for UCSD dataset.

Receiver Operating Characteristics (ROC) is a plot of True Positive Rate (TPR) versus False Positive Rate (FPR) at varied thresholds. Since the optimum thresholds for the methods are not known, the FPR values at the ideally required TPR of 1.0 obtained by the different methods has been shown in third column of Table 3. To make the analysis more meaningful, the TPR values obtained by the methods at the cost of 0.25 FPR (since TPR is generally 0.0 at 0.0 FPR) has been placed in the fourth column of Table 3. It can be seen that STC and the method in (Rao et al., 2017) outperform others against UCSD and Anomalous Walking Patterns datasets respectively.

Figure 6. Sample snapshots of the detected anomalous events in the different dataset videos, by the method of (Rao et al., 2017)

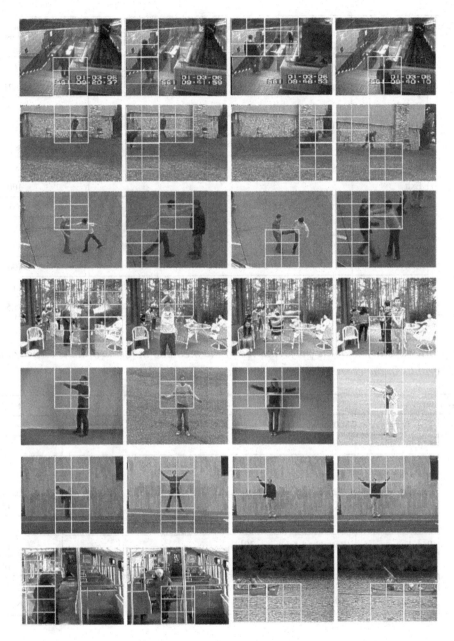

Precision-Recall (PR) curve is the plot of precision (the fraction of detected unusual queries that are truly unusual) versus recall (the fraction of truly unusual queries detected) at varied decision making thresholds. For the same reason of not knowing the optimum thresholds, the recall values of the methods at their maximum precision and precision values at their maximum recall are used for comparative analysis in Table 4. The method in (Rao et al., 2017) produces better results on the Subway Surveillance and Spatio-temporal Anomaly Detection (Train video sequence) datasets.

Table 1. Comparative analysis of the performance of the methods in terms of their detection rates (results taken from corresponding references)

Dataset		Method	Detection Rate (%)
UCSD	Ped. 1	MDT	75
	Ped. 2		75
	Ped. 1	Bag of LBPs	67.75
	Ped. 2		82.8
	Ped. 1	STC	85
	Ped. 2		87
Subway Surveillance	Entrance	Local Optical Flow	81
	Exit		100
	Entrance	Dynamic Sparse Coding	90
	Exit		100
	Entrance	STC	90
	Exit		100
	Entrance	(Rao et al., 2017) (Rao, 2016)	Not used
	Exit		95.5

Table 2. Comparative analysis of the performance of the methods in terms of their EER values derived from the ROC graphs in the corresponding references

Dataset		Method	EER (%)
UCSD	Ped. 1	MDT	25
	Ped. 2		25
	Ped. 1	Bag of LBPs	32.25
	Ped. 2		17.2
	Ped. 1	STC	15.0
	Ped. 2		13.0
	Ped. 1	(Roshtkhari & Levine, 2013)	15.0
	Ped. 2		14.0
	Ped. 1	(Cheng, Chen, & Fang, 2015)	23.7
	Ped. 2		Not used

Considering Contextual Information for Behaviour Understanding

Identifying the genuine unusual activities requires correct understanding of the human behavior in the event, for which considering the contextual information becomes very much essential. This is because, it is said that it is nearly impossible to correctly understand the human behavior without considering the context where it is observed (Roshtkhari & Levine, 2013). In other words, a behavior which is suspi-

Table 3. Comparative analysis of the performance of the methods in terms of their TPR and FPR values derived from the ROC graphs in the corresponding references

Dataset		Method	FPR at TPR=1.0	TPR at FPR=0.25
UCSD	Ped. 1	MDT	0.79	0.76
	Ped. 2		0.8	0.79
	Ped. 1	Bag of LBPs	0.96	0.6
	Ped. 2		0.88	0.87
	Ped. 1	STC	0.61	0.9
	Ped. 2		0.53	0.93
	Ped. 1	(Roshtkhari & Levine, 2013)	0.56	0.89
	Ped. 2		0.48	0.94
	Ped. 1	(Cheng, Chen, & Fang, 2015)	1.0	0.79
	Ped. 2		Not used	Not used
Anomalous Walking Patterns		IBC	0.47	0.91
		STC	0.48	0.91
		(Rao et al., 2017) (Rao, 2016)	0.35	0.98

Table 4. Comparative analysis of the performance of the methods in terms of their Precision-recall values derived from the PR graphs in the corresponding references

Dataset	Method	Recall at Maximum Precision		Precision at Maximum Recall	
		Recall	Precision	Recall	Precision
Subway Surveillance (Exit)	STC	0.0	1.0	1.0	0.64
	(Rao et al., 2017) (Rao, 2016)	0.93	0.93	1.0	0.79
Spatio-temporal Anomaly Detection (Train video sequence)	STC	0.0	1.0	1.0	0.15
	(Rao et al., 2017) (Rao, 2016)	0.038	1.0	1.0	0.15

cious in one context may not be so in another context. This important but not often considered attribute has been taken into account only in four of the above approaches i.e., in (Roshtkhari & Levine, 2013; Boiman & Irani, 2007; Roshtkhari & Levine, 2013; Rao et al., 2017). In all these works, the authors used the ensembles of spatio-temporal video volumes/patches (which may represent an activity) after dense sampling and ensemble construction, to understand the spatio-temporal relationship among the volumes. This gives desired the contextual information aiding in the more accurate inference of an unusual activity. In fact, the authors of (Roshtkhari & Levine, 2013; Rao et al., 2017) claim that the superior performance of their method was due to the consideration of contextual information in the scene which made it possible to learn complicated behaviors.

Unsupervised Learning for Adaptation to Changing Environments

Commonly, an automated surveillance system is initialized with a training set to differentiate abnormal from normal behaviors. But, it is said that it is almost impossible to have a training set for all the normal behaviors in all contexts, as the behaviors may change with the changing contexts and over time (Wiliem et al., 2012). As a result, any new usual event will remain to be unusual for such systems provided the event is manually set as a normal one. Similarly, a suspicious event which may turn into a regular event in the future will be falsely detected as suspicious until manual intervention. Such a system fails to adapt to the changes in the environment or to a new one. This is undesirable in an intelligent surveillance system. Hence, an unsupervised learning capability is required so that the system once initialized is able to learn to differentiate normal from abnormal behaviors on its own in the long run without manual training. This property has been incorporated in five of the above papers (Adam et al., 2008; Roshtkhari & Levine, 2013; Zhao et al., 2011; Rao et al., 2017).

In (Adam et al., 2008), the authors used a cyclic buffer in the monitors to store each of the new observations while oldest observation is removed. The monitors compute the likelihood for each new observation with respect to the likelihood of those in the buffer to infer the anomaly. A new (usual) event which occurs repeatedly will fill up the buffer. The likelihood of this event also increases accordingly to the level of a usual event.

Zhao et al. (Zhao et al., 2011) made use of an automatically learnt event dictionary for unsupervised learning of usual/unusual events. The idea was to first learn and create an initial dictionary using the initial portion of the actual video itself, and then update this learnt dictionary using each newly observed event. The updation of the dictionary is done using projected stochastic gradient descent.

Roshtkhari et al. (Roshtkhari & Levine, 2013), in their approach, used an online unsupervised incremental technique which updates the probability distribution functions of the normal events. This allows the method to adaptively learn newly observed normal patterns. In (Roshtkhari & Levine, 2013) as new data are observed, the learnt codebooks are updated using the previous frames. This process is performed continuously and the detection thresholds are updated correspondingly based on the previously learnt codebooks.

In (Rao et al., 2017) the frequency of the codewords in different positions of the ensembles in the training is incremented, updated and used to obtain the volume posterior probabilities when a query is processed and the frequency values are carried forward for the next query, in order to learn.

Real-Time Performance

It is also necessary that the system detects the desired events in real-time i.e., as they occur. This plays a major role in timely management of unusual event affected situation or in prevention of perilous acts from happening. Among the methods considered for this survey, five of the approaches (Adam et al., 2008; Xu et al., 2015; Roshtkhari & Levine, 2013; Rao et al., 2017) have been developed to work in real-time. The authors of (Adam et al., 2008) say that the method of Local Optical Flows is computationally non-demanding, thus allowing real-time working. However, this claim has not been supported with the required statistics. In the work of (Xu et al., 2015) the KL divergence function used runs very fast thus making rare event detection in real-time.

In the case of (Roshtkhari & Levine, 2013), the authors claim that the method STC performs real-time abnormality detection and localization, requiring on an average of only 0.22 seconds of computational time per frame processing, for Pedestrian 1, Pedestrian 2, Subway videos and walking patterns. This speed up is due to grouping of volumes using codebook which reduces the dimensions of the search space (database) and the memory required for it, thereby considerably reducing the computational time for computing similarity, and the use of pdf reduces the computational time required for determining the similarity of the volume compositions.

The work in (Rao et al., 2017) is also capable of real-time processing of frames for anomaly detection requiring an average of only 0.17 seconds of computational time per frame processing of the query belonging to Subway Surveillance dataset (Adam et al., 2008). This can be attributed to the reasons mentioned above, additionally to the employment of non-overlapping volumes and ensembles, and to the use of a simpler codebook construction process.

CONCLUSION

In the present day scenario, when crimes jeopardizing social life are on the rise, public safety and security are one of the top priority issues in front of us. Visual Sensor Networks are already in the frontline when it comes to finding a solution towards this problem, through visual surveillance. However, developing an efficient surveillance system is a challenging task. There are certain issues to be dealt with so as to allow the surveillance system serve its true purpose and to its full extent. The primary challenge among them is the development of an approach for identifying unusual activities efficiently. Review of literature revealed that there are some important attributes which determine the level of performance of an unusual event detection mechanism, such as being able to work in real-world contexts, adapt to any changing scenes, identify the truly suspicious activities, work in real-time. In this chapter, an attempt has been made to give the readers, an insight into some of the important research works directed towards achieving these properties along with their test results and quantitative comparative analysis. Future research directions have also been presented with a hope that it will benefit researchers towards developing a better surveillance system.

FUTURE RESEARCH DIRECTIONS

It is hard to conclude as to which of the above discussed algorithms are superior in their ability to detect anomalous behaviors and be highly suitable for surveillance applications since the methods have been proved to achieve best results against specific datasets. Hence, detection models that are efficient in simultaneously capturing a wide range of anomalies will be highly appreciated in order to capture the entire set of suspicious behaviors that are of interest to ensure public security. It is also an important requirement that an unusual event detection approach is applicable to any real world context whose definition varies extremely broadly. Hence, there is always scope for research towards development of an approach with 100% accuracy in any given scenario ranging from a simple residential context to a highly critical context such as an airport, military facility etc. Such a method should have an adaptive inference mechanism to operate successfully in changing scenarios. However, it is generally the case that the unusual activity detection approach relies on a minimum acceptable similarity value fixed as the threshold (Roshtkhari & Levine, 2013). Such a single experimentally determined threshold cannot guarantee the detection of genuine anomalies in every context of deployment. In (Rao et al., 2017) an attempt was made towards this objective with the proposal of three context-based adaptive inference mechanisms which adaptively determine the threshold for the given context. Nevertheless, the robustness and performance of the method could be improved through the employment of a single unified inference framework which adapts to change of contexts.

Real-time detection of anomalous events has already been attempted and achieved in some of the works. Nonetheless, there is scope to go beyond this towards the prediction of the anomalous events i.e., early recognition of unfinished unusual activities as opposed to recognition of completed events. This is of particular importance in surveillance applications which are required to prevent crimes and dangerous activities from occurring. Research works have already been presented which speak about prediction of human activities (Ryoo, 2011; Yu, Yuan, & Liu, 2012; Li & Fu, 2014) which can be used as basis for anomalous event prediction.

Diverting to energy constraint in visual sensors, it is well known that the lifetime of battery-operated camera nodes is limited by their energy consumption, which is proportional to the amount of work a VSN node performs i.e., energy required for sensing, processing, and transmitting the data (Marcus & Marques, 2012). Given the large amount images captured by the camera nodes, both processing as well as transmitting them are quite costly in terms of energy as it requires large bandwidth for transmission data. Hence focus is to be laid on developing simple anomaly detection algorithms for the sensors and transmit only the anomalous frames to the centralized location instead of all the captured frames.

Since the data streams recorded and being transmitted are mostly sensitive, they need to be secure throughout when they travel through the network right from their point of capture. However, the security problems and their solutions are unique only for one context and not for all. In turn, the context of deployment depends on the efficiency of the surveillance system. This is another point of consideration for future research. Also, there are other limitations that have been mentioned for some of the approaches in this chapter which can be researched upon further.

REFERENCES

Adam, A., Rivlin, E., Shimshoni, I., & Reinitz, D. (2008). Robust real-time unusual event detection using multiple fixed-location monitors. *IEEE Transactions on Pattern Analysis and Machine Intelligence*, *30*(3), 555–560. doi:10.1109/TPAMI.2007.70825 PMID:18195449

Boiman, O., & Irani, M. (2007). Detecting irregularities in images and in video. *International Journal of Computer Vision*, *74*(1), 17–31. Retrieved from http://www.wisdom.weizmann.ac.il/~vision/Irregularities.html doi:10.1007/s11263-006-0009-9

Cheng, K. W., Chen, Y. T., & Fang, W. H. (2015). Gaussian Process Regression-Based Video Anomaly Detection and Localization With Hierarchical Feature Representation. *IEEE Transactions on Image Processing*, *24*(12), 5288–5301. doi:10.1109/TIP.2015.2479561 PMID:26394423

Computer Vision Pattern Recognition (CVPR). Performance Evaluation of Tracking and Surveillance (PETS). Retrieved from http://www.cvg.rdg.ac.uk/PETS2001 http://www.cvg.rdg.ac.uk/PETS2006

Fisher, R. (2007). BEHAVE: Computer-assisted prescreening of video streams for unusual activities. *The EPSRC project GR S, 98146*. Retrieved from http://homepages.inf.ed.ac.uk/rbf/ BEHAVE/

Gong, S., Loy, C. C., & Xiang, T. (2011). Security and surveillance. In *Visual Analysis of Humans* (pp. 455–472). Springer London. doi:10.1007/978-0-85729-997-0_23

Gorelick, L., Blank, M., Shechtman, E., Irani, M., & Basri, R. (2011, November). Actions as space-time shapes. Retrieved from http://www.wisdom.weizmann.ac.il/~vision/SpaceTimeActions.html

Guo, H., Wu, X., Wang, H., Chen, L., Ou, Y., & Feng, W. (2015, August). A novel approach for global abnormal event detection in multi-camera surveillance system. *Proceedings of the 2015 IEEE International Conference on Information and Automation* (pp. 73-78). doi:10.1109/ICInfA.2015.7279261

Huang, J. Y., & Lee, W. P. (2014). A smart camera network with SVM classifiers for crowd event recognition. *Proceedings of the World Congress on Engineering*.

Idrees, H., Saleemi, I., Seibert, C., & Shah, M. (2013). Multi-source multi-scale counting in extremely dense crowd images. *Proceedings of the IEEE Conference on Computer Vision and Pattern Recognition* (pp. 2547-2554). doi:10.1109/CVPR.2013.329

Iscen, A., Armagan, A., & Duygulu, P. (2014). What is usual in unusual videos? Trajectory snippet histograms for discovering unusualness. *Proceedings of the IEEE Conference on Computer Vision and Pattern Recognition Workshops* (pp. 794-799). doi:10.1109/CVPRW.2014.123

Javan Roshtkhari, M., & Levine, M. D. (2013). Online dominant and anomalous behavior detection in videos. *Proceedings of the IEEE Conference on Computer Vision and Pattern Recognition* (pp. 2611-2618). doi:10.1109/CVPR.2013.337

Laptev, I., & Caputo, B. (2011). Recognition of human actions. Retrieved from http://www.nada.kth.se/cvap/actions/

Li, K., & Fu, Y. (2014). Prediction of human activity by discovering temporal sequence patterns. *IEEE Transactions on Pattern Analysis and Machine Intelligence*, *36*(8), 1644–1657. doi:10.1109/TPAMI.2013.2297321 PMID:26353344

Loy, C. C., Xiang, T., & Gong, S. (2009, September). Modelling Multi-object Activity by Gaussian Processes. Proceedings of BMVC (pp. 1–11).

Mahadevan, V., Li, W., Bhalodia, V., & Vasconcelos, N. (2010, June). Anomaly detection in crowded scenes. Proceedings of CVPR (Vol. 249, p. 250).

Marcus, A., & Marques, O. (2012). An eye on visual sensor networks. *IEEE Potentials*, *31*(2), 38–43. doi:10.1109/MPOT.2011.2178279

Mould, N., Regens, J. L., Jensen, C. J. III, & Edger, D. N. (2014). Video surveillance and counterterrorism: The application of suspicious activity recognition in visual surveillance systems to counterterrorism. *Journal of Policing. Intelligence and Counter Terrorism*, *9*(2), 151–175. doi:10.1080/18335330.2014.940819

Rao, T. N. (2016). A smart visual surveillance system for better crime management. Unpublished master's thesis, National Institute of Technology Karnataka, Surathkal, Karnataka, India.

Rao, T. N., Girish, G. N., & Rajan, J. (2017). An improved contextual information based approach for anomaly detection via adaptive inference for surveillance application. *Proceedings of International Conference on Computer Vision and Image Processing* (pp. 133-147). Springer, Singapore. doi:10.1007/978-981-10-2104-6_13

Roshtkhari, M. J., & Levine, M. D. (2013). An on-line, real-time learning method for detecting anomalies in videos using spatio-temporal compositions. *Computer Vision and Image Understanding, 117*(10), 1436–1452. doi:10.1016/j.cviu.2013.06.007

Ryoo, M. S. (2011). Human activity prediction: Early recognition of ongoing activities from streaming videos. *Proceedings of the 2011 IEEE International Conference on Computer Vision (ICCV)* (pp. 1036-1043). IEEE.

Ryoo, M. S., & Aggarwal, J. K. (2012). UT-Interaction dataset. *ICPR contest on Semantic Description of Human Activities (SDHA)*. Retrieved from http://cvrc.ece.utexas.edu/SDHA2010/HumanInteraction.html

Soro, S., & Heinzelman, W. (2009). A survey of visual sensor networks. *Advances in Multimedia, 2009,* 1–21. doi:10.1155/2009/640386

Unusual crowd activity dataset. (n. d.). University of Minnesota. Retrieved from http://mha.cs.umn.edu/movies/crowdactivity-all.avi.5

Vezzani, R., & Cucchiara, R. (2010). Video surveillance online repository (visor): An integrated framework. *Multimedia Tools and Applications, 50*(2), 359–380. Retrieved from http://www.openvisor.org doi:10.1007/s11042-009-0402-9

Wang, X., Ma, X., & Grimson, W. E. L. (2009). Unsupervised activity perception in crowded and complicated scenes using hierarchical bayesian models. *IEEE Transactions on Pattern Analysis and Machine Intelligence, 31*(3), 539–555. doi:10.1109/TPAMI.2008.87 PMID:19147880

Wiliem, A., Madasu, V., Boles, W., & Yarlagadda, P. (2012). A suspicious behaviour detection using a context space model for smart surveillance systems. *Computer Vision and Image Understanding, 116*(2), 194–209. doi:10.1016/j.cviu.2011.10.001

Xu, J., Denman, S., Fookes, C., & Sridharan, S. (2011, December). Unusual event detection in crowded scenes using bag of LBPs in spatio-temporal patches. *Proceedings of the 2011 International Conference on Digital Image Computing Techniques and Applications (DICTA)* (pp. 549-554). doi:10.1109/DICTA.2011.98

Xu, J., Denman, S., Fookes, C., & Sridharan, S. (2015, April). Detecting rare events using Kullback-Leibler divergence. *Proceedings of the 2015 IEEE International Conference on Acoustics, Speech and Signal Processing (ICASSP)* (pp. 1305-1309). doi:10.1109/ICASSP.2015.7178181

Yu, G., Yuan, J., & Liu, Z. (2012, October). Predicting human activities using spatio-temporal structure of interest points. *Proceedings of the 20th ACM international conference on Multimedia* (pp. 1049-1052). ACM. doi:10.1145/2393347.2396380

Yuan, J., Liu, Z., & Wu, Y. (2011). Discriminative video pattern search for efficient action detection. *IEEE Transactions on Pattern Analysis and Machine Intelligence, 33*(9), 1728–1743. Retrieved from http://research.microsoft.com/en-us/um/people/zliu/actionrecorsrc/ doi:10.1109/TPAMI.2011.38 PMID:21339530

Zaharescu, A., & Wildes, R. (2010, September). Anomalous behaviour detection using spatiotemporal oriented energies, subset inclusion histogram comparison and event-driven processing. In European Conference on Computer Vision (pp. 563–576). Springer Berlin Heidelberg. Retrieved from http://www.cse.yorku.ca/vision/research/spatiotemporal-anomalous-behavior.shtml doi:10.1007/978-3-642-15549-9_41

Zhao, B., Fei-Fei, L., & Xing, E. P. (2011, June). Online detection of unusual events in videos via dynamic sparse coding. *Proceedings of the 2011 IEEE Conference on Computer Vision and Pattern Recognition (CVPR)* (pp. 3313-3320). doi:10.1109/CVPR.2011.5995524

Zhong, H., Shi, J., & Visontai, M. (2004, June). Detecting unusual activity in video. *Proceedings of the 2004 IEEE Computer Society Conference on Computer Vision and Pattern Recognition CVPR '04* (*Vol. 2*, pp. 819-826).

Zhou, S., Shen, W., Zeng, D., & Zhang, Z. (2015, April). Unusual event detection in crowded scenes by trajectory analysis. *Proceedings of the 2015 IEEE International Conference on Acoustics, Speech and Signal Processing (ICASSP)* (pp. 1300-1304). doi:10.1109/ICASSP.2015.7178180

Chapter 2

Approaches for Image Database Retrieval Based on Color, Texture, and Shape Features

Kratika Arora
Sant Longowal Institute of Engineering and Technology, India

Ashwani Kumar Aggarwal
Sant Longowal Institute of Engineering and Technology, India

ABSTRACT

With an ever-increasing use and demand for digital imagery in the areas of medicine, sciences, and engineering, image retrieval is an active research area in image processing and pattern recognition. Content-based image retrieval (CBIR) is a method of finding images from a huge image database according to persons' interests. Content-based here means that the search involves analysis of the actual content present in the image. As the database of images is growing day by day, researchers/scholars are searching for better techniques for retrieval of images with good efficiency. This chapter first gives an overview of the various image retrieval systems. Then, the applications of CBIR in various fields and existing CBIR systems are described. The various image content descriptors and extraction methods are also explained. The main motive of the chapter is to study and compare the features that are used in Content Based Image Retrieval system and conclude on the system that retrieves images from a huge database with good precision and recall.

INTRODUCTION

The extensive use of digital images is on rise with each passing day, fuelled by the rapid expansion of digital image content in today's world of internet. Professionals of different fields are trying to make use of the opportunity to distantly access and manipulate stored images for providing better service to the clients. Professions such as advertising, engineering, law enforcement, fashion designing, graphic designing, medicine, crime prevention, publishing and architectural designing are making extensive use of digital image databases for maintaining record of images and use them when necessary. This leads

DOI: 10.4018/978-1-5225-2848-7.ch002

to demand of a system that can rapidly and effectively retrieve images which are similar and are also relevant. For many years, researchers have been working on the retrieval processes. Hence the image retrieval systems are used for searching, browsing and retrieving images from large image databases. These image retrieval systems can be classified into three categories.

- Keyword Based Image Retrieval (KBIR)
- Content Based Image Retrieval (CBIR)
- Semantic Based Image Retrieval (SBIR)

Keyword Based Image Retrieval uses metadata such as notes, keywords, remarks, annotations, tags, captions, or descriptions linked with the image. These descriptions are man-made and are very subjective. Moreover manual addition of tags in each image is time-consuming, tedious and error prone as image description may vary from person to person. Also, it may not provide the whole information describing the image (Gong et al., 1994). For example, if the image contains an object such as a bus or a car, the user uses his knowledge and adds tags describing the type, the model name, the size and the color. In this case there may be some details which can be missed like object orientation or surrounding objects. Hence the image search initiated using keyword based retrieval system leads to the image retrieval problem wherein the search results may be irrelevant and are not acceptable.

The Content Based Image Retrieval uses an advanced approach compared to Keyword Based Image Retrieval systems (Zhang et al., 2003). In these systems, a query image is given as an input and images similar to the query image are retrieved from the stored database according to persons' interest. Content based here means that the search involves the actual content present in the image which can be color, texture, shape or any other useful information that can be obtained from the image. In traditional content based image retrieval systems, the visual content of the images in the database are extracted and described by multi-dimensional feature vectors. Here features used can be low level or high level. The low-level features are based on the global image statistics. Since these features are determined for the complete image, they do not separate the items from the background. Hence, they produce good results when queried for the same image or most similar image like pictures having slight variation, modified by adding some text or a frame. When the query demands on finding images containing the same or similar objects, low level features are not sufficient and the high-level feature algorithms are needed. An example of this system is shown in the Figure 1 and 2. Figure 1 is the query image given by the user and Figure 2 is the retrieved images using content based image retrieval system.

Figure 1. Query image

Figure 2. Retrieved images of content based image retrieval system

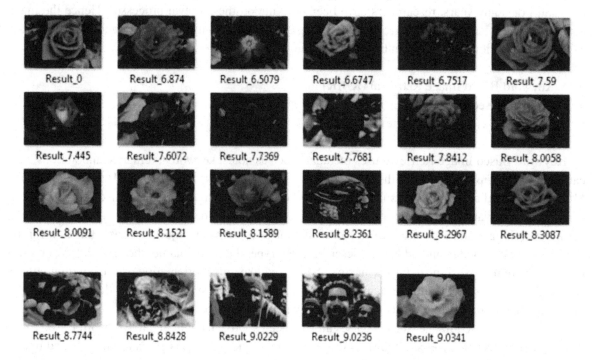

Semantic-Based Image Retrieval uses the combination of the above retrieval methods; keyword based image retrieval and content based image retrieval and merges textual keywords with image features. There is a gap between the image description by some algorithm and a human perception known as semantic gap (Singh et al., 2012). SBIR methods use phrases i.e. short sentence instead of simple or one line keywords. For example, "find the bright sky images" instead of following keywords: "white," "sun," "orange." Mostly the semantic features are extracted from the image features and text is transformed into semantic features. They are further mapped onto semantics of database images.

Objective

The main motive of the chapter is to study the features that are used in Content Based Image Retrieval system and conclude on the system that retrieves images from a huge database as per user's requirements with good precision, recall and F1-measure. Also, to compare and analyze various color, texture and shape feature extraction methods.

Applications of CBIR

There is a wide range of applications for CBIR technology identified by many researchers (Eakins & Graham, 1999). Substantial uses include engineering and architectural design, crime prevention, journalism, advertising, fashion and interior design, the military, medical diagnosis, education and training, geographical information and remote sensing systems, face finding, web searching, etc.

A close look at many of these areas reveal that the research groups are developing systems, and at the same time practitioners are experimenting with the technology, yet few examples of fully operational CBIR systems can be found. The current state of play in each of the application areas is as follows.

Crime Prevention

All the lawyers and advocates working in law enforcement agencies generally maintain files of visual evidence, including past suspects' fingerprints, facial photographs (known as mugshots), and shoeprints (Wen & Yu, 2005). Whenever some crime is committed, they can compare the evidence from the crime scene with record in their archive files for its similarity. This can be treated as an example of identity instead of similarity matching, though all such images vary naturally with time, the discrimination is of less importance. Practically more relevant is difference between systems designed for verifying the identity of a known person and those capable of searching an entire database to find the closest matching record.

Engineering and Architectural Design

Engineering and architectural design shares many number of similar features. The use of stylized two dimensional(2D) and three dimensional(3D) models to represent design objects, the need to visualize designs for the benefit of non-technical clients and the need to work within externally-imposed constraints, often financial. Such constraints mean that the designer should be aware of the previous designs, particularly if these can be adapted to the problem at hand (Chen, 2006). Hence to search design archives for previous examples which are similar or meet specified suitability criteria is valuable.

Journalism and Advertising

Newspapers and certain stock shot agencies keep repository of photographs to demonstrate advertising copy or articles. These repositories can be large and expensive to maintain if detailed keyword indexing and retrieval is provided. Broadcasting corporations face even a bigger problem of dealing with thousands of hours of archive video footage, which are very difficult to annotate without automatic assistance. This area is one of the prime importance of CBIR technology, though not in the form originally envisaged. In the early development years of CBIR technology, there were high hopes that the technology would provide efficient and effective retrieval of still images from photo libraries, eliminating or reducing the need for manual keyword indexing. Disillusionment set in as it was realized that the CBIR techniques under development are of little significance for retrieval by semantic content. In stock shot agencies, the retrieval systems are most likely based on manual key wording for many years, though a few are experimenting with the use of CBIR software instead of keyword indexing.

Fashion and Interior Design

Similarities can also be seen in the other fields, including fashion and interior design (Ward, 2008). In this, again the designer has to work within externally-imposed constraints, such as selection of materials. The ability to search a group of fabrics to find a combination of color or texture is increasingly recognized as a useful aid to the design process. So far very less development activity has been reported in this area. Several attempts are made to use general-purpose CBIR packages for specific tasks such as matching color of items from electronic versions of mail-order catalogues and identifying textile samples bearing a desired pattern but no commercial use is made at present.

Military

Applications of imaging technology in military are best developed, though least publicized. Examples include recognition of enemy aircraft from radar screens, identification of targets from satellite photographs and provision of guidance systems for cruise missiles (Dufaux et al., 2007). Though these almost certainly represent only limited examples, many of the surveillance techniques used in crime prevention can also be relevant with respect to the military field.

It can be concluded that application of CBIR lies in all fields where one needs to find an image of his interest from a large image repository. Because of its demand, it is still one of the most active research areas in image processing and researchers are still finding ways to develop an effective and accurate image retrieval system that can be used for images of all classes.

Existing CBIR Systems

From historical perspective, first use of CBIR goes back to Kato, 1992 in early nineties where he implemented the first automated image retrieval system using color and shape features. Since Kato's pioneer work many prototypes of CBIR systems have been developed, and some of them have been used in the commercial market. Some of the existing CBIR systems have been explained below.

Google Search by Image

With Google's search by image tool, user can now begin search with an actual image seen on the web or on the computer to search for similar images or to find out more information about that specific image instead of searching image with a word or a phrase. After the image has been uploaded the search results will be displayed. Google attempts to find the original creator of the image based on search results and also displays images that are visually similar. This can also be very helpful for finding additional images for a similar set. Beneath the similar image results, it also gives a list of pages that have the same image on them. This image retrieval tool is widely used by students and professionals of all fields. However, it is not very accurate as it gives irrelevant images in the search result.

Multimedia Analysis and Retrieval Systems (MARS)

The MARS project at the University of Illinois is integrated relevance feedback architecture for content based image retrieval. This is an interactive image retrieval system that achieves the relevance feedback at all levels: feature representation and similarity measure. The person's query is automatically refined by the retrieval system based on user's relevance feedback (Huang et al., 1997).

Surfimage

This is an example of European CBIR technology from INRIA, France by Nastar, 1998. It works similar to the MARS system, using multiple types of image feature which can be combined in different ways. It also offers sophisticated users' relevance feedback facilities.

QBIC(TM)

With the on-line collections of images growing larger day by day, more tools are needed to efficiently organize, manage and navigate through them. Due to this need IBM has developed a system called Query by Image Content (QBIC) which allows queries of large image databases based on visual image content using properties such as percentage of color, color layout and textures occurring in the images. These queries use the visual properties of images, so anyone can match colors, textures and their positions without describing images in words. But for example, a query using a blue bus on a yellow background will match a yellow bird on a similar blue background. So, often content based queries are combined with keyword, tags and text to get a powerful retrieval method for image database.

VisualSEEk

It is a highly functional system for searching images by visual features from an image database. The VisualSEEk system is novel since the user forms the queries by spatial arrangements of color regions. The system finds the images that contain the most similar arrangements of similar regions. Prior to the queries, the system automatically extracts and indexes salient color regions from the images. By utilizing efficient indexing techniques, region sizes and relative spatial locations, a variety of complex joint color/spatial queries may be computed.

It can be seen that there are various CBIR systems which are used in the commercial market and still it is an emerging topic of the era since its application lies in various domain.

Working of CBIR

In a simple CBIR system shown in Figure 3, to retrieve images user gives the retrieval system example images or sketched figures called as query. The system then transforms these examples into its internal representation called as feature vectors. For the similarity measure/distance measure, distances between the feature vectors of the query or sketch and those of the images in the database are then computed. Commonly used similarity measures are Euclidean distance, Manhattan distance, Canberra distance. After the distance measure the retrieval is performed with the help of an indexing scheme. The indexing scheme provides a proficient way to search for the image database. In order to generate perceptually and semantically more meaningful retrieval results, recent retrieval systems have incorporated users' relevance feedback to modify the retrieval process. The success of the CBIR system depends mainly on the approach used to extract the image features as well as the distance metrics used for finding the similarity measure between the query image and the images in the database. Also, studies made on experiments show that the method based on the combination of one or more features has higher retrieval accuracy than the other methods based on single feature extraction.

Figure 3. Block diagram of CBIR

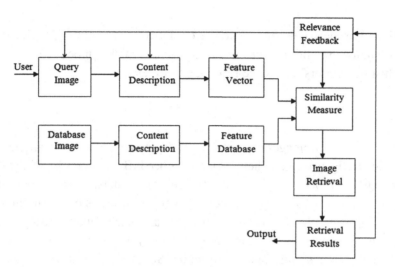

Image Content Descriptors

In an image descriptors are the initial step for finding the similarity between the pixels contained in a digital image and what humans recall after observing that image. Image content includes both visual and semantic content. Visual content can be very general or domain specific. General visual content includes color, texture, shape, spatial relationship, etc. Domain specific visual content like human faces is application dependent and may involve domain knowledge. Semantic content is obtained either by textual annotation or by complex inference procedures based on visual content. A good visual content descriptor should be invariant to the accidental variance introduced by the imaging process for example the variation of the illuminant of the scene. These visual content descriptors namely color, texture and shape are called low level features whereas objects like car, chair, camera, book, etc., present in an image are called as high level features. The general visual content descriptors or the low-level features are described below.

Color

The use of color in an image retrieval process is motivated by certain factors. Firstly color (Swain & Ballard, 1991) is a very dominant descriptor that simplifies the process of object recognition and extraction from an image or a scene. Secondly capability of humans to perceive thousands of color shades and intensities, compared to about only two dozen shades of gray. Color features are comparatively easy to extract and are valuable for indexing and searching of color images from image databases.

Types of Color Model

One of the important facets before applying any color extraction method is the selection of color model. A color model is a specification of a coordinate system in which each color is represented by a single point. There is no agreement on which is the best. However, one of the desirable characteristics of an appropriate color space for image retrieval is, it should be uniform (Mathias, 1998) which means that the measured proximity between the colors must have a direct relation with the psychological similarity among them. The various color models used in image retrieval systems are explained below.

RGB Color Model

RGB model is a widely used color model for image display based on the Cartesian coordinate system. Each color in RGB model appears as primary spectral components of Red, Green and Blue. All colors in this model are points on or inside the cube and are defined by the vectors extending from origin. Figure 4 is the schematic of RGB color model. Primary colors i.e. red, green and blue are at three corners of the cube. Secondary colors i.e. cyan, magenta and yellow are at the other three corners. Black is at the origin and white is at the corner farthest from the origin. Points of equal RGB values (gray scale) extend from black to white along the line joining these two points.

HSV Color Model

In HSV color model three color components are Hue, Saturation and Value (brightness). Figure. 5 is the schematic of HSV color model in which hue is an attribute associated with the dominant wavelength in a mixture of light waves. It represents the dominant or pure color perceived by an observer. Calling an object red, yellow or pink, is specifying hue. Saturation means relative purity or the amount of white light mixed with hue. Pure spectrum colors like red and green are fully saturated whereas colors such as pink which is a mixture of red and white are less saturated. Brightness embodies the achromatic notion of intensity and is one of the main factors for color sensation. HSV color model is widely used in image processing; hence other models are converted to HSV before processing.

Figure 4. Schematic of RGB color model

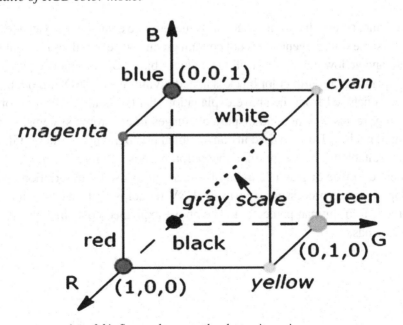

For a more accurate representation of this figure, please see the electronic version.

Figure 5. Schematic of HSV color model

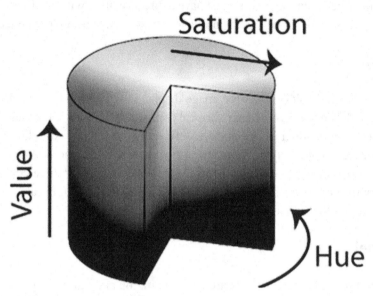

For a more accurate representation of this figure, please see the electronic version.

CMY/CMYK Color Model

In CMY color model three color components are secondary colors: Cyan, Magenta and Yellow. Figure 6 gives the schematic of CMY/CMYK color model. This color model is primarily used for printing purpose. Conversion from RGB to CMY is a very easy process which can be performed by the Equation 1.1.

$$[CMY] = 1 - [RGB] \tag{1.1}$$

This equation demonstrates that light reflected from a surface coated with cyan does not contain red (i.e. C=1-R). In the same way, magenta does not contain green and yellow does not contain blue. Adding the cyan, magenta and yellow colors for printing produces black. So, to produce pure black which is a dominant color in printing, a fourth color black is added giving rise to CMYK model.

Thus, it can be concluded from the above explanation that the main application of the RGB color model is for sensing, representation, and display of images in electronic systems, such as computers and televisions though it has also been used in conventional photography. Further, RGB and CMY color models are ideally suitable for hardware implementation purpose. RGB color model is used for image capture by a camera or image display in a monitor screen but its use for description of color is limited. Hence for developing image processing algorithms HSV model is preferred which describes color in terms that are practical for human perception. The above explained color models are used in various color extraction methods.

Figure 6. Schematic of CMY/CMYK color model

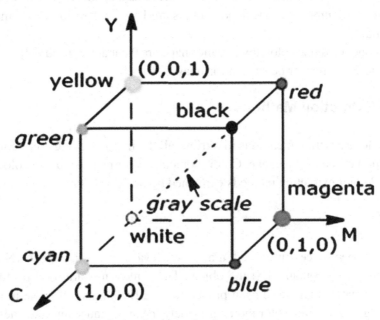

*For a more accurate representation of this figure, please see the electronic version.

Texture

Texture is another content descriptor which is visual and gives the tactile quality of a surface (Chang & Kuo, 1993). It contains information about the structural arrangement of the pixels and their relation to the surrounding pixel. It is the property of virtually all surfaces including flowers, bricks, skin, fabric, etc. There are three levels at which texture analysis can be discussed: On the structural level, texture is the primitives of the image and their placement rules. On a statistical level, a set of statistics value extracted from the image. On the spectral level, set of coefficients in the transform domain is texture. With the aid of above levels the texture can be identified but it may not agree with the human perception of evaluating the texture. Reasons for this include semantic gap and human perception. Statistical methods include Fourier power spectra, Tamura feature, co-occurrence matrices, shift-invariant principal component analysis, Wold decomposition and M-resolution filtering techniques such as Gabor and wavelet transform, describes texture by the statistical distribution of the image intensity.

Shape

The third feature shape can also be used for the image retrieval process (Tegolo, 1994). Shape of an image may not refer to the shape of an image but to the shape of some particular area or object in the image. Depending on the application, sometimes user requires the shape representation to be invariable to rotation, translation and scaling. Shape features of objects or areas have been used in many CBIR systems. Unlike color and texture features, shape features are generally described after image has been segmented into parts or objects. Shape features are categorized as area based and boundary based. Boundary based uses only the outer boundary of the shape whereas area-based shape features use entire shape area. The shape is represented through clubbed geometric cues such as corners, joints and polygonal areas extracted from an image. Such a clubbing may serve as a spatial layout or as a rough sketch by additional processing. Commonly used shape features are Fourier descriptors, moment invariants and edge based histogram.

Thus, it can be concluded that color, texture and shape are the features used for describing the content of the image and these can further be exploit for image retrieval.

Color Feature Extraction Methods

The objective of color extraction method is to retrieve all the images having color composition same as the color composition of the query image. Color moments, color histogram and color coherence vector are the widely-used color extraction methods explained below.

Color Moments

Color moments have been successfully used in many retrieval systems like QBIC (Niblack et al., 1993) especially when the image contains just the object. These measures are used to differentiate images based on their color features and have been proved to be efficient and effective in representing color distributions of images. The three color moment namely mean, variance and skewness are used for image retrieval. These can be determined globally for the complete image or locally by dividing an image into sub-blocks. Mathematically, these three moments are defined as:

$$\mu_{r,i} = \frac{1}{N} \sum_{j=1}^{N} I_{i,j} \tag{1.2}$$

$$\sigma_{r,i} = \sqrt{\frac{1}{N} \sum_{j=1}^{N} \left(I_{i,j} - \mu_{r,i} \right)^2} \tag{1.3}$$

$$\acute{A}_{r,i} = \sqrt[3]{\frac{1}{N} \sum_{j=1}^{N} \left(I_{i,j} - \mu_{r,i} \right)^3} \tag{1.4}$$

where N represents number of pixels present in an image and I_{ij} represents the value of ith color component for the image pixel j and $\mu_{r,i}$, $\sigma_{r,i}$ and $\rho_{r,i}$ are the mean, variance and skewness of ith color component of region r respectively. Using the 3rd order moment in addition i.e. skewness, compared to using only the 1st and 2nd order moments improves the performance. But sometimes it makes the representation more sensitive to illumination changes, decreasing the overall performance.

Since, only nine numbers (three moments for each of the three color components) are used to represent the color content of every image, color moments becomes a compact representation compared to all other color methods. To overcome this instead of finding moments for the whole image, the image can be partitioned into regions and moments for each region can be computed.

Color Histogram

Histogram gives the distribution of number of pixels present in an image (Brunelli & Mich, 2011). These are easier in computation and are effective in describing both the local and global colour distribution in an image. For huge image database, histogram comparison saturates the discrimination. For solving such problem, the joint histogram technique can be used. As the colour histogram doesn't takes spatial information into account, thus different images can have similar color histogram. This problem becomes especially acute for large databases. To increase the discrimination power, many improvements are designed to consider spatial information. A simple approach includes dividing an image into sub-parts and computing the histogram for every sub-part separately. This division can be simple as vertical or horizontal partition, or as complex as an area or even object segmentation. Also, increase in the no. of sub-parts increases the information content and also the memory and computational time at the same time.

Color Coherence Vector

Pass and Zabith, 1996 used a different way of incorporating spatial information into the color histogram, introducing color coherence vectors (CCV). In this each histogram bin was partitioned into two types, i.e. coherent if it belongs to a large uniformly-colored region or incoherent if it does not. Let α_i denote the number of coherent pixels in the ith color bin and β_i denote the number of incoherent pixels in an image. Then, the CCV of the image is defined as the vector: $(\alpha_1, \beta_1), (\alpha_2, \beta_2), ..., (\alpha_N, \beta_N)$. Here $(\alpha_1 + \beta_1), (\alpha_2 + \beta_2), ..., (\alpha_N + \beta_N)$ is the color histogram of the image. It has been shown that CCV provides better retrieval results than the color histogram, especially for images which have either mostly uniform color or mostly texture regions due to its additional spatial information. In addition, for both the color histogram and color coherence vector representation, the HSV color space provides better results than any other color spaces.

Texture Feature Extraction Methods

In texture extraction methods, the image in the database whose texture is similar to the query image is retrieved. The various texture extraction methods are Gabor filter, Haar wavelet, and gray level co-occurrence matrix. In the following section, Gabor filter features and Haar wavelet transforms for extraction of texture are discussed.

Gabor Filter Features

Dimai, 1999 used the Gabor filter to extract features of image, especially the texture features. It is optimal in minimization of the joint uncertainty in frequency and in space and is often used as a scale and orientation tunable edge and bar/line detector. There are many approaches which are designed to characterize texture of images based on Gabor filters.

A two- dimensional Gabor function is:

$$g\left(x,y\right)=\frac{1}{2\pi\sigma_x\sigma_y}\exp\left[-\frac{1}{2}\left[\left(\frac{x}{\sigma_X}\right)^2+\left(\frac{y}{\sigma_y}\right)^2\right]+2\pi jWx\right] \qquad (1.5)$$

where, σ_x and σ_y represents the standard deviations of Gaussian envelopes along the x and y direction respectively. A list of Gabor filters is obtained by appropriate rotations and dilations of g(x, y):

$$g_{mn}\left(x,y\right)=a^{-m}g\left(x'-y'\right) \qquad (1.6)$$

$$x'=a^{-m}\left(x\cos\theta+y\sin\theta\right) \qquad (1.7)$$

$$y'=a^{-m}\left(-x\sin\theta+y\cos\theta\right) \qquad (1.8)$$

the number of orientations and scales. The scale factor a-m ensures that energy is independent of m.

Given an image I(x´, y´), its Gabor transform is defined as:

$$W_{mn}\left(x',y'\right)=\int I\left(x',y'\right)*g_{mn}\left(x'-x1,y'-y1\right)dx'dy' \qquad (1.9)$$

where * is complex conjugate. Mean μ_{mn} and standard deviation σ_{mn} of |Wmn | is f given by:

f = [μ_{00}, σ_{00}, …, μ_{mn}, σ_{mn},] which represents the texture feature vector of the image.

Haar Wavelet Transforms

Wavelets give a multi-resolution approach for texture classification and analysis. For a two-dimensional (2D) image, wavelet transform computation applies recursive filtering and sampling. At every sub level, the image is decomposed into four frequency sub-bands, LL, HH, HL, and LH where H is the high frequency and L is the low frequency. Let a data set X1, X2, …, Xn contain M elements, so there will be M/2 averages and M/2 wavelet coefficient values. The average is stored in the 1st half of the M element array and the coefficient is stored in the 2nd half of the M element array. The averages are the input in the next step in the calculation. For a 1D Haar transform of an array of M elements, determine the average of every pair, and find the difference between every pair and divide it by 2. Now fill the 1st half with the averages, the 2nd half of the array with coefficients. Repeat the process till a single average and a single coefficient are determined. For a 2D Haar transform, compute 1D Haar wavelet decomposition for every row of the original pixel values, then compute1D Haar wavelet decomposition for every column of the row-transformed pixels. RGB components are extracted from the images. Now apply the 2D Haar transform to every color matrix.

A feature vector is determined from every image present in the database. Set of all the features is organized in a database index. When similar image has to be searched with a query image, a feature vector is again extracted from the query image and is then matched against the feature vectors in the index.

Measure between feature representation of the query image and feature representation of the database image is determined if it is small, then it is considered similar. In this way, Haar wavelet can be used for matching images from the database.

Shape Feature Extraction Methods

Shape is also one of the features that can be used for the images having similar or most similar shape. Commonly used shape feature extraction methods namely Fourier descriptors and edge based histogram are discussed below.

Fourier Descriptors

It describes the shape of an area or object with Fourier transform of its edge or boundary. Considering the contour of a 2D object as a sequence of successive pixels (x_s, y_s), where $0 \le s \le N\text{-}1$ and N is the no. of pixels in the boundary. Then the three types of contour representations centroid distance, curvature and complex coordinate function can be defined. The distance between boundary pixels and the centroid (x_c, y_c) of the object is centroid distance given by:

$$R(s) = \sqrt{\left(x_s - x_c\right)^2 + \left(y_s - y_c\right)^2} \qquad (1.10)$$

The curvature C(s) at a point 's' along the contour is the rate of change in tangent direction of the contour having $\theta(s)$ as turning function of the contour, given by:

$$C(s) = \frac{d}{ds}\theta(s) \qquad (1.11)$$

The complex coordinate is obtained by representing coordinates of the boundary pixels as complex numbers given by:

$$Z(s) = \left(x_s - x_c\right) + j\left(y_s - y_c\right) \qquad (1.12)$$

The Fourier transforms of these three types of contour representations generates three sets of complex coefficients, representing the shape in the frequency domain. Lower frequency coefficients signify the general shape while higher frequency coefficients signify shape details. For achieving rotation invariance, only the amplitudes of the complex coefficient are used and the phase component is discarded. For scale invariance, the amplitude of the coefficient is divided by the amplitude of DC component or the first non-zero coefficient. The translation invariance is obtained directly from the contour representation.

The Fourier descriptor of the curvature is given by:

$$F_K = \left[|\,F_1\,|,|\,F_2\,|,|\,F_3\,|,|\,F_4\,|\right] \qquad (1.13)$$

The Fourier descriptor of the centroid distance is given by:

$$f_R = \left[\left| \frac{F_1}{F_0} \right|, \left| \frac{F_2}{F_0} \right|, \ldots, \left| \frac{F_{\frac{M}{2}}}{F_0} \right| \right] \tag{1.14}$$

where Fi represents ith component of Fourier transform coefficients. Since the curvature and centroid distance functions are real, only the positive frequency axes are considered. The Fourier descriptor of the complex coordinate is given by:

$$f_Z = \left[\left| \frac{F_{-\left(\frac{M}{2}-1\right)}}{F_1} \right|, \left| \frac{F_{-1}}{F_1} \right|, \left| \frac{F_2}{F_1} \right|, \ldots, \left| \frac{F_{\frac{M}{2}}}{F_1} \right| \right] \tag{1.15}$$

where F_1 is the first non-zero frequency component used for normalizing the transform coefficients.

Edge Based Histogram

Edges in images make up a salient feature for representation of their content. Also, the human eyes are receptive to edge features for image perception. One way to represent such an important edge feature is using histogram. An edge orientation histogram represents the frequency and the directionality of the brightness changes in the image. The basic idea is to build a histogram with the directions of the gradients of the edges (borders or contours).

Similarity Measurement

Instead of exact matching, content-based image retrieval determines the visual similarities between a query image and images in database. Hence the retrieval result is not a single image but a list of images ranked by their similarities with the query image. Many similarity measures have been developed for image retrieval based on empirical estimates of the distribution of features in recent years. Different similarity/distance measure affects the retrieval performance of an image retrieval system significantly. Commonly used similarity measures are given below:

Euclidean Distance

If each dimension of image feature vector is independent of each other and is of equal importance, the Euclidean distance or L2 norm is appropriate for calculating the distance between two images. The Euclidean distance EuDist(A, B) is defined as:

$$EuDist(A, B) = \sqrt{\sum_{i=1}^{n} \left(A_i - B_i \right)^2} \tag{1.16}$$

where, A_i denotes the ith element of feature vector A of query image and B_i denotes the ith element of feature vector B of images in database each of dimension n. It is the most widely used metric for image retrieval. For instance, MARS system used Euclidean distance to compute the similarity between texture features.

Manhattan Distance

The Manhattan distance or L1 norm is also known as city block metric. It is another widely used distance measure in image processing given by mathematical expression below:

$$ManDist\left(A, B\right) = \sum_{i=1}^{n} \mid X_i - B_i \mid \tag{1.17}$$

where, ManDist(A, B) denotes Manhattan distance, Ai denotes the ith element of feature vector A of query image and Bi denotes the ith element of feature vector B of images in database each of dimension n.

Canberra Distance

The Canberra distance is another measure used for similarity comparison. It allows the feature set to be in unnormalized form. The Canberra distance CanDis(A, B) is defined as:

$$CanDis\left(A, B\right) = \sum_{i=1}^{n} \frac{\mid A_i \mid - \mid B_i \mid}{\mid A_i \mid + \mid B_i \mid} \tag{1.18}$$

where, A_i denotes the ith element of feature vector A of query image and B_i denotes the ith element of feature vector B of images in database each of dimension n.

Performance Indices

The performance of the CBIR system is evaluated in terms of performance parameters namely precision, recall and F1-measure. These performance indices can be defined with the help of data in the confusion matrix as explained in the following.

Confusion Matrix

A confusion matrix is a table that is often used to describe the performance of a retrieval system on a set of test data for which the true values are known. The following table gives the confusion matrix.

Table 1. Confusion Matrix

Images	Relevant	Irrelevant
Retrieved	True Positive (Tp)	False Positive (Fp)
Not Retrieved	False Negative (Fn)	True Negative (Tn)

Here, Tp represents the number of relevant images that are retrieved, Fp represents the number of irrelevant images that are retrieved, Fn represents the number of relevant images that are not retrieved and Tn represents the number of irrelevant images that are not retrieved by the system.

Precision

Precision is one of the main parameter to evaluate the performance of the retrieval system. It is defined as the fraction retrieved that is relevant. It measures the ability of the system to retrieve only the models that are relevant. It can be computed in terms of Tp and Fn given in confusion matrix using Equation 1.19.

$$(P) = \frac{\text{Number of relevant images retrieved}}{\text{Total number of images retrieved}} = \frac{T_p}{T_p + F_p} \times 100\% \qquad (1.19)$$

Recall

Recall is defined as the fraction relevant that is retrieved. It measures the ability of the system to retrieve all the models that are relevant. It can be computed in terms of Tp and Fn given in confusion matrix using Equation 1.20.

$$(R) = \frac{\text{Number of relevant images retrieved}}{\text{Total number of relevant images in database}} = \frac{T_p}{2T_p + F_p} \times 100\% \qquad (1.20)$$

Precision equal to 100% means nothing but the whole truth and recall equal to 100% means the whole truth.

F1-Measure

F1 measure is also used for evaluating the performance of the image retrieval system. It is defined as the weighted harmonic mean of precision and recall given by Equation 1.21.

$$F1 = \frac{2 \times P \times R}{P + R} \qquad (1.21)$$

Discussion

There are various techniques developed which are used in image retrieval systems. The developed techniques are tested on database of 1000 images consisting of 10 categories with each category consisting of 100 images picked randomly from Wang database. The experiments can be performed in two ways. In the first case single feature extraction method is applied i.e. only color, texture and shape. In the second case experiments are performed using combination of the three techniques. Results are captured in both the cases and performance of the system is determined. It can be seen from Equation 19 that precision increases, as number of images retrieved decreases and from Equation 20 that recall increases, as number of relevant images in the database decreases. The comparative study of the methods based on the previous research papers is shown below.

The first system by Lai in 2011, used a user-oriented approach based on interactive genetic algorithm. Color attributes, the entropy based on the gray level co-occurrence matrix and the edge histogram of an image were used. Furthermore, to reduce the gap between the retrieval results and the users' expectation, the IGA was employed to help the users identify the images that are most satisfied to the users' need. In the second system by Malik in 2012, combination of quantized histogram texture in DCT domain were used. The statistical texture features were extracted from quantized histogram in the DCT domain using only DC and first three AC coefficients of the DCT blocks of an image having more information. In the

Table 2. Average of Precision Value

Class	2011 Lai et al.	2012 Malik et al.	2013 Bounthanh et al.
Africans	61	92	90
Beach	93	86	90
Building	85	68	85
Buses	71	89	100
Dinosaurs	100	100	100
Elephants	80	76	90
Flowers	82	100	100
Horses	79	93	100
Mountains	56	47	70
Food	99	66	85
Average	80.6	81.7	91.0

Table 3. Average of Recall Value

Class	2011 Lai et al.	2012 Malik et al.	2013 Bounthanh et al.
Africans	12	18	18
Beach	18	17	18
Building	17	16	19
Buses	14	18	20
Dinosaurs	20	20	20
Elephants	16	15	18
Flowers	16	20	20
Horses	15	18	20
Mountains	11	9	14
Food	19	13	17
Average	15.8	16.4	18.4

third system by Bounthanh in 2013 combination of all three i.e. color, shape and texture features were used to achieve higher retrieval efficiency. The color feature was extracted by quantifying the YUV color space and the color attributes like the mean value, the standard deviation, and the image bitmap of YUV color space was represented. The texture features were obtained by the entropy based on the gray level cooccurrence matrix and the edge histogram descriptor of an

image. The shape feature descriptor was derived from Fourier descriptors (FDs) and the FDs derived from different signatures. When computing the similarity between the query image and target image in the database, normalization information distance was used for adjusting distance values into the same level. And then the linear combination was used to combine the normalized distance of the color, shape and texture features to obtain the similarity as the indexing of image. It can be seen from the table that in the third system in which combination of color, texture and shape is used, precision and recall are better than the first and second system. Furthermore, experimental results also indicated that a weight variation achieved higher retrieval efficiency.

Limitation

There are various other areas to work with for the further improvement of the content based image retrieval systems. The existing techniques may be used to improve the quality of image retrieval and the understanding of user intentions. An approach that combines two different approaches to image retrieval, together with active use of context information and interaction can further be used. The problem of bridging the semantic gap between high level query which is normally in terms of an example image and low level features of an image such as color, texture, shape and object force to apply techniques to reduce the semantic gap. The image retrieval methods in this chapter have used WANG database. The methods can be tested on different database. Also, the research is limited to feature based, it can be extended to other enhanced high level features.

Content Based Image Retrieval in Medical Imaging

Content Based Image Retrieval in medical is one of the major areas in Computer Vision and Image Processing. CBIR can be used to locate radiology images in large radiology image databases. Medical images are usually fused, subject to high inconsistency and composed of different minor structures. So there is a necessity for feature extraction and classification of images for easy and efficient retrieval. Every day large volumes of different types of medical images such as dental, endoscopy, skull, MRI, ultrasound, radiology are produced in various hospitals as well as in various medical centers. Medical image retrieval has many significant applications especially in medical diagnosis, education and research fields. Medical image retrieval for diagnostic purposes is important because the historical images of different patients in medical centers have valuable information for the upcoming diagnosis with a system which retrieves similar cases, making diagnosis more accurate and decide on appropriate treatment. There are several reasons why there is a need for additional, alternative image retrieval methods apart from the steadily growing rate of image production. It is important to explain these needs and to discuss possible technical and methodological improvements and the resulting clinical benefits. The goals of medical information systems have often been defined to deliver the needed information at the right time, the right place to the right persons in order to improve the quality and efficiency of care processes. Such a goal needs more than a query by patient name, series ID or study ID for images. For the clinical decision making process it is beneficial and important to find other images of the same modality, the same anatomic region of the same disease. Although part of this information is normally contained in the DICOM headers and many imaging devices are DICOM compliant at this time, there are still some problems. DICOM headers have proven to contain a fairly high rate of errors, for example for the field anatomical region, error rates of 16% have been reported (Kohnen et al., 2002). This can hinder the correct retrieval of all wanted images. Clinical decision support techniques such as case based reasoning (LeBozec et al., 1998) or evidence based medicine (Boissel et al., 2003) can even produce a stronger need to retrieve images that can be valuable for supporting certain diagnosis. It could even be imagined to have Image Based Reasoning (IBR) as a new discipline for diagnostic aid. Decision support systems in radiology (Kahn et al., 1994) and computer aided diagnostics for radiological practice as demonstrated at the RSNA (Radiological Society of North America) (Kaplan et al., 1996) are on the rise and create a need for powerful data and metadata management and retrieval. Horsch in 2003, developed an initiative to identify important tasks for medical imaging based on their possible clinical benefits. Still, the problems and advantages of the technology have to be stressed to obtain acceptance and use of visual and text based access methods up to their full potential. Besides diagnostics, teaching and research especially are expected to improve through the use of visual access methods as visually interesting images can be chosen and can actually be found in the existing large repositories. The inclusion of visual features into medical studies is another interesting point for several medical research domains. Visual features do not only allow the retrieval of cases with patients having similar diagnoses but also cases with visual similarity but different diagnosis. In teaching it can help lecturers as well as students to browse educational image repositories and visually inspect the results found. This can be the case for navigating in image atlases. It can also be used to cross correlate visual and textual features of the images. Thus, it can be concluded that application of content based image retrieval in medical is not limited and the researchers are still developing new methods to further improve the image retrieval process.

FUTURE RESEARCH DIRECTIONS

Content Based Image Retrieval has been a very active research area since 1990's; there are still many challenging issues due to the variation and complexity of image data. Although it provides an intelligent and automatic solution for efficient searching of images, the majority of current techniques are based on low level features which are used in the current work. The similarity measures between visual features do not necessarily match human perception but user demands it to be in semantically and perceptually similar images. Also, the retrieval results of low level feature based approaches are generally unsatisfactory and often unpredictable. To solve these problem high level features can further be used.

CONCLUSION

Image retrieval systems used for searching, browsing and retrieving images from huge image databases is one of the most active research areas in the recent years. In this chapter complete overview of content based image retrieval is given. The application area in which it is used and existing CBIR systems is described. There are mainly three features of an image namely color, texture and shape which are used for image matching. Different feature extraction methods are presented in detail. These features can be used separately and can further be combined for image retrieval. It is found from the experiments that when the combination of color, texture and shape is used for image retrieval, system is more accurate.

REFERENCES

Boissel, J. P., Cucherat, M., Amsallem, E., Nony, P., Fardeheb, M., Manzi, W., & Haugh, M. C. (2003). Getting evidence to prescribers and patients or how to make EBM a reality. *Proceedings of the Medical Informatics Europe Conference (MIE '03)*, St. Malo, France.

Bounthanh, M., Attachoo, B., Hamamoto, K., & Bounthanh, T. (2013). Content-based image retrieval system based on combined and weighted multi-features. *Proceedings of the 2013 13th International Symposium on Communications and Information Technologies (ISCIT)*. doi:10.1109/ISCIT.2013.6645900

Brunelli, R., & Mich, O. (2011). Histograms Analysis for Image Retrieval. *Pattern Recognition, 34*(8), 625–1637.

Chang, T., & Kuo, C. C. J. (1993). Texture analysis and classification with tree-structured wavelet transform. *IEEE Transactions on Image Processing, 2*(4), 429–441. doi:10.1109/83.242353 PMID:18296228

Chen, C.C. (2006). Using Tomorrow's Retrieval Technology to Explore the Heritage: Bonding Past and Future in the Case of Global Memory Net. *Proceedings of the World Library and Information Congress*, Seoul, Korea.

Dimai, A. (1999). Rotation Invariant Texture Description using General Moment Invariants and Gabor Filters. *Proc. of the 11th Scandinavian Conf. on Image Analysis* (pp. 391-398).

Dufaux, F., Ouaret, M., & Ebrahimi, T. (2007). Mobile multimedia/image processing for military and security applications. sensors, and command, control, communications, and intelligence (C3I). *Technologies for Homeland Security and Homeland Defense VI., 10*, 358.

Eakins J. P. & Graham M. E. (1999). Content-based image retrieval, a report to the JISC Technology Applications programme.

Gong, Y., Zhang, H., Chuant, H., & Skauuchi, M. (1994). An image database system with contents capturing and fast image indexing abilities. *Proceedings of IEEE International Conferences on Multimedia Computing and Systems*, Boston, Massachusetts, USA (pp. 121–130). doi:10.1109/MMCS.1994.292444

Gueld, M. O., Kohnen, M., Keysers, D., Schubert, H., Wein, B. B., Bredno, J., & Lehmann, T. M. (2002). Quality of DICOM header information for image categorization. *Proceedings of the International Symposium on Medical Imaging* (pp. 280-287).

Horsch, A., & Thurmayr, R. 2003. How to identify and assess tasks and challenges of medical image processing. *Proceedings of the Medical Informatics Europe Conference (MIE '03)*, St. Malo, France.

Kahn, C. E. Jr. (1994). Artificial intelligence in radiology. Decision support systems. *Radiographics, 14*(4), 849–861. doi:10.1148/radiographics.14.4.7938772 PMID:7938772

Kaplan, B., & Lundsgaarde, H. P. (1996). Toward an evaluation of an integrated clinical imaging system: Identifying clinical benefits. *Methods of Information in Medicine, 35,* 221–229. PMID:8952308

Kato, T. (1992). Database architecture for content-based image retrieval. In *SPIE/IS&T 1992 symposium on electronic imaging: science and technology* (pp. 112–123). International Society for Optics and Photonics.

Lai C. C. & Chen Y. C. (2011). A user-oriented image retrieval system based on interactive genetic algorithm. *IEEE Trans. Measurement, 60*(10).

LeBozec, C., Jaulent, M. C., Zapletal, E., & Degoulet, P. (1998). Unified modeling language and design of a case based retrieval system in medical imaging. *Proceedings of the Annual Symposium of the American Society for Medical Informatics (AMIA)*, Nashville, TN, USA.

Long, F., Zhang, H., & Feng, D. D. (2003). Fundamentals of content-based image retrieval. In *Multimedia Information Retrieval and Management* (pp. 1–26). Springer Berlin Heidelberg. doi:10.1007/978-3-662-05300-3_1

Malik, F., & Baharudin, B. (2012). Effective content-based image retrieval: combination of quantized histogram features in the DCT domain. *Proceedings of the International Conference on Computer on Information Science* (Vol. 1, pp. 425-430).

Mathias, E. (1998). Comparing the influence of color spaces and metrics in content-based image retrieval. *Proceedings of International Symposium on Computer Graphics, Image Processing, and Vision* (pp. 371 -378). doi:10.1109/SIBGRA.1998.722775

Nastar, C., Mitschke, M., Boujemaa, N., Meilhac, C., Bernard, H., & Mautref, M. (1998). Retrieving images by content: the surfimage system. In *Advances in Multimedia Information Systems* (pp. 110–120). Berlin, Heidelberg: Springer. doi:10.1007/3-540-49651-3_11

Niblack, C. W., Barber, R., Equitz, W., Flickner, M. D., Glasman, E. H., Petkovic, D., . . . Taubin, G. (1993). QBIC project: querying images by content, using color, texture, and shape. *Proceedings of the Symposium on Electronic Imaging: Science and Technology* (pp. 173-187). International Society for Optics and Photonics. doi:10.1117/12.143648

Pass, G., & Zabith, R. (1996). Histogram refinement for content-based image retrieval. *Proceedings of the IEEE Workshop on Applications of Computer Vision* (pp. 96-102). doi:10.1109/ACV.1996.572008

Rui, Y., Huang, T. S., & Mehrotra, S. (1997). Content-based image retrieval with relevance feedback in MARS. *Proceedings of International Conference on Image Processing* (Vol. 2, pp. 815- 818). doi:10.1109/ICIP.1997.638621

Singh, A., Shekhar, S., & Jalal, A. S. (2012). Semantic based image retrieval using multi-agent model by searching and filtering replicated web images. *Proceedings of the 2012 World Congress on Information and Communication Technologies* (WICT) (pp. 817-821).

Swain, M. J., & Ballard, D. H. (1991). Color indexing. *International Journal of Computer Vision, 7*(1), 11–32. doi:10.1007/BF00130487

Tegolo, D. (1994). Shape analysis for image retrieval. *Proc. of SPIE, Storage and Retrieval for Image and Video Databases -II*, San Jose, CA (pp. 59-69). doi:10.1117/12.171781

Ward, A. A., McKenna, S. J., Buruma, A., Taylor, P., & Han, J. (2008). Merging technology and users: applying image browsing to the fashion industry for design inspiration. *Proceedings of the International Workshop on Content-Based Multimedia Indexing CBMI '08* (pp. 288-295). IEEE. doi:10.1109/CBMI.2008.4564959

Wen, C. Y., & Yu, C. C. (2005). Image retrieval of digital crime scene images. *Forensic Sci. J., 4*(1), 37–45.

Chapter 3
Block–Based Motion Estimation:
Concepts and Challenges

Shaifali Madan Arora
MSIT, India

Kavita Khanna
NCU, India

ABSTRACT

Recent years have witnessed a great technological evolution in video display and capturing technologies leading to the development of new standards of video coding including MPEG-X, H.26X and HEVC. The cost of computations, storage and high bandwidth requirements makes a video data expensive in terms of transmission and storage. This makes video compression absolutely necessary prior to its transmission in order to accommodate for different transmission media's capabilities. Digital video compression technologies therefore have become an important part of the way we create, present, communicate and use visual information. The main aim behind a video compression system is to eliminate the redundancies from a raw video signal. The tradeoff involved in the process of video compression is between the speed, quality and resource utilization. The current chapter explores the techniques, challenges, issues and problems in video compression in detail along with the major advancements in the field.

INTRODUCTION

Recent years have established a great technological evolution in video display and capturing technologies. Ease in accessibility of digital technology has made it possible to use digital camera, cable, sound, and video by the common people in day today applications. Revolutionary development in mobile phones has made video production a common task. Gone are the days when video production was possible only for specialized studios. In fact, digital video has paved way towards the development of various challenging real-time applications.

The transmission of video involves the conversion of analog video into its corresponding digital domain. In a NTPC signal 30 frames (Huckfield, 1992) are transmitted per second in 4:2:2 YUV format with 858×525 luminance samples, $429 \times 525 \times 2$ chrominance samples, and 8 bits per samples.

DOI: 10.4018/978-1-5225-2848-7.ch003

bit rate = 30 × 8 × ((858 × 525) + (429 × 525 × 2)) = 216.216 Mbps

As above mentioned bit rate, transmission rate of 216 Mbps is required for a single digital television signal in NTPC format (Barbero et al., 1992). But for practical applications this bit rate is very high. Consider the example of local area networks (LANs) for which the data transmission rate is on the order of 10 Mbps, and for wide area networks (WANs) this transmission rate is even lower than this. Although high bandwidth data networks are developing, still distributing an uncompressed video bit stream over these networks is quite expensive. This clearly indicates that the video data must be compressed (encoded) before its transmission in order to adjust as per the varying capabilities of different transmission media.

So transmission of video data is expensive with respect to the number of computations, requirement of storage space and bandwidth. Video compression techniques therefore have become a fundamental part of the way the visual information is created, presented and communicated.

The use of video data has shown its growing applicability in digital television, personal computers, hand held devices and other multimedia applications, and it seems that this growth is not slowing down. Need of pervasive, good-quality digital video with high compression has become the aim of companies, researchers and standard bodies (Richardson, 2003). It has therefore emerged as an important field for research and development for the last three decades.

Digitization of synthetic/ real-time video scenes was an inevitable step. Digital video is easier to transmit, virtually immune to noise, and is capable of providing an interactive interface to users. Digital video coding has outperformed analog video coding in terms of higher compression rates without much deterioration of subjective video quality (Mistretta et al., 1981). It thus eliminates the high band-width requirement of transmitting analog videos. This significant feature has led to the development of many application areas for example, video playback using compact disk, set-top box, P2P video delivery, video conferencing over IP networks, mobile TV broadcasting, and video surveillance. Thus, the specifically designed nature of video applications has helped towards the development of various video compression techniques with different quality, size, power consumption, performance and cost.

Latest advancement in the technology of mobile phones has given us a new generation of small devices which can process videos with limited power supply and channel bandwidths (O'Hara et al., 2007). The enormous use of video information in these devices has raised the need for efficient video compression.

Also, the new emerging technologies such as 3-D television, high definition (HD) and ultra HD videos have resulted in the transmission and processing of large amounts of video data (Javidi & Okano, 2002). All these emerging video applications and availability of limited bandwidth of networks has made video compression a fundamental and essential component of a video processing system. The diagrammatic representation of a video processing system is shown in figure 1.

Figure 1. Video Processing system

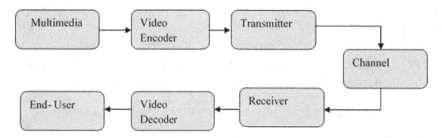

Figure 1 show that a basic video processing or a video coding system comprises of an encoder which converts a raw input video sequence in to its compressed form which may be used for transmission or for storage. The decoder on the other hand performs the opposite function to encoder. Video compression forms an integral part of any video processing system as large amount of information is involved in raw video signal.

A video compression system (Atkinson, 1994; Gall, 1991) is based on removing redundancies from a raw video signal. The need is to achieve a tradeoff between the quality of compressed video, speed of transmission, utilization of resources and power consumption. An image can be compressed by removing the spatial redundancy present between neighboring pixels. In a video scene, 15-60 image frames are transmitted per second. There exists very small difference i.e. very high correlation between neighboring frames. Coding the difference between neighboring frames can reduce temporal redundancy and provide significant compression. However, when a sequence of frames contains rapidly moving objects, involves camera zoom or sudden scene changes then similarity between neighboring frames is reduced and compression is affected negatively. Video compression systems avoid this problem in two ways: either by tracking object movement and compensating for it during the prediction and differencing process or by switching to an alternate coding system when there is insufficient inter frame correlation to make predictive coding advantageous.

Video compression is achieved in three steps in order to reduce data redundancy (Gall, 1992). First, the temporal redundancy in successive frames is reduced by estimating the motion between successive frames. In this process a motion estimation (ME) technique is employed to find the motion distance for the blocks in the current frame, where blocks could be defined as specific partitions of the frame. Then with this motion information, the residual between the current encoded frame and the previous frame is compensated and this is called motion compensation (MC). Second step reduces the spatial redundancy within each frame by applying transform coding. Third step is to apply, entropy coding, which aims to reduce statistical redundancy over the residue and compression data.

Motion estimation is the key component of a video compression system and takes 80-90% time in the process of encoding/compressing the video frames. Fortunately, only the encoder must estimate motion in terms of motion vectors (MV). The decoder uses these MVs and simply accesses the areas of the reference frames that were used in the encoder to form the prediction residuals. Because of this, any specific motion estimation algorithm is not included in most of the video compression standards and proposes an optimization problem. Therefore, immense research is going on in field of motion estimation from the past three decades to optimize this process by reducing the computations and improving the video quality (Sullivan & Ohms, 2010).

EVOLUTION IN VIDEO CODING STANDARDS

Since 1980s, when the technology was in its early stages, different types of video coders were being developed; coding standards have played an important role in spreading the technology by providing powerful interoperability among various products, while allowing enough flexibility for ingenuity in optimizing and fitting a given application. International Telecommunications Union-Telecommunication standardization sector (ITU-T, 2011), International Organization for Standardization (ISO) (http://www.iso.org/2013) in conjunction with the International Electro technical Commission (IEC), Video Coding Experts Group (VCEG), Moving Pictures Expert Group (MPEG) are continuously and collaboratively working towards the development of new standards for improving the coding rates for meeting the overwhelming technological advancements.

Raw video is composed of a sequence of image frames and thus the principle of video compression is based on the concepts of image compression. There has been significant progress in the image and video coding since 1980s. In 1984, International Telegraph and Telephone Consultative Committee came up with H.120 (Tawbi et al., 1993) video coding standard. This standard was based on Differential Pulse Code Modulation, scalar quantization and variable-length coding techniques for point-to-point data communication transmission. The standard achieved good spatial resolution with 2 Mbits/s but resulted in poor temporal quality.

In late 1980s an improvement over H.120 was given which was built on the Discrete Cosine Transform. In line to this, the Joint Photographic Experts Group (JPEG) also suggested appreciable compression of static images which was also based on DCT (Wallace, 1992). Various lossy compression methods like run-length encoding (Murayama et al., 1980), Huffman coding (Golomb, 1980) and arithmetic coding (Langdon et al., 1981) were explored in late 1980's.

In 1990, ITU gave another standard as H.261 which was considered as a benchmark in practical digital video coding. Thereafter all the standards are based on the design of H.261. H.261 was preliminary designed for transmitting videos over ISDN lines, with multiples of 64 kbit/s data rates and QCIF (176×144-pixel) or CIF (352×288-pixel) resolution. It was a revolutionary method based on hybrid video coding scheme. It uses 4:2:0 data sampling such that the number of luminance samples is double then that of chrominance samples. The idea is based on the better sensitivity of human eye towards light intensities than to color. This standard was the first one to use an array (16×16) of luma samples called Macro Block (MB). Temporal redundancy was reduced with the help of inter-picture prediction whereas spatial redundancy was reduced with the help of transform coding with an 8×8 DCT.

In 1990s, the Motion Picture Experts Group (MPEG) came up with a new standard as MPEG-1. It was designed with an aim to attain a video quality at 1.5Mbit/s and resolution at 352x288/240-pixel. MPEG-1 (ISO-IEC, 1993) standard was designed on the framework of H.261. The main target of MPEG-1 was to achieve efficiency in compression as the main focus of this standard was on to the storage applications of video.

MPEG-1 decoders could be easily adapted to multimedia on personal computers. The biggest disadvantage of MPEG-1 was that it could work only for progressive- scan images i.e. images which are non-interlaced. The missing feature of compressing interlaced images in MPEG-1 led to the development of MPEG-2 in 1994. It achieved a milestone in digital television broadcasting and DVD-Video (Eckart & Chad, 1995). Subsequently MPEG-3 was developed for coding of High Definition (HD) TV. Later MPEG-3 was merged in to MPEG-2 because the desired functionality could be provided through MPEG-2 as well.

The goal to achieve more compression led to the development MPEG-4 visual (ISO/IEC, 1999) and H.264 Advanced Video Coding (AVC) (Wiegand et al., 2003) standards. These standards aimed to double the compression rate in comparison to the previous standards while maintaining the video quality. MPEG-4 is based on object oriented processing and could work for lower as well as higher bit rates thus providing a flexible visual communication. On the other hand, H.264 was designed on the basis of existing technology to make it more efficient and robust. Due to this, it has been adopted in majority of video coding applications like iPod, play station and in TV broadcasting standards. Development of new video coding standards is centered on the extending standards rather than coming up with a totally new one.

The major drawback of the existing standard H.264/AVC is that it does not provide the compression ratios desired for the HD or ultra HD videos transmission with the available facilities. This drawback has increased the need to develop new coding standards which can increase the compression rate. Consequently, new standard named High Efficiency Video Coding (HEVC) have been started by the standardization bodies ITU-T VCEG and ISO/IEC MPEG with a target to reduce the coding rates by half while maintaining the same video quality (Sullivan et al., 2012).

Lot of research has been done in the field by researchers from industry and academics and some copy-right standards have been proposed which are based on similar concepts. The underlying idea behind all the existing compression standards is the hybrid coding approach enabling the transmission, storage and broadcast digital video. Table 1 summarizes the important features of the existing video coding standards.

OVERVIEW OF VIDEO CODING OR COMPRESSION

Compression aims to reduce the amount of data required for conveying the desired information. Compression is based on the basic principle behind information i.e. any information has some sort of inherent ordering and patterning in itself. This order and patterning represents the crux of information and thus could be easily transmitted with lesser data then the original one.

Compression can be divided into two main types; lossless compression and lossy compression. The concept of lossless data compression utilizes the statistical redundancy to represent data without losing the information. These algorithms are implemented in applications where exactly same reconstruction of received signal is required as that of transmitted signal or information. In contrast, using lossy compression, the exact replica of the sequence cannot be recovered. In this case, high compression ratio is possible but at the cost of loss of some information. The compression rates of lossy compression schemes are about 95% higher than the schemes based on lossless compression (Said & William, 1996). Lossy compression schemes exploit the sensitivity of human eye which is subtle to the brightness of objects more than the color variations. These schemes also utilize the fact that the visual system of human beings does not perceive subtle details in an image. So, these details could be neglected so as to reduce the size of the image without making any visible errors in the reconstructed image. Raw video contains immense amount of data. Lossy compression techniques are applied to significantly reduce the size of video data at the expense of quality.

Table 1. Properties of various Image/Video coding standards

Standard	Application	Bit Rate
JPEG	Continuous-tone still-image compression	Variable
H.261	Video telephony and teleconferencing over ISDN	p x 64 kb/s
MPEG-1	Video on digital storage media (CD-ROM)	1.5 Mb/s
MPEG-2	Digital Television	> 2 Mb/s
H.263	Video telephony over PSTN	< 33.6 kb/s
MPEG-4	Object-based coding, synthetic content, interactivity	Variable
H.264	From Low bitrate coding to HD encoding, HD-DVD, Surveillance, Video conferencing.	Variable

CONCEPTS OF VIDEO COMPRESSION

An analog system involves the generation of an analog video signal from the camera which is obtained by scanning a scene from left to right and from top to bottom making up an image frame. The number of lines to be scanned per frame is based on the bandwidth, flicker and resolution. Video is nothing but sequence of image frames taken one after the other that to human eye it seems a continuous scene where every frame amounts to the dissemination of light, energy and wavelength over a finite area. Every digital frame comprises of a prescribed number of rows and columns of digital values which are known as picture elements or pixels. So, the pixel elements, at any specific point, represent the quantized values of the brightness of a given color. The total number of pixels in a frame represents the spatial resolution of the frame. More the spatial resolution of a frame, clearer will be details covered.

Frame Rate

As described earlier a video is sequence of image frames. The number of images displayed per second is known as the frame rate. Frame rates are used to adjust audios and pictures in a movie, television, or any video. The Society of Motion Picture and Television Editors (SMPTE) group is responsible for the standardization of frame rates. Higher frame rate signifies smooth videos displays to the users whereas lower rate accounts to erratic displays. The commonly used frame rates are 24, 25 and 30 frames per second (fps). Each frame rate has its own utility for example the frame rate for motion pictures is 24 fps whereas a HD video can use up to 60 fps. A simple personal computer or graphics hardware has the potential of displaying 10-15 frames per second.

Frame Dimensions

An image frame is represented by the width × height of a frame and is expressed in terms of number of pixels. Some common formats are given in Table 2.

Representation of Video Signals – RGB, YUV Format

The RGB format is one of the popular means of representing color images. Three basic color components Red (R), Green (G) and Blue (B) are used to represent each sample point in any visual information,

Table 2. Frame Dimensions used in different applications

S. No.	Standard	Frame Size
1	Quarter Common Intermediate Format (QCIF) - Standard for video conferencing systems.	176 × 144
2	Common Intermediate Format (CIF) - Standard resolution for video conferencing systems to convert from PAL to NTSC or vice versa.	352 × 288
3	DV is a standard resolution for digital video recording in consumer products according NTSC standard.	720 × 480
4	PAL is a composite video standard similar to NTSC, mainly used in Europe, Asia and Australia.	720 × 576
5	HDTV-720, High Definition Television with 1M Pixel.	1280 × 720
6	HDTV-1080, High Definition Television with 2M Pixel.	1920 × 1080

which are combined in different proportions to synthesize a color. Each value is represented using 8-bits, making 256 levels to represent each color component. In another format to represent digital video, the luminance (brightness) Y and chrominance (color) C information can be represented separately. Weighted sum of the three colors R, G and B is calculated to find the luminance component Y. Color differences Cr, Cb, and Cg can be calculated by finding the difference between the luminance and each primary component as given in following equations:

$$Cr = Wr(R - Y), Cb = Wb(B - Y), Cg = Wg(G - Y) \tag{1}$$

where Wr, Wb, and Wg are weights.

As can be observed from above equations out of three color signals, the two signals are linearly independent whereas the third one can be represented as a linear combination of the other two. Therefore, luminance Y and any two of the color signals are used to express the original color. PAL, SECAM, and NTSC are the three main standards for analog color television (Wu et al., 2006). These standards use Y as luminance, U as blue color difference which is similar to Cb defined above and V as the red color difference which is similar to Cr defined above, to represent a color, known as YUV (Klaue et al., 2003) which has an edge over the RGB format. Further, human visual system (HVS) is more sensitive to brightness than to chrominance, therefore the chrominance signals can be expressed with a lower resolution than the luminance. This representation achieves data compression to a certain degree but without degrading the visual quality. One of the YUV format is 4:4:4, in which each pixel position at full resolution has both luminance and chrominance samples. In another format, i.e. 4:2:2, chrominance samples are sub-sampled in horizontal direction whereas in 4:2:0 format, chrominance samples are sub-sampled in both vertical and horizontal directions. 4:2:0 is the most widely used format in entertainment applications like a DVD video.

Along with the increase in technological advancements in terms of storage, transmission and processor the advances in compression technology has made it possible for a common man to produce, store, transmit and use videos in day today applications.

Different Type of Video Frames

A video is nothing but large number of image fames presented per second. Principle of video compression is based on encoding one reference image frame and the difference of subsequent fames w.r.t this reference frame. A video consists of various scene changes in its entire span and there will not be correct

Table 3. Comparison of bit rates before and after compression

Application	Data Rate	
	Uncompressed	**Compressed**
Video Conference *352 x 240 @ 15 fps*	30.4 Mbps	64 - 768 kbps
CD-ROM Digital Video *352 x 240 @ 30 fps*	60.8 Mbps	1.5 - 4 Mbps
Broadcast Video *720 x 480 @ 30 fps*	248.8 Mbps	3 - 8 Mbps
HDTV *1280 x 720 @ 60 fps*	1.33 Gbps	20 Mbps

prediction using previous frame as reference frame when there is such scene change. Therefore, entire video is divided into group of pictures (GOPs) with one group continues until there is scene change which is followed by next GOP in that order (Frey & Son, 2000). These GOPs consists of I, P and B pictures which are briefed as follows.

1. **I Frames:** Frames encoded using intra-frame coding technique only are called I frames. First frame of a video sequence is an I frame which is coded spatially without any reference to another frame in sequence. Pictures with scene change are also coded as I frames.
2. **P Frames:** A future frame could be predicted by an encoder by starting from an intra- frame. This is commonly named as a P frame. This frame could also be predicted with other P frames, but in a forward time manner. Consider an example of a group of pictures consisting of only 6 frames. Suppose the ordering of frames is given as I, P, P, P, P, P, I, P, P, P, P, ... Now each P frame in this sequence could be predicted from its immediately preceding frame irrespective of whether it is a P frame or an I frame.
3. **B Frames:** B-frames are referred to as bi-directional interpolated prediction frames. These frames could be predicted using both forward and backward predictions. Consider an example of a group of pictures consisting of only 6 frames. Suppose the ordering of frames is given as I, B, P, B, P, B, I, B, P, B, P, B, ... As discussed previously, all the I frames are coded spatially whereas the P frames are predicted with the help of previous I and P frames. In this example, all the B frames are coded with the help of a forward prediction from previous P or I frame, and also from a backward prediction from a succeeding I or P frame.

TECHNIQUE TO ACHIEVE VIDEO COMPRESSION

Video compression can be attained by utilizing the similarities or replication that may exist in a video signal. There could be two types of redundancy in a video signal:

1. **Spatial Redundancy:** It refers the type redundancy which exists in every frame.
2. **Temporal Redundancy:** It refers to the type of redundancy which exists between the neighboring frames. This type of redundancy can be removed with the help of motion estimation and compensation. Various objects could be same in the successive video frames. Motion estimation aims to find the movement of these objects and find the vectors that represent the estimated motion. Motion compensation refers to the compression that could be achieved by exploiting the estimated motion.

Figure 2. MPEG GOP- Order in which Video Frames are sent

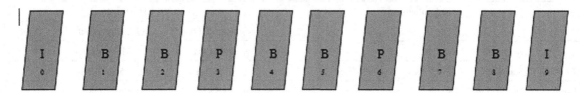

Motion estimation and compensation are efficient techniques to remove the temporal redundancy which exists because of high correlation in the consecutive frames. Various algorithms have been proposed in literature to estimate motion between successive frames.

VIDEO ENCODER

A video encoder uses inter and intra frame coding techniques (Sugiyama,1991) to reduce temporal and spatial redundancy. The block diagram of a general video encoder is given in figure 3(a) which uses the discrete cosine transform (DCT)/Discrete wavelet transform (DWT), quantization and variable size run length coding for intra-frame coding whereas concept of motion estimation is used for inter-frame coding.

Intra Frame Coding

Intra-frame coding (Gonzales et al.,1990) deals with the cases in which video compression is accomplished with respect to the information contained within the current frame only. It doesn't consider the information of any other frame in the video. So, with this technique temporal processing is not done outside of the current frame. It is very similar to the Joint Photographic Experts Group (JPEG) image encoder for coding still images except at the quantization stage which is uniform for video encoder. The main processing blocks for intra frame coding are – quantization, DCT, and run length/variable length coder which is summarized below.

First step is to segment the input image into blocks of size N×N. Second step is to transform the input image into frequency domain. A significant benefit achieved from transformation is that it tends to reduce statistical correlation between the input samples with a result that the most pertinent characteristics of the input samples are reduced into lesser number of variables. Karhunen-Loève transform (KLT) (Tarres & Kirlin, 1990) and discrete cosine transform (DCT) are famous examples of such type of transformations.

Figure 3. Intra Frame Encoder and Decoder

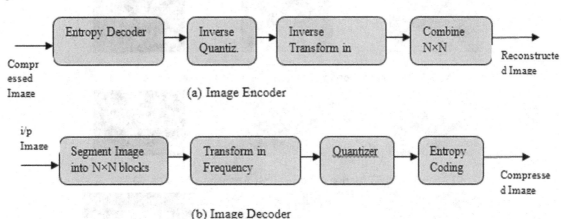

Inter Frame Coding

Inter-frame coding utilizes motion estimation in videos in order to remove temporal redundancy. In most real video sequences, consecutive frames are very similar to each other (until there is scene change) except movement of some objects within these frames. Figure 4 depicts the two consecutive frames and their differences for three sequences containing slow, medium and fast motion activities. As it can be observed from figure 4, that there exists very small difference in frames; also, multiple objects are moving randomly in different directions. So for estimating the motion it is not feasible to take the complete frame as a single unit.

The solution is thus to divide each frame of the video into fixed size blocks, called macroblocks (MB) and motion of each object is estimated at macroblock level. Standard macroblock size is 16×16 as it gives a tradeoff between computation complexity and quality parameters. In MPEG-4 and H.264 standards variable block sizes from 4×4 to 16×16 are used.

Search Window plays a very important role in the determination of motion vectors in motion estimation. The best match for a block in the current frame is obtained by searching for it in the reference frame within a predefined search window as shown in figure 5. In case of fast motion, a large search window may be required to find accurate motion vectors and for slow or medium motion, smaller search window may give good results. Therefore, correct choice of the window size may lead to reduction in the amount of computations needed to find the motion vectors without compromising with the quality. Full search method is the most accurate method of searching as it exhaustively searches all points in the search window and thus needs very high computations.

Further, the block which gives the minimum error is determined as the best match. Location of best matching block within the search window in the reference frame with reference to the location of candidate block in the current frame is known as the motion vector.

Figure 4. Difference in two continuous image frames

CLASS A - Slow Motion "Akiko test seq Frames 10-11"

CLASS B - Medium Motion "Foreman Test Sequence Frame 10-11"

CLASS C - FAST Motion " Flower Test Sequence Frames 10-11"

Third step is the quantization of the transformed values. In the quantization process, rounding off of the less significant digit is done. Usually the rounding precision is restrained by a step size that indicates the smallest representable value increment. Quantization is not invertible as it leads to many-to-few mapping which definitely leads to some loss of integrity.

Finally, in the fourth step the samples are encoded. It involves the representation of discrete-valued source symbols in order to exploit the advantage of the relative probabilities of the various possible values of each source symbol. A famous entropy code is the variable-length code (VLC) (Chan et al., 1990). It establishes a tree-structured code table in which the more likely values are represented using short binary strings and less likely values with longer. Huffman code method is a well-known method which tends to produce optimal variable length code. Arithmetic coding is a comparatively new technique which produces more optimal results than the VLC.

The best matching block is determined by finding the difference of the analogous pixels in the current and the reference frame. This difference is then squared and summed over the entire block and is decided upon as the similarity measure. The best matching block is the one having minimum summation. To save the computations involved in finding the squares, mean absolute difference (MAD) based block matching criterion is used. It involves the comparison of corresponding pixels from each block and then summing up their absolute differences. Lower MAD indicates the better match which leads to choosing of the block with minimum MAD as the best match. Another most popularly used criterion is sum of absolute difference (SAD) in which mean calculation is skipped. The block with minimum SAD gives the best matching block.

Motion vectors of all blocks in the current frame are calculated and a predicted frame is generated from the reference frame with the help of these motion vectors. Finally, the distinction between the predicted frame and the actual frame, known as residue error, is coded for transmission/storage purposes. This whole process for encoding a video frame is depicted in figure 6. First frame in a GOP, which is I-frame, is coded by the image encoder. Then consecutive frames P or B are encoded by the motion estimator and compensator units. Motion estimation is the most crucial part of any video encoder. It is used for removal of temporal redundancy and takes more time for processing.

Figure 5. Motion Estimation Based on Block Matching

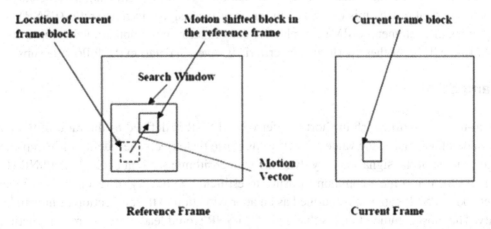

Figure 6. Video Frame Encoder

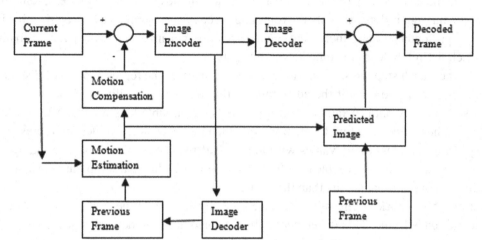

Full search (FS) algorithm provides the optimum solution for motion estimation but its high computational complexity is the main bottleneck so that FS cannot be implemented in real time applications. ME is left as the optional part in most of the video standards and is therefore a hot research area for past three decades. Numerous fast ME algorithms have been given in the past. The speed and accuracy of a ME algorithm depends upon certain important factors such as - block matching criterion, motion estimation algorithm, search window size, block size selection, motion estimation based on detecting the edges of objects in video data and accelerating motion estimation by zero motion prejudgment. In this thesis, new fast ME algorithms are proposed to fasten the process of ME.

PERFORMANCE OF MOTION ESTIMATION CRITERION

Designing a fast motion estimation algorithm tends to make a compromise between the search speed and video quality. Full search algorithm although gives the best quality but its main drawback is its search speed. To compare the performance of motion estimation algorithms, following parameters need to be checked – video quality which is expressed in terms of peak signal to noise ratio (PSNR), structural similarity index measurement (SSIM), search efficiency in terms of computational complexity and size of residual frame. Each of these performance criteria is given in detail in the following subsections.

PSNR and SSIM

Peak signal-to-noise ratio which in short is referred as PSNR is defined as the ratio of the maximum possible value of a signal to the value of corrupting noise that affects the fidelity of its representation. The range of most of the signals is very dynamic so logarithmic scale in decibels is PSNR (Huynh & Ghanbari, 2008). It is a most common measure to estimate the quality of reconstructed image/video from an encoder. PSNR can also be defined as an approximation to the perception of human beings for the quality. The most common trend is that a higher PSNR would lead to higher reconstruction quality but there may be exception to it.

Peak signal to noise ration provides a subjective way to measure the quality of video produced from an encoder and is defined as:

$$PSNR = 10\log_{10}\frac{Max^2}{MSE}$$ (2)

In the above equation, Max represents the maximum possible pixel value in the video frame. MSE i.e the mean square error is the difference of the original frame to that of the motion compensated frame. The optimum possible results in terms of PSNR are given by a full search (FS) algorithm as this algorithm is based on finding the best matching block by comparing the candidate block to all the blocks in the search window. This algorithm thus serves as a standard for evaluating the performance of other algorithms.

Another parameter to evaluate image/ video quality is SSIM. SSI measures the similarity amidst two images. SSIM is dissimilar to MSE (Mean Square error) and PSNR as it considers the perceived change in structural information for image degradation which is unlike PSNR and MSE which are based on estimating the perceived errors. Structural information signifies the strong dependencies in pixels due to their spatial closeness. Such spatial dependencies sustain crucial information about an object's structure in any visual scene. A frame in a video is divided into blocks of fixed size i.e. N×N for simulations. SSIM between the two blocks say block A and block B can be measured using the following equation:

$$SSIM\left(A,B\right) = \frac{2\left(u_A u_B + c1\right)\left(2\sigma_{AB} + c2\right)}{\left(u_A^2 + u_B^2 + c1\right)\left(\sigma_A^2 + \sigma_B^2 + c2\right)}$$ (3)

Here block A is in the original video frame whereas block B is in the motion compensated frame. Also, u_A and u_B represent the average of each of the respective blocks; σA_2 and $\sigma B2$ are covariance each of the blocks; σAB is covariance between the two blocks and cn=$(_k nl)_2$ is a constant obtained from k1, $_k 2$ and l where k1 = 0.01, k2 = 0.03 and l = 255.

Search Efficiency

Search efficiency refers to the computational complexity which is measured with reference to the average number of search points needed per block to estimate the MVs. Full search algorithm compares all blocks from the reference frame in a given search window to find the best match point. Therefore, it requires very large number of search points. Fast motion estimation algorithms lessen these search points but provide suboptimum solutions. The goal of any motion estimation algorithm is to lessen the search points so that search process can be fastened and to provide the best possible quality.

Representation of Residual Frame

Another parameter to analyze the performance of any motion estimation algorithm is the size of residual frame. Residual frame is the difference between the actual frame and the motion compensated frame. This residual frame is encoded using efficient entropy encoding schemes and is measured in terms of number of bits required to represent a pixel. If an algorithm is able to predict accurate motion vectors, then the distinction between the actual frame and the motion compensated frame will be less and so few bits will be needed to encode the residual frame. The MVs given by FS algorithm are optimum and thus it requires the optimum number of bits and so it is used as a benchmark for analyzing the other fast motion estimation algorithms.

CHALLENGES IN DESIGNING MOTION ESTIMATION ALGORITHMS

The major challenge in designing a motion estimation algorithm is to attain global minima with a minimum number of search points while maintaining the video quality as close to that of FS. The accuracy and speed of the motion estimation directly affects the performance of an algorithm and subsequent coding. However, these two are opposite factors and thus pose a challenging optimization problem. Subsequently a large number of algorithms have been designed in the last three decades but provide sub-optimum solutions. There are various factors that can directly affect the speed and accuracy of ME and are discussed here in brief.

Block Matching Criteria

Block Matching criterion gives a means to find the best matching of the current block within the SW in the given reference frame. The criterion should be such that it should give accurate results even for contrast variations in the scene. Some of the block matching criterion and their comparisons are discussed in this section.

Eric Chan et al (Chan et al.,1994) proposed a simple criterion in that is based upon the comparison of each pixel of the target block to its corresponding pixel in the candidate block and then classifying each pixel pair as moving or not depending on whether the absolute difference between pixels is less than some predefined threshold. Total numbers of moving pixels are counted in a block and the block with maximum number of moving pixels in a given SW is the best matching block. The chosen threshold value has major impact on the performance and the threshold selection depends on the scene itself. Although this criterion requires very less hardware but dependency on threshold restricts its use in practical implementation.

$$k = \left| Pc_{ij} - Pc_{ij} \right|$$

(4)

$$\text{If } k < T \begin{cases} Pixel\, categorised\, as\, moving \\ \quad\quad otherwise\, not \end{cases}$$

where Pc and Pr are the pixels from the current and reference blocks. T is the threshold to categorize the moving pixels. In order to remove the use of threshold, T. Koga et al. proposed another block matching criteria (eqn. 4) named as mean square difference (MSD) in which the difference between the corresponding pixels in current and reference block is squared and summation of these squares over entire block is taken as similarity measure. The block for which this summation is minimal is the best match block. This technique gives good results but calculations involved in finding squares increases the computational cost.

$$MSD = \frac{1}{N^2} \sum_{i=0}^{N-1} \sum_{j=0}^{N-1} \left(C_{ij} - R_{ij} \right)^2 \tag{5}$$

where C_{ij} and R_{ij} are the blocks from the current block and the reference block respectively.

MH Fadzil et al (Fadzil & Dennis, 1990) suggested mean absolute difference (MAD) in equation 5 similar to MSD but square is replaced by absolute values and is the most preferred criteria because of its simplicity and easy to implementation.

$$MAD = \frac{1}{N^2} \sum_{i=0}^{N-1} \sum_{j=0}^{N-1} \left| C_{ij} - R_{ij} \right| \tag{6}$$

Integral projection based block matching criterion was introduced by Huang et al (Huang et al., 2006) which is claimed to be less susceptible to noise than others. In this, pixels from each column and each row of the block are summed up. Advantage of this technique is that values calculated for a particular candidate block can be reused in calculating the integral projections for overlapping candidate blocks, thus reducing computational cost. This criterion works better for exhaustive search but may not be useful for suboptimal searches.

Shigang Wang et al (Wang et al., 1999) suggested vector matching criterion which is a variant of MAD. It is focused on the individual error term rather than the average value over the entire block as in MAD. In this technique, a macro block is subdivided into smaller size blocks (authors have taken 2x2 size) and matching is performed at these sub block levels using conventional MAD criterion with a predetermined threshold value. Each macro block is treated as a vector and all its sub blocks as its components. A best match block represents vector which has maximum number of components with their matching error less than a threshold value. To further improve the quality of MAD block variances were included as another important feature.

Smooth constrained mean absolute difference (SC-MAD) suggested by Xuan Jing et al. (Jing Et al., 2003) reduces the number of bits required at encoder. A residue block, obtained by taking absolute difference between the current block and the reference block is divided in to four sub blocks. Difference between the maximum and the minimum residue error in each sub block is added which is then used as another factor along with conventional MAD as a distortion measure.

Joon-Seek Kim et al (Kim et al.,1992) suggested statistically adaptive block-matching criterion (SABMC) to resolve the average variation problem that occurs in the conventional BBME algorithms. This criterion considers time-varying average and shape that represents the fluctuation of pixel values. Bing Xiong et al (Xiong & Zhu, 2009) proposed integral picture representation of a video frame which gave a new direction in this field. In this technique, blocks are divided into sub blocks and a candidate sub block is searched in the reference frame within the search area using its integral sum representation. Further, consideration of block variances along with sum of absolute difference of block using integral frame representation was suggested and substantial gain in computation over conventional MAD was claimed with almost same quality. This work was enhanced by adding contrast between sub blocks of a given block as inter-block feature. Here only the sub block sum feature was used as intra-block feature and contrast was used as an inter-block feature. Total four features were used to find the best matching block - block sum, horizontal contrast, vertical contrast and diagonal contrast. Further multilevel structure has been proposed which is based on these features for achieving a tradeoff between computation loads and coding efficiency.

Another approach robust to contrast variations in the input sequence is based on mapping pixel intensities in reference and current frames and matching is performed over these mapped pixels (Purwar et al., 2011). The block matching criterions discussed in this sub-section can be applied with different block motion estimation algorithms.

Sub Sampled Pixels on Matching-Error Computations

In order to reduce the computations associated with the block distortion (which is measured in terms of sum of absolute difference) calculation, various types of sub sampling can be applied to the current and reference block. Matthias Bierling (Bierling, 1981) have suggested that every second pixel in a block is selected in both horizontal and vertical direction for finding the cost function. Liu et el (Liu & Andre, 1993) proposed a set of four patterns with 4:1 subsampling instead of the fixed decimation pattern and these patterns are altered during the search process to reduce the influence of sub sampling on the ME accuracy. Byung C Song et al (Song & Jong, 1998) proposed hierarchical partial distortion search (HPDS) algorithm which uses hierarchical sub-sampling with three levels of hierarchy. At each level, the number of candidate MVs has been taken into account decreases and the number of pixels taken for the MDP calculation increases. These two parameters can be adjusted to balance the speed and the accuracy of the ME process.

Yankang Wang et al (Wang et al., 2000) proposed globally adaptive pixel decimation (GAPD) that applies Hilbert scan to convert a 2D block into a 1D Hilbert sequence. Adaptive thresholding is employed to select pixels belonging to the edge and highly structured regions which are used for the BDM calculation. Chung-Neng Wang (Wang et al., 2003) proposed pixel decimation scheme based on N-queen lattice which is obtained by placing N queens on a chessboard. Only pixels at the positions occupied by the queens are selected for the distortion calculation. The scheme guarantees that at least one pixel is selected from each row, column and diagonal. Fixed 4:1 subsampling pattern is compared with a 4−queen pattern.

Avishek Saha (Saha et al., 2008) proposed several decimation patterns based on the boundary approach (observation that new objects enter an MB through its boundary regions) and N-queen lattices. Genetic algorithms are employed for the optimal pattern selection. Such computation reduction methodology can be incorporated into other algorithms and can give higher computational gain.

Accelerating ME by Zero Motion Prejudgment (ZMP)

A large number of blocks in two consecutive video frames contain zero or very little motion. In most of the real world video sequences more than 70% of the MBs are static which do not need the remaining search. If the static macro blocks are predicted by ZMP procedure before starting the ME, significant reduction of computation is possible and the remaining search is faster and saves memory. It has been found that distortion measure of stationary blocks is very small as compared to moving blocks. Therefore for finding a block to be stationary, its block distortion is compared with a predetermined threshold Ts. If it is below Ts, the block is categorized as stationary and search is terminated thereafter assigning MVs as (0,0). Threshold with which the block distortion is compared plays an important role in ZMP and can be fixed as well as dynamic. Concept of using a threshold value for detection of stationary blocks is given in (Zeng et al., 1997). Hang et al suggested to use fixed threshold (Hang et al., 1997) for early detection of stationary blocks, but didn't propose a global value for fixed threshold. To alleviate the need of extra memory and calculations involved in using adaptive threshold Nie and Ma (Nie & Ma, 2002) conducted experiments on various sequences and suggested the idea of fixed threshold. Fixed threshold is simple to implement and is also used in (Luo et al., 2015; Nie & Ma, 2001) to identify stationary blocks. The major disadvantage of using fixed threshold is that SAD based prediction error of zero motion blocks is different for different parts of a frame and different frames in a sequence. It is therefore difficult to select an appropriate fixed threshold that is applicable in all situations.

G. De Haan (Haan, 1992) proposed the concept of block hopping to identify stationary blocks. The threshold used is periodically adjusted so as to use the capacity of hardware as efficiently as possible. Shi et al (Shi et al., 1998) have also used adaptive thresholding for pre-judgement of MVs for very slow motion video sequences. Yang et al (Yang et al., 2002) have given a reference threshold algorithm which is based on finding whether the macro block in the previous frame is zero motion or not. If the block is not a zero motion block then constant threshold is used for ZMP. The values of constant and reference threshold have been determined experimentally.

Some of the recent approaches have used dynamic threshold for motion estimation using ZMP which is more generalized than the previously defined fixed thresholds. Ishfaq Ahmed (Ahmed et al., 2006) has used adaptive threshold which enables a faster and robust detection of stationary blocks. It is based on the idea of using the maximum or minimum of SAD values of adjacent blocks as the threshold, depending on whether all or one of the adjacent blocks (upper, upper-right and left) have motion vector (0, 0). Ismail et al (Ismail et al., 2007) have given two early search termination techniques- adaptive early search termination (AEST) and dynamic early search termination (DEST). AEST is based on identifying the low, medium and high SAD fields and assigning the thresholds accordingly. DEST is based on using the average SAD values of the previous stationary blocks. In yet another attempt to increase the accuracy of this threshold. They have given a better model to evaluate the threshold dynamically. The technique is based on finding the initial search centers (ISC) before the ZMP process and threshold is dependent upon the average of the SAD values of all previous stationary blocks and the SAD value between the current and ISC block. Recently Shaifali et al, (Shaifali et al., 2016) proposed a new two level zero motion prejudgment technique to enhance the accuracy in zero motion prejudgment.

Adaptive Selection of Search Window (SW) Size

In an image an object occupies more than one block and motions of these neighboring blocks are highly correlated. Also in the blocks of consecutive frames due to the inertia of the moving objects, there is correlation among MV. If the MVs of the previously computed blocks are all large, then it is very much possible that the current block may have large MV. However, the fact is, high probability of large motion vector does not mean that a large SW is required. The size of the search area effects the calculation for finding motion vector. Adaptively adjusting SW according to the information given by previously encoded syntax element, also known as adaptive search range (ASR) algorithm, can efficiently reduce the computational complexity of ME. Compared with heuristic search pattern (HSP) algorithms like diamond/hexagon search, ASR algorithms are more fundamental, flexible and hardware-oriented. A lot of research has been done to adjust the search window size and is summarized in this sub section.

Hwang-Seok Oh et al (Oh et al., 2000) proposed to reduce the computational complexity of the full search block-matching algorithm for low bit-rate video coding. The proposed method exploits the correlation of successive video frames and adjusts the size of search area depending on the displaced block difference and the block classification information in the previous frames of the block.

Most of the search range or area adjustment are based upon the MV information from neighboring blocks to predict the shape and the size of the SW. Predictive search area (A smaller or bigger search range) can not only reduce the execution time required but also improves the accuracy of ME.

Toru Yamada et al (Yamada et al., 2005) proposed an adaptive search range decision algorithm for use with both frames and individual blocks. It offers both fast and accurate motion estimation. Sumeer Goel et al in (Goel et al., 2005) reduced the computational cost for finding motion vector by reducing the search space without significant loss in quality. A new adaptive reduction of search area for the block-matching algorithm has been presented.

Anand paul suggested adaptive window size selection (Anand et al., 2006) in which, appropriate search window for each block is determined on the basis of MVs and prediction errors obtained for the previous block.

Mohammed Golam Sarwer et al. (Sarwar & Wu, 2009) suggested a novel adaptive search area decision method by utilizing the information of the previously computed motion vectors (MVs). Selection of the search area is based on the direction of picture movement of the previously computed blocks. Authors suggested significant improvement in coding speed with negligible objective quality degradation in comparison to the FS motion estimation method adopted by H.264/AVC reference software.

In latest fast motion search algorithms, a motion vector predictor (MVP) is obtained from the motion vectors (MVs) of spatially and temporally neighboring blocks, which is called the predictive MV set. By exploiting the relationship between the variance of the predictive MV set and the SR, an adaptive SR selection algorithm is proposed by Chung-Cheng Lou (Lou et al., 2010). A larger variance implies lower accuracy of the MVP and thus a larger SR.

Anand Paul (Paul, 2015) used threshold values for changing different search range from average SAD of designated region of block. Unwanted computations are eliminated by effectively switching from one search range to another. Local characteristics of the motion are utilized for selecting the search range.

Byung-Gyu Kim et al. (Kim et al., 2015) applied an efficient adaptation method to control the search ranges of the motion estimation process according to block modes from the base layer, where the full motion vector search is used. This adjustment is also extended to the adaptive search range in the base layer.

Chang-Hung Tsai et al (Tsai et al, 2010) proposed a group of macroblock (GOMB) based motion estimation (ME) algorithm supporting adaptive search range (ASR) for H.264 video coding and performing ME to greatly reduce both the computational complexity and memory bandwidth while maintaining good video quality.

Zhiru Shi et al (Shi et al. 2011) proposed Simulated Annealing Adaptive Search (SAAS) to reduce the computational load. The basic idea of the proposed scheme is based on adjusting search pattern not only for each frame but also for each block. Initially, the adaptive search pattern is performed by statistical analysis of previous frame's motion vector correlation. Then the search pattern is adjusted for each block according to the predicted motion vector. According to motion vector correlation statistics information, search region is adaptively divided and Simulated Annealing (SA) mechanism is adopted to select search power for each region and to avoid trapping into local minima.

Varying Block Size for Improving the Quality of Video

The performance of the ME is affected by the size of the blocks. Small block sizes have good approximation to the natural object boundaries and also to real motion. But a large amount of raw motion information is produced with small block sizes. This increases the number of transmission bits. From performance point of view, small blocks also suffer from object ambiguity problem, which means similar objects may appear at multiple locations inside a picture and may lead to incorrect displacement vectors and random noise problem. Large block size on the other hand may produce less accurate motion vectors since a large block may likely contain pixels moving at different speeds and directions. The employment of the variable block size techniques show a significant change in quality of the video and are therefore implemented in advance video coding standards like H.264. But in H.264 encoder, the most time-consuming component is variable block-size motion estimation (VBSME). A lot of research is done and is still going on to fasten this process. A large number of new algorithms have been proposed for reducing the computations and adaptively selecting the block sizes. Concept of variable block size was suggested for compressing an image. An image is segmented into regions of different sizes, classifying each region into one of several perceptually distinct categories, and using a distinct coding procedure for each category. The important regions in the image have been isolated; the remaining parts of the image can be coded at a lower rate than would be otherwise possible. Jung Woo Lee et al (Lee et al., 1995) suggested a new quadtree based approach for VBSME. In this approach, a fast tree optimization technique is used to reduce the computational complexity of the algorithm so that it can be run in real time in appropriate hardware. A new adaptive block-size transform (ABT) was proposed for coding of high resolution and interlaced video in the emerging video coding standard H.264/AVC. The basic idea of inter ABT is to align the block size used for transform coding of the prediction error to the block size used for motion compensation. Zhi Zhou et al. (Zhou et al., 2014) suggested fast VBSME based on merge and split procedure. The algorithms take advantage of the correlation of MVs of the different block-size modes, to achieve good computation reduction. Libo Yang et al. (Yang et al., 2005) suggested an early termination algorithm to fasten VBSME. Recently (Suliman & L, 2016; Shaifali et al., 2016) a new adaptive partitioning scheme and decision criteria is proposed which utilizes more effectively the motion content of a frame in terms of the size, shape of the blocks and uses less number of partition blocks. Recently, Shaifali et al (Shaifali & Navin, 2014) proposed a comparison of the block based motion estimation techniques and in (Shaifali & Navin, 2014) comparisons for fast medium and slow moving video sequences have been done.

Improvement in Quality of BBME by Considering the Edges of Objects in Video

Intensity based BMAs are widely used for exploiting temporal redundancies in video coding. But blocks located on boundaries of moving objects are not estimated accurately. As human eyes are sensitive to edge details, therefore edge detecting techniques when included with ME improves the quality of the video. Yui-Lam chan et al. (Chan & Siu, 1997) suggested a novel approach which incorporates edge matching techniques to accurately predict the motion of moving objects such that the motion compensated frames are tied more closely to the physical features. Accurate MVs of edge blocks can be used to develop an efficient block motion estimation algorithm. But the computationally expensive process of edge detection has made these techniques inevitable in real time applications.

Muhammad Bilal Ahmad et al (Ahmad et al., 2000) proposed an efficient algorithm for accurately determining the motion vectors using the edge matching criteria. This method gives good motion estimation, and the motion compensated frames are very close to the original frames. This new method reduces the computational requirements significantly and gives good results as compared to the intensity based full search algorithm.

BASIC PROBLEMS ASSOCIATED WITH BLOCK BASED VIDEO CODING

The major problem which arises with video compression is the distortions which are added to the video because of lossy compression. This section describes the most common artifacts that have emerged with the various coding tools and standards (Andreas, 2012):

1. **Blocking Artifacts:** These are caused because of partitioning of frame in to equal size or variable size blocks. Since each of the macro block is coded separately it leads to perceivable edges at the borders.
2. **Mosquito Noise Artifact:** Also, known as Gibb's effect, this artifact appears at the borders of the objects. It occurs as a result of quantization of high frequency components as well as the prediction errors which appear while inter-frame prediction is used for coding of blocks.
3. **Blurring Artifact:** It is the attenuation of high frequency components which may be a result of filtering or quantization.
4. **Ringing Artifacts:** This is also a common artifact which is evident around sharp edges and results from the inadequate approximation of steep edges.
5. **Staircase Artifact:** This artifact is most nearly related to the ringing artifact with the difference that it results from inadequate approximation of diagonal edges.

CONCLUSION

A detailed review of the basic concepts in video coding, development of video coding standards and BBME techniques has been discussed in this chapter. Full search motion estimation algorithm gives the optimum results for BBME but suffers from high computation load. Various fixed pattern search algorithms that reduce the computational load of FS but give suboptimum results have been discussed in detail. Further improvement in efficiency and accuracy of BBME algorithms can be done by predicting the motion vectors using spatio-temporal correlation between neighboring blocks and frames. Algorithms designed using these approaches and sub-pixel decimation have also been discussed in detail. There are various factors which when incorporated with any fast ME algorithm can further reduce computations and enhance its accuracy like block matching criteria, variable block and window size, zero motion prejudgment and edge detection.

REFERENCES

Ahmad, I., Zheng, W., Luo, J., & Liou, M. (2006). A fast adaptive motion estimation algorithm. *IEEE Transactions on Circuits and Systems for Video Technology, 16*(3), 420–438. doi:10.1109/TCSVT.2006.870022

Ahmad, M. B., Kim, D. Y., Roh, K. S., & Choi, T. S. (2000). Motion vector estimation using edge oriented block matching algorithm for video sequences. *Proceedings of the 2000 International Conference on Image Processing* (Vol. 1, pp. 860-863). IEEE. doi:10.1109/ICIP.2000.901095

Arora, S. M., & Rajpal, N. (2014). Comparative analysis of motion estimation algorithms on slow, medium and fast video sequences. *Proceedings of the 2014 International Conference on Optimization, Reliability, and Information Technology* (pp. 422-427). IEEE. doi:10.1109/ICROIT.2014.6798367

Arora, S. M., & Rajpal, N. (2014). Survey of fast block motion estimation algorithms. *Proceedings of the 2014 International Conference on Advances in Computing, Communications and Informatics* (pp. 2022-2026). IEEE. doi:10.1109/ICACCI.2014.6968599

Arora, S. M., Rajpal, N., & Khanna, K. (2016). A new approach with enhanced accuracy in zero motion prejudgment for motion estimation in real-time applications. *Journal of Real-Time Image Processing*.

Atkinson, W. (1994). U.S. Patent No. 5,335,299. Washington, DC: U.S. Patent and Trademark Office.

Barbero, M., & Stroppiana, M. (1992). Data compression for HDTV transmission and distribution. *Proceedings of the IEE Colloquium on Applications of Video Compression in Broadcasting*.

Bierling, M. (1988). Displacement estimation by hierarchical blockmatching. In *Visual Communications and Image Processing'88: Third in a Series* (pp. 942–953). International Society for Optics and Photonics. doi:10.1117/12.969046

Cafforio, C., Rocca, F., & Tubaro, S. (1990). Motion compensated image interpolation. *IEEE Transactions on Communications, 38*(2), 215–222. doi:10.1109/26.47856

Chan, E., Rodriguez, A. A., Gandhi, R., & Panchanathan, S. (1994). Experiments on block-matching techniques for video coding. *Multimedia Systems, 2*(5), 228–241. doi:10.1007/BF01215400

Chan, M. H., Yu, Y. B., & Constantinides, A. G. (1990). Variable size block matching motion compensation with applications to video coding. *Communications, Speech and Vision, IEE Proceedings, 137*(4). doi:10.1049/ip-i-2.1990.0029

Chan, Y.-L., & Siu, W.-C. (1997). Block motion vector estimation using edge matching: An approach with better frame quality as compared to full search algorithm. *Proceedings of 1997 IEEE International Symposium on Circuits and Systems ISCAS'97 (Vol. 2*, pp. 1145-1148). IEEE.

De Haan, G. (1992). Motion estimation and compensation: An integrated approach to consumer display field rate conversion [PhD diss.]. TU Delft, Delft University of Technology.

Eckart, S., & Fogg, C. E. (1995). ISO-IEC MPEG-2 software video codec. *Proceedings of the IS&T/SPIE's Symposium on Electronic Imaging: Science & Technology*. International Society for Optics and Photonics, .

Fadzil, M. A., & Dennis, T. J. (1990). A hierarchical motion estimator for interframe coding. *Proceedings of the IEE Colloquium on Applications of Motion Compensation.*

Frey, M., & Nguyen-Quang, S. (2000). A gamma-based framework for modeling variable-rate MPEG video sources: the GOP GBAR model. *IEEE/ACM Transactions on Networking, 8*(6), 710-719.

Goel, S., Ismail, Y., & Bayoumi, M. A. (2005). Adaptive search window size algorithm for fast motion estimation in H. 264/AVC standard. *Proceedings of the 48th Midwest Symposium on Circuits and Systems.* IEEE. doi:10.1109/MWSCAS.2005.1594412

Golomb, S. W. (1980). Sources which maximize the choice of a Huffman coding tree. *Information and Control, 45*(3), 263–272. doi:10.1016/S0019-9958(80)90648-8

Gonzales, C. A., Allman, L., McCarthy, T., Wendt, P., & Akansu, A. N. (1990). DCT coding for motion video storage using adaptive arithmetic coding. *Signal Processing Image Communication, 2*(2), 145–154. doi:10.1016/0923-5965(90)90017-C

Hang, H.-M., Chou, Y.-M., & Cheng, S.-C. (1997). Motion estimation for video coding standards. *The Journal of VLSI Signal Processing, 17*(2), 113–136. doi:10.1023/A:1007994620638

Huang, Y.-W., Chen, C.-Y., Tsai, C.-H., Shen, C.-F., & Chen, L.-G. (2006). Survey on block matching motion estimation algorithms and architectures with new results. *Journal of VLSI Signal Processing Systems, 42*(3), 297–320. doi:10.1007/s11265-006-4190-4

Huckfield, D. M. (1992). Post production applications of video compression in broadcasting. *Proceedings of the IEE Colloquium on Applications of Video Compression in Broadcasting.*

Huynh-Thu, Q., & Ghanbari, M. (2008). Scope of validity of PSNR in image/video quality assessment. *Electronics Letters, 44*(13), 800–801. doi:10.1049/el:20080522

International Orgranization for Standardization. (n. d.). Retrieved from http://www.iso.org/

International Telecommunications Union. (n. d.). Retrieved from http://www.itu.int/ITU-T/

Ismail, Y., Elgamel, M., & Bayoumi, M. (2007). Adaptive techniques for a fast frequency domain motion estimation. *Proceedings of the 2007 IEEE Workshop on Signal Processing Systems* (pp. 331-336). IEEE. doi:10.1109/SIPS.2007.4387567

ISO-IEC. (1993). *I. S. 11172 (MPEG-1). Coding of moving pictures and associated audio for digital storage media up to about 1.5 Mbit (Technical report).* Motion Picture Experts Group.

ISO/IEC MPEG-4 Visual Version 1 Coding of audio-visual objects—Part 2: Visual. (1999, April).

Javidi, B., & Okano, F. (Eds.). (2002). *Three-dimensional television, video, and display technologies.* Springer Science & Business Media.

Jing, X., Zhu, C., & Chau, L.-P. (2003). Smooth constrained motion estimation for video coding. *Signal Processing, 83*(3), 677–680. doi:10.1016/S0165-1684(02)00482-6

Kim, B.-G., Reddy, K., & Ahn, W. H. (2009). Dynamic search-range control algorithm for fast interframe coding in scalable video coding. *Optical Engineering (Redondo Beach, Calif.), 48*(9), 097002–097002. doi:10.1117/1.3212684

Kim, J.-S., & Park, R.-H. (1992). A fast feature-based block matching algorithm using integral projections. *IEEE Journal on Selected Areas in Communications, 10*(5), 968–971. doi:10.1109/49.139002

Klaue, J., Rathke, B., & Wolisz, A. (2003). *Evalvid–A framework for video transmission and quality evaluation. In Computer performance evaluation. Modelling techniques and tools* (pp. 255–272). Springer Berlin Heidelberg. doi:10.1007/978-3-540-45232-4_16

Langdon, G., & Rissanen, J. (1981, June). Compression of black-white images with arithmetic coding. *IEEE Transactions on, 29*(6), 858–867. doi:10.1109/TCOM.1981.1095052

Le Gall, D. (1991). MPEG: A video compression standard for multimedia applications. *Communications of the ACM, 34*(4), 46–58. doi:10.1145/103085.103090

Le Gall, D. J. (1992). The MPEG video compression algorithm. *Signal Processing Image Communication, 4*(2), 129–140. doi:10.1016/0923-5965(92)90019-C

Lee, J. (1995). Optimal quadtree for variable block size motion estimation. *Proceedings of the International Conference on Image Processing* (Vol. 3, pp. 480-483). IEEE.

Liu, B., & Zaccarin, A. (1993). New fast algorithms for the estimation of block motion vectors. *IEEE Transactions on Circuits and Systems for Video Technology, 3*(2), 148–157. doi:10.1109/76.212720

Lou, C.-C., Lee, S.-W., & Jay Kuo, C.-C. (2010). Adaptive search range selection in motion estimation. *Proceedings of the 2010 IEEE International Conference on Acoustics Speech and Signal Processing (ICASSP)* (pp. 918-921). IEEE. doi:10.1109/ICASSP.2010.5495282

Luo, J., Yang, X., & Liu, L. (2015). A fast motion estimation algorithm based on adaptive pattern and search priority. *Multimedia Tools and Applications, 74*(24), 11821–11836. doi:10.1007/s11042-014-2280-z

Mistretta, C. A., Crummy, A. B., & Strother, C. M. (1981). Digital angiography: A perspective. *Radiology, 139*(2), 273–276. doi:10.1148/radiology.139.2.7012918 PMID:7012918

Murayama, N., Taniguchi, H., Konishi, A., & Matsuda, H. (1980). U.S. Patent No. 4,207,599. Washington, DC: U.S. Patent and Trademark Office.

Nie, Y., & Ma, K.-K. (2002). Adaptive irregular pattern search with zero-motion prejudgement for fast block-matching motion estimation. *Proceedings of the 7th International Conference on Control, Automation, Robotics and Vision ICARCV '02* (Vol. 3, pp. 1320-1325). IEEE.

O'Hara, K., Mitchell, A. S., & Vorbau, A. (2007). Consuming video on mobile devices. *Proceedings of the SIGCHI conference on Human factors in computing systems*. ACM. doi:10.1145/1240624.1240754

Oh, H.-S., & Lee, H.-K. (2000). Block-matching algorithm based on an adaptive reduction of the search area for motion estimation. *Real-Time Imaging, 6*(5), 407–414. doi:10.1006/rtim.1999.0184

Paul, A. (2015). Adaptive search window for high efficiency video coding. *Journal of Signal Processing Systems for Signal, Image, and Video Technology, 79*(3), 257–262. doi:10.1007/s11265-013-0841-4

Paul, A., Wang, J. F., Wang, J. C., Tsai, A. C., & Chen, J. T. (2006). Projection based adaptive window size selection for efficient motion estimation in H. 264/AVC. *IEICE Transactions on Fundamentals of Electronics, Communications and Computer Science, 89*(11), 2970–2976.

Purwar, R. K., Prakash, N., & Rajpal, N. (2011). A matching criterion for motion compensation in the temporal coding of video signal. *Signal, Image and Video Processing, 5*(2), 133–139. doi:10.1007/s11760-009-0149-9

Richardson, I.E. (2003). H. 264 and MPEG-4 Video Compression. England: Wiley.

Saha, A., Mukherjee, J., & Sural, S. (2008). New pixel-decimation patterns for block matching in motion estimation. *Signal Processing Image Communication, 23*(10), 725–738. doi:10.1016/j.image.2008.08.004

Said, A., & Pearlman, W. A. (1996). An image multiresolution representation for lossless and lossy compression. *IEEE Transactions on Image Processing, 5*(9), 1303–1310. doi:10.1109/83.535842 PMID:18285219

Sarwer, M. G., & Jonathan Wu, Q. M. (2009). Adaptive search area selection of variable block-size motion estimation of H. 264/AVC video coding standard. *Proceedings of the 11th IEEE International Symposium on Multimedia ISM'09* (pp. 100-105). IEEE. doi:10.1109/ISM.2009.53

Shi, Y.-G., Zhang, Y., & Wu, L.-N. (1998). Adaptive thresholding for motion estimation prejudgement. *Electronics Letters, 34*(21), 2016–2017. doi:10.1049/el:19981380

Shi, Z., Fernando, W. A. C., & Kondoz, A. (2011). Adaptive direction search algorithms based on motion correlation for block motion estimation. *IEEE Transactions on Consumer Electronics, 57*(3), 1354–1361. doi:10.1109/TCE.2011.6018894

Song, B. C., & Ra, J. B. (1998). Hierarchical block-matching algorithm using partial distortion criterion. Proceedings of Photonics West '98 on Electronic Imaging (pp. 88-95). International Society for Optics and Photonics, . doi:10.1117/12.298403

Sugiyama, K. (1991). *U.S. Patent No. 4,985,768*. Washington, DC: U.S. Patent and Trademark Office.

Suliman, A., & Li, R. (2016). Video Compression Using Variable Block Size Motion Compensation with Selective Subpixel Accuracy in Redundant Wavelet Transform. In Information Technology: New Generations (pp. 1021-1028). Springer International Publishing. doi:10.1007/978-3-319-32467-8_88

Sullivan, G. J., & Ohm, J.-R. (2010). *Recent developments in standardization of high efficiency video coding (HEVC)*. International Society for Optics and Photonics. doi:10.1117/12.863486

Sullivan, G. J., Ohm, J.-R., Han, W.-J., & Wiegand, T. (2012). Overview of the high efficiency video coding (HEVC) standard. *IEEE Transactions on Circuits and Systems for Video Technology, 22*(12), 1649–1668. doi:10.1109/TCSVT.2012.2221191

Tawbi, W. (1993). Video compression standards and quality of service. *The Computer Journal, 36*(1), 43–54. doi:10.1093/comjnl/36.1.43

Torres-Urgell, L., & Lynn Kirlin, R. (1990). Adaptive image compression using Karhunen-Loeve transform. *Signal Processing, 21*(4), 303–313. doi:10.1016/0165-1684(90)90100-D

Tsai, C.-H., Tan, K.-J., Su, C.-L., & Guo, J.I. (2010). A group of macroblock based motion estimation algorithm supporting adaptive search range for H. 264 video coding. *Proceedings of 2010 IEEE International Symposium on Circuits and Systems (ISCAS)* (pp. 1891-1894). IEEE. doi:10.1109/ISCAS.2010.5537919

Unterweger, A. (2012). *Compression artifacts in modern video coding and state-of-the-art means of compensation.* In *Multimedia Networking and Coding* (p. 28).

Wallace, G. K. (1992). The JPEG still picture compression standard. *Consumer Electronics, IEEE Transactions on, 38*(1), xviii–xxxiv. doi:10.1109/30.125072

Wang, C.-N., Yang, S.-W., Liu, C.-M., & Chiang, T. (2003). A hierarchical decimation lattice based on N-queen with an application for motion estimation. *IEEE Signal Processing Letters, 10*(8), 228–231. doi:10.1109/LSP.2003.814403

Wang, S., & Chen, H. (1999). An improve algorithm of motion compensation MPEG video compression. *Proceedings of the IEEE International Vehicle Electronics Conference IVEC'99* (pp. 261-264). IEEE. doi:10.1109/IVEC.1999.830680

Wang, Y., Wang, Y., & Kuroda, H. (2000). A globally adaptive pixel-decimation algorithm for block-motion estimation. *IEEE Transactions on Circuits and Systems for Video Technology, 10*(6), 1006–1011. doi:10.1109/76.867940

Wiegand, T., Sullivan, G. J., Bjontegaard, G., & Luthra, A. (2003). Overview of the H. 264/AVC video coding standard. *IEEE Transactions on Circuits and Systems for Video Technology, 13*(7), 560–576. doi:10.1109/TCSVT.2003.815165

Wien, M. (2003). Variable block-size transforms for H. 264/AVC. *IEEE Transactions on Circuits and Systems for Video Technology, 13*(7), 604–613. doi:10.1109/TCSVT.2003.815380

Wu, Y., Hirakawa, S., Reimers, U. H., & Whitaker, J. (2006). Overview of digital television development worldwide. *Proceedings of the IEEE, 94*(1), 8–21. doi:10.1109/JPROC.2005.861000

Xiong, B., & Zhu, C. (2009). Efficient block matching motion estimation using multilevel intra-and inter-subblock features subblock-based SATD. *IEEE Transactions on Circuits and Systems for Video Technology, 19*(7), 1039–1043. doi:10.1109/TCSVT.2009.2020260

Yamada, T., Ikekawa, M., & Kuroda, I. (2005). Fast and accurate motion estimation algorithm by adaptive search range and shape selection. *Proceedings of the IEEE International Conference on. Acoustics, Speech, and Signal Processing ICASSP'05* (Vol. 2). IEEE. doi:10.1109/ICASSP.2005.1415550

Yang, J.-F., Chang, S.-C., & Chen, C.-Y. (2002). Computation reduction for motion search in low rate video coders. *IEEE Transactions on Circuits and Systems for Video Technology, 12*(10), 948–951. doi:10.1109/TCSVT.2002.804892

Yang, L., Yu, K., Li, J., & Li, S. (2005). An effective variable block-size early termination algorithm for H. 264 video coding. *IEEE Transactions on Circuits and Systems for Video Technology, 15*(6), 784–788. doi:10.1109/TCSVT.2005.848306

Zeng, B., Li, R., & Liou, M. L. (1997). Optimization of fast block motion estimation algorithms. *IEEE Transactions on Circuits and Systems for Video Technology, 7*(6), 833–844. doi:10.1109/76.644063

Zhou, Z., Sun, M.-T., & Hsu, Y.-F. (2004). Fast variable block-size motion estimation algorithm based on merge and slit procedures for H. 264/MPEG-4 AVC. *Proceedings of the 2004 International Symposium on Circuits and Systems ISCAS'04 (Vol. 3)*. IEEE. doi:10.1109/ISCAS.2004.1328849

Chapter 4
Computed Tomography Brain Images Semantic Segmentation

Poonam Fauzdar
GLA University, India

Sarvesh Kumar
GLA University, India

ABSTRACT

In this paper we applianced an approach for segmenting brain tumour regions in a computed tomography images by proposing a multi-level fuzzy technique with quantization and minimum computed Euclidean distance applied to morphologically divided skull part. Since the edges identified with closed contours and further improved by adding minimum Euclidean distance, that is why the numerous results that are analyzed are very assuring and algorithm poses following advantages like less cost, global analysis of image, reduced time, more specificity and positive predictive value.

INTRODUCTION

Image segmentation, a process to analyse the peculiarities and provide a strong basis for quantative and qualitative comparison of human pathology images and functions. All pixels of same label in a image share same format related to visual characteristics, so image segmentation process is more or less assign these labels to pixels during analysis. The image partitioning into homogeneous regions based on a set of characteristics, are the key features are very advantageous for computer vision applications and image analysis for abnormalities. Clustering is one of the methods available for image segmentation along with others like threshold based, edge based, region based, watershed based, feature based, background based algorithms etc. for this purpose. Clustering is defined as process for classifying pixels of any type of images based on similarity according to gray-level intensity, edge intensity, feature vector table, pixel colour etc.

Still in today era medical image segmentation or clustering remains one of the major challenges for researchers (Zacki, Fauzi & Besar 2011). Numerous different concepts and theories are proposed and implemented for segmentation of images considering various application areas but unsatisfactory results

DOI: 10.4018/978-1-5225-2848-7.ch004

have been brushed during analysis of abnormalities in special cases of medical images during classification of affected areas by different existing algorithm. Similar data is considered as statistics for classification of fundamental information employed in such a way that correspondent regions are grouped together as compare to dissimilar data that differ due to unique features (Cheng, Cheng & Koschan, 2011). Applications areas that include digital figures processing, need accurate and commonly used techniques for clustering procedure which partition prominent regions from original image and distinguish borders of all objects present in whole image and its basis for search are indices of dissimilarity, similarity or outer regions from all data points or pixels. The real idea of segmentation algorithms is to simplify the illustration of an image into distinguished regions that move towards more accurate and précised information analysis (Subash & Thangavel, 2012).

However, the problem is that the performance of algorithm for image segmentation and analysis would be improved by modernization of any of already proposed set method classic velocity accuracy.

This chapter includes a comprehensive survey of existing image segmentation algorithms and propose an approach to segment an affected eccentric tissues of medical brain images along with a process of segmentation for distinguishing any abnormalities such as blood draining, blood clots, ventricles misaligned, abnormal behaviour of cells of brain images on a standard database of computed tomography brain images "MINAC". This chapter helps to understand the issues in existing algorithm like long execution time and low accuracy.

Background

Segmentation of cranial binary structures in CT images represent an important step in identification of significant regions that in turn provide indication for divergent behaviour from healthy medical images of human body. X-ray images, Bone scan images, Ultrasound images, Mammogram images, MRI images etc. are found to be less compatible for diagnosis by both patients and doctors. These scan images lacks accuracy because of many reasons like metal implants or scan taken when the patient is not able to remain motionless due to issues like body pain, health, age etc., so CT scan images are most preferred for diagnosis because CT images are taken under controlled environment many times and they show every angle of images for detecting abnormalities and they provide high probability of accuracy and good detection of spastic, classifications and drains. The real idea of segmentation algorithms is to simplify the illustration of an image into distinguished regions that move towards more accurate and précised information analysis. Mainly medical image segmentation is typically used to locate distinct objects and boundaries of abnormal behavior tissues in main images. In recent scenario, growing attention has been put on robust techniques like clustering, segmentation, classification in data and image analysis. The main application areas of specific recent pattern recognition are related to medical images, remote sensing etc. For example: One major application that include mining information, extract autonomous and useful patterns from large collection of content in data warehouses or data marts. It involves the use of sophisticated online analytical processing tools to discover previously unknown, valid recent patterns and relationships between them in large data usage sets. Data mining consists of unique process of recognizing patterns from already managed data, it also includes analysis, classification and rule prediction. The CT scan images are more comfortable than other scanning techniques of abnormalities classification and does not have any side effects on human body because it does scanning without using radiation. Basic fundamental behind this scanning is employed using theories of radio wave movement and magnetic fields. There are different types of algorithm were developed for brain tumour detection.

Despite colossal extent of research that has been done, and the innumerable segmentation techniques that have been appliance, most of the methods still illustrate it as a strong active domain research area including different applications and proposal for a unified image segmentation procedure remains an open problem till date.

The chapter organized in different sections. The first section covers introduction and background. The second section includes study of previous and current research applications of medical image processing. Next section includes fundamentals of design and implementation. After that, simulation results are being discussed in the next section and finally concludes with future prospects explained.

LITERATURE REVIEW

Medical image analysis is either done by segmentation process or clustering to find significant regions as it provides the basis of quantitative study of human body anatomy and internal functions. In past decades manual segmentation procedure is employed for analysis of affected areas of medical data is examined as more time consuming process so automated segmentation nowadays gained over it for image processing (Boss and Thangavel, 2012). Segmentation of the cranial structures in CT images exhibit a very influential step in the identification of significant and affected areas that reveal the presence of abnormalities. MRI images are often used for the purpose of segmenting damaged regions. So computed tomographic images are considered as second scanning option for patients who are incompatible with MRI such as in case of metal implants (those who are unable to remain motionless during checkup due to pain, old age, or any other situation related to medical mishappening) (Banumathi, Pethalakshm, 2012).

Multi-Level Set Thresholding Method

W. Mimi Diyana and W. Zaki propose a procedure to remove gray level values inconsistency in MRI images, radiography, computed tomography images, etc. The gray level in colour pictures is the preeminent problem that come across during different methodologies performance that tends to object segmentation within the same intensity level by different functions. So implicitly, the limitation has been overcome by directing towards multi-level segmentation based on calculating threshold parameter values which can be implied for both global and local intracranial heteroclites segmentations. According to this algorithm it is a multi step process in which firstly for global segmentation, clustering has been exploited by fuzzy logic to extract dissimilar and similar skull regions and other regions of interest and outer cranial structures are extracted from an image background and then in the further levels of the intracranial segmentation, author have applied double level or multi level thresholding technique based on multithresholding OTSU concept (Zaki & Fauzi, 2011).

The algorithm comparative analysis is mentioned in table 1 and equations used in algorithm are as follows:

1. The probability to find grey level regions in an image by equation is

$$P(j) = Fj/N \tag{1}$$

where Fj are number of pixel to be considered.

2.   Individual specified class frequencies are computed as

$$S1(t) = \sum_{i=1}^{q} P(j) \text{ and } S2(t) = \sum_{i=1}^{q} P(j) \tag{2}$$

3.   Class variances and individual class variances are calculated as:

$$\mu 2(r) = \sum_{i=1}^{t} \left(i - \beta(\mathrm{r})2 \; \mathrm{P(j)}/\mathrm{S1(t)}\right) \tag{3}$$

4.   Symmetrical features is given by formula

$$T1 = \left[Nnsf\{left\} - Nnsf\{right\}\right]\Big/\left[Nnsf\{left\} \; + \; Nnsf\{right\}\right] \tag{4}$$

where Nnsf are total number of pixel in right and left side of brain image midline.

Watershed Segmentation Method

The method was appliance by Lamia Jaffar mainly rely on the theory to find optimal decomposition into two parts one that is optimal design and other its complementary part out of original image. It is a robust segmentation operant introduced from the subject area of mathematical etiology (Sun & Sonka, 2013). This approach is applied to segment the image into drainage areas and lines and the gradient pixel magnitude intensities go through transformation to produce a topographic surface. Natural application of this concept allows the users to detect the main edges so that they can be preserved and outer images can be smoothened. Since the edges identified with closed contours and further improved by adding physiographic gradient, that is why the numerous results that are analyzed are very assuring and algorithm poses following advantages like less cost, global analysis of image, unwanted contours or noise removal, over segmentation problem solved etc. (Sun & Sonka, 2013; Zaki & Fauzi, 2011).

Table 1. Comparative analysis of different abnormalities

Abnormalities	No. of Images	Symmetrical feature 1	Symmetrical feature 2	Intensities	Location
Calcification	60	--	--	yes	yes
Bleeding	80	Yes	--	yes	--
Normal case	519	Yes	yes	yes	--
Misaligned tissues	61	--	yes	--	--

Expectation Maximization Method

This method was appliance by R.Ravindraiah mainly rely on the theory to divide regions into clusters by identifying the most likely indexed pixel parameters from whole known distribution with some unknown data. Data pixels identified as feature vectors for each pixel and maximum expected pixels that belong to pixels are hidden variables, these pixel identifications need prior knowledge for procedure but does not need any training. In this approach unsampled original data is processed into characterized into similar or dissimilar groups. It initially starts by calculating mean value, standard deviation parameters, covariance values and then procedure is followed iteratively to segment the image for abnormalities. It is among the most significant algorithms for estimation of maximum density pixels of image (Zaki & Fauzi, 2011). The algorithm comparative analysis with other techniques is mentioned in table 2.

Background Recognition and Perceptual Organization Method

Author proposed a novel outdoor scene image segmentation method related to on background knowledge and recognition with perceptual reasoning. The algorithm distinguishes the background image regions to capture non-conflicting structural relationship between the existing constituent parts and then group them according to specific classification due to perceptual laws. The image is perceived into two parts one is outdoor scenes that are unstructured objects like car, grass, trees and front part is a structured object such as the people, buildings, etc. Since it is impossible to know all classes of background objects so this algorithmic procedure depends solely upon the visual real-life perception of human mind and accordingly groupings are formed without any prior knowledge. This algorithm achieves accuracy and quality segmentation for images which consist of natural outdoor scenes (Cheng, Cheng & Koschan, 2011).

The algorithm comparative analysis with other techniques is mentioned in table 3 and table 4 and equations used to calculate parameters are mentioned as follows:

1. Weight Function used in POM are calculated as

$$Q\left(x,y\right) = e^{-\theta \, *n(Pi \, - \, Pa)} \tag{5}$$

where (x,y) belongs to I and I belongs to boundary length R

Table 2. Comparative analysis of various algorithms

Algorithms	Results			
	Rejected	Below Average	Good	Excellent
Multi Level Set	1	7	2	140
Expectation Maximum	38	16	29	67
Watershed	22	4	11	113

2.   Boundary Complexity of image is measured by

$$Ci = 1\!\!\Big/ M \sum_{i=1}^{n} \mathrm{B}\big(\mathrm{s},\mathrm{k}\big) * \ \mathrm{Q}\big(\mathrm{x},\mathrm{y}\big) \qquad\qquad (6)$$

Fuzzy C Means Algorithm

Author proposed an approach based on Fuzzy Logic. It is a problem-solving technology that involves control system methods that tends to implementation of systems like very small and embedded micro-controllers and large multi-channel networking computers meant for data acquisition and control systems. Clustering by fuzzy technique implies that every pixel has a degree of correlation to neighbouring pixels regions in separate clusters instead than belonging wholly to just one cluster (Boss & Thangavel, 2012). Many papers propose mammogram images, computed tomography images and magnetic resonance image segmentation using Fuzzy C Means clustering algorithm. The filtering technique is employed for pre-processing of image based on median values, to reduce noise normally in an image. The features are clustered by K-Means and FCM algorithms in order to segment the region of interests for further classification. The performance of fuzzy reasoning is compared and analyzed as compared to K means segmentation according to accurate and low cost (Corso, Yuille, Sicotte & Toga, 2007).

FPCM (Fuzzy Possibilistic C-Means)

M. Gomathi proposes a technique of image segmentation based on customization of conventional Fuzzy logic for length measurement and allow the labelling of pixel regions effected by possibilistic parti-

Table 3. Comparative analysis of performance for different background classes

Classes classification	Test set		
	Test set Gould09	Test set Pom	Full Dataset
Foreground	9.3	27.8	26.8
Mountain	20.4	28.8	33.0
Building	11.8	29.6	30.2
water	37.6	58.8	44.9
Grass	26.4	42.9	40.5
Road	28.01	38.76	42.5
Sky	32.5	46.1	49.1

Table 4. Comparative analysis of feature extraction parameters

Abnormality Classification	Arthritis Detection	Stress fracture
Area covered	0.0279	0.0045
Magnitude of Major axis	0.2326	0.0992
Magnitude of Minor Axis	0.1740	0.06391

tion of whole image, in presence of neighbouring pixels and prevent noise effect during segmentation. Rather than including one term in calculation of objective function, a second value is also incorporated influencing the membership to be more high valued without any limit. In conventional Fuzzy C Means clustering is based solely on dispensation of pixel attributes in component space and dimensional distribution of pixels are not taken into examination. Fuzzy Possibilistic C-Means clustering algorithm is appliance mainly for colored images of any type and features because firstly local geographical similarity measure is considered for initial clustering and membership function, then fuzzy clustering is applied for more customized inter pixel association intrisincity of membership function (Ganesam & Rajini, 2010).

Fuzzy possiblistic algorithm modified the standard membership function calculated for forming clusters in standard Fuzzy C Means to below defined possiblistic membership function. It is calculated by equation:

$$\min\left[\left(Rm\left(x,y,z\right)\right) = \sum_{i=1}^{c}\sum_{k=1}^{n}\mu\mathrm{lk}\ \mathrm{plk}^{2} + \sum_{i=1}^{c}\partial\sum_{k=1}^{n}\left(1\text{-}\mu\mathrm{lf}\right)^{\mathrm{m}}\right] \tag{7}$$

where P_{lk} is distance between kth data and lth cluster in the center, μ_{lf} represents degree fuzziness, a positive integer ∂ is used for calculation and the algorithm comparative analysis with other techniques is mentioned in table 5.

Graph Based Segmentation With Computer Aided Refinement

Author proposed an novel approach for simultaneous segmentation approach for 4D images in two steps that is in first step graph based segmentation of images is employed and after that user inspect the outcome and improve the errors within the reckoning framework of computer aided applications. As we know CT Images 4D contain both volume and time, so it become very tedious to manually segment the abnormalities for analysis. This approach works basically for automated segmentation of right and left part of images from midline shift where sub cage detection is done for initial segmentation by RASM (Recent advances in sliding modes) and automated initialization and inspiration and expiration of images are calculated by observing graphs. After all the process RASM matching and transformation take place by OSF graph and shape priors. The second refinement process is optimal for users as it can be per the need, it is to utilized quickly correct small segmented errors so that, it will not produce disaster errors for segmentation. This approach led to a very quantative segmentation because of Optimal surface finding (OSF graph) refinement (Sun & Sonka, 2013). Flowchart of graph based segmentation algorithm is shown in figure 1.

Table 5. Indices comparison of standard proposed FCM algorithms

Indices	Algorithms		
	Fuzzy Possiblistic C Means	**Standard Fuzzy C Means**	**Modified Fuzzy C Means**
FN ratio	3.40	8.50	5.30
FP ratio	12.80	20.15	16.50
Similarity feature	92.50	86.03	89.50

Figure 1. Flowchart of graph based segmentation algorithm

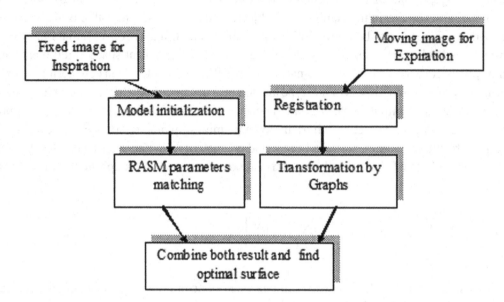

Weighted Shape Based Averaging Technique

Subrahmanyam present a new approach to improve the accuracy of image segmentation is to match the atlas images and standard images .It is based on spatially diversified and similar neighbourhood preceding model and edge preserving evenness with the concept of already existing algorithms and the algorithm proceeds by collecting numerous voting methodologies where the major areas of voting agrees with local average pixel values of atlas images, general weighted voting conforms on the weight of atlases by counting vote of images. Local weighted images are different from global weighted because it is based on local similarity and shape based averaging and voting perceive the fusion problem from different perspective. Shape based method basically transform atlas images by measuring the deep and far away Euclidean distance from the contours of each pixel (Mujmdar, Sivaswamy, Kishore &Varma, 2013).

Liver Segmentation by K Means

Shraddha Sagwan proposed an algorithm that describe a new liver segmentation procedure for the need of transplantation surgery that is one of measure of cure liver tumours. Liver images are segmented not only for computation of total volume but also for information regarding diagnosis of medical abnormalities problem of patients. Basically, the algorithms work towards liver segmentation is still considered a convoluted and challenging problem because of many features like squat contrast, obscure edges, inconsistent shapes, complex features etc. So, the author tried a variational model to successfully overcome the abovementioned problems that reflect the ideology of probability distribution of intensity and volume appearance propagation. K Means is the simplest algorithm that proceeds by firstly considering initial k centroids of each image, then Euclidean distance is calculated, each data point of a given dataset related to the nearest centroids combined to form clusters and then again process iteratively with new centroids until no more changes are observed. The image segmentation is carried out by author by employing and combining modified K Mean procedure with localized contouring algorithm to find five separate regions for computed tomography liver image (Sangwar & Peshaattiwar, 2013).

The algorithm can be summarized as follows:

1. Apply in first step standard K Means procedure.
2. In next step additional images are added to complete the standard structure.
3. Now Region Growing technique is applied on image obtained in second step.
4. Next points are plotted to liver volume through canny edge detection technique.
5. At last parameters are evaluated for performance evaluation.

Integrated Segmentation Using Interpolation on Infrequent Data

Adeline proposes a method for solving two most inherently related problems of images that is segmentation of uneven regions and interpolation. The concept of interpolation of data is used most preferably for segmenting information as compare to pixel intensities for better, accurate and robust performance and also support 2D slices of images of any orientation, position, size etc. with spatial configuration. The proposed algorithm is valid for artificial data, MRI scan, CT scans, X ray and to prove better results when the method is employed by first interpolating the volume of images and then segmentation is iteratively processed over total image volume. More specifically interpolation based techniques are more accurate in case of images with large gaps as the method accounts even global shape of object and work better even at extreme end points even when objects lie outside image slices shown in figure 2. The author studied many segmentation approaches for experimentation and choose piecewise constant algorithm as most appropriate approach for validated framework on any kind of data made up of constant piecewise regions and the algorithm comparative analysis with other techniques is mentioned in table 6. Algorithm is first started by a registration process of images by MRF method which then integrates the intensity and matching gradient constraints for finding matching points and interpolating adjacent area of images (Paiement, Mirmehdi, Xie & Hamilton, 2014).

Figure 2. Slices of sparse data

Table 6. Comparative analysis of interpolation approaches

Algorithms	Image data set	Feature used in Interpolation
Modelling approach	3D Images	Modelling and continuity
Sequential segmentation using interpolation	2D images	Surface based interpolation
Sequential interpolation of image followed by segmentation	3D Images	Image pixel based interpolation
Level set algorithm	3D levelset	Diffusion techniques

Parathyroid Tumours Clustering Using Linear Dynamic System

Author proposed an algorithm for detection of Parathyroid tumours in MRI images for classification of adenomas and carcinomas. The image tissues are designed as continuous productive system to evaluate system parameters operating on curves of particular voxels and their time series analysis testifies to be very useful methodology for extracting features still in presence of noise and uncertain behaviour. This method has been employed in different applications like video sequencing, mobile object tracking, data centre modelling etc. to segment out information about feature vectors. The algorithm proceeds by time series analysis to extract related features from curves of time intensity for each voxel and categorise the dynamic behaviour of tissues in presence of inhomogeneties. The parametric variables associated with straight analysis is independently estimated for every imaging voxels to better classify healthy and tumour clustered classes by employing M step, then E step and at last fuzzy clustering (Jayender, Ruam, Narayan, Agrawal, Jolesz & Mamata, 2013).

The linear Dynamic system analysis is computed by equations:

$$X1 = \partial A + E\mu \tag{8}$$

$$X\left(n+1\right)Ixn + E\mu\left(n=1\right) \tag{9}$$

$$Yn = Cxn + Vn \tag{10}$$

Segmentation Using T Mixture Model

The author proposes an algorithm in concern to device a semi-automated medical images segmentation because manual methods are very tedious to perform and fully automated algorithms lacks human intervention. As segmentation approaches for medical images are becoming day by day standard techniques for visualizing abnormal structures and estimated size comparisons. The algorithm employed semi-automatic approach based primarily on classification of regions and boundaries. Region based techniques quickly result in segmentation by assigning membership functions to voxels according to homogeneous statistics but for in homogeneity it results in inaccurate segmentation because of irregular boundaries.

So, further boundary based algorithms are employed to align irregular boundaries by minimizing energy variables that quantifies feature vector gradient near the edges. Basically, the algorithm proceeds by seed initialization and deformation of images implicitly (Palagan &Leena, 2011).

Neuro Fuzzy Classifier Based Image Segmentation

Aram Tariq appliance a approach for lung cancer diagnosis through computer aided techniques and the algorithm comparative analysis with other techniques is mentioned in table 7. The basic steps employed for detection are lung image segmentation and image enhancement. It is based on automated approach because automated approach as compare to manual segmentation are very beneficial for cancer detection and provide efficient performance in terms of both time and cost. Lung nodules basic shape are almost round or oval shaped that have sharp margins with 3 cm length that is why larger masses if detected are easily referred malignant masses. The first step of lung segmentation firstly convert original image into gray scale image, background is extracted based on gradient mean value and at end segmentation is result of optimal threshold. In second step, morphological operations are carried out for post processing, morphological opening on threshold image, morphological closing applied to enhance borders, morphological thinning of extracted image, pulmonary lobes are identified, border reconstruction by computing Euclidean distance and at last filling is applied for getting post processed image (Tariq, Akram & Javed, 2013).

Atlas Image Labelling and Segmentation

Kaifung Du proposed a methodology for labelling of subcortial structures and cerebral regions of brain CT images. There are numerous studies available about labelling of MRI images but very less literature is available for labelling of subcortial structures of CT Images. Atlas based labeling process starts by propagating labels of query images from the atlas with registration and multi atlas fusion strategies for labelling are analysed through stages single, similar and stable. In first strategy similarity in query image and atlas images are analysed to compute preferred images. In second step one atlas is chosen out from both images with minimum SSD. In third step MV Stage label assigned to voxels on the basis of majority voting. Finally, stable expectation maximization is employed between the iterations and an atlas is chosen out of all query images present in database (Belaid, Jaafar & Mourou, 2012).

Table 7. Comparative analysis of various algorithms

Algorithms	Accuracy (%)
Nodule detection using Genetic Neuro network	94
Two step process of Nodule detection	89.6
Automated nodule detection algorithm	85.3
Automated detection using reconstruction	88.6
Proposed Fuzzy Neuro classifier procedure	95

Image Segmentation by Morphological Transform

B Sridhar present a method for automatic and quantative detection of breast cancer. The computer based technologies use is increasing day by day in scientific fields and employed for solving problems of computer vision. The author employed one of the computing method that is curvelet transform that is directional transform for optimal representation of edges in different angles and scale. In first step normalized value of curvelet transform is calculated by multiplying value of difference operator, spatial frequency, mean in addition to mean value of distorted image. Thirdly the algorithm employ a wrapping fast transform by an equation. Then computed value of threshold is applied an image and inverse the function to convert into spatial domain from curvelet functions. Finally, imaginary part is removed from original image to enhance gray scale of images. Implementation of proposed approach take the raw image and curvelet transform is applied to convert the image into spatial domain and threshold value is used for normalization (Lu, 2008).

Nonlinear Diffusion Tensor Technique for Medical Image

Vinh Q Dang proposes a non-invasive magnetic technique that characterize microstructural biological tissues to localize white matter lesion of brain tumors. Diffusion tensor technique is employed to produce maps which is computed based on voxels by adjusting signal intensities as a function of related data parameters. The purpose of this proposed algorithm is to use GPU hardware for estimation of tensor map by accelerating through non-linear regression. Moreover, this procedure need a related programming efforts to utilize all present resources to result in non-productive environment for domain scientist. LMA algorithm is also utilized in simulating a curve fitting procedure to solve the problem of non-linear function minimization. The algorithm steps proceed by computing the Jacobian function, which is used to calculate error gradient and cross product. Secondly update the calculated parameters and recalculate the errors. Iterate the steps until the convergence criteria meet the exit condition (Zhou, Chang & Liu, 2008).

Unsupervised Segmentation of Heterogeneous Populated Brain Images

Annemie Ribbons proposes an algorithm to study neurological diseases in magnetic resonance brain images. It is basically a data driven framework that perform atlas instructed segmentation of different set of brain images and form homogenous clusters subgroups. Furthermore, it is analysed that subgroups formed by unsupervised framework is similar to clinical method of determining subgroups in case of brain morphology that indicate that the method is able to detect heterogeneous modes in whole population and led to new achievements in disease detection and cure. Since it is a combinational and hypothesis driven approach and result in minimal requirement of previous knowledge so it become a important tool for analysis of changes due to aging. The algorithm proceeds through steps from model assumptions, solve posterior problem, expectation step, Maximization step, clustering and finally model variations. In this paper author presented a probalistic unified framework that segment the image into clusters depending on tissue classes without any prior knowledge and integrating the concepts of image atlases, registration and segmentation produces a comprehensive result as compare to other conventional segmentation method (Hwang & Li, 2008).

Design and Implementation of Proposed Work

Segmentation of outer cranial structures in CT images represent a necessary step for diagnosis. Mammogram images, MRI images etc. are found to be less compatible for identification of significant regions that in turn provide indication for divergent behaviour from healthy medical images of human body. Different scan images lack accuracy because of many reasons like metal implants or scan taken when the patient is not able to remain motionless due to issues like body pain, health, age etc., so CT scan images are most preferred for diagnosis because CT images are taken under controlled environment many times and they show every angle of images for detecting abnormalities. Conventionally medical image segmentation is often used to position distinct objects and boundaries of abnormal behaviour tissues in main images. In this paper, the author applies an approach for segmenting brain tumour regions in a computed tomography images by proposing a multi-level fuzzy technique with quantization and minimum computed Euclidean distance applied to morphologically divided skull part. Since the edges identified with closed contours and further improved by adding minimum Euclidean distance, that is why the numerous results that are analyzed are very assuring and algorithm poses following advantages like less cost, global analysis of image, reduced time, more specificity and positive predictive value. The image partitioning into homogeneous regions based on a set of characteristics, are the key features are very advantageous for computer vision applications and image analysis for abnormalities. Clustering is one of the methods available for image segmentation along with others like threshold based, edge based, region based, watershed based, feature based, background based algorithms etc. for this purpose. Still in today era medical image segmentation or clustering remains one of the major challenges for researchers. Numerous different concepts and theories are proposed and implemented for segmentation of images considering various application areas but unsatisfactory results have been brushed during analysis of abnormalities in special cases of medical images during classification of affected areas by different existing algorithm. Many segmentation procedures have been proposed including a method to remove gray level values inconsistency in MRI images, radiography, computed tomography images etc. (Zaki, Fauzi, 2011). The method was appliance by Lamia Jaffar mainly rely on the theory to find optimal decomposition into two parts one that is optimal design and other its complementary part out of original image. It is a robust segmentation operant introduced from the subject area of mathematical etiology (Cheng, Cheng, & Koschan, 2011). One more method that mainly rely on the theory to divide regions into clusters by identifying the most likely indexed pixel parameters from whole known distribution with some hidden data (Boss & Thangavel, 2012). A novel outdoor scene image segmentation method related to on background knowledge and recognition with perceptual reasoning is also proved to be beneficial for segmentation (Corso, Yuille, Sicotte & Toga, 2007). A technique of image segmentation based on customization of conventional Fuzzy logic for length measurement and allow the labelling of pixel regions effected by possibilistic partition of whole image, in presence of neighbouring pixels (Yan, Ying & Li, 2011). Subrahmanyam present a new approach to improve the accuracy of image segmentation is to match the atlas images and standard images. It is based on spatially diversified and similar neighbourhood preceding model and edge preserving evenness with the concept of already existing algorithms (Mujumdar, Sivaswamy, Kishore & Varma, 2013).

Colour Image Segmentation Using Euclidean Distance

N Selvarasu applies an approach for segmentation of colour images to detect the abnormalities in medical thermograph images. The flowchart of color image segmentation is shown in figure 3 and the algorithm stated as follows:

1. **First Step is to Choose Kind of Images by Infrared Thermography Concept:** It is a non-destructive technique for medical image testing and diagnosis. Actually, thermal images are better option for diagnosis because even small temperature range can be easily noticed and reflection of human physiocology is easily analysed for normal and abnormal behaviour.
2. **Now Fracture is Detected by Scanning Thermographs:** Thermographs (thermal maps) are formed by imaging technique that can be captured for small region of interest or for whole human body structure. The low intensity regions in a image are represented by dark spots(shades)and remaining brightly shaded portion represents high intensity.
3. **Next Image Processing by Euclidean Distance:** Since colour in a image appears to be most promising factor for specific object identification and extraction of region of interest from thermographs. The algorithm is employed by choosing a average colour and then characterize regions on the basis of RGB values, then homogenous pixels are clustered together. Let us suppose the average pixel values are denoted by letter p ' and similar pixel is represented by letter 'q ', so the Euclidean distance is computed by formula:

$$D\left(q,p\right)=\left[\left(qr-pr\right)^2+\left(qg-pg\right)^2+\left(qb-pb\right)^2\right]^{1/2} \qquad (11)$$

where r, g, b are intensities values.

4. **Now Apply Feature Extraction Technique:** Firstly, hotspot pixel are chosen as average intensity values and based on above calculated Euclidean distance comparison is done on threshold value that is if threshold value remain greater than calculated distance then the chosen pixel remain to be hotspot pixel. Then after this rest of the pixel are set to zero and values for minor axis, area per cm square and major axis are.

Pattern Matching Using Linear Distances Applied on Fuzzy Sets

Joakim Lindblad proposes an approach to solve applications of image classification and pattern matching using set to distances procedure applied on fuzzy set and gray level image data. Author proposes four types of distances, two distances are computed by integration of alpha cuts and other two distance transform are computed based on fuzzy set. The advance applications of defined distance measures are considered to be most imperative tool for image clustering, image segmentation, medical disease analysis and pattern recognition. This paper presents four novel fuzzy logic in combination to set distance measure and based on them different classes of fuzzy set is classified. The proposed methods for distance measures are appraised both in theoretical concepts and image applications, where their exceptional performance is proved with results. The generic and elastic distances implementation perform excellently

Figure 3. Flowchart of colour image segmentation

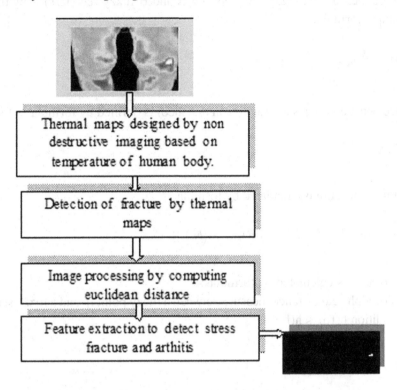

when applied directly on gray scale pixels of any type of images, where they abducted, in one measure, both shape and intensity variations of objects. This enables concurrent matching of structural texture of objects and deferent shapes, providing a both influential and efficient image analysis tool. The distance computation proceeds as follows

1. Set to set distances computation integrate shape and membership of intensities and various distances are calculated as follows:
    a. Distance transform of a crisp set is defined and computed as follows:

$$B \subset Y \text{ is defined as } DTC[B](w) = \min w \in X \left\{ d(w, z) \mid z \in B \right\} \tag{12}$$

    b. Fuzzy logic based distance transform (FLDT) consider fuzzy sets and formulated as follows:

$$B \text{ is FLDT}[B](x) = \text{MIN} \left\{ dB(x, y) \mid y \in \text{supp}(B) \right\} \tag{13}$$

    c. The shortest distance measure i.e. path based distance calculated between two points
        1. c. A is the length lg of a shortest path

$$\text{Distance}(q,s) = \min \pi(p,q) \lg(\pi(q,s)) \tag{14}$$

d. A distance measure on fuzzy sets between A and B fuzzy sets defined by this fuzzification by principal formula:

$$\delta(X,Y) = \int_0^1 d(X^a, Y^a) \, da \tag{15}$$

e. Distance between crisp sets (Euclidean distance) is defined by formula as follows:

$$DCE(A,B) = \inf a \in B d(A,b) \tag{16}$$

Hausdorff distance measure is calculated by formula

$$HDH(A,B) = \max\left(\sup a \in A \ D(a,Y), \sup b \in B \ D(b,X)\right) \tag{17}$$

2. Point to set distance is calculated by formulas:
    a. The inside alpha cut distance measure between a fuzzy point fp and a fuzzy set fs so that agree with condition h(fp) ≤ h(fs)) is

$$d^a(fp, S) = \int_{fp}^h (fp) d(fp, \alpha fs) \, da \tag{18}$$

    b. Bidirectional alpha distances are defined as:

$$d^\beta(p, W) = d^\beta(p, W) + d^\beta(p, W) \tag{19}$$

where p denotes fuzzy point and W denotes fuzzy set.

Table 8 shows performance of algorithms due to various distance measures.

Table 8. Evaluation of performance of algorithms based on various distance measures

Parameters for distance computation	Error Rate (%)	
Distance(α) SMD	1.3	Algorithm based on inward symmetry
Distance (π) SMD	1.1	
Distance(α) SSMD	1.0	
Distance (π) SSMD	1.1	
Distance(α) SMD	1.0	Algorithm based on bidirectional asymmetry
Distance (π) SMD	1.0	
Distance(α) SSMD	1.0	
Distance(π) SSMD	1.2	

Fuzzy C Means Algorithm

It is a problem-solving technology that involves control system methods that tends to implementation of systems like very small and embedded microcontrollers and large multi-channel networking computers meant for data acquisition and control systems. Clustering by fuzzy technique implies that every pixel has a degree of correlation to neighbouring pixels regions in separate clusters instead than belonging wholly to just one cluster (Boss & Thangavel, 2012). The filtering technique is employed for pre-processing of image based on median values, to reduce noise normally in an image. The features are clustered by K Means and FCM algorithms in order to segment the region of interests for further classification. The performance of fuzzy reasoning is compared and analyzed as compared to K Means segmentation according to accurate and low cost. Flowchart of Fuzzy C mean algorithm is shown in figure 4 with an example of original brain image and segmented image as shown in figure 5 and figure 6.

Fuzzy C Means algorithm are as follows:

1. Initialize the clusters, the fuzzy parameters greater than 1, and exit condition.
2. Initialize partition matrix to default initial values.
3. Initialize loop variable l = 0.
4. Compute the cluster centroids to calculate objective function.
5. For each pixels of a given image, design a matrix of the membership values.
6. If the value of objective function calculated iteratively is not more than the exit condition then stop else increase k by 1 and iteratively follow step 4to 6.
7. At last proceed with defuzzification and image segmentation.

Figure 4. Flowchart of Fuzzy C Means algorithm

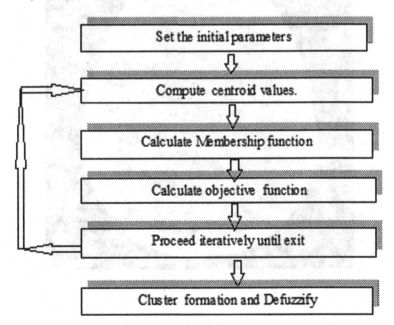

Figure 5. Original Brain image

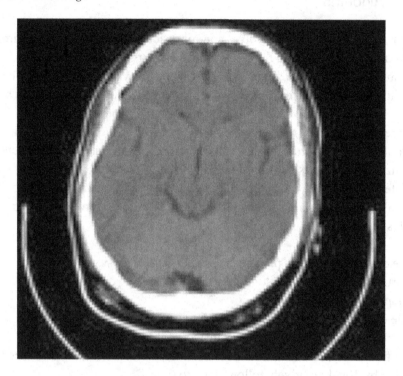

Figure 6. Black and white Clustered Image

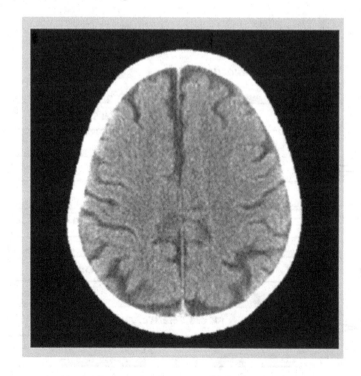

Multi-Level Set Segmentation Algorithm

W. Mimi Diyana proposes an algorithm by applying multiple levels on Fuzzy C Means Algorithm to extract an outer cranial abnormalities present in brain images background and second part i.e. skull and further a two-level Otsu multi-thresholding approach is tested over data to separate the intracranial structure into brain matters, fluid regions and other similar areas. This concept is further used by other authors to remove the problem of gray levels. The gray level in colour images is the preeminent problem encountered during the different methodologies that gravitated to object segmentation within the similar and matched intensities by different functions. So implicitly, the limitation has been overcome by approaching towards multi-level segmentation based on threshold parameters which can be implied for both global and local intracranial heteroclites segmentation. Subsequently, the algorithm is a multi-step procedure in which primarily for global segmentation, clustering has been exploited by fuzzy logic to extract dissimilar and similar skull regions and other regions of interest, which is intracranial and extracted from background part and then in the further levels of the intracranial segmentation, author have applied two-level fuzzy levels in addition to threshold parameters based technique defined in multi-thresholding Otsu algorithm and summarized comparative analysis in table 9. The multi-level set algorithm with its implemented results including the proposed method are shown in figure 7 and figure 8.

Figure 7. Flowchart of Multi Level Set algorithm

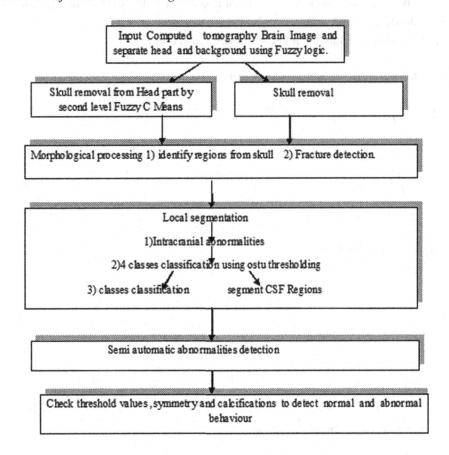

Table 9. Distinguished features of abnormal CT images

Abnormalities	No. of Images	Symmetrical feature 1	Symmetrical feature 2	Intensities	Location
Calcification	60	---	---	yes	yes
Bleeding	80	yes	---	yes	---
Normal case	519	yes	yes	yes	--
Misaligned tissues	61	---	yes	---	---

The algorithm is summarized as:

1. Input computed tomography brain image.
2. Separate head and background by applying first level Fuzzy C Means.
3. Next separate skull into two skull and scalp to identify region of interest and fracture detection.
4. Next from scalp and intracranial local segmentation is employed into 4 classes of segmentation using 1 level Otsu thresholding.
5. Then segment 4 classes into 3 classes using 2nd Ostu thresholding and CSF regions.
6. In next step 3 classes of segmentation is further divided for pixel intensity feature extraction and supervised midline point identification.
7. Threshold values are calculated to find normal and abnormal behavior and midline identification is used for calcification and stop.
8. From step 3 the skull is analyzed for fracture detection and stop.

The equations for different evaluation parameters are

$$\text{Sensititvity}\left(SN\right) = tp\big/\left(tp + fn\right) \tag{20}$$

$$\text{Specificity}\left(SP\right) = tn\big/\left(tn + fp\right) \tag{21}$$

$$PCC = \left(tp + tn\right)\big/\left(tp + fp + tn + fn\right) \tag{22}$$

$$PPV = tp\big/\left(tp + fp\right) \tag{23}$$

$$AUC = fp\big/\left(fp + tp\right) \tag{24}$$

The above parameters are defined as follows:

Figure 8. (a) Original image (b) Manually segmented part (c) Output from Morphological operation (d) Tumour detection in red color (e) Proposed segmented result(f) manual segmented result

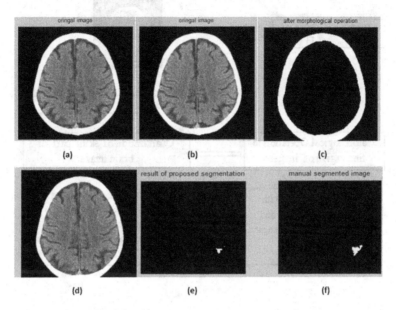

1. The sensitivity parameter measures the percentage of actual positives values which are correctly identified.
2. The measurement of the percentage of negative values which are correctly identified is known as specificity.
3. 3. Percentage of correct classification (PCC) is quantitative measure that is calculated by comparing the intracranial segmentation outcomes.
4. Positive predictive value is termed as the ratio of true positives out of all positive outcomes.

Proposed Algorithm

In this section, we describe basic logic of fuzzy connectivity, morphological operation, segmentation by multi-thresholding, quantization of image, predicting Euclidean distance extract highest distance and finally merge to find ROIs. Conventionally, all the theory and algorithms led to very accurate brain tumour segmentation. The flowchart as shown in figure 9 represents the proposed method.

The algorithm proceeds as follows:

I. Fuzzy C Means

It is a problem-solving technology that involves control system methods that tends to implementation of systems like very small and embedded microcontrollers and large multi-channel networking computers meant for data acquisition and control systems.

II. Morphological Processing

Figure 9. Represents a flowchart representation of the proposed method

Morphological processing is defined as a process of clipping out preeminent mass area from images and this process is employed due to numerous reasons like extraction of small objects from whole image, evacuation of noise, separation of connected components (regions of interest), characterize proper shape and texture. In our proposed algorithm Sobel edge detection is applied before morphological process because it helps in extracting intracranial part from whole skull. Figure 10 shows the fuzzy means algorithm's performance.

III. Quantization

The preeminent areas identified due to the change in pixel intensity seems to appear divergent from normal behaviour of tissues and asymmetric in nature. Thus, quantization is performed by comparing parts of intracranial structure from midline and algorithm is shown by flowchart.

Figure 10. Fuzzy C Means algorithm

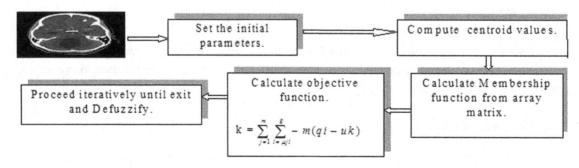

```
1) For frequency i=0 to i=255
2) T=0,Foll=0;
3) For n=1 to n=p
   For y=1 to y=q
```

$$\left\{ if \ \ i < I(x,y) < i + p \qquad T = T + 1 \ , Foll \ = Foll \ + I(x,y) \ \ otherwise \ T = T + 0\right\}$$

```
END FOR ; END FOR
4)  Fcf = Foll/T  END FOR
```

IV.   Euclidean distance

In our proposed algorithm next step is to calculate Euclidean distance. Suppose we have n number of objects present in a image, so by taking mean of all frequency for each object by formula:

$$Mn = \sum_{h=1}^{h=m} Ih * 1 / m \tag{25}$$

where m represents the no. of pixel in ith object and Ii represent its frequency. Next calculate central frequency as follows:

$$Mc = \sum_{h=1}^{h=m}\sum_{q=1}^{q=n}\left(I\left(h,q\right) * 1\!\!/mn\right) \tag{26}$$

So, final predicted distance value is calculated by equation Edist (m) = Mc-Mn and Object having maximum Euclidean distance will be predicted as tumour part.

RESULTS AND DISCUSSIONS

In this experiment, we have arranged set of 35 brain images from a reputed hospital and tested our proposed algorithm on the dataset. The result shows that the computational time is 0.0022869, Sensitivity and Specificity parameters value for algorithm is 0.82759and 0.999. Two more parameters are calculated that denote the predictive value and correct classification i.e. PPV and PPC shows better results as compare to multilevel set algorithm to be 0.64438 and 0.99802 respectively. The performance of the proposed algorithm step by step is shown in figure 11 and figure 12.

The processing of proposed algorithm is carried out by following steps shown above. In first row original image is processed by applying first level Fuzzy C Means followed by morphological processing of image. Further based on intensities histograms are drawn to find out maximum intensity pixels. Lastly Iterative Euclidean distance measure is applied to calculate maximum distance regions to detect tumour.

The comparative analysis data under different parameters is appliance in table 10.

Figure 11. Original Image, Morphological Imag, Segmented Image Quantization plot and Edge Detection (from left to right)

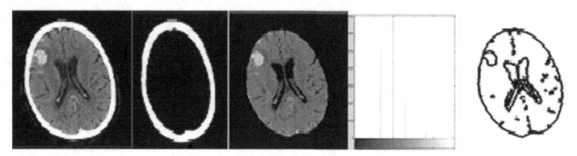

Figure 12. Maximum Distance Segmented Tumour detected Comparision of segmented and manual part (from left to right)

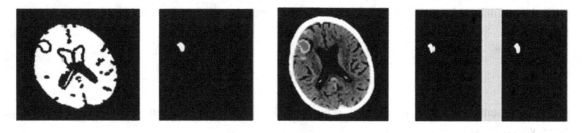

Table 10 describes summary of comparative analysis of original algorithm and proposed algorithm evaluation on five different parameters of sensitivity, specificity, PCC, PPV and total time taken. Table 11 describes parameters value for 21 different samples of image from original database.

CONCLUSION

Terminology and important issues in image segmentation are first presented. Current segmentation approaches are then reviewed with an emphasis on the advantages and disadvantages of these methods for medical imaging applications. In our proposed work, Euclidean distance based computed tomography brain images segmentation has successfully quantified, covered 99% cases and extracted the abnormities and tested on arranged set of 35 brain images from a reputed hospital and tested our proposed algorithm on the dataset. The result shows that the computational time, sensitivity, specificity, positive predictive

Table 10. Comparative analysis of MLSA and Proposed algorithm

Algorithms	Evaluation Parameters				
	Specificity	Sensitivity	PPC	PPV	Time
MLSA	0.99647	0.29787	0.99298	0.29787	1.7338
Proposed work	0.99821	0.64438	0.99802	0.64438	0.016821

Table 11. Evaluation parameters values for different samples

Image Samples	Time	SN	SP	PCC	PPV
Sample 1	0.016821	0.64438	0.99821	0.99644	0.64438
Sample2	0.0029757	0.85496	0.99913	0.99826	0.85496
Sample3	0.0026921	0.87702	0.99811	0.99628	0.87702
Sample 4	0.017051	0.54103	0.99769	0.9954	0.54103
Sample5	0.0025097	0.75207	0.99908	0.99817	0.75207
Sample6	0.0026408	0.64762	0.99887	0.99774	0.64762
Sample7	0.0023023	0.88486	0.99316	0.98708	0.88486
Sample8	0.002366	0.0	0.99742	0.99485	0.0
Sample9	0.0023895	0.85111	0.99886	0.99774	0.85111
Sample10	0.0022701	0.0	0.99632	0.99266	0.0
Sample11	0.0021506	0.0	0.9977	0.99541	0.0
Sample12	0.0022305	0.72067	0.99924	0.99848	0.72067
Sample13	0.017473	0.69178	0.99931	0.99863	0.69178
Sample14	0.0022063	0.7027	0.99882	0.99765	0.7027
Sample15	0.0022635	0.83024	0.99902	0.99805	0.83024
Sample16	0.0047284	0.58462	0.99835	0.99671	0.58462
Sample17	0.019443	0.8905	0.98939	0.98066	0.8905
Sample18	0.018423	0.8905	0.98939	0.98066	0.8905
Sample19	0.0023976	0.0	0.98979	0.97978	0.0
Sample20	0.017153	0.62304	0.9989	0.99781	0.62304
Sample21	0.016865	0.89604	0.99936	0.99872	0.89604

value and precision for chances to cure parameters value for algorithm is 0.0022869, 0.82759, 0.999, 0.016821 and 0.64438. The proposed technique is employed by considering threshold value and average pixel intensities. All parameters sensitivity, specificity, time taken, PPC and PPV for medical images with abnormality as hotspot presents better result as compare to multi-level set algorithm by combining multi-level with Euclidean distance measure and Quantization. In this project, I have presented a critical assessment of the current status of semi-automated, manual and automated methods for the segmentation of phenomenal medical images.

Future Scope

So refinement of proposed algorithm by considering both structure information and spatial information of medical images for segmentation is an active area for further research to produce more promising outcomes. Since clustering procedures are widely used because of unsupervised learning behaviour and process does not employ use of any training data so numerous adaptive clustering techniques can be easily continued towards 3D volumetric images in addition for multi-channel images also. Future research in the segmentation of medical images will contend towards improving then accuracy, precision for cure and total computation time analysed during segmentation process, and method that reduces the time taken in manual segmentation methods. Computational efficiency is very preeminent feature in real time processing applications and computerized segmentation methods have already validated their vast utility in research application areas and are now increasingly in use for computer aided diagnosis and radiotherapy planning. It is unlikely that automated image segmentation will replace physicians from analysis but it will be still a crucial process to segment biomedical images.

REFERENCES

Ganesan, P., & Rajini, V. (2010, November 13-15). A Method to Segment Color Images based on Modified Fuzzy-Possibilistic-C-Means Clustering Algorithm. *Recent Advances in Space Technology Services and Climate Change, 5*, 157–163.

Anna Palagan, C., & Leena, T. (2011, April 8-10). Brain Structure Segmentation of Magnetic Resonance Imaging Using T– Mixture Algorithm, Electronics Computer Technology (ICECT). *Proceedings of the 3rd International Conference* (Vol. 3, pp. 446-450).

Banumathi, A., & Pethalakshm, A. (2012, February). Refinement of K-Means and Fuzzy C-Means. *International Journal of Computers and Applications, 39*(17), 11–17. doi:10.5120/4911-7441

Belaid, L. J., & Mourou, W. (2012, August). Image segmentation: A Watershed transformation algorithm. *Image Analysis & Stereology, 28*(2), 93–102. doi:10.5566/ias.v28.p93-102

Cheng, C., Koschan, A., Cheng, C., & Koschan, A. (2011, September). Outdoor Scene Image Segmentation Based on Background Recognition and Perceptual Organization. *IEEE Transactions on* Image Processing, *21*(3), 1007–1019. PMID:21947522

Corso, J. J., Yuille, A. L., Sicotte, N. L., & Toga, A. W. (2007, October). Detection and segmentation of pathological structures by the extended graph-shifts algorithm. In *Medical Image Computation Aided Intervention* (Vol. 1, pp. 985–994). PMID:18051154

Cosic, D., & Loncaric, S. (1996, October). Two methods for ICH segmentation. *Proceedings of ISBME* (pp. 63–66).

Flandrin, P. (1992, March). Wavelet analysis and synthesis of fractional Brownian motion. *IEEE Transactions on Information Theory, 38*(2), 910–917. doi:10.1109/18.119751

Gering, D., Grimson, W., & Kikinis, R. (2005, January). Recognizing deviations from normalcy for brain tumor segmentation, in Proceedings of International Conference Medical Image Computation Assist. *Intervention (Amstelveen, Netherlands), 5*, 508–515.

Gonzalez, R. C., & Woods, R. E. (2007). Image processing. Digital image processing, 2.

Gurcan, M.N., Sahiner, B., Petrick, N., Chan, H.P., Kazerooni, E.A., Cascade, P.N., & Hadjiiski, L. (2002). Lung nodule detection on thoracic computed tomography images: Preliminary evaluation of a computer aided diagnosis system. *Proceedings of Medical Physics, 29*(11), 2552-2558.

Hung, C.-C., Kulkarni, S., & Kuo, B.-C. (2011, June). A New Weighted Fuzzy C-Means Clustering Algorithm Remotely Sensed Image for Classification. *IEEE Journal of Selected Topics in Signal Processing, 5*(3), 543–553. doi:10.1109/JSTSP.2010.2096797

Hwang, J.-N., & Li, H. (2008, September). Surface reconstruction from non-parallel curve networks, Neural Networks for Signal Processing. *Computer Graphics Forum, 27*(2), 155–163.

Jayender, J., Ruan, D. T., Narayan, V., Agrawal, N., Jolesz, F. A., & Mamata, H. (2013, April 7-11). Segmentation of Parathyroid Tumors from DCE-MRI using Linear Dynamic System Analysis, Biomedical Imaging (ISBI). *Proceedings of IEEE 10th International Symposium* (pp. 1469-1472).

Lee, Y., Hara, T., Fujita, H., & Itoh, S. (2001). Automated detection of pulmonary nodules in helical CT images based on an improved template matching technique. *Transactions on Medical Imaging, 20*(7), 595-604.

Mujumdar, S, Sivaswamy, J., Kishore, L.T., & Varma R. (2013, March 28-30). Auto-Windowing of Ischemic Stroke Lesions in Diffusion Weighted Imaging of the Brain. *Proceedings of the Medical Informatics and Telemedicine conference (ICMIT)* (pp 1-6).

Nyul, L. G., Udupa, J. K., & Zhang, X. (2000, February). New variants of a method of MRI scale standardization. *IEEE Transactions on Medical Imaging, 19*(2), 143–150. doi:10.1109/42.836373 PMID:10784285

Paiement, A., Mirmehdi, M., Xianghua Xie, , & Hamilton, M. C. K. (2014, January). Integrated Segmentation and Interpolation of Sparse Data. *IEEE Transactions on Image Processing, 23*(1), 110–125. doi:10.1109/TIP.2013.2286903 PMID:24158475

Pan, Z., Yin, X., & Wu, G. 2004, September Segmentation-based interpolation of 3-D medical images. In *Computational Science and Its Applications, LNCS* (Vol. *3044*, pp. 731–740). doi:10.1007/978-3-540-24709-8_77

Pentland, A. P. (1984, November). Fractal-based description of natural scene. *IEEE Transactions on Pattern Analysis and Machine Intelligence, 6*(6), 661–674. doi:10.1109/TPAMI.1984.4767591 PMID:22499648

Quddus, A., & Basir, O. (2012, May). Semantic image retrieval in magnetic resonance brain volumes. *IEEE Transaction Information Technology Biomedical Imaging, 16*(3), 348–355. doi:10.1109/TITB.2012.2189439 PMID:22389157

Sangwar, S., & Peshaattiwar, A.A. (2013, September 21-23). Segmentation of CT images using K Means algorithm. *Proceedings of International Conference On Advanced Electronic Systems* (pp. 6 – 9).

Subash Chandra Boss, R., & Thangavel, K. (2012, March 21-23). Mammogram Image Segmentation Using Fuzzy Clustering. *Proceedings of the International Conference on Pattern Recognition* (pp. 290 – 295).

Sun, S., & Sonka, M. (2013, April 7-11). Graph based 4D Lung Segmentation in CT Images with expert guided computer aided refinement. *Proceedings of IEEE 10th International Symposium* (pp. 1312 – 1315). doi:10.1109/ISBI.2013.6556773

Tariq, A, Akram, M.U., & Javed, M.Y. (2013, April 16-19). Lung Nodule Detection in CT Images using Neuro Fuzzy Classifier. Proceedings of the IEEE Fourth International Workshop on Computational Intelligence in Medical Imaging (CIMI) (pp. 49-53).

Wang, Z. B., & Lu, R. H. (2008, December 12-14). A New Algorithm for Image Segmentation Based on Fast Fuzzy C-Means Clustering, Computer Science and Software Engineering. Proceedings of the 2008 International Conference on Computer Science and Software Engineering (V*ol. 6*, pp. 14-17).

Yedla, M., & Pathakota, S. R. (2010, September). T M Srinivasa, Enhancing KMeans Clustering Algorithm with Improved Initial Center. *International Journal of Computer Science and Information Technologies, 1*, 121–125.

Yu, C. Y., Li, Y., Liu, A. L., & Liu, J. H. (2011, August 24-26). A Novel Modified Kernel Fuzzy C-Means Clustering Algorithm on Image Segmentation. *Proceedings of the 14th IEEE International Conference on Computational Science and Engineering* (Vol. 3, pp. 621 – 626).

Zaki, W. M. D. W., Fauzi, M. F. A., Besar, R., & Ahmad, W. M. W. (2011, November 21-24). Qualitative and Quantitative Comparisons of Hemorrhage Intracranial Segmentation in CT Brain Images. Proceedings of 10th IEEE Region Conference (pp. 369 – 373).

Zhou, J., Chang, S., & Pappas, Q. L. G. (2008, May 14-17). A novel learning based segmentation method for rodent brain structures using MRI. *Proceedings of 5th IEEE International Symposium on* Biomedical Imaging (pp. 61–64).

Zhou, J., & Hung, C. C. (2007, August). A Generalized Approach to Possibility Clustering. *International Journal of Uncertainty, Fuzziness and Knowledge-based Systems, 15*(Suppl. 2), 110–132. doi:10.1142/S0218488507004650

Zook, J. M., & Iftekharuddin, K. M. (2005, January). Statistical analysis of fractal-based brain tumor detection algorithms. *Magnetic Resonance Imaging, 23*(5), 671–678. doi:10.1016/j.mri.2005.04.002 PMID:16051042

Chapter 5
Cross-Domain Usage in Real-Time Video-Based Tracking

Satbir Singh
Delhi Technological University, India

Rajiv Kapoor
Delhi Technological University, India

Arun Khosla
Dr. B.R. Ambedkar NITJ, India

ABSTRACT

This chapter emphasizes on the approach to include information from different type of sensors into the visible domain real time tracking. Since any individual sensor is not able to retrieve the complete information, so it is better to use information from distinct category of sensors. The chapter firstly enlightens the significance of introducing the cross-domain treatment into video based tracking. Following this, some previous work in the literature related to this idea is briefed. The chapter introduces the categorization of the cross-domain activity usage for real time object tracking and then each category is separately discussed in detail. The advantages as well as the limitations of each type of supplemented cross domain activity will be discussed. Finally, the recommendation and concluding remarks from the authors in lieu of future development of this cutting-edge field will be presented.

INTRODUCTION

Tracking in the simplest form can be defined as the problem of estimating the trajectory of an object as it moves around a scene. Earlier ways of tracking an object in a video sequence included application of an intelligent tracking algorithm on the image frame information contained in the video sequence. This technique worked well for some time, but a new research field evolved due to handicapping of the visual information in locating the object individually under certain conditions like low vision, background similarity, occlusions, limited range of view etc. This new practice intruded data and information from different modes of information and merged the new information to obtain a robust tracking estimate in

DOI: 10.4018/978-1-5225-2848-7.ch005

the visible domain itself. Addition of the different sensor's information to camera information is not a simple process since it involves different complex stages such as calibration of data for cross domain usage, appointment of a suitable fusion algorithm that is handy for decision making, recovering the missing information from individual domains and cancellation of mutual information from sensors. Because of numerous advantages and proven results of efficient tracking by the use of cross domain intruded tracking, it is need of the hour to be aware of this upcoming technology. Also, there is an urgent need for intelligent video systems to replace human operators to monitor the areas under surveillance. Applications of a Robust Object tracking includes: Motion-based recognition, Automated surveillance, Video indexing, Human-computer interaction, Traffic monitoring, Vehicle navigation and various controlling applications including Accident Avoidance, Automatic Guidance, Head Tracking for Video Conferencing etc. Due to loss of information from a unique domain only, few challenges that emerge for a healthy tracking include occlusion, shape deformation of object, changes in lighting conditions, shadow effect, illumination variations, real-time processing requirements, loss of information caused by projection of 3D world on 2D image etc. Since generally an event or activity consists of rich multimodal information, one can use information from different modes themselves. The chapter will aim at covering the role of following domains mingled with the visible imagery to obtain an efficient real time tracking of objects:

1. Usage of Thermal Imagery in Visible video tracking
2. Usage of Audio information in visible video tracking
3. Usage of RADAR's information in visible video tracking
4. Usage of LIDAR's information in visible video tracking.

BACKGROUND

Due to limitations occurring in tracking using visible information only, various techniques started to evolve that complement the video tracking procedure using help of secondary information from distinct modes.

To enhance the vision capabilities, earlier multi vision and stereo tracking was made use. (Bakhtari, Naish, Eskandari, Croft, & Benhabib, 2006) carried an experiment to increase the quality of a surveillance system using 1 static overhead camera and 4 mobile cameras. But here only a single target's position and orientation were surveyed in this basic research. A method to carry out multiple people detection and tracking using stereo vision was presented by (Muñoz-Salinas, García-Silvente, & Carnicer, 2008). In this method depth, color and gradient information was used to track people in complex situations using a multiple particle filter algorithm. Each particle filter was corresponded to an individual target. Although the approach was able to perform well in conditions like occlusions, peoples jumping and running, shaking hands and swapping their positions etc., but could not provide a solution related to disguised vision conditions. For increasing the vision capabilities of a single camera, a multi camera technique was proposed by (Lin & Huang, 2011) in which the field of view (FOV) for object detection and tracking was enhanced by the concept of overlapping and non-overlapping FOV of distributed cameras. Kalman filter was used for tracking of objects and a homography mapping technique was used to provide a unique continuous tracking result. Though various problems of the single visible sensor track were tried to remedies through incorporation of the multiple camera views, which made the tracking more accurate, but still there was scope of improvements for the case where the information in the visible light form is itself inefficient to properly characterize the scene and the object.

The thermal domain is helpful to visible mode by its ability to remain unaffected during low/night vision and inconsistent illumination conditions. (Treptow, Cielniak, & Duckett, 2005) presented an approach that made use of thermal imagery along with gray scale imagery for locating, tracking and identifying a target in a mobile robot application. Major emphasis was on acquiring the information in case of illumination variations and locating the information of a faraway target. In both these cases, it is very hard to obtain the skin color/visible information. Though the work introduced a handy approach, but the robot was only able to localize the face of target that was in closest proximity of it or having the maximum probability and the other targets could not be detected. An optimum wavelet data fusion technique was proposed and compared with other data fusion techniques for combined usage of visible and thermal imagery in (Hanif & Ali, 2006). This technique was shown to be equally effective with face recognition as well as for non-face images. This method used Gabor filter and was effective variations in lightning conditions but was not mended for real time video use. A 'product of experts' type technique was used by (Conaire, O'Connor, & Smeaton, 2008) in which individual experts for each thermal and visible spectrum were involved. The thermal expert used investigating hints like thermal brightness and visible expert used the information like luminosity, edge orientation etc. After individual tracking, finally the combined estimate was formulated by product of these beliefs. But the method was inappropriate for disguised and challenging vision conditions. Moreover, no feedback mechanism was present to analyze individual expert's decision during unfavorable conditions. (Stolkin, Rees, Talha, & Florescu, 2012) introduced a new concept of rapidly relearning background models to get an accurate weighting for the individual domains for their participation into the fusion based tracking. The method also promised to detect the effect of camouflaging in the respective domains. A similar kind of approach was extended and used in (Talha & Stolkin, 2014) in which color based particle filters and intensity based histograms in thermal imagery were used in conjunction for tracking under camouflaging conditions. Besides the abovementioned techniques for introduction of thermal domain imagery into the visible hints, the following paragraphs provide the background of rest type of cross domain usage in the video based tracking.

Due to limited field of view of the visible camera and important features of speaking target provided by the audio mode the collaboration of these two can be useful for localization the active speaking target in the visible preview. (Strobel, Spors & Rabenstein, 2001) proposed a decentralized Kalman filter based recursive fusion method in features from both the domains were provided for estimating a merged global track. But as the Kalman filter is limited only to the linear motion estimation, so an advanced fusion method for maneuvering in the non-linear fashion was the limitation of this method. An improvement over this was presented by (Gatica-Perez, Lathoud, McCowan, Odobez, & Moore, 2003) in which the probabilistic importance particle filters were deployed for the audio-visual fusion. This method concentrated on the idea to incorporate random search based particle filter can be for audio visual fusion based tracking. Extending the work for multi-speaker localization and tracking, (Daniel Gatica-Perez, Lathoud, Odobez, & McCowan, 2007) proposed a distinct observation model based Markov Chain Monte Carlo particle filter (MCMC-PF). Use of 3 cameras along with a circular array of 8 microphones was used for tracking the different speaker's movement. In audio domain source localization technique was used and human head's shape and spatial structure was taken as cue for the visible domain. This method yet had several issues to solve for more complex cases like complex clutters, noisy audio conditions and working with the assumption of a single audio source to be tracked. Association between target and measurements using a well-known particle filter was applied by (Lim & Choi, 2009) in Robotics. The practically implemented application was used to judge and track a speaking target from a number of targets present in the scene. The optimal association was made using cross correlation based likelihood of the incoming sound signal in audio domain and the target visual cues. The accuracy of the system was meant to be improved for real scenario application. Another innovative approach to an improved tracking using audio visual fusion was presented by (Shivappa, Rao, & Trivedi, 2010). The authors adopted a multiple iterative decoding technique to fuse hypothesis from individual domain trackers to form a multiple iterative decoding – audio visual tracker. In the visible domain, a simple foreground object detection technique using background subtraction was used to find the feature state vectors in the visible domain. Audio information was in the form of a Time Difference of Arrival (TDOA) based estimate. A total of 4 cameras and 24 microphones were used in total to produce the track by fusion. Global track estimates were found from the corresponding local track estimates from individual domains. The method proposed to use a rough self –calibrated scheme for sensors and hence was said to be very less sensitive to accurate sensor calibrations. Although the method was more effective than the particle filtering approach in terms of accuracy but it had limitation of slow processing (2.5 times slower than particle filter) and hence cannot be recommended for real time tracking purpose.

Detection using light waves reflected from laser devices can also complement the vision based tracking. Moreover, Light-based tracking is fast and covers a larger geographical area with least cost. Some research work had already been suggested in this direction. (Chakravarty & Jarvis, 2006) proposed to fuse the laser information and view information of a low resolution panoramic camera and then track the object using a particle filter framework. A color model of each target to be tracked was maintained using a background subtraction algorithm. Depth information from laser is used to counter the situation of occlusions. But the tracking using this method didn't work well when the object was far away from the robot due to poor resolution and also the track was only possible when the robot maintained a stationary position. A method for tracking in a real-world scenario (especially for outside scenes) was proposed by (Song, Cui, Zhao, & Zha, 2008). A probabilistic detection based Particle filter was used to estimate the track position using the fused information of Light and visible camera in a Bayesian Framework. The method when compared with the state of art methods fared better in terms of accuracy as well as computational complexities. But the algorithm required an additional modification with increasing number of targets to be tracked. (Spinello, Triebel, & Siegwart, 2009) presented a research work for detecting and tracking multi class objects. Cars and Pedestrians (representing two different classes of objects) were distinctly tracked in the same video sequence using the fusion of camera and Laser range scanner. The classification used Implicit Shape Model for image mode and Conditional Random fields for Laser data points. Kalman Filter was used for tracking. The multi-class method was constrained to recognize the linear motion of different classed objects due to inefficiency of Kalman filter in non-linear tracking. To deal with the interacting targets in case of multi- target tracking, a technique was proposed by (Song, Shin, & Jeon, 2012) that introduced an online learning procedure using the cross-domain information to obtain robust track estimates under frequently interacting conditions. The learning was done while the targets were not in a close proximity and the system was updated for target interacting cases. Laser was used alone when objects are not close to each other and video domain was used to learn the system. But, the method failed to work correctly in case where two persons having similar appearance were walking together. But since this type of fusion is a recently evolving technology, efforts can be made to make this technology compatible and tangible for common man use.

In early days, RADAR systems were giant sized were mainly used in aerospace and military operations. But due to technological advancements, the size and the cost of RADAR had reduced considerably. So, now the usage of RADAR has a bright scope in field autonomous driving and vehicle navigation. Since RADAR provides the radial information of the target object, so it is used in conjunction with the camera to provide an accurate estimation of the target object. An example to this type of tracking was presented by (Sugimoto, Tateda, Takahashi, & Okutomi, 2004). It was a typical case of driver assistance system in which obstacle avoidance and running control of car was assessed by continuous tracking through the fusion of millimeter-wave RADAR and a camera. Calibration between two sensors was provided through homography projections in which the clustered data from RADAR was projected to image frame to get information regarding obstacles. The method lacked in approach to handle the running of vehicle in crowd/noisy conditions because no measure was taken in it to remedies such kind of real situations artifacts. For improving the accuracy, a Multiple Integrated Probability based data associations technique was implemented by (Kim & Jeon, 2014). In this the two physical sensors complementing each other fused their observations together in the framework of multiple Kalman filters for object tracking. The CCD camera helped in expanding the bearing angle range for a cheap millimeter-wave RADAR module for tracking under multi-person scenario. (Germa, Lerasle, Ouadah, Cadenat, & Devy, 2009) also proposed a human tracking through a robot using the fusion of information through radio waves and visible pan-tilt camera. The algorithm used for fusion is particle filter that enables the merging of the asserted data obtained from camera and RFID detection system mounted on the robot. Once the robot after identified the target, it followed its motion as a tracking system. The system proposed had a complex hardware approach and would be even more complex if used for multiple people tracking. Currently the usage of the proposed work was intended for single user tracking.

Thus, the previous literature study has shown that the field of cross domain usage in visible tracking is a challenging and revolutionary task to uplift the surveillance and tracking applications. Different modes have been amalgamated to provide the supplementary information to the visible camera cues. Work has been done in the thermal/visible, audio/visible, RADAR/visible and LIDAR/visible mode as mentioned in above section. The following section of the chapter will discuss in detail that how the usage of information from distinct modes can be incorporated to visual tracking.

CROSS DOMAIN USAGE IN VISIBLE TRACKING

Due to the inefficiency of the visible domain tracking, an extra aid from different sources such as sound, temperature, light, radio frequency waves etc. can be incorporated. This process itself requires some thought provoking fusion strategies, so that efficient fusion of information takes place for a robust track estimate. These strategies of merging the information depend upon the choice of the sensors used and the type of information being acquired by the tracker. This section presents the in-depth details of the specific supplemented cross domain usage added to visible camera tracking.

1. Use of Thermal Imagery in Real Time Video Tracking

Visible camera mainly depends on the colour content of the object and surroundings. Thermal / IR camera only captures the thermal image of the object. Thermal image is only related with the temperature value of the object. High temperature objects possess rich information content, whereas low temperature objects do not possess significant information in thermal image. Since both the domains lie in the image plane, it is easiest to calibrate the information obtained from these cross domains. By combining the target features of visible colors information and heat signatures, tracking can be made more robust, since objects of scene clutter and distracters are less likely to share common feature values with the target in

Figure 1. OSU Dataset sequence 2 (a) visible Image, (b) Thermal Image

(a)   (b)

both spectra simultaneously (Talha & Stolkin, 2014). The addition of information from the thermal imagery has already been incorporated for various image fusion applications to improve the quality of the image. This temperature information from the secondary domain can be amalgamated in to the primary visible domain by either pixel level, feature level or decision level for the process of object tracking.

In figure 1 from a well- known registered dataset, it is clear captures the thermal image of the object. Thermal image is only related with the temperature value of the object. High temperature objects possess rich information content, whereas low temperature objects do not possess significant information in thermal image. Since both the domains lie in the image plane, it is easiest to calibrate the observations.

a. Usage at Pixel Level

This is the most basic approach of directly including the aid of pixel intensity from the thermal image to improve the result in the visible tracking. By doing this the quality of the image frame is improved, which directly helps in tracking the target in the final fused image. Various approaches of simple image fusion like: simple averaging technique, wavelet transforms, pyramid fusion schemes, (Zhou, Wang, Li, & Dong, 2016) can be used for this kind of intra domain fusion.

But this approach of cross domain usage is very rarely employed in real time video applications like tracking, because of their time-consuming behavior.

b. Usage at Feature Level

Usage at feature level involves invoking the information from feature vectors obtained from different type of information sensors rather than the pixel level information merging. So, rather than complete

Figure 2. Block Diagram of fusion at pixel level

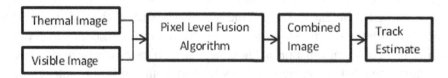

Figure 3. Block Diagram of fusion at Feature level

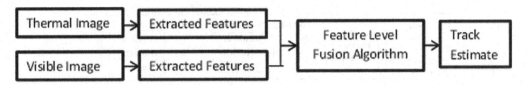

data from the required region, only few features values can be used, which can be helpful in reducing the computational complexity and reduce the rime to process. (Conaire et al., 2008) proposed a spatiogram based bi-modal fusion tracking. Spatiogram corresponds to spatial histograms. Mean shift framework was used for estimating new position of object. Each mode tracker produced a likelihood measure known as expert. The final likelihood score was determined through product of individual experts. It lacked an adaptive approach to fusion, since multiplication alone gives robust results.

c. Usage at Decision Level

This type of cross domain information usage is the advanced level of fusion, in which the final decision is taken based upon the individual decisions obtained from each sensor independently. Very thought provoking fusion algorithms are required for this type of tracking, since the outcome has to be obtained by just fetching information from decisions of the tracks alone. (Xiao, Yun, & Wu, 2014) presented a tracking before fusion method. Improved Particle filter tracking was used in visible domain. Template matching criteria was used for thermal imagery domain. A novel fusion rule is proposed to estimate the final track after obtaining the individual tracks. An anti-jumping scheme and an occlusion avoiding scheme is also presented in the research work. Both feature level and decision level usage is generally employed for the real time thermal aided visible domain tracking.

Methodology of tracking using decision level fusion of method described above is presented here in Figure 5 for providing more understandings to readers.

In the proposed approach, an independent tracking was performed in Visible and Infra-red domain of the scene. Visual feature included the RGB color value which was used to obtain the Bhattacharya distance to give weights to different particles of a particle filter. Template Matching was introduced in the infra-red domain, where initially the object to be tracked was chosen as reference window was matched throughout the images of all the frames for maximum correlation value. Equation (1) describes the template matching criteria for obtaining the correlation value.

Figure 4. Block Diagram of fusion at Decision level

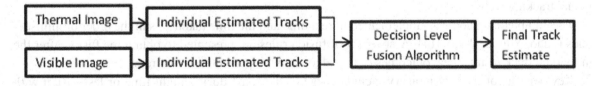

Figure 5. Methodology of Decision Level Fusion (Xiao, Yun, & Wu, 2014)

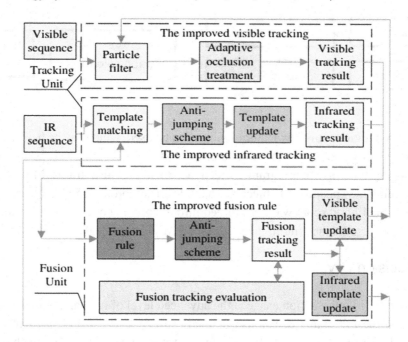

$$C(l,m) = \frac{\sum_{l',m'} Temp(l',m') . \mathrm{Im}\,age(l+l',m+m')}{\sqrt{\sum_{l',m'} \left[Temp(l',m')\right]^2 \sum_{l',m'} \left[\mathrm{Im}\,age(l+l',m+m')\right]^2}} \tag{1}$$

where, the initial target region chosen for tracking was used as template Temp which slid across the whole image Image to calculate the IR (Infra-Red) image weight value denoted by C. Further, an Adaptive occlusion treatment was also incorporated to enhance the efficiency of the algorithm. To end with, the final state was estimated by fusing the information obtained from visual and infra-red counterparts. After obtaining the individual tracking estimate in both the domains, the final estimate was obtained through the fusion rule given by eq. (2):

$$S_f = \gamma_{vis} S_{vis} + \gamma_{IR} S_{IR} \tag{2}$$

where, S_{vis}, S_{IR} and S_f represents the tracking state estimate through individual visible domain, individual Infra-red domain and Multi modal fusion of these respectively. γ_{vis} and γ_{IR} represents the modified weights of the states after a conditioning strategy depending upon the difference in their individual tracking weight values.

The complete method was implemented in real time and the time taken was in the order of milliseconds (Xiao, Yun, & Wu, 2014). A novel set of fusion rules are presented to obtain the fusion after the individual track results. Few outcomes of this algorithm are presented in figure 6.

Key benefits of thermal imagery include usage of the same during night time or less vision with negligible effects as compared to the visible counterpart of imagery. This is very helpful for surveil-

Figure 6. Outcomes of performance improvement by adding thermal imagery as cross domain aid(a) visible Imagery outcome, (b) Thermal Imagery outcome, (c) Outcome using fusion of cross domain information (Xiao, Yun, & Wu, 2014)

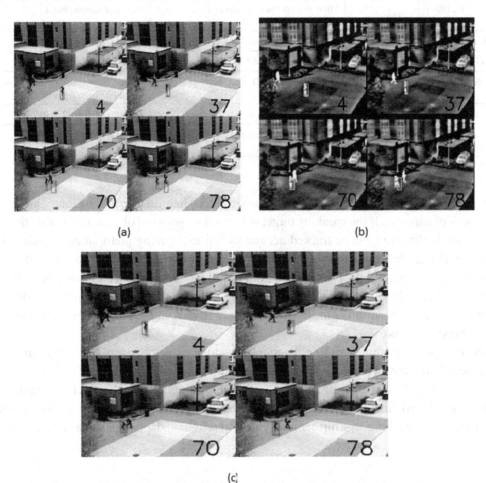

lance applications. Moreover, in case of human target tracking, background illumination variations and inconsistent cloth texture can act as artifacts to tracking, but the thermal domain usage is unaffected from it. So, due to above advantages, usage of thermal information into video based tracking result in a very motivated field to work upon. Few works involving this strategy are listed in Table 1.

The limitation of this type of tracking is the high cost of the thermal/Infrared sensors/cameras that can capture a high quality thermogram of the scene under observation. The following subsection deals with the audio assisted visual tracking.

2. Use of Audio Information in Real Time Video Tracking

Another important source of information is audio domain that is particular handy in tracking a speaking target or a sound producing source. It is a wonderful aid to the visible domain tracking, especially under conditions of occlusions, background light variations; object's clothing colour change etc. Recent

Table 1. Various Tracking schemes for thermal-visual tracking

Research	Sensors used	Algorithms used
Palmeri(Palmerini, 1997)	Micro camera class devices and thermographic cameras	Extended Kalman Filter
(Torabi & Mass, 2010)	1 thermal and 1 visible camera	Sum-rule silhouette
(Talha & Stolkin, 2014)	1 Colour camera and 1 Thermal camera	Particle Filter
(Xiao, Yun, & Wu, 2014)	IR camera and a CCD Camera	Particle filter, correlation analysis and weighted fusion algorithm
(Conaire et al., 2008)	1 Infra-red Camera, 1 Visible Camera	Product of Expert Beliefs
(Stolkin et al., 2012)	1 FLIR Thermal Camera and 1 Colour Camera	Bayesian Fusion

researches have shown that audio domain's information can be helpful also to remediate 'limited field of view' drawback of cameras. If the speaking target to be tracked goes out of view of camera, then through its sound signal its direction can be tracked accurately without having pictorial cues. (Kilic, Barnard, Wang et al., 2015) demonstrated the above said fact. In his work, a case was taken that if one talking person to be tracked in a multi people scenario goes out of sight of camera and is not available for providing any of the visual features for few frames. The algorithm updating and learning was stopped from the moment the user went out of sight. Hence the visual tracker alone didn't provide accurate results. The case is shown in Figure 7.

But now, the speech attribute can be utilized in this situation as the line of arrival of target speaking person can be referred for locating the position and updating the algorithm.

The approach introduced fusion of audio and visual information to rectify the tracking that resulted in ambiguous results when the tracking was performed using the visual information alone. The audio assisted robust visual tracking was further amalgamated with an adaptive particle filter that adaptively

Figure 7. Visual Tracking outcome of sequence 11 of AV 16.3 Dataset (Kilic, Barnard, Wang et al., 2015)

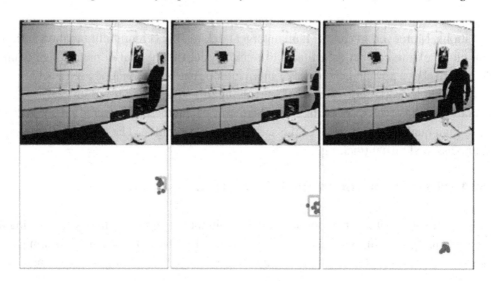

Figure 8. Audio Assisted Visual Tracking outcome of sequence 11 of AV 16.3 Dataset (Kilic, Barnard, Wang et al., 2015)

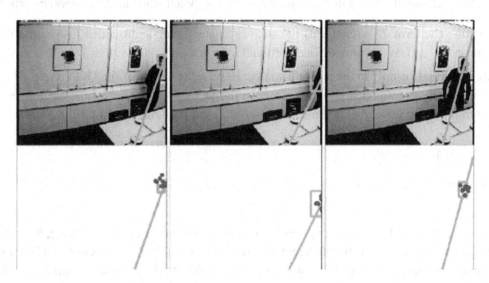

decides the number of particles it has to choose for tracking. The proposed algorithm improved the tracking when one user went out of view of camera for some time and again was introduced into the scene. Based on the direction of arrival (DOA) of the audio signal obtained from that user, particles were again provided new weights and the state output of the tracker was modified. After attaining the DOA information, a 2D DOA line was drawn on the image frame for helping the ordinary particle filter in the visible domain in finding the target's correct location. The main aim was to relocate the distributed particles around the DOA line and then re-calculate the weights of the relocated particles according to their distance to the DOA line (V Kilic & Barnard, 2013). The line was drawn by using calibrated information from the microphones arrays and cameras or alternatively by estimation techniques such as microphone self-calibration (Crocco, Del Bue, Bustreo, & Murino, 2012) and combined microphone and camera calibrations (Legg & Bradley, 2013). After drawing the DOA lines, a perpendicular Euclidean distance, $S_t^{(N)}$ of all the propagated particles in the visible tracker was found out using eq. (3) as:

$$S_t = \left[S_t^{(1)}, \ldots\ldots\ldots\ldots, S_t^{(N)} \right] \tag{3}$$

where, t stands for t^{th} frame and n = 1, 2, …, N. N is the total no. of particles propagated. The normalized distance $\hat{s}_t = \left[\hat{s}_t^{(1)}, \ldots\ldots\ldots\ldots, \hat{s}_t^{(N)} \right]$ is then used to relocate the particles distribution (Klee, Gehrig, & McDonough, 2006) by the fusion rule mentioned in eq. (4)

$$\hat{E}_t^{(n)} = E_t^n \oplus \hat{s}_t^{(n)} D_t C_t \tag{4}$$

where, $\oplus$ stands for element wise addition and C_t is the parameter to control the effect of audio and is found by taking the Bhattacharya distance between the estimated state and the reference object in the visible domain. The term $\hat{E}_t^{(n)}$ represents the state estimated using audio aided fusion into the visual tracker estimate E_t^n. Array C_t provides a directional information having values $[\cos(\alpha_t)\,0\,\sin(\alpha_t)\,0\,0]^T$ so that update in the state is only in the position values. Here, represents (α_t) the DOA angle. The emphasis of the fusion process was that particles closer to the DOA line in terms of the Euclidean distance must get high importance weights in the audio assisted visual particle filter algorithm

$$\hat{w}_t^{(n)} = \left(e^{\left(\lambda \left| B^{(n)^2} \right| \right)} \right) \frac{\left\| s_t \right\|_1}{s_t^{(n)}}, \tag{5}$$

Here, the likelihood is found in an exponential manner as shown by eq. (5). In (Kilic, Barnard, Wang et al., 2015), although one can get two different direction of arrival (DOA) lines for two different speakers by the calibrated formulas, to assist the visual particle tracker with the audio information, but there will be ambiguity in deciding that which sound corresponds to which user. Specially, in case of multiple users, getting lot of DOA lines for various audio sources will create ambiguity unless on knows regarding the audio features of our desired target. A few audio-visual fusion schemes are listed in the following Table 2.

Aids of Audio assisted Visual tracking include:

1. Assistance in case of limited field of view of camera
2. Provides additional hints in case of occlusion or similar structure clutter presence
3. Invariant to lighting variations in the scene
4. Provides additional features to characterize the object like Pitch, intensity of sound, direction of arrival of sound and time taken for sound arrival etc.

Table 2. Various Tracking schemes for audio-visual tracking

Research	Sensors used	Algorithms used
(Kilic, Barnard, Wang et al., 2015)	2 Circular Microphone arrays and 3 cameras	Audio Assisted Adaptive Particle Filter
(Checka, Wilson, Siracusa, & Darrell, 2004)	2 cameras and 4 microphone arrays	Particle Filter
(Gehrig, Nickel, Ekenel, Klee, & McDonough, 2005)	4 cameras and 16 Microphone in array	Kalman Filter, Distributed Kalman Filter
(Lim & Choi, 2009)	1 stereo camera and 3 microphones	Particle Filter
Nickel, Gehrig, Stiefelhagen et al.,	4 Cameras and 3 Microphones	Adaptively weighted particle filter
(Megherbi, Ambellouis, Colôt, & Cabestaing, 2005)	1 camera and 1 microphone	Data association using belief theory
(D'Arca, Hughes, Robertson, & Hopgood, 2013)	1 camera and 16 microphones	Kalman Filter
(Shivappa et al., 2010)	4 cameras and 24 microphones	Multilevel Iterative decoding (MID)
(Kim, Choi, & Kim, 2007)	3 microphones, 1 camera	Integration using visual tracking after sound DOA

Some limitations associated with audio information are:

1. This tracking assistance is confined only to case of speaking target or a sound producing source and hence additional computational cost of merging the audio information is useless for the complete video duration.
2. There is a new problem known as audio clutters that may arise if the noise is present along with the speaking target to be tracked.
3. Again if multiple speakers speak at same time that can happen during conversation, conference or lectures, so there is an additional treatment required to tackle this issue of audio occlusion.

3. Use of RADAR Information in Real Time Video Tracking

RADAR stands for radio detection and ranging. In early days, RADAR was big sized and costly equipment that was mainly used in Aerospace science. But, recent electronics technology made current RADAR systems small and cheap. Due to which, these are now preferred in commercial vehicle navigation systems. There are several researches available today which have insisted the use of RADAR systems along with the pictorial information for driver assistance systems, obstacle detection etc. The details of the methodology adopted and key effects of introducing RADAR into the real time visible domain tracking will be explained in the chapter.

A combined system involving millimeter-wave RADAR and a CCD camera was proposed in (Sugimoto et al., 2004). The authors introduced a calibration method of two sensors via homography. The transformation between the RADAR scanning plane and the image plane was modeled using homographic projections. The information acquired using the RADAR sensor was visualized on the 2D image as shown by Figure 9.

Figure 9. Transformation between RADAR and Image Planes

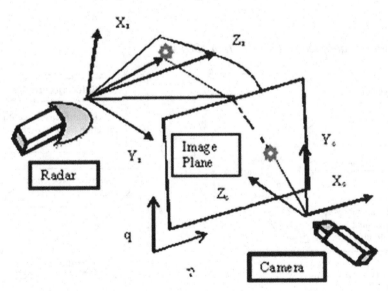

The RADAR coordinates $\left(X_r, Y_r, Z_r\right)$ and the camera coordinates $\left(X_c, Y_c, Z_c\right)$ were transformed into image plane (p, q). The proposed method was tested for real life vehicle mounted system. The data was acquired by the RADAR and camera simultaneously and the result of RADAR clustering for objects was displayed on the image plane. The clusters were proposed to be tracked throughout the test using Kalman filter. But the observational factors such as multiple reflections, diffraction, etc. make the method vulnerable to errors. So, the main disadvantage of this method was its ineffectiveness to noise and spurious measurements from false targets. Another method to remedies this work was presented by (Kim & Jeon, 2014) in which the noise and cluttering effect's removal was the major advancement. It used RADAR module IMA RS 3400. The methodology of the applied procedure is shown by Figure 10.

A Multi-object integrated probabilistic data association was employed here to render the effect of false targets such as clutters or echoes. This algorithm was based on the Gaussian mixtures of individual IPDA (integrated probabilistic data association) and could be treated as the extension for multi target case. The working was mainly emphasized on key aspects such as: Measurements and Geometry of sensors, Calibration of sensors involving homography, Kalman Filtering based Fusion, MIPDA (Multiple Object Integrated Probabilistic Data Association) based Multi object tracking.

a. Measurements and Geometry of Sensors

RADAR Sensor: The Sivers IMA RS 3400 module was used to measure the radial distance of objects. This module is a step frequency continuous wave (SFCW) radar module and was used to measure the phase difference between the echo signal and the radiated signal. The phase difference was expressed as: $O = \cos(\phi)$, where ϕ can be calculated in terms of the radiated RF frequency can be calculated using the equation (6):

$$\phi\left(f_R\right) = 2\pi \frac{2x}{v} f_R \tag{6}$$

Figure 10. Methodology adopted by (Kim & Jeon, 2014)

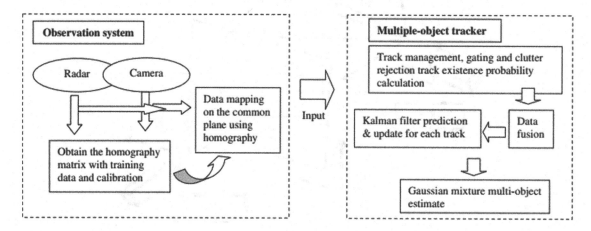

and the radial distance information of the target was estimated by the relation $x = f_c / (2W)$. Here 2x was taken as the round-trip distance of the reflecting object. For finding the radial distance information, frequency domain analysis is used. The required output O from the radar module can be obtained using equation (7) and given by:

$$O(n) = \cos\left(\phi_0 + 2\pi \frac{2x}{v} \frac{n}{N} W\right) \tag{7}$$

where W is the bandwidth = 1500 MHz, ϕ_0 is the phase value at the starting RF signal frequency of the sweeping and n is the frequency point index ranging form $n = 0, 1, 2, ..., N - 1$. The frequency was linearly increased from 24 GHz to 25.5 GHz with a step of 1500 MHz and total no. of steps = N. Equation (8) states the calculated fast Fourier transform of output:

$$\sum(f) = fft(O(n)) = \frac{1}{2}\left[\Delta\left(f - \frac{2x \times W}{v}\right) + \Delta\left(f + \frac{2x \times W}{v}\right)\right] \tag{8}$$

where, f indicates the normalized index in the frequency transformed domain.

CCD Camera: The CCD camera sensor was used to provide the XZ plane information of the object. CCD with VGA (Video Graphics Array) sensor (640 X 480) pixels was used and had framing speed of 30 fps. To analyze the position of object, initial hints were taken from the Radar's poor resolution bearing angle information and the final estimate i.e. a bounding box around the object was drawn with the help of a blob detector.

b. Calibration of Sensors

Since the information obtained from diverse sources is of different form, so to obtain a similar representation of the information, the radar observations were redrawn to the image plane and information fusion was further applied. Figure 9 illustrates the idea of transformation from another domain to the required domain. For calibration purpose, a homography matrix based approach (Sugimoto et al., 2004) was used. The radar coordinates $\left(X_r, Y_r, Z_r\right)$ and the camera coordinates $\left(X_c, Y_c, Z_c\right)$ were transformed into image plane (p, q). The transform relation between the radar coordinates and the image was modeled using affine homography and with an assumption of setting the radar plane in $Y_r = 0$. The following relation in equation (9) provides the homography modelling for conversions:

$$w\begin{bmatrix} p \\ q \\ 1 \end{bmatrix} = \begin{pmatrix} ah_{11} & ah_{12} & ah_{13} \\ ah_{21} & ah_{22} & ah_{23} \\ 0 & 0 & 1 \end{pmatrix}\begin{bmatrix} X_r \\ Z_r \\ 1 \end{bmatrix} \tag{9}$$

Taking the value of w = 1, the above linear algebraic equations are converted to homogeneous linear least square problem which could be solved using Singular Value Decomposition (SVD).

c. Kalman Filtering Based Fusion

After proper calibration of the two different domains of information into a single information domain, the fusion process of the different information was carried out through the Kalman filter. Two approaches of information fusion were discussed viz. centralized fusion and decentralized fusion and an equivalence of them is proved. The centralized fusion scheme was used here, in which a simple augmented observation system was thought of by concatenating the individual measurements from sensors respectively. The fused augmented output was found with the help of equation (10)

$$P_t = M_t X_t + u_t \tag{10}$$

Here, M_t is the combined measurement matrix from radar and image mode. The term u_t corresponds to the noise counterpart. Value of M_t and u_t is given by the eq. (11) and (12)

$$M_t = \left[\left(M_t^1 \right)^T \left(M_t^2 \right)^T \right]^T, u_t = \left[\left(u_t^1 \right)^T \left(u_t^2 \right)^T \right]^T \tag{11}$$

$$u_t \sim \mathbb{N}\left(u_t; 0, \sigma_t \right), \sigma_t = diag\left(\sigma_t^1, \sigma_t^2 \right) \tag{12}$$

Here, σ_t resembles the variance term of noise. Succeeding working of Kalman Filter for tracking is same apart from the alteration provided by substitution of above fused terms into the basic Kalman Filter Equations.

d. MIPDA Based Data Association for Multi Object Tracking

A Multi-object integrated probabilistic data association is further employed to render the effect of false targets such as clutters or echoes. This algorithm is based on the Gaussian mixtures of individual IPDA (integrated probabilistic data association) proposed by (Musciki, Evans, & Stankovic, 1994) and can be treated as the extension for multi target case. The gated probability and the object existence probability are the two parameters considered for track management and data association under cluttered environments.

The computational time of the above proposed method is quite lucrative since it takes very less time (0.002 sec elapsed time for Intel Core 2 Duo, 2.67 GHz, 3 GB RAM) as compared with previous methods (Kim & Jeon, 2014). The results obtained while combined tracking using the above categorized sensors were provided and are shown in the Figure 11.

There is still a lot of scope for advancements in field related to Radar fusion. The ground clutters remained a problem even in the mentioned work of. Some new techniques of fusion can also be developed that are less dependent upon the complex calibration process. But this type of tracking can be very useful for autonomous vehicle driving purposes in field of autotronics.

Benefits of RADAR information: A cheap RADAR module provides the visible imagery mode with radial distance information; the RADAR signals are less affected by noises such as fog, dust, snow, etc. and can detect trapped objects; has a high distance resolution.

Figure 11. Outcomes of combined tracking using RADAR and visual camera (a) RADAR observations, (b) CCD camera track outputs, (c) combined 3D estimate of object providing distance measure along with position coordinates (D. Y. Kim & Jeon, 2014)

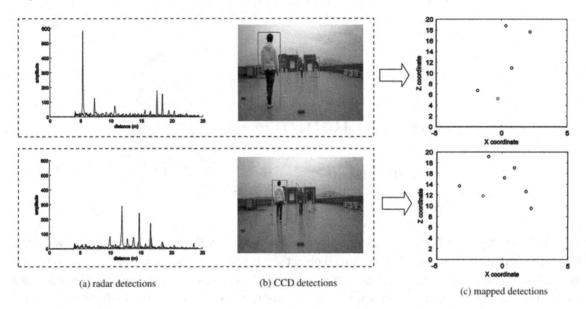

(a) radar detections   (b) CCD detections

(c) mapped detections

Drawbacks of using the RF information are the noise hindrance, ground clutters and reflections, multiple reflections and other RF related chaos encountered in RF communication. Also, the calibration of RADAR information into image is a complex process as compared to the rest domains of information. So, a smart calibration method should be designed to map both the domains.

4. Use of LIDAR Information in Real Time Video Tracking

LIDAR stands for Light detection and Ranging and is similar to the functioning of RADAR (Radio Detection and Ranging), the waves used for transmission and reception is the only difference. In LASER based tracking, target is represented by several points. The point representation helps to identify and classify different type of clutters/objects. An illustration to this is provided by the help of Figure 12.

Since it is fast and cheap and covers a lot of geographic area easily, LIDAR is widely used in different remote sensing applications.

Fusion of LIDAR and visible camera leads to a robust tracking approach since both modes complement each other with the type of information provided (Douillard, Fox, & Ramos, 2007). A camera provides dense appearance information, but it does not give a sense of scale, whereas a LIDAR gives accurate geometric information, but only at sparse locations, and much of the appearance information cannot be captured (Kwak, Kim, Min, & Park, 2014). The calibration procedure required for amalgamation between these two sensor modalities was made possible in (Kwak, Huber, Badino, & Kanade, 2011), (Zhang & Pless, 2004), (Li, Liu, Dong, Cai, & Zhou, 2007), (Wasielewski& Strauss, 1995) by finding corresponding features in the LIDAR and camera data.

(Kwak et al., 2014) proposed a new fusion method for tracking that included two modes of tracking, one in visible domain and by camera and other through a single- line scanning LIDAR sensor. In this

Figure 12. An illustration to working of Laser Detection and Ranging

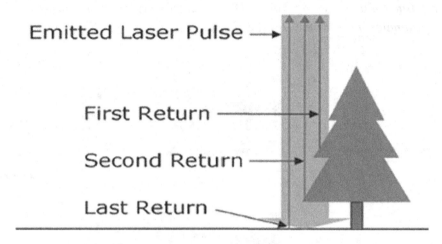

method, the relative pose between the two sensors was obtained by the approach of (Kiho Kwak et al., 2011). The approach consisted of two steps: (i) object segmentation by boundary detection and (ii) data association by integer programming. The segmentation of objects was based on boundary detection task. The features from both the modalities were fed as input to a SVM (State Vector Machine) classifier. Integration of these features in the classifier leaded the way to the feature level fusion of different modalities. Features were retrieved from the projected LIDAR measurements and image patches surrounding the LIDAR measurements. The LIDAR features described by eq. (13), (14), and (15), included distance $dist_i$ between the points, range difference l_i of the points and surface orientation th_i for two consecutive LIDAR measurement points Pt_i and Pt_{i+1} were defined as:

$$dist_i = \left\| Pt_i - Pt_{i+1} \right\|_2 \tag{13}$$

$$l_i = \left| r_i - r_{i+1} \right| \tag{14}$$

$$th_i = \arccos \frac{a.b}{\|a\|\|b\|} \tag{15}$$

where, a is the vector between Pt_i and Pt_{i+1}, and b is the vector between the mid-point of Pt_i and Pt_{i+1} and the sensor origin. While considering the image features, histograms of the regions I_i and I_{i+1} corresponding to the LIDAR movements Pt_i and Pt_{i+1} were firstly calculated. Two derived features viz. intersection distance of colored histograms of these patches and normalized sum of square differences (Criminisi, Blake, Rother, Shotton, & Torr, 2007) of intensity images were modeled further. The data association step was performed by solving an integer programming problem (K. Li et al., 2008) that maximizes the likelihood between the matching pairs. Result of the data association was the formation of a likelihood vector given by eq. (16).

$$cx_v = Sim_L \left(Z_p, Z_q \right) Sim_I \left(I_p, I_q \right) \tag{16}$$

where, Sim_L represents the similarity measure from the LIDAR sensor information and Sim_I from the image sensor information and I is the image patch corresponding to LIDAR cluster Z. The similarity $Sim_L \left(Z_p, Z_q \right)$ between two segmented LIDAR clusters is obtained by first finding the Bhattacharyya distance of two probability distributions Pb_p and corresponding to Z_p and is given by: $Sim_L \left(Z_p, Z_q \right) = \exp(-D_{BH})$. The similarity measure in the image mode is obtained by finding the modified Bhattacharya measure (Comaniciu, Ramesh, & Meer, 2003), given by eq. (17), between normalized color histograms $Hist_p$ and $Hist_q$ related to image patch regions I_p and I_q and is given by:

$$Sim_I \left(I_p, I_q \right) = \sqrt{1 - \sum_{K+1}^{K} \sqrt{H_p\left(k\right), H_q\left(k\right)}} \tag{17}$$

where K indicates the total no. of bins of histogram. The performance of the proposed algorithm was compared with an adaptive breakpoint detector method proposed in (Borges & Aldon, 2004). List of common techniques coming under this category are tabulated in the following Table 3.

Benefits of LIDAR assisted tracking can be listed as:

1. A very cost effective product to acquire information specially over large areas
2. Easy to integrate its information with other information sources
3. Insensitive to environmental changes and night time conditions.
4. Low computational requirements
5. Speed of LASER is very fast.

The shortcoming of using this technology into tracking is that since in impenetrable situations containing a crowded scene containing lots of people, it will be difficult to acquire an accurate Laser signal

Table 3. Various Tracking schemes for Lidar-visual tracking

Research	Sensors used	Algorithms used
(X. Song et al., 2008)	1 LASER scanner LMS291 and 1Camera	Bayesian Fusion
(X. Song et al., 2013)	2 Single row LASER Scanners and 1 Camera	Online training of classifiers and mergers
(Chakravarty & Jarvis, 2006)	1 Camera and Laser sensor mounted on top of it	PF and Gaussian Background subtraction
(Spinello et al., 2009)	1 monocular camera and 1 Laser range finder	Conditional Random Fields, Implicit Shape Model, Kalman Filter
(Canedo-Rodríguez et al., 2016)	1 laser., 5 Cameras, 1 Wifi card, a d 1 magnetic compass	Particle filter

back without any restriction or influence from surrounding objects. Moreover, similar type of object like multiple humans having almost similar structure and standing nearby in a scene will not provide different information for a LIDAR sensor, so one will have to rely only upon the visible sensor for this case.

So, in the end of this section, it can be stated that it is possible to overcome the shortcomings of a alone visual tracker by the inserting the aid of information from distinct sources. For this, an intelligent technique is required that can decide the use of a particular category of information according to the requirement of tracking application and capable of efficiently merging the information from different modes to produce a robust tracking estimate in one domain.

FUTURE RESEARCH DIRECTION

Since improvement will always be a scope for any trending field. So, this inter domain information exchange for tracking in video sequence can be advanced thorough the practices mentioned in the following points:

1. Various other form of information such as seismic signal information that is fastest and most sensitive is yet to be worked upon for fusion with the video camera signal to be applied to an object tracking information.
2. Development of classes of fusion algorithms those are optimal for handling the inclusion of specific type of information respectively.
3. Cross domain interaction of more than two different types of information sources is yet to be practiced in the real-time object tracking applications.
4. Researches should be made to develop hardware systems that are independently compatible for acquiring simultaneous real time data from different mode of information.
5. Various calibration techniques are needed to be proposed in future that can map one form of information to another form optimally for application of union based tracking algorithms.

CONCLUSION

Due to the increasing use of information capturing from multiple sources in object tracking application, it was need of the hour to appraise the various methods indulged into these types of accomplishments. The chapter included the specific needs, implementation work plans, benefits, and future pathways for the different fusion strategies present for object tracking based upon aid from distinct sources of information. Almost all the cross-domain inclusion tracking activities viz. thermal, RADAR and LIDAR are real time implementable except audio signal fusion because it takes time to improve the SNR of the signal received from audio sources generally. After introducing the topic and its need, extensive literature background covering the different worked out techniques of various cross domain activities was presented. After this, details of individual fusion strategies for performing object tracking were discussed that covered the implementation, advantages and limitations. The common technologies like audio-visual fusion and thermo-visual fusion along with the future technologies involving the fusion of the visual information with the genre of radio frequency waves and light waves were the topic of prime focus in the chapter. The use of RADAR is inevitably helpful in automatic vehicle guidance systems and various traffic monitoring situations, since these provide the distance information of the target through the use of basic Doppler Effect in RADAR's. LIDAR on the other hand uses the similar basics as that of RADAR but through the use of light waves. All of the above mentioned multi domain techniques possess several advantages when compared with the single sensor tracking. The comparison of these fusion strategies is majorly based on the tracking application involved. For example, audio domain inclusion is mainly done in closed room, lecture hall and conference proceedings to track the speaking target, whereas RADAR and LIDAR schemes are helpful in tracking involving vehicular communications and open area situations. Thermal imagery can be incorporated in both indoor as well as outdoor scenes to help the visual tracking in vision disguised conditions. Few suggestions related to possible future improvements to the trending approach were presented in the future research direction subsection. The use of source of information such as seismic sensors and SONAR's etc. is negligible at present which needs to be brought in use in near future for obtaining a robust and accurate tracking under all possible circumstances.

REFERENCES

Bakhtari, A., Naish, M. D., Eskandari, M., Croft, E. A., & Benhabib, B. (2006). Active-vision-based multisensor surveillance - An implementation. *IEEE Transactions on Systems, Man, and Cybernetics. Part A, Systems and Humans*, *36*(5), 668–679. doi:10.1109/TSMCC.2005.855525

Borges, G. A., & Aldon, M. J. (2004). Line extraction in 2D range images for mobile robotics. *Journal of Intelligent and Robotic Systems: Theory and Applications*, *40*(3), 267–297. doi:10.1023/B:JINT.0000038945.55712.65

Canedo-rodríguez, A., Álvarez-santos, V., Regueiro, C. V., Iglesias, R., Barro, S., & Presedo, J. (2016). Particle filter robot localisation through robust fusion of laser, WiFi, compass, and a network of external cameras. *Information Fusion*, *27*, 170–188. doi:10.1016/j.inffus.2015.03.006

Chakravarty, P., & Jarvis, R. (2006). Panoramic vision and laser range finder fusion for multiple person tracking. *Proceedings of the IEEE International Conference on Intelligent Robots and Systems* (Vol. 1, pp. 2949–2954). doi:10.1109/IROS.2006.282149

Checka, N., Wilson, K. W., Siracusa, M. R., & Darrell, T. (2004). Multiple person and speaker activity tracking with a particle filter. *Proceedings of the 2004 IEEE International Conference on Acoustics Speech and Signal Processing* (Vol. 1, pp. 881-884). doi:10.1109/ICASSP.2004.1327252

Comaniciu, D., Ramesh, V., & Meer, P. (2003). Kernel-based object tracking. *IEEE Transactions on Pattern Analysis and Machine Intelligence*, *25*(5), 564–577. doi:10.1109/TPAMI.2003.1195991

Conaire, C. Ó., OConnor, N. E., & Smeaton, A. (2008). Thermo-visual feature fusion for object tracking using multiple spatiogram trackers. *Machine Vision and Applications*, *19*(5–6), 483–494. doi:10.1007/s00138-007-0078-y

Criminisi, A., Blake, A., Rother, C., Shotton, J., & Torr, P. H. S. (2007). Efficient dense stereo with occlusions for new view-synthesis by four-state dynamic programming. *International Journal of Computer Vision*, *71*(1), 89–110. doi:10.1007/s11263-006-8525-1

Crocco, M., Del Bue, A., Bustreo, M., & Murino, V. (2012). A closed form solution to the microphone position self-calibration problem. *Proceedings of the IEEE International Conference on Acoustics, Speech and Signal Processing ICASSP* (pp. 2597–2600). doi:10.1109/ICASSP.2012.6288448

D'Arca, E., Hughes, A., Robertson, N. M., & Hopgood, J. (2013). Video tracking through occlusions by fast audio source localisation. *Proceedings of the 2013 IEEE International Conference on Image Processing* (pp. 2660–2664). doi:10.1109/ICIP.2013.6738548

Douillard, B., Fox, D., & Ramos, F. (2010). A spatio-temporal probabilistic model for multi-sensor multi-class object recognition. In Springer Tracts in Advanced Robotics (Vol. 66, pp. 123–134). doi:10.1007/978-3-642-14743-2_11

Gatica-Perez, D., Lathoud, G., McCowan, I., Odobez, J.-M., & Moore, D. (2003). Audio-visual speaker tracking with importance particle filters. *Proceedings 2003 International Conference on Image Processing* (Vol. 3, pp. 25-28). doi:10.1109/ICIP.2003.1247172

Gatica-Perez, D., Lathoud, G., Odobez, J.-M., & McCowan, I. (2004). Audio-Visual Tracking of Multiple Speakers in Meetings. *IEEE Transactions on Audio, Speech, and Language Processing, 15*(72), 601–616.

Germa, T., Lerasle, F., Ouadah, N., Cadenat, V., & Devy, M. (2009). Vision and RFID-based person tracking in crowds from a mobile robot. *Proceedings of the 2009 IEEE/RSJ International Conference on Intelligent Robots and Systems IROS '09* (Vol. 3, pp. 5591–5596). doi:10.1109/IROS.2009.5354475

Hanif, M., & Ali, U. (2006). Optimized visual and thermal image fusion for efficient face recognition. *Proceedings of the 2006 9th International Conference on Information Fusion, FUSION*.

Kilic, V., & Barnard, M. (2013). Audio constrained particle filter based visual tracking. In *Acoustics, Speech and Signal Processing* (pp. 3627–3631).

Kilic, V., Barnard, M., Wang, W., & Kittler, J. (2015). Audio assisted robust visual tracking with adaptive particle filtering. *IEEE Transactions on Multimedia, 17*(2), 186–200. doi:10.1109/TMM.2014.2377515

Kim, D. Y., & Jeon, M. (2014). Data fusion of RADAR and image measurements for multi-object tracking via Kalman filtering. *Information Sciences, 278*, 641–652. doi:10.1016/j.ins.2014.03.080

Kim, H. D., Choi, J. S., & Kim, M. (2007). Human-Robot Interaction in Real Environments by Audio-Visual Integration. *Intl. J. of Control Automation and Systems, 5*(1), 61–69.

Kim, H. D., Choi, J. S., & Kim, M. (2007). Human-Robot Interaction in Real Environments by Audio-Visual Integration. *Intl J of Control Automation and Systems, 5*(1), 61–69.

Klee, U., Gehrig, T., & McDonough, J. (2006). Kalman filters for time delay of arrival-based source localization. *EURASIP Journal on Applied Signal Processing, 2006*, 1–16. doi:10.1155/ASP/2006/12378

Kwak, K., Huber, D. F., Badino, H., & Kanade, T. (2011). Extrinsic calibration of a single line scanning lidar and a camera. *Proceedings of the IEEE International Conference on Intelligent Robots and Systems* (pp. 3283–3289).

Kwak, K., Huber, D. F., Jeongsook, C., & Kanade, T. (2010). Boundary detection based on supervised learning. *Proceedings of the 2010 IEEE International Conference on Robotics and Automation (ICRA)* (pp. 3939–3945). doi:10.1109/ROBOT.2010.5509379

Kwak, K., Kim, J.-S., Min, J., & Park, Y.-W. (2014). Unknown multiple object tracking using 2D LIDAR and video camera. *Electronics Letters*, *50*(8), 600–602. doi:10.1049/el.2014.0355

Legg, M., & Bradley, S. (2013). A Combined Microphone and Camera Calibration Technique With Application to Acoustic Imaging. *IEEE Transactions on Image Processing*, *22*(10), 4028–4039. doi:10.1109/TIP.2013.2268974 PMID:23797248

Li, G., Liu, Y., Dong, L., Cai, X., & Zhou, D. (2007). An algorithm for extrinsic parameters calibration of a camera and a laser range finder using line features. *Proceedings of the IEEE International Conference on Intelligent Robots and Systems* (pp. 3854–3859).

Li, K., Miller, E. D., Chen, M., Kanade, T., Weiss, L. E., & Campbell, P. G. (2008). Cell population tracking and lineage construction with spatiotemporal context. *Medical Image Analysis*, *12*(5), 546–566. doi:10.1016/j.media.2008.06.001 PMID:18656418

Lim, Y., & Choi, J. (2009). Speaker selection and tracking in a cluttered environment with audio and visual information. *IEEE Transactions on Consumer Electronics*, *55*(3), 1581–1589. doi:10.1109/TCE.2009.5278030

Lin, D.-T., & Huang, K.-Y. (2011). Collaborative pedestrian tracking and data fusion with multiple cameras. *IEEE Transactions on Information Forensics and Security*, *6*(4), 1432–1444. doi:10.1109/TIFS.2011.2159972

Megherbi, N., Ambellouis, S., Colôt, O., & Cabestaing, F. (2005). Joint audio-video people tracking using belief theory. *Proceedings of the IEEE International Conference on Advanced Video and Signal Based Surveillance AVSS '05* (pp. 135–140). doi:10.1109/AVSS.2005.1577256

Muñoz-Salinas, R., García-Silvente, M., & Medina Carnicer, R. (2008). Adaptive multi-modal stereo people tracking without background modelling. *Journal of Visual Communication and Image Representation*, *19*(2), 75–91. doi:10.1016/j.jvcir.2007.07.004

Musciki, D., Evans, R., & Stankovic, S. (1994). Integrated Probabilistic Data Association. *IEEE Transactions on Automatic Control*, *39*(6), 1237–1241. doi:10.1109/9.293185

Nickel, K., Gehrig, T., Stiefelhagen, R., & McDonough, J. (2005). A joint particle filter for audio-visual speaker tracking. *Proceedings of the 7th International Conference on Multimodal Interfaces ICMI '05*. doi:10.1145/1088463.1088477

Palmerini, G. B. (2014). Combining thermal and visual imaging in spacecraft proximity operations. *Proceedings of the IEEE International Conference on Control Automation Robotics and Vision (pp. 383–388).* doi:10.1109/ICARCV.2014.7064336

Premebida, C., Ludwig, O., & Nunes, U. (2009). LIDAR and vision-based pedestrian detection system. *Journal of Field Robotics*, *26*(9), 696–711. doi:10.1002/rob.20312

Shivappa, S. T., Rao, B. D., & Trivedi, M. M. (2010). Audio-visual fusion and tracking with multilevel iterative decoding: Framework and experimental evaluation. *IEEE Journal of Selected Topics in Signal Processing*, *4*(5), 882–894. doi:10.1109/JSTSP.2010.2057890

Singh, M. P. (2015). Norms as a basis for governing sociotechnical systems. *Proceedings of the IJCAI International Joint Conference on Artificial Intelligence* (pp. 4207–4211).

Song, H., Shin, V., & Jeon, M. (2012). Mobile node localization using fusion prediction-based interacting multiple model in cricket sensor network. *IEEE Transactions on Industrial Electronics*, *59*(11), 4349–4359. doi:10.1109/TIE.2011.2151821

Song, X., Cui, J., Zhao, H., & Zha, H. (2008). A Bayesian Approach: Fusion of Laser and Vision for Multiple Pedestrians Tracking. *International Journal (Toronto, Ont.)*, *3*(1), 1–9.

Song, X., Zhao, H., Cui, J., Shao, X., Shibasaki, R., & Zha, H. (2013). An Online System for Multiple Interacting Targets Tracking: Fusion of Laser and Vision, Tracking and Learning. *ACM Transactions on Intelligent Systems and Technology*, *4*(1), 1–21. doi:10.1145/2414425.2414443

Spinello, L., Triebel, R., & Siegwart, R. (2009). A trained system for multimodal perception in urban environments. *Proc. of The Workshop on People Detection and Tracking (ICRA)*, Kobe, Japan.

Stolkin, R., Rees, D., Talha, M., & Florescu, I. (2012). Bayesian fusion of thermal and visible spectra camera data for region based tracking with rapid background adaptation. *Proceedings of the IEEE International Conference on Multisensor Fusion and Integration for Intelligent Systems* (pp. 192–199). doi:10.1109/MFI.2012.6343021

Strobel, N., Spors, S., & Rabenstein, R. (2001). Joint audio-video object localization and tracking, A Presentation of General Methodology. *IEEE Signal Processing Magazine*, *18*(1), 22–31. doi:10.1109/79.911196

Sugimoto, S., Tateda, H., Takahashi, H., & Okutomi, M. (2004). Obstacle detection using millimeter-wave RADAR and its visualization on image sequence. *Proceedings of the International Conference on Pattern Recognition* (Vol. 3, pp. 342–345). doi:10.1109/ICPR.2004.1334537

Talha, M., & Stolkin, R. (2014). Particle filter tracking of camouflaged targets by adaptive fusion of thermal and visible spectra camera data. *IEEE Sensors Journal*, *14*(1), 159–166. doi:10.1109/JSEN.2013.2271561

Torabi, A., & Mass, G. (2010). Feedback scheme for thermal-visible video registration, sensor fusion, and people tracking. *Proceedings of the IEEE computer society conference Computer Vision and Pattern Recognition Workshop* (pp. 15–22).

Treptow, A., Cielniak, G., & Duckett, T. (2005). Active people recognition using thermal and grey images on a mobile security robot. *Proceedings of the 2005 IEEE/RSJ International Conference on Intelligent Robots and Systems IROS* (pp. 3610–3615). doi:10.1109/IROS.2005.1545530

Wasielewski, S., & Strauss, O. (1995). Calibration of a multi-sensor system laser range finder/camera. *Proceedings of the IEEE Intelligent Vehicles Symposium* (pp. 472–477). doi:10.1109/IVS.1995.528327

Xiao, G., Yun, X., & Wu, J. (2016). A new tracking approach for visible and infrared sequences based on tracking-before-fusion. *International Journal of Dynamics and Control*, *4*(1), 40–51. doi:10.1007/s40435-014-0115-4

Zhang, Q., & Pless, R. (2004). Extrinsic Calibration of a Camera and Laser Range Finder (improves camera calibration). *Proceedings of IROS* (Vol. *3*, pp. 2301–2306).

Zhou, Z., Wang, B., Li, S., & Dong, M. (2016). Perceptual fusion of infrared and visible images through a hybrid multi-scale decomposition with Gaussian and bilateral filters. *Information Fusion, 30*, 15–26. doi:10.1016/j.inffus.2015.11.003

Chapter 6
Electrical Impedance Tomography:
A Real-Time Medical Imaging Technique

Ramesh Kumar Meena
NIT Jalandhar, India

Abdullah Bin Queyam
NIT Jalandhar, India

Sarwan Kumar Pahuja
NIT Jalandhar, India

Amit Sengupta
IIT Delhi, India

ABSTRACT

Presently, non-invasive techniques are in vogue and preferred standard clinical approach because of its limitless advantages in monitoring real time phenomenon occurring within our human body without much interference. Many techniques such as ultrasound, magnetocardiography, CT scan, MRI etc., are used for real time monitoring but are generally not recommended for continuous monitoring. The limitations created by above used techniques are overcome by a proposed technique called non-invasive bio-impedance technique such as Electrical Impedance Technique (EIT). EIT imaging technique is based on internal electrical conductivity distribution of the body. The reconstruction of cross sectional image of resistivity required sufficient data collection by finite element method using MATLAB software. The EIT technique offers some benefits over other imaging modalities. It is economical, non-invasive, user friendly and emits no radiation thus appears to be one of the best fit technology for mass health care to be used by the basic health worker at a community level.

1. INTRODUCTION

Non-invasive techniques are the standard clinical approach because of its use in long term monitoring of the patients as well as industrial subject (Kumar et al., 2013). Alternatively, many techniques are used in medical area for patient monitoring like ultrasound, magnetocardiography (MCG), computerised tomography (CT) scan, magnetic resonance imaging (MRI) etc., but are generally not recommended for hours long monitoring and real time monitoring. Due to these limitations in real time monitoring, patient

DOI: 10.4018/978-1-5225-2848-7.ch006

as well as medical personnel face inconvenience (Kumar et al., 2013). The restrictions created by above used techniques is overcome by a proposed method called non-invasive bio-impedance technique, such as, electrical impedance tomography and impedance plethesmosraphy (Holder, 2005). Many research groups have established EIT prototypes system and done lots of experimental study and clinical studies (Holder, 2005). Validation of EIT data was an important part in most of these studies. Regional distribution of ventilation has been associated to other medical techniques (Holder, 2005). Various studies also established that EIT technique associates the potential to occur as a useful of real time monitoring tool for clinical filed.

Formerly bio impedance measurement became a general method to determine the features of body tissue. With knowledge of the bio impedance of various points about an object testing, the interior conductivity distribution can be projected. This method is known as electrical impedance tomography (Holder, 2005). EIT was developed over 70 years ago for non-medical purposes by the Sheffield group. It is an imaging modality and also known as bio impedance imaging or tomography. In this the study of passive electrical properties of the biological tissues is done (Patterson, 2005). EIT is based on two main concepts. First, the fact that there is a large resistivity difference between a different types of tissue in human body which permits for the use of this resistivity difference to form anatomical images of that cross-section of human body. Second, there is clear dissimilarity between normal and pathological tissues which can be easily identified by measuring the resistivity difference or electrical distribution (Holder, 2005; Patterson, 2005).

Many studies also established that EIT technique associates the potential to emerge as a useful of real time monitoring tool for clinical filed. Presently, many EIT prototype are available for data acquisition of the object, such as, through the DSP kit switching, controller with multiplexer, multiplexer switching, electronic switching etc. similarly, many image reconstruction algorithms have been developed to check the field distribution in closed object. Such as that, using FEM, Neural Network, GUI based, EIDORs toolkit, several mathematical algorithms are available at present (Patterson, 2005). Many phantom studies are done which shows that EIT can be implemented in medical or industrial application. Subsequently, many other studies show trial of EIT technique on human volunteers at different-2 body locations such as brain, joints of body, abdomen etc. The EIT technique presented desired outcomes on a set of experiments done on many phantoms and has been compared. Results clearly presented that the electrical impedance tomography efficiently can be used to detect related to bio-physiological and morphological parameters of the human body and can be beneficial for medical mass healthcare applications. And the advantage of this technique is radiation free, non-invasive, inexpensive and portable monitoring to patients.

For impedance measurement of the three-dimensional resolution may be improved by using an arrangement of electrodes around the surface of the object or the concerned subject (Vauhkonen, 2004). Electric current may be fed sequentially through different combination available electrode pairs and the corresponding output voltage is measured sequentially by all remaining electrode pairs (Kumar et al., 2016). It is possible to create an image of the impedance of different regions of the object by the use of reconstruction algorithms. This imaging method is called impedance imaging. A 3D image is usually constructed from the 2D slice images of the object this method is also called impedance tomography and ECCT (electric current computed tomography). Thus, impedance tomography is an imaging method which may be used to accompaniment positron emission tomography (PET), X-ray scan, CT scan, ultrasonography imaging, and others (Kumar et al., 2013).

2. BACKGROUND AND HISTORY

Nowadays, the aim of medical research is to improve the tools and analytical instruments, develop new techniques for medical diagnosis, non-invasive and long-term monitoring method for medical diagnosis (Patterson, 2005). Currently, many non-invasive techniques are used in medical field some of which is not used for long time monitoring of the body while some may be used for long term monitoring of the body, like electrical impedance technique (Holder, 2005). The main concept of electrical impedance technique is to studying the internal properties of a medium or subject by imposing a current, calculating the voltage distribution, and concluding the inner resistivity of the object (Kumar et al., 2013; Holder, 2005). This idea of electrical impedance tomography was proposed by Holder, D. S. and Patterson for electrical impedance tomography imaging.

2.1. Bio-Impedance of Body

Bio impedance denotes to the electrical properties of a biological tissue, calculated the voltages when the current flows through in tissue. This impedance changes with frequency and different tissue types and varies sensitively with the fundamental study of the tissues (Holder, 2005). Different mechanisms and structures of the internal cell or tissue explanation for the biological system's electrical properties. Basically, two types of electrical properties in body have been found, such as, passive and active electrical properties (Atefi et al., 2015). Active electrical properties of the living organisms contain ionic pumps inboard the action potentials or plasma layer and passive electrical properties of the body tissue have permitted the development of electric sources and tools for reduction of pain, the treatment and diagnosis (Atefi et al., 2015).

2.2. Cell Electrical Properties

Cells are the building blocks of living tissue. Body fluids like blood such as the intracellular and extracellular space contain ions. The ions in these liquids fabricate an electrolyte that can take away the DC ionic current after applying an Exterior voltage (Holder, 2005). The medium around the cells is filled with extracellular fluid, which is divided from the intercellular space by the plasma layer (Atefi et al., 2015). The intercellular space includes the organelles, cytosol, protoplasm and the nucleus of the cell, Intercellular and extracellular fluids and the cell membrane into the ingredient that account for cell and tissue electrical properties (Holder, 2005).

The plasma membrane combination of lipids and proteins. In Lipids have a hydrophobic and a hydrophilic side. The hydrophobic sides attract each other, forcing the hydrophilic sides to the exterior and keeping the hydrophobic side's internal structure (Holder, 2005). This structure is known as the lipid bi-layer. The conductivity of the lipid bi-layer is very poor and is mostly considered as a dielectric and lipid bi-layer and intracellular and extracellular medium all together act as a capacitor (Holder, 2005).

2.3. Electrical Cell Model

The basic properties of the tissue are resistance and capacitance. In bio impedance Resistance is a measure of the amount to which opposes the flow of the electrons or, in liquid solution as in alive tissue, the flow of ions among its tissues cells. Cells contain three components and may be exhibited as a group of electronic components (Atefi et al., 2015).

The R_e is represented as a resistor for extracellular Space, and the Membrane (C_m) and the intracellular space (R_i) is modelled as a capacitor and resistor respectively. Both the extracellular space and intracellular space are extremely conductive, because they consist of salt ions (Holder, 2005). The cell membrane capacitor C_m, in parallel with membrane resistance R_m. Because the membrane conductivity is poor, the membrane resistance can be ignored, and the can be simplified to the model in Figure 1.

The lipid membrane of cells is an insulator, which stops the current at lower frequencies from entering the cells. On lower frequencies, nearly about the all current flows through the extracellular space only, so the total impedance is mostly resistive and is equally to the extracellular space (Holder, 2005; Atefi et al., 2015). As this is generally less of the total tissue, the total resulting impedance is comparatively high. On Higher frequencies, the applied current can cross the capacitance of the Membrane cell and so enter the intracellular space as well (Holder, 2005). Then cell has penetration to the conductive ions in both the intra and extra cellular spaces, so the total Impedance is lower (Atefi et al., 2015).

2.4. Impedance Measurement

The impedance of values is generally recorded with (Agcl) silver electrodes. The Simple arrangement of electrodes is to place at either end of a cylinder-shaped of the tissue (Patterson, 2005). Than a constant current is insert through the electrodes and the Impedance is calculated from the voltage measurement. The weakness of this method is that the impedance measured comprise not only the Tissue, but also have include of the electrodes (Holder, 2005). The bio impedance can be authentic, but needs that a standardization process is achieved first to set up Electrode impedance (Kumar et al., 2013; Holder, 2005). These then need to be subtracted from the whole Impedance measured, and it should be a reasonable hypothesis that the electrode Impedances do not change amid the calibration and test process. Mainly bio impedance technique is impedance plethysmogrpahy and electrical impedance tomography. Both techniques are non-invasively and safe (Kumar et al., 2013).

Figure 1. the equivalent of the cell electrical model (a) and (b), as well as the simplified model Neglecting R_m (c)

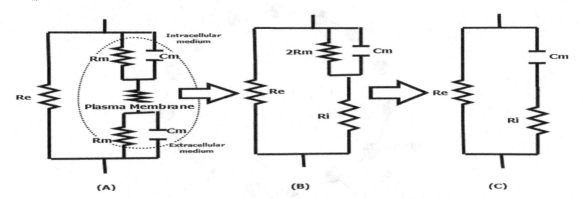

3. IMPEDANCE PLETHYSMOGRPAHY

Impedance plethysmogrpahy, is a non-invasive (Kumar et al., 2013) medical technique that measures small changes in electrical impedance of the body surface (Anderson et al., 1980). These measurements reflect blood volume variations, and can indirectly show the existence or absence of veins blockage. IPG is introduced by NYBOER (NYBOER et al. in 1950), it has received increasing attention in the last two decades as a noninvasive method for assessing cardiac, pulmonary, cerebral, and other functions in the human (Malmivuo & Plonsey, 1995). The IPG introduces a high frequency and low current signal between two electrodes which is measured of Electrical resistance using another electrodes pairs (Anderson et al., 1980). Anatomic features were selected as the most appropriate locations for comparing changes within and across patients.

In Plethysmogrpahy technique is injecting a small current pulse into subject using two Ag-Agcl skin electrodes, as current electrodes, and then calculating the potential difference amid these two current electrodes using two others Ag-Agcl skin electrodes, as voltage electrodes, that act as voltage sensors. Electrical resistance of the tissue is then calculated by using the voltage difference between the electrodes, which is caused by the passage of the current through the tissue (Mhaligji et al., 2012). Changing the voltage the body, then also related to resistance of the body, of which directly reflect the blood volume and human body mostly contributed by blood conductivity (Anderson et al., 1980).

4. ELECTRICAL IMPEDANCE TOMOGRAPHY

Electrical impedance tomography (EIT) is a non-invasive imaging technique (Kumar, 2013). This imaging technique can use for industrial and medical subjects (Holder, 2005). This imaging technique is based on internal conductivity distribution of the subject and reconstructing the image from the electrical measurements of electrodes attached to the subjects (Edic et al., 1995). Shown the Figure 2. This electrode is connected to the phantom (phantom may be used medical or industrial) inserted the some

Figure 2. EIT Basic Concept and Electrode configuration

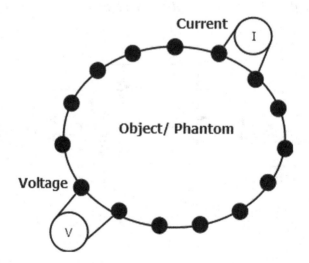

current pattern into the subject (Babaeizadeh et al., 2006). A particular current is inserted into the subject through some electrodes and measure the voltages from the other electrodes. The current (AC) range is used in milliampere and frequency vary from 10 kHz to 100 kHz (Holder, 2005; Kumar et al., 2015). An image reconstruction method is formerly used to calculate the internal conductivity distribution from the boundary data of the phantom (Bera & Nagaraju, 2009). As shown the Figure 3 of EIT system. In EIT, the position of the current pattern is rotated around the phantom/object and therefore the current is consecutively applied to all others electrode pairs (Kumar et al., 2015).

5. METHODS OF DATA ACQUISITION

The electric impedance may be measured either conventionally through basic originate electric approaches. The traditional electric methods are discussed first (R Kumar et al., 2016). According to impedance plethysmogrpahy, also in Electrical impedance tomography, the current pulse is inserting to the object and the voltage is measured through different pairs of electrodes. In the following we explained some of the data acquisition methods of EIT that are used (R Kumar et al., 2016; Anderson et.al., 1980).

5.1. Neighboring Method

In this method, the current location is applied on two neighbouring electrodes and measuring voltages from all other remaining adjacent electrode sets (Malmivuo & Plonsey, 1995). As Shown in Figure 4, the applied current location is on electrode 1 and 2, after that calculating the voltage measurements from the other electrode pairs, like 3-4,3-5, 3-6, 3-7, 3-8, 3-9, … After that changing the current location on next neighboring electrode pair 2 and 3. Again calculating the voltage measurement 4-5,4-6,4-7,4-8, 4-9… like that for next current location. then again changing the current location and calculating the voltage measurement (Malmivuo & Plonsey, 1995; Rahim et al.,2003).

In this method, 13 voltage measurements are obtained for single current location and all these 13 measurements are independent (According to 16-electrode system). Each of them is assumed to represent

Figure 3. Electrical Impedance Tomography System

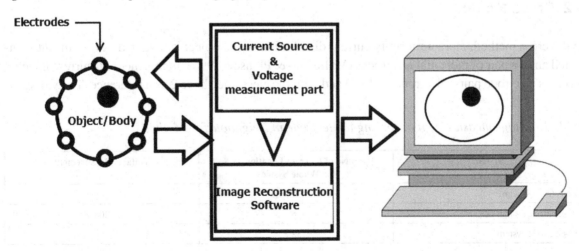

Figure 4. Neighbouring Method

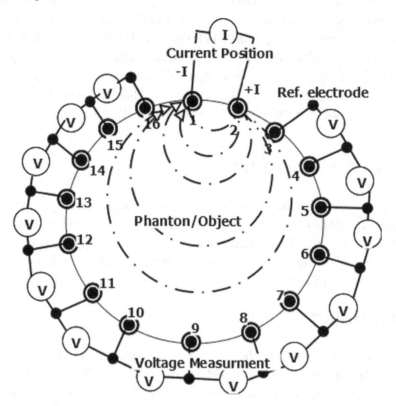

the impedance amidst the equipotential lines intersecting the measurement electrodes. For a 16-electrode system, $16 \times 13 = 208$ voltage measurements are acquired (R Kumar et al, 2016). Because of reciprocal, those measurements in which the current electrodes and voltage electrodes are exchange produce identical measurement outcomes. Therefore, only 104 measurements are independent. As shown the Table 1. For an EIT system, {N (N-3)} (N = No of electrode) voltage measurements are obtained (Malmivuo & Plonsey, 1995; Kumar, 2016).

5.2. Cross Method

In the cross method, more uniformity current distribution of the object is obtained as the current is injected amid a pair of more afar electrodes (Malmivuo & Plonsey, 1995). In this method, current injected on cross electrode pairs (electrode no 1 - 3) and with the electrode above 2 as a reference. The voltage is

Table 1. voltage measurement according to electrode in Neighbouring Method

System	No of Current Location (for Whole System)	Voltage Measurement
8-electrode system	8	40
16-electrode system	16	208
32-electrode system	32	928

measured sequentially for all other electrodes pairs, like 2-4,2-5, 2-6, 2-7, 2-8, 2-9, ... After that changing the current location on next crossed electrode pair 1 and 5. Again define another reference electrode for this current location and calculating the voltage measurement 2-3,2-4,2-6,2-7, 2-8... like that for next current location. then again changing the current location and calculating the voltage measurement (Malmivuo & Plonsey, 1995) As Shown in Figure 5. this method does not have as decent sensitivity in the periphery as does the Neighboring method but has better sensitivity over the whole region (Kumar et al., 2016) (Malmivuo & Plonsey, 1995).

In this method, 13 voltage measurements are obtained for single current location (According to 16-electrode system) and 7×13 = 91 voltage measurements are obtained. In this method have two ways of current inserting of the object, oddly and evenly. Any one we used. And obtained current location and voltage measurement shown in Table 2 according to system (Kumar et al. 2016).

Figure 5. Cross Method

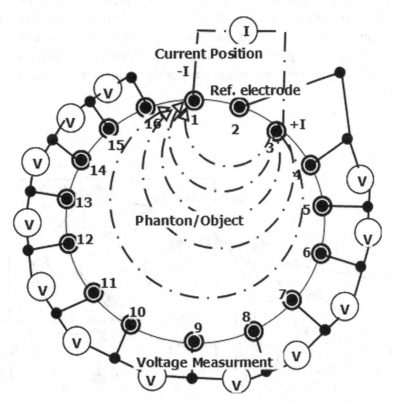

Table 2. Voltage measurement according to electrode in Cross Method

System	No of Current Location (Odd and Even)	Voltage Measurment
8-electrode system	3 or 3	15 or 15
16-electrode system	7 or 7	91 or 91
32-electrode system	15 or 15	435 or 435

5.3. Opposite Method

In this method, current is inserted through two opposite's electrodes (as shown in Figure 6). The electrode adjacent to the current-injecting electrode is used as the voltage reference. Voltage is measured from all other electrodes except the current electrodes, voltage measurements (Malmivuo & Plonsey, 1995; R Kumar et al., 2016). As Shown in Figure 6, the applied current location is on electrode 1 and 9, after that a define the reference electrode like electrode 2 is reference electrode and calculating the voltage measurements from the other electrode pairs, like 2-3,2-4, 2-5, 2-6, 2-7, 2-8, ... After that changing the current location on next opposite electrode pair 2 and 10. Again define another reference electrode for this current location and calculating the voltage measurement 3-4,3-5,3-6,3-7, 3-8, 3-9... like that for next current location. then again changing the current location and calculating the voltage measurement (R Kumar et al., 2016). The current distribution in this method is more uniform and, therefore, has an excellent sensitivity (Malmivuo & Plonsey, 1995).

In this method, 13 voltage measurements are obtained for single current location and all these 13 measurements are independent (According to 16-electrode system). For a 16-electrode system, 8×13 = 104 Potential measurements are acquired (Malmivuo & Plonsey, 1995; Rahim et al., 2003). And obtained current location and voltage measurement shown in Table 3 according to system. The current distribution in this method is more uniform compared to other methods, therefore, has a good sensitivity (Rahim et al., 2003)

Figure 6. Opposite Method

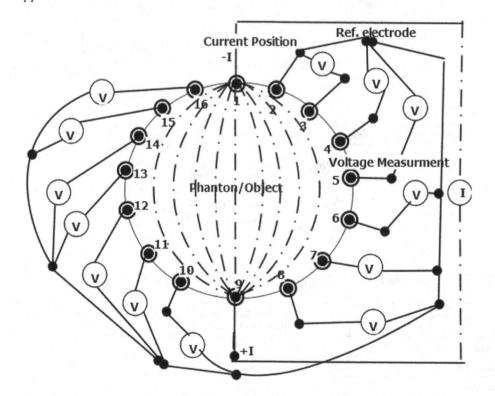

Table 3. voltage measurement according to electrode in Opposite Method

System	No of Current Location (for Whole System)	Voltage Measurement
8-electrode system	4	20
16-electrode system	8	104
32-electrode system	16	464

5.4. Adaptive Method

In the above-mentioned methods, current has been inserted with a pair of electrodes and voltage has been measured similarly (Kumar et al., 2016). In the adaptive method, current is injected through all electrodes. Because current applying through all the electrodes pairs of the object with feeding current range is -5 to +5 mA, as numerous independent current generators are required for calibration. After that measured the voltages from object with respect to a single grounded electrode (Malmivuo & Plonsey, 1995).as shown in Figure 7.

If the volume conductor is cylinder-shaped with rounded cross-section, the inserted current must be proportional to cos θ to acquire a homogeneous current distribution (Rahim et al., 2003). The voltages are measured with respect to a single grounded electrode. For 16 electrodes system, the 15 voltage measurements obtained for a single current distribution of the system. The next current distribution is

Figure 7. Adaptive Method

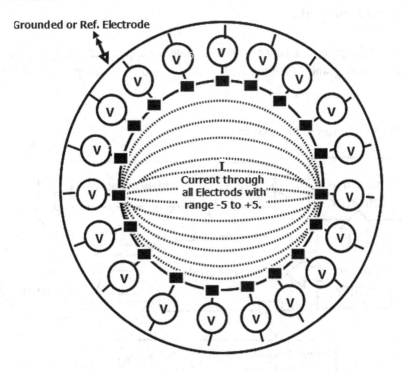

Table 4. voltage measurement according to electrode in Adaptive Method (Malmivuo & Plonsey, 1995)

System	No of Current Location (for Whole System)	Voltage Measurement
8-electrode system	4	28
16-electrode system	8	120
32-electrode system	16	496

then rotated one electrode increment, so 8 different-2 current distributions are obtained, yielding 8×15 = 120 independent voltage measurements. Shown in Table 4 according to system and no. of electrode attached to object (Malmivuo & Plonsey, 1995; Babaeizadeh et al.2006; Rahim et al., 2003).

6. HARDWARE OF EIT

EIT system is a combination of two parts; the first part is hardware (Mhalighi et al., 2012) (current source, Data acquisition, display part) and others are image reconstruction algorithm (Lui et al. 2014). The hardware part of EIT system is a combination of digital and analog circuits, an array of electrodes which performances as EIT-sensors (Xu et al., 2007) and a computer. In the analog section of hardware include an accurate current source and a data acquisition part (R Kumar et al., 2016). And In digital part contains microcontroller unit and also can be used the programmable (Arpinar et.al., 2001). In Figure 8 shows the basic block diagram of EIT system

6.1. Phantom and Electrode

In the construction of the phantom, firstly to find a material appropriate (R Kumar et.al, 2016) for an electrical impedance tomography imaging and analysis used to develop a reliable quantitative data

Figure 8. Basic Block Diagram of EIT System

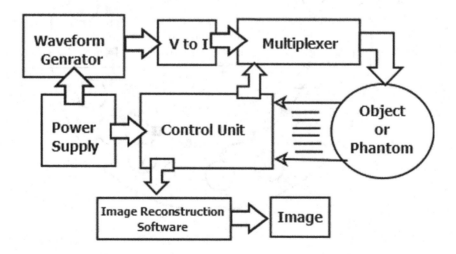

processing protocol for phantom scanning. Phantom like an object or modal, it has similar properties of the object. An array of electrodes, attached to the surface of the phantom (Bera & Nagaraju, 2011). The array of the electrode must be used in ring and equally space between two electrodes. The no. of electrode may be used 4, 8, 16, and 32 like that. If we used high number of electrode, then better quality of image is obtained of the phantom. Many types of electrode used in EIT system (Kumar et al., 2016; Soleimani, 2006). e.g. AgCl, steel, iron type, etc.

6.2. Waveform Generator and V to I Converter

A waveform generator is used for generating a constant sinusoidal alternating voltage signal. Many ways is used for signal wave generation, like using MAX038, XR2206, ICL8038 and using controller, use resistor DAQ card etc. created single must be low voltage with high frequency variation and have signal output impedance must be high (Bera & Nagaraju, 2009a, 2011b). After that this voltage signal to convert into constant current to inject into the surface of the phantom (R Kumar et al., 2016). The voltage to current convertor is combination of operational amplifier circuit. Many combinations of operational amplifier are available at present, like Holland circuit (Mhalighi et al., 2012), two or three operational amplifier Combination. The inserting current must have milliamp and frequency is kHz to MHz (Kumar et al, 2013; Malone et al., 2014).

6.3. Multiplexer

Multiplexer's panel used is developed for current switching of the electrode to object. The multiplexers may be used analog as well as digital according to suitability (Kumar et al., 2016; Mhalighi et al., 2012). Multiplexers are used to develop an automatic switching system for current to inject into the adjacent pair of electrodes after completing one set of voltage measurements of the object (Arpinar & Eyuboglu, 2001). For multiplexer is required of digital bits to controlling and operating. Multiplexers to switch the current in the electrodes are created by microcontroller and are fed into the multiplexers linked to the surface electrodes of the object/phantom (Mhalighi et al., 2012).

6.4. Control unit

The control unit is a central part of the EIT system. It is controlling the multiplexer part (R Kumar et al., 2016). (current position and voltage position) to determine of the voltage measurements of each electrode pairs, also communicating with a computer and matching with operating software platform for data transaction through RS-232 (Mhalighi et al., 2012). Serial communication is one of the procedures that are supported through several types of computer and therefore connecting the computer, controller and cable. And also connecting to ADC and controlling the some interrupted signals (Mhalighi et al., 2012).

6.5. Demodulation and ADC

The demodulator is another significant part of the EIT system for voltage measurement from the surface of the phantom (R Kumar et al., 2016). Before the voltage measurement, the electrode voltages should be demodulated. The voltage demodulation means receiving sample from of the analog signal of the voltage waveform and making the electrode voltages for calculating, essentially after the demodulation part only measured the sampled values of the voltages data (Arpinar & Eyuboglu, 2001). And Analog to digital convertor is used for converting analog to digital and interfacing to the PC. Hence it should be rehabilitated from analog to digital value by ADC and transmitted to a microcontroller in the control unit (Mhalighi et al., 2012).

7. EXPERIMENTAL ANALYSIS AND VALIDATION

In experimental setup, first we have to take some phantom and construct an image for it by putting electrodes over its circumference of the phantom and applying current to electrodes and finding the voltage for another electrode. The electrodes may use of Needle-type or Iran nail type, Agcl and also required an AC source (Bera & Nagaraju, 2009). This current source is a simple combination of operational amplifiers which converts the voltage signal to current signal. The current range must be mA with (10 KHz to 100 KHz) KHz frequency (Kumar, 2013; Holder, 2005; Bera & Nagaraju, 2009). In this experiment combination of two section. In one section, we creating a current source (it consists of waveform generator and voltage to current convertor) and second voltage measurement part, measurements have been made manually using multimeter and CRO (R Kumar et al., 2016). The outputs of the measurement are displayed on cathode ray oscilloscope. As shown in Figure 9 of Experimental Setup Block Diagram (Kumar et al, 2015).

We have taken Papaya for the phantom it is more analogues to the stomach of the human body also other phantoms are used like cabbage and electrode are inserted over its circumference (Bera & Nagaraju, 2009), as shown. Figure 10. Then an applied current from a current source then a the potential is calculated to another electrode through the multimeter using the opposite to the EIT methods. In this experiment used Current is 0.6 mA to 1 mA with Frequency 30 kHz to 50 kHz (Halter et al., 2015; Malone et al., 2014).

In this experiment, analysis of obtaining data from the different current pattern/position. For each position, thirteen measurements have been made manually using multimeter and CRO (Kumar et al., 2015). The outputs of the measurement are displayed on cathode ray oscilloscope and also compare the output voltage to the position of electrodes, as shown.in Figure 9 of the Experimental Setup Block Diagram. In experiment 1 and 2 shown the impedance distribution according to one position of current

Figure 9. Experimental Setup Block Diagram

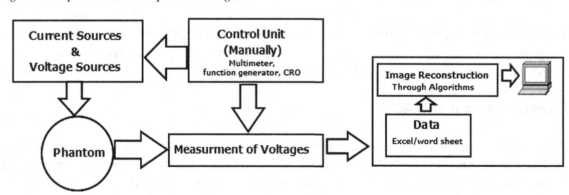

And other two experiment shown in the impedance distribution according to the whole position of current for the system (Kumar et al., 2015a, 2016b). as shown. Figure 10.

(Kumar et al., 2015) (A) – Phantom I (Cabbage), (B) Phantom II (Papaya), (C) impedance chart for one current location of the Phantom I, according to opposite methods. (D) impedance chart for one current location of the Phantom II, according to opposite methods. (E) impedance chart for whole system (for All current location) of the Phantom II.

8. ALGORITHMS OF IMAGE RECONSTRUCTION

Image reconstruction algorithm is a most significant part of a whole EIT system. The Resistivity of the image is reconstructed from the data collected from the phantoms using mathematical algorithms (Seok et al., 2014). These algorithms start with an initial conductivity, and the voltages are calculated from the different electrode positions of the object. Calculated voltages are compared with the homogeneous data (Mengxing et al., 1998; Wang et al., 2011; Stasiak et al., 2007; Abbaszadeh et al., 2013; Bahrani, 2012; Jehl et al., 2014; Pursiainen & Hakula, 2006; Bera et al., 2011). To estimate the resistivity distribution, that is, to solve the inverse problem and the forward problem of EIT has to be solve. The forward problems and inverse problems are solved through an FEM mesh of triangular nodes and elements (Seok et al., 2014). Forward problem is solved by a known current injection pair, current amplitude and a given conductivity of the homogeneous medium (Abbaszadeh et al., 2013). Som we say that the forward problem is the procedure for calculating the boundary potential based on impedance distribution of the object. And the inverse problem is the process for calculating the impedance distribution of the object, based on boundary potential on the surface of the object (Stasiak et al., 2007). Several different mathematical approaches used for the forward and inverse problem have been developed.

It is described how the Laplace equation is driven by the Maxwell equations (Pursiainen & Hakula, 2006). A typically low frequency is used for EIT system. Therefore, this problem approximated to be

Figure 10. Phantom and Experimental results of the phantoms

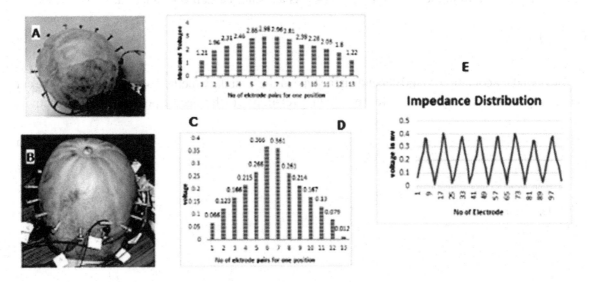

quasi-static, that is, EIT made of quasi-static approximation (Bahrani, 2012). Hence, the electrostatic forms of Maxwell's laws are employed in EIT.

The Laplace equation is a general equation in electrostatic problems which is derived from the electric potential (Abbaszadeh et al., 2013; Bahrani, 2012; Jehl et al., 2014; Pursiainen & Hakula, 2006; Bera et al., 2011).

It starts from KCL written for current density vector J . This equation (1) is Also known as current continuity equation.

$$\nabla.J = 0 \tag{1}$$

This equation expresses that in the absence of independent electric charges, the summation of outward and inward current at any point or any closed surface inside the domain Ω is zero. The point form of the Ohm's Law provides the relation between the Electric field vector and the current density (Pursiainen & Hakula, 2006).

$$J = \sigma.\text{E} \tag{2}$$

where

σ represents the conductivity. J is the current density, E is electric field intensity.

With quasi-static assumption in force, the Electric field would be curl-free; hence it is possible to write the electric field in the form of the gradient of a scalar potential as:

$$\text{E} = -\nabla\varphi \tag{3}$$

where ϕ is the electric field potential?

Finally, substituting the Ohm's law into the KCL and replacing the electric field with the gradient of the electric potential from the equation (2) (3) (4). As a result, the Laplace equation.

$$\nabla.\left(\sigma\nabla\varphi\right) = 0 \tag{4}$$

The boundary condition would depend on the type of the boundary method used for the EIT. The current density at the boundary would have the following relation with the electric potential and conductivity.

$$\varphi\big|\;\big|\partial\text{A} = \varphi\left(\chi,\gamma\right) \tag{5}$$

$$\sigma\frac{\partial\varphi}{\partial\eta}\big|\;\big|\partial\text{A} = J_0 \tag{6}$$

where

$\varphi\left(\chi,\gamma\right)$ is measured voltage.

J_0 is current density on boundary.

∂A is represent the boundary of the object.

The forward problem is defined as "impedance distribution $\Rightarrow$ boundary potential" for the object, and an inverse problem can be defined as "boundary potential $\Rightarrow$ impedance distribution". The forward problem is well-posed, but the inverse problem is non-linear and extremely ill-posed (Wang et al., 2011).

8.1. Forward Problem Using Finite Element Method

Many numerical approaches are used for solving the forward problem. Such as that, the finite element method (FEM), partial differential equations (PDE), the boundary element method (BEM), finite difference method (FDM). The forward solver based on first order FEM for whole electrode modal (Pursiainen & Hakula, 2006).

The FEM is the most common technique presently used for the numerical solution of EIT problems. We can also use some numerical methods for EIT problems like the finite difference method and finite volume method. Compared to the FEM, these two methods have the benefit that more efficient solvers can be employed. Also, it can be applied to a system for any geometric shapes or boundary conditions (Bahrani, 2012).

Forward problem solving by finite element method includes the following process, shown in Figure 11.

The resulting global equation can be obtained from governing equation using FEM.

Also, we can say that this equation defines a relation between the measured potential and conductivity. The global equation (7) is shown below.

$$\left[\varphi\right] = \left[K\right]\left[\sigma\right] \tag{7}$$

where $\sigma, \varphi, \mathrm{K}$ is a vector of conductivity, voltage measurement, transformation matrix relating, ϕ respectively. If the vector of conductivity and transformation matrix is known, the global equation can be solved using FEM (Pursiainen & Hakula, (2006; Bahrani,2012; Gagnon et al., 2010; Bera & Nagaraju, 2013). This process is called the 'forward problem.'

8.2. Inverse Problem

The inverse problem is non-linear and extremely ill posed for EIT. It is used to reconstruct the conductivity distribution from the boundary potential. This problem is also called reconstruction and the process of recovering an image from the obtained data of EIT system is 'Reconstruction' process (Bahrani, 2012). Many reconstruction algorithms can be used for inverse problem, such as that, Tikhonov regularization method, Gauss-Newton Algorithm, Jacobian matrix, etc.

The resulting global equation (8) for inverse problem can be obtained from governing equation (4) using FEM and from the global equation (7) we get.

Figure 11. Forward Problem Process Using FEM

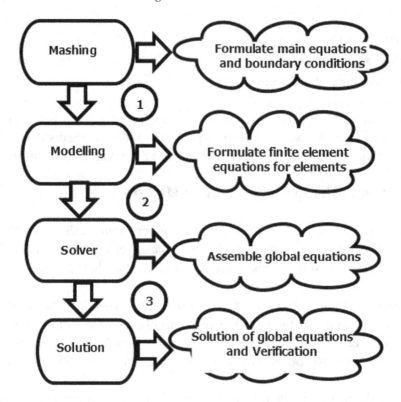

$$\sigma = \mathrm{K}^{-1}\varphi \qquad\qquad\qquad (8)$$

Where $\sigma, \varphi, \mathrm{K}$, is a vector of conductivity, voltage measurement, transformation matrix respectively. So, we can say that the transformation matrix and voltage measurement are known and calculate the conductivity (Bahrani, 2012; Jehl et al., 2014). This process is called the 'inverse problem.'

9. RESULT

The final stage for simulation outcomes in the 2D image. Shown in figure 12 is based on EIDORs toolkits of finite element methods. In the number of finite elements are rises, then image becomes clearer. The existing set of MATLAB functions delivers a platform for fast prototyping of deferent-2 reconstruction schemes in EIT.

10. APPLICATION

Many application of electrical impedance tomography technique used for biomedical and industrial filed. Such as given below.

In medical application, such as that,

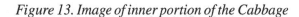

Figure 12. Image of inner portion of the Papaya   *Figure 13. Image of inner portion of the Cabbage*

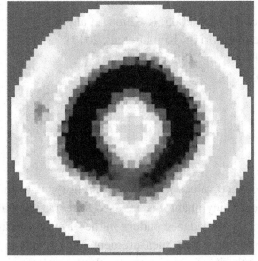 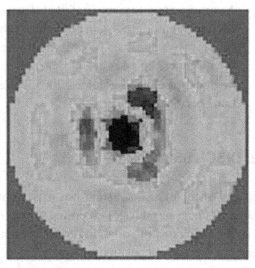

*For a more accurate representation of these figures, please see the electronic version.

- Study of lung ventilation and Monitoring (Holder, 2005).
- Feto-maternal monitoring and Evaluation of the Morphological & Physiological parameters for Fetal (Kumar et al., 2013).
- Modality of imaging for the body (Holder, 2005; Griffiths, 1986).
- The investigation of the human brain and monitoring (Gagnon et al., 2010; Kumar and Anwar, 2014)
- Monitoring of gastric emptying (Holder, 2005).
- Breast investigation (Halter et al., 2015).
- Monitoring of gastric emptying (Holder, 2005).
- Monitoring of the Muscular Contractions, Swelling in muscles (Dosinas et al., 2006).
- Sports medicine / home care (Griffiths, 1986; Negishi & Tong, 2011).

In industrial application, such as that,

- On-line monitoring of process plant (Jia et al., 2010).
- Process control, industrial tanks monitoring.
- Monitor mixtures of conductive fluids in vessels or pipes (Jia et al., 2010).
- Chemical Processes (Metal Corrosion)
- Laboratory design, and educational usage (Kumar et al., 2016; Dosinas et al., 2006)

11. FUTURE TRENDS

Electrical impedance tomography (EIT) is a newly imaging technique. This technique is used non-invasively (Kumar et al., 2013), so continues increased the uses of medical and non-medical applications and at present many researcher working on this technique (Kumar et al., 2013) [1-5]. Such as that.

- A therapy optimization tool (Kumar et al., 2013; Holder, 2005).
- A consultant tool for medical filed (Patterson, 2005).
- On line monitoring system of medical or nonmedical (Holder, 2005; R Kumar et al., 2016).
- Non-invasive approach supports continuous bedside monitoring (Kumar et al., 2013).
- Breath-by-breath assessment of therapy measures (Patterson, 2005).
- Regional compliance (Holder, 2005; Patterson, 2005).
- Lung perfusion (Holder, 2005).

12. DISCUSSION

The aim of the experimentation was to accumulate impedance values from the different types of the phantom (Papaya, Cabbage) according to no. of electrodes. Many phantoms are used for experimental work according to aim, suitability of the application. Also, the impedance pattern in the form of the bar graph for one current position and line graph is shown for whole system measurements. So, we can say that, the image reconstruction accuracy and resolution of the image in EIT generally depends on the phantom conformation parameters like, no of electrodes, electrode materials, phantom height, phantom type, electrode width, electrode array position, electrode materials, phantom diameter, electrode geometry etc. and also depends on implemented parts of the hardware like controller and multiplexer module and other parts EIT system. And also to studied to examine the phantom responses for different electrode geometry and compare to other author graphs of the phantom responses.

13. CONCLUSION

It has been observed that the image of the human body impedance varies from 700 to 1000 ohm. The array of electrodes is placed around the area of the object. The constant current a reference resistance are those point on which accuracy of the impedance easily by proposed methodology that can be further converted to images using the MATLAB tools. The proposed methods are non-invasive methods a dose not face any problem from any kind of after effects of radiation. The images obtained from electrical impedance are required to validate from the original shape of the body organ.

In this paper, a basic data acquisition methods of EIT system. It is capable of making measurement at much higher rates and today image reconstruction algorithm provides higher resolution as previous a robustness to electrode errors with reduced image relics and also improve interference system, reduced noise. It provides a new bio-medical imaging modality that is radiation free, inexpensive and portable. EIT system requires improvement in basis use & technical points like EIT data, and images should be accessible in usual formats. Reconstruction software should have a spontaneous. Automated approaches are required to enhance clinical decision making for data analysis and interpretation.

REFERENCES

Abbaszadeh, J., Rahim, H. A., Rahim, R. A., Sarafi, S., Nor Ayob, M., & Faramarzi, M. (2013). Design procedure of ultrasonic tomography system with steel pipe conveyor. *Sensors and Actuators. A, Physical*, *203*, 215–224. doi:10.1016/j.sna.2013.08.020

Anderson, F. Jr, Penney, B. C., Patwardhan, N. A., & Wheeler, H. B. (1980). Impedance plethysmography: The origin of electrical impedance changes measured in the human calf. *Medical & Biological Engineering & Computing, 18*(2), 234–240. doi:10.1007/BF02443300 PMID:7392690

Arpinar, V. E., & Eyuboglu, B. M. (2001). Microcontroller controlled, multifrequency electrical impedance tomograph. *Annual Reports of the Research Reactor Institute, 3,* 2289–2291.

Atefi, R. (2015). *Electrical Bio impedance Cerebral Monitoring: From Hypothesis and Simulations to First Experimental Evidence in Stroke Patients.* Stockholm, Sweden: Royal Institute of Technology, School of Technology and Health.

Babaeizadeh, S., Brooks, H., Isaacson, D., & Newell, J. C. (2006). Electrode boundary conditions and experimental validation for BEMBased EIT forward and inverse solutions. *IEEE Transactions on Medical Imaging, 25*(9), 1180–1188p. doi:10.1109/TMI.2006.879957 PMID:16967803

Bahrani, N. (2012). 2 1/2 D Finite Element Method for Electrical Impedance Tomography Considering the Complete. Carleton University, Ottawa, Canada.

Bedenbaugh, P. H. (2011). Deep brain stimulation for phantom perceptions. *Proceedings of the 2011 5th International IEEE/EMBS Conference on Neural Engineering NER '11* (pp. 712–717).

Bera, T. K., Biswas, S. K., Rajan, K., & Jampana, N. (2011). Improving the image reconstruction in Electrical Impedance Tomography (EIT) with block matrix-based Multiple Regularization (BMMR): A practical phantom study. *Proceedings of the 2011 World Congress on Information and Communication Technologies WICT '11* (pp. 1346–1351). doi:10.1109/WICT.2011.6141444

Bera, T. K., & Nagaraju, J. (2009). A study of practical biological phantoms with simple instrumentation for Electrical Impedance Tomography (EIT). *Proceedings of the 2009 IEEE Instrumentation and Measurement Technology Conference* (pp. 511–516).

Bera, T. K., & Nagaraju, J. (2011). A chicken tissue phantom for studying an electrical impedance tomography (EIT) system suitable for clinical imaging. *Sensing and Imaging, 12*(3-4), 95–116. doi:10.1007/s11220-011-0063-4

Bera, T. K., & Nagaraju, J. (2013). A MATLAB-Based Boundary Data Simulator for Studying the Resistivity Reconstruction Using Neighbouring Current Pattern. *Journal of Medical Engineering.*

Bera, T. K., & Nagaraju, J. A. (2009). Stainless Steel Electrode Phantom to Study the Forward Problem of Electrical Impedance Tomography. *Sensors & Transducers Journal, 104,* 33–40.

Dosinas, A, Vaitkunas, M., & Daunoras, J. (2006). Measurement of human physiological parameters in the systems of active clothing and wearable technologies. *Elektronika Ir Elektrotechnika, 7*(7), 77–82.

Edic, P. M., Saulnier, G. J., Newell, J. C., & Isaacson, D. (1995). A Real-Time Electrical Impedance Tomograph. *IEEE Transactions on Bio-Medical Engineering, 42*(9), 849–859. doi:10.1109/10.412652 PMID:7558059

Gagnon, H., Cousineau, M., Adler, A., & Hartinger, A. E. (2010). A resistive mesh phantom for assessing the performance of EIT systems. *IEEE Transactions on Bio-Medical Engineering, 57*(9), 2257–2266. doi:10.1109/TBME.2010.2052618 PMID:20550982

Griffiths, H. (1988). A phantom for electrical impedance tomography. Clinical Physics and Physiological Measurement, 9(4A), 15.

Halter, R. J., Hartov, A., Poplack, S. P., diFlorio-Alexander, R., Wells, W., Rosenkranz, K. M., & Paulsen, K. D. (2015). Real-Time electrical impedance variations in women with and without breast cancer. *IEEE Transactions on Medical Imaging, 34*(1), 38–48. doi:10.1109/TMI.2014.2342719 PMID:25073168

Hinz, J., Hahn, G., & Quintel, M. (2008). Electrical impedance tomography. *Der Anaesthesist, 57*(1), 61–69. doi:10.1007/s00101-007-1273-y PMID:17934702

Holder, D. S. (2005). *Electrical Impedance Tomography Methods, History and Applications. Institute of Physics Publishing Bristol and Philadelphia, Book.* USA: Institute of Physics Publishing.

Jehl, M., Dedner, A., Betcke, T., Aristovich, K., Klofkorn, R., & Holder, D. (2014). A Fast Parallel Solver for the Forward Problem in Electrical Impedance Tomography. *IEEE Transactions on Bio-Medical Engineering, 62*(1), 126-137.

Jia, J., Wang, M., Schlaberg, H. I., & Li, H. (2010). A novel tomographic sensing system for high electrically conductive multiphase flow measurement. *Flow Measurement and Instrumentation, 21*(3), 184–190p. doi:10.1016/j.flowmeasinst.2009.12.002

Kumar, , P., & Anwar, M.I. (2014). Brain Tumor and CAD Through MRI by using Wavelet Transform and Genetic Algorithm. *Journal of Information Engineering and Applications, 4*(4), 52–60.

Kumar, R., Kumar, S., & Sengupta, A. (2016). A Review: Electrical Impedance Tomography System and Its Application. *Journal of Control & Instrumentation, 7*(2), 14–22p.

Kumar, R., Pahuja, S. K., & Sengupta, A. (2015). Phantom based Analysis and Validation using Electrical Impedance Tomography. *Journal of Instrumentation Technology and Innovation, 5*(3), 17–23p.

Kumar, S., Anand, S., & Sengupta, A. (2013). Development of a non – invasive point of care diagnostic tool for fetal monitoring using electrical impedance based approach. *Proceedings of the 2013 IEEE PHT* (pp. 16–18).

Lu, L., Liu, L., & Hu, C. (2014). Analysis of the Electrical Impedance Tomography Algorithm Based On Finite Element Method and Tikhonov. *Proceedings of the 2014 International Conference on Wavelet Analysis and Pattern Recognition (ICWAPR)* (pp. 36-42).

Malmivuo, J.A, & Plonsey, R. (1995). *Impedance Tomography*.

Malone, E., Jehl, M., Arridge, S., Betcke, T., & Holder, D. (2014). Stroke type differentiation using spectrally constrained multifrequency EIT: Evaluation of feasibility in a realistic head model. *Physiological Measurement, 35*(6), 1051–1066. doi:10.1088/0967-3334/35/6/1051 PMID:24844796

Mengxing, T., Xiuzhen, D., Mingxin, Q., Feng, F., Xuetao, S., & Fusheng, Y. (1998). Electrical impedance tomography reconstruction algorithm based on general inversion theory and finite element method. *Medical & Biological Engineering & Computing, 36*(July), 395–398. doi:10.1007/BF02523205 PMID:10198520

Mhalighi, M., Vosoughi, V. B., Mortazavi, M., Hy, W., & Soleimani, M. (2012). The practical design of low-cost instrumentation for industrial electrical impedance tomography (EIT). *Proceedings of the IEEE I2MTC Conference* (pp. 1259–1263).

Negishi, M., & Tong, T. (2011). Constable RT. Tomography: A Simulation Study. *IEEE 2011*, *30*(3), 828–837.

Nyboer, J., Kreider, M. M., & Hannapel, L. (1950). Electrical impedance plethysmography; a physical and physiologic approach to peripheral vascular study. *JOAHA. Circulation*, *2*(6), 811–821p. doi:10.1161/01. CIR.2.6.811 PMID:14783833

Patterson, R. P. (2005). Electrical Impedance Tomography: Methods, History, and Applications (Institute of Physics Medical Physics Series). *Physics in Medicine and Biology*, *50*(10), 2427–2428. doi:10.1088/0031-9155/50/10/B01

Pursiainen, S., & Hakula, H. (2006). A High-Order Finite Element Method for Electrical Impedance Tomography. *PIERS Online*, *2*(3), 260–264. doi:10.2529/PIERS050905044807

Rahim, R. A., Huei, L. Y. I., San, C. K. O. K., Fea, P. J. O. N., & Lean, L. C. (2003). Initial result on electrical impedance tomography. *Engineering*, *39*(D), 105–112.

Seok, B., Youn, K., & Kim, S. (2014). Image reconstruction using adaptive mesh refinement based on adaptive thresholding in electrical impedance tomography. *Nuclear Engineering and Design*, *270*, 421–426. doi:10.1016/j.nucengdes.2013.12.063

Soleimani, M. (2006). 92006). Electrical impedance tomography system: An open access circuit design. *Biomedical Engineering Online*, *5*(1), 28. doi:10.1186/1475-925X-5-28 PMID:16672061

Stasiak, M., Sikora, J., Filipowicz, S. F., & Nita, K. (2007). Principal Component analysis and artificial neural network approach to electrical impedance tomography problems approximated by multi-region boundary element method. *Engineering Analysis with Boundary Elements*, *31*(8), 713–720. doi:10.1016/j. enganabound.2006.12.003

Vauhkonen, P. J. (2004) Image Reconstruction in Three-Dimensional Electrical Impedance Tomography [Doctoral Dissertation]. Department of applied physics, University of Kuopio.

Wang, Q., & Wang, H. (2011). Image reconstruction based on expectation maximization method for electrical impedance tomography (EIT). *Proceedings of the 2011 IEEE International Conference on Imaging Systems and Techniques* (Vol. 1, pp. 50–54). doi:10.1109/IST.2011.5962175

Xu, G., Wang, R., Zhang, S., Yang, S., Justin, G. a., Sun, M., & Yan, W. (2007). A 128-electrode three dimensional electrical impedance tomography system. *Proceedings of the Annual International Conference of the IEEE Engineering in Medicine and Biology* (pp. 4386–4389). doi:10.1109/IEMBS.2007.4353310

KEY TERMS AND DEFINITIONS

Bio Impedance: It is a normally used technique for approximating body composition, and in specific fat of the body and determines the electrical impedance, opposition of the flow of an electric current over the body tissues, then, compute and estimation of body mass and, other important parameter of the body.

Eidors: It is to encourage collaboration between groups working on Diffusion based Optical Tomography and Electrical Impedance Tomography, in non-medical and medical backgrounds. EIDORS is an imaging package for image reconstruction in electrical impedance tomography and diffuse optical tomography.

Forward Problem: It is the procedure for calculating the boundary potential based on impedance distribution of the object/subject.

Inverse Problem: It is the process for manipulative the impedance distribution based on boundary voltages/potential of the object.

Phantom: A depiction, part of which is given a diaphanous effect so as to allow representation of details else hidden from view, as the inside workings of a mechanical device.

Plethysmography: It is a technique for measuring variations of the body and the size of an organ, on the basis of the amount of blood passing through or present in the part.

Tomography: Is a technique for displaying an image (in form of slice) of a cross section through a medical or industrial object.

Chapter 7
Hardware Realization of Antifogging System

Amruta Laxman Deshmukh
SGGS, India

Satbir Singh
Delhi Technological University, India

Balwinder Singh
Centre for Development of Advanced Computing (C-DAC), India

ABSTRACT

There are many reasons for invisibility of objects on road in daylight, majority of them are Fog (con-densed water droplets in atmosphere), smog (soot particles in air). This reduced visibility is one of the prime factors responsible for accident of vehicles and disadvantage in surveillance system. This chapter takes account of a method that comprises of a complete embedded system for the process of restoring the captured foggy images. Use of a novel 'Mean Channel Prior' algorithm for defogging is presented. Further detailed step by step explanation is given for hardware implementation of MATLAB code. Hardware consists of raspberry pi which is an ARM7 Quad Core processor based mini computer model. System serves as portable, low cost and low power processing unit with provision of interfacing a camera and a display screen.

INTRODUCTION

There are many reasons for invisibility of objects on road in daylight, majority of them are fog (con-densed water droplets in atmosphere), smog (soot particles in air). For any object to be visible our eyes should sense the light reflected from that object. Visibility of objects on road is highly dependent on the concentration of condensed water droplets in air. Condensation of water droplets in air can result into the appearance of haze to almost zero visibility. This reduction in visibility is the main reason for accident of vehicles. In foggy atmospheric conditions, images lose contrast and defogging algorithms can be used to improve image quality of foggy images. This means that defogging algorithms have ap-

DOI: 10.4018/978-1-5225-2848-7.ch007

plication in various camera based driver assistance systems and surveillance system. Picture captured in foggy atmospheric condition gets affected due to attenuation of light received by camera from the scene point along the line of site.

This chapter presents prototype model of image defogging system. In that camera, raspberry pi and screen are involved to capture image, as image processing unit, and to display enhanced image respectively. It works on power supplied by raspberry pi and supplies image data to raspberry pi through USB cable. One can also use raspberry pi's special camera module available in market but its little costly. So, this prototype uses USB webcam to serve as image input device. It is a fact that amount of scattering of reflected light from an object depends upon distance of object from camera so, for testing practicality of the algorithm, we applied it on previously captured images of different foggy road scenes inhibiting different foggy conditions.

Background

In this section literature survey related to presented topic is discussed.

(Pomyen 2015) had done master of science thesis on signal and image processing with MATLAB on Raspberry pi platform. From this literature, we came to know that raspberry pi surves as hardware platform for image processing. His application was to read barcode. The limitation of this model is its compilation time, which is in few minutes. This model required few minutes for computation. Author had suggested that use of simulink blocks to create a model increases complexity of model and processing time so, to reduce processing time it's good to use MATLAB scripts for simulink blocks.

The Dark channel prior algorithm was awarded best paper for "Single Image Fog Removal". That's why we are including it in our chapter for comparison of our work. The famous DCP Dark channel prior algorithm for fog removal by (He, Sun & Tang, 2011) is based on the fact that every haze free image has at least one pixel having minimum values in R or G or B channels, this can't be true all the time. DCP had used soft matting technique to refine transmission map that uses sparse function and it is an integral part of the its code. So, as simulink does not support sparse function it is impossible to use this algorithm to deploy in simulink model based system. So it's hardware implementation is not possible.

(Kang, Kim & Lee 2015) had designed pixel-based median channel prior (MCP) single image defogging algorithm. K. He et al. method DCP had low intensity in one color channel therefore generates halo effect in final result so, needed post-processing. This algorithm did not used any post processing technique and had low complexity. This work had been done using platform of Visual Studio 2013 to see output and programming had been done using Open CV.

(Li, Wang, Zheng, Zheng, 2014) had presented a method for haze removal from single image. It removed haze from image using dark channel which is content-adaptive and then post enhancement was applied to it for resolving problems of dark channel prior i.e. holo-effects, etc. Author had clearly mentioned necessity of further effort to use his designed method into applications that too work in real-time, such as in-vehicle vision systems surveillance systems.

The same problem regarding atmospheric conditions like haze, mist, fog is discussed in paper Single image fog removal based on local extrema (Zhao, Xiao, Yu & Xu, 2015).

Proposed novel image defogging method utilized atmospheric scattering model fog removal from image. It by applying local extrema method found out pyramid levels to estimate atmospheric vail. Finally manipulated contrast details through manipulation algorithm. It failed to give method to implement it on hardware.

New fog removal method (Ning, Li, Dong, Zhang & Shi, 2015). The method based on the disinhibition properties of retinal neurons concentric receptive field whose function is three Gaussians. Firstly, we enhance original fog image by using contrast limited global histogram equalization. Secondly, a local image enhancement method is carried out to restore the image's details and deepness information. This method worked well but no sufficient information is given regarding its hardware implementation.

In paper (He, Zhao, Zheng et al., 2016), the goal of the developed algorithm was to obtain an optimal transmission map as well as to remove hazes from a single input image. To solve the problem, the author meticulously analyzes the optical model and recasts the initial transmission map under an additional boundary prior. That means this algorithm is based on two assumptions, so it cannot work once the assumption is broken.

From present literature, we can see that until now there is no proper hardware implementation is available for image defogging algorithms. The proposed work presents prototype of antifogging system.

FOG AND HAZARDS

This section will introduce the fog, its formation, types of fog and how it affects the real life of common man.

1. **Factors Affecting Visibility of Atmosphere:** There are many factors that affect visibility in open atmosphere. Factors can be classified as following:
    a. Depending on number of obscuring particles present in the atmosphere.
    b. Position of the sun with respect to position of object to be viewed and observer at the time of viewing.
    c. The difference of contrast between the object to be viewed and background of that object (at the time of viewing).
    d. The level of brightness present at night time.
    e. Size of object to be viewed.

At the time of sunrise and sunset effect of sun is significant than rest of the day. Obscuring particles present in the atmosphere are mainly whether dependent.

2. **Whether Phenomena Affecting Transparency of Atmosphere:**
    a. Precipitation
    b. Fog
    c. Mist
    d. Haze
    e. Smog
    f. Dust storms and Sandstorms
3. **Atmospheric Fog:** After precipitation fog is major atmospheric phenomenon that affects day to day activities like transportation due to its effect on transparency of atmosphere. Fog is basically a type of cloud and moisture in the fog is often generated locally. It mostly appears in winter. Relative humidity of fog is 100%. Formation of fog is possible when the difference between dew point and temperature goes below 2.5 °C or 4 F. Visibility of objects on road is highly dependent

on the concentration of condensed water droplets in air. Condensation of water droplets in air can result into the appearance of haze to almost zero visibility. Mist, fog, haze are different things. All these reduce visibility of scene. Differences between fog mist and haze with respect to visibility and relative humidity are listed in Table 1. Majorly fog is present near watery areas like lake, ocean, nearby moist ground.

a.   Types of Fog:

    i.   **Radiation Fog:** This type of fog is also called as ground fog. It generally occurs at night, when earth's surface cools the shallow layer of moist air near the ground to its dew point or below. This condenses nearby air layers into fog. This type of fog forms mainly under calm weather. Its mechanism is shown in Figure 1(a).

    ii.   **Advection Fog:** When warm air flows over relatively cooler moist surface it starts moving horizontally, then there is high possibility of formation of activation fog as shown in Figure 1(b). This type of air flow cools the surface below its dew point and results in the formation of advection fog. It can be formed at any time and it is persistent. This type of fog is common along coastlines.

    iii.   **Upslope Fog:** When air flows over higher topographical conditions, because of the topographic barrier it is forced to rise in altitude in higher topographical areas and cooled by adiabatic expansion. This type of fog specially found on the windward slopes of mountains and hills as shown in Figure 1(d).

    iv.   **Evaporation Fog:** Evaporation fog forms due to evaporation of warm water from earth surface into cold air. Due to evaporation, additional water vapor gets added into nearly saturated air so, air reaches to its due point and fog forms. When warm water droplets of rain falls on cool air nearer to the ground surface 'frontal fog' forms and due to flowing of cold air above warmer water surface 'steam fog' forms. Mechanism of this type of fog is shown in Figure 1(c).

Table 1. Comparison between fog, mist and haze

	Sr. No.	**Visibility**	**Relative Humidity**
1.	Fog	< 1 km (5/8 statute mile)	Nearly 100%
2.	Mist	> 1 km (5/8 statute mile)	Below than 95%
3.	Haze	< 1 km	Greater than 95%

Figure 1. Representation of mechanism of (a) radiation fog (b) Representation of mechanism of advection fog (c) evaporation fog (d) upslope fog ("Using FCOG," 2015)

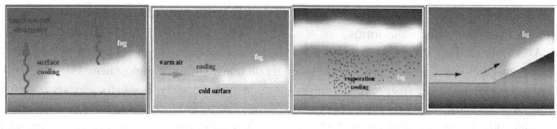

Figure 1:   (a)   (b)   (c)   (d)

4. **Real Life Problems Due to Atmospheric Fog:** Fog effects human life in many ways. It also effects road, train and air traffic significantly. According to news 145 people gone dead in accident due to fog in Uttar Pradesh on Dec 31 in 2014, 32 trains are rescheduled by railway department many are delayed and 80 cancelled due to fog (Using TNN,2014).

It concludes no fog means no delay in flight and fog means delay in flight. Following Table 2 and 3 shows impact of whether on road traffic and operational decisions and whether related crash statistics. Speed of traffic, accident risk and travel time gets effected due to fog on the road. Passenger's safety depends on driver's capability, speed limit control applied on the vehicle's engine or road side speed indications. Even though fog contributed 1% to 3% in total crashes due to bad whether, its crash count is very significant. No of crashes due to fog are 174446 (USDT, 2015).

5. **Remedies Used by People While Driving in Foggy Environment:** People slow down their speeds, stay focused on the road and always use headlights but, these remedies are not sufficient for safety of individual. People also use right-side pavement line and highway rules suggest using fog lamps. These are bright focused lights fitted behind and front of the vehicle. Due to its bright and focused beam driver detects vehicle in front of its own vehicle. But it does not give any clear idea about road side obstacles.

SOLUTIONS AND RECOMMENDATIONS

1. Role of Image Processing in Image Noise Reduction

Digital image processing plays very important role in improving pictorial information given by scene data for human interpretation and for autonomous machine perception. Digital image processing has many applications such as storing of image and data for transmission in business related applications, remote sensing, medical imaging, industrial automation, acoustic imaging and Forensic sciences (Kumar

Table 2. Impact of whether on road traffic and operational decisions (USDT, 2015)

Road Whether Variable	Impact on Roadway	Impact on Traffic Flow	Operational Impact
Fog	Visibility distance	Traffic speed Speed variance Travel time delay Accident risk	Driver capabilities/behavior Road treatment strategy Access control Speed limit control

Table 3. Whether related vehicle crash statistics (USDT, 2015)

Road Weather Condition	Whether Related Crash Statistics	
	No. of Crashes	Percentage of 10 Years
Fog	1,74446	1% of vehicle crashes 3% of whether related crashes 1% of crash injuries 3% of whether related injuries 2% of crash fatalities 9% of whether related fatalities

& Shaik, 2016). For example, 60% pixels of image are noisy that means 60% pixels of original image is replaced by random gray values varying from black to white. Noise reduction algorithms i.e. image restoration algorithms are used to remove noise from image and to get original image back. These algorithms use different types of noise reduction methodologies for example neighborhood approach. In this approach, we calculate RGB values for center pixel by taking average values of its neighboring pixels. This reduces the noise level of image and makes it soft (Kumar & Shaik, 2016).

There are many image processing algorithms designed for particular noise reduction application. The proposed work uses new image defogging algorithm to remove fog from captured image. MATLAB is used for implementation of algorithm.

2. Comparison of Different Hardware Platforms

1. Here we have chosen raspberry pi due to following advantages over others.
2. It has maximum RAM and operating frequency than others
3. It has moderate cost
4. Sufficient port pins are available
5. Direct USB camera support
6. HDMI compatibility
7. Good processor ARM
8. Ethernet compatibility
9. Easy to use Linux-based OS (Raspbian)

This research work provides prototype design of Image Defogging system.

3. Methodology of Image Defogging System

Figure 2 shows work flow of proposed system is explained. As whole system is powered by a main power supply, at first we have to power on raspberry pi and display screen. Then raspberry pi provides power to attached USB camera module. Then camera starts capturing images and feed to processing unit, where mean channel prior algorithm is applied on image and results are produced. This defogged image is displayed on attached display screen. To turn off the system its need to power off raspberry pi.

1. **Hardware Description:** Figure 3 shows hardware modules used in image antifogging system. In this work a Raspberry Pi 2 model B is used. A specification of this model is described as follows:
   a. **Raspberry Pi:** This model of RPi is based on Broadcom BCM2836 SoC (System on chip) and all modules are shown in Figure 4.
      i. It uses ARM7 quad core processors at 900 MHz clock speed. This is a 32-bit SOC.
      ii. 900 MHz clock frequency provides good performance
      iii. **Ethernet Port:** Pi2 model B has 10/100 Base T ethernet socket. This is RJ45 standard Ethernet port.
      iv. This model requires any heat sink and it is provided with its casing.
      v. It includes 1GB on chip CPU RAM.
      vi. It supports variable size SD card. There is no hard drive on RPi. Connected SD card is the only memory used to store everything in RPi.

Figure 2. Work flow of proposed system

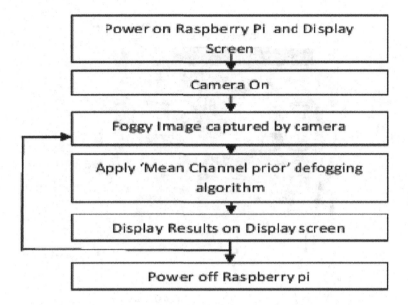

Figure 3. Block diagram of the antifogging system

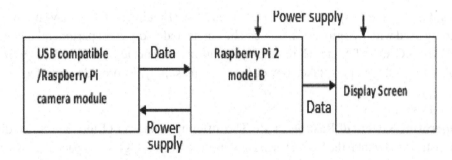

vii. **Video Output:** It consists of HDMI port for video output.

viii. It has 1GB RAM and supports variable sized GB SD Card.

ix. **Audio Output:** 3.5 mm jack for audio. It is capable to drive amplified speaker.

x. **USB:** 4 USB 2.0 port in 2 pairs. These ports are operated on 100 mA current.

b. **USB Camera Module:** Webcam is type of video camera and used to capturing images by using some software with the help of computers. Captured images or videos can be saved and can send to process running on one computer network to others by using some sources e.g. email, internet etc. USB cables are generally used for connection of USB webcam to the computer. Webcam is work on the principle of digital camera, charge coupled device using a small lens with light detectors are used inside it. CCD converts the images into digital formats of arrays of ones and zeros, which can easily understand by the computer. Digital camera having inbuilt memory but webcam do not have any in built memory or flash therefore cable and system memory is used for storing the captured images and process to destination. In this proposed system, USB Camera QHM 495LM is used for capturing foggy image and is interfaced to the RPi module by using raspberry pi supporting packages of Simulink.

Figure 4. Raspberry Pi 2 Model B

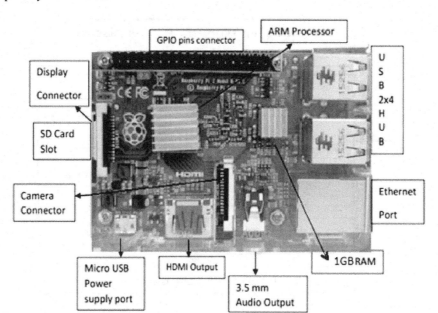

c. **Display Screen:** Display screen used here is LCD (Liquid crystal display) monitor that commonly used with traditional CPU. It can be connected to different peripheral devices via DVI, HDMI, VGA, LVDS etc. Here display monitor is connected via HDMI to VGA converter cable to raspberry pi. It takes power from mains supply. Pi provides data feed to screen for display.

2. **Software Description:**

a. **Operating System of Raspberry Pi:** The different versions of Linux are called distributions or distros. They take the Linux kernel and its other technologies and package it with their own software, software repositories, branding and perhaps even a desktop environment. Debian is an example of one of these distros. Raspbian is most recommended distro for Raspberry Pi. It's easy to maintain, and terminal can be used for simple commands. It seems like normal desktop OS. It provides good user interfaces for user, it also provides different ways to access data one through user interface other is through its Linux terminal. The major advantage of choosing Raspbian over the other distros is the teaching material and educational material included on the distro. This OS also supports overclocking limits which are recommended, any future official hardware add-ons as well and the Raspberry Pi camera. Major benefit for new comers willing to use Raspbian is that a lot of tutorials, third-party hardware run off, projects are available as per standard. These available materials make easier to learn coding or one can replicate it. Raspbian is quite light and fast. It also provides facilities of accessing web browser. The proposed work uses Raspbian Wheezy as its operating system.

b. **Steps for Completing a Project in Simulink:**

i. Building the model: New model with hierarchical subsystems is built using predefined functional blocks in library and it is saved with .slx extension.

ii.   Simulating the model: Simulink environment (http://in.mathworks.com/products/simulink/ features.html-simulating_the_model) simulates the created model as per the dynamic behavior of that model.

iii. Analysis of Simulation Results: Simulation results are generated after the completion of simulation and debug is also possible in this environment.

iv.   Managing Projects: Many types of code are generated as C code, executable and software components.

v.   Hardware connection: Deployment of Simulink model on embedded system is done using hardware support packages. To make this system possible Simulink support packages for Raspberry Pi hardware were used.

c.   **Installation Steps for MATLAB/Simulink Support Packages on Raspberry Pi Hardware:** For running MATLAB code on raspberry pi hardware requires MATLAB/Simulink support packages for raspberry Pi hardware. Following are steps for downloading and successfully installing it on raspberry Pi.

i.   **Step 1:** Choosing Hardware support packages from Add-Ons list: In MATLAB software packages for different hardware platforms are available that are shown in Figure 5.

ii.   **Step 2:** Choosing from downloading options for support package installation: Different downloading options are available for each support package that are shown in Figure 6.

Four options are available install from internet, download from internet, install from folder and un-install. First option directly installs support packages in MATLAB without storing it on PC.

Second option enables downloading of complete support packages and storing in PC for further use. In the proposed work download from internet option was chosen. After downloading, support packages can be repeatedly installed from folder where it was previously downloaded by choosing 'Install from folder' option.

iii. **Step 3:** Selecting support packages for both image acquisition as well as Simulink model running on raspberry Pi.

There are two support packages available for Raspberry Pi hardware that are shown in Figure 7, each of them should be selected for further installation.

Figure 5. Available options in add-ons list of MATLAB

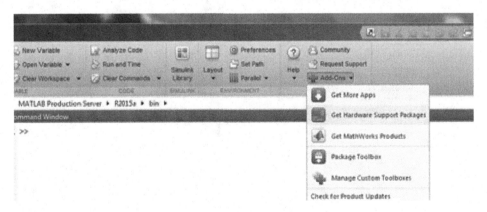

Figure 6. Available downloading options for support packages

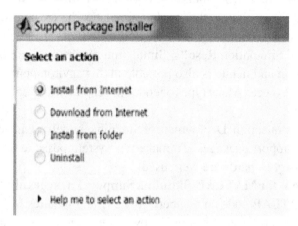

Figure 7. Available hardware support packages for Raspberry Pi

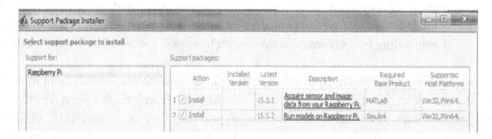

   iv.   **Step 4:** Installing support packages
   v.   **Step 5:** Downloading of Raspbian Wheezy with Raspberry pi support packages

Progress in operating system download is shown in Figure 8.

   vi.   **Step 6: Conformation of Installation -** After the completion of installation process support package installer gives conformation message.

Figure 8. Downloading process of operating system of raspberry pi

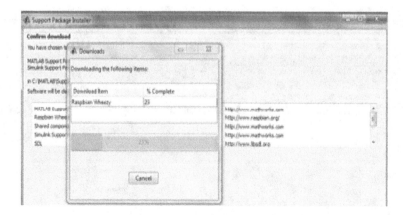

vii. **Step 7: Selecting Required RPi Board -** There are multiple raspberry pi board options available in firmware updating stage. These options are shown in Figure 9.

viii. **Step 8: Selection of Network -** There are three options for communication of PC having MATLAB with RPi board. First is through LAN. Choosing of this option, setups network configuration parameters of RPi board using settings of connected LAN. Second option creates direct connection of computer with raspberry pi module through cable it gets IP address by itself. Third option is manually setting network parameters. All these options are shown in Figure 6.

ix. **Step 9: Selecting Drive and Uploading Firmware -** After downloading and installing hardware support packages, they need to be loaded to SD card. This process is shown in Figure 10.

4. Steps for Firmware Update of Raspberry Pi

Step 1: Choosing update firmware option - It is good if we update the firmware periodically, for this process options are given under Simulink Tools.

Step 2: Selecting available packages - Again, from available hardware support packages each package has to be selected while updating firmware that is shown in Figure 7. Rest steps are same as step 4 to step 9 of Simulink support package installation steps.

5. About MATLAB/Simulink Support Packages of Raspberry pi

As shown in Figure 11 there are 11 blocks present in Simulink Library for 'Simulink support package for raspberry Pi hardware'. In this thesis work video capture and video display blocks from support package are used.

Figure 9. Available options of raspberry pi

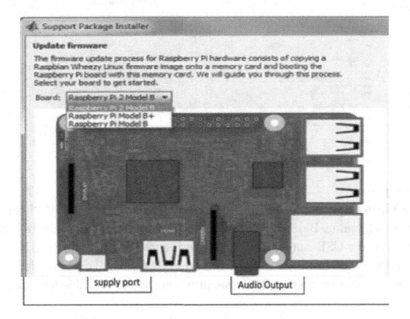

Figure 10. loading firmware to SD card

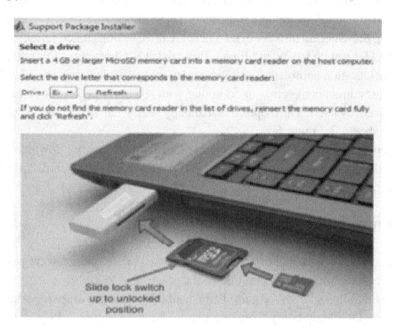

Figure 11. Simulink support package for raspberry Pi hardware in Simulink Library

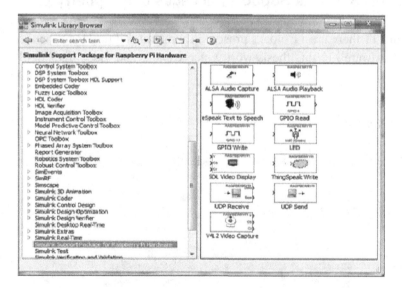

1. **Block Description:**
   a. **V4L2 Video Capture Block:** V4L2 stands for Video for Linux Two API, it is a driver framework. This Simulink Block is provided in Raspberry Pi support package to capture live video from attached a USB camera. It is shown in Figure 11. The output can be taken in RGB or YCbCr format. In this thesis, we have used RGB format. This block feeds input image to further blocks for processing. There are different choices available for aspect ratio of image.

b. **SDL Video Display:** SDL stands for Simple Direct media Layer for multimedia library. This Simulink Block is provided in Raspberry Pi support package to display video on attached display screen. It is shown in Figure 11. Aspect ratio of display is same as aspect ratio of V4L2 image capture block. The input can be taken in RGB or YCbCr format. In this thesis, we have used RGB format. This block can be used as output and it is only one per Simulink model.

2. **Foggy Image Database:** We used standard data base of diverse road scenes (Foggy Road Image DAtabase) FRIDA (Tarel, Hautière, Cord, Gruyer & Halmaoui 2010), FIRIDA2(Tarel, Hautière, Caraffa, Cord, Halmaoui & Gruyer 2012) comprises of synthetic images of 18 urban road scenes. FRIDA2 (Tarel, Hautière, Caraffa, Cord, Halmaoui & Gruyer, 2012) comprises synthetic images of 66 diverse road scenes. For all 66 different images depth maps and the ground truth images are available for research purpose. Foggy images and their corresponding ground truth images are shown in Figure 12. It is a systematic way to check performance of visibility and contrast restoration algorithms. This database allowed us researchers to rate our own visibility enhancement algorithms.

3. **Proposed Image Defogging Algorithm:** Figure 13 shows flow of used image defogging algorithm. Detailed explanation of proposed algorithm:

a. **Calculation of Mean Channel:** Proposed algorithm calculates mean of minimum values of RGB (Red Green Blue) in local patch to get better quality of dark channel. As intensity of pixels in small patch have small variations so by taking mean of minimum values of all three channels of each pixel gives better quality of dark channel. In this desertion work it is called as mean channel. Mean channel $J_{(x)}^{mean}$ $J_{mean}(x)$ calculated by following equation:

$$J_{(x)}^{mean} = \underset{y\varepsilon\,\Omega(x)}{mean}\left[\underset{c\varepsilon(r,g,b)}{\min} I^c(y)\right] \tag{1}$$

Figure 12. FRIDA2 Synthetic road image database (a)Foggy image database (b) Ground truth image database (Tarel, Hautière, Caraffa, Cord, Halmaoui & Gruyer 2012)

Figure 13. Flowchart of image defogging algorithm

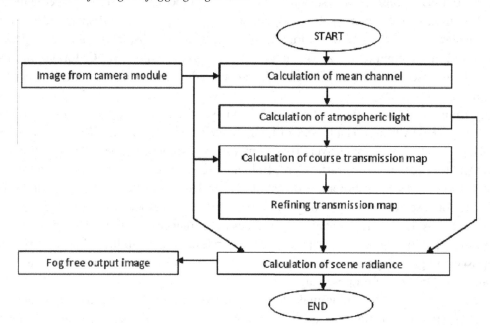

where, $I^c(y)$ is a RGB color channels of I and $\Omega(x)$ is a patch of pixels which is centered at x and of size 15.

b. **Estimating the Atmospheric Light:** After calculating hazy pixels in input image, we need to calculate the light reflected by hazy pixels i.e. atmospheric light. In most of the single image methods atmospheric light A^c_L is supposed to be equal to the RGB values of most hazy pixel of dark channel but it is not true in all cases. So, to calculate atmospheric light firstly we selected top 0.1% brightest pixels of the dark channel, then we switch back to the original RGB values of these pixels and consider the brightest pixel as atmospheric light.

c. **Estimating Coarse Transmission Map:** The transmission map obtained by following equation 2 and is important because it is considered as function of distance of object i.e. scene point from the camera lenses. As the distance of different objects in scene are different from camera so their corresponding transmission maps formed are different for different objects and different scenes. In small patch $\Omega(x)$ assumption is that transmission due to haze is constant. Transmission map $\tilde{t}(x)$ is estimated by following equation:

$$\tilde{t}(x) = 1 - \omega \, \underset{y \varepsilon \Omega(x)}{mean} \left(\min_{c} \frac{I^c(y)}{A} \right) \qquad (2)$$

where, w is a factor that is called weighting factor and its value varies according to its application. It keeps feeling of depth in image by not removing the fog thoroughly from image. It this paper it is set to be 0.95. $\tilde{t}(x)$ Refer to refined transmission map, $I^c(y)$ is original foggy input image in RGB, A is atmospheric light.

d. **Refining the Transmission Map:** Transmission map is important because it is a function of the distance of the scene from the camera and as different objects in the scene are at different distances the transmission map is different for different objects and different scenes. In the obtained transmission map from equation 3 edges of object in the images are sharp so to make edges of transmission map smooth transmission map refining is required. Here median filter is used to refine the transmission map.

e. **Estimating Scene Radiance:** Scene radiance can be estimated by putting refined transmission map, atmospheric light and the original hazy input image in equation 2. We obtain the following equation of scene radiance.

$$J(x) = \frac{I^c(y) - A}{\tilde{t}(x)} + A \tag{3}$$

$J(x)$ refers to haze free colored image, $I^c(y)$ is original colored foggy input image, A refers to atmospheric light, $\tilde{t}(x)$ refined transmission map.

Results of Algorithm According to Performance Matrices

Qualitative Analysis

Qualitative results are obtained by applying fog removal algorithms on foggy images. The Dark channel prior, Median Channel Prior and newly designed mean channel prior algorithms are applied on database of synthetic foggy images (Tarel, Hautière, Caraffa, Cord, Halmaoui & Gruyer 2012) and corresponding results are shown in figure 14.

Figure 14. Qualitative comparison results of FRIDA2 database(a) Original image, (b) defogged image using Dark Channel Prior, (c) defogged image using Median Channel Prior, (d) defogged image using mean channel prior algorithm

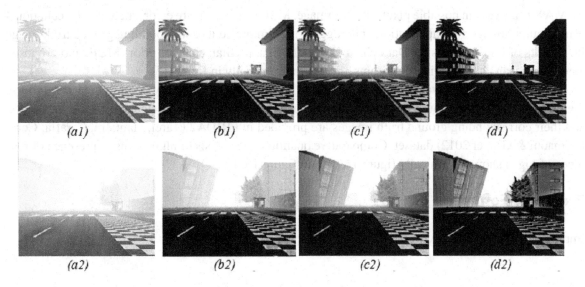

Quantitative Analysis

Qualitative analysis of defogged image is important to check for its comparative analysis with other algorithms. There are many performance analysis metrics are available, such as peak signal to noise ratio(PSNR), Mean Square error(MSE), the Feature Similarity Metric (FSIM), Normalized Color Difference (NCD), Contrast Gain, Color Naturalness Index, Perceptual Quality. Quantitative analysis of proposed algorithm was done by applying it on FRIDA2 (Tarel, Hautière, Caraffa, Cord, Halmaoui & Gruyer 2012) dataset (whose ground truth is also available) and by comparing results with ground truth images of corresponding foggy images.

- **Mean Square Error:** It can be considered as risk function corresponding to the expected value of squared losses. It is used to compare different image algorithms. Lower the value of MSE better the algorithm. MSE was calculated by following equation:

$$MSE = \frac{1}{n} \sum_{i=1}^{n} \left(I^c(i) - I_g^c(i) \right)^2 \tag{4}$$

I^c is output colored image after application of defogging algorithm and I_g^c is its corresponding colored ground truth image.

- **Peak Signal to Noise Ratio:** PSNR can be seen as an approximation to human perception of reconstruction quality. Higher the PSNR value higher the quality of image reconstruction. This gives support to the conclusion drawn by mean square error. PSNR is calculated by following equation:

$$PSNR = 10 \log_{10} \left(\frac{MAX_I^2}{MSE} \right) \tag{5}$$

MAX is maximum possible pixel value of image, MSE is mean square error calculated by equation 4 using I output image after application of defogging algorithm and its corresponding ground truth image Ig. Results of PSNR values for Dark channel prior (DCP), Median channel prior (MCP) and proposed algorithm mean channel prior algorithms are shown graphically in figure 15.

The proposed fog removal algorithm was further tested on four different types of fog that are uniform fog, heterogeneous fog, cloudy fog and cloudy heterogeneous fog. Foggy images for these types of fog and their corresponding ground truth images are provided in FRIDA2 (Tarel, Hautière, Caraffa, Cord, Halmaoui & Gruyer 2012) dataset. Comparative quantitative analysis of algorithms in presence of four types of fog is shown graphically figure 16 (a) and figure 16 (b).

Prototype Formation

Implementation of MATLAB Code in Raspberry Pi Hardware

Figure 15. Comparative results of image defogging algorithms based on (a)Mean square error and (b) Peak Signal to Noise Ratio

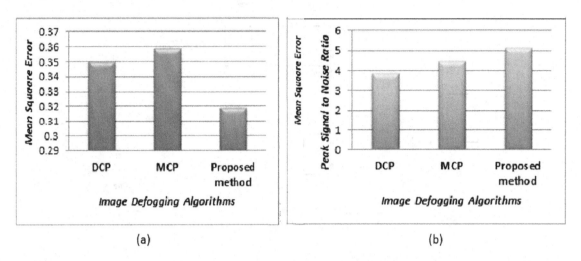

(a)   (b)

Figure 16. (a) Performance of algorithms based on mean square error in different types of fog. (b) Performance of algorithms based on peak signal to noise ratio in different types of fog

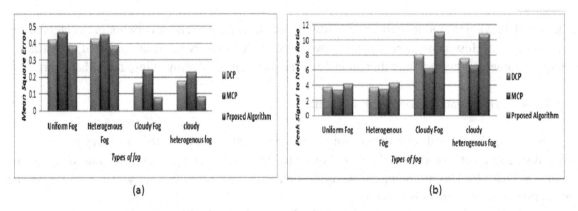

(a)   (b)

*For a more accurate representation of this figure, please see the electronic version.

Step 1: Creating simulink Model.

Figure 17 Shows Simulink model of proposed work. 1ˢᵗ MATLAB function from left receives input image in separate RGB format and converts it into single image I, then dark channel J was formed from input foggy image, atmospheric light A was calculated by receiving inputs I and J from respective blocks, then transmission map was calculated in MATLAB function blocks 3,4,5. In MATLAB function block transmission map was refined and scene radiance was estimated by taking transmission map, atmospheric light and input foggy image. The output defogged image then passed to SDL Video Display block by separating it into RGB channels.

Step 2: Built Simulink model.

Figure 17. Simulink Model of proposed system

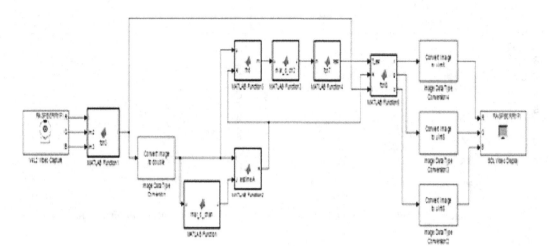

Created Simulink model was run and built, then used for deployment on hardware.

Step 3: Configuring network parameters.

Before deploying the model into target hardware, it is important to check network parameters of connected hardware. Host name, user name, Password and built directory name are required to be filled. If network parameter is correct only then model will be successfully deployed into target hardware.

Step 4: Deploying Simulink module in target hardware.

This step sends required support files for running Simulink model into the raspberry pi.

Hardware setup of prototype is shown in Figure 18. This prototype requires 7 seconds to process image of size 320x240. This prototype can be used as surveillance system, but to use it as driver assistance system further improvement is needed.

FUTURE RESEARCH DIRECTIONS

This work can be further extended to make it real time and to work during night. Also, the work can be integrated with other driver assistance systems. This system can be made RealTime by coding it into Python, use of Simulink support packages of Raspberry Pi is responsible for unwanted time delay.

CONCLUSION

Till now there is no system available in market that provides fog free vision to vehicle's driver driving on foggy road. This system is step forward for making such system and will be useful to detect presence

Figure 18. Hardware setup of image antifogging system

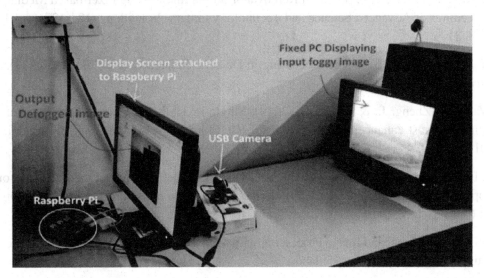

and absence of obstacles on road in front of the vehicle and can also be used as surveillance system. System is portable, low cost and low power. Mean channel prior image defogging algorithm that is used in this system has lowest mean square value and highest peak signal to noise ratio in foggy condition as compared to DCP (He, Sun & Tang, 2011) and MCP (Kang, Kim & Lee, 2015).

This system can be made RealTime by coding it into Python, use of Simulink support packages of Raspberry Pi is responsible for unwanted time delay.

ACKNOWLEDGMENT

The authors express their sincere thanks to Centre of Advanced Development and Computing, Mohali for providing support in the proposed research work.

REFERENCES

Kidsgeo.com. (n. d.). Fog – Clouds On Ground. Retrieved September 5. 2015. from http://www.kidsgeo.com/geography-for-kids/0110-fog.php

He, K., Sun, J., & Tang, X. (2011). Single Image Haze Removal Using Dark Channel Prior. *IEEE Transactions on Pattern Analysis and Machine Intelligence*, *33*(12), 2341–2353. doi:10.1109/TPAMI.2010.168 PMID:20820075

He, L., Zhao, J., Zheng, N., & Bi, D. (2016). Haze Removal using the Difference-Structure-Preservation Prior. IEEE Transactions on Image Processing, 26(3), 1063-1075.

Kang, H., Kim, Y., & Lee, Y. (2015). Fast Removal of Single Image using Pixel-based Median Channel Prior. Proceedings of Advanced Science and Technology Letters (Vol. 98. pp. 124-127). doi:10.14257/astl.2015.98.31

Kumar A. & Shaik F. (2016). Image Processing in Diabetic Related Causes (illustration 39). *Forensic and Medical Bioinformatics*, *56*, 62.

Li, B., Wang, S., Zheng, J., & Zheng, L. (2014). Single image haze removal using content-adaptive dark channel and post enhancement. *IET Journal IET Computer Vision*, *8*(2), 131–140. doi:10.1049/iet-cvi.2013.0011

Ning, X., Li, W., Dong, X., Zhang, L., & Shi, Y. (2015). A image fog removal method based on human visual property. *Proceedings of the 8th International Congress on Image and Signal Processing* (*CISP*), Shenyang (pp. 178-183). doi:10.1109/CISP.2015.7407871

Pomyen, S. (2015). Signal and Image Processing with Matlab on Raspberry Pi Platform [MSc. Thesis]. Tampere university of technology, Finland.

Tarel, J. P., Hautière, N., Caraffa, L., Cord, A., Halmaoui, H., & Gruyer, D. (2012). Vision Enhancement in Homogeneous and Heterogeneous Fog. *Intelligent Transportation Systems*, *4*(2), 6–20.

Tarel, J. P., Hautière, N., Cord, A., Gruyer, D., & Halmaoui, H. (2010). Improved Visibility of Road Scene Images under Heterogeneous Fog. *Proceedings of IEEE Intelligent Vehicles Symposium (IV'10)* (pp. 478 – 485). doi:10.1109/IVS.2010.5548128

The Times of India. (2014 December 31). Fog again affects rail. air traffic: 32 trains rescheduled 80 cancelled. Retrieved from http://timesofindia.indiatimes.com

U.S. Department of Transportation- Federal Highway Administration. (2015). How Do Weather Events Impact Roads? Retrieved October 12. from http://www.ops.fhwa.dot.gov/_weather/q1_roadimpact.html

Whiffen, B., Delannoy, P., & Siok, S. Fog: Impact on Road Transportation and Mitigation Options. Retrieved September 9, 2015. from http://www.chebucto.ns.ca/Science/AIMET/archive/whiffen_et_al_2003.pdf

Zhao, H., Xiao, C., Yu, J., & Xu, X. (2015). Single image fog removal based on local extrema. IEEE/CAA Journal of Automatica Sinica, 2(2), 158-165.

Chapter 8
Image Retrieval Techniques Using Content–Based Local Binary Descriptors:
A Survey

Rakesh Asery
Dr B. R. Ambedkar National Institute of Technology Jalandhar, India

Puneeta Marwaha
Dr. B. R. Ambedkar National Institute of Technology Jalandhar, India

Ramesh Kumar Sunkaria
Dr. B. R. Ambedkar National Institute of Technology Jalandhar, India

Lakhan Dev Sharma
Dr. B. R. Ambedkar National Institute of Technology Jalandhar, India

ABSTRACT

In this chapter authors introduces content-based image retrieval systems and compares them over a common database. For this, four different content-based local binary descriptors are described with and without Gabor transform in brief. Further Nth derivative descriptor is calculated using (N-1)th derivative, based on rotational and multiscale feature extraction. At last the distance based query image matching is used to find the similarity with database. The performance in terms of average precision, average retrieval rate, different orders of derivatives in the form of average retrieval rate, and length of feature vector v/s performance in terms of time have been calculated. For this work a comparative experiment has been conducted using the Ponce Group images on seven classes (each class have 100 images). In addition, the performance of the all descriptors have been analyzed by combining these with the Gabor transform.

INTRODUCTION

As of late the computerized library's storage capacity have grown explosively because of the development in field of web and advanced picture securing innovations. The difficulties produced before advanced picture database is storage, way to research, remote detection, education, and other applications given to the users (Rui, Huang & Chang, 1999; Smeulders, Worring, Santini et al., 2000; Kokare, Chatterji,

DOI: 10.4018/978-1-5225-2848-7.ch008

& Biswas, 2002; Liu, Zhang, Lu et al., 2007). For efficient seek numerous streamlined procedures have been created that can consequently recover the query picture from the colossal database. To address this issue, one of the regularly embraced arrangements is Content-based Image ordering and recovery (CBIR). This CBIR framework has been identified in two classifications based on the ordering procedures utilized for highlight extraction from the database pictures, which are: text-based and content based. These elements extracted from every image are put away as a record highlight vector. As shown in Figure 1, the vector utilizing a coordinating foundation of every file vector is used to find some best coordinating image to the query image.

In text-based recovery framework, pictures are defined with a printed portrayal and as indicated by comparability in view of content based database management systems (DBMS) the clients literary question picture is recovered. This approach has two essential imperfections. In the first place is the boundless level of work required for manual match for both little and immeasurable picture database. The second is the explanation mistake because of colossal substance in the image and the subjectivity of human discernment. These flaws may bring about purposeless matches in further recovery forms.

To conquer the text-based recovery framework shortcomings, content-based image ordering and recovery (CBIR) framework was proposed in the mid-1980s (Smeulders, Worring, Santini et al., 2000; Huang, Kumar, Mitra et al., 1997). In CBIR, based on different descriptor calculations, by using picture visual features, as color, shapes, texture have been proposed. It is exhausting to find a superior stable documentation of an image for all perceptual subjectivity, since picture representation additionally relies on upon conditions like change, scaling changes, and so forth. Along these lines, a consistent representation of an image is still an open research issue. A wide writing assessment in CBIR framework is exhibited in (Smeulders, Worring, Santini et al., 2000; Liu, Zhang, Lu et al., 2007; Huang, Kumar, Mitra et al., 1997; Moghaddam, Khajoie & Rouhi, 2003).

Figure 1. Basic idea framework for CBIR

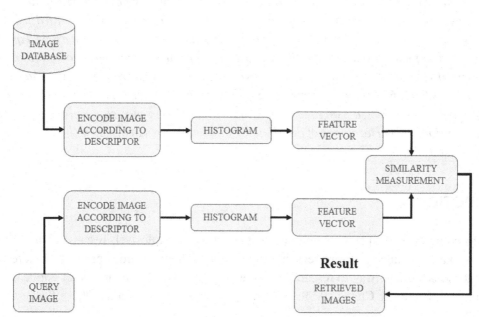

Background

Local binary descriptor (LBD), is a computationally efficient and effective strategy for surface database classification and recovery framework. Timo Ojala et al. proposed a method on grayscale images and rotational invariant adaptation of surface database by applying LBDs (Ojala, Pietikainen, & Maenpaa, 2002) for surface classification (Pietikäinen, Ojala, & Xu, 2000; Guo, Zhang, & Zhang, 2010). Liao et al. built up another methodology which involves dominant local binary pattern (DLBP) and circularly symmetric Gabor filter reactions based supplementary components (Liao, Law, & Chung, 2009). Zhenhua Guo et al. built up an option cross breed plan, with division of picture for local variation LBD texture elements and utilized LBD histograms arrangement for coordinating (Guo, Zhang, & Zhang, 2010). Different variations of LBDs, as finished displaying of LBDs descriptor (Guo, Zhang, & Zhang, 2010), and nearby examples joint appropriation with Gaussian blends (Lategahn, Gross, Stehle et al., 2010) are produced for rotational invariant adaptation of surface database classification.

The LBD descriptor was effectively utilized for the examination and acknowledgment of outward appearance, as proposed in (Ahonen, Hadid, & Pietikainen, 2006; Zhao & Pietikainen, 2007). Timo Ahonen et al. portioned face pictures for LBD highlight extraction and adjusted component vector was utilized as a face descriptor (Ahonen, Hadid, & Pietikainen, 2006). Guoying Zhao et al. built up another methodology with volume local binary patterns (VLBP), considered the LBD on three orthogonal planes (LBD-TOP) for Dynamic texture (DT) (Zhao & Pietikainen, 2007). Xi Li et al. built up the heat kernel based LBD (HKLBD) descriptor on multiscale for face representation (Li, Hu, Zhang et al., 2010). At the last face classification structure was finished with a Support Vector Machine (SVM) classifier.

Guoying Zhao et al. (2009) proposed a system for recognizing talked segregated expressions, construct exclusively in light of visual information, nearby spatiotemporal descriptors from the LBD. From mouth regions, Spatiotemporal LBDs extracted for ascertaining segregated expression sequences. Su et al. (2010) built up another strategy for pixel-based illustrations recovery, organized neighborhood structured local binary Haar pattern (SLBHP). To encode the extremity of the difference between gathered grayscale estimations of nearby rectangles, SLBHP was utilized, which is an amalgam of LBD and Haar wavelet for realistic recovery. The LBD has been additionally utilized for shape localization (Huang, X., Li, S. Z., & Wang, Y., 2004), foundation, demonstrating and moving articles identification (Heikkila & Pietikainen, 2006), multi-texture image segmentation (Li & Staunton, 2008), district of interest portrayal (Heikkilä, Pietikäinen, & Schmid, 2009), and biomedical picture recovery (Unay, Ekin, & Jasinschi, 2010). Shiv Ram Dubey et al. (2016) proposed a method for image description with multichannel decoded LBDs and introduced adder- and decoder-based two schemas for the combination of the LBDs from more than one channel.

Xiaoyang Tan et al. (2010) tended to the face acknowledgment under difficult lighting condition issue, presented new local ternary patterns (LTP) descriptor. LTD is a sum up variation of the LBD descriptor that is less sensitive to noise. Ni Liu et al. (2015) extended conventional LTD-based classifiers towards learning. Authors combined both the fixed circular LTD structure and the long-range learned LTDs to address the problem short-range local structures disappeared for some textures.

Baochang Zhang et al. (2010) proposed a technique to encode directional example highlights, local derivative descriptor (LDD), by further extending the LBDs to high-arrange nearby example portrayal for nth-request LDDs. Zhen Lei et al. (2011) proposed a novel system, first the face picture is decayed into different introduction and scale reactions by convolving multiorientation and multiscale Gabor filters, a second analysis using neighbor pixel relationship for different scale and introduction reactions utilizing LBDs. Nisha Chandran et al. (2015) proposed strategies for implementing LDD on GPGPUs for extracting parallelism from LDP algorithm and showed that by porting LDD algorithm on CUDA a speedup of the order of 36X can be achieved as compared to its sequential counterpart for images.

Subrahmanyam Murala et al. (2012) created local tetra designs (LTrDs), another methodology for picture ordering and recovery. In view of the headings LTrPs figures the connection between the referenced pixel and its neighbors, utilizing the first-request subsidiaries as a part of horizontal and vertical bearings.

Anu Bala et al. (2016) developed a local texton XOR patterns (LTXOR) feature descriptor with help of texton co-occurrence matrix (Gonde, Maheshwari, & Balasubramanian, 2010), in which textons pattern collected from 2x2 subblock of image according to pattern of the textrons. At last exclusive OR (XOR) operation performed on the textron pattern between the center pixel and its surrounding neighbors.

The LBD, the LTD, and LTXOR descriptors are encoded by appropriation of edges, and give two (positive or negative) directions data and LDD encoded two directional patterns and LTrDs enhanced these strategies for differentiating the edge data in four directions.

The rest of the structure of this chapter is sorted out as takes after: In Section, "Local patterns descriptors", a compact investigation of local descriptors (LBD, LTD, LDD, and LTrDs), and a framework of system is presented. In Section, "rotational and multiscale feature extraction", we present the idea of multi-orientation and multiscale highlight extraction, and separation based query image coordinating. Next Segment presents results of the experiments. Finally, in last Section, conclusions are attracted and conceivable future scopes are presented.

LOCAL PATTERN DESCRIPTORS

1. Technique Framework

The flowchart of the CBIR image recovery method as appeared in Figure 1. The process is given as:

Calculation: Query image as input information; Retrieval result as output;

1. Stack the information image, and changes over it into 2-D gray scale.
2. For every pixel, direction is ascertained from the first-arrange subsidiaries.
3. Compute the second-arrange direction data from encompassed neighbors.
4. Isolate the second-arrange designs into further sections as per the middle pixel's heading (according to used descriptor).
5. Histograms are seen from these binary patterns.
6. The center pixel magnitude response is calculated (for LTrD).
7. Calculate the magnitude response patterns, and their histogram (for LTrD).
8. The middle pixel extent reaction is computed.
9. Arrange the histograms reaction observed in past strides.
10. Histogram reaction utilized as the feature vector.
11. For matching the query image highlight vector correlation with the database picture.
12. From the database, in view of the most extreme matches the pictures are recovered.

Similar approach is applied for these descriptors with Gabor transform, on Gabor wavelet sub-bands (rotational and multiscale feature extraction) for GLD (Gabor local descriptor).

2. Non-Directional Descriptors

The LBD and the LTD descriptor are considered as a non-directional pattern because these descriptors don't provide directional information.

a. LBD Descriptor

The LBD descriptor was proposed by Timo Ojala et al. (2002) for surface pictures classification. By considering the inside pixel as reference, the LBD descriptor is ascertained by contrasting its grayscale quality and its neighbors, as presented in Figure 2, as take after

$$LBD_{J,R} = \sum_{j=1}^{J} 2^{(j-1)} \times f_1 \left(G_j - G_0 \right) \tag{1}$$

$$f_1(z) = \begin{cases} 1 & if \quad z \geq 0 \\ 0 & if \quad z < 0 \end{cases} \tag{2}$$

Figure 2. Case of figuring LBP and ternary pattern (upper and lower) for getting the LTP for the 3×3 example. For the upper ternary example, holding 1 and substituting 0 for - 1 and 0 in ternary example. For the lower ternary example, supplant 1 with - 1 and 0 for 1 and 0 in ternary example

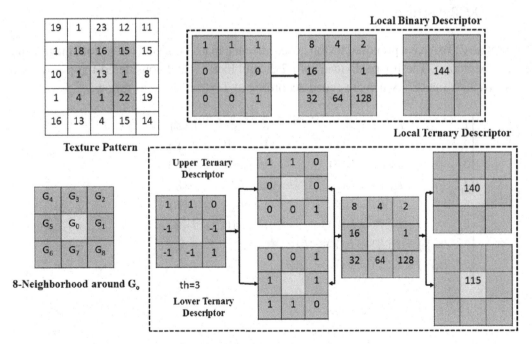

Here G_0 is a grayscale estimation of the referenced focus pixel, G_j is a grayscale estimation of its encompassed neighbors, J is the aggregate number of encompassed neighbors, and R is the neighboring pixels radius.

Limitation: It easily encodes gray scale image into two bits 0 and 1, but not provide directional information of image so need to further improvement.

    b.   LTD descriptor

Xiaoyang Tan et al. (2010) extended the LBD descriptor to three worth codes, LTD descriptor, in which gray levels in a zone of width ±th referenced center pixel G_0 around are doled out to zero, the ones above (G_0 + th) are allotted in 1 and those underneath (G_0−th) to -1 after supplanting $f_1(y)$ in (1) by $f_2(G_j, G_0, th)$ in light of

$$f_2(G_0, G_0, th) = \begin{cases} +1 & if\ G_j \geq G_0 + th \\ 0 & if\ |G_j - G_0| < th \\ -1 & if\ G_j \leq G_0 - th \end{cases} \tag{3}$$

Here "th" is a client specified limit, the LTD technique is described in Figure 2 and the threshold was set to 3. LTD descriptor codes are more impervious to noise, point by point examination can be found in (Tan & Triggs, 2010).

Limitation: Comparatively encodes gray scale image in a better way, into three bits -1, 0 and 1, but don't provide directional information of image so need to further improvement.

    c.   LTXOR descriptor

Gonde et al. (2010) have proposed texton co-occurrence matrix coded from texton image which used for feature extraction. The image divided into 2x2 subblocks I_s and considered the positions of gray values as "W, X, Y, and Z" which are coded according to Textron shape as follow:

$$TXOR(a,b) = \begin{cases} 1, & Is(W) = Is(X) & \&\ Is(Y) \neq Is(Z) \\ 2, & Is(X) = Is(Z) & \&\ Is(W) \neq Is(Y) \\ 3, & Is(Y) = Is(Z) & \&\ Is(W) \neq Is(X) \\ 4, & Is(W) = Is(Y) & \&\ Is(X) \neq Is(Z) \\ 5, & Is(W) = Is(Z) & \&\ Is(X) \neq Is(Y) \\ 6, & Is(X) = Is(Y) & \&\ Is(W) \neq Is(Z) \\ 7, & Is(W) = Is(X) = Is(Y) = Is(Z) \\ 0, & Is(W) \neq Is(X) \neq Is(Y) \neq Is(Z) \end{cases} \tag{4}$$

Local texton XOR patterns proposed by Anu Bala et al. (2016) in which these eight different Textron shapes considered for the texton image generation as shown in Figure 3.

After calculating the texton pattern, we perform the XOR operation between the center pixel of texton and its surrounding neighbor texton pixels. The local texton XOR patterns are coded as:

$$LTXOR_{J,R} = \sum_{j=1}^{J} 2^{(j-1)} \times f_3 \left(TXOR\left(G_j\right) \otimes TXOR\left(G_0\right) \right) \tag{5}$$

$$f_3\left(x \otimes y\right) = \begin{cases} 1 & x \neq y \\ 0 & else \end{cases} \tag{6}$$

where $TXOR(G_0)$ is the shape of texton referenced focus pixel, $TXOR(G_j)$ is a shape of texton for the neighbor pixel and $\otimes$ represents the XOR operation between the variables. Figure 4 shows the detailed representation of LTXOR descriptor for a given image.

3. Directional Descriptors

These patterns represented after encoding the directional information of the image and also provide higher order derivatives.

a. LDD Descriptor

Baochang Zhang et al. (2010) encoded the LDDs descriptor for face recognition. They encoded directional pattern highlights by further extending the LBDs to high-arrange local pattern depiction for n^{th}-request LDDs after considering the LBD descriptor as the non-directional first-request neighborhood design descriptor. The LDD gives more definite data highlights as compared to LBD.

The nth-order LDD is figured from the $(n-1)^{th}$-order subsidiaries, along 0°, 45°, 90°, and 135° directions, allotted as $I_D^{(n-1)}(G_0)|_{D=0°,45°,90°,135°}$. At that point n^{th}-order LDD is processed as

Figure 3. Eight Textron shape

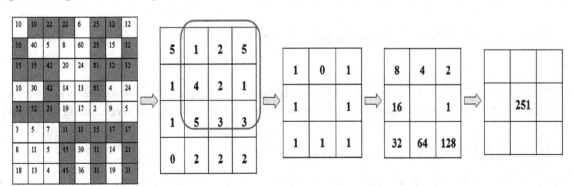

Figure 4. LTXOR pattern calculation from Eight Textron shape

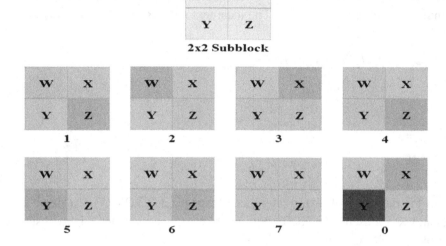

$$LDD_D^n\left(G_0\right) = \sum_{j=1}^{J} 2^{(j-1)} \times f_3\left(I_D^{n-1}\left(G_0\right) - I_D^{n-1}\left(G_j\right)\right)\Big|_{J=8} \qquad (7)$$

$$f_3\left(w,x\right) = \begin{cases} 1 & if \ \ w.x \ge 0 \\ 0 & if \ \ w.x < 0 \end{cases} \qquad (8)$$

Similarly, remaining 90°, and 135° directional patterns calculated as shown in Figure 5, the LDD bits are

$$\begin{aligned}
0^0 &\rightarrow \ LDD_{0^0}^2\left(G_0\right) = 10011100 \\
45^0 &\rightarrow \ LDD_{45^0}^2\left(G_0\right) = 00011101 \\
90^0 &\rightarrow \ LDD_{90^0}^2\left(G_0\right) = 10101000 \\
135^0 &\rightarrow \ LDD_{135^0}^2\left(G_0\right) = 11001001
\end{aligned} \right\} = LDD^2(G_0) \qquad (9)$$

$$LDD^2(G_0) = 10011100000111011010100011001001$$

The case for the LDD estimation and detailed discussion can be found in (Zhang, Gao, Zhao et al., 2010).

Limitation: Provide better result compare to previously existing descriptor after encoded gray scale image along 0°, 45°, 90°, and 135° directions. But for more significant retrieval, further encoding is required.

b.   LTrDs Descriptors

Subrahmanyam Murala et al. (2012) proposed LTrDs, new approach received from neighborhood designs descriptor (LBD, LTD, and LDD). They encoded directional pattern highlights by the first-order

Figure 5. Count of derivative pattern bits for the middle pixel "10" for 0°, 45° direction corresponding to neighbors. Direction of (red) the middle pixel and (sky) that it's neighboring pixels

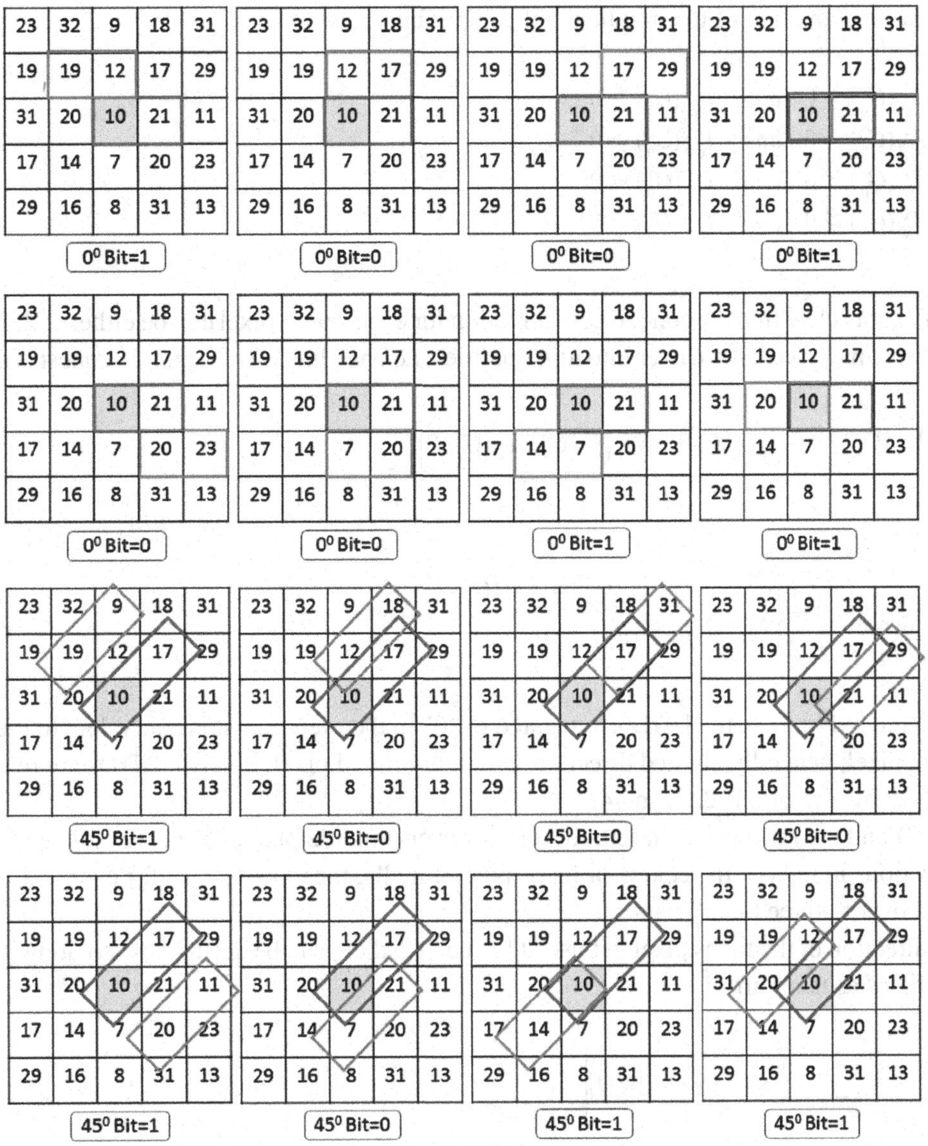

Each cell below shows the same 5×5 pixel grid:

23	32	9	18	31
19	19	12	17	29
31	20	10	21	11
17	14	7	20	23
29	16	8	31	13

Row 1 labels: 0° Bit=1 | 0° Bit=0 | 0° Bit=0 | 0° Bit=1

Row 2 labels: 0° Bit=0 | 0° Bit=0 | 0° Bit=1 | 0° Bit=1

Row 3 labels: 45° Bit=1 | 45° Bit=0 | 45° Bit=0 | 45° Bit=0

Row 4 labels: 45° Bit=1 | 45° Bit=0 | 45° Bit=1 | 45° Bit=1

subordinates along 90° and 0° directions are indicated the vertical and flat neighborhoods of focus pixel. The first-order subsidiaries indicated as $I_\theta^1(G_0)|_{\theta=0°,90°}$. The four conceivable courses can be either 1, 2, 3, or 4, as in (12) for every middle pixel, and in the long run, the image is isolated into four directions.

Let G_h and G_v signify the flat and vertical neighborhoods of G_0, individually. At that point, the first-request subsidiaries at the inside pixel can be composed as

$$I_{0°}^1\left(G_0\right) = I\left(G_h\right) - I\left(G_0\right)$$

(10)

$$I^1_{90^0}\left(G_0\right) = I\left(G_v\right) - I\left(G_0\right) \tag{11}$$

After that, the direction of the middle pixel can be figured as

$$I^1_{DR} = \begin{cases} 1 & I^1_{0^0}(G_0) \geq 0 \quad and \quad I^1_{90^0}(G_0) \geq 0 \\ 2 & I^1_{0^0}(G_0) < 0 \quad and \quad I^1_{90^0}(G_0) \geq 0 \\ 3 & I^1_{0^0}(G_0) < 0 \quad and \quad I^1_{90^0}(G_0) < 0 \\ 4 & I^1_{0^0}(G_0) \geq 0 \quad and \quad I^1_{90^0}(G_0) < 0 \end{cases} \tag{12}$$

From (12), it is clear that the conceivable direction for each center pixel can be either 1, 2, 3, or 4, and eventually, the image is changed over into four qualities, i.e., headings. The second-request is defined as:

$$LTrD^2\left(G_0\right) = \left\{f_4\left(I^1_\theta\left(G_0\right),I^1_\theta\left(G_1\right)\right),....,f_4\left(I^1_\theta\left(G_0\right),I^1_\theta\left(G_J\right)\right)\right\}\Big|_{J=8} \tag{13}$$

$$f_4\left(I^1_{DR}\left(G_0\right),I^1_{DR}\left(G_J\right)\right) = \begin{cases} 0 & I^1_{DR}\left(G_0\right) = I^1_{DR}\left(G_J\right) \\ I^1_{DR}\left(G_J\right) & else \end{cases} \tag{14}$$

As appeared in Figure 6, the LTrD is relegated to "0" in the event that it is equivalent to the direction of the inside pixel, generally allotted direction of neighborhood pixel. So also, LTrDs are registered for every pixel having directions 2, 3, and 4.

From (13) and (14), we get 8-bit tetra design for every middle pixel. Then, we isolate all examples into four sections in light of the course of focus pixel. Finally, the tetra designs for every part (heading) are changed over to three binary patterns.

Let the direction of the focus pixel got used (12) be "1"; then, can be defined by isolating it into three paired examples as takes after:

$$LTrD^2\Big|_{DI=2,3,4} = \sum_{j=1}^{J} 2^{(j-1)} \times f_5\left(LTrD^2\left(G_0\right)\right)\Big|_{DI=2,3,4} \tag{15}$$

Figure 6. Count of tetra pattern bits for the middle pixel heading "1" utilizing the direction of neighbors. Direction of (green) the middle pixel and (orange) that it's neighboring pixels

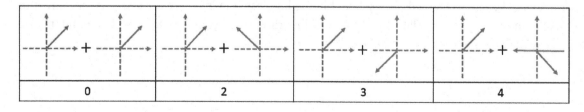

$$f_4\left(LTrD^2\left(G_0\right)\right)\Big|_{DI=\phi} = \begin{cases} 1 & if & LTrD^2(G_0) = \phi \\ 0 & else \end{cases} \tag{16}$$

where φ=2, 3, 4.

Similarly, the other three tetra designs for staying three directions of focus pixels are calculated. In this way, we get 12 (4x3) binary examples.

Guo et al. (2000) utilized the extensible part of the neighborhood contrast operator to propose the size LBP, alongside the sign LBP for texture classification. They demonstrated that, in spite of the fact that the sign segment separates more valuable information as contrasted and the extent segment, misusing the blend of sign and size parts can give better insights, which are not clear in any one individual segment. This idea has motivated the authors to propose the thirteenth twofold pattern by utilizing the extents of flat and vertical first-request subordinates utilizing

$$M_{I^1}\left(G_j\right) = \sqrt{\left(I_{0^0}^1\left(G_0\right)\right)^2 + \left(I_{90^0}^1\left(G_j\right)\right)^2} \tag{17}$$

$$LMP = \sum_{j=1}^{J} 2^{(j-1)} \times f_1\left(M_{I^1}\left(G_j\right) - M_{I^1}\left(G_0\right)\right)\Big|_{J=8} \tag{18}$$

Tetra pattern: 3 0 4 2 3 2 0 0;
Pattern_1: 0 0 0 1 0 1 0 0; Pattern_2: 1 0 0 0 1 0 0 0; Pattern_3: 0 0 1 0 0 0 0 0;
Magnitude Pattern: 0 1 0 1 0 0 1 1;

For the local pattern with J neighborhoods, mixes of LBDs are conceivable, bringing about the element vector length of 2J. The computational expense of this component vector is high. So as to lessen the computational cost, we consider the uniform examples (Kokare, Biswas, & Chatterji, 2007). The uniform pattern alludes to the uniform appearance design that has restricted discontinuities in the roundabout twofold representation. In this chapter, those examples that have not exactly or equivalent to two discontinuities in the roundabout double representation are alluded to as the uniform examples, and the rest of the examples are alluded to as non-uniform. Thus, the unmistakable uniform examples for a given inquiry picture would be J(J-1) + 2 .The conceivable uniform examples for J = 8 can be seen in (Kokare, Biswas, & Chatterji, 2007). In the wake of recognizing the local pattern (the LBD, the LTD, the LDD, or the 13-binary pattern form LTrD), the entire picture is spoken to by building a histogram utilizing

$$HG\left(l\right) = \frac{1}{r \times c} \sum_{m=1}^{r} \sum_{n=1}^{c} f_5\left(LDTN\left(m,n\right), l\right) \tag{19}$$

$$l \in \left[0, J \times \left(J - 1\right) + 2\right]$$

Figure 7. Case to acquire the tetra and magnitude designs. For creating a tetra pattern, the bit is coded with the direction of a neighbor when the direction of the middle pixel and its neighbor are distinctive, something else "0." For the greatness design, the bit is coded with "1" when the size of the inside pixel is not exactly the extent of its neighbor, generally "0." Direction of (red) the middle pixel and (sky) that it's neighboring pixels

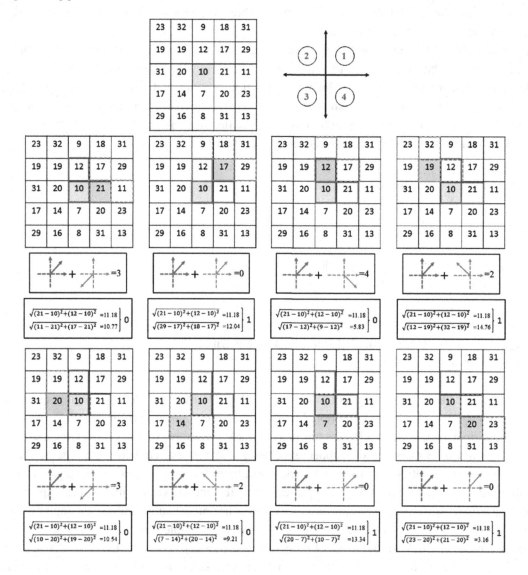

$$f_5(c,d) = \begin{cases} 1 & if \quad c = d \\ 0 & else \end{cases} \tag{20}$$

where r*c speaks to the information picture size.

Figure 7 shows the conceivable local pattern moves direction about an LTrD for direction "1" of the middle pixel. The LTrD is coded to "0" when it is equivalent to the direction of focus pixel, generally coded toward neighborhood pixel. Utilizing similar analogy, LTrDs are ascertained for focus pixels having directions 2, 3, and 4. For the neighborhood pixel "21", we watch the direction "3" and magnitude "10.77". Because the area pixel and the middle pixel direction are not same so, relating LTrD bit coded "3". Next, for the area pixel "17", we watch direction "1" and magnitude "12.04". Since the middle pixel and the area pixel direction are same, relating LTrD bit coded "0". From the specimen design the inside pixel magnitude is "11.18", which is greater than the first neighborhood pixel magnitude. In this way, comparing LMP bit coded "0" as appeared in Figure 7. Utilizing similar relationship, LTrD and LMP for other residual neighborhood pixels are encoded direction about the tetra design "3 0 4 2 3 2 0 0" and the magnitude pattern "0 1 0 1 0 0 1 1". After that, we confine tetra design into three binary patterns as takes after: Considering the encoded tetra design, for the first pattern keeping "2" where the tetra pattern esteem is "1" and else "0", i.e., "0 0 0 1 0 1 0 0". Similarly, the other two paired examples "1 0 0 0 1 0 0 0" and "0 0 1 0 0 0 0 0" are processed for tetra design values "3" and "4," separately. Similarly, tetra designs for focus pixels having directions 2, 3, and 4 are registered. In this way, with four tetra designs, 12 paired examples are acquired. The thirteenth paired example is acquired from the magnitude of the first-arrange subordinates.

c. N^{th} Derivative Descriptor

For further computation of the third-subordinate derivative, or tetra design (here consider tetra pattern), for every one of the four directions the second-arrange subsidiaries, indicated as $I_\theta^2(G_j)|_{\theta=45\circ,90\circ,135\circ,180\circ}$ are figured. Utilizing these second request subordinates, the third-arrange tetra design $LTrD(G_0)$ is defined as

$$LTrD^3(G_0) = \left\{ f_4(I_\theta^2(G_0), I_\theta^2(G_1)), ..., f_4(I_\theta^2(G_0), I_\theta^2(G_J)) \right\}\Big|_{J=8} \tag{21}$$

Utilizing the same relationship, the authors summed up plan for the nth-request LTrD can be defined by utilizing past $(n-1)^{th}$-request subsidiaries in every one of the four directions

$$LTrD^n(G_0) = \left\{ f_4(I_\theta^{(n-1)}(G_0), I_\theta^{(n-1)}(G_1)), ..., f_4(I_\theta^{(n-1)}(G_0), I_\theta^{(n-1)}(G_J)) \right\}\Big|_{J=8} \tag{22}$$

The higher request LTrDs have given more deep information, as compared with the lower order, because they also encode intermediate pixels detailed direction patterns. Be that as it may, the principle downside is that as the request of LTrDs expands the affectability to commotion is likewise expanding, so it has been seen by contrasting second request LTrD and higher request, the second-arrange LTrD gives better performance (refer to comes about with discussion section).

ROTATIONAL AND MULTISCALE FEATURE EXTRACTION

Gabor Transform is utilized for recurrence and directional data to surface investigation. For pattern recognition, the GT is likewise used to examine the effectiveness of every single existing encoder for applications in pattern recognition. In this manner, we compare all the existing techniques with the GT.

1.   GT

Spatial usage of the GT given by Subrahmanyam Murala et al. (2009) and connected Gabor filters on the picture to different scale at different introduction, a while later got a variety of extents. A grayscale picture Gabor capacity, tweaked by an unpredictable sinusoid, is a Gaussian part. From the recurrence of sinusoid wave ω increased by a Gaussian envelope with the standard deviations σ_k and σ_l, the GT can be gotten as takes after:

$$\psi(k,l) = \frac{1}{2\pi\sigma_k\sigma_l}\exp\left\{(\frac{-1}{2})(\frac{k^2}{\sigma_k^2} + \frac{l^2}{\sigma_l^2}) + 2\pi j\omega k\right\} \tag{23}$$

The input of the Gabor filter is the convolution of test picture I_T with the Gabor window, and figured as

$$GT_{pq}(k,l) = \sum_s\sum_t I_T(k-s,l-t)\psi_{pq}^*(s,t) \tag{24}$$

2. Gabor Descriptor

After getting the output from GT, all the descriptors encoded. Here we connected the GT with four scales h (h=1, 2, 3, 4) and two directions 0°, and 90° on an offered picture to figure subordinates in four directions. After that, the nth-request Gabor LTrDs (GLTrDs) descriptors are registered by performing past (n−1)[th]-order subordinates in light of:

$$GT_{h,0^0}^{n-1}(G_0) = GT_{h,0^0}^{n-2}(G_0) - GT_{h,0^0}^{n-2}(G_h) \tag{25}$$

$$GT_{h,90^0}^{n-1}(G_0) = GT_{h,90^0}^{n-2}(G_0) - GT_{h,90^0}^{n-2}(G_v) \tag{26}$$

The nth-request GLTrD can be defined as

$$GLTrD^n(G_0) = \left\{\begin{array}{l} f_4\left(GT_{h,\theta}^{(n-1)}(G_0), GT_{h,\theta}^{(n-1)}(G_1)\right), \\ f_4\left(GT_{h,\theta}^{(n-1)}(G_0), GT_{h,\theta}^{(n-1)}(G_2)\right), \\ ..., f_4\left(GT_{h,\theta}^{(n-1)}(G_0), GT_{h,\theta}^{(n-1)}(G_J)\right) \end{array}\right\}\Bigg|_{J=8} \tag{27}$$

Besides, the 12 paired patterns at every scale are figured given to (15), and the 13th parallel example is computed by (18).

3. Distance Based Query Matching

The inquiry picture Q_I coded as the feature vector $F(Q) = (F_1(Q), F_2(Q), ..., F_N(Q))$ is figured from highlight extraction. Utilizing the same similarity, the database every photo is coded by the element vector F(DB) = (F$_{k1}$(DB), F$_{k2}$(DB), ..., F$_{kN}$(DB)), k = 1, 2, 3, ..., |DB|. Our motivation is to take over the inquiry picture and select the best pictures like the questionable picture. Utilizing the distance estimation between the database pictures and the query picture, we select top coordinated pictures from the database pictures. With a specific end goal to coordinate the photos in the database, we utilize the distance metric similitude, figured as takes after:

$$DMM(Q, DB) = \sum_{a=1}^{N} \left| \frac{F_{ka}(DB) - F_a(Q)}{1 + F_{ka}(DB) + F_a(Q)} \right| \tag{28}$$

where F$_{kN}$(DB) is the ath feature of the kth picture in database |DB|.

RESULTS WITH DISCUSSIONS

To contemplate the effectiveness of the existed approach, investigations were performed on PONCE picture databases (Lazebnik, Schmid, & Ponce, 2004). The performance is discussed about in the accompanying subsections on these databases. The shorter terms utilized as a part of the examination of the outcome are taking over:

TrD1: LTrD 2nd-order Descriptor without and with GT.
TrD2: LTrD 3rd-order Descriptor without and with GT.
TrD3: LTrD 4th-order Descriptor without and with GT.
DD1: LDD 2nd-order Descriptor without and with GT.
DD2: LDD 3rd-order Descriptor without and with GT.
DD3: LDD 4th-order Descriptor without and with GT.
TD: LTD without and with GT.
BD: LBD without and with GT.

For investigation, Ponce's database (DB) is utilized, which is comprises of 161 pictures delineating 8 protests in various stances against a practically uniform foundation and 51 test messed pictures containing rescaled, turned, incompletely impeded and contrastingly enlightened occurrences of the articles. For this analysis, we have chosen 700 pictures each class size N$_{cl}$ = 100, to frame DB database. These photos choose from 7 different classes, in particular, Admiral, Egret, Mandarin, Owl, Puffin, Toucan, and Wood duck, with a determination varying from 230×200 to 800×863. Figure 8 speaks in the example pictures of DB database (one picture from each class). Every image in the DB database is utilized as the inquiry image for this trial.

The framework has fittingly recovered the required image from the database if the resultant image identified with the same class as that of the inquiry image, otherwise, the framework has neglected to find the related image from the database.

The effectiveness of the descriptors is measured as average precision (AP %), and the average recall (AR %) or the average retrieval rate (ARR %). For the query picture IM$_Q$, the precision is ascertained in view of:

Figure 8. Sample pictures (one picture every class) of PONCE DB database

$$P\left(IM_Q, n\right) = \frac{1}{n} \sum_{p=1}^{|DB|} \left| \delta\left(\psi\left(IM_p\right), \psi\left(IM_Q\right)\right)\right|$$
$$Rank\left(IM_p, IM_Q\right) \le n$$

(29)

where "n" means the quantity of recovered resultant image and |DB| is the image database size. Ψ(c) is the class of "c", and Rank(IMp, IM_Q) gives back the image rank IMp (for the inquiry image IMQ) among all images of |DB|, as

$$\delta\left(\psi\left(IM_p\right), \psi\left(IM_Q\right)\right) = \begin{cases} 1 & if & \psi\left(IM_p\right) = \psi\left(IM_Q\right) \\ 0 & if & \psi\left(IM_p\right) \ne \psi\left(IM_Q\right) \end{cases}$$

(30)

Recall is given as

$$R\left(IM_Q, n\right) = \frac{1}{N_{cl}} \sum_{p=1}^{|DB|} \left| \delta\left(\psi\left(IM_p\right), \psi\left(IM_Q\right)\right)\right|$$
$$Rank\left(IM_p, IM_Q\right) \le n$$

(31)

The AP (%) for the eth similarity class of the given database picture are ascertained as

$$P_{Avg}^{e}(n) = \frac{1}{N_{cl}} \sum_{p \in N_{cl}} P\left(IM_p, n\right) \tag{32}$$

Finally, the overall AP (%) and the AR (%) for the complete reference database images are computed utilizing (33) and (34), separately, as

$$P_{Avg}^{Tot}(n) = \frac{1}{|DB|} \sum_{p=1}^{|DB|} P\left(IM_p, n\right) \tag{33}$$

$$ARR = \frac{1}{|DB|} \sum_{p=1}^{|DB|} R\left(IM_p, n\right)\Big|_{n \leq 120} \tag{34}$$

Utilizing the same relationship, the average recall is likewise defined. Figure 9 speaks to class precision and recall of the existing descriptors with and without GT on the database DB.

Figure 9. Class wise comparison of existing descriptors in type of Precision (P) without (A) and with GT (B) and in types of Recall (R) without (C) and with GT (D) on DB database

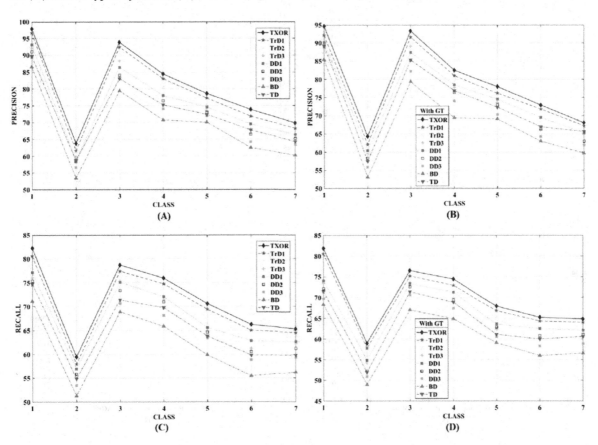

For higher estimations of AP (%) and AR (%), the outcomes are thought to be better. From Figure 9, it can be observed that LTrD descriptor gives better result contrasted with alternate strategies in each of the ten classes.

Figure 10 represents the exploratory consequences of the existing descriptors as AP (%) and ARR (%) as indicated by the recovered images.

Figure 11 speaks to the execution examination of LTrD, and LDP descriptors between different orders as AP(%) and AR(%), with and without GT. From these figures, it is presumed that in term of AP, and AR (or ARR) as compared with existing descriptors, LTrD significantly enhances recovery comes about on Ponce database images.

Table 1, summarizes all systems as AP(%) and AR(%) with and without GT. As observed from Table 1 and Figure 9-11, it is noticeable that the LTrD surpasses the other existing descriptors.

Run time is additionally a critical factor in numerous applications. For this chapter, technique utilizes just basic closed-form image operations so it is significantly more productive than ones that require costly iterative advancements. The Matlab implementation of these descriptors to process a 600x722 pixel takes time as shown in Table 2, Ponce Group image on a 2.10-GHz i3, permitting images preprocessing to be performed continuously and in this manner giving the capacity to handle substantial image databases.

Figure 10. Performance comparison of the existing descriptors in terms of AP(%) without (A) and with GT (B) and ARR(%) without (C) and with GT (D) on DB database

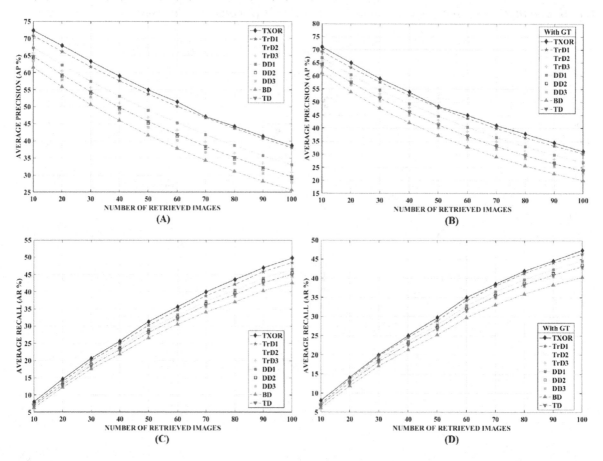

Figure 11. Performance comparison between different orders of existing descriptors in terms of Average Precision (P) without (A) and with GT (B) and in terms of Average Recall (R) without (C) and with GT (D) on DB database

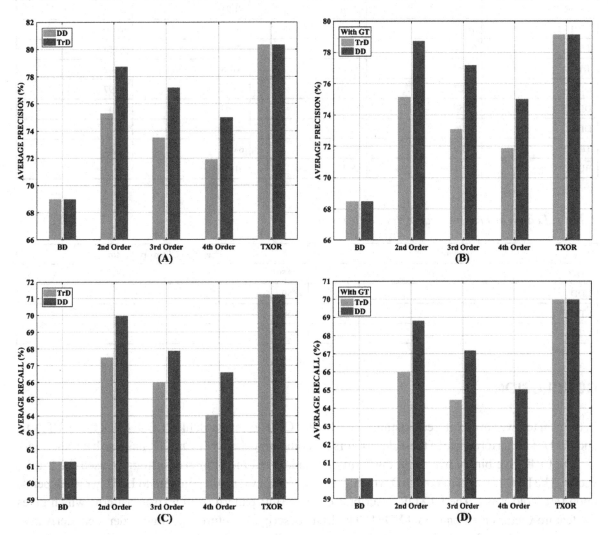

Table 2 speaks to the LBD, LTD, LDD, and LTrD strategies for a given inquiry picture with a component vector length vs simulation time.

From Figure 9-11, and Tables 1 and 2, it can be seen that the length of the component vector LTrD is 13, 6.5, and 3.25 times of LBD, LTD, and LTrD descriptors, respectively. The LTXOR is outruns from others as:

1. In the type of average precision on Ponce database LBD by 16.42%, LTD by 10.02%, LDD by 6.69% and LTrD by 2.04%;
2. In the type of average recall on Ponce database LBD by 16.28%, LTD by 9.74%, LDD by 5.54% and LTrD by 1.80%;

Table 1. AP (%) and ARR (%) for the 10 DTD texture database DB classes

Descriptor	AP (%)	AP GT (%)	AR (%)	AR GT (%)
TXOR	80.31	79.10	71.21	69.96
TrD1	78.70	77.45	69.95	68.80
TrD2	77.16	74.55	67.87	67.14
TrD3	74.97	73.65	66.58	65.02
DD1	75.27	75.10	67.47	65.97
DD2	73.50	73.07	65.99	64.44
DD3	71.86	71.06	64.03	62.36
TD	73.00	72.78	64.89	63.62
BD	68.98	68.46	61.24	60.13

Table 2. Length of Feature Vector V/s Performance

Descriptor	Length of Feature Vector
LTrD	13*59
LDD	4*59
LTD	2*59
LBD	59

CONCLUSION

In the chapter, we have explored existing technique for CBIR framework like, LBD, LTD, LDD, LTXOR and LTrD. The performance of these descriptors, by combining them with the GT, has also been analyzed.

The LBD give binary pattern in the form of 1 and 0, and then uniform histogram used for feature vector. The LTD is extension of LBD which gave better retrieval result compare to LBD, which depends upon threshold value. The LTXOR descriptor encode XOR pattern from textron patterns which gives the feature vector based on the LTXORP. The LDD descriptor captures the high-order local derivative variations and according to direction give local pattern. The LTrD gives the local binary pattern based on the direction of pixels that are calculated in 0^0 and 90^0 derivatives. The magnitude of the binary pattern is collected using magnitudes of derivatives.

The execution examination of LBD, LTD, LDD, and LTrD descriptors on pictures of the database has been detailed below.

1. For Ponce database as compared with LBD, LTD, LDD, LTrD and LTXOR descriptors, the average precision (AP %) has significantly enhanced from 68.97%, 73.00%, 75.27% and 78.70% to 80.31% respectively.
2. For Ponce database as compared with LBD, LTD, LDD, LTrD and LTXOR descriptors, the average recall (AR %) has significantly enhanced from 61.24%, 64.89%, 67.47% and 69.95% to 71.21% respectively.

FUTURE RESEARCH DIRECTIONS

In this chapter, some cases in the LTXOR descriptor are ignored so by using that case for three pixel combination definitely we get efficient results. For LTrD only flat and vertical pixels have been utilized for subsidiary figuring. Results can be further enhanced by considering the corner to corner pixels, means the diagonal pixels for derivative calculations with flat and vertical directions. The effectiveness of the technique can be further modified by expanding the radius of neighboring pixels. Because of the viability of the proposed strategy, it can be additionally reasonable for other pattern recognition applications, for example, face recognition, fingerprint recognition, and so on.

REFERENCES

Ahonen, T., Hadid, A., & Pietikainen, M. (2006). Face description with local binary patterns: Application to face recognition. *IEEE Transactions on Pattern Analysis and Machine Intelligence*, 28(12), 2037–2041. doi:10.1109/TPAMI.2006.244 PMID:17108377

Bala, A., & Kaur, T. (2016). Local texton XOR patterns: A new feature descriptor for content-based image retrieval. *Engineering Science and Technology, an International Journal*, 19(1), 101-112.

Chandran, S. N., Gangodkar, D., & Mittal, A. (2015, May). Parallel implementation of local derivative pattern algorithm for fast image retrieval. *Proceedings of the 2015 International Conference on Computing, Communication & Automation (ICCCA)* (pp. 1132-1137). IEEE. doi:10.1109/CCAA.2015.7148545

Dubey, S. R., Singh, S. K., & Singh, R. K. (2016). Multichannel Decoded Local Binary Patterns for Content-Based Image Retrieval. *IEEE Transactions on Image Processing*, 25(9), 4018–4032. doi:10.1109/TIP.2016.2577887 PMID:27295674

Gonde, A. B., Maheshwari, R. P., & Balasubramanian, R. (2010, December). Texton co-occurrence matrix: a new feature for image retrieval. *Proceedings of the 2010 Annual IEEE India Conference (INDICON)* (pp. 1-5). IEEE. doi:10.1109/INDCON.2010.5712603

Guo, Z., Zhang, L., & Zhang, D. (2010). Rotation invariant texture classification using LBP variance (LBPV) with global matching. *Pattern Recognition*, 43(3), 706–719. doi:10.1016/j.patcog.2009.08.017

Guo, Z., Zhang, L., & Zhang, D. (2010). A completed modeling of local binary pattern operator for texture classification. *IEEE Transactions on Image Processing*, 19(6), 1657–1663. doi:10.1109/TIP.2010.2044957 PMID:20215079

Heikkila, M., & Pietikainen, M. (2006). A texture-based method for modeling the background and detecting moving objects. *IEEE Transactions on Pattern Analysis and Machine Intelligence*, 28(4), 657–662. doi:10.1109/TPAMI.2006.68 PMID:16566514

Heikkilä, M., Pietikäinen, M., & Schmid, C. (2009). Description of interest regions with local binary patterns. *Pattern Recognition*, 42(3), 425–436. doi:10.1016/j.patcog.2008.08.014

Huang, J., Kumar, S. R., Mitra, M., Zhu, W. J., & Zabih, R. (1997, June). Image indexing using color correlograms. *Proceedings of the 1997 IEEE Computer Society Conference on Computer Vision and Pattern Recognition* (pp. 762-768). IEEE.

Huang, X., Li, S. Z., & Wang, Y. (2004, December). Shape localization based on statistical method using extended local binary pattern. *Proceedings of the Third International Conference on Image and Graphics (ICIG'04)* (pp. 184-187). IEEE.

Kokare, M., Biswas, P. K., & Chatterji, B. N. (2007). Texture image retrieval using rotated wavelet filters. *Pattern Recognition Letters*, *28*(10), 1240–1249. doi:10.1016/j.patrec.2007.02.006

Kokare, M., Chatterji, B. N., & Biswas, P. K. (2002). A survey on current content based image retrieval methods. *Journal of the Institution of Electronics and Telecommunication Engineers*, *48*(3-4), 261–271. doi:10.1080/03772063.2002.11416285

Lategahn, H., Gross, S., Stehle, T., & Aach, T. (2010). Texture classification by modeling joint distributions of local patterns with Gaussian mixtures. *IEEE Transactions on Image Processing*, *19*(6), 1548–1557. doi:10.1109/TIP.2010.2042100 PMID:20129862

Lazebnik, S., Schmid, C., & Ponce, J. (2004, September). Semi-local affine parts for object recognition. *Proceedings of the British Machine Vision Conference (BMVC'04)* (pp. 779-788). The British Machine Vision Association (BMVA).

Lei, Z., Liao, S., Pietikainen, M., & Li, S. Z. (2011). Face recognition by exploring information jointly in space, scale and orientation. *IEEE Transactions on Image Processing*, *20*(1), 247–256. doi:10.1109/TIP.2010.2060207 PMID:20643604

Li, M., & Staunton, R. C. (2008). Optimum Gabor filter design and local binary patterns for texture segmentation. *Pattern Recognition Letters*, *29*(5), 664–672. doi:10.1016/j.patrec.2007.12.001

Li, X., Hu, W., Zhang, Z., & Wang, H. (2010). Heat kernel based local binary pattern for face representation. *IEEE Signal Processing Letters*, *17*(3), 308–311. doi:10.1109/LSP.2009.2036653

Liao, S., Law, M. W., & Chung, A. C. (2009). Dominant local binary patterns for texture classification. *IEEE Transactions on Image Processing*, *18*(5), 1107–1118. doi:10.1109/TIP.2009.2015682 PMID:19342342

Liu, N., Gimel'farb, G., & Delmas, P. (2015, November). Combined ternary patterns for texture recognition. *Proceedings of the 2015 International Conference on Image and Vision Computing New Zealand (IVCNZ)* (pp. 1-6). IEEE. doi:10.1109/IVCNZ.2015.7761509

Liu, Y., Zhang, D., Lu, G., & Ma, W. Y. (2007). A survey of content-based image retrieval with high-level semantics. *Pattern Recognition*, *40*(1), 262–282. doi:10.1016/j.patcog.2006.04.045

Moghaddam, H. A., Khajoie, T. T., & Rouhi, A. H. (2003, September). A new algorithm for image indexing and retrieval using wavelet correlogram. *Proceedings of the 2003 International Conference on Image Processing ICIP '03* (Vol. 3, pp. III-497). IEEE. doi:10.1109/ICIP.2003.1247290

Murala, S., Gonde, A. B., & Maheshwari, R. P. (2009, March). Color and texture features for image indexing and retrieval. *Proceedings of the IEEE International Advance Computing Conference IACC '09* (pp. 1411-1416). IEEE. doi:10.1109/IADCC.2009.4809223

Murala, S., Maheshwari, R. P., & Balasubramanian, R. (2012). Local tetra patterns: A new feature descriptor for content-based image retrieval. *IEEE Transactions on Image Processing*, *21*(5), 2874–2886. doi:10.1109/TIP.2012.2188809 PMID:22514130

Ojala, T., Pietikainen, M., & Maenpaa, T. (2002). Multiresolution gray-scale and rotation invariant texture classification with local binary patterns. *IEEE Transactions on Pattern Analysis and Machine Intelligence*, *24*(7), 971–987. doi:10.1109/TPAMI.2002.1017623

Pietikäinen, M., Ojala, T., & Xu, Z. (2000). Rotation-invariant texture classification using feature distributions. *Pattern Recognition*, *33*(1), 43–52. doi:10.1016/S0031-3203(99)00032-1

Rui, Y., Huang, T. S., & Chang, S. F. (1999). Image retrieval: Current techniques, promising directions, and open issues. *Journal of Visual Communication and Image Representation*, *10*(1), 39–62. doi:10.1006/jvci.1999.0413

Smeulders, A. W., Worring, M., Santini, S., Gupta, A., & Jain, R. (2000). Content-based image retrieval at the end of the early years. *IEEE Transactions on Pattern Analysis and Machine Intelligence*, *22*(12), 1349–1380. doi:10.1109/34.895972

Su, S. Z., Chen, S. Y., Li, S. Z., Li, S. A., & Duh, D. J. (2010). Structured local binary Haar pattern for pixel-based graphics retrieval. *Electronics Letters*, *46*(14), 996–998. doi:10.1049/el.2010.1104

Tan, X., & Triggs, B. (2010). Enhanced local texture feature sets for face recognition under difficult lighting conditions. *IEEE Transactions on Image Processing*, *19*(6), 1635–1650. doi:10.1109/TIP.2010.2042645 PMID:20172829

Unay, D., Ekin, A., & Jasinschi, R. S. (2010). Local structure-based region-of-interest retrieval in brain MR images. *IEEE Transactions on Information Technology in Biomedicine*, *14*(4), 897–903. doi:10.1109/TITB.2009.2038152 PMID:20064763

Zhang, B., Gao, Y., Zhao, S., & Liu, J. (2010). Local derivative pattern versus local binary pattern: Face recognition with high-order local pattern descriptor. *IEEE Transactions on Image Processing*, *19*(2), 533–544. doi:10.1109/TIP.2009.2035882 PMID:19887313

Zhao, G., Barnard, M., & Pietikainen, M. (2009). Lipreading with local spatiotemporal descriptors. *IEEE Transactions on Multimedia*, *11*(7), 1254–1265. doi:10.1109/TMM.2009.2030637

Zhao, G., & Pietikainen, M. (2007). Dynamic texture recognition using local binary patterns with an application to facial expressions. *IEEE Transactions on Pattern Analysis and Machine Intelligence*, *29*(6), 915–928. doi:10.1109/TPAMI.2007.1110 PMID:17431293

Chapter 9
Invariant Model Combining Geometry and Appearance for Facial Detection and Gender Classification From Arbitrary Viewpoints

Mokhtar Taffar
University of Jijel, Algeria

Serge Miguet
LIRIS, Université de Lyon 2, UMR CNRS 5205, France

ABSTRACT

In this chapter, we tackle in the same process the problems of face detection and gender classification, where the faces present a wide range of the intra-class appearance are taken from arbitrary viewpoints. We try to develop complete probabilistic model to represent and learn appearance of facial objects in both shape and geometry with respect to a landmark in the image, and then to be able to predict presence and position of the appearance of the studied object class in new scene. After have predicted the facial appearance and the geometry of invariants, geometric hierarchical clustering combines different prediction of positions of face invariant. Then, the algorithm of cluster selection with a best appearance localizes faces in the image. Using a probabilistic classification, each facial feature retained in the detection step will be weighted by a probability to be male or female. This set of features contributes to determine the gender associated to a detected face. This model has a good performance in presence of viewpoint changes and a large appearance variability of faces.

DOI: 10.4018/978-1-5225-2848-7.ch009

INTRODUCTION

The face image analysis has become a field of study in the world. One of the most common visual trait classification task is to determine the gender from images of face. We try to treat the face detection and gender classification simultaneously. Several models exist which perform detection with high accuracy, but not across all views of face.

Local Haar wavelets can be computed very efficiently and is proved useful for frontal face detection using boosted classifiers (Viola & Jones, 2001). The integral image approach is less effective in coping with arbitrary viewpoints. It needs a series of classifiers or a set of detectors to model the in-plane deformation parameters such as the image scale and orientation and the out-of-plane viewpoint changes (Toews & Arbel, 2006).

Contrary to global features, the local feature approaches give robust invariance to illumination, viewpoint and orientation changes. Thus, they offer opportunity for further performances to detect faces and to classify their gender.

Local invariant features (Lowe, 2004; Kadir & Brady, 2001; Mikolajczyk & Schmid, 2004; Yu & Morel, 2009; Herbert, Tinnr, & Gool, 2006) are widely used in object recognition, stitching images in panorama and scene reconstruction, etc. (Hartley & Zisserman, 2000; Lowe, 1999; Schmid & Mohr, 1997; Mikolajczyk & Schmid, 2002; Tuytelaars & Van Gool, 2000; Fergus, Perona, & Zisserman, 2003). They have a high capability to capture appearance information. They allow to select the sparse appearance patches of objects, as faces. Thus, it becomes possible to model the faces and to learn their appearance variability through a model that embeds features and that presents invariant properties.

Using the co-occurrence statistics of features with interest trait, we train a classifier to recognize the gender of faces in terms of visual traits. The gender of a face can be inferred from a collection of image features which define the traits of gender.

The human vision uses a wide range of visual traits to describe objects in images. In general, databases used for learning of the appearance of an object class with low supervision contain many images but small numbers of instances of a single object of class (Toews & Arbel, 2009). These databases focus on labeling the object identity and its location but provide little information regarding further traits, and also the number of images may be insufficient for learning traits. In the case of the face class, it is a limit to use these databases for learning and classifying traits through many different instances of face class. In the interest of comparison, most approaches train and test on the FERET database (Color FERET Face Database, 2009), which contains detailed labels for visual traits such as sex and age.

The model of face class appearance is based on learning of the relationship between the appearance of facial patches and the geometry of face invariant, denoted FI. The visual facial features that have contributed to infer face are then used to recognize its gender. The FI is a common geometric landmark to all face features; it connects them across all different viewpoints. The extraction of such invariants directly from an image is complex (Burns, Weiss, & Riseman, 1993). We have boosted this geometric structure by a probabilistic model in order to capture the multimodal nature of face and to learn the geometric transformations that link facial appearance to instances of FI through images.

The face detection process uses a probabilistic model and the geometric transformations to infer a face instance in the form of a FI in a new image even in the presence of changes in illumination and head pose, see Figure 1. A clustering of invariants is performed to correct the geometric error and efficiently locate the face appearance. The proposed clustering algorithm, based on the features appearance and using the Ward criterion, presents simplicity, a low cost, and an accurate localization. Then, a cluster is selected

197

Figure 1. Face labeled by face invariant FI (yellow arrow). FI is learned from faces images (around the circle) in the database. The red arrows draw the geometric transforms and appearance similarity between features in the request image and the facial features of the model

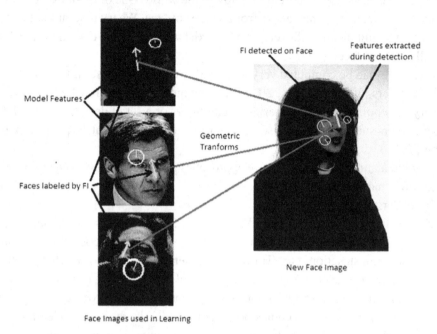

which corresponds to a set of visual traits that represent the best facial appearance. The features that have not contributed to detect the face will be discarded; they contain little or no information regarding facial appearance. The remaining facial features fed the probabilistic classifier to decide the gender of face. The gender of each feature is determined by computing its gender appearance probability; this allows to recognize with accuracy the gender of each facial appearance occurrence. The expected features with high gender likelihood affect the final result of gender classification of face.

The facial model needs a low degree of supervision, as learning on some hundreds of images, and can accept complex assumptions on face parameters, e.g., rich multimodality of faces. It is able to learn, detect the multimodal facial appearance (i.e. sunglasses, expression, wink), and recognize the gender of faces even when a partial occlusion occurs in significantly cluttered images.

Experimentation proves that the entire model learned from a few images is simultaneously efficient to detect faces and correctly classify their gender, all in the presence of viewpoint changes and large intra-class variability (i.e. ethnicity, beard, etc.).

RELATED WORKS

Objects Appearance Modeling

The objects appearance modeling remains an active area of research (Fergus, Perona, & Zisserman, 2003; Agarwal, Awan, & Roth, 2004; Bart, Byvatov, & Ullman, 2004; Dorko & Schmid, 2003; Fei-Fei, Fergus,

& Perona, 2003) due to the difficulty to learn a wide range of appearance variability characterizing the natural objects. Many approaches with models of specific object appearance have been learned from a single image (Lowe, 2001; Moreels, Maire, & Perona, 2004; Rothganger, Lazebnik, Schmid, & Ponce, 2003; Torralba, Murphy, & Freeman, 2004) and used for object detection and recognition.

A popular paradigm tries to solve the problem by modeling the objects as a collection of local features (Ullman, Vidal-Naquet, & Sali, 2002; Lowe, 1999; Weber, Welling, & Perona, 2000; Burl, Weber, & Perona, 1998; Pope, & Lowe, 2000). The difficulty lies in learning the model parameters. It needs to explore a huge space to determine the visual traits best suited to the recognition and learn the wide intra-class variability and all possible viewpoints of the face. Most approaches select regions of interest of an object and represent the object by only these descriptions of local regions. For face classification purpose, from a collection of features that are presumably appreciated as facial appearance, the task is then to model and learn simultaneously face appearance, spatial relations, and co-occurrence held by these visual features (Helmer & Lowe, 2004). Toews et al. (Toews & Arbel, 2006) used an object class invariant which combines geometry and appearance of the object class through a probabilistic learning to detect object instances on new images. In (Taffar, Miguet, & Benmohammed, 2012), the facial appearance has been described by a face model which has a great capability to capture the facial appearance variability and to localize face with accuracy, such approach is robust to clutter, occlusion, and affine transformations in image.

Gender Classification

In face image analysis, determining gender of face using the facial trait classification is still a challenge task. The greater part of publications of gender classification highlights the state-of-art on the general trait classification. The trait learning is done by using the spatially global feature representations such as templates (Kim, Kim, Ghahramani, & Bang, 2006), principal components (Moghaddam & Yang, 2002), independent components (Jain, Huang, & Fang, 2005), or image intensities directly (Baluja, & Rowley, 2007). While most approaches utilize intensity data, 3D information may also improve the sex classification (O'Toole, Vetter, Troje, & Bulthoff, 1997). In this context, many works have explored the capacity of different machines learning such as neural networks (Gutta, Wechsler, & Phillips, 1998), SVMs (Moghaddam & Yang, 2002), and boosted classifiers (Baluja, & Rowley, 2007). In the last decade, trait classification based on local features has emerged, such as those using local regions (BenAbdelkader & Griffin, 2005) or Haar wavelets (Shakhnarovich, Viola, & Moghaddam, 2002).

The majority of approaches of gender classification are based totally on single viewpoints, i.e., frontal faces (Makinen & Raisamo, 2008). They assume that, prior to classification, some environment constraint such as background distraction must be respected, and faces or facial features precisely localized. They reported low error rates and used different images of the same person in both classifiers training and testing (Yang, Li, & Ai, 2006). As facial features arising from different frontal images of the same person are highly correlated, one cannot know whether the low classification error reported reflects the ability of the classifier to generalize to new faces unseen or never before seen or simply a classification by recognition.

In the literature, few works have addressed gender classification of faces from an arbitrary viewpoint or in the presence of partial occlusion. In (Toews & Arbel, 2009), the approach is multi-viewpoint, invariant to rotation, but the mean error rate reported increases when the angle pose of face changes in the interval varying from 22 degrees to profile position. It has also reported that the combination of OCI model (Toews & Arbel, 2006) with a Bayesian classifier gives the best results with a classification error rate of about 16.3%. In (Shakhnarovich, Viola, & Moghaddam, 2002), the authors proposed an approach for a general trait classification based on image features, which can be localized in the presence of partial occlusion, and using the boosted classifiers of Haar wavelet features (Viola & Jones, 2001). The approach is single viewpoint (frontal faces), intolerant to rotation, and the reported error rate of 0.21 reflects the increased difficulty of the task to combine views. The results obtained are based on proprietary training and testing, on the databases in which the faces with ambiguous gender or the in-plane orientations greater than 30 degrees are manually removed, as such a direct comparison cannot be made with our approach.

Motivation

The facial appearance modeling is always an active research area due to the complexity to capture the large variability of appearance characterizing the face class. A drawback of appearance approaches based on global features is that they attempt to infer or detect a stable 2D configuration of visual features in the plan, thus they are inherently single-viewpoint. To extend these models to account for changes in viewpoint, we will require more detectors at different viewpoints/poses (Mikolajczyk, Schmid, & Zisserman, 2004), which complicates the model size, adding learning and fitting (Zhang & Koch, 2012).

The appearance models based on local invariant features can be efficiently learned and used to detect face instances in the images which present severe geometric deformations and illumination changes.

Excepted integral image (Shakhnarovich, Viola, & Moghaddam, 2002), most approaches try to remove background clutter (e.g., by applying the predefined facial masks) to localize precisely facial features and faces (e.g., manually specifying the eye locations, frontal alignment of face) prior to classify faces. These approaches offer small interest regarding classification performance and accuracy. This performance drops fast when localization of faces and facial features needed for classification is nontrivial due to the large variability of the face shape, the wide range of illumination, and pose changes (Toews & Arbel, 2009). The purpose of this work is to overcome the limits reached by the local regions (Abdelkader & Griffin, 2005) and Haar wavelets (Yang, Li, & Ai, 2006) approaches and address the problem of gender classification of faces from arbitrary viewpoints or in the possible presence of partial occlusion.

In object recognition tasks based on local visual traits, some approaches extract image region descriptors to perform image matching in order to detect and recognize objects in the scene. These image patches capture well the appearance of objects but less with rich multimodal nature of faces (e.g., expression, ethnicity, etc.). In (Taffar, Miguet, & Benmohammed, 2012), a face model has been used to overcome the difficulty of the facial description against the appearance variability when the changes occur in viewpoints and/or illuminations. Furthermore, using features matching based on a metric of appearance similarity involves major difficulties in face detection and gender classification. It is necessary to enhance the representation of local appearance by a model that learns the geometric relations that connect local features, and links them to the appearance in a high-level representation. Because it is not feasible to learn unexpected variability of all faces, the idea is to improve the learning by a convenient probabilistic model for the face class. Thus, the face model based on a probabilistic matching, on few facial features detected, should be computationally efficient and sufficiently discriminating to localize face with success and recognize its gender.

Facial Appearance Modeling

We adapt a model of face appearance (Taffar, Miguet, & Benmohammed, 2012) and we expand a probabilistic formulation based on facial traits to simultaneously address the face detection and gender classification in order to make them reliable to changes of face viewpoints. The new model is a montage of elements belonging to both appearance-based description techniques (Lindeberg, 1998; Mikolajczyk & Schmid, 2002; Harris & Stephens, 1988) and approaches of learning for object recognition (Moreels, Maire, & Perona, 2004). Conceptually such model allows representing a large variability of face appearance with high tolerance to viewpoint changes. The new point reported by the proposed model is that it selects the facial features using a probabilistic matching of appearance and it uses the information relating the geometry of features for more accurate face localization. Then, compute the gender appearance probability of each facial feature allows to determine the sex of face with best prediction.

Invariant Feature Model

The facial feature model is based on the local scale-invariant feature (Lowe, 2004; Yu, & Morel, 2009) description which has mainly both geometric and appearance components. The model of feature denoted $f : \left\{ f_i^b, f_i^g, f_i^a, f_i^s \right\}$, representing the presence, geometry, appearance and sex of a facial feature related to the face class. Thus, the value of a facial feature includes four measures:

- Binary flag f_i^b corresponding to the presence of feature on face, e.g., $f_i^{b=1}$ for facial trait
- 3-parameter geometric structure f_i^g, representing the geometry of a feature. The geometric parameters consist of location (x,y), scale σ, and direction θ of feature, denoted $g = \left\{ (x,y), \sigma, \theta \right\}$
- Vector f_i^a describing the image appearance at f_i^g, it is a 128-value vector, corresponding to bins of oriented gradients histogram of image first derivatives quantized into 8x4x4=128 bins over orientation and (x, y) position
- Binary parameter f_i^s corresponding to sex of feature (e.g., $s = 1$ for male and $s = 0$ for female).

The parameter f_i^b is used to learn and distinguish facial features to those belonging to background (e.g., b=0). Only one occurrence of $f_i^{b=1}$ may be sufficient to predict the position of the invariant in the image.

The face is represented by a set of features and the spatial relations that link these features. The idea is to combine geometry and appearance of different descriptors in order to localize the face and to recognize its gender with only occurrence of few facial feature instances in new image.

One invariant descriptor does not characterize the same local region on different faces (e.g., left eye, nose, or cheeks …) but rather it describes the same facial appearance anywhere on faces.

Face Invariant Model

The face invariant model (Taffar, Miguet, & Benmohammed, 2012), noted FI, is a geometric landmark. It has a high capability to infer the complex multimodality of the facial appearance in the presence of illumination and viewpoint changes. The face invariant (FI) consists of two measures:

- A binary flag b relates to the presence of the invariant within image
- A 3-parameter vector $g = \{(x,y), \sigma, \theta\}$, including location, scale, and angle, represents the invariant geometry in the image

An instance of FI is denoted as $inv : \{inv^b, inv^g\}$, it does not contain appearance information. Schematically it is a line segment from nose tip to forehead, as in Figure 2. An invariant arrow associated to a face illustrates the position, size, and direction in terms of location, scale, and orientation of face. In an image, all features are geometrically relating to the FI by a geometric transformation. This transformation links the appearance component of features to the geometry with respect to invariant through a probabilistic model. Any facial feature is able to infer the location of inv, anywhere in the image. We learned the model and used it to detect face instances then to classify their gender from still images.

The geometric relationship between a feature model and FI is defined by the ratio of scales, difference of angles, and pixels Euclidean distance between positions. The leaning model embeds this geometric relationship. Some spatial constraints and of appearance enhance the performances of detection and classification. A 3-parameter geometric thresholding which includes scale, angle, and length allows to bound the variability due to the illumination and viewpoint changes, to image distortion, and to morphologic deformations of face.

PROBABILISTIC FORMULATION

Facial Localization

The model learning of FI is based on the following assumptions,

Figure 2. Face labeled by face invariant FI (yellow arrow). FI, as geometric landmark, links local facial features (red circles), among them and to FI, through geometric transforms (gray arrows). The visual traits hold the facial appearance and its variability. When appearance similarity occurs between the features of a test image and the facial features of the probabilistic model, the latter, combining the features appearance to geometry of FI, can predict a FI representing a face in new image

Face invariant (FI) denoted: *inv*

Invariant Feature Model
(Local Scale-Invariant Feature)

Geometric Tranformation
(from feature to invariant)

- f_i^b, f_i^a, and f_i^s are statistically independent of f_i^g given inv
- f_i^g is statistically dependent of inv^g given f^b and inv^b
- f^a and f^s are statistically dependent given f^b
- $\left(f^a, f^s\right)$ and inv are statistically independent given f^b

The learning consists to determine the likelihood term $p\left(f_j \mid inv\right)$, e.g., $p\left(f_j \mid inv\right) = p\left(f_j \mid inv^b, \; inv^g\right)$, expressed as:

$$p\left(f_j \mid inv\right) = p\left(f_j^b, f_j^g, f_j^a, f_j^s \mid inv\right) = p\left(f_j^b, f_j^a, f_j^s \mid inv\right) p\left(f_j^g \mid inv\right)$$
$$= p\left(f_j^a, f_j^s \mid f_j^b\right) p\left(f_j^b \mid inv^b\right) p\left(f_j^g \mid inv^b, inv^g\right)$$

In detection, given a set of *n* image features $\left\{f_i\right\}$ which are conditionally independent given $\left\{inv_i\right\}$, we individually quantified the probability of each inv_i given an image feature f_i by using Bayes rule. We formulated the expression as:

$$p\left(inv_i \mid f_j\right) = \frac{p\left(inv_i\right) p\left(f_i \mid inv_i\right)}{p\left(f_j\right)}$$

where $p\left(inv_i\right)$ and $p\left(f_i\right)$ are a prior over invariant (geometry and occurrence) and facial feature respectively, and $p\left(f_i \mid inv_i\right)$ is the likelihood of f_i given inv_i. The meaning of $p\left(inv_i \mid f_j\right)$ can be understudied as

$$p\left(inv_i \mid f_j\right) = p\left(inv^b, inv^g \mid f_j^b, f_j^g, f_j^a, f_j^s\right)$$
$$= p\left(f_j^b \mid f_j^a\right) p\left(inv^b \mid f_j^b\right) p\left(inv^g \mid inv^b, f_j^g, f_j^b\right)$$

where $p\left(f_j^b \mid f_j^a\right)$ is the estimation likelihood of feature presence f_j^b given its localized appearance evaluated as facial, the likelihood term $p\left(inv^b \mid f_j^b\right)$ is the probability of invariant presence inv^b given feature presence, and $p\left(inv^g \mid inv^b, f_j^g, f_j^b\right)$ is the likelihood over the invariant geometry given the extracted feature geometry.

1.   Appearance

The appearance of a visual image feature f_j is evaluated according to the density of the model feature f_i. Each f_i is modeled by a Gaussian with a mean μ_i^a and covariance $\sum_i^a$. Thus, appearance likelihood $p\left(f_i^a \mid f_i^b\right)$ is represented as a Gaussian distribution in the appearance space. Furthermore, the appearance agreement of feature pairs $\left(f_i \mid f_j\right)$ can be evaluated by setting parameters $\mu_i^a, \sum_i^a$ to

maximize likelihood of $p\left(f_i^{b=1} \mid inv^{b=1}\right)$ and then the likelihood ratio $r\left(f_i \mid inv\right)^b = \dfrac{p\left(f_i^{b=1} \mid inv^{b=1}\right)}{p\left(f_i^{b=1} \mid inv^{b=0}\right)}$.

2.   Presence

The probability $p\left(f_i^{b=1} \mid inv^{b=1}\right)$ of occurrence of a model feature given the hypothesis of occurrence of the invariant is represented as a discrete multinomial distribution with event count parameters $\pi_i = \left\{\pi_i^1, \ldots, \pi_i^4\right\}$. The $p\left(f_i^{b=1} \mid inv^b\right)$ is poorly sample. In learning, to avoid feature redundancy, f_i which have no mutual information with other features $\left\{f_j\right\}$, given geometry of inv, are retained.

3.   Geometry

During learning, the geometric likelihood $p\left(f_i^g \mid inv^b, inv^g\right)$ models the geometric error of a 3-parameter linear transform from feature to invariant. It is represented as a Gaussian distribution with mean and covariance parameters μ_i^g, Σ_i^g. This is a manner to evaluate the spatial agreement of feature pairs $\left(f_i \mid f_j\right)$ with respect to (*wrt*) invariant geometry inv^g. The geometric error is characterized in a scale-invariant space by normalizing translation to the scale of invariant.

Gender of Facial Appearance

Using the co-occurrence statistics of features with a trait of interest, we train a classifier via a supervised learning. The model learning of gender classifier is based on assumption that is f^a and f^s are statistically dependent given $f^{b=1}$. The presence occurrence of facial feature f_i is noted $t_i = f_i^{b=1}$, this means that the event of presence of the face invariant $inv^{b=1}$ occurs. Moreover, we use a discrete random variable f_i^s over 2 trait values to predict the gender of feature, where s is sex in $\left\{s_1 = 0, \ s_2 = 1\right\}$, e.g., $f_i^{s=0}$ for female.

The gender of a facial feature f_i is evaluated according to the density of its appearance f_i^a. Given hypothesis of facial appearance occurrence f_i^a, each f_i^s is modeled by a discrete distribution with event count parameters $\pi_i = \left\{\pi_i^1, \ldots, \pi_i^4\right\}$. Thus, gender likelihood $p\left(f_i^s \mid f_i^a\right)$ is represented as a binomial distribution in the gender space. The gender agreement of feature to facial appearance $\left(f_i^s, f_i^a\right)$ can be evaluated by maximizing likelihood $p\left(f_i^s \mid f_i^a, f_i^{b=1}\right)$, then the likelihood ratio $\dfrac{p\left(f_i^s \mid f_i^a\right)}{p(f_i^{\neg s} \mid f_i^a)}$ determines the gender of f_i.

For a training image, where N facial features t_i are conditionally independent given characteristic f^s, the model learning involves estimating, for each t_i, the conditional probability $p\left(t_i \mid f_i^{s_j}\right)$ formulated as

$$p\left(t_i \mid f_i^{s_j}\right) = \frac{p\left(t_i\right) p\left(f_i^{s_j} \mid t_i\right)}{p\left(f_i^{s_j}\right)} = \frac{p\left(t_i\right)}{p\left(f_i^{s_j}\right)} p\left(f_i^{s_j} \mid t_i\right)$$

For recognition of sex of face, under the assumption that the facial features t_i are conditionally independent given f^s, an EM (Expectation-Maximization) classifier $\varphi\left(f^s\right) = \varphi\left(\{f_i^s\}\right)$ establishes the trait classification given N image feature occurrences $\{t_i\}$, that can be expressed as

$$\varphi\left(f^s\right) = \varphi\left(f_i^{s_j}\right) = \frac{p\left(f^{s_j} \mid \{t_i\}\right)}{p\left(f^{\neg s_j} \mid \{t_i\}\right)} = \frac{p\left(f^{s_j}\right)}{p\left(f^{\neg s_j}\right)} \prod_i^N \frac{p\left(t_i \mid f_i^{s_j}\right)}{p\left(t_i \mid f_i^{\neg s_j}\right)}$$

The terms $\dfrac{p\left(f^{s_j}\right)}{p\left(f^{\neg s_j}\right)}$ and $\dfrac{p\left(t_i \mid f_i^{s_j}\right)}{p\left(t_i \mid f_i^{\neg s_j}\right)}$ are estimated during learning.

An optimal EM classification is to choose trait value f^{s^*} maximizing $\varphi\left(f^s\right)$

$$f^{s^*} = argmax_{f^s} \left\{\varphi\left(f^s\right)\right\}$$

LEARNING PROCESS

Learning to Detect

For training process, we consider a set of face images containing feature observations $\left\{\left(f_i^a, f_i^g\right)\right\}$ and a manually labeled hypothesis inv^g. The advantage of model is that it learns with weak supervision, only some hundreds of images are sufficient to provide the high performances. It requires simplified assumptions, such as a small number of features of multimodal appearance (i.e., sunglasses, sex) and different face viewpoint data.

- Modeling facial appearance is achieved by labeling the face by an invariant inv^g, and getting its values of geometric 3-parameters. Thus, it is sufficient to model faces over a 180 degrees range of viewpoint.
- Extract a set of visuals traits, and efficiently choice a small set of features $\{f_i\}$ to increase their independence and obtain a wide range of representation of geometry and appearance.
- These traits must be geometrically informative regarding to *inv*, asymmetric on face relating to invariant landmark to avoid geometric redundancy, and non-redundant in terms of appearance.
- All the coordinates of features in the same image are brought back to the referential of the invariant presents on the face. Thus, it becomes easy to deduce the geometric transformation that link features $\{f_i^g\}$ to invariant inv^g, (e.g., $F\left(\{f_i^g\}\right) = inv^g$), and to compute the invariant location on the test image with high accuracy.

In probability terms, learning is a model parameters estimation of a set of features $\left(\left\{ f_i^a, f_i^g \right\}, \; inv^g \right)$ related to the geometry of *inv* and an evaluation of the missing geometric data $\left\{ \left(f_i^g, inv^g \right), \; \left(f_i^b, inv^b \right) \right\}$ under presence hypothesis. The construction of probabilistic model consists to:

1. Collects a set of invariant samples $\left\{ inv^b \right\}$ to compute the geometric likelihood $p\left(f_i^g \mid inv^b, inv^g \right)$, each feature has a Gaussian density with a mean μ_i^g and covariance matrix Σ_i^g.

2. Generates trait samples $\left\{ f_i^b \right\}$ to calculate appearance likelihood $p\left(f_i^a \mid f_i^b \right)$. By evaluating the appearance agreement of features, reject features with no facial appearance (e.g., $f_i^{b=0}$). Ideally, it is to achieve a maximum likelihood ratio $r\left(f_i, inv \right)^b$. As features with low $r\left(f_i, inv \right)^b$ provide modest information about *inv*, they are not taken to learn the model parameters.

Even after learning, dependencies exist between database features which slightly affect the predicted geometric values of invariants in Eq. (2). These dependencies are related to spatial overlap of features f_i with respect to their respective inv_i. A good estimation of the joint probability should take account of this assumption.

Learning to Gender Classify

The idea is to detect the facial traits before they should be used to classify the gender of face in natural cluttered image. These tasks are embedded within a general model of facial appearance derived from local invariant features captured from arbitrary viewpoints and with a possible presence of partial occlusion. We consider a set of facial visual traits $\left\{ \left(f_i^a, f_i^s \right) \right\}$.

The training process consists to estimate $\dfrac{p\left(f^{s_j} \right)}{p\left(f^{\neg s_j} \right)}$ and $\dfrac{p\left(f_i^a \mid f_i^{s_j} \right)}{p\left(f_i^a \mid f_i^{\neg s_j} \right)}$ in Eq. (5). Each learned feature bears information regarding sex. Also, many features, although very common in the face class, are uninformative regarding sex. Features with high likelihood ratios are important to classification and are highly informative with respect to a particular trait value $f_i^{s_j}$, as illustrated in Figure 3.

We use these likelihood ratios to quantify the relationship between the learned features and the face traits in new image to decide their gender, as in Figure 4. The proportion of male and female features in the learning model is a male:female ratio of approximately 3:2. A feature is claimed as strongly male if its likelihood of co-occurring with the male sex in training images is greater than 2/3 to be female and inversely. A given face instance consists of a set of local features in which a subset is reflective of either sex. It is this subset which determines the gender of face.

- The term $\dfrac{p(t_i \mid f_i^{s_j})}{p(t_i \mid f_i^{\neg s_j})}$ expresses the likelihood ratio of trait value presence of gender s_j versus absence $\neg s_j$ coinciding with observed feature t_i

Figure 3. Different instances of the same local feature bearing gender information (white circles), from data set of features where the male:female ratio is approximately 3:2. The forehead feature shown in (a) occurs in 30 males and three females and is indicative of male trait. The cheek feature in (b) occurs in zero males and eight females and is indicative of female trait. The nasal feature in (c) occurs in 16 males and 10 females and bears no or weak information regarding sex

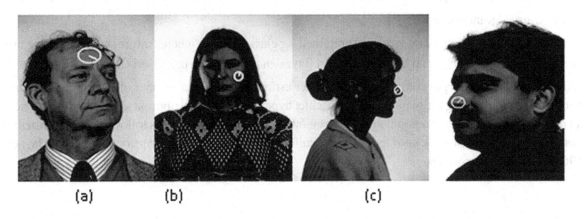

Figure 4. Sex classification of faces, from sex of the local visuals traits (colored circles), is based on probabilistic matching. Of 21 model features detected in (a), 16 are strongly male and one is strongly female, suggesting a male face. Of 15 features detected in (b), 9 are female and two are male, suggesting a female face. Many features, common to two sexes, have low importance for classification

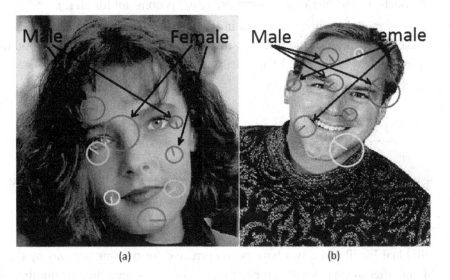

Using a supervised learning, the likelihood ratio estimation is based on observed occurrences of model features t_i and trait labels $f_i^{s_j}$ for each image. Discrete class-conditional likelihoods $p\left(t_i \mid f_i^{s_j}\right)$ can be represented as binomial distributions, parameterized by event counts (Jordan, 1999). During training, $p\left(t_i \mid f_i^{s_j}\right)$ is estimated using the definition of conditional probability

$$p\left(t_i \mid f_i^{sj}\right) = \frac{p\left(t_i, f_i^{sj}\right)}{p\left(f_i^{sj}\right)}$$

The term $p\left(f_i^{sj}\right)$ is a prior over sex; it corrects bias (Toews & Arbel, 2009). $p\left(t_i, f_i^{sj}\right)$ is the probability of observed joint events $\left(t_i, f_i^{sj}\right)$.

The model consists of many local traits retained for classification, where feature occurrences are rare events. The term $p\left(t_i, f_i^{sj}\right)$ can be estimated via Bayesian maximum a posteriori (MAP) which is stable and tend toward (converge) conservative parameter estimates while the number of data samples is low, but involves regularizing estimates using a Dirichlet hyperparameter distribution (Jordan, 1999). Dirichlet regularization involves prepopulating event count parameters with samples following a prior distribution. Where no relevant prior knowledge exists, uniform or maximum entropy prior can be used (Jaynes, 1968). The estimator we use is

$$p(t_i \mid f_i^{sj}) \approx \frac{n_{i,j}}{p(f_i^{sj})} + d_{i,j}$$

where $n_{i,j}$ is the number of occurrence of the joint event $\left(t_i, f_i^{sj}\right)$, e.g., $n_{i,0}$ for $\left(t_i, f_i^{sj=0}\right)$, $p\left(f_i^{sj}\right)$ is the frequency of trait value f_i^{sj} in the training data, and $d_{i,j}$ is the Dirichlet regularization parameter used to populate event counts. In the case of a uniform prior, $d_{i,j}$ is constant for all i, j.

The occurrences of model features identified in training images along with FERET sex labels are used to estimate likelihood ratios of the EM classifier of traits. In estimating likelihood ratios via Eq. (11), we used an empirically determined Dirichlet regularization parameter of $d_{i,j} = 2$, which maximizes training set classification performance.

- A prior ratio $\dfrac{p\left(f^{sj}\right)}{p\left(f^{\neg sj}\right)}$ of trait value presence s_j versus absence $\neg s_j$ (e.g., male versus not male),

  controlling classifier bias toward different trait values. We estimate the equivalent likelihood ratios
  $log \dfrac{p\left(f^{sj}\right)}{p\left(f^{\neg sj}\right)}$.

Although individual likelihood ratios have been corrected for training set bias by the estimator in Eq.(11), the EM classifier in Eq.(7) will still exhibit bias due to the fact that the number of features f_i and their corresponding likelihood ratios associated with different traits are often unequal. To reduce bias in Eq.(7), the proportionality constant in Eq.(11) can be obtained by normalizing over values of f_i, but not required for likelihood ratios.

Given a set of q features to classify, $log\ \varphi\left(s\right)$ will be higher a priori for trait values associated with a larger number of features or with features bearing higher likelihood ratios.

This bias can be controlled by setting $log\dfrac{p\left(f^{s_j}\right)}{p\left(f^{\neg s_j}\right)}$ for each trait value s_j such that the expected value

of $log\ \varphi\left(f^{s_j}\right)$ based on a set of q features is zero.

$$E\left[log\ \varphi\left(f^{s_j}\right)\right] = E\left[log\left(\frac{p\left(f^{s_j}\right)}{p\left(f^{\neg s_j}\right)}\right) + \sum_i^q log\left(\frac{p\left(t_i\mid f_i^{s_j}\right)}{p\left(t_i\mid f_i^{\neg s_j}\right)}\right)\right] = 0$$

and thus,

$$log\frac{p\left(f^{s_j}\right)}{p\left(f^{\neg s_j}\right)} = -E\left[\sum_i^q log\frac{p\left(t_i\mid f_i^{s_j}\right)}{p\left(t_i\mid f_i^{\neg s_j}\right)}\right] = -qE\left[log\left(\frac{p\left(t_i\mid f_i^{s_j}\right)}{p\left(t_i\mid f_i^{\neg s_j}\right)}\right)\right]$$

where the expectation on the right-hand side of Eq. (10) is taken with respect to the conditional probability of t_i given invariant occurrence $inv^{b=1}$:

$$E\left[log\frac{p\left(t_i\mid f_i^{s_j}\right)}{p\left(t_i\mid f_i^{\neg s_j}\right)}\right] = \sum_i p\left(t_i\mid f_i^a, inv^{b=1}\right) log\frac{p\left(t_i\mid f^{s_j}\right)}{p\left(t_i\mid f^{\neg s_j}\right)}$$

Thus, term $log\dfrac{p\left(f^{s_j}\right)}{p\left(f^{\neg s_j}\right)}$ is the product of the expected likelihood ratio for trait s_j calculated during

training from Eq. (11), and the number of facial features q of detected face retained for classification.

Localization Process

Viewpoint invariant face localization is performed by identifying the FI instances in each of the testing images. The learning model captures the facial appearance $\left\{f_i^a\right\}$ and the geometric transformation that binds features $\left\{f_i^g\right\}$ to invariant inv^g. It predicts with high accuracy the invariant location in the test image. Thus, invariant detection is achieved in two steps appearance selection and geometric localization.

Appearance Classification

Appearance Prediction

The EM prediction allows to decide one by one if the features are face or not. The idea is to find a cluster of features that have appearance agreement with a face. This set of data observations $\left\{f_i^{b=1}\right\}$ is formed from features that agree on facial appearance by estimating appearance likelihood $p\left(f_i^a\mid f_i^b\right)$ results of a true face or background. The image features are submitted to appearance classifier and those with high facial appearance probability $p\left(f_i^a \mid f_i^{b=1}\right)$, e.g., $p\left(f_i^a \mid f_i^{b=1}\right) > p\left(f_i^a \mid f_i^{b=0}\right)$, are selected which represent a strong probability of the facial presence, as shown in Figure 5.

The best facial appearance localization is performed by maximizing the Bayes decision ratio $\dfrac{p\left(f_i^a \mid f_i^{b=1}\right)}{p\left(f_i^a \mid f_i^{b=0}\right)}$ during learning. Also, features with high agreement to facial appearance $p\left(f_i^a \mid f_j^a\right)$ in the learning model are evaluated; they correspond to a clustering of visual traits with facial appearance.

Appearance Vote

We refine the set of visual traits because the results of EM classification sometimes conserve few further cluttered features due to the nature of appearance descriptor.

The set of features formed is submitted to a voting algorithm based on the appearance matching in the learning model. This probabilistic matching allows to decide for each feature if it is facial or not. It presents a high cost computation but also high accuracy.

For each image feature f_i that match in the model, its facial (resp. background) appearance probability is computed. This probability is based on the value of the appearance distance from f_i to model trait f_j, noted $d\left(f_i, f_j^{b=1}\right)$ (resp., $d\left(f_i, f_k^{b=0}\right)$), where f_j and f_k are respectively the model features in the facial and background appearance spaces, and b is the facial presence parameter, e.g., $b=0$ for face absence. The similitude used to fit the descriptors is defined in term of Mahalanobis distance.

When f_i match, it is voted that is closest and agrees to the facial (resp. background) appearance model relatively to an appearance threshold Γ^a. Thus, f_i is kept and its amount of vote as face $v_i^{b=1}$ (resp. as clutter $v_i^{b=0}$) is increased. Finally, each f_i is weighted by the vote values and the best minimal distances of facial and background appearance.

Figure 5. Features extracted 22 on FERET image in the center from original image on the left. There are 11 remain traits in the right image classified as facial by an EM classification

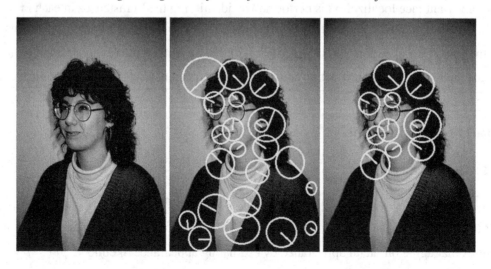

The face appearance probability of f_i, denoted $p\left(f_i \mid f_j^{b=1}\right)$, is calculated as follow:

$$p\left(f_i \mid f_j^{b=1}\right) = \frac{d\left(f_i, f_k^{b=0}\right)}{d\left(f_i, f_j^{b=1}\right) + d\left(f_i, f_k^{b=0}\right)}$$

Thus, the feature is declared to belong to face if $p\left(f_i \mid f_j^{b=1}\right) > p\left(f_i \mid f_k^{b=0}\right)$.

This has an aim to reject features which have weak resemblance to a face appearance and retain only these with a high facial appearance probability. They procure strong invariance to lighting and viewpoint variations, see Figure 5 where facial appearance features are selected with accuracy and where almost all features are located on the face.

The features with high facial probability are kept to participate to the prediction of the position of the face invariant. They are enough discriminative to easily predict the facial presence.

Finally, the face appearance probability $p\left(\{f_i\} \mid f^{b=1}\right)$ of all image features is computed as follow:

$$p\left(\{f_i\} \mid f^{b=1}\right) = \frac{\prod_{i=1}^{n} v_i^{b=1} p\left(f_i \mid f^{b=1}\right)}{\prod_{i=1}^{n} v_i^{b=1} p\left(f_i \mid f^{b=1}\right) + \prod_{i=1}^{n} v_i^{b=0} p\left(f_i \mid f^{b=0}\right)}$$

Decide the presence of face is resolute if $p\left(\{f_i\} \mid f^{b=1}\right) > p\left(\{f_i\} \mid f^{b=0}\right)$.

Geometric Localization

Invariants Prediction

The invariant localization is performed by evaluating hypothesis whether each voted image feature results independently to a true invariant $inv = \left\{inv^g, inv^{b=1}\right\}$ or negative sample (e.g., $inv = \left\{inv^g, inv^{b=0}\right\}$).

The idea is to generate an invariant for each retained facial feature that is geometrically present on face, e.g., $p\left(inv^{b=1} \mid f_i^{b=1}\right) > p\left(inv^{b=0} \mid f_i^{b=1}\right)$.

For each facial feature f_i in the test image that probabilistically matches to the best model feature f_j, the corresponding invariant model is expected, e.g., $p\left(inv_i^{b=1} \mid f_i^{b=1} = f_j^{b=1}\right) > p\left(inv_i^{b=0} \mid f_i^{b=1} = f_k^{b=0}\right)$, where f_j and f_k are respectively the features with best matching in the facial and background appearance spaces. Thus, a set of invariant assumptions are engendered, they form the set of predicted invariants, see Figure 6. This probabilistic method allows to obtain different hypothesis on the geometric parameters of invariants with location error relative to $1/\sigma$ (σ is the invariant scale).

Then, each invariant and its corresponding facial trait are maintained by estimating the invariant geometric likelihood to be on face according to the feature geometry, e.g., $p\left(inv_i^g \mid inv_i^{b=1}, f_i^g\right)$.

By combining several hypotheses on the invariants, the location of face can be determined with accuracy, e.g., $p\left(inv^g \mid \left\{inv_i^g, inv_i^{b=1}\right\}\right)$.

For each feature f_i, an invariant inv_i is predicted through Bayes rule as

$$p\left(inv_i \mid f_i\right) = \frac{p\left(inv_i\right)p\left(f_i \mid inv_i\right)}{p\left(f_i\right)}$$

Furthermore, an invariant hypothesis inv_i satisfies the ratio of Bayes rules:

$$\rho\left(inv_i\right) = \frac{p\left(inv_i \mid f_i\right)}{p\left(\neg inv_i \mid f_i\right)} = \frac{p\left(inv_i\right)}{p\left(\neg inv_i\right)} \frac{p\left(f_i \mid inv_i\right)}{p\left(f_i \mid \neg inv_i\right)}$$

$$= \frac{p\left(inv_i{}^g, inv_i{}^{b=1}\right)}{p\left(inv_i{}^g, inv_i{}^{b=0}\right)} \frac{p\left(f_i \mid inv_i{}^g, inv_i{}^{b=1}\right)}{p\left(f_i \mid inv_i{}^g, inv_i{}^{b=0}\right)} > 1$$

The terms $\dfrac{p\left(inv_i\right)}{p\left(\neg inv_i\right)}$ and $\dfrac{p\left(f_i \mid inv_i\right)}{p\left(f_i \mid \neg inv_i\right)}$ are estimated during learning.

In other word, we have individually evaluated hypotheses for which each data observation f_i in new image is or not the result of a true model invariant FI. The image feature f_i for which $\rho\left(inv_i\right) > 1$, one instance inv_i is generated, then its geometry is deduced from the learned invariant of the corresponding model feature that probabilistically matches with f_i. Finally, one or more invariant occurrences can be expected. The ratio $\dfrac{\rho\left(inv_i\right)}{\rho\left(\neg inv_i\right)}$ is an estimation of false detection rate.

Spatial Constraints and Geometric Agreement

Each retained invariant agrees geometrically with the corresponding facial visual trait with respect to (*wrt*) the constraints of learned geometric model. The 3-paramaters geometric threshold Γ^g (containing

Figure 6. Face invariants prediction. The bottom line images show the predicted invariants for the corresponding features in the top line images

position $\Gamma^{g:(x,\,y)}$, scale $\Gamma^{g:\sigma}$, and orientation $\Gamma^{g:\theta}$) is used to check the spatial configuration of each engendered invariant to its respective image feature that holds a facial presence, as show in Figure 7.

We identified a set of features $\left\{f_i^g\right\}$ that produce similar hypotheses $\left\{inv_i^g\right\}$. An optimization can be reached as $inv = \underset{inv_i^g}{argmax}\left\{\rho\left(inv_i\right)\right\}$, this allows to avoid performing search over all combinations of one-to-one pairings from model features to observed data, or to no observation at all (in which case $\dfrac{p\left(f_i\mid inv\right)}{p\left(f_i\mid\neg inv\right)}\simeq 1$).

After have checking the geometric agreement, we use a metric (Taffar & Benmohammed, 2011) that allows us to compute the distance of each invariant to its respective image feature. By taking into account of the facial symmetry, and regarding to the geometric position of the facial trait, this distance must agree to a geometric threshold relatively to the learning model. Thus, the geometric clustering of invariants can be doing.

Invariants Clustering

The idea is to perform the geometric hierarchical clustering to all predicted invariants on image, see Figure 8. The ascendant clustering algorithm of invariants based on minimum linkage (Ward) criteria uses a distance between invariant vectors (Taffar & Benmohammed, 2011) defined below. The Ward criterion increases the inter-class inertia and thus in variance for the cluster being merged. Thus, one or more clusters of invariants are formed. Each cluster has one or more invariants instances represented by their geometric parameters. The invariants not clustered are rejected with their respective image features. Each remaining cluster is a potential presence of face. Thereafter, we will see that the algorithm of best cluster based on the appearance of facial visual features is applied to select the best cluster of invariants that is this cluster which localizes face in image. This selection is optional by causality that the image can present most than one face.

Figure 7. Remaining invariants (in the left image) agree geometrically regarding to their respective features (in the right image)

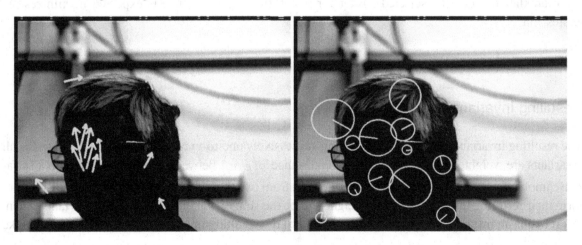

Figure 8. Geometric clustering eliminates invariants that have not been clustered and no agree geometrically, in the top line images, and yields clusters that detect face in bottom images

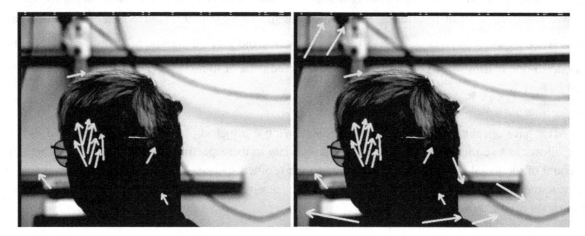

Cluster Selection

To determine the cluster of m invariants with the best facial appearance, we compute the appearance probability $p(c_k)$ of each cluster $c_k = \left\{ inv_i \mid \left\{ inv_i^{b=1}, f_i^{b=1} \right\} \right\}$ based on appearance of the corresponding features $\left\{ f_i^a \right\}$ and expressed as

$$p(c_k) = p\left(\left\{f_i^a\right\} \mid \left\{f_i^{b=1}, \; inv_i\right\}\right) = \prod_{i=1}^{m} p\left(f_i^a \mid f_i^{b=1}, \; inv_i\right)$$

where inv_i is an invariant belonging to cluster c_k, and f_i is the corresponding feature to inv_i in the image.

The optimal selection of best cluster of invariants is to choose the one for which the cluster value $c*$ maximizing $p(c_k)$.

In another manner, the selected cluster for which the facial presence is expected maximizes the expression

$$c* = argmax_{c_k} \left\{ p(c_k) \right\}$$

Resulting Invariant

The resulting invariant is formed by computing successively one-to-one pairings invariants. Initially, all invariants are weighted by a value of one. The distance $d(v_1, v_2)$ between two invariant vectors (Taffar & Benmohammed, 2011) is defined below. We start from two invariants that have minimum distance to form their resulting invariant which its weight will be the sum of weights of these two invariants. Then, if it remains an invariant with a minimum distance to the resulting invariant, they will be used to make a new resulting invariant, and so on. Figure 9 shows the resulting invariant computed to localize face in image.

Given two invariant vectors $v_1\left(o_1, e_1\right)$ and $v_2\left(o_2, e_2\right)$, where the pairs of points $\left(o_1, e_1\right)$ and $\left(o_2, e_2\right)$ are the origin and extremity points of v_1 and v_2 respectively, the metric used to compute the distance $d\left(v_1, v_2\right)$ between v_1 and v_2 is expressed as:

$$d\left(v_1, v_2\right) = \frac{d_e\left(o_1, o_2\right) + d_e\left(e_1, e_2\right)}{d_e\left(o_1, e_1\right) + d_e\left(o_2, e_2\right)}$$

where, $d_e\left(o_1, o_2\right)$ is the Euclidean distance from point o_1 to o_2, and $d_e\left(o_1, e_1\right)$ represents the scale of the invariant v_1.

The geometric parameters of the resulting invariant are computed as in (Taffar & Benmohammed, 2011). The location coordinates are obtained by taking the average of weighted coordinates of invariants, and thus it is possible to deduce the amount of the invariant scale. The value of orientation angle is calculated by using vector computation.

Geometric Prediction of Location

Another approach to do a geometric prediction of face location is to provide estimation in only one step.

This step allows doing simultaneously an appearance-based invariants clustering and a resulting invariant localization.

The idea is to predict the geometry of invariants and by consequence to determine their location parameters by using a probabilistic approach based on some assumptions in the learning model. To determine the clusters of invariant, we perform an ascendant hierarchical clustering of visual features corresponding to the invariants. The invariant clustering is based on appearance metric of features and used the Ward criterion. The Ward linkage criterion increases in variance for the cluster being merged.

Figure 9. After clustering, the resulting invariant computed on the best cluster of invariants in the right image allows to localize the face in the left image

For each cluster $c_k = \{f_i\}$ of n features that agree to facial appearance and to geometry of invariants in the learned model, the presence of the resulting invariant inv_{C_k} for c_k in new image can be estimated by the likelihood ratio of Bayes decision:

$$p\left(inv_{C_k} \mid \{f_i\}\right) = \frac{p\left(inv_{C_k}\right) p\left(\{f_i\} \mid inv_{C_k}\right)}{p\left(\{f_i\}\right)} = p\left(inv_{C_k}\right) \prod_i^n \frac{p\left(f_i \mid inv_{C_k}\right)}{p\left(f_i\right)}$$

where $p\left(f_i \mid inv_{C_k}\right)$ is estimated by $p\left(f_i \mid inv_i\right)$ for each feature in the learning model, and $p\left(inv_{C_k}\right)$ is a prior on invariant.

We evaluate collectively the hypotheses for which the features of cluster c_k result directly over a resulting face invariant inv_{C_k}. This geometric prediction deduces the location of the resulting invariant for each cluster. Each resulting invariant is a proof of a facial presence in this location of the image, as shown in Figure 10.

Gender Classification Process

The contribution of this part of paper is in how the parameters of the model are learned and used to recognize the gender. In the following we present a manner to use the maximum likelihood parameters of model.

Under the assumption that the facial features t_i are conditionally independent given characteristic f^s, an EM classifier $\varphi\left(f^s\right)$ establishes the most expected trait classification given a set of N feature occurrences $\{t_i\}$, that for one image, can be expressed as

Figure 10. Face detected in the left image. Only one feature has contributed to invariant localization in the right image

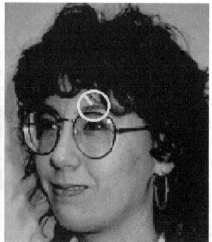

$$\varphi\left(f^{s}\right) = \frac{p\left(f^{s} \mid \{t_{i}\}\right)}{p\left(f^{\neg s} \mid \{t_{i}\}\right)} = \frac{p\left(f^{s}\right)}{p\left(f^{\neg s}\right)} \prod_{i}^{n} \frac{p\left(t_{i} \mid f_{i}^{s}\right)}{p\left(t_{i} \mid f_{i}^{\neg s}\right)}$$

equivalent to,

$$log \; \varphi\left(f^{s}\right) = log \frac{p\left(f^{s}\right)}{p\left(f^{\neg s}\right)} + \sum_{i}^{n} log \frac{p\left(t_{i} \mid f_{i}^{s}\right)}{p\left(t_{i} \mid f_{i}^{\neg s}\right)}$$

In (23), the two terms $\frac{p\left(f^{s}\right)}{p\left(f^{\neg s}\right)}$ and $\frac{p\left(t_{i} \mid f_{i}^{s}\right)}{p\left(t_{i} \mid f_{i}^{\neg s}\right)}$ have been estimated during learning step. The term

$\frac{p\left(f^{s}\right)}{p\left(f^{\neg s}\right)}$ expresses a prior ratio of trait value presence f^{s} versus absence $f^{\neg s}$ (e.g., male versus not male),

controlling classifier bias toward different trait values. $\frac{p\left(t_{i} \mid f_{i}^{s}\right)}{p\left(t_{i} \mid f_{i}^{\neg s}\right)}$ is the likelihood ratio of trait value

presence f^{s} versus absence $f^{\neg s}$ coinciding with observed feature t_{i}, it expresses the false gender recognition rate as face f^{s}.

The optimal EM classification is to choose trait value f^{s*} maximizing $log \; \varphi\left(f^{s}\right)$

$$f^{s*} = argmax_{f^{s}} \left\{log \; \varphi\left(f^{s}\right)\right\}$$

Another approach consists dealing with the traits of unknown face which are classified either as male or female features by computing the gender probability of each of them.

Based on assumption that traits $\{t_{i}\}$ are conditionally independent, the male probability of face, denoted $p\left(\{t_{i}\} \mid f^{s_{j}=1}\right)$, is obtained as follow:

$$p\left(\{t_{i}\} \mid f^{s_{j}=1}\right) = \prod_{i=1}^{n} p\left(t_{i} \mid f_{i}^{s_{j}=1}\right)$$

equivalent to,

$$log \; p\left(\{t_{i}\} \mid f^{s_{j}=1}\right) = \sum_{i=1}^{n} log \; p\left(t_{i} \mid f_{i}^{s_{j}=1}\right)$$

In representation space, the gender distribution with respect of the facial appearance presence can be estimated as,

$$p\left(\{t_i\} \mid f^{s_j=1}\right) = \frac{\prod_{i=1}^{n} k_{i,1}\, p\left(t_i \mid f_i^{s_j=1}\right)}{\prod_{i=1}^{n} k_{i,0}\, p\left(t_i \mid f_i^{s_j=0}\right) + \prod_{i=1}^{n} k_{i,1}\, p\left(t_i \mid f_i^{s_j=1}\right)}$$

where $k_{i,s}$ is the weight of t_i of gender f^s. It corresponds to the number of model features which have voted for t_i as gender f^s. It is obtained from voting procedure. It expresses the importance to classify the gender of t_i in f^s class. Thus, the face is declared as male if $p\left(\{t_i\} \mid f^{s_j=1}\right) > p\left(\{t_i\} \mid f^{s_j=0}\right)$.

EXPERIMENTATION

Experimental Considerations

Some parameters have been experimentally fixed by testing their impact on the effective localization of invariant and so for gender classification. These parameters are concerned by appearance, geometric, and clustering thresholds.

In order to localize the expected facial appearance and avoid as possible as the false positive detection, the appearance threshold Γ^a is set to 0.4. Thus, only features with a reasonable facial appearance are preselected.

For a geometric agreement and a symmetric consistency of invariants, the value of threshold Γ^g is set on 3-parameters that correspond to position, scale and rotation. The location parameter of threshold $\Gamma^{g:(x,y)}$ is a pixel distance that should be less than inverse of invariant scale ($1/\sigma$ pixels), the scale parameter of threshold $\Gamma^{g:\sigma}$ is a difference in scale of $log(2.0)=0.3$ of number of octaves in image, and the direction parameter of threshold $\Gamma^{g:\theta}$ offers 10 degrees tolerance in orientation. With such a geometric thresholding all invariants retained must agree geometrically within image.

The hierarchical clustering permits to correct the geometric error of invariants that have undergone weak geometric transforms and facial distortions. The clustering threshold Γ^c preset the minimum distance of invariant to its cluster relatively to the invariant scale.

Data Considerations

The learning of invariant model involves a set of images, about 500, belonging to different parts of databases, PIE (Face Research Group, 2009), CMU-profile (CMU Face Group, 2009), FERET (Color FERET Face Database, 2009), and also some negative images not containing faces.

The model learning involves 9,893 features (8,436 facial features, where 5,624 men, 2,812 women, and 1,457 background features); they are chosen well, deemed to be informative with respect to FI, and not redundant, because learning is done in the presence of significant clutter in images.

For the purpose of experimentation, the test images belong to environments of different contexts. They exhibited different geometric transforms, a variety of viewpoints, as well as large appearance variability (illumination, expression, race, glasses, etc.). This allows us to evaluate the performance of FI model. Then, to compare the results with these of OCI model combined with Bayes classifier (Toews & Arbel, 2009) and BOW (Bag-Of-Words) model (Dance, Willamowski, Fan, Bray, & Csurka, 2004).

Face Localization

The principal aim of this experiment is to show that the invariant model is able to detect facial appearance in the presence of viewpoint changes. Facial localization is performed by determining the FI instances in each of the testing images. First, a set of features are extracted from new image, then detection is achieved by controlling an agreement of these visual traits with model features under both geometric and appearance aspects.

The performance of FI model is evaluated after have fixed the values of thresholds Γ^g and Γ^a. The detection trials estimate the optimum value of clustering threshold Γ^c for a high precision of facial localization, then to show that the FI model is tolerant to viewpoint changes.

Figure 11 plots the precision and recall for facial detection in presence of viewpoint changes and facial appearance variability, for different values of Γ^c. It draws the capacity of face invariant model to infer new face instances. The performance value grows and reaches the face detection rate of 89.67%, thus the chosen thresholds are cut. Table 1 results of detection rate on a total of 400 face images of a variety of viewpoint of different databases.

The next detection trials have been performed when the changes of the angle view of face varies as 0°, 30°, 45°, 60° and 90°. Table 2 summarizes results by varying the angles of view of faces of different databases images.

Figure 11. Precision and recall for face detection, in presence of viewpoint changes, evaluated for different values of Γ^c

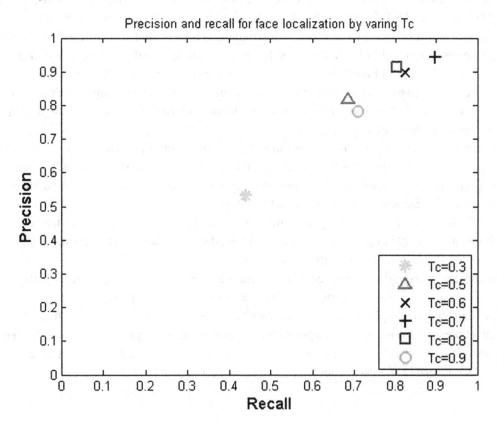

Table 1. Result of face detection rate on 400 images in presence of viewpoint changes and high appearance variability of faces, for the value Γ^c =0.7

	Databases		
	FERET	**CMU-Profiles**	**PIE**
Images tested	220	80	100
Face detection rate (%)	85	88.75	95
False positive rate (%)	12.5	5	3

Table 2. The face detection rate obtained for Γ^c =0.7 and by varying the angles of view shows that the FI model is invariant to face pose

Viewpoint angles	Facial	0°-30°	30°-45°	45°-60°	60°-90°	Profile
Face detection rates (%)	77.56	89.10	76.15	80.38	89.63	82.95

As shown in Figure 12, the detection error rate EER (equal error rate) obtained is less than 12% where the performance decreases when viewpoint change occurs at 45°±10°.

A comparison of performances was done between three models: FI (Taffar, Miguet, & Benmohammed, 2012), Haar wavelets classifier (Viola, & Jones, 2001) based on integral image features and embedding frontal and profile classifiers, and OCI (Toews, & Arbel, 2006). The detection tests were performed on a set of 400 images of FERET database in two protocols. The first test protocol is done with 200 images where the faces are frontal, and the second with remain 200 images that present viewpoint changes.

Table 3 presents the results of face detection for the three models on the same protocol and depict the accurate quality of FI model based on a clustering algorithm of invariants when the viewpoint of faces increase. The model gives a good satisfaction and performs very well on images with high intra-class variability. It provides best performances than global feature approaches which need a pretreatment of images, appearance and spatial constraints.

In general, the FI model performs better than OCI model. Contrary to Haar classifier that has high detection performance for the frontal or profile pose of faces and decreases drastically when the faces present a severe change in viewpoint. The detection rate of FI model remains relatively stable even when the angles of pose of faces vary between 30 and 60 degrees.

Figure 13 shows the face detection rate curves comparing our FI model, Haar detector, and OCI model where an acceptable improvement has been obtained and by consequence its impact on the gender classification EER which is shown in the next section.

Facial appearance classification based on local features is capable of coping with a significant degree of viewpoint changes and partial occlusion, as only a subset of features is required.

Figure 14 gives an example of experimental results of a correct face invariant localization where the face in image presents some degree viewpoint changes that varies from profile views (70-90 degrees) to frontal views (0°-20°) and also where face occlusion can occur. By image, few features have contributed to localize face invariant. We have counted in average 4 correct inliers by face.

Figure 12. Detection error as a function of the degree of viewpoint. For each interval of viewpoint angle, detection trials are performed using the invariant trained on 500 images. The points and error bars indicate the mean and the standard deviations of the detection error. Detection error starts at 12.7% with facial images and rises to approximately 19.5% for an angle around of 50°

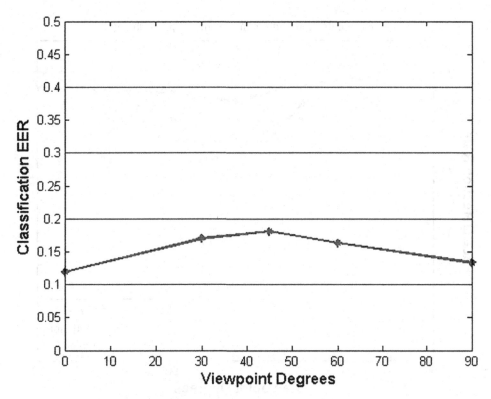

Table 3. Comparison of face detection performances of FI, Haar cascade classifier (which embeds frontal and profile classifiers), and OCI models when face viewpoint changes occur

	Frontal view	**0°-30°**	**30°-60°**	**60°-90°**	**Profile view**
Number of images	200	56	37	42	65
FI model	90.51	86.13	80.84	83.56	85.35
Haar detector	96.60	80.32	57.78	76.17	90.14
OCI model	83.65	74.48	64.27	75.21	79.55

The appearance classification generally performs well in trials on FERET imagery. This suggests that EM classification generalizes more readily to the context of cluttered imagery. A comparison to others classifiers like SVM or Decision Tree is recommended. Figure 15 illustrates correct face detection results where the faces present some degree viewpoint changes and their lighting has wide range.

Figure 13. The curve on face detection rate draws the quality of FI model vs. OCI model and Haar detector when the poses of faces vary from frontal to profile views. The experiment is done on 400 testing image of FERET database, illustrates the rate of about 89.67% of FI model and its stability for viewpoint changes even when a possible partial occlusion can occur

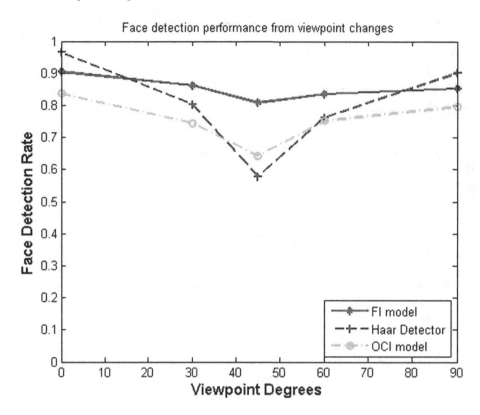

Figure 14. Examples of FI localization in cluttered scenes containing faces in arbitrary viewpoints and partial occlusion. The detection is done for angles view of 45 and 90 degrees (right to left)

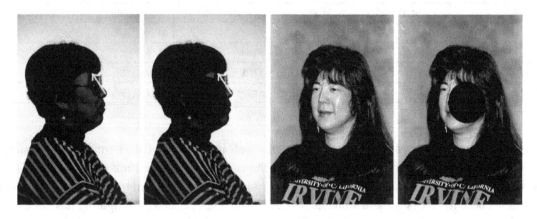

Figure 15. Face localization with accuracy on images from different databases in which faces occur with different viewpoints and appearances

Gender Classification from Arbitrary Viewpoints

The sex classification of faces is based on the probability of sex of traits from arbitrary viewpoints, a wide range of appearance variability. We report the gender classification performance on faces correctly detected while varying the amount of appearance threshold.

Once a FI instance is detected in a new image, facial features associated to FI are then used to determine sex using the EM classifier in Eq. (23). As faces are either male or female, determining face sex is a two-class problem and, thus, $\varphi(male) = \varphi(female)^{-1}$. A single-threshold Φ on $\varphi(f^s)$ can be used such that faces are classified as either male if $log\ \varphi(male) > \Phi$ or as female if $log\ \varphi(male) < \Phi$. Classification results are reported in terms of log likelihood ratio of gender recognition where the probabilities of classifying males and females are different.

First, we give results of the simultaneous tasks of face detection and sex classification in the presence of viewpoint changes on a subset of images from different databases.

Table 4 details the results on gender recognition task where the faces are already detected in the same process. The faces in images present distortions, some degree viewpoint changes and their intra-class variability is drastic.

The next trials are based on three random partitions of the data into 400 training and 404 testing images. They give 372 valid recognitions, 38 false positives, and the remaining number corresponds to 26 true negatives. A sex recognition rate of 92.1% is reached.

Only few features, in average 2 by image, are sufficient to contribute to recognize the sex of face, the remaining features have equal probabilities to be male or female, thus they are uninformative to sex classification.

Table 4. Gender classification results on images, with faces correctly detected and which have large presence of viewpoint changes and appearance variability

	FERET	**CMU-Profiles**	**PIE**
Faces Detection Rate	87.13	89.54	90.96
Gender Classification Rate	93.25	92.18	90.52

The next gender classification tests performed on the FERET database are distributed over three ranges of viewpoint involving 400 subjects, ranging from frontal to profile views.

Although, faces take the arbitrary viewpoints, an EER of 10.6 percent is obtained for over a 180 degree range of face pose. The error rate for profile views is two times that of frontal views, reflecting the difficulty of classifying non-frontal faces, and the results are shown in Table 5. This appears to be due to the fact that non-frontal views generally contain fewer model features. The EER 6.4% for frontal views is somewhat comparable to than error rates obtained by other frontal face classifiers (4-10 percent) (Baluja & Rowley, 2007; Yang, Li, & Ai, 2006; Jain, Huang, & Fang, 2005; Moghaddam & Yang, 2002; Gutta, Wechsler, & Phillips, 1998).

The classification error degrades smoothly with an increase in the degree of viewpoint, demonstrating the capacity of local feature-based classification to cope with missing features.

From the face detection results obtained in the previous section where an acceptable improvement has been achieved, the gender classification error EER has been reduced to 9% against 16% for OCI model combined with a Bayesian classifier (Toews & Arbel, 2009). Figure 16 depict an analysis of classification performance in the presence of pose changes.

For the comparison trials, we use the FI model with a probabilistic gender classifier which alternatively embedded different classification methods. Experimentation tests combinations of model (e.g., OCI (Toews & Arbel, 2009), BOW (bag-of-words) (Dance, Willamowski, Fan, Bray, & Csurka, 2004), and FI (Taffar, Miguet, & Benmohammed, 2012)) and classifier (e.g., SVM, Bayesian, and EM) are illustrated in table 6.

The gender classification equal error rate (EER) has been improved to 11.6% against 16.3% for OCI model based on Bayesian classification and 23.5% for BOW (bag-of-words) model combined to Bayesian classifier. In general, FI model using an EM classifier has good performance rate. This suggests that the features geometrically localized within an invariant reference frame have contributed for good sex classification.

In order to illustrate that the degradation of sex classification performance is related to the detection precision, we evaluate sex classification on the sets of 50, 100, and 200 faces detected with the highest precision. A set of 200 faces, which is manually determined to contain 130 males and 70 females, is

Table 5. The Data Distribution and Mean EERs for Three Ranges of Face Viewpoint in All Trials Based on 400 Training Images

Viewpoint range	**0° - 20°** **(Frontal)**	**20° - 70°**	**70° - 90°** **(Profile)**
Data (%)	27.4	47.2	25.3
Mean EER (%)	6.4	13.5	11.8

Figure 16. Gender classification error as a function of the degree of viewpoint. For each interval of viewpoint angle, classification trials are performed using the gender classifier trained on 400 images. The points and error bars indicate the mean and the standard deviations of the classification error for the indicated angles. Classification error starts at about 8.7% with facial and profile images and rises to approximately 18.9% for an angle of 50°

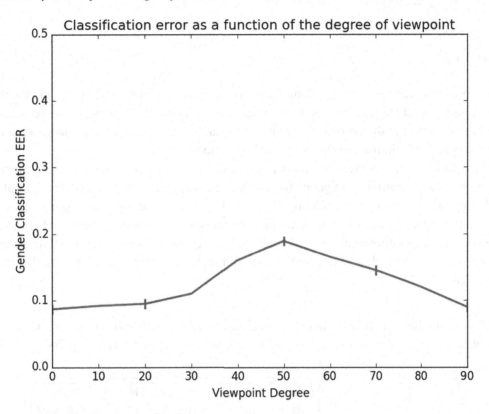

Table 6. The Sex Classification EERs comparison for FI, BOW, and OCI Models combined with different Classifiers like EM, SVM, and Bayesian

Models	Classifiers	EERs
OCI	Bayesian	16.3% ± 0.9%
BOW	Bayesian	23.5% ± 1.3%
FI	Bayesian	15.5% ± 0.6%
FI	EM	11.6% ± 0.7%
FI	SVM	20.8% ± 0.4%

selected. Note the bias toward the male sex, from inspection the male:female ratio over the entire CMU profile data set appears to be approximately 2:1.

The experimentation demonstrates that the probabilistic formulation is useful and has high capability to recognize gender of new face instances, all in images exhibiting a wide range of facial appearance.

Figure 17 illustrates the precision-recall characteristic of detection when faces present viewpoint changes, along with sex classification error rates at the indicated values of precision.

Classification performance generally degrades with decreasing detection precision, as both are linked to the number of images features extracted in each localized face. Figure 18 shows an example of the result of a correct gender classification on face (e.g., woman) image.

CONCLUSION

By making use of recent research extending local invariant feature-based techniques to modeling face class appearance and of the evolution of face recognition methods, the approach adopted is able to explicitly address and tackle the problems of objects appearance recognition based on visual traits from arbitrary viewpoints and in the presence of partial occlusion.

With this work, we have presented a model of face class appearance which has two parts related to contexts surrounding learning (both geometry and appearance) and recognition (detection followed by gender classification). This model, with high tolerant to viewpoint and especially to intra-class appearance variability, is based on geometric invariant defined across instances of faces and combining appearance and geometry information of local features. The experimentation reveals that the probabilistic formulation and geometric clustering give to the model high capability to localize and classify the sex of new face instances.

Figure 17. The precision-recall characteristic of detection and localization based on 200 faces of the CMU database. The sex classification EERs are displayed for the top 50, 100, and 200 detected faces

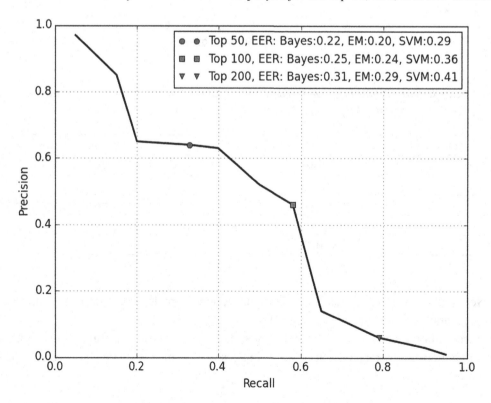

Figure 18. One facial feature in the left image has been used to localize invariant and retained to determine the gender probability of face, with an appearance probability of 18.62% to be man and 81.38% of woman appearance probability

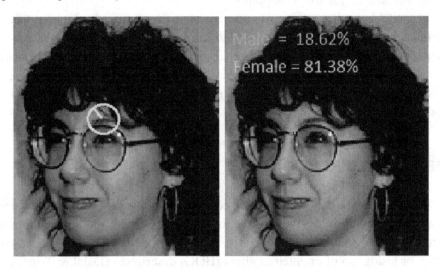

Figure 19. An example of correctly localized and classified faces in a scene that presents viewpoint variations on images from CMU-profile and FERET databases. White arrows overlaying the central image indicate correctly identified FIs. Features overlaying thumbnails indicate instances of model features involved in localization and gender classification for each face. Blue features indicate male characteristics and pink features are female, where the color saturation is proportional to the magnitude of the log likelihood ratio. The successful classification is possible despite the high degree of occlusion in the rightmost face

A learned model capture well intra-class appearance variability and any viewpoint change in-plane geometric transformation. These properties of FI avoid to use a huge variety of descriptors required by many approaches to learn all possible viewpoints.

The invariant model has a low degree of supervision, as in significant cluttered face images even containing partial occlusion, yet the model is able to learn, detect and recognize the gender of the rich multimodal appearance of face images exhibiting viewpoint changes, by using a reasonable number of descriptors. Its magnitude remains approximately constant with respect to the size of face in the image. Of course, this model can be applied to another object class. In general, the time taken to detect and recognize gender of face is quite low.

FUTURE RESEARCH DIRECTIONS

Future work will involve testing the model to detect and recognize another type of objects, like cars and tumors for medical application. We will try to combine invariant model, scale invariant feature with integral image feature (Viola & Jones, 2001), local binary patterns (LBP) (Ojala, Pietikäinen, & Mäenpää, 2002), or histogram of oriented gradient (HOG) descriptors (Dalal & Trigg, 2005) for high performance to detect face and classify its gender. Obviously, the probabilistic model based on these combined features will obey to other rule. We also intend to use another type of local descriptor or try to improve the existing one. We will test others classifiers which have proved their high quality in the literature. Finally, another potential application to evaluate this approach is to localize and classify the face features presented through video frame like publicity.

REFERENCES

Agarwal, S., Awan, A., & Roth, D. (2004). Learning to detect objects in images via a sparse, part-based representation. *PAMI, 26*(11), 1475–1490. doi:10.1109/TPAMI.2004.108 PMID:15521495

Baluja, S., & Rowley, H. A. (2007). Boosting Sex Identification Performance. *International Journal of Computer Vision, 71*(1), 111–119. doi:10.1007/s11263-006-8910-9

Bart, E., Byvatov, E., & Ullman, S. (2004). View-invariant recognition using corresponding object fragments. *Proc. ECCV Conference* (pp.152–165).

BenAbdelkader, C., & Griffin, P. (2005). A Local Region-Based Approach to Gender Classification from Face Images. *Proc. IEEE Conf. Computer Vision and Pattern Recognition.*

Burl, M., Weber, M., & Perona, P. (1998). A probabilistic approach to object recognition using local photometry and global geometry. *Proceedings of the ECCV Conference*, Freiburg, Germany (pp.628–641). doi:10.1007/BFb0054769

Burns, J., Weiss, R., & Riseman, E. (1993). View variation of pointset and line-segment features. *PAMI, 15*(1), 51–68. doi:10.1109/34.184774

CMU Face Group. (2009). *Frontal and profile face databases*. Retrieved 2009, from http://vasc.ri.cmu.edu/idb/html/face/

Color FERET Face Database. (2009). *FERET Evaluation Project*. Retrieved 2009, from www.itl.nist. gov/iad/humanid/colorferet

Dalal, N., & Trigg, B. (2005). Histograms of Oriented Gradients for Human Detection. *Proceedings of the CVPR Int'l Conference* (pp.886-893). doi:10.1109/CVPR.2005.177

Dance, C., Willamowski, J., Fan, L., Bray, C., & Csurka, G. (2004). Visual Categorization with Bags of Keypoints. *Proc. ECCV Workshop, Statistical Learning in Computer Vision.*

Dempster, A., Laird, N., & Rubin, D. (1976). Maximum likelihood from incomplete data via the EM algorithm. *Journal of the Royal Statistical Society. Series A (General), 39*, 1–38.

Dorko, G., & Schmid, C. (2003). Selection of scale-invariant parts for object class recognition. Proceedings of ICCV (pp.634–640).

Face Research Group. (2009). *CMU Pose, Illumination, and Expression (PIE) database*. Retrieved 2009, from http://www.ri.cmu.edu/projects/project 418.html

Fei-Fei, L., Fergus, R., & Perona, P. (2003). A bayesian approach to unsupervised one-shot learning of object categories. *Proceedings of ICCV* (pp. 1134–1141).

Fergus, R., Perona, P., & Zisserman, A. (2003). Object class recognition by unsupervised scale-invariant learning. Proceedings of CVPR03, Madison, Wisconsin (pp. 264–271).

Gutta, S., Wechsler, H., & Phillips, P. (1998). Gender and Ethnic Classification of Human Faces Using Hybrid Classifiers. *Proc. Int'l Conf. Automatic Face and Gesture Recognition* (pp. 194-199). doi:10.1109/AFGR.1998.670948

Harris, C., & Stephens, M. (1988). A combined corner and edge detection. *Proc. of Alvey Vision Conference* (pp.147–151).

Hartley, R., & Zisserman, A. (2000). *Multiple view geometry in computer vision*. Cambridge University Press.

Helmer, S., & Lowe, D. G. (2004). Object Class Recognition with Many Local Features. *Proceedings of the Conference on Computer Vision and Pattern Recognition Workshop* (*Vol. 12*, pp.187). doi:10.1109/CVPR.2004.409

Herbert, B., Tinnr, T., & Gool, L. V. (2006). SURF: Speeded Up Robust Features. Proceedings of ECCV, *LNCS* (Vol. *3951*, pp. 404–417).

Jain, A., Huang, J., & Fang, S. (2005). Gender Identification Using Frontal Facial Images. *Proc. IEEE Int'l Conf. Multimedia and Expo* (pp.1082-1085).

Jaynes, E. (1968). Prior Probabilities. *IEEE Trans. Systems, Science, and Cybernetics, 4*(3), 227–241. doi:10.1109/TSSC.1968.300117

Jordan, M. I., Ghahramani, Z., Jaakkola, T. S., & Saul, L. K. (1999). An Introduction to Variational Methods for Graphical Models. *Machine Learning, 37*(2), 183–233. doi:10.1023/A:1007665907178

Kadir, T., & Brady, M. (2001). Saliency, scale and image description. International Journal of Computer Vision, *45*(2), 83–105. doi:10.1023/A:1012460413855

Kim, H.-C., Kim, D., Ghahramani, Z., & Bang, S. Y. (2006). Appearance-Based Gender Classification with Gaussian Processes. *Pattern Recognition Letters*, *27*(6), 618–626. doi:10.1016/j.patrec.2005.09.027

Lindeberg, T. (1998). Feature detection with automatic scale selection. *International Journal of Computer Vision*, *30*(2), 79–116. doi:10.1023/A:1008045108935

Lowe, D. (2001). Local feature view clustering for 3D object recognition. Proceedings of CVPR (pp.682–688).

Lowe, D. G. (1999). *Object Recognition from Local Scale-Invariant Features. Proceedings of ICCV* (pp. 1150–1157). Corfu, Greece: . doi:10.1109/ICCV.1999.790410

Lowe, D. G. (2004). Distinctive Image Features from Scale-Invariant Keypoints. International Journal of Computer Vision, *60*(2), 91–110. doi:10.1023/B:VISI.0000029664.99615.94

Makinen, E., & Raisamo, R. (2008). Evaluation of Gender Classification Methods with Automatically Detected and Aligned Faces. *IEEE Trans. PAMI*, *30*(3), 541–547. doi:10.1109/TPAMI.2007.70800 PMID:18195447

Mikolajczyk, K., & Schmid, C. (2002). An Affine Invariant Interest Point Detector. Proceedings of ECCV (pp. 128-142).

Mikolajczyk, K., & Schmid, C. (2004). Scale and affine invariant interest point detectors. International Journal of Computer Vision, *60*(1), 63–86. doi:10.1023/B:VISI.0000027790.02288.f2

Mikolajczyk, K., Schmid, C., & Zisserman, A. (2004). Human detection based on a probabilistic assembly of robust part detectors. Proceedings of ECCV (pp. 69–81).

Moghaddam, B., & Yang, M. (2002). Learning Gender with Support Faces. *IEEE Transactions on Pattern Analysis and Machine Intelligence*, *24*(5), 707–711. doi:10.1109/34.1000244

Moreels, P., Maire, M., & Perona, P. (2004). Recognition by probabilistic hypothesis construction. Proceedings of ECCV '04 (pp. 55–68).

Ojala, T., Pietikäinen, M., & Mäenpää, T. (2002). Multiresolution gray-scale and rotation invariant texture classification with local binary patterns. *IEEE Transactions on Pattern Analysis and Machine Intelligence*, *24*(7), 971–987. doi:10.1109/TPAMI.2002.1017623

OToole, A. J., Vetter, T., Troje, N. F., & Bulthoff, H. H. (1997). Sex Classification Is Better with Three-Dimensional Structure than with Image Intensity Information. *Perception*, *26*(1), 75–84. doi:10.1068/p260075 PMID:9196691

Pope, A., & Lowe, D. G. (2000). Probabilistic models of appearance for 3D object recognition. *IJCV*, *40*(2), 149–167. doi:10.1023/A:1026502202780

Rothganger, F., Lazebnik, S., Schmid, C., & Ponce, J. (2003). 3D object modeling and recognition using affine-invariant patches and multi-view spatial constraints. Proceedings of CVPR (pp. 272–277).

Schmid, C., & Mohr, R. (1997). Local Grayvalue Invariants for Image Retrieval. *IEEE PAMI*, *19*(5), 530–534. doi:10.1109/34.589215

Shakhnarovich, G., Viola, P. A., & Moghaddam, B. (2002). A Unified Learning Framework for Real Time Face Detection and Classification. *Proc. Int'l Conf. Automatic Face and Gesture Recognition*. doi:10.1109/AFGR.2002.1004124

Taffar, M., & Benmohammed, M. (2011). *Generic Face Invariant Model for Face Detection. In Proc. IP & C Conf.* (Vol. 1, pp.42-50). doi:10.1007/978-3-642-23154-4_5

Taffar, M., Miguet, S., & Benmohammed, M. (2012). Viewpoint Invariant Face Detection. *Proc. NDT Conference* (pp. 390–402).

Toews, M., & Arbel, T. (2006). Detection over Viewpoint via the Object Class Invariant. *Proc. Int'l Conf. Pattern Recognition* (Vol. 1, pp.765-768). doi:10.1109/ICPR.2006.444

Toews, M., & Arbel, T. (2009). Detection, Localization, and Sex Classification of Faces from Arbitrary Viewpoints and under Occlusion. *IEEE Trans. on PAMI*, *31*(9), 1567–1581. doi:10.1109/TPAMI.2008.233 PMID:19574619

Torralba, A., Murphy, K. P., & Freeman, W. T. (2004). Sharing features: efficient boosting procedures for multiclass object detection. Proceedings of CVPR (pp. 762–769).

Tuytelaars, T., & Van Gool, L. (2000). *Wide Baseline Stereo Matching Based on Local Affinely Invariant Regions* (pp. 412–425). BMVC. doi:10.5244/C.14.38

Ullman, S., Vidal-Naquet, M., & Sali, E. (2002). Visual features of intermediate complexity and their use in classification. *Nature Neuroscience*, *5*(7), 1–6. PMID:12055634

Viola, P., & Jones, M. (2001). Rapid Object Detection Using a Boosted Cascade of Simple Features. *Proc. IEEE CVPR Conf.* (pp. 511–518). doi:10.1109/CVPR.2001.990517

Weber, M., Welling, M., & Perona, P. (2000). Unsupervised learning of models for recognition. *ECCV Conference*, Dublin, Ireland (pp. 18–32).

Yang, Z., Li, M., & Ai, H. (2006). An Experimental Study on Automatic Face Gender Classification. *Proc. Int'l Conf. Pattern Recognition* (pp. 1099-1102).

Yu, G., & Morel, J. M. (2009). A Fully Affine Invariant Image Comparison Method. *Proc. IEEE International Conference on Acoustics, Speech, and Signal Processing (ICASSP)*, Taipei. doi:10.1109/ICASSP.2009.4959904

Zhang, L., & Koch, R. (2012). Line Matching Using Appearance Similarities and Geometric Constraints. In *Pattern Recognition, LNCS* (Vol. *7476*, pp. 236–245).

Chapter 10
Intelligent Control of Vehicles' Number Plates on Toll Gates in Developing Nations

Tawanda Mushiri
University of Johannesburg, South Africa

Charles Mbohwa
University of Johannesburg, South Africa

Simbarashe Sarupinda
CUT, Zimbabwe

ABSTRACT

Developing nations have implemented toll gates in their countries major trunk highways as a move towards the improvement in fiscal levels. However, several problems have arisen in the toll collection system that has been implemented. The system exists as an incomplete system in comparison to internationally acclaimed systems and methods. This chapter therefore seeks to introduce an automated toll collection system which has enhanced security features and intelligent vehicle classification methods. Utilising machine intelligence and computer vision methods in the system, the researchers intend to develop the automated and intelligent toll collection system for developing nation's tollgates. The mechatronic system will combat security loopholes and enhance the efficiency of the toll collection process.

1. INTRODUCTION

Tolling as a method of financing the transportation system is becoming more common in the United States. Neither the traveling public nor State Departments of Transportation want vehicles to stop or slow down to pay to use a toll facility. To this end, several technologies, collectively called Electronic Toll Collection (ETC), have been developed in the last 15 years, allowing drivers to move in and out of toll systems without delay. Open Road Tolling (ORT), with all-electronic toll collection, is now the preferred practice, being more efficient, environmentally friendly, and safer than manual toll collection.

DOI: 10.4018/978-1-5225-2848-7.ch010

Whilst technological advances have been realised in various areas of the Zimbabwean society, some areas are still lagging and these urgently require attention. Of note is the development of toll gates which were introduced in Zimbabwe in order to aid in maintaining road maintenance and fiscal levels. To date over 57 million dollars has been collected through the nation's toll collection system. However, several inconsistencies and issues have surrounded the implementation of the toll collection system. There are three main reasons why tolling, or road pricing, is implemented (Wikipedia: Road Pricing, 2006):

- **Finance/Revenue Generation:** To recoup the costs of building, operating and maintaining the facility. Road pricing is becoming a more appealing means of funding transportation, since revenues from federal and state gas taxes have not kept up with growth in demand for infrastructure. Moreover, toll financing allows projects to be built sooner instead of waiting for tax revenues to accumulate.
- **Demand Management:** To moderate the growth in demand on the transportation system, and to encourage more use of public transportation and carpooling. For example, vehicles are charged to enter inner London, England, as a way of regulating the demand in the region.
- **Congestion Management:** To place a price on limited roadway space in proportion to demand. In this application, the toll increases with the level of congestion. In the absence of such pricing, drivers do not appreciate the costs they impose on others as a result of the congestion they cause.

1.1. Background of the Problem

The method of collection is still manual for the various classes of the vehicles which pass through a toll collection point. Historically, toll counters have been installed in various highways within Zimbabwe's road networks. Such have allowed for the demographic modelling of traffic density on the networks. These toll data loggers have aided in determining the possible lifespan of a highway given the traffic density recorded for the system. The collection of toll fees is dependent upon the operator's presence at the toll collection site. In instances when harsh weather conditions arise, the toll collection officers tend to leave some sites unattended and this results in a loss of revenue which is significant on a national level when analysed cumulatively. Within the area of coverage, the patrol vehicle is used and the patrol officer will perform spot audits and inspections of the activities on the toll site. It has however occurred that the present system has safety loopholes for the toll operators and this arises from the ergonomics of the present system. Auditing of the toll collection system is usually a tedious process for the auditors in revenue collection. Fraudulent behaviour has gone unnoticed and this has occurred in instances which the local press could substantiate on. High volumes of traffic stimulate a congested environment on toll gate sites as the human operator's responsiveness is based on mental alertness and agility as well as fatigue levels (This is mainly evident during public holidays).

Zimbabwe is yet to develop and automate a toll collection system which caters for various challenges that the manual system presently faces as cited above. The inefficiency of the previous system will require to be addressed through such a system. At present investment is being made towards the enhancement of service on the toll gates and the whole infrastructure.

1.2. Statement of the Problem, Aim and Objectives

Manual toll collection, fraud and inefficiency exist in Zimbabwe's toll collection system. The aim of this research is to design an automatic and intelligent mechatronic system for toll collection which caters for local demands and specifications. The formulation of solutions to the problem will be dependent on the following objectives.

1. Developing an automated solution to the toll collection procedure.
2. Inco-operating recognition and vision elements to aid system intelligence.
3. Analysing system performance against the human operator and optimising it to a desired threshold.
4. Selecting appropriate and reliable vehicle classification, enforcement and identification methods for the system.
5. Ensuring the design of a secure method of toll fee collection.

1.3. Justification

Efforts to engage international partners have been unfruitful for the transport ministry and the revenue collection department. This is with respect to the toll gate design and system deployment. However, a compromise in competency and standard has been realized in the resultant systems. The present toll collection system is heavily dependent on the human operator and the ability of the operator to work for longer hours in the shift. It is difficult to make a full audit of transactions on the present system. Operations such as auditing are performed in post time and cannot be executed in real time. Thus, enforcement on toll sites is low. An intelligent system will thus enhance security on the toll sites and secure fiscal deposits acquired at various toll sites. This will reduce issues of theft and corruption in the toll collection system.

The present collection process is monotonous. Whilst it may appear easy, the toll operator experiences monotony with the way repetitive operations are undertaken on toll collection sites. Unfriendly weather conditions inhibit human operator's ability to articulate on the demands of work thus collection is performed on the detriment of the collection officer in question. Heat waves and the general influence of weather elements have impacted the toll operators negatively. Increased exposure of operators to ultraviolet radiation has long term negative effects. Automated processing stimulates the growth of higher performance levels in most systems. Deploying automation in non-automated functions for manufacturing processes increases the pace of operation for the toll collection site. This can therefore be realized in the toll collection scenario as well. Enhanced functionality of a toll site where complex tasks and operations are present may be applied through the introduction of machine intelligence within the system and its functions. The development of the toll collection system greatly stimulates the growth of intellectual property for the institution and the world at large.

1.4. Research Scope

The scope of the research will be with respect to the following subject areas

- The development of an automatic toll collection system to replace the manual toll collection methods and systems presently in use.
- The creation of mechatronic solutions to enhance the toll collection system's functionality.

- Improving fiscal transparency through intelligent mechatronic functions that will be used in auditing of the operators' transactions in the toll collection process.
- Creating fool proof methods of collection which are secure and efficient.
- Developing algorithms for machine intelligence mainly computer vision.
- Appraising automation and intelligence hardware for the system.

2. LITERATURE REVIEW

The researchers will explore the various systems and methodologies used in the toll collection system. The chapter shall entail the review of various cases where electronic and computer based technologies are used in toll collection. Standardisation issues and system development and management techniques will be considered for review as well in order to develop an insight into automatic and intelligent toll collection.

2.1. The Implementation of Toll Collection Systems in Zimbabwe

With effect from the 8th of August 2009 road tolls were introduced on Zimbabwe's roads. Charges range from 1 to 5 US$ per vehicle. Payable at points on the city to city trunk roads and at entry points into the country. Collection is done by ZIMRA agents (customs and excise) in conjunction with Zimbabwe Republic Police roadblocks. To commence the system, 22 tollgates were set up on all the country's major highways charging motorists a fee to boost government coffers and help rehabilitate the collapsing and dangerous road network. Vehicles are classified in the following classes with corresponding charges being outlined in Figure 1. The image depicts vehicular classes and their respective toll fees. It can be seen that ordinary cars are charged $2 per entry, Commuter Omnibuses $2, Maxi Buses $3, Commercial

Figure 1. Toll charges for vehicle classes in Zimba

Lorries $4, and Haulage Trucks $5. The charges are applicable per entry on the toll collection site. The Herald, on 26 August 2011 reported that a ZIMRA staffer was jailed for theft and the ZIMRA employee was yesterday convicted of stealing tollgate receipt books. The projected losses were stated to amount to USD 1.7 million.

Prelude to the acceptable definition of an intelligent system, it has been attainable through Russell and Norwig (1995) that Artificial Intelligence (AI) is an essential basis for building intelligent systems and AI has two main directions. These inclinations are humanistic AI (HAI) - that studies machines that think and act like humans, and rationalistic AI (RAI) that examines machines that can be built on the understanding of intelligent human behaviour. In the current information technology era, the use of automations and intelligent systems is becoming more and more widespread (Anishiya and Joans, 2011). Therefore, following the notion by Russel and Norwig (1995), it can be construed that automated functions derived from human behaviour and containing elements of the intelligent system becoming automated intelligent systems. However, in the field of mechatronics, Rezvski, (2003) established that an automated mechatronic system is capable of handling materials and energy, communicating with its environment and is characterised by self-regulation, which enables it to respond to predictable changes in its environment in a pre-programmed fashion. An overwhelming majority of current mechatronic systems belong to this category.

Rezvski (2003) also established a notion on intelligent systems stating that an intelligent mechatronic system is capable of achieving given goals under conditions of uncertainty. In contrast to automated systems, which are, by definition, pre-programmed to deliver given behaviour and are therefore predictable, intelligent systems may arrive at specified goals in an unpredictable manner. They are endowed with flexibility, which means they are capable of responding to frequent changes in their environments without being re-programmed. This qualitative difference in their behaviour is a result of the separation of the domain knowledge from the mechanism for problem solving.

2.2. Software Used in Developing Intelligent Systems

It has been established through various scholarly articles that Intelligence can be designed into a system using traditional Artificial Intelligence methods such as expert systems, fuzzy logic or neural networks, but the most cost-effective and powerful implementation is through the use of distributed artificial intelligence, where a community of intelligent agents decides on the optimal or near-optimal action through a process of negotiation. Implementation and design of intelligent systems has been investigated in various institutions and research centers and the major developments and implementations can be undertaken in MATLAB, C, C++, FORTRAN, Python and other programming languages. The dependency required for a software package to undertake intelligent system development is the ability of the programming software to perform mathematical computations as most intelligent systems are modelled using mathematical constructs. Mapping of neural networks, neural network layers and perceptrons has been successfully developed through the MATLAB programming environment and a specialised software toolbox for Neural Networks is present in recent versions of MATLAB.

For the purposes of attaining set goals for the toll collection system to be developed, the researcher sought to investigate computer vision as a possible application for automating classification and recognition functions in the toll collection system. The derived intelligence of the toll collection system would thus be investigated in the line of applicability in computer vision sense. Various approaches and reviews have been done in the area of computer vision application and algorithm development and harnessing the technological applications in computer vision may prove handy for the purposes of automating various human oriented functions in toll collection systems. Perceptual psychologists have spent decades trying to understand how the visual system works and, even though they can devise optical illusions to tease apart some of its principles, a complete solution to this puzzle remains elusive (Marr, 1982; Palmer, 1999; Livingstone, 2008). The taxonomy below shows the transients and dynamics of topics in computer vision thus illustrating the present importance of computer vision in industry and its untapped benefits. Researchers in computer vision have been developing mathematical techniques for recovering the three-dimensional shape and appearance of objects in imagery. We now have reliable techniques for accurately computing a partial 3D model of an environment from thousands of partially overlapping photographs. Given a large enough set of views of a particular object or facade, we can create accurate dense 3D surface models using stereo matching as in Figure 2. We can track a person moving against a complex background We can even, with moderate success, attempt to find and name all of the people in a photograph using a combination of face, clothing, and hair detection and recognition. However, despite all of these advances, the dream of having a computer interpreting an image at the same level as a two-year old (for example, counting all of the animals in a picture) remains elusive (Szeliski, 2010).

Szeliski acknowledges that computer vision applications may appear to be error prone and difficult but application of it is not impossible thus it has been established that computer vision has been applied in the areas that are shown in Figure 3. Optical character recognition (OCR) involves reading handwritten postal codes on letters and automatic number plate recognition (ANPR); Machine inspection: Encompasses rapid parts inspection for quality assurance using stereo vision with specialized illumination to measure tolerances on aircraft wings or auto body parts or looking for defects in steel castings using X-ray vision; Object recognition is undertaken for automated checkout lanes; Fully automated construction of 3D models from aerial photographs used in systems such as Bing Maps; Medical imaging: Registering pre-operative and intra-operative imagery or performing long-term studies of people's brain morphology as they age; Automotive safety: Detecting unexpected obstacles such as pedestrians on the street, under conditions where active vision techniques such as radar or lidar do not work well. Some scholars have however investigated on automotive safety where fully automated driving has been accomplished and this includes the recent work of Miller et al. where a robot was designed which was

Figure 2. Timeline of Computer Vision topics

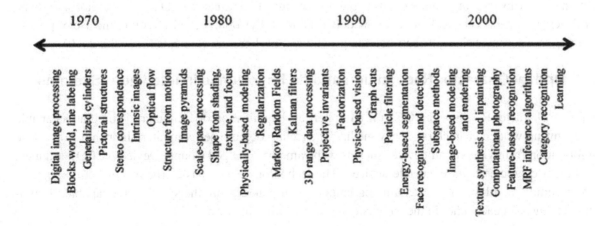

Figure 3. Industrial applications of computer vision

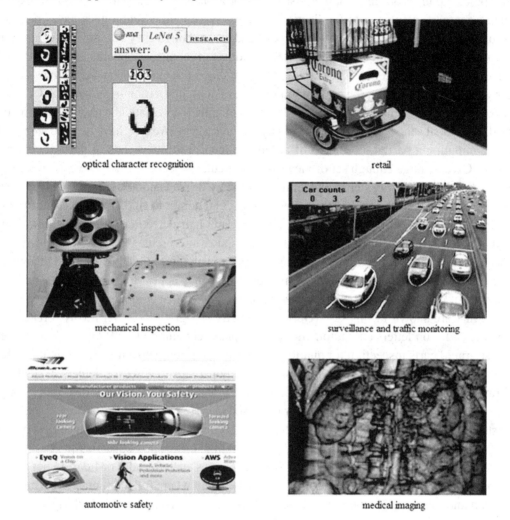

capable of undertaking fully automated driving. Merging computer-generated imagery (CGI) with live action footage by tracking feature points in the source video to estimate the 3D camera motion and shape of the environment. Such techniques are widely used in Hollywood; they also require the use of precise matting to insert new elements between foreground and background elements (Szeliski, 2010).

2.3. Optical Character Recognition and its Importance in Intelligent Systems

Optical Character Recognition (OCR) is an upper level application of computer vision that is capable of capturing written characters off any media. The technology utilises computer algorithms to capture information from video input devices such as web cameras, Charged Couple Devices (CCD), scanners and other character capture capable devices. The technology encompasses the use of both high-level programming and low level programming languages in making sure the systems are capable of communicating with each other in the hardware and information platforms.

2.3.1. Historical and Present Developments of OCR Systems

The engineering attempts at automated recognition of printed characters started prior to World War II. But it was not until the early 1950's that a commercial venture was identified that justified necessary funding for research and development of the technology. This impetus was provided by the American Bankers Association and the Financial Services Industry. They challenged all the major equipment manufacturers to come up with a "Common Language" to automatically process checks. After the war, check processing had become the single largest paper processing application in the world. Although the banking industry eventually chose Magnetic Ink Recognition (MICR), some vendors had proposed the use of an optical recognition technology. However, OCR was still in its infancy at the time and did not perform as acceptably as MICR. The advantage of MICR was that it is relatively impervious to change, fraudulent alteration and interference from non-MICR inks. The "eye'' of early OCR equipment utilized lights, mirrors, fixed slits for the reflected light to pass through, and a moving disk with additional slits. The reflected image was broken into discrete bits of black and white data, presented to a photo-multiplier tube, and converted to electronic bits. The "brain's" logic required the presence or absence of "black" or "white" data bits at prescribed intervals. This allowed it to recognize a very limited, specially designed character set. To accomplish this, the units required sophisticated transports for documents to be processed. The documents were required to run at a consistent speed and the printed data had to occur in a fixed location on each and every form.

2.3.2: The Derived Importance of OCR in Intelligent Systems.

Through the above discussions, it can be established therefore that optical character recognition algorithms play an integral role in intelligent systems. The OCR technology may aid a system in automating and optimizing various data capture scenarios where the human operator would need to be replaced. The OCR engines act as "eyes" to intelligent machines and systems which require implementation of machine vision. OCR technologies have had their functionality extended to other sectors of intelligent systems. Martinsky, (2007) outlines that integration efforts in information technologies has caused the demand for processing vehicles as conceptual resources in information systems. OCR has been extended to Automatic Number Plate Recognition (ANPR) technology whose application extends to vehicle traffic and security applications in parking, access control, border control and tracking of stolen cars. Thus, it has been derived for the purposes of this project that OCR technology is the primary driver in ANPR systems. The resultant intelligence as viewed by Martinsky arises due to the fact that a vehicle information system has to get its data between reality and the system by special intelligent equipment or a human agent which are able to recognise vehicles by their number plates. So, it can be concluded therefore that OCR can be extended to ANPR systems which comprise a practical application of artificial intelligence.

2.4. Data Storage and Retrieval Systems for Toll Collection Systems

2.4.1. Archive Traffic Data Management Systems (ADMS)

Sharan and Ramadurai (2011) studied on ADMS systems and thus brought the idea of data retrieval systems that can be implemented in transportation systems. They define ADMS as a collection of hardware and software that work together to store traffic flow data, and other relevant data of importance in the transportation system. Whilst their study had inclinations to management systems as per se, their contribution is valuable as it sheds light on the various technological data storage and retrieval technologies in use in transportation systems. Such systems have been used in the acquisition of demographic data using various means to count vehicles and obtain statistical data from highways. Data obtained from the systems will then be analysed in real time and as archive data so as to assist engineers and planners to make informed decisions in the traffic sector. The information concerning the various systems worldwide has been summarised in the Figures 4 and Figure 5 which follow.

2.4.2. Vehicle Classification Methods for Toll Collection Systems

Vehicle classification can be executed using various components which may be either automated or manual in nature. For toll collection systems, automatic vehicle classification involves the use of various components and processes in the determination of a vehicle configuration. Once determined, the vehicle configuration can be used for apportioning a suitable toll fee. Traditionally, automatic vehicle classification has been achievable by the use of different types of sensors and transducers which enumerate the physical characteristics of vehicles. Outputs from the devices would then go through an Automatic Vehicle Classification (AVC) processor to distinguish a vehicle class. (Source Placeholder) mentions that AVC systems are used to verify the classifications assigned by toll collectors whilst in electronic toll collection systems, the AVC technology is used to pre-process a toll fee which is due and the associated vehicle classification as well.

Figure 4. ADMS systems courtesy of Sharan and Ramad

	Israel	Illinois	The Netherlands	Belgium	Turkey	Italy
Scope of the system	Citywide City of Tel Aviv	Statewide	Nationwide	Statewide State of Flanders	Citywide City of Istanbul	Citywide City of Bologna
Organization responsible for the ADMS	Transportation Research Institute, Technion on behalf of the Tel Aviv municipality	University of Illinois at Chicago	Rijkswaterstaat-Centre for Transport and Navigation	Traffic Centre Flanders	Istanbul Metropolitan Municipality	Comune di Bologna (Municipality of Bologna, Italy)
Types of traffic detectors used for data collection	• Induction Loop detectors • CCTV	• Induction Loop detectors • RADAR • GPS devices on public transit	• Induction Loop detectors • Infrared detectors • GPS devices on public transit	• Induction Loop detectors • Video Image Processing • CCTV • GPS devices on automobiles	• Induction Loop detectors • Video Image Processing • CCTV • RADAR • Microwave detectors	• Induction Loop detectors • Video Image Processing • GPS on public transit • GPS devices on automobiles
Types of data collected and stored in the ADMS	• Incident data • Entire signal program library • Operation schedules and actual signal cycle and green duration	• Incident data • Construction data • Dynamic Message Sign Text	• Incident data	• Weather data, Incident data • Construction data	• Weather data • Incident data • Construction data	• Incident data
Data aggregated before archival?	Yes	Yes	Yes	Yes	Yes	Yes
Communication networks to transfer field data to the ADMS	• Wired Area Network • Copper Wires	• Wired Area Network • Wireless Area Network • Cellular Network	• Wired Area Network	• Wired Area Network	• Wired Area Network • Cellular Network • 3G Cellular Network	• Wired Area Network • Cellular Network • 3G Cellular Network

Figure 5. ADMS systems and other information access

	Israel	Illinois	The Netherlands	Belgium	Turkey	Italy
Data Transmission Protocols employed	• Proprietary Protocols	• Extensible Markup Language (XML) • Hypertext Transfer Protocol (HTTP)	• Data Exchange (DATEX) II	• File Transfer Protocol (FTP)	• Real Time Streaming Protocol (RTSP) • Raw Binary Data	• FTP • Proprietary Protocols
Database software	• SQL Server	• PostgreSQL	• ORACLE	• ORACLE • SQL Server	• SQL Server	• ORACLE • MYSQL • Microsoft Access
Traffic parameters calculated by the system	• Flow • Level of Service per link	• Travel Time	• Vehicle Miles Travelled • Vehicle Hours Travelled • Travel Time • Speed • Delay • Flow • Delay due to congestion	• Vehicle Hours Travelled • Speed • Occupancy	• Travel Time • Speed • Flow • Occupancy	• Travel Time • Delay • Flow • Queues at signalized intersections • Modal Split
Applications of the ADMS	• Bottleneck identification • Incident management • Planning analyses • Analyses of traffic management activities	• Web based Advance Traveller Information System	• Bottleneck identification • Incident Management • Planning analyses • Bottleneck analyses	• Travel time prediction	• Travel time prediction • Incident management • Advance Traveller Information System (ATIS) - Variable Message Sign	• Bottleneck identification • Incident Management • ATIS - Variable Message Sign • Planning analyses • Traffic signal optimization

2.4.3. Hardware Based Electronic Vehicle Classification Methods

Radar

Defined as Radio Detection and Ranging, it is regarded as one of the non-intrusive methods of vehicle classification. The technology encompasses the use of Radio Waves in the Detection and Ranging of an oncoming object. Radar detection is a speed-based detector that transmits speed data to the host when vehicles pass through the cone of detection. These detectors normally use Doppler technology to provide speed data. They can provide volume and occupancy data along with speed data, depending on the manufacturer. Use of radar detectors requires an FCC license by the manufacturer. It is used primarily for flow monitoring of the limited access highway system by Highway Operations. Radar-based vehicle detection and speed measurement techniques mostly mature and are widely used, but in comparison the development of vehicle classification remains premature in laboratory. There are three major kinds of target classification techniques using microwave radars: Doppler signature, height profile, and combination of distance and Doppler. Techniques based on Doppler signatures are used to divide targets into several macro groups such as aircrafts, vehicles, creatures, and so on, but have not been used specifically for vehicle classification. Techniques based on height profiles, and on the combination of distance and Doppler information require complicated high-resolution radar devices, which are usually expensive, and thus limit their applications (Fang et al, 2007).

On the other hand, the simple-structured low-cost continuous wave (CW) radars can provide Doppler information for vehicle detection and speed measurement, but are rarely applied to classification because only the speed information can be easily drawn and used. However, systems proposed by Fang et al. where vehicle detection and classification is done using unmodulated continuous waves (CW) have proven to be of sufficiently high accuracy (up to 95%) for detection and classification.

Induction Loop Method

Two methods exist and these have different configurations. The first approach is ordinarily called the loop whilst the second method is called the preformed loop. Loop detectors consist of an amplifier located in the controller cabinet and coiled wires in the pavement, which create an electrical field. It is the most widely used type of vehicle detection because of the flexibility of design. Loop detectors can be used to sense vehicle presence, passage, lane occupancy, speed and volume. On the other hand the preformed loop is similar to a loop detector described above, but not imbedded in the pavement. It has been found to be suitable in bridge decks and overhead beams.

Microwave Method

Microwave detectors are mounted above the ground and beam a cone shaped area to an approaching vehicle which reflects some of the microwave energy back to the detector thereby providing a momentary contact closure (pulse) to indicate that a vehicle has been detected. This type of detection can be considered in areas where detector pavement installation is not possible, in instances where pavement is in poor condition or right-of-way is limited. Some trends in microwave technologies for vehicle classification include Unmodulated Continuous-wave Radar. According to Fang et al (2007) such a technology is of a low cost, works in all weather and lighting conditions, and is promising in both research and application. The microwave radars for traffic applications mostly work on X-band (around 10 GHz) or K-band (around 24 GHz), with fixed antennae. Depending on the system type, they can usually be divided into pulse Doppler (PD) radars, unmodulated CW radars, and Frequency-Modulated CW (FMCW) radars. Some scholars report that existing systems, which are based on FMCW radar provide capabilities of measuring parameters such as traffic volume, vehicle presence, lane occupancy, vehicle speed and queue length.

Infrared Detectors

Infrared detectors operate by detecting the infrared rays that are reflected by vehicles passing along the road. Infrared waves are part of the electromagnetic spectrum with wavelengths higher than that of the visible region and are usually between 0.7 and 1.0 μm. These detectors may either be active or passive in their operation. The active detector technology uses a transmitter and a receiver, the transmitter emits the infrared rays and the receiver component of the detector looks for these rays reflected from the vehicles. Whereas for a passive infrared device the receiver component is present and it tries to detect the rays that are reflected by the vehicles whose original source is either sunlight or other infrared energy sources (Sharan & Ramadurai 2011).

The detectors are non-intrusive and may be installed either above or on the roadside segment. Some of the flow parameters that can be identified by the infrared detectors are vehicle speed, length, height, count and class. Klein et al (2006) state that infrared sensors are utilised for signal control, volume, speed, and class measurement, detection of pedestrians in crosswalks, and transmission of traffic information to motorists.

2.5. Weigh in Motion Techniques

These are pressure-sensitive devices generally placed in frames installed in the roadbed and used to determine the axle weight of vehicles. Many of the sensors used in weigh-in-motion devices are the same as those used in treadles. They differ in that treadles utilize a series of sensors to detect the direction of axle movements.

1. **Bending Plates:** These devices utilize a bending plate to determine the axle weight of a vehicle. The device generates an electric current when subjected to pressure caused by an axle crossing the plate.
2. **Capacitive Strip:** The degree of pressure on strip as axle crosses strip allows calculation of axle weight.
3. **Piezoelectric Sensors:** These devices utilize special material inside a tube. The material generates a varying electrical current proportional to the weight of the axle crossing the sensor.

Magnetic Detector Method

There are four types of magnetic detectors; the standard magnetic detector, directional magnetic detector (no longer available), magnetometer, and self-powered vehicle detector (SPVD). The standard magnetic detector cannot sense vehicles moving less that 8km/hr; therefore, cannot provide presence detection. The SPVD is similar to the magnetometer; however, it does not require cable to connect the sensor to the amplifier. The magnetometer and SPVD can provide either pulse or presence detection.

Software Based Vehicle Classification Methods

The software based vehicle classification methods involve the use of a specialised software for real-time and archive data analysis and image processing. The image processing may be undertaken on video clips attained from CCTV cameras during the operation of the security point. The methods and use will be discussed under the categories which follow.

Automatic Number Plate Recognition (ANPR)

Automatic Number Plate Recognition is the technical method of artificial vision (OCR) that allows the recognition of number plates in images of vehicles. Historically, it has been applied on security systems to control accesses of vehicles and car parks.

Nowadays, the ANPR technology has improved its reliability. Some systems are able to offer recognition rates between 95 and 98%. Also, some ANPR equipment are able to recognise the number plate of vehicles that drive up to 200km/hr.

Generally, the ANPR technology can be bought in two modalities:

- The ANPR engine
- The ANPR equipment (Hardware and recognition engine)

Utilizing video processing and capture, the ANPR engine can recognize the number plate directly from the images stored in a hard disk. This type of software allows the user to take to good use images that have been obtained from other systems like CCTV or cameras. The ANPR equipment incorporates all the hardware necessary to capture the images of the vehicles and to recognise the number plate. Moreover, it incorporates the ANPR engine. The ANPR equipment are designed to offer the maximum reliability in all environmental conditions.

Depending on each case the ANPR equipment or ANPR engine will have different uses and advantages. The merits and demerits arise from functionality, robustness and design parameters that the manufacturers implement in their systems. However, their performance is based entirely on the strength of the processing algorithms incorporated in the software engine.

2.6. The Development of Algorithms for Image Processing and Vehicle Identification Systems

Scholars like Duan et al, (2005) outlined that the problem of automatic vehicle number plate recognition is being studied since the 1990's. This follows the perception from Lee et al. (1999) who had related work in vehicle identification systems through image processing technologies. Algorithms such as the Hough Transform would thus be used in the system with results being obtained where a number plate region would be identified as two parallel lines. The Standard Hough Transform (SHT) uses the parametric representation of a line. The SHT measures the angle of the line clockwise with respect to the positive x-axis and produces a resultant matrix from its input. In MATLAB, the Hough Transform algorithm quantizes the rho values to the nearest number in the rho vector. The rho vector depends on the size of the input image and the user-specified rho resolution. The block increments a counter (initially set to zero) in those accumulator array cells represented by (*rho, theta*) pairs found for each pixel. This process validates the point (*R, C*) to be on the line defined by (*rho, theta*). The block repeats this process for each logical true pixel in the image. The Hough block outputs the resulting accumulator matrix.

Another approach was based on the morphology of objects in an image where a focus on some salient properties of vehicle plate images such as their brightness, contrast, symmetry and angles was used in the identification process of the system (Gonzalez, 2002) (Bai and Liu, 2004). Due to these features, this method could be used to detect the similar properties in a certain image and locate the position of number plate regions. Clark and Mirmehdi (2000) discuss a third approach which was based on statistical properties of text. In this approach, text regions were discovered using statistical properties of text like the variance of grey level, number of edges and edge densities in the region. This approach was commonly used in finding text in images, and could well be used for discovering and designating candidate number plate areas as they include alphabets and numerals.

There have been a number of other methods relating to this problem focusing on detecting number plates using artificial intelligence and genetic algorithms. These systems used edge detection and edge statistics and then Artificial Intelligence (AI) techniques to detect the location of the number plate-designate area. It has however occurred that the systems outlined in prior discussion have limitations in terms of their dependencies on various parameters which include ambient conditions in which the system exists.

2.7. Parts of the Generic ANPR System

Most ANPR units are comprised of the Capture Unit and the Process Unit. These have been included and described in Figure 6.

1. The Capture Unit- It has the camera housing, the camera and Infrared focus.
2. Processing Unit- It has an embedded computer, a frame grabber and recognition engine.

Automation hardware for toll collection systems includes coin collection machines and token collection machines. These have been used in the actual collection of the toll charge on toll plazas and toll sites. However, the use of transponders and video enforcement devices has allowed for the automation of various highway routes in some countries without human interaction.

Many methods can be used to single out a vehicle in Zimbabwe. The methods that follow international security protocols include identifying a vehicle by its engine and chassis numbers. These two numbers are reconciled and considered as a tamper proof mechanism to shield motorists from various vehicle fraud instances. On a local base this vehicle information is extended to the vehicle number plate and full information concerning a vehicle's identification particulars is stored in a database at the Central Vehicle Registry department. The number plate becomes an authentic record of ownership which should not be altered in any instant as it provides identification of the vehicle to its owner.

Compounding from the above scenario, the Zimbabwean number plate becomes an official record of identity for the vehicles that are of local ownership. Since 2006, a new class of number plates was issued which has more security features and of a better identification criteria that the older systems that have been in use as in Figure 7. Figure 8 follows with government number plates.

Figure 6. A typical number plate recognition system

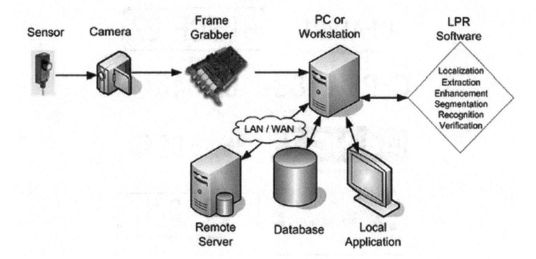

Figure 7. Private vehicle number plates old and new

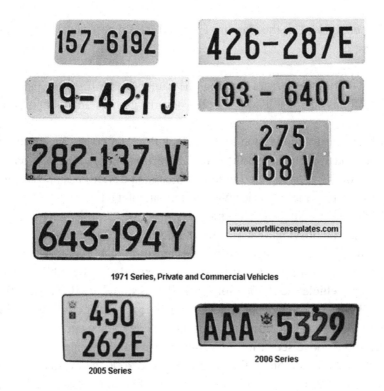

Figure 8. Number plates of government public service and diplomate

IDEF8 Human-System Interaction Design Method

The IDEF8 Human-System Interaction Design Method is used to produce high quality designs of the interactions that do, or should, occur between users and the systems they operate. IDEF8 is not a graphical user interface design method, that is, it is not used to describe screen placement or the size of buttons or windows. It is used to help the system developer capture the interactions that must flow between the system and its users. Systems are collections of objects which perform one or more functions to accomplish a particular goal. The system is not necessarily a computer or a computer program. Human-system interactions are designed at three levels of specification in the IDEF8method. The first level defines the philosophy of system operation and produces a set of models and textual descriptions of overall system processes. The second level of design specifies role-cantered scenarios of system use. The third level of IDEF8 design is for detailing and refinement of the human-system design. At this level of design, IDEF8provides a library of metaphors used to help users and designers specify the desired behaviour in terms of other objects whose behaviour is more familiar. Metaphors provide a model of abstract concepts in terms of familiar, concrete objects and experiences. For example, a light switch metaphor might be used to specify user's interactions involving two possible options. Among the products of this level of design is a human-system interaction mock up with which to test user requirements, formulate user interface strategies (e.g., selecting preferred input and feedback devices), and so forth. Once validated, the products of IDEF8 application are used by system developers (e.g., programmers) to build implementations. Much of IDEF8's language constructs come directly from the IDEF3 Process Description Capture method because of IDEF8's need for a mechanism to capture and organize process information at multiple levels of abstraction and detail. Specialized language extensions distinguish IDEF8 design models, which are prescriptive in nature, from IDEF3 descriptive representations. The fundamental goals of the IDEF8 method are to promote good design practice for human-in-the-loop systems to realize higher quality implementations in less time and at a reasonable cost. IDEF8 seeks to help users produce good human-system interaction designs and consequently higher quality systems by:

1. Facilitating user-focused data collection
2. Enabling direct user involvement in design activities
3. Focusing efforts on early validation of designs using mock-ups and prototypes
4. Promoting more productive iterations through the design process

Technology design considerations in toll collection systems.

Five major factors have been highlighted as critical components for the design of toll collection systems. These technological parameters influence the resultant system architecture for toll collection systems. These have been outlined in the diagram of Figure 9.

Description of design parameters

1. Accuracy
2. Operations
3. Standards
4. Functionality
5. Reliability

Figure 9. Toll collection system design parameters

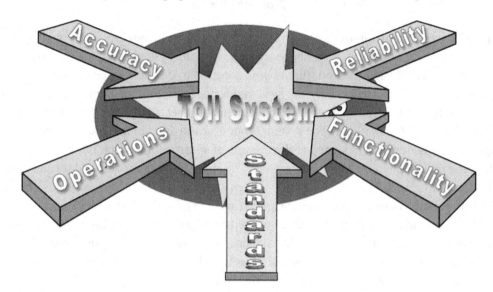

2.8. Case Studies of Implemented Toll Collection Systems

2.8.1. Canada

The ETC system used in Canada is known as the Canada 407 Express toll route (ETR). It is one of the most sophisticated toll roads in the world (Khali, 2007). The Canada 407 ETR is a closed-access toll road, which means that there are gantries placed at the entrance and exit points of each toll. In this system, cameras are equipped with Optical Character Recognition (OCR). The OCR cameras are used to photograph license plate numbers of vehicles that do not have transponders. The toll bill will then be sent directly to the registered address of the vehicle owners. Other than that, two laser beam scanners are placed above the roadway to detect the types of vehicles passing through the gantries. Nevertheless, this toll road bears a very high infrastructure cost, and the users are the ones who help recover the cost through increments in their toll bills (Kamarulazizi and Ismail, 2010). Figure 10 shows the Canadian ETR electronic toll collection system.

2.8.2. Poland

The ETC system used in Poland has been proposed by the Motor Transport Institute along with the University of Technology in Warsaw and Dublin as shown on Figure 11. This system is called the National Automatic Toll Collection System (NATCS), and consists of the National Automatic Toll Collection Centre (NATCC), control gates, and on-board units (OBU). The NATCS uses a combination of mobile telecommunication technology (GSM) with satellite-based Global Positioning System (GPS). Using GPS technology, the OBUs determine the kilometres that have been driven, calculate the toll fees and rates, and then transmit the information to the NATCS computer centre. Each vehicle will be charged

Figure 10. Canada ETR electronic toll Collection system

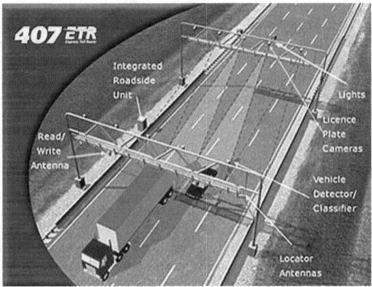

from the highway entrance up until the end of the highway. In order to identify the plate numbers of trucks, the system has control gates equipped with digital short range communication (DSRC) detection equipment and high resolution cameras (Gabriel, 2009). Due to the technical specifications, this system incurs a high cost for motorists.

Figure 11. Poland electronic toll Collection system

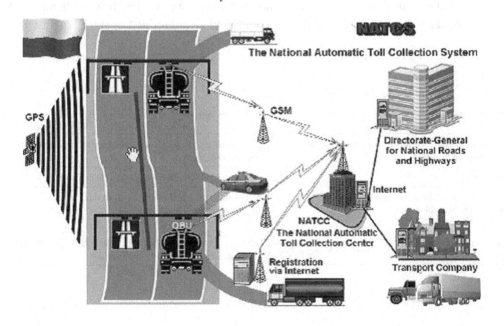

2.8.3. Philippines

The ETC system used in the Philippines has been implemented at the South Luzon Expressway (SLEX) since August 2000. The ETC is referred to as the E-PASS system, which uses Trans core technology. Here, electronic transponders are placed in front of a vehicle's rear-view mirror. Each time a vehicle enters the toll booth, the tag is read by the receiver, automatically identifying the account and debiting the toll fee amount from the corresponding account. Once the amount has been debited, the control gate will lift and the vehicle is allowed to pass through (Crispin, et al. 2005).

3. DESIGN METHODOLOGY AND SYSTEM AUDIT

In order to satisfy previously stated aims and objectives the researcher selected various implementation tools and methods which best fit mechatronic system development metrics. The methodology has been utilised in order to fulfil the desired system goals and tasks. The methodology has been structured to show the information that is necessary to simulate the functionality of the automated and intelligent toll collection system with respect to system functionality as in Table 1.

3.1. Enumeration of Methodology Steps and Activities

MATLAB preliminary experiments in Computer Vision and character recognition (OCR).

MATLAB has toolboxes for Image Acquisition and Image Processing. These toolboxes contain functions that can be used for processing and acquiring images from image capture devices and instruments. Preliminary system development has been designed and undertaken using various toolboxes and methods available for system development. These experiments assisted the researcher to incorporate recognition and computer vision elements to aid system intelligence which is one of the main project objectives. The fact that the design process is iterative in nature implies that the establishments from the experimentation stages for system design can be compounded and refined in stages of system design.

Table 1. Design Methodology Structure

Design Step	Objectives to Be Accomplished
1. MATLAB preliminary experiments in Computer Vision and character recognition.(OCR)	Inco-operating recognition and computer vision elements to aid system intelligence.
2. Interface Design	Developing an automated solution to the toll collection procedure.
3. MATLAB experiments for system performance 4. Software System Modelling 5. Hardware System Modelling	Analysing system performance against the human operator and optimising it to a desired threshold
6. Hardware Design appraisal 7. Software system appraisal	Selecting appropriate and reliable vehicle classification, enforcement and identification methods for the system.

Interface Design

Graphical user interfaces (GUI) are important for most modern systems since they link the human operator to the system and provide a platform for the control of deployed hardware in the system. The resultant interface design must suit constructs of the IDEF8 methodology for user interface design. Thus the researcher designed a user interface using the MATLAB programming GUI programming environment. Continuous refinement, modification and optimisation was performed so as at aid in quality and functional enhancements for the toll collection system user interface.

Software System Modelling

The software system for the toll collection procedure has been mapped using various software tools. However Unified Modelling Diagrams (UML) have been used for the purposes of software system modelling as they provide a fit and adequate basis for software system modelling.

Hardware System Modelling

The hardware system constitutes various hardware components which include image capture hardware, computers and toll fee collection equipment. The possible architectures can be mapped from the models that will be developed in the hardware system modelling steps. Mechatronic integration activities are the central basis for hardware system conceptual modelling.

Software System Design

The design of the automation software and user interfaces has been done in MATLAB using GUI tools available in MATLAB's programming environment. The software system design encompasses software deployment activities for system devices and hardware. The software system design activities include:

1. Optical Character Recognition Engine Design
2. Number Plate Capture software design
3. Image Processing algorithms
4. Secure Database system design
5. Graphical User Interface coding
6. Billing system integration and design

MATLAB Experiments for System Performance

This step assisted the researcher in analysing the performance of the system based on various hardware and software architectures and platforms. The hardware platforms include supporting computer operating environments for the image acquisition equipment. The experiments often bring to light a failure mode of the system and ways in which the failure modes of the system may be combated. The experiments necessitate the analysis of system performance against the human operator and modify the performance to the desired threshold.

Software System Appraisal

Software system appraisal entails the selection and optimisation of the software system variables and evaluating acceptable run times. The appraisal methods for software runtimes in MATLAB have been necessitated by the use of MATLAB programming environment timers. Various platforms for software development have performance issues and confinements related to the software architecture thus appraisal is essential at such a juncture.

Hardware Design Appraisal

This process encompasses selecting appropriate and reliable vehicle classification, enforcement and identification methods for the system. Decision matrices have been utilised for the purposes of appraisal as the Quality Function Deployment (QFD) analysis is an essential component for appraisal.

Systems Audit Formulation

For the purposes of solution formulation and analysis, a brief system audit has been included so as to provide the basis from which the requirements for system design shall emanate from. The audit includes various functions and structures that are present in the collaborative toll collection effort in Zimbabwe.

Systems Audit Framework

The brief systems Audit has been undertaken using the following guideline which has been utilised so as to identify the available system's operational parameters and equipment from those that are presently available.

Toll Collection Sites

Toll collection sites have been set up on various parts of the country. The sites have different infrastructure and their traffic densities differ as well. This implies that the robustness of the hardware to be deployed at the various sites will thus vary since the load on the system to be developed will be different for the toll sites. Apparently, the general demographics are that two toll collection officers man the toll collection site in conjunction with six (6) security officers. A total of $49 000 is released monthly in security costs.

Existing Toll Collection Infrastructure

The temporary tollgate structures that are in place have power support systems in place. On each toll site there has to be:

1.   Diesel or Petrol Generator
2.   Solar Cell System
3.   Connection to National Grid
4.   Communication infrastructure in the form of wireless GPRS coverage or optic fibre.

3.2. Existing Procedures and Practices

Toll Collection Procedure

The operator identifies an oncoming vehicle and visually classifies the vehicle. The operator thus selects a ticket type for the vehicle that has been classified and issues a ticket detached from the ticket book to the motorist who would have paid an appropriate toll charge.

Site Patrol

These are undertaken by patrol officers who visit various sites within their area of jurisdiction and conduct deployment of officers on the toll collection sites. No specialised surveillance hardware has been selected at the toll collection sites at present.

Operator Shifts

Operators work on a shift basis and are assigned to a specific site which they in turn man for the entire duration, depending on the type of shift (day or night shift).

3.3. Potential Risks Exposed to Toll Collection Officers

Security Risk

Regardless of the presence of police officers on the toll collection site, the toll collection officers are at risk of armed robberies as the toll collection officer carries the money collected in a pouch that is perched over the operator's shoulder. There are no vaults or security screens that have been installed where the collection officer is guaranteed of a completely secure operating environment.

Environmental Risk

Exhaust fumes are emitted each time a vehicle passes through a toll collection point. Combustion products are harmful if inhaled by a human operator and continuous exposure to the fumes may prove lethal in the long run for the toll collection officers. It has been evidently observed that a huge amount of toxic emissions are present at toll gates as toll gate pillars are blackened by smoke particles. Longer waiting times at toll sites contribute greatly to localised exhaust emission related pollution.

4. SYSTEM DESIGN

It is the researcher's goal that previously stated objectives be fulfilled in order to satisfy the demands of the project and the system design steps have been outlined in the Table 2 that follows.

A system is characterised by inputs, processes and outputs. Thus, for the toll collection system design metrics to be met fully, its inputs, processes and outputs have been considered in the system design phase and sections which follow. This has necessitated the system design to be organised in terms of justifi-

Table 2. Design step and objectives to be accomplished

Design Step	Objectives to be accomplished
1. MATLAB experiments in Computer Vision and character recognition (OCR)	Inco-operating recognition and computer vision elements to aid system intelligence.
2. Interface Design	Developing an automated solution to the toll collection procedure.
3. MATLAB experiments for system performance 4. Software System Modelling 5. Hardware System Modelling	Analysing system performance against the human operator and optimising it to a desired threshold
6. Hardware Design appraisal 7. Software system appraisal	Selecting appropriate and reliable vehicle classification, enforcement and identification methods for the system.

able processes, algorithms and sub-functions for the system components at input, processing and output stages as in Figure 12. MATLAB experiments in computer vision and Optical character recognition assist the researcher in attaining appropriate machine vision elements to aid in the system's intelligent functions. Since the system shall undertake perception or image capture from the received input image, MATLAB experiments will assist in developing proper design parameters for use in the toll collection system. The general algorithm for Number Plate Character Recognition has been structured in the section which follows.

1. Receive pre-processed Binary Large Objects (Blobs)
2. Compare processed blobs with characters in template
3. Concatenate characters that have been matched with those in character recognition template.
4. Output identified characters into text file.

The toll collection system seeks to automate the toll collection procedure that has been in place. Factors of merit for a reliable read rate have been delimited to computer vision system design therefore essential algorithms in Image processing and Image Analysis have been utilised which are available within the MATLAB programming environment.

4.1. Algorithms for Hardware Control, Integration and Image Capture

To necessitate system initialisation and hardware trigger mechanisms, several algorithms have been utilised which necessitate hardware installation and integration to the toll collection system. Whilst a suitable cash collection methodology is yet to be appraised, it has been assumed that the toll collection system requires a cashless transaction method where a prepayment system has to be appraised. Thus, hardware for the purposes of cash collection and its initialisation has been omitted from the hardware control algorithms included in this section.

Figure 12. Generic toll collection system

1. Presence
2. Image capture

To necessitate the process of automating the toll collection system using computer vision elements, a live video stream has to be initiated for the system to attain the required image sequences and data. Thus to achieve this, the algorithm has been developed to initiate the image capture hardware.

1. Find driver software for installed hardware
2. Initialise image capture hardware and send it to a memory buffer
3. Display the live image stream.

An image is the core source for any Computer Vision system, treating an image as a matrix and each row in the image as a dimensional vector simplify the implementation of complex operations on images. This can be done in the 255 colour bitmap space or the binary image space.

- **Image Transformation and Conversion:** The process of scaling images from different size (width - height) and type (colour - Grayscale - binary). Most of the scaling operations are carried out using Nearest Neighbour Interpolation. Image format conversion normally requires two steps of creating a temporary memory, and copying corresponding data pixel.
- **Blurring Technique:** Using Gaussian blur, convolving image with Gaussian kernel or Gamma correction to pre-process all image pixels, making it easier to apply a subsequent colour intensity thresholding to filter the interesting regions.
- **Erosion:** The process of removing a defined structuring element from the image, pixel by pixel, this operation is particularly useful in shrinking blobs in pixel, hence, helps to eliminate small distracting noise from the image.
- **Dilation:** The opposite process of Erosion, where a structuring element will be added to the image pixel by pixel with the objective to grow the all blobs found in images, hence, helps to clarify the shapes of dim objects.
- **Ultimate Erosion:** An iteration of several Erosion steps will be carried out until the targeted blob starts to disappear, this method is particularly useful in the case of finding image skeleton for blobs in images.
- **Opening:** Based on Erosion and Dilation, consists of an Erosion followed by a Dilation, general purpose is to first eliminate distracting blobs, then signify those blobs that can go through the Erosion filtering.
- **Closing:** Opposite to Opening, consists of a Dilation followed by Erosion, aiming to clarify important segments of each blob, while removing those redundant and small parts.
- **White Top Hat:** With the purpose to obtain the small particles in images, this process consists of an Opening operation followed by a subtraction of the Opened output from the original image, the result image will contain those parts that have been eliminated over from the opening.
- **Edge Detection:** The objective of all Edge Detection algorithms is to get the parts on the boundary of all blobs from the image, those parts are also known as Contours, and are really useful for detecting lines in the images, or performing layered operations. Several popular algorithms for detecting edges in images are Sobel, Prewitt, Roberts, Laplacian of Gaussian (LoG) and Canny. In the context of the design stages for the automated and intelligent toll collection system, the

different edge detection techniques have been utilised in the experimentation phase where the techniques were evaluated for effectiveness

- **Line Detection:** Collections of all edges can be put into a Hough Transform to identify all lines with matched parameters (length, width, and angle). The analysis operation is mostly based on the correlation of pixels among other, those pixels with the maximum Hough analysis amplitude will be judged as the extremes of some lines.
- **The Aspect Ratio (Also Called Elongation or Eccentricity):** Can be found by scanning the image and finding the minimum and maximum values on the row and columns where the object lies. This ratio is defined in terms of rows and columns which are denoted by c and r. The Axis of Least Second Moments provides information about the orientation of the object.

4.2. Interface Design

In order for the toll collection system to be fully appreciated, precepts from the IDEF8 models have been used in the design of a standardised interface for the toll collection system. A data flow model diagram has been utilised here so as to illustrate the flow of information between various stages of the expected toll collection system. This falls in line with the requirements that have been found to be beneficial for the system users.

Interface Requirements

The general requirements of the system are:

1. The interface should provide a live video capture screen
2. The interface has to provide the user interactive functions which necessitate successful capture of a number plate using optical character recognition.
3. Through the interface a customer must get a receipt tendered from the OCR engine.
4. The flow of traffic should be regulated such that the flow of traffic will not outweigh the performance of the system as highlighted in Figure 13.

Description of the Data Flow Model Diagram

The data flow model diagram is a standard software modelling tool that can be utilised to model how a software system will execute its functions. This tool illustrates the flow of data acquired and how the data can be translated into useful information.

1. The toll operator captures data acquired from the number plate recognition system and saves the data in a plates.txt file.
2. The file would have been generated by the OCR engine and saved in the text file format.
3. The data from the text file requires to be archived in a database file that will be retrieved by the toll collection patrol officers.
4. Such information retrieved in system stages above can be used for auditing and toll verification procedures.

Figure 13. Data flow model diagram

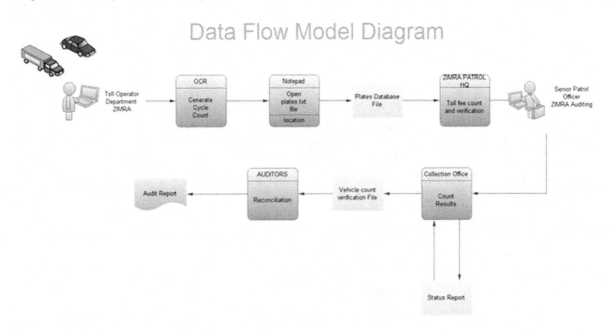

4.3. MATLAB Parameters for Character Recognition Engine Design

To undertake experiments in MATLAB, a computer was setup with the following operational parameters as in Table 3:

The character recognition engine is expected to process and interpret binary image matrix data and recognise characters from the binary information. Various methods can be utilised but in this instance correlation has been used as the main tool to foster the character recognition process. The objective of the OCR engine is to register the existence of text in the binary image and output corresponding characters that would have been recognised from the system.

The input that is processed by the OCR engine is binary image input. This is matrix array which has a representation of the processed number plate image as in Figure 14.

Table 3. Optical Character Recognition parameters

Parameter	Set Variable
Programming Environment	MATLAB R2010b
Computer Hardware	2.8 GHz Intel Celeron Processor, 1GB RAM,
Hardware Interface	Universal Serial Bus 2.0
Image acquisition hardware	1. Tech-com USB webcam; Resolution up to 20MegaPixels with drivers 2. Nikon Digital Camera; 10MegaPixel 3. Blackberry Pearl 8110 mobile phone camera

Figure 14. OCR engine algorithm flow chart

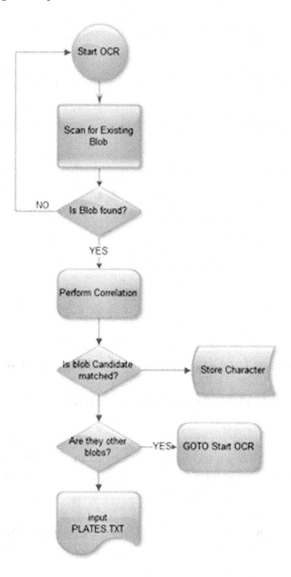

1.   Receive Binary large objects (blobs).
2.   Compare blob with letter template.
3.   If blob with maximum correlation is found output corresponding letter.

The recognition engine for alphabetic characters for the Zimbabwean number plate are designed using the FS-Schrift font. Thus, the formulation of the OCR character set has been done using the alphanumeric character set in FS-Schrift as in Figure 15. For the recognition engine to have a reference set of system characters, the system should have singled out characters which will be used by the OCR engine in performing correlation calculation for desired blobs received. Such characters have been cropped to pixel dimensions of 24X42 pixel aspect ratios as highlighted in Figure 16.

Figure 15. Zimbabwean Number plate alpha-numeric character

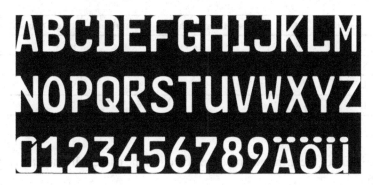

Figure 16. Scaled binary image for OCR

4.4. OCR General Code

Optical character recognition design has been developed using correlation principles. The approach in correlation for optical character recognition is such that each character in the templates binary is compared with the captured blob regions that are sent for correlation and matching.

Mathematical Constructs of Optical Character Recognition Using Correlation

Binary data in the image matrices is utilised for the computation of the matched blob is returned to the word file and character concatenation is undertaken for the matched characters as shown in Annexure 1.

4.5. System Design

Presence Detection Method Appraisal

To come up with a suitable presence detection method, the following rank matrix was developed. The desirable features have a higher score on the evaluation scale whilst the undesirable features take a lower score on the ranking matrix. A score of 1 to 10 has been used for the selection of the hardware units under consideration as in Table 4.

In order to grab frames from the live video stream, a frame grabbing trigger mechanism can be incorporated to the system. The trigger mechanism initiates image capture the moment a vehicle reaches a proximity defined to give a clearly captured image. The range where the hardware capture device produces a clear and acceptable image value is the one where the location of the trigger sensor may be placed. The circuit design for the camera trigger can be developed from a microcontroller interfaced with infrared sensors. The general functionality is such that when the vehicle reaches the desired capture

Table 4. Presence detection QFD table

Detection Method	Sensitivity	Cost	Ease of maintenance	Durability	Ease of installation	Total Score
1. Laser	10	8	7	8	9	42
2. Induction Loop	8	4	7	6	4	29
3. Radar	10	5	8	8	9	40
4. Microwave	10	5	7	8	9	39

zone and crosses the beam of the infrared presence detectors the camera immediately captures the image of the car in Table 5.

Due to the existence of various enforcement techniques, barriers can be implemented which will be utilised as authentication zones for the toll collection system. The working principle of the system is such that the barrier will be connected within the system through wired or wireless media and will facilitate a stopping zone where the toll user will reduce speed or stop momentarily before the barrier as the system undertakes automated toll collection functions. The barrier may be gate which actuates upon receiving an authorisation signal from the automated toll collection system software engines. The gate should have a real-time communication connection which enables real time instruction and communication from the computer controlling the toll site.

4.6. Lighting and Illumination System Design

Computer vision systems require illumination levels to be consistent and reliable since the level of illumination influences the quality of the resultant images. Various techniques have been put into consideration as the toll site is operated on a day and night basis. Therefore, it is necessary to operate the computer vision system with illumination induced in it. It will be desirable for the system to be of low energy consumption therefore greater weight is preferred for the toll collection system to be energy efficient as in Table 6.

The location of sensors and actuators on the toll collection site is of integral importance as the performance of the resultant system may be justified by these. The system requires a power source, the processing computer, artificial illumination equipment and operator consoles. The imaging system has to prevent the availability of shadows on desired number plate regions thus proper assessment of site configuration is integral so as to facilitate maximum system performance. It is envisaged that the performance of the computer vision equipment is reliant on the site configuration. Various setups have initially been considered but the desirable configuration should be compatible with experimental setup and outcomes obtained from the simulation. The location of sensors is dependent on the deployment hardware.

Table 5. Computer usage for different trigger mechanisms

Method	Computer hardware Usage	Implication
Continuous trigger	High	High hardware usage slows down system performance.
Infrared trigger	Low	Faster processing times are achieved and performance is high.

Table 6. Lighting equipment methods and appraisal

Lighting Method	Energy Consumption per desired unit light intensity	Durability	Running Cost
Floodlights	High	Low	High
Infrared illumination	Low	High	Low
Fluorescent	Low	High	Medium
Incandescent	Medium	Low	

5. SYSTEM DATA INPUT

When a vehicle reaches the required proximity, its presence has to be detected in order to trigger the toll collection system. The system requires a pulse or electrical system so as to initiate the image capture and the automatic toll collection system processing engine. Various images were captured at different illumination levels and these were utilised as the image sample for the number plates that require processing within the number plate recognition system. The sample aids in identifying a robust technique for number plate recognition as it is a key component for the toll collection system. Parameters that have been varied in the captured images include the following:

1. Illumination level
2. Camera resolution
3. Captured image size
4. Camera orientation
5. Distance from image source

The above parameters affect the algorithm development for the various cases as the effect of noise, distortion and clarity are altered each time one of the above parameters is varied. Still images have been used for the development of the Number plate recognition engine and also for evaluating the effectiveness of the Optical Character Recognition engine including all algorithms.

5.1. System Processes and Data Generated

In order to acquire varied image samples with varied illumination and camera resolution, the researcher utilised natural lighting conditions for evaluation of field variables. This aids in attaining the performance of the system without the need for artificial illumination equipment. The attained field sample and data can be seen in Figure 17.

5.2. Image Pre-Processing Outcomes

The image processing activities in MATLAB can be executed in multiple stages with outcomes of each image processing stage being outputted into the MATLAB workspace. The resultant matrix value can be called for visualization either in the form of a graph or output that is passed to the video screen as an image. The algorithms used for image processing and the data that is generated from them has been

Figure 17. Filed samples for system simulation

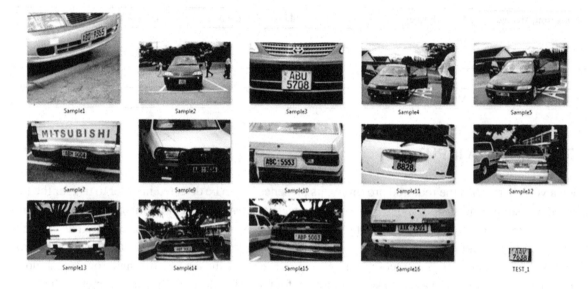

included below. Each stage of the image processing stages and its outcomes has been included in the section that follows.

Data Generated Through the Imread Function

The imread function reads a grayscale or colour image from the file specified by the string pointing to the file and its file extension. The return value returned by the function is an array containing the image data. If the file contains a grayscale image inputted as an M-by-N array. If the file contains a true colour image, the image will be an M-by-N-by-3 array as in Figure 18. The matrix values for each acquired pixel value in the image can be seen in part below the image with vehicles and the returned variable, *capimage,* and its matrix dimensions are shown on the left pane in the screenshot above. In the above instance the captured images are those that have been attained using the digital camera in the process of attaining field samples for use in the experimentation phase of the system design. Pixel gradations are shown which give the image aspect ratio or size in pixel dimensions. For the purposes of simulation of this system, 640 X 480 image sizes have been utilised for experimentation and code testing.

5.3. Modelling and Simulation of the Design

In order to assess the functionality of the system, the researcher utilised a design which is based on the following parameters:

1. Natural lighting conditions have been used.
2. Stationary vehicles are used for sampling, experimentation and system design.
3. Process design was conducted off site.

The simulation of the chosen design has been outlined in the sections that follow.

Figure 18. Read function and output plot in MATLAB

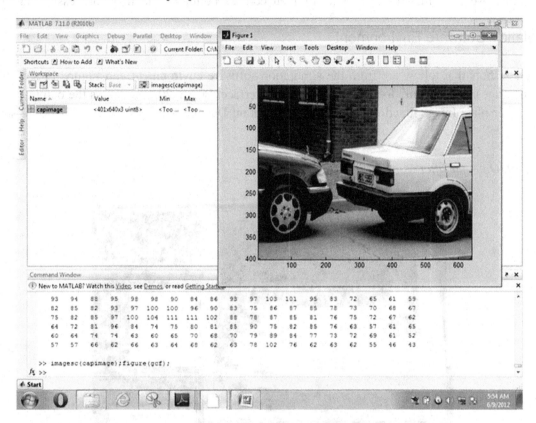

Simulation Setup

The setup was utilised in order to come up with the results for the simulated toll collection system setup.

Simulation Devices

1. Webcam for image capture
2. Computer with computer vision software.
3. Computer with database management software.

Description of Simulation Procedure

The following steps outline the procedural steps that comprise the simulation.

1. Initialise image acquisition hardware.
2. Process Number Plate captured using the image capture devices.
3. Send number plate information to a text file
4. Import information from the captured number plates into a database.
5. Process database information for the purposes of billing and customer clearance.

Runtimes were recorded for the time to complete code execution for the image processing activities.

Simulation Software Environment

The screenshots that follow are from the simulation software environment and Figure 19 shows the outcome after using the initialise camera button in interface, Figure 20 now shows the output on capture number plate Image function and Figure 21 resultant Databases in MS Access. Figure 22 shows

Figure 19. Outcome after using initialize camera

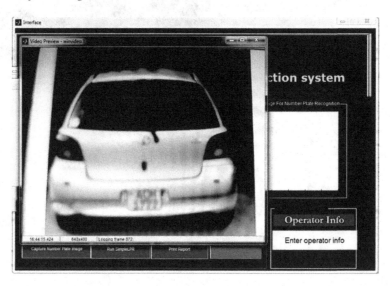

Figure 20. Output on capture number plate image function

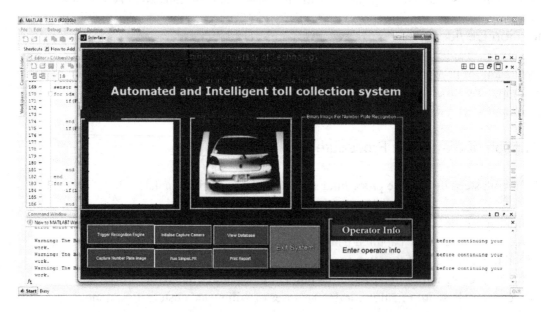

Figure 21. Resultant image database in MS access

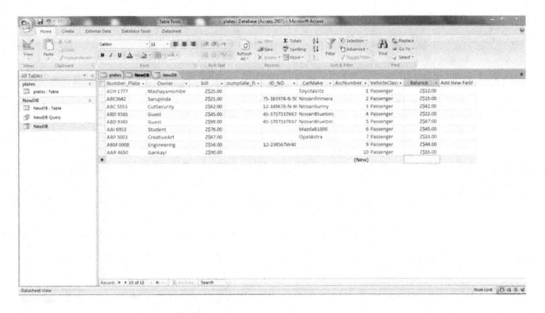

Figure 22. Plates database query area for new entries

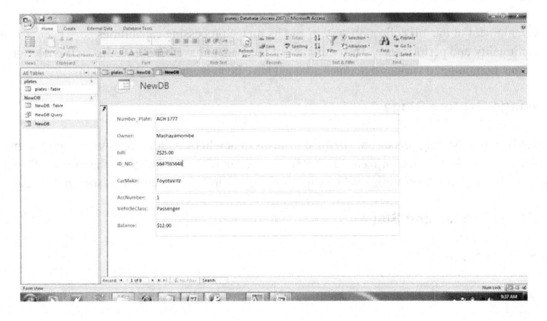

the plates database query area for new entries with parameters for entry. Figure 23 is now the Entity relationship diagram for the database used for plate registration and verification. The above outcome is obtained from the database. It is the interface function for entering a new database query. The entity relationship diagram shows the linkages in the databases. In this case the reference link is the number plate that would have been passed in the system.

Figure 23. Entity relationship diagram for data

6. RESULTS AND DISCUSSIONS

The development of the toll collection system and its image processing capabilities have been assessed for functionality and performance. The outcomes of the system have been included in this section and discussions pertaining to various outcomes attained have been included in this section.

6.1. Image Capture Stage

MATLAB values for image capture are defined in terms of height by width. The system captures images from a live video stream by capturing a snapshot from the frames being acquired by the camera. The snapshot is a still image of the oncoming vehicle approaching the toll collection site as shown on Figure 24.

6.2. Image Processing Stage

Image Conversion

The captured image is then converted to a grayscale image prior conversion to binary image format as in Figure 25.

Image Filtering

The top hat morphological operation is undertaken immediately after the conversion of the image to the grayscale colour space as in Figure 26. The image acquired after the top hat operation is then converted into a black and white image using a threshold value. In this instance a threshold value that has been identified through experimentation was 0.3. The outcome from the application of thresholding has been shown in Figure 27.

Figure 24. Captured image from live video

Figure 25. Grayscale image outcome

Figure 26. Outcome of Top hat morphological operation

Figure 27. Black and white filter outcome

Number Plate Region Identification

After all the pre-processing of the image to filter out backgrounds the next stage will be to determine the number plate region and identify its position in the captured image in Figure 28. The corresponding horizontal projection can be viewed in Figure 29. It is an outcome from the Sobel Edge detection algorithm to ascertain the probable region of a number plate. The horizontal and vertical edge sum has been attained by summing the vertical and horizontal edge detection.

6.3. Statistical Image Filtering to Ascertain Number Characters in Image

Image properties have been determined for the captured number plate images and these have been used to determine whether blobs in an image are alphanumeric characters or not. Bounding box, Orientation and Image eccentricity are important features that the number plate recognition segment of the toll collection has utilised to find number plate characters. Through experimentation and continuous analysis, pre-set values were attained for Eccentricity and Orientation which are peculiar to the captured number plate regions in the Zimbabwean number plates. The attained values have allowed the researcher to define proper number plate recognition parameters which give an accurate determination of pixel values and their properties.

Statistical Regions Filters

The following command is used to ascertain the regions in a binary image and show their properties.

stats2 = regionprops (cc, 'Orientation','Area','Perimeter','BoundingBox')

Figure 28. Vertical edge projection

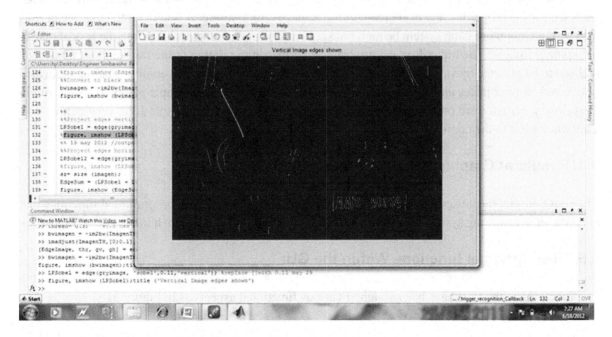

Figure 29. Horizontal edge detection and projection

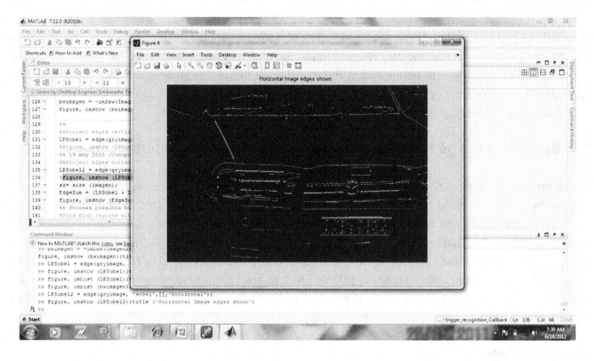

In this case the filter has been used to determine orientation, area, perimeter and bounding box properties for the binary image under processing. The second filter has been designed as follows.

Number Plate Recognition Outcomes

The number plate regions that were recognised properly using the computer vision algorithms have been analysed for the properties that made recognition a success or a failure. It is anticipated that the performance of a computer vision system be high but some environmental factors stimulate the loss of clarity of captured images. The toll collection system's performance in relation to the failure modes has been realised to be affected by various critical failure mode attributes such as uneven illumination, deformed or defaced number plates and shadows. However various regions for the sample plates that were run in the primary system were only recognised fully when verified using the Simple LPR verification tool. This was owing to the nonrobust nature of the algorithms in use.

6.4. Resultant Graphical User Interface (GUI)

The resultant graphical user interface (GUI) is an interface with icons and programmed functions that aid the user in acquiring system functions and communicating with the system hardware as in Figure 30.

6.5. Description of functions Within the GUI

The functions in the GUI have been assigned various functional aspects as in Figure 31.

Figure 30: Final user interface for toll collection

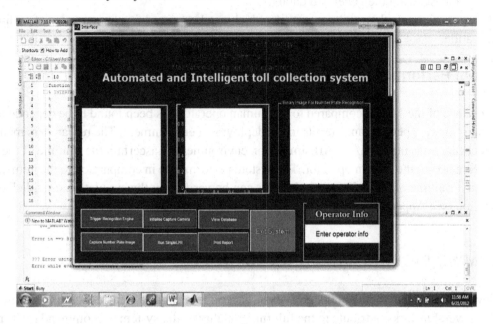

Figure 31. Resultant database and queries

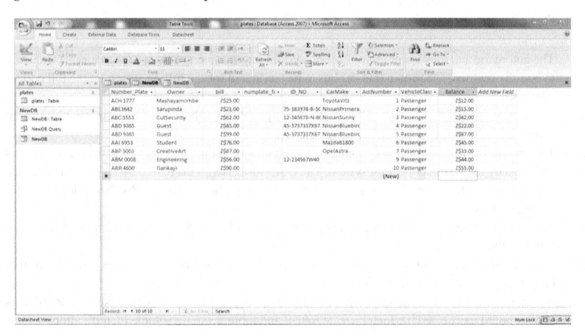

1. Trigger recognition engine: triggers the computer vision recognition engine and processes.
2. Capture number plate image: captures the displayed number plate image from the video in the workspace.
3. Initialize capture camera: Initializes connected image capture device.
4. Run simple LPR: Runs the offline number plate verification file for the system.

5.   View Database: open the generated database.
6.   Print report: Outputs the resultant text file which can be printed for the purposes of auditing and verification.

6.6. System Performance as Compared to Human Operator

The performance of the system compared to the human operator has been found to be dependent on the hardware and software performance levels in the deployment environment. The researchers managed to use the timer functions in the MATLAB simulation environment to ascertain the runtime of the system and comparing it with the human operator. The system performance in comparison to the human operator produced a runtime of 3.708576 seconds. This can be verified in the simulation provided with this documentation (see Appendix 1).

7. RECOMMENDATIONS AND CONCLUSION

Having developed a system for toll collection whose backbone is number plate recognition, it is important to note that several factors contribute to the full functionality of the system. Recommendations pertaining to the application of the system and its deployment have been included in the section which follows.

7.1. Recommendations

1.   The automatic and intelligent toll collection system requires a cashless approach for its efficiency to be fully realised. Electronic transfer has to be facilitated for the billing system in the toll collection system.
2.   It is recommended that infrared illumination equipment be utilised in conjunction with infrared cameras for the purposes of quality image capture.
3.   The system has to be deployed on an embedded hardware platform to aid in increased robustness and security for the toll collection system. The DSE-400D is a 2 Port RS-232/422/485 Serial device server from Quatech capable of such a deployment. The platform provided by the device is tamper proof and robust.
4.   Automated barriers may be incorporated into the system for purposes of enforcement and ease of image capture.
5.   Further tests and recognition engine code refinement are necessary prerequisites since the system has limited robustness in the present setup.
6.   In order to enhance reliability, the system might require assistive technologies such as RFID tags and on-board units (OBU) which provide robust and more accurate vehicle identification.

8. CONCLUSION

The development of the toll collection system has been largely a success owing to the accomplishment of the objectives in the toll collection system design stages. To a greater extent the development of a local solution for toll.

REFERENCES

Kalbande, D. R., Deotale, N., Singhal, P., Shah, S., & Thampi, G. T. (2011). An Advanced Technology Selection Model using Neuro Fuzzy Algorithm for Electronic Toll Collection System. *(IJACSA). International Journal of Advanced Computer Science and Applications*, *II*(4), 97–104.

Anishiya, P., & Joans, S. M. (2011). Number plate recognition for indian cars using morphological dilation and erosion with the aid of ocrs. *Proceedings of the 2011 International Conference on Information and Network Technology (IPCSIT)*.

Atkociunas, E., Blake, R., Juozapavicius, A., & Kazimianec, M. (2005). Image Processing in Road Traffic Analysis. *Nonlinear Analysis: Modelling and Control, 10*(4), 315–332.

Chuang, Y. Y., Agarwala, A., Curless, B., Salesin, D. H., & Szeliski, R. (2002). Video matting of complex scenes. *ACM Transactions on Graphics, 21*(3), 243-248.

Clark, P., & Mirmehdi, M. (2000). Finding Text Regions using Localised Measures. *Proceedings of the 11th British Machine Vision Conference* (pp. 675-684).

Crispin, D. D. E., Aileen, U. M., Ricardo, G. S., Jim, J. M., & Hilario, S. P. (2005). Allocation of Electronic Toll Collection Lanes at Toll Plazas Considering Social Optimization of Service Times and Delays. *Proceedings of the Eastern Asia Society for Transportation Studies* (pp. 1496–1509).

Duan, T. D., Du, T. H., Phuoc, T. V., & Hoang, N. (2005). Building an Automatic Vehicle License-Plate Recognition. *Proceedings of the International Conference in Computer Science* (pp. 59-63).

Duan, T. D., Duc, D. A., & Du, T. L. H. (2004). Combining Hough Transform and Contour Algorithm for detecting Vehicles License-Plates. *Proceedings of 2004 International Symposium on Intelligent Multimedia, Video and Speech Processing* (pp. 747-750). doi:10.1109/ISIMP.2004.1434172

Electronic Toll Collection System. (n, d.). Retrieved from http://ntl.bts.gov/lib/jpodocs/edldocs1/13480/ch5.pdf

Fang, J., Meng, H., Zhang, H., & Wang, X. (2007). A Low-cost Vehicle Detection and Classification System based on Unmodulated Continuous-wave Radar. Proceedings of the 2007 IEEE Intelligent Transport Systems Conference, Seattle, WA, USA (pp. 715-720).

Fritz, W. (2006). *Intelligent Systems*. New Horizons Press.

Gabriel, N., Mitraszewska, I., & Tomasz, K. 2009. The Polish Pilot Project of Automatic Toll Collection. *Proceedings of the 6th International Scientific Conference*.

Gonzalez, R. C., & Woods, R. E. (2002). *Digital Image Processing*. Englewood Cliffs, New York: Prentice Hall.

Hongliang, B., & Changping, L. (2004). A Hybrid License Plate Extraction Method Based on Edge Statistics and Morphology. *Proceedings of the 17th International Conference on Pattern Recognition*.

Rudas, I. J., & Fodor, J. (2008). Intelligent Systems. *International Journal of Computers, Communications & Control*, 3(3), 132–138.

Jack, O. (2006). Future of Vehicle and Roadside Intelligent Transport Systems. *Proceedings of the 2nd IEE Conference on Automotive Electronics.*

Kamarulazizi, K., & Ismail, D. W. (2010). Electronic Toll collection System using passive RFID technology. *Journal of Theoretical and Applied Information Technology, 2,* 70-76.

Krishnakumar, K. (2003). *Intelligent systems for aerospace engineering – an overview.* NASA.

Lee, J. C. (1999). Automatic Character Recognition for Moving and Stationary Vehicles. Proceedings of the International Joint Conference on Neural Networks IJCNN'99 (Vol. 4, pp. 2824-2828.

Livingstone, M. (2008). *Vision and Art: The Biology of Seeing.* New York: Abrams.

Marlin, T. E. (1995). *Process Control, Designing Processes and Control Systems for Dynamic performance.* McGraw-Hill.

Marr, D. (1982). *Vision: A Computational Investigation into the Human Representation and Processing of Visual Information.* San Francisco: W. H. Freeman.

Martinsky, Ondrej. 2007. *Algorithmic and Mathematical principles of Automatic Number Plate Recognition systems.*

Minea, M., Grafu, M., Cormos, F. D., & Ciprian, A. 2007. Reliable Integrated Communications for Urban Intelligent Transport Systems. *Proceedings of the 8th International Conference on Telecommunications in Modern Satellite, Cable and Broadcasting Services.* doi:10.1109/TELSKS.2007.4376090

Opiola, J. (2006). *Toll Collection Systems- Technology Trend Impact on PPP's & Highways' Transport.* Washington, U.S.A: World bank.

Palmer, S. E. 1999. Vision Science: Photons to Phenomenology. Cambridge, Massachusets: The MIT Press.

Persad, K., Walton, C. M., & Hussain, S. (2007). Toll Collection Technology and Best Practices. Vehicle/License Plate Identification for Toll Collection Application.

Pressman, R. S. (1982). *Software Engineering: A Practitioner's approach.* New York: McGraw-Hill.

Revski, G. (2003). On Conceptual Design of Intelligent Systems. In *Mechatronics 13* (pp. 1029–1044). Uxbridge, U.K.: Elsevier Ltd.

Russel, P., & Norvig, S. (1995). *Artificial Intelligence: A Modern Approach.* New Jersey: Prentice Hall.

Sharan, D., & Gitakrishnan, R. (2011). Archive traffic Data Management Systems- A study on the feasibility and implementation in Indian Urban Areas.

Szeliski, R. (2010). *Computer Vision Algorithms and Applications.* Springer.

Tang, W.C., & Ho, T.V. (2007). *Electronic Toll Collection System.* US 7233260 B2.

The Association Of Automatic Identification And Data Capture Technologies. (2000). *Optical Character Recognition (OCR).* Pittsburg, USA: AIM Inc.

Thi, H. T. (2007). *A robust traffic surveillance system for detecting and tracking vehicles at nighttime.* University of Technology, Sydney.

APPENDIX

1.   Appendix 1: Software Disk with simulation software and previous versions illustrating the experiments and development stages of the automated and intelligent toll collection system have been included in the disk.
2.   Appendix 2: Supporting modules Included in the simulation

```
Create templates (create_templates.m)
%CREATE TEMPLATES
%Letter
A=imread('letters_numbers\A.bmp');B=imread('letters_numbers\B.bmp');
C=imread('letters_numbers\C.bmp');D=imread('letters_numbers\D.bmp');
E=imread('letters_numbers\E.bmp');F=imread('letters_numbers\F.bmp');
G=imread('letters_numbers\G.bmp');H=imread('letters_numbers\H.bmp');
I=imread('letters_numbers\I.bmp');J=imread('letters_numbers\J.bmp');
K=imread('letters_numbers\K.bmp');L=imread('letters_numbers\L.bmp');
M=imread('letters_numbers\M.bmp');N=imread('letters_numbers\N.bmp');
O=imread('letters_numbers\O.bmp');P=imread('letters_numbers\P.bmp');
Q=imread('letters_numbers\Q.bmp');R=imread('letters_numbers\R.bmp');
S=imread('letters_numbers\S.bmp');T=imread('letters_numbers\T.bmp');
U=imread('letters_numbers\U.bmp');V=imread('letters_numbers\V.bmp');
W=imread('letters_numbers\W.bmp');X=imread('letters_numbers\X.bmp');
Y=imread('letters_numbers\Y.bmp');Z=imread('letters_numbers\Z.bmp');
%Number
one=imread('letters_numbers\1.bmp');  two=imread('letters_numbers\2.bmp');
three=imread('letters_numbers\3.bmp');four=imread('letters_numbers\4.bmp');
five=imread('letters_numbers\5.bmp'); six=imread('letters_numbers\6.bmp');
seven=imread('letters_numbers\7.bmp');eight=imread('letters_numbers\8.bmp');
nine=imread('letters_numbers\9.bmp'); zero=imread('letters_numbers\0.bmp');
%*-*-*-*-*-*-*-*-*-*-*-
letter=[A B C D E F G H I J K L M...
    N O P Q R S T U V W X Y Z];
number=[one two three four five...
    six seven eight nine zero];
character=[letter number];
templates=mat2cell(character,42,[24 24 24 24 24 24 24 ...
    24 24 24 24 24 24 24 ...
    24 24 24 24 24 24 24 ...
    24 24 24 24 24 24 24 ...
    24 24 24 24 24 24 24 24]);
save ('templates','templates')
clear all
Code for Clipping and Cropping an Image Region for Processing.
```

```
function imgn=clip(imagen)
%Crops a black letter with white background.
%Example:
% imagen=imread('metal.bmp');
% imgn=clip(imagen);
% subplot(2,1,1);imshow(imagen);title('INPUT IMAGE')
% subplot(2,1,2);imshow(~imgn);title('OUTPUT IMAGE')
if ~islogical(imagen)
    imagen=im2bw(imagen,0.99);
end
a=~imagen;
[f c]=find(a);
lmaxc=max(c);lminc=min(c);
lmaxf=max(f);lminf=min(f);
imgn=a(lminf:lmaxf,lminc:lmaxc);%Crops image
```

Code to Read Lines in System

```
function [fl re]=lines(im_texto)
% Divide text in lines
% im_texto->input image; fl->first line; re->remain line
% Example:
% im_texto=imread('TEST_3.jpg');
% [fl re]=lines(im_texto);
% subplot(3,1,1);imshow(im_texto);title('INPUT IMAGE')
% subplot(3,1,2);imshow(fl);title('FIRST LINE')
% subplot(3,1,3);imshow(re);title('REMAIN LINES')
im_texto=clip(im_texto);
num_filas=size(im_texto,1);
for s=1:num_filas
    if sum(im_texto(s,:))==0
        nm=im_texto(1:s-1,:); % First line matrix
        rm=im_texto(s:end,:);% Remain line matrix
        fl = clip(nm);
        re=clip(rm);
        %*-*-*Uncomment lines below to see the result*-*-*-*-
        %         subplot(2,1,1);imshow(fl);
        %         subplot(2,1,2);imshow(re);
        break
    else
        fl=im_texto;%Only one line.
        re=[ ];
    end
```

```
end

function img_out=clip(img_in)
[f c]=find(img_in);
img_out=img_in(min(f):max(f),min(c):max(c));%Crops image
```

Code for Reading Letters

```
function letter=read_letter(imagn,num_letras)
% Computes the correlation between template and input image
% and its output is a string containing the letter.
% Size of 'imagn' must be 42 x 24 pixels
% Example:
% imagn=imread('D.bmp');
% letter=read_letter(imagn)
global templates
comp=[ ];
for n=1:num_letras
    sem=corr2(templates{1,n},imagn);
    comp=[comp sem];
end

vd=find(comp==max(comp));

%*-*-*-*-*-*-*-*-*-*-*-*-*-
if vd==1
    letter='A';
elseif vd==2
    letter='B';
elseif vd==3
    letter='C';
elseif vd==4
    letter='D';
elseif vd==5
    letter='E';
elseif vd==6
    letter='F';
elseif vd==7
    letter='G';
elseif vd==8
    letter='H';
elseif vd==9
    letter='I';
```

```
elseif vd==10
    letter='J';
elseif vd==11
    letter='K';
elseif vd==12
    letter='L';
elseif vd==13
    letter='M';
elseif vd==14
    letter='N';
elseif vd==15
    letter='O';
elseif vd==16
    letter='P';
elseif vd==17
    letter='Q';
elseif vd==18
    letter='R';
elseif vd==19
    letter='S';
elseif vd==20
    letter='T';
elseif vd==21
    letter='U';
elseif vd==22
    letter='V';
elseif vd==23
    letter='W';
elseif vd==24
    letter='X';
elseif vd==25
    letter='Y';
elseif vd==26
    letter='Z';
    %*-*-*-*-*
elseif vd==27
    letter='1';
elseif vd==28
    letter='2';
elseif vd==29
    letter='3';
elseif vd==30
    letter='4';
```

```
elseif vd==31
    letter='5';
elseif vd==32
    letter='6';
elseif vd==33
    letter='7';
elseif vd==34
    letter='8';
elseif vd==35
    letter='9';
else
    letter='0';
end
```

Annexure 1

```
%storage matrix word from image
word=[ ];
re=imagen;
%Opens plates.txt as file for write
fid = fopen('plates.txt', 'at');
% Load templates
load templates
global templates
% Compute the number of letters in template file
num_letras=size(templates,2);
while 1
%Fcn 'lines' separate lines in text
    [fl re]=lines(re);
    imgn=fl;
%Uncomment line below to see lines one by one
    imshow(fl);pause(1.5)
%-------------------------------------------------------------
% Label and count connected components
    [L Ne] = bwlabel(imgn);
for n=1:Ne
        [r,c] = find(L==n);
% Extract letter
        n1=imgn(min(r):max(r),min(c):max(c));
% Resize letter (same size of template)
        img_r=imresize(n1,[42 24]);
%Uncomment line below to see letters one by one
        imshow(img_r);pause(2)
```

```
%-----------------------------------------------------------------
% Call fcn to convert image to text
        letter=read_letter(img_r,num_letras);
% Letter concatenation
        word=[word letter];
end
%fprintf(fid,'%s\n',lower(word));%Write 'word' in text file (lower)
    fprintf(fid,'Plate Number:%s \n Date: %s \n',word,date);%Write 'word' in
text file (upper)
% Clear 'word' variable

ord=[ ];
%*When the sentences finish, breaks the loop
if isempty(re) %See variable 're' in Fcn 'lines'
break
end
end
fclose(fid);
%Open 'plates.txt' file
winopen('plates.txt')
```

Chapter 11
Medical Image Fusion in Spatial and Transform Domain:
A Comparative Analysis

Alka Srivastava
Sant Longowal Institute of Engineering and Technology Punjab, India

Ashwani Kumar Aggarwal
Sant Longowal Institute of Engineering and Technology Punjab, India

ABSTRACT

Nowadays, there are a lot of medical images and their numbers are increasing day by day. These medical images are stored in the large database. To minimize the redundancy and optimize the storage capacity of images, medical image fusion is used. The main aim of medical image fusion is to combine complementary information from multiple imaging modalities (e.g. CT, MRI, PET, etc.) of the same scene. After performing medical image fusion, the resultant image is more informative and suitable for patient diagnosis. There are some fusion techniques which are described in this chapter to obtain fused image. This chapter presents two approaches to image fusion, namely spatial domain Fusion technique and transforms domain Fusion technique. This chapter describes Techniques such as Principal Component Analysis which is spatial domain technique and Discrete Wavelet Transform and Stationary Wavelet Transform which are Transform domain techniques. Performance metrics are implemented to evaluate the performance of image fusion algorithm.

1. INTRODUCTION

Medical imaging field demands images which have high resolution and higher information content, for necessary disease diagnosis and visualization. Therefore, in practical scenarios more complementary information is required for necessary disease diagnosis purpose. Multimodal medical image fusion algorithms and devices have shown notable achievements in improving clinical accuracy of decisions based on medical images. The selection of the imaging modality for a targeted clinical study requires

DOI: 10.4018/978-1-5225-2848-7.ch011

medical insights specific to organs under study. It is practically impossible to capture all the details from one imaging modality that would ensure clinical accuracy and robustness of the analysis and resulting diagnosis. Medical images to be fused are taken from different modalities, i.e. CT scan, MRI scan, PET scan, etc. These modalities are used for different purposes as described below. Figure 1 shows medical image of different modalities.

1.1. Imaging Modalities

In medical imaging, Computed Tomography (CT), Magnetic Resonance Imaging (MRI), Positron Emission Tomography (PET), Single Photon Emission Computed Tomography (SPECT) and other modes of medical images reflect human information from various angles. CT scan can clearly reflect the anatomical structure of bone tissues. It provides detailed cross sectional views of all types of tissues. SPECT scan can highlight the lesion of tissues and organs and provide information about blood flow and temperature of body parts. PET scanning can show blood flow, oxygen and glucose metabolism in the tissues of the brain. MRI can clearly reflect the anatomical structure of soft tissues, organs and blood vessels.

In the clinical diagnosis and treatment, the problems regarding comparison and synthesis of images like CT-PET, MRI-PET and CT-MRI were frequently encountered. In order to provide more useful information for clinical diagnosis, there is a need to combine more useful information from different source images. Combining complementary information from different images of the same lesion area is known as image fusion. A CT image gives distinct contours of bones but it cannot show clear image of ligaments which is needed for differentiating tumor from scar tissues. MRI shows the shape of both ligaments and bones but fails to produce distinct contours of the bones. Fusion of CT-MRI images is used to assist in planning surgical procedure. Combining PET with CT or MRI gives both anatomic and metabolic information. This is very useful in showing detailed views of moving organs or structures with higher anatomical variation which is used to detect lung cancer. Combination of MRI-PET images is used in detecting brain tumors, SPECT-CT is useful in abdominal studies and Ultra Sound (US)-MRI for vascular blood flow test (Azzwai, 2009).

Figure 1. CT scan and MRI scan of same scene

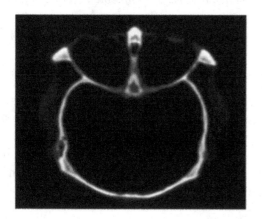 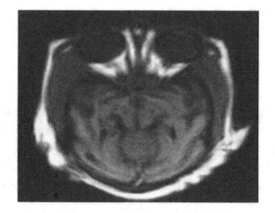

1.2. Objective

The main motive of the chapter is to study about Medical Image Fusion and their classification. Medical Image Fusion's method is classified in to two domains i.e. spatial domain and transform domain. The disadvantage of spatial domain technique is that they produce spatial distortion in the fused image. To eliminate the disadvantages of spatial domain fusion techniques, transform domain fusion techniques are used. Some of techniques which fall under this domain have been studied. The performance of Medical Image Fusion's methods is calculated in terms of various parameters. Based on the various performance parameters, comparative analysis is done.

2. ADVANTAGES OF IMAGE FUSION

Image Fusion is used in many areas due to the several advantages which are described below (Sharma, 1999).

1. **Improved Reliability:** The fusion of multiple measurements can reduce noise and therefore improve the reliability of the measured quantity.
2. **Robust System Performance:** Redundancy in multiple measurements can help in systems robustness. In case one or more sensors fail or the performance of a particular sensor deteriorates, the system can depend on the other sensors.
3. **Compact Representation of Information:** Image fusion leads to compact representations. For example, in remote sensing, instead of storing images from several spectral bands, it is comparatively more efficient to store the fused information.
4. **Extended Range of Operation:** Multiple sensors that operate under different operating conditions can be deployed to extend the effective range of operation. For example, different sensors can be used for day/night operations.
5. **Extended Spatial and Temporal Coverage:** Information of fused image from sensors that differ in spatial resolution can increase the spatial coverage. The same is true in case of the temporal dimension.
6. **Reduced Uncertainty:** Information of fused image from multiple sensors can reduce the uncertainty associated with the sensing or decision process.

3. APPLICATIONS OF MEDICAL IMAGE FUSION

There are several applications of image fusion as discussed earlier. Some of them are in the field of medical image fusion for medical diagnosis which is mentioned below.

3.1. Neurology

In neurology, for neurosurgical monitoring and planning through preoperative, intra-operative and post-operative assessment of therapeutic interventions is done through fusion of CT, PET, MRS and MRA/MRV with MRI scans (Haller et al., 1999). Also, in image guided neurosurgery system fusion of preoperative MRI and intra-operative US (ultra sound) are done to detect brain tissue deformation during craniotomy and monitor extent of lesion removal (Comeau et al., 2009). Fusion of MRI and SPECT for the synthesis of high resolution 3D (three dimensional) functional brain images is done for the monitoring of Alzheimer's disease.

3.2. Cardiology

Quantitative measurements of coronary vessels in 3D and 4D based on X-ray angiography and IVUS facilitates volumetric and velocity measurements to monitor atherosclerosis (Olszewski et al., 2000, Wahle et al., 1999). Tagged MRI and F18-FDG PET fusion system helps in the assessment of myocardial viability in patients with coronary heart disease (Belhloul et al., 1998). Accurate diagnosis and staging are essential for the optimal management of cancer patients. Fusion of positron emission tomography with 2-deoxy- 2-[fluorine-18] fluoro- D-glucose integrated with computed tomography (F18-FDG PET/CT) has emerged as a powerful imaging tool for the detection of various cancers.

3.3. Oncology

MRI scan, CT scan, and PET scan fusion helps in tumor segmentation and localization for radiation therapy.

3.4. Other Fields

Fusion of ultra sound and X-ray images from the same volume of interest helps in breast pathologies (Hernandez et al., 1996). Endoscopic video fusion with CT and/or MRI helps in the visualization of structures and access paths in ENT surgery (Truppe et al., 1996).

4. WORKING OF MEDICAL IMAGE FUSION

The block diagram to explain the medical image fusion is shown in figure 2. The mandatory step in this block diagram is preprocessing. It requires registration of source images. Image registration is a procedure to correlate the traits between the source images. It is performed by mapping points from one image to corresponding points of other images. In addition to this it also involves conversion of RGB image to gray scale image. The pre-processed image is then decomposed into various multi-resolution techniques. Image contains information at different levels, called as resolution. Analyzing the image at only one resolution is not sufficient to identify all the information present in the image. So, an image is decomposed into various resolution levels/bands. The obtained sub-bands may be completely combined using the appropriate fusion rule (Bhateja et al., 2015).

This is followed by reconstruction of the fused sub-bands back into original form. The selection of the fusion rule is dependent upon nature of application and the specific requirements pertaining to object restoration in the final image.

Figure 2. General block diagram of 'Multimodal Medical Image Fusion'

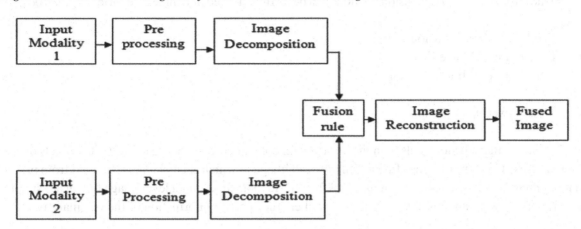

5. CLASSIFICATION OF IMAGE FUSION METHODS

Image Fusion algorithms can be broadly classified into two categories i.e. spatial domain fusion techniques and transform domain fusion techniques. In spatial domain image is directly used whereas in transform domain image is transformed to other domains (Redondo et al., 2009). These techniques are described below.

5.1. Spatial Domain Fusion Techniques

Spatial domain techniques directly deal with the image pixels. These pixel values are manipulated to achieve the desired result. These techniques are based on gray level mappings, where the type of mapping used depends on the criterion chosen for enhancement. The fusion techniques such as averaging, Brovey method, principal component analysis (PCA) and intensity hue saturation (HIS) based methods fall under this category. Another important spatial domain fusion technique is the high pass filtering based technique.

The disadvantage of spatial domain technique is that they produce spatial distortion in the fused image. To eliminate the disadvantages of spatial domain fusion techniques, transform domain fusion techniques are used.

5.2. Transform Domain Fusion Techniques

In transform domain techniques, image is first transformed to frequency domain. The transformation is based on the manipulation of the orthogonal transform of the image rather than the image itself. Transformation domain techniques are suited for processing the image according to the frequency content. The fusion techniques such as discrete wavelet transform (DWT), stationary wavelet transform (SWT), and curvelet transform etc. fall under the transform domain techniques.

On the basis of level, image fusion methods can be further divided into three categories as given below:

- Pixel Level Image Fusion
- Feature Level Image Fusion
- Decision Level Image Fusion

I.   Pixel Level Image Fusion

Pixel level image fusion deals with the information content corresponding to individual pixels of the input images. This type of image fusion generates an image in which each pixel is estimated from pixels in input images. It is also called as signal level fusion. Advantages of pixel level image fusion are simple and straight forward and disadvantage is that, it alters the spectral information of the original image.

II.   Feature Level Image Fusion

In feature level image fusion, the input image is divided into various regions depending upon the features like texture, edges, boundaries, etc., and then fusion is done. Feature used can be extracted either by calculating separately from source images or by simultaneous processing of the images. It is also called as object level fusion.

III.   Decision Level Image Fusion

In decision level image fusion, image fusion is done by decision. It is also called as symbol or highest level image fusion. Decision level represents probabilistic decision information based on the voting or fuzzy logic, employed on the output of feature level processing on the images.

As Compared to feature and decision level, pixel level methods are more suitable for medical imaging as they can preserve spatial details in fused images.

6. PIXEL LEVEL METHODS

In the field of Medical image fusion, pixel-level fusion becomes the primary method since it can preserve original information of source images as much as possible, and the algorithms are computationally efficient and easy to implement, most image fusion applications employ pixel level based method (Redondo et al., 2009). There are most commonly used methods of pixel-level image fusion, PCA (principal component analysis), wavelet transforms image fusion etc.

6.1. Principal Component Analysis

Principal component analysis (PCA) is a vector space transform often used to reduce multidimensional data sets to lower the dimensions for analysis. It is the simplest and most useful of the true eigenvector-based multivariate analyses, because its operation is to reveal the internal structure of data in an unbiased way. If a multivariate dataset is visualized as a set of coordinates in a high-dimensional data space (1 axis per variable), PCA supplies the user with a 2D picture, a shadow of this object when viewed from its most informative viewpoint. This dimensionally-reduced image of the data is the ordination diagram of the 1st two principal axes of the data, which when combined with metadata (such as gender, location etc) can rapidly reveal the main factors underlying the structure of data (Pure et al., 2013).

The PCA involves a mathematical procedure that transforms a number of correlated variables into a number of uncorrelated variables called principal components. It computes a compact and optimal description of the data set. The first principal component accounts for variance in the data as much as possible and each succeeding component accounts for the remaining variance possible. First principal component is taken along the direction with the maximum variance. The second principal component is constrained to lie in the subspace perpendicular to the first. Within this subspace, this component points the direction of maximum variance. The third principal component is taken in the maximum variance direction in the subspace perpendicular to the first two and so on. PCA is also called as Karhunen-Loève transform or the Hotelling transform. The PCA does not have a fixed set of basis vectors like in FFT, DCT and wavelet etc. and its basis vectors depend on the data set. The mathematical representation of PCA is described below.

Let X be a d-dimensional random vector having zero empirical mean and V be the orthonormal projection matrix then matrix $\Upsilon = V^T X$ with the following constraints. The covariance of Υ, i.e., $\mathrm{cov}(\Upsilon)$ is a diagonal and inverse of V is equivalent to its transpose ($V^{-1} = V^T$) (Pradnya et al., 2013). Using matrix algebra

$$
\begin{aligned}
\mathrm{cov}(\Upsilon) &= E\{\Upsilon\Upsilon^T\} \\
&= E\{(V^T X)(V^T X)^T\} \\
&= E\{(V^T X)(X^T V)\} \\
&= V^T E\{XX^T\} V \\
&= V^T \mathrm{cov}(X) V
\end{aligned}
\tag{1}
$$

where E denotes the expected value.

Multiplying both sides of Equation (1) by V, Equation 2 is obtained.

$$
V \mathrm{cov}(\Upsilon) = VV^T \mathrm{cov}(X) V = V \mathrm{cov}(X) V
\tag{2}
$$

V can be written as V= [V_1, V_2, ..., V_d] and

$$
\mathrm{cov}(\Upsilon) = \begin{pmatrix} \Upsilon_1 & \cdots & 0 \\ \vdots & \ddots & \vdots \\ 0 & \cdots & \Upsilon_d \end{pmatrix}
\tag{3}
$$

Substituting Equation (1) in Equation (2) gives

$$
[\Upsilon_1 V_1, \Upsilon_2 V_2, ..., \Upsilon_d V_d] = [\mathrm{cov}(X) V_1, \mathrm{cov}(X) V_2, ..., \mathrm{cov}(X) V_d]
\tag{4}
$$

This can be rewritten as

$$Y_i V_i = \mathrm{cov}(X)V_i \tag{5}$$

where I = 1, 2, ..., d and V_i is an eigenvector of cov(X).

6.1.1. PCA Algorithm

The basic steps involve in principal component analysis algorithm is discussed below.

Let the source images (images to be fused) be arranged in two-column vectors. The steps followed to project this data into 2-D subspaces are

1. Organize the data into column vectors. The resulting matrix Z is of dimension 2 x n.
2. Compute the empirical mean along each column. The empirical mean vector M_e has a dimension of 1 x 2.
3. Subtract the empirical mean vector M_e from each column of the data matrix Z. The resulting matrix X is of dimension 2 x n.
4. Find the covariance matrix C of X i.e. C=XX^T mean of expectation = cov(X)
5. Compute the eigenvectors V and eigen value D of C and sort them by decreasing eigen value. Both V and D are of dimension 2 x 2.
6. Consider the first column of V which corresponds to larger eigen value for computation of P_1 and P_2 as:

$$P_1 = \frac{V(1)}{\Sigma V} \text{ and } P_2 = \frac{V(2)}{\Sigma V} \tag{6}$$

where V(1) and V(2) are the first and second element of that column which corresponds to larger eigen value and ΣV is summation of eigen vector matrix.

6.1.2. Image Fusion Using PCA

The information flow diagram of PCA-based image fusion algorithm is shown in Figure 3. The input images to be fused $I_1(x, y)$ and $I_2(x, y)$ are arranged in two column vectors and their empirical means are subtracted. The resulting vector has a dimension of n x 2, where n is length of each image vector. Compute the eigenvector and eigen values for this resulting vector and then find the eigenvectors corresponding to the larger eigen value. The normalized components P_1 and P_2 (i.e., $P_1 + P_2 = 1$) using Eqn. (7) are computed from the obtained eigenvector. The fused image (I_f) is given by:

$$I_f = P_1 I_1(x, y) + P_2 I_2(x, y) \tag{7}$$

Figure 3. Information flow diagram employing PCA

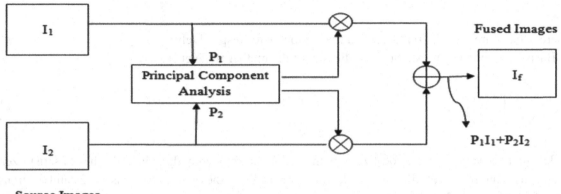

6.2. Wavelet Transform

Wavelet theory is an extension of fourier theory in many aspects and it was introduced as an alternative to short-time Fourier transform (STFT) (Chui, 1992). In fourier theory, the signal is decomposed into sine and cosine components but in wavelet theory, the signal is projected onto a set of wavelet functions. Fourier transform provides good resolution in frequency domain whereas wavelet transform provides good resolution in both frequency and time domain. The wavelet theory was introduced as a mathematical tool in 1980s; from then it has been extensively used in image processing. It provides a multi-resolution decomposition of an image in a bi-orthogonal basis which results in a non-redundant image representation. The basis is called wavelets and the functions which are used, are generated by translation and dilation of the mother wavelet. In Fourier analysis, the signal is decomposed into sine waves of different frequencies whereas in wavelet analysis, the signal is decomposed into scaled (dilated or expanded) and shifted (translated) versions of the chosen mother wavelet. A wavelet as the name implies is a small wave that grows and decays essentially in a limited time period. For a wavelet to be a small wave, it must satisfy two basic properties:

(i) Time integral must be zero.

$$\int_{-\infty}^{\infty} \psi(t)dt = 0 \tag{8}$$

(ii) Square of wavelet integrated over time must be unity.

$$\int_{-\infty}^{\infty} \psi^2(t)dt = 1 \tag{9}$$

Wavelet transform of a 1-D signal f(x) onto a basis of wavelet functions (W) is defined as:

$$W_{a,b}(f(x)) = \int_{x=-\infty}^{\infty} f(x)\psi_{a,b}(x)dx \tag{10}$$

where a and b are the dilation factor and translation factor respectively.

Basis is obtained by translation and dilation of the mother wavelet as:

$$\psi_{a,b} = \frac{1}{\sqrt{a}}\psi\left(\frac{x-a}{b}\right) \tag{11}$$

The mother wavelet would localize in both spatial and frequency domain and it has to satisfy zero mean constraint. In case of discrete wavelet transform (DWT), the dilation factor is a = 2^m and the translation factor is b = n*2^m, where m and n are integers.

The information flow in one level of two dimensional (2D) image decomposition is illustrated in figure 4. Wavelet separately filters and down samples the two dimensional (2D) data, (image) in the vertical and horizontal directions (separable filter bank). The input (source) image is I(x, y) filtered by low pass filter L and high pass filter H in horizontal direction and then down sampled by a factor of two (keeping the alternative sample) to create the coefficient matrices I_L(x, y) and I_H(x, y).

These coefficient matrices I_L(x, y) and I_H(x, y) are both low pass and high pass sub images filtered in vertical direction and down sampled by a factor of two to create four sub bands (sub images) I_{LL}(x, y), I_{LH}(x, y), I_{HL}(x, y) and I_{HH}(x, y) (Shah et al., 2014). The I_{LL}(x, y), contains the average image information corresponding to low frequency band of multi scale decomposition. It can be considered as smooth and sub sampled version of the source image I(x, y) representing the approximation of source image.

Figure 4. One level of 2-D image decomposition

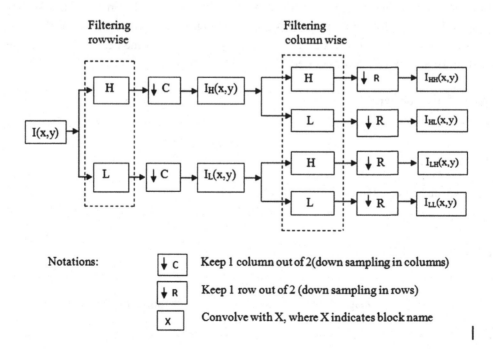

I(x, y), I_{LH}(x, y), I_{HL}(x, y), and I_{HH}(x, y), are detailed sub images which contain directional (horizontal, vertical and diagonal) information of the source image I(x, y), due to spatial orientation. Multi-resolution could be achieved by recursively applying the same algorithm to low pass coefficients from the previous decomposition (Gonzalo et al., 2004; Mitra, 2005).

Inverse 2-D wavelet transform is used to reconstruct the image I(x, y), from sub images I_{LL}(x, y), I_{LH}(x, y), I_{HL}(x, y), and I_{HH}(x, y) as shown in Figure 5. This involves column up sampling (inserting zeros between samples) and filtering using low pass L% and high pass filter H% for each sub images. Row up sampling and filtering with low pass filter L% and high pass filter H% of the resulting image and summation of all matrices will construct the image I(x, y).

6.2.1. Image Fusion Using Wavelet Transform

The most common form of transform type image fusion algorithms is the wavelet fusion algorithm, due to its simplicity and its ability to preserve the time and frequency details of the images to be fused. Wavelet transform fusion is more formally defined by applying the wavelet transforms (WT) of the two registered input images and then decomposing these images into lower sub bands and higher sub bands. To fuse these images, appropriate fusion rule is applied and then the inverse wavelet transform (IWT) is computed, to reconstruct the fused image (Sasi et al., 2013).

The wavelet fusion algorithm of two registered images I_1(x, y) and I_2(x, y) is shown in Figure 6. It can be represented by the following equation,

$$I_f\left(x,y\right) = W^{-1}\left[\psi\left\{W\left(I_1\left(x,y\right)\right), W\left(I_2\left(x,y\right)\right)\right\}\right] \tag{12}$$

Figure 5. One level of 2-D image reconstruction

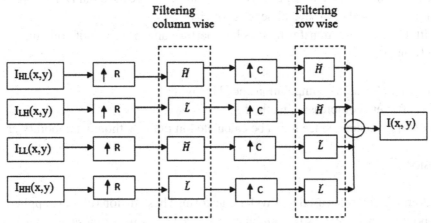

Notations:

$\uparrow$C   Insert 1 column of zeros in between column (up sampling in columns)

$\uparrow$R   Insert 1 row of zeros in between rows (up sampling in rows)

Figure 6. General representation of fusion process in wavelet transforms

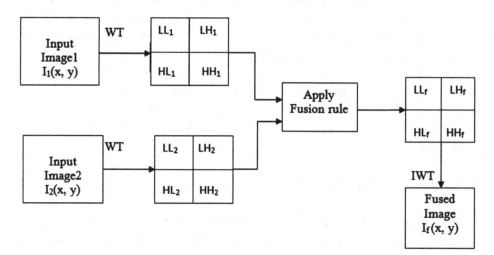

where W, W[1] and ψ are the wavelet transform operator, the inverse wavelet transform operator and the fusion rule, respectively. When wavelet transform is applied to input image1, it decomposes into LL_1, LH_1 (lower sub bands) and HL_1, HH_1 (higher sub bands). The same process is repeated for input image 2 and obtained sub bands are LL_2, LH_2, (lower sub bands) HL_2, HH_2 (higher sub bands), then fusion rule is applied to fuse both the input images. There are several wavelet fusion rules that can be used for the selection of wavelet coefficients from the wavelet transforms of the images to be fused explained. The most frequently used fusion rule is the maximum frequency rule which selects the coefficients that have the maximum absolute values. After applying the fusion rule, the LL_f, LH_f, HL_f, HH_f four sub bands are obtained. To reconstruct the image, inverse wavelet transform is applied. The wavelet transform concentrates on representing the image in multi-scale and it is appropriate for representing linear edges. In wavelet transform, Haar, Daubechies, Symlet etc. wavelets are used but DWT with Haar based fusion method is assessed best due to several benefits of Haar.

DWT with Haar wavelet transform gives best performance in terms of computation time due to the following advantages.

1. It is very simple and its computation speed is high.
2. HWT is efficient compression method.
3. It is memory efficient, since it can be calculated in place without a temporary array.

6.2.2. Fusion Rule

There are several fusion rules used in wavelet transform. These fusion rules are applied after the decomposition of both the input images (Brahmbhatt et al., 2013). Some of these are explained below.

6.2.2.1. Simple Average Method

Simple Averaging is the linear based method. This method is used for smoothing the image i.e. it provides better region in fused image than the input images. It is defined as

$$F(i,j) = \left[P_A(i,j) + P_B(i,j)\right]/2 \tag{13}$$

where F (i, j) is the fused image, P_A(i, j) and P_B(i, j) are different medical input images.

6.2.2.2 Maximum Selection Method

This scheme just picks coefficient in each sub band with largest magnitude. A selection process is performed wherein, for every corresponding pixel in the input images, the pixel with maximum intensity is selected, and is put as the resultant pixel of the fused image F (i, j). It is defined as

$$F(i,j) = Max\left[w\left(I_1(x,y)\right), w\left(I_2(x,y)\right)\right] \tag{14}$$

where F (i, j) is the fused image, I_1(x, y) and I_2(x, y) are different medical input images.

6.2.2.3. Minimum Selection Scheme

This scheme just picks coefficient in each sub band with smallest magnitude. A selection process is performed wherein, for every corresponding pixel in the input images, the pixel with minimum intensity is selected and is put in as the resultant pixel of the fused image F(i, j).

$$F(i,j) = Min\left[w\left(I_1(x,y)\right), w\left(I_2(x,y)\right)\right] \tag{15}$$

where W is the wavelet transform I_1(x, y) and I_2(x, y) are the input images.

After reviewing various papers, it was found that discrete wavelet transform is preferred for medical fusion purpose. There are various advanced wavelet transforms e.g. contourlet transform, curvelet transform, and non-subsample contourlet transform which are also used in medical image fusion. They give better performance of the fused image. But these transforms are very expensive and hence not commonly used for fusion purpose. Discrete wavelet transform is easy and efficient method for medical image fusion as it provides the relevant information of input image with low cost and less complexity.

6.3. Discrete Wavelet Transform

Two dimensional DWT is very useful in image processing because the image data is discrete and the spatial and spectral resolution is dependent on frequency. Discrete Wavelet Transform (DWT) (Udomhunsakul et al., 2011) also converts the image from the spatial domain to frequency domain. Figure 7 shows the frequency distribution of DWT. The image is divided into vertical and horizontal lines representing the first-order of DWT and the image is separated in four parts LL_1, LH_1, HL_1 and HH_1. These four parts represent four frequency areas in the image. For the low- frequency domain LL_1 is sensitive to human eyes. In the frequency domain, LH_1, HL_1 and HH_1 have more detail information than LL_1.

After applying average as fusion rule, DWT- Average selection method is explained below.

Figure 7. Frequency distribution of DWT

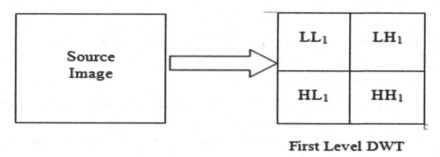

6.3.1. Discrete Wavelet Transform-Averaging Selection Method

In Discrete Wavelet Transform-Averaging Selection method, (DWT-Avg.) initially two different modality medical images (1 and 2) are considered as input. The input images are decomposed into lower sub band and higher sub bands (LL, LH, HL, HH) using discrete wavelet transform with haar filter. The lower sub band coefficients and higher sub band coefficients are fused using average method given in eq. (13). Finally, the inverse discrete wavelet transform is applied. The resultant image is a fused image. The block diagram of this method is shown in figure 8.

DWT suffers from certain disadvantages like loss of edge information due to down-sampling, blurring effect and high storage cost etc. In order to eliminate these disadvantages, stationary wavelet transform (SWT) technique is used.

Figure 8. Block diagram for DWT-Avg

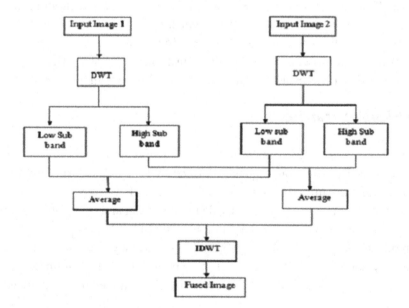

6.4. Stationary Wavelet Transform

The Discrete Wavelet Transform is not a time invariant transform. The way to restore the translation invariance is to average some slightly different DWT, called un-decimated DWT, to define the stationary wavelet transform (SWT). It does so by suppressing the down-sampling step of the decimated algorithm and instead up-sampling the filters by inserting zeros between the filter coefficients. Algorithms in which the filter is up sampled are called "à trous", which means "with holes". In the decimated algorithm, the filters are applied first to the rows and then to the columns. But in this case, undecimated algorithm is used in which the four images produced (one approximation and three detail images) are at half the resolution of the original but of same size as the original image. The approximation images from the undecimated algorithm are therefore represented as levels in a parallelepiped, with the spatial resolution becoming coarser at each higher level, but the size remains same. Stationary Wavelet Transform (SWT) is similar to Discrete Wavelet Transform (DWT), the only difference is that in SWT process of down-sampling is suppressed which means it is translation-invariant (Gao et al., 2008).

The 2D Stationary Wavelet Transform (SWT) is based on the idea of no decimation. It applies the Discrete Wavelet Transform (DWT) and omits both down-sampling in the forward and up-sampling in the inverse transform. More precisely, it applies the transform at each point of the image and saves the detail coefficients and uses the low frequency information at each level. The Stationary Wavelet Transform decomposition scheme is illustrated in figure 9, where I_i, G_i, H_i represent source images, low-pass filter and high-pass filter, respectively.

6.4.1. SWT Algorithm

The basic algorithm of stationary wavelet transform is explained below (Pradnya et al., 2013).

Figure 9. SWT decomposition scheme

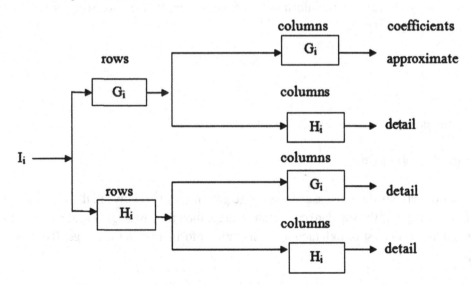

1. Decompose the two source images using SWT at one level resulting in three detail sub bands and one approximation sub band (HL, LH, HH and LL bands).
2. Compute the average of approximate parts of images.
3. Find the absolute values of horizontal parts of the image by subtracting second part of image from first.

$$D = \left| H_1 L_2 \right| - \left| H_2 L_1 \right| \geq 0 \tag{16}$$

where D denotes the difference and $H_1 L_2$, $H_2 L_2$ are the horizontal part of image.

4. Make element wise multiplication of D and horizontal part of first image and then subtract another horizontal part of second image multiplied by logical not of D from first for the fusion of horizontal part.
5. Find D for vertical and diagonal parts and obtain the fused vertical and details of image.
6. Obtain the fused image by taking inverse stationary wavelet transform.

7. PERFORMANCE PARAMETERS

Performance evaluation is necessary for qualitative and quantitative analysis of the image fusion techniques. The performance parameters or the quality metrics namely entropy, standard deviation, root means square error and peak signal to noise ratio are explained in the following section (Mohamed et al., 2011; Teng et al., 2010; Cui et al., 2009)

7.1. Entropy

Entropy is one of the most important quantitative measures in image fusion. A digital image consists of pixels arranged in rows and columns. Each pixel in image is defined by its position and gray scale level. Higher entropy indicates more informative image. For an image consisting of L gray levels, the entropy of an image is defined as.

$$H = \sum_{i=1}^{L} p(i) \log_2 p(i) \tag{17}$$

where p (i) is the probability of each gray scale level.

7.2. Standard Deviation

Standard deviation reflects discrete case of the image grey intensity relative to the average. It represents the contrast of an image. If the standard deviation is large, then the image grey scale distribution is scattered and the image's contrast is high then it means more information in the image. It can be defined as given in eq 18.

$$\sigma = \sqrt{\dfrac{\sum_{i=1}^{M}\sum_{j=1}^{N}\left[F\left(i,j\right) - \overline{f}^{\,2}\right]}{M * N}} \tag{18}$$

where F (i, j) is the grey value of fused image at point (i, j). $\overline{f}$ is the mean value of grey-scale image fusion and M×N is the size of image.

7.3. Root Mean Square Error (RMSE):

Root Mean Square Error (RMSE) presents the error between the reconstructed image and the original image as a percentage of the mean intensity of the original image. The RMSE is given by.

$$RMSE = \sqrt{\dfrac{1}{M * N}\sum_{x}\sum_{y}\left[I_{true}\left(x, y\right) - I_{fused}\left(x, y\right)\right]^{2}} \tag{19}$$

where $I_{true}(x, y)$ is the reference image, $I_{fused}(x, y)$ is the fusion image and M, N are the dimensions of the images.

7.4. Peak Signal to Noise Ratio (PSNR):

Peak signal to noise ratio is most commonly used a measure of quality of reconstruction of loss compression codec's (e.g., for image compression). The signal in this case is the original data of the image, and the noise is the error introduced by compression. When comparing compression codes it is used as an approximation to human perception of reconstruction quality, therefore in some cases one reconstruction may appear to be closer to the original than another, even though it has a lower PSNR (Chu, 1992). A higher PSNR will normally indicate that the reconstruction is of higher quality.

The PSNR is calculated by using the following formula.

$$PSNR = 10 * \log_{10}\left(\dfrac{M * N}{RMSE}\right) \tag{20}$$

where M, N are the dimensions of the image. PSNR is generally expressed in decibel i.e. db

8. RESULT AND DISCUSSION

There are various techniques which are used for fusion of medical images. These medical images have been taken from database which is shown in Figure 10, these images are of two modalities i.e. PET scan and MRI scan, called source images.

These source images are fused with the help of three techniques which is discussed above in this chapter. Performance parameters of these techniques are calculated and results are shown in Table 1.

Figure 10. Source image (dataset)

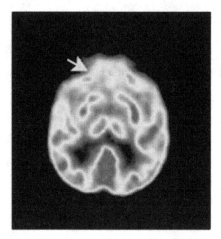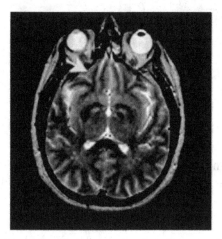

*For a more accurate representation of this figure, please see the electronic version.

From the Table 1, it is seen that different results are obtained for Entropy. Higher entropy indicates images are more informative. For this dataset, fused image entropy is more than any of source images means better quality of image fusion. Standard deviation is better for SWT technique means that resultant image shows more contrast in case of SWT technique. Form this table it is clear that SWT technique performs well as compared to PCA and DWT.

9. FUTURE RESARCH

The motive of this chapter is to fuse two medical images these medical images are two dimensional, further it can be extended to fuse three dimensional images. Also, more than two modalities and video clips can be used for fusion purpose which will further help in patient diagnosis.

10. CONCLUSION

It can be concluded that Medical image fusion helps in patient diagnosis. Medical image fusion techniques are classified in two domains, i.e. spatial domain and transform domain. Spatial transform techniques have disadvantage of spatial distortion in fused image which is removed by transform domain techniques.

Table 1. Results for Dataset image for Different Techniques

Techniques	Performance Parameters	
	Entropy	Standard Deviation
PCA	5.0617	49.3252
DWT(avg.)	5.3150	59.5236
SWT	5.4493	60.6561

In this chapter, PCA is used as spatial domain techniques whereas DWT and SWT are used as transform domain techniques. But DWT technique suffers from certain disadvantages like loss of edge information, blurring effect and high storage cost. These disadvantages of DWT are removed by SWT. The limitation of this chapter, this work is experimented only on three modalities i.e. CT, MRI and PET.

REFERENCES

Al-Azzawi, N., & Abdullah, W. A. K. W. (2009). Medical Image Fusion Schemes using Contourlet Transform and PCA Based. *Proceedings of the Annual International Conference of the IEEE* (pp. 5813-5816). Engineering in Medicine and Biology Society.

Belhloul, F., Janier, M., Croisille, P., Poirier, C., & Boudraa, A. (1998, November). Automatic assessment of myocardial viability based on PET-MRI data fusion. *Proc. of 20th International Conference of the IEEE Engineering in Medicine and Biology Society*, Hong Kong, China.

Bhateja, V., & Satapathy, S. C. (2015, September). Multimodal Medical Image Fusion for Computer Aided Diagnosis.

Brahmbhatt, K. N., & Makwana, R. M. (2013). Comparative study on image fusion methods in spatial domain. *International journal of advanced research in engineering and technology*.

Chui, C. (1992). *An Introduction to Wavelets*. New York: Academic Press.

Comeau, R. M., Sadikot, A. F., Fenster, A. F., & Peters, T. M. (2000, April). Intraoperative ultrasound for guidance and tissue shift correction in image-guided neurosurgery. *Medical Physics*, *27*(4), 787–800. doi:10.1118/1.598942 PMID:10798702

Cui, Z., Zhang, G., & Wu, J. (2009, April). Medical Image Fusion Based on Wavelet Transform and Independent Component Analysis. *Proceedings of the International Joint Conference on Artificial Intelligence (JCAI '09)*, Hainan Island (pp. 480-483). doi:10.1109/JCAI.2009.169

Gao, Q., Zhao, Y., & Lu, Y. (2008). Despecking SAR image using stationary wavelet transform combining with directional filter banks. *Applied Mathematics and Computation*, *205*(2), 517–524. doi:10.1016/j.amc.2008.05.026

Haller, J. W., Ryken, T., Madsen, M., Edwards, A., Bolinger, L., & Vannier, M. W. (1999). Multimodality image fusion for image-guided neurosurgery. *Proc. of 13th International Symposium on Computer Assisted Radiology and Surgery (CARS '99)*, Paris, France.

Hernandez, A., Basset, O., Magnin, I., Bremond, A., & Gimenez, G. (1996, November). Fusion of ultrasonic and radiographic images of the breast. *Proc. of IEEE Ultrasonics Symposium*, San Antonio, TX. doi:10.1109/ULTSYM.1996.584316

Jalili-Moghaddam, M. (2005). *Real-time multi-focus image fusion using discrete wavelet transform and Laplacian pyramid transform*. Goteborg, Sweden: Chalmess University of Technology.

Mirajkar Pradnya, P., & Ruikar, S. D. (2013, July). Image Fusion Based on Stationary Wavelet Transform. *International Journal of Advanced Engineering Research and Studies*.

Mirajkar Pradnya, P., & Ruikar, S. D. (2013, July). Image Fusion Based on Stationary Wavelet Transform. *International Journal of Advanced Engineering Research and Studies*.

Mohamed, M. A., & El-Den, B. M. (2011). Implementation of Image Fusion Techniques for Multi- Focus Images Using FPGA. *Proceedings of the 28th National radio science conference*.

Olszewski, M. E., Long, R. M., Mitchell, S. C., & Sonka, M. (2000, April). Quantitative measurements in geometrically correct representations of coronary vessels in 3-D and 4-D. *Proc. 4th IEEE Southwest Symposium on Image Analysis and Interpretation*, Austin, TX. doi:10.1109/IAI.2000.839611

Pajares, G., & De La Cruz, J. M. (2004). A Wavelet-based Image Fusion tutorial on Pattern Recognition.

Pure, A. A., Gupta, N., & Shrivastava, M. (2013, July). An Overview of Different Image Fusion Methods for Medical Applications. *International journal of scientific & engineering research*, *4*(7).

Redondo, R., Sroubek, F., Fischer, S., & Cristobal, G. (2009). Multifocus image fusion using the log-Gabor transform and a Multisize Windows technique. *Information Fusion*, *10*(2), 163–171. doi:10.1016/j.inffus.2008.08.006

Sasi, A., Parameswaran, L., & Sruthy, S. (2013). *Image Fusion technique using DT-CWT*. IEEE.

Shah, S. K., & Shah, D. U. (2014, March). Comparative Study of Image Fusion Techniques based on Spatial and Transform Domain. *International Journal of Innovative Research in Science, Engineering and Technology, 3*(3).

Sharma, R. K. (1999). Probabilistic Model-based Multisensor Image Fusion [PhD thesis]. Oregon Graduate Institute of Science and Technology, Portland, Oregon.

Teng, J., Wang, S., Zhang, J., & Wang, X. (2010, October). Neuro-fuzzy logic based fusion algorithm of medical images. *Proceedings of the 2010 3rd International Congress on Image and Signal Processing (CISP)* (Vol. 4, pp. 1552-1556). IEEE.

Truppe, M. J., Freysinger, W., Gunkel, A. R., & Thumfart, W. F. (Jan. 1996). Remote-guided surgical navigation in ENT surgery. *Proc. of Medicine Meets Virtual Reality IV*. San Diego, CA: Healthcare in the Information Age - Feature Tools for Transforming Medicine.

Udomhunsakul, S., Yamsang, P., Tumthong, S., & Borwonwatanadelok, P. (2011, July). Multiresolution Edge Fusion using SWT and SFM. *Proceedings of the World Congress on Engineering* (Vol. 2).

Wahle, A., Prause, G. P. M., Von Birgelen, C., Erbel, R., & Sonka, M. (1999, October). Fusion of angiography and intravascular ultrasound in vivo: Establishing the absolute 3-D frame orientation. IEEE Transactions on Bio-Medical Engineering, 46(10), 1176–1180. *PubMed, 1999*. doi:10.1109/10.790492

Chapter 12
Moving Object Classification in a Video Sequence Using Invariant Feature Extraction

S. Vasavi
V. R. Siddhartha Engineering College, India

Reshma Shaik
V. R. Siddhartha Engineering College, India

Sahithi Yarlagadda
V. R. Siddhartha Engineering College, India

ABSTRACT

Object recognition and classification (human beings, animals, buildings, vehicles) has become important in a surveillance video situated at prominent areas such as airports, banks, military installations etc., Outdoor environments are more challenging for moving object classification because of incomplete appearance details of moving objects due to occlusions and large distance between the camera and moving objects. As such, there is a need to monitor and classify the moving objects by considering the challenges of video in the real time. Training the classifiers using feature based is easier and faster than pixel-based approaches in object classification. Extraction of a set of features from the object of interest is most important for classification. Textural features, color features and structural features can be chosen for classifying the object. But in real time video, object poses are not always the same. Zernike moments have been shown to be rotation invariant and noise robust due to Orthogonality property.

1. INTRODUCTION

Object recognition and classification (human beings, animals, buildings, vehicles) has become important in a surveillance video situated at prominent areas such as airports, banks, military installations etc., Outdoor environments are more challenging for moving object classification because of incomplete appearance details of moving objects due to occlusions and large distance between the camera and moving

DOI: 10.4018/978-1-5225-2848-7.ch012

objects. As such, there is a need to monitor and classify the moving objects by considering the challenges of video in the real time. Training the classifiers using feature based is easier and faster than pixel-based approaches in object classification. Extraction of a set of features from the object of interest is most important for classification. Textural features, color features and structural features can be chosen for classifying the object. But in real time video, object poses are not always the same. Zernike moments have been shown to be rotation invariant and noise robust due to Orthogonality property.

1.1. Motivation

Visual surveillance and monitoring moving objects is required in many prominent and public areas such as banks, railway stations, airports, buses and military applications. Data that is collected from these Surveillance cameras have to be monitored either manually or using intelligent systems. Human operators monitoring manually for long durations is infeasible due to monotony and fatigue. As such, recorded videos are inspected when any suspicious event is notified. But this method only helps for recovery and does not avoid any unwanted events. "Intelligent" video surveillance systems can be used to identify various events and to notify concerned personal when any unwanted event is identified. As a result, such a system requires algorithms that are fast, robust and reliable during various phases such as detection, tracking, classification etc. This can be done by implementing a fast and efficient technique to classify the objects that are present in the video in the real time.

1.2. Problem Statement

Basic video analysis operations such as object detection, classification and tracking require scanning the entire video. But this is a time-consuming process and hence we require a method to detect and classify the objects that are present in the frames extracted from a real time video. Moments are used to classify objects present in a frame. Various forms of moment descriptors such as Moment Invariants, Geometric Moments, Rotational Moments, Orthogonal Moments, and Complex Moments have been extensively employed as pattern features in scene recognition, registration, object matching as well as data compression. Zernike moments have been shown to be superior to the others in terms of their insensitivity to image noise, information content, and ability to provide faithful image representation. In this chapter, Zernike moments based moving object classification is performed. Zernike moment has the rotation invariance property only, translation and scaling invariance should be achieved before applying the extraction features set. Zernike moment's method has less computational complexity than geometric moment's method. Zernike Moments is a feature extraction method from an image by which we can extract global features like amplitude and angle.

1.3. Background

The field of computer vision requires understanding of key terms such as color spaces, key frame extraction, foreground subtraction, feature extraction, blob detection, Bag of Visual Words (BoV), Occlusions, Binarization, filtration and classification as described in the following sections.

1.3.1. Color Spaces

Color is a phenomenon that relates to the physics of light, chemistry of matter, geometric properties of object and human visual perception. Color is a purely psychological phenomenon. Color model is also called as Color Space or Color System. A color model is a mathematical model and it describes in the way colors can be represented as tuples of numbers, as four or three values of color components. There are different types of color spaces that are Red Green Blue (RGB), Cyan Magenta Yellow Key/Black (CMYK), Hue Saturation Value (HSV), Hue Saturation Intensity (HIS), etc. from which RGB color space and HSV color space are most commonly used.

1.3.1.1. RGB Color Space

In the RGB model, each color appears in its primary spectral components of red, green, and blue. RGB model is based on a Cartesian coordinate system. RGB image is an image in which each of the red, green, and blue images are an 8-bit image. The term full-color image is used often to denote a 24-bit RGB color image as shown in figure 1.

1.3.1.2. HSV Color Space

The HSV color space model represents the Hue, Saturation and Value in 24 bit colors and arranges the colors in a more virtually appropriate modeling. The Hue value is in between 0 and 360 degree rotated along the axis while the Saturation is the distance from the axis, and the Value is a value along the axis where the axis is extended from H: 0, S: 0, V: 0 (Poorani, Prathiba, & Ravindran, 2013). As hue varies from 0 to 1.0, the corresponding colors vary from red through yellow, green, cyan, blue, magenta, and back to red, so that there are actually red values both at 0 and 1.0 as shown in figure 2. As saturation

Figure 1. RGB color space (Poorani, Prathiba, & Ravindran, 2013)

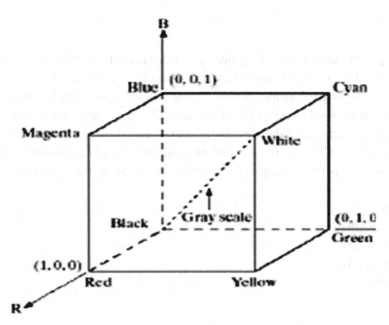

Figure 2. HSV color space (Poorani, Prathiba, & Ravindran, 2013)

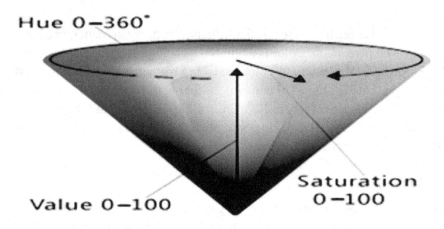

varies from 0 to 1.0, the corresponding colors (hues) vary from unsaturated (shades of gray) to fully saturated (no white component). As value, or brightness, varies from 0 to 1.0, the corresponding colors become increasingly brighter.

1.3.3. Binarization

Binarization is the process of converting pixel image into a binary image. A number of techniques have been proposed on binarization towards moving object detection and human gait recognition (Chaki, Nabendu, Shaikh et al., 2014). Basing on the criteria used for calculation of threshold value, binarization methods can be categorized in to different groups. Otsu, Sauvola and Niblack are based on image variance. Entropy based methods are proposed by Johannsen and Kapur. Bernsen proposed a thresholding approach based on image contrast. Kittler consider error measure in calculating the optimal threshold.

1.3.4. Filteration

Filteration is the process of removing the noisy data from the image. During filtration, each pixel is adjusted with the net effect of neighboring pixels. For linear filters, the output values are linear combinations of the pixels in the original image, as such smoothness increases greatly removing noise and non-linear filters reduce noise levels without simultaneously blurring edges. Image filtering can be done as Smoothing (Low pass filters) and Edge detection, Sharpening (High pass filters). There are three kinds of non-linear filters: Max, Min and Median. Median is the best way of filtering that provides sharp edges and removes the noise. Existing techniques for filtration are (Ganguly, Bhattacharjee, & Nasipuri, 2014):

- Linear Filters.
  - Gaussian filter
  - Average Filter
  - Laplacian Filter
  - Mean filter
- Non-linear Filters

- ○ Median Filter
- ○ Max Filter
- ○ Min Filter
- ○ Adaptive Filter

1.3.5. Blob Detection

In computer vision, blob detection methods are based on detecting regions in a digital image that differs in the properties, such as brightness, color compared to surrounding regions.

1.3.6. Edge Detection

From the filtered binary image, edges can be easily detected by making use of different edge detection techniques Prewitt, Sobel, Canny and Robert. Edge detection is the internal work done in blob detection. It makes use of sharpening filters also called as masks. Existing Edge Detection Techniques are classified as follows (Lakhani, Minocha & Gugnani, 2016):

- Prewitt.
- Sobel.
- Canny.
- Zero cross.
- Robert.

The Gradient values of SOBEL edge detection operator (Fermüller & Pollefeys, 2015) are shown in table 1and table 2.

Survey on various edge detection methods is given in (Das, 2016). Prewitt edge operator is simpler to implement computationally than the Sobel operator but it produces a somewhat nosier result. Canny edge detector is the most powerful edge detector that performs edge linking by incorporating the weak signal that are connected to the strong pixels.

Finding connected components in binary image is important for object recognition. This works in 2 ways: Figure 3 presents the 4 - connected neighborhood and figure 4 presents 8- connected neighborhood.

1.3.7. Feature Extraction

Classification of image objects is performed by extracting features using Zernike moments. Fruits Zernike introduced Zernike moments based on the theory of Orthogonal Polynomials and Teague first introduced the use of Zernike moments to overcome the shortcomings of information redundancy pres-

Table 1. Gradient value for x – coordinate

-1	0	+1
-2	0	+2
-1	0	+1

Table 2. Gradient value for y – coordinate

-1	-2	-1
0	0	0
+1	+2	+1

Figure 3. 4- Connected neighborhood   *Figure 4. 8- Connected neighborhood*

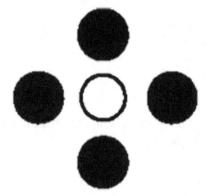   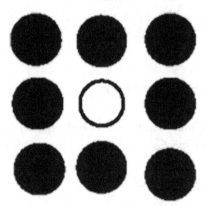

ent in the popular geometric moments (Teh & Chin, 1988). Zernike moments are a class of orthogonal moments and have been shown effective in terms of image representation. Zernike moments, a type of moment function, are the mapping of an image onto a set of complex Zernike polynomials. As these Zernike polynomials are orthogonal to each other, Zernike moments can represent the properties of an image with no redundancy or overlap of information between the moments.

The Zernike moments are calculated using the equation 1:

$$m_{pq} = \sum \sum x^p y^q f(x, y) \tag{1}$$

where p is the order of the Zernike moment.

q is the repetition.
(x, y) is the pixel position.
f(x,y) is the orthogonal function.

1.3.8. Image Classification Methods

Image Classification methods can be roughly divided into two broad families of approaches: (a) Learning-based classifiers also known as parametric methods require learning phase. (b) Nonparametric classifiers require no learning and classification decision is based on Nearest-Neighbor distance estimation of the data. Support Vector Machine (SVM) classifier performs classification by constructing hyper-planes in a multidimensional space that separates cases of different class labels as shown in figure 5.

The k-Nearest Neighbor algorithm (k-NN) is a non-parametric method used for classification and also for regression. The training samples are stored as n- dimensional numeric attributes. When a test sample is given, the k-nearest neighbor classifier searches the k training samples which are closest (Euclidean distance) to the unknown sample. Euclidean distance between two points X_1(x1, x2, ..., xn) and X_2(x1, x2, ..., xn) is given in equation 2.

Figure 5. Two possible separating hyper planes and their associated margins [Jiawei han and Micheline Kamber,(2006)]

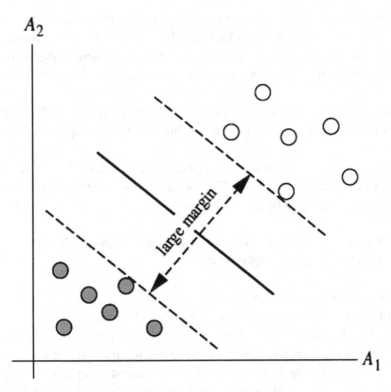

$$dist\left(X_1, X_2\right)\sqrt{\sum_{i=1}^{n}\left(x1i - x2i\right)^2} \tag{2}$$

Bagging and Boosting techniques improves the prediction accuracy of classifier. Given a training data set, D, for iteration i (i = 1, 2, ..., k), a training set, Di, of d tuples is sampled with replacement from the original set of tuples, D. A classifier model, Mi, is learned for each training set, Di. To classify an unknown tuple, X, each classifier, Mi, returns its class prediction, which counts as one vote. The bagged classifier, M_i, counts the votes and assigns the class with the most votes to X.

In boosting, a series of k classifiers is iteratively learned. After a classifier Mi is learned, the weights are updated to allow the subsequent classifier, Mi+1, to classify the tuples that were misclassified. The final boosted classifier, M*, combines the votes of each individual classifier, where the weight of each classifier's vote is a function of its accuracy.

1.3.9. Bag of Visual Words (BoV)

In the field of computer vision, BoV approach can be applied to object classification, by considering image features as words. Bag of words is a sparse vector of occurrence counts of words that is a sparse histogram over the vocabulary. In computer vision, a bag of visual words is a vector of occurrence counts of a vocabulary of local image features.

1.3.10. Occlusion

Occlusion can be explained by taking few examples, if you are developing a system which tracks objects (people, cars), occlusion occurs if an object hides another object. Like two persons walking past each other, or a car that drives under a bridge. The challenge and the problem in the above cases is what we do when an object is hidden or disappears and reappears again. Occlusion is of two kinds.

1. Self-occlusion (one object occludes another), Ex: During tracking, smaller size object (Bicycle) is covered by the large object (Lorry) due to the difference in their speed and velocity as shown in figure 6.
2. Inter object occlusion (structure in the background occludes the tracked object in the foreground). Ex: During tracking, foreground object (Bicycle) is covered by the background object (Flexi banners or iron gates) as shown in figure 7.

The main objective of proposed approach is to classify the objects in a Video taken from the CCTV footage on highways having dynamic background.

1. Extracting 29 fps from the video.
2. Identifying object locations by using blobs (regions) in the frames.
3. Preprocessing the identified blobs by having each blob with constant resolution (256*256).
4. Extract the features of the objects using Zernike moments and store them as a file.
5. Classification is done by training the classifiers: k-Nearest Neighbor (k-NN), Support Vector Machine (SVM), Bagging and Boosting in combination with both k-NN and SVM
6. Performance analysis of various classifiers using measures such as Classification Accuracy Rate (CAR), Precision, Recall and F-measure.

Figure 6. Self-occlusion (Pepik, Stark, Gehler et al., 2013)

Figure 7. Inter object occlusion (Pepik, Stark, Gehler et al., 2013)

2. LITERATURE REVIEW

2.1. Occlusion Detection and Handling: A Review (Chandel & Vatta, 2015)

This paper deals with the problem of handling occlusion in object tracking under different categories. It provides a summarizing study for handling occlusions under different scenarios. Authors showed various Image processing, Computer vision and Machine Learning techniques for occlusion. It is observed by the authors that, when both the objects, occluded and occluder are being tracked by the same algorithm, it does not perform well in handling occlusions. According to them, shape is the best feature that helps to match occluded part of the object with the same object in the next frame. Geometric patterns and machine learning techniques helps in effective handling of occlusions. Even though Histogram of Gradient (HOG) is good for object detection, is not effective for handling occlusion. Authors concluded that, if the detected features are better, the occlusion estimation will be better.

2.2. Multiclass Object Classification In Video Surveillance Systems Experimental Study (Elhoseiny, Bakry & Elgammal, 2013)

In this paper, detection and segmentation is done on the dynamic objects through a motion detection module.

- **Object Detection:** In surveillance systems, monitoring and detection are important. For stationary camera, the background modeling is the most efficient approach having low false alarm and high accuracy. Dynamic objects are detected by using non-parametric kernel density Estimation (KDE) approach as shown in figure 8. For this step, the outcome is the series of connected foreground areas. These are further segmented into blobs.

Figure 8. Experimental framework for multiclass object classification (Elhoseiny, Bakry, & Elgammal, 2013)

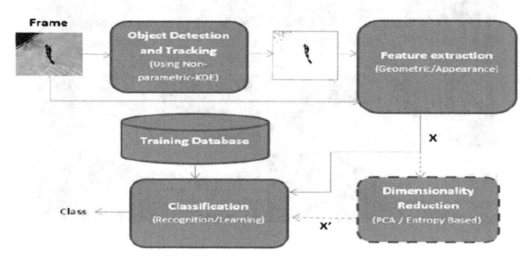

- **Feature Extraction:** This phase is to find the effectiveness of several feature descriptors and evaluate the performance of different machine learning techniques on the extracted features. It takes input from the detected foreground regions. The features are extracted based on the following methods (Elhoseiny, Bakry, & Elgammal, 2013).
  - HOG Features
  - Luminance Symmetry
  - Central Moments
  - Angular Radial Transform (ART) Moments
  - Cumulants
  - Horizontal and Vertical Projection ($HP_{i,+}$, $VP_{+,j}$)
  - Morphological Features
- **Dimensionality Reduction:** This technique is used for increasing the robustness of data analysis. The two main categories for dimensionality reduction are: Feature transform (supervised/unsupervised) and Feature selection. Principal Component Analysis (PCA), as an unsupervised feature transform method and Entropy Based Discretization (EBD) is used as a feature selection method.
- **Extracting Training Samples:** For training purposes, features are extracted from VIRAT dataset and frames are chosen to classify five classes: namely Human, Car, Vehicle objects and Bicycle objects. The four constraints described in [Mohamed Elhoseiny, AmrBakry, and Ahmed Elgammal,(2013)] were considered in training phase, while only the first three are considered on the test videos.
- **Object Classification:** For training, a list of pairs $\left\{(x_i, y_i)\right\}_{i=1}^{N}$ where $x_i \in R^d$ is the feature vector, and $y_i \in \{1, 2, ..., K\}$ is the sample label. Let $X = [x1, x2, ..., x_N]^t$ is N×d matrix and $Y = [y1, y2, ..., y_N]^t$ is N dimensional column vector.
- **Dataset Used:** Virat dataset

Advantages

1. 71.4% accuracy was achieved based on HOG features.
2. SVM and AdaBoost classification techniques performed well for recognizing objects.
3. Geometric features perform significantly better in surveillance systems.

Disadvantages

1. In Surveillance Systems, the experiments shows that using appearance features like HOG features did not perform well and is less discriminating for recognizing object classes.
2. PCA technique violates the real time requirements of surveillance systems.
3. The effect of changing the weak classifiers count for the training and test accuracy for every category significantly increases the processing time by using AdaBoost classification.

2.3. Feature Extraction Using Zernike Moments (Rao, Prasad, & Kumar, 2013)

This work evaluated Zernike moments for various patterns of objects that are cursive in nature as shown in figure 9. Feature extraction of patterns for vowels and consonants in cursive script Telugu using Zernike moments is considered in comparison with Hu's seven moments.

1. Converts gray-scale image into the binary numeral image as shown in figure 10(a).
2. Then unit circle mapped image bitmap onto NxN pixel image as shown in figure 10(b).
3. Compute the distance as shown in Equation 3.

$$d = \sqrt{\left(x^2 - \overline{x}\right)^2 \frac{1}{2} + \left(y^2 - \overline{y}\right)^2}$$
(3)

Compute the distance vector ρ and angle θ for any (x, y) pixel in f (x, y) in polar coordinates as shown in Equation 4 and Equation 5.

Figure 9. Computation of Zernike moments (Rao, Prasad, & Kumar, 2013)

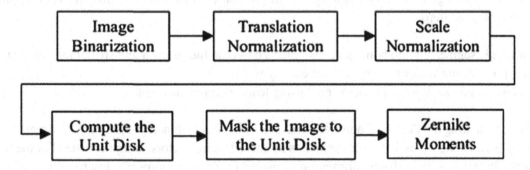

Figure 10. (a) NxN pixels (b) Unit Circle Mapped image bitmap onto NxN pixel size image (Rao, Prasad, & Kumar, 2013)

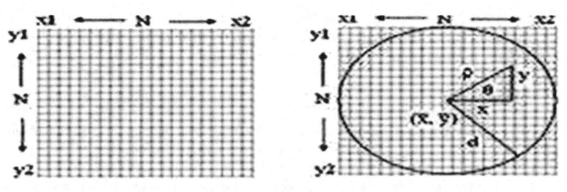

$$\theta = \tan^{-1} \frac{\left|x - \bar{x}\right|}{\left|y - \bar{y}\right|} \tag{4}$$

$$\rho = \sqrt{\left(x - \bar{x}\right)^2 + \left(y - \bar{y}\right)^2 \Big/ d} \tag{5}$$

4. Complex polynomials $\{V_{nm}(x, y)\}$ which form a complete orthogonal set over the unit disk
5. Then compute Zernike moment of order n and repetition m for function f(x, y)

Zernike moments themselves are invariant to image rotations. So, image reconstruction is easy. This work mainly focused on the extraction of the features of the plain TELUGU characters. Computational complexity is high.

2.4. Zernike Moments and SVM For Shape Classification in Very High Resolution Satellite Images (Mahi, Isabaten & Serief, 2014)

In this paper, a Zernike moments-based descriptor is used as a measure of shape information for the detection of buildings from Very High Spatial Resolution (VHSR) satellite images. Their approach comprised of three steps.

1. Image is segmented into homogeneous objects based on the spectral and spatial information
2. Zernike feature vector is computed for each segment
3. SVM-based classification is performed using feature vectors as input

After calculating the Zernike feature vectors, a class label is assigned to each of the segments in the image by performing a classification method using these feature vectors as inputs instead of the image segments. In this way, only shape information measured by Zernike moment's descriptor is used in the classification process. SVM classification is performed on the extracted Zernike feature vectors. This system doesn't include the textural and the spectral information in the classification process. In order to increase the building identification accuracy, adaptive mean shift algorithm can be used in segmentation stage.

2.5. Weighted Bag of Visual Words for Object Recognition (Biagio, Bazzani, Cristani et al., 2014)

This paper uses Bag of Visual words strategy for object recognition, which is used to represent an image as a vector of counts using a learned vocabulary. Following are the steps used for object recognition:

- **Feature Extraction:** Grid of pixel locations with spacing of 4 pixels in both x, y directions are defined on the image. Around these pixel locations, patches of different sizes (12×12, 18×18, 24×24, 30×30 pixels) are extracted. On each patch, Scale Invariant Feature Transform (SIFT) descriptor is calculated, generating a set of local descriptors for each image.
- **Codebook Creation:** In this step, the local descriptors are used to generate a codebook with K words, by Gaussian Mixture Model (GMM) clustering. This result in a weighted histogram, where the height of each bin depends on the number of associated codes retrieved in the image, and on their related weights. This is called Weighted Bag of Visual words (WBoV) as described in figure 11.
- **Encoding:** The salience of each patch is included in this step to guide the exploration of the image. Two specific encoding schemes weighted Vector Quantization(VQ) and weighted Fisher Vector (FV) are applied. Expectation- Maximization algorithm for GMM is used on the SIFT feature vectors.

Weighted VQ encodes a set of feature vectors extracted from an image by associating each element to the closest word in the vocabulary, where the association is weighted by the corresponding α_i. Bag of visual feature representation is defined as a vector $v = [v_1, v_2, ..., v_K]$, given in Equation 6 (Biagio, Bazzani, Cristani et al., 2014)

$$V_k = \sum_{i=1}^{NI} \alpha_i \delta\left(x_i, \mu_k\right) \tag{6}$$

If α_i is set to be always 1, then the standard VQ is obtained. FV is an extension of VQ where first and second order statistics are also considered.

- **Spatial Pyramid Matching:** In this step, the image is partitioned into increasingly finer spatial sub-regions and Weighted BoV is computed from each sub-region, following a spatial pyramid scheme. Typically, $2r \times 2r$ sub-regions, with $r = \{0, 1, 2\}$ are used.
- **Weighted Histogram:** All the Weighted BoV extracted from each sub region is pooled and concatenated together, generating the final Weighted BoV representation of the image. Finally, classification is done using one-vs-all linear SVM.
- **Datasets Used:** Caltech-101, Caltech-256, VOC2007 datasets

Figure 11. Object recognition pipeline [Marco San Biagio, Loris Bazzani, Marco Cristani, Vittorio Murino(2014)]

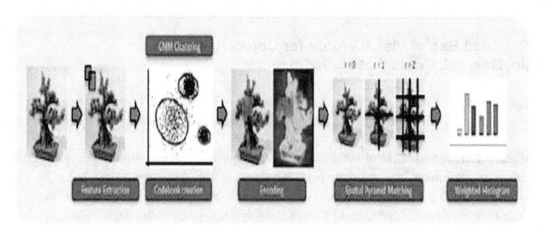

Advantages

1. Weighting the BoV representation is always beneficial for both VQ and FV.
2. This technique gives the robustness to spatial translations of features, the efficiency to compute it, and its competitive performance in different image categorization tasks.
3. This bag of visual words method performs well with both dense and sparse patches on challenging recognition datasets.

Disadvantages

1. Some pairs of images of Caltech-256 are correctly classified using the weighted BoV approach but miss-classified with the classic BoV.
2. Some examples are miss-classified using the weighted BoV representation but classified correctly using the classic BoV.

2.6. Occlusion Handling in Videos Object Tracking: A Survey (Materka & Strzelecki, 1998)

This paper mainly describes about the problems related to occlusion and the methods to overcome occlusion during object tracking in a real-time video monitoring. Following paragraph summarizes the survey made by the authors.

Occlusion is of two kinds. 1. Self-occlusion (one object occludes another), 2. Inter Object occlusion (structure in the background occludes the tracked object in the foreground). Many challenges still remain while tracking objects, this can arise due to the object motion, changing appearance patterns of objects and the scene, non-rigid object structures and most significantly is handling occlusion of tracked object. Handling occlusion in single object environment is a straight forward task but handling occlusion in multi object environment becomes more complicated. Now-a-days inter object occlusion is a challenging problem especially when the targets are identical.

The severity of occlusion is explained in three categories. During non-occlusion, the tracked object appears as a single blob having all tracking features. This can be avoided by using template matching and mean shift algorithms. When partial occlusion is happened, some of the key features of the tracked object are hidden from the camera during tracking and can be avoided by using mean shift method. Full occlusion happens when the tracking is completely invisible while knowing that object has not left the area of the view of the camera can be avoided using Kalman filter technique. These occlusions can be handled with the help of optimal camera placement method (camera is mounted on the ceiling of a room, which is, when a birds-eye view of the scene is available).

- **Dataset Used:** PETS, ETISEO dataset

2.7. Depth Aided Tracking Multiple Objects under Occlusion (Chen, Feris, Zhai et al., 2012)

This paper describes the tracking method aiming at detecting objects and maintaining their label or identification over the time. The key factors of this method are to use depth information and different strategies to track objects under various occlusion scenarios.

Depth Estimation

1. Block matching algorithms (color image, depth image)
2. Foreground segmentation and Shadow cancellation (for static image - absolute difference method, dynamic object - GMM)
3. Blob detection, extraction
4. Occlusion detection
5. Object tracking (without occlusion, under occlusion)

- **Dataset Used:** Any video dataset

Disadvantage

1. This approach works only under indoor environments and moving object velocity should be low.

2.8. Drawbacks of Existing Methods

1. Object classification is done only on the fixed classes and gives accurate results only when the classes are more specific.
2. HOG features did not perform well and is less discriminating for recognizing object classes.
3. RGB and Ohta histograms are severely degraded when the illumination source is not kept constant.
4. Most of the existing methods work only under indoor environments.
5. More redundancy in the case of Hu's moments.
6. SVM classification accuracy is low.

7. Accuracy is low for Hu's moments.
8. Hu's moments are more complex.

The proposed approach considers the training dataset consisting of various types of image samples and the features are extracted from those samples, which is used to train the classifier. To classify the objects, video is divided into frames. Zernike moment features are extracted and BoV is constructed. K-NN, SVM, Bagging classifiers is used for classification.

3. PROPOSED SYSTEM

This section presents the detailed functionality of the proposed system to perform moving object classification in a video sequence. Our proposed method gives solution to the drawbacks that are already mentioned in the previous section. The main phases in moving object classification are:

1. **Frame Extraction:** Frames are extracted from the video at the rate of 29 frames per second.
2. **Binarization:** Converting RGB image to binary image
3. **Blob Detection:** Object detection and recognition test bed are built so as to result in higher performance.
4. **Preprocessing:** Preprocessing is done on each identified blob to have a constant resolution (256*256).
5. **Feature Extraction:** Various features such as appearance features and geometric features are considered.
6. **Classification:** Based on classifiers such as k-NN, SVM, Bagging and Boosting classification performance will be evaluated using precision, recall, error rate and accuracy.

Architecture

Figure 12 and 13 presents the proposed architecture for training and testing data to perform object classification using Zernike moments.

Otsu's thresholding method is used in the proposed system. It automatically performs histogram shape-based image thresholding for the reduction of a gray-level image to a binary image. The algorithm assumes that the image for thresholding contains two classes of pixels (e.g., foreground and background) and then calculates the optimum threshold separating those two classes so that their combined spread (intra-class variance) is minimal. It exhaustively searches for the threshold that minimizes the intra-class variance, defined as the weighted sum of variances of the two classes as shown in Equation 7 and Equation 8.

$$q_1(t) = \sum_{i=0}^{t} P(i) \tag{7}$$

$$q_2(t) = \sum_{i=t+1}^{255} P(i) \tag{8}$$

and the class means are given by Equation 9 and Equation 10:

Figure 12. Architecture for Training

Figure 13. Architecture for Testing

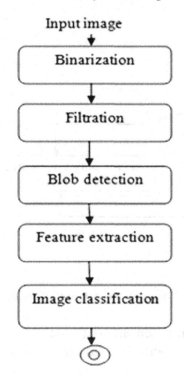

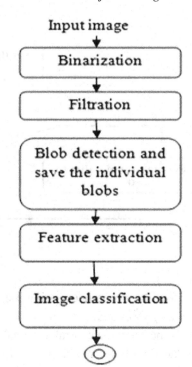

$$\mu_1(t) = \sum_{i=0}^{t} i * P(i) \Big/ q_1(t) \qquad (9)$$

$$\mu_2(t) = \sum_{i=i+1}^{255} i * P(i) \Big/ q_2(t) \qquad (10)$$

Thresholding is a process of converting a grayscale input image to a bi-level image by using an optimal threshold. In thresholding, the color-image or gray-scale image is reduced to a binary image. Figure 14 presents the flowchart of binarization process. In this system, the threshold value of 0.9 is taken during the experimentation.

Filteration is the process of removing the noisy data from the image. It can be done in many ways – either linear or nonlinear filtering. Median Filters are used in the proposed system. It is a nonlinear digital filtering technique, often used to remove noise. It is widely used because, under certain conditions, it preserves edges while removing noise. It is mainly used to remove salt and pepper noise. The median filter considers each pixel in the image in turn and looks at its nearby neighbors to decide whether or not it is representative of its surroundings. Instead of simply replacing the pixel value with the mean of neighboring pixel values, it replaces it with the median of those values. The median is calculated by first sorting all the pixel values from the surrounding neighborhood into numerical order and then replacing the pixel being considered with the middle pixel value. (If the neighborhood under consideration contains an even number of pixels, the average of the two middle pixel values is used.) Figure 15 presents the

Figure 14. Binarization of input image

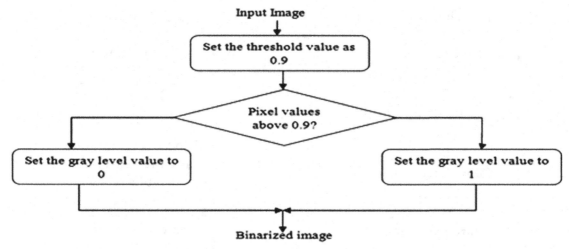

flowchart for filtration process using median filters and Table 3 presents calculation of median value for a pixel neighborhood.

As it can be seen, the central pixel value of 150 is rather unrepresentative of the surrounding pixels and is replaced with the median value: 124. A 3×3 square neighborhood is used here: larger neighborhoods will produce more severe smoothing.

Blob Detection, by now, we get the neatly filtered binary image from which the edges can be easily detected by making use of different edge detection operators such as Prewitt, Sobel, Canny and Robert. Sobel Edge detection is used in the proposed system. Figure 16 presents the flowchart for blob detection.

Feature extraction process uses Zernike moments to extract the features of the blobs. Figure 17 presents the flow chart for feature extraction.

In classification, we will construct the .xlsx files to store the features extracted from Zernike moments separately for both the training images and testing images. These files are given as input to different classifiers like k-NN, SVM and Bagging and Boosting algorithms.

Table 3. Calculating the median value of a pixel neighborhood

123	125	126	130	140
122	124	126	127	135
118	120	150	125	134
119	115	119	123	133
111	116	110	120	130

Neighborhood values:
115, 119, 120, 123, 124, 126, 127, 150
Median value: 124

Figure 15. Filtration of binary image

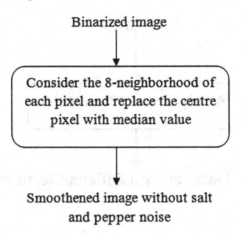

Figure 16. Detection of Blobs

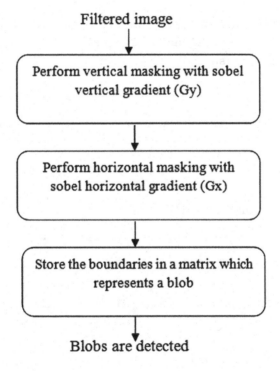

3.1. Algorithm for Moving Object Classification

The following three algorithms describe the detailed working of the proposed approach. Algorithm1 states the feature extraction process to construct the training data; Algorithm2 is used for extracting features to construct testing data and Algorithm3 describes the classification performed on training and testing data.

Figure 17. Feature Extraction

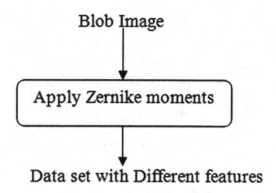

Input: Captured video (.mp4 or .avi or any other format)
Output: An object classified into a particular class (Humans, Vehicle{bicycle, bike, auto, bus, car}, other objects {bag, lunchbox etc.})

Algorithm 1: Constructing feature set for training the classifier
Input: Sample images 1…n (n-total no of images)
Output: Features (train dataset)

```
    //Feature Extraction
for 1: n do
resize the image
binarization with threshold value of 0.9
filteration by median filter
sobel edge detection
blob detection with 8 neighborhood
perform regionprop
{
    r(1)  =  [];                    %Clear 1st entry as it's the outside rectangle.
    MaxArea  =  60;                 %Select largest area you want to keep.
    r  =  r([r.Area] >MaxArea);     %Detect cells larger than some value.
    L  =  length(r);
}
Store each blob as separate image
Implement feature selection by calling Zernike Moments and construct BoV;

//Zernike Moments
v = v+1;
    k = 1;
    M  =  zeros(1);
M(k) = u;
    k = k+1;
```

```
for n = 0:5
     if mod(n,2) =  = 0
        st = 0;
     else
        st = 1;
     end
     for m = st:+2:n
        [S,A,P] =  Zernikmoment(single,n,m);
        M(k) = real(S);
        M(k+1) = imag(S);
         k = k+2;
     end
end

function [Z, A, Phi]  =  Zernikmoment(p,n,m)
N  =  size(p,1);
x  =  1:N; y  =  x;
[X,Y]  =  meshgrid(x,y);
R  =  sqrt((2.*X-N-1).^2+(2.*Y-N-1).^2)/N;
Theta  =  atan2((N-1-2.*Y+2),(2.*X-N+1-2));
R  =  (R< = 1).*R;
Rad  =  radialpoly(R,n,m);                         % get the radial polynomial
Product  =  p(x,y).*Rad.*exp(-1i*m*Theta);
Z  =  sum(Product(:));                             % calculate the moments
cnt  =  nnz(R)+1;            % count the number of pixels inside the unit circle
Z  =  (n+1)*Z/cnt;                            % normalize the amplitude of moments
A  =  abs(Z);                          % calculate the amplitude of the moment
Phi  =  angle(Z)*180/pi;      % calculate the phase of the moment (in degrees)
function rad  =  radialpoly(r,n,m)
rad  =  zeros(size(r));                      % Initialization
for s  =  0:(n-abs(m))/2
 c  =  (-1)^s*factorial(n-s)/(factorial(s)*factorial((n+abs(m))/2-
s)*factorial((n-abs(m))/2-s));
rad  =  rad + c*r.^(n-2*s);
end
write(f1); //f1 represents a file of train dataset
end
```

Algorithm 2: Constructing testing data
Input: Video (.mp4 or .avi)
Output: Features Extracted (test dataset)
if (video) then
Extract frames (1..m) from video;
Perform blob detection;

```
end
if(occluded objects) then
        Blob refinement;
end
//Feature Extraction
for 1: y do //total no of blobs identified
 Implement feature selection;
 write(f2); //f2 represents a file of test dataset
end
```

Algorithm 3: Classification
Input: Training and Testing datasets
Output: Assigns a class label C ∈ $C_1, C_2, C_3,$
Train the classifier using f1; //f1 – training data
Upload f2 for testing; //f2 – testing data
for 1...i do //i – no of rows (data samples) in f1
 for 1...j do //j – no of rows (data samples) in f2
        if (features in f1 is nearly ∈features in f2) then
                Assigns (1..m) ∈ C;
 end
end

3.2. Implementation and Results

MAtrix LABoratory (Matlab) and Rapidminer tool are used for implementing moving object classification algorithm. It is a multi-paradigm numerical computing environment and fourth-generation programming language. A proprietary programming language developed by Math Works, MATLAB allows matrix manipulations, plotting of functions and data, implementation of algorithms, creation of user interfaces, and interfacing with programs written in other languages, including C, C++, Java, Fortran and Python (David Houcque,2005). Common usage of the MATLAB application involves using the Command Window as an interactive mathematical shell or executing text files containing MATLAB code. MATLAB is used for binarizing the image, filtering the salt and pepper noise, blobs detection and feature extraction purposes. RapidMiner is a software platform developed by the company of the same name that provides an integrated environment for machine learning, data mining, text mining, predictive analytics and business analytics. RapidMiner provides data mining and machine learning procedures including: data loading and transformation (Extract, transform and load (ETL)), data pre-processing and visualization, predictive analytics and statistical modeling, evaluation, and deployment (Kotu & Deshpande, 2014). RapidMiner is written in the Java programming language. RapidMiner provides a GUI to design and execute analytical workflows. RapidMiner is used for training and testing various classifiers.

3.2.1. Dataset Used

Training

To train the classifier, we have taken the different samples of human, 2-wheeler, 3-wheeler, 4-wheeler and other objects at different views. Total 133 samples are taken to form the training dataset as shown in Figure 18.

Testing

A real-time video between Hyderabad to Vijayawada highway is considered as an input. This video is taken as it includes all the objects (human, 2-wheeler, 3-wheeler, 4-wheeler, and other objects) and it has dynamic background as shown in Figure 19.

3.2.2. Performance Measures

Performance is calculated for the different classification algorithms (k-NN, SVM, Bagging with k-NN, Bagging with SVM, Bagging with Decision tree) as shown in Figure 20 depending on the parameters given below:

Figure 18. Training dataset

Figure 19. Video considered for testing

Figure 20. Experimental setup in Rapidminer for classification

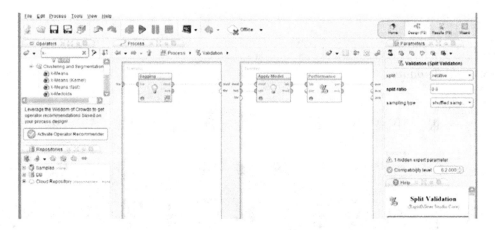

1. **Confusion Matrix:** The confusion matrix is also known as contingency table or error matrix. It is a specific table that allows the visualization of the classification performance of the proposed algorithm as mentioned in the Table 4. In the confusion matrix, 'a' and 'b' are class labels and:
    a. P indicates True Positives
    b. FP indicates False Positives
    c. TN indicates True Negatives
    d. FN indicates False Negatives

2. **Precision:** It is the ratio of the number of matched objects retrieved to the total number of irrelevant and relevant matched objects retrieved and it is defined as in Equation 11 (Han & Kamber, 2006).

Table 4. Confusion Matrix [Jiawei Han and Micheline Kamber,2006]

	a	b
actual a = 0	TP	FN
actual b = 1	FN	TP

$$\text{Precision} = \frac{tp}{tp + fp} * 100\% \tag{11}$$

where, tp: true positives, is the number of relevant matched objects retrieved fp: false positive, is the number of irrelevant matched objects retrieved

3. **Recall:** It is the ratio of the number of relevant matched objects retrieved to the total number of relevant matched objects present. It is defined as in Equation. 12 (Han & Kamber, 2006).

$$\text{Recall} = \frac{tp}{tp + fn} * 100\% \tag{12}$$

where, tp: true positive, is the number of relevant matched objects retrieved fn: false negatives, is the number of relevant matched objects not retrieved

4. **Error Rate:** It measures the average magnitude of the error.
5. **Classification Accuracy Rate (CAR or Accuracy):** The accuracy is measured using all the prediction values that are correct that is TP (true positives), FP (false positive), TN (true negative) and FN (false negative). It is defined as in Equation. 13 (Han & Kamber, 2006).

$$\text{accuracy} = \frac{tp + tn}{tp + tn + fp + fn} * 100\% \tag{13}$$

3.2.3. Comparison

The following tables from 5 to Table 9 present the different classification results for National Highway video. Table 5 presents Classifier Accuracy Rate (CAR), Precision and Recall values for k-NN Classifier. Table 6 presents for SVM Classifier. Table 7 presents the results for Bagging with k-NN Classifier. Table 8 presents the results for Bagging with SVM Classifier. Finally, Table 9 presents CAR, Precision and Recall values for Bagging with Decision Tree

It is observed from these tables from 5 to Table 9 that, k-NN, SVM and bagging with k-NN could predict well for vehicles class, whereas Bagging with SVM could predict all the three classes, human class is predicted well by bagging with decision tree.

F-Measure is the harmonic mean of precision and recall. It is calculated using the Equation 14.

Table 5. CAR, Precision and Recall values for k-NN Classifier

Accuracy:86.67%				
	True Vehicle	True Human	True Other	Class Precision
Pred. Vehicle	3	0	0	100.00%
Pred. Human	0	7	1	87.50%
Pred. Others	1	0	3	75.00%
Class Recall	7.005%	100.00%	75.00%	

Table 6. CAR, Precision and Recall values for SVM Classifier

Accuracy:80.00%				
	True Vehicle	True Human	True Other	Class Precision
Pred. Vehicle	2	0	0	100.00%
Pred. Human	1	7	1	77.78%
Pred. Others	1	0	3	75.00%
Class Recall	50.00%	100.00%	75.00%	

Table 7. CAR, Precision and Recall values for Bagging with k-NN Classifier

Accuracy:86.67%				
	True Vehicle	True Human	True Other	Class Precision
Pred. Vehicle	3	0	0	100.00%
Pred. Human	0	6	1	85.71%
Pred. Others	0	1	4	80.00%
Class Recall	100.00%	85.71%	80.00%	

Table 8. CAR, Precision and Recall values for Bagging with SVM Classifier

Accuracy:100.00%				
	True Vehicle	True Human	True Other	Class Precision
Pred. Vehicle	3	0	0	100.00%
Pred. Human	0	7	0	100.00%
Pred. Others	0	0	5	100.00%
Class Recall	100.00%	100.00%	100.00%	

Table 9. CAR, Precision and Recall values for Bagging with Decision Tree

Accuracy:66.67%			
	True Vehicle	True Human	True Other	Class Precision
Pred. Vehicle	3	0	2	60.00%
Pred.Human	0	4	0	100.00%
Pred.Others	0	3	3	50.00%
Class Recall	100.00%	57.14%	60.00%	

$$F_1 = 2 * \left(precision * recall \right) / \left(precision + recall \right) \tag{14}$$

Table 10 to Table 12 compares F-Measure values of Bagging with k-NN, SVM and Decision Tree with Zernike order as n = 4, 5, 6.

It can be observed that, when n = 4, Bagging with k-NN performed well. When n = 5 and 6, Bagging with SVM outperformed all the other combinations.

Table 10. F_Measure values for various classifiers with Zernike order as n = 4

	k-NN	SVM	Bagging With k-NN	Bagging With SVM	Bagging With Decision Tree
Human	85.71%	82.35%	83.33%	87.50%	76.92%
Vehicle	75%	40%	100%	80%	85.71%
Other	75%	75%	83.33%	88.88%	60%

Table 11. F_Measure values for various classifiers with Zernike order as n = 5

	k-NN	SVM	Bagging With k-NN	Bagging With SVM	Bagging With Decision Tree
Human	93.33%	87.50%	85.71%	100%	72.72%
Vehicle	85.71%	66.67%	100%	100%	75%
Other	75%	75%	80%	100%	54.55%

Table 12. F_Measure values for various classifiers with Zernike order as n = 6

	k-NN	SVM	Bagging With k-NN	Bagging With SVM	Bagging With Decision Tree
Human	93.33%	87.50%	85.71%	92.30%	71.43%
Vehicle	85.71%	66.67%	100%	100%	75%
Other	75%	75%	80%	90.90%	24.99%

In our experimentation, we have taken the Zernike moment order as $n = 5$ and repetition as $m = 2$. Table 13 presents the comparison of performance of various classifiers for different orders of Zernike moments with respect to the Zernike moment order, $n = 5$.

When the order is taken as $n = 4$, the accuracy of k-NN classifier decreased to 80% whereas for the order $n = 6$, it is same as that for $n = 5$.

When the order is taken as $n = 4$, the accuracy of the SVM classifier decreased to 73.33% whereas for the order $n = 6$, it is same as that for $n = 5$.

When the order is taken as $n = 4$ or $n = 6$, the accuracy of Bagging and Boosting in combination with k-NN classifier is same as that for $n = 5$. In combination with SVM classifier, the accuracy is decreased for both $n = 4$ and $n = 6$. Where as in combination with Decision Tree, the accuracy is increased to 73.33% and for $n = 6$, the accuracy is decreased to 60%.

In the testing phase, each image contains multiple objects. If the image contains occluded objects, the objects that are occluded will be detected as a single blob thereby reducing the performance i.e., the

Table 13. Comparison of performance of various classifiers for different orders of Zernike moments

	k-NN	SVM	Bagging With k-NN	Bagging With SVM	Bagging With Decision Tree
n = 4	Decreased	Decreased	Remains constant	Decreased	Increased
n = 6	Remains constant	Remains constant	Remains constant	Decreased	Decreased

number of blobs doesn't match the actual number of objects in an image. If the image doesn't contain occlusion, each object will be detected as a separate blob and the Zernike moments will be calculated for those blobs. Table 14 presents snapshot of the F_Measure values for various classifiers with different Zernike moment orders for the occlusion case.

Table 15 and Table 16 presents snapshot of class labels obtained using k-NN and SVM classifier respectively. k-NN classifier performed well when compared to SVM.

Table 17 compares F_Measure values for various classifiers with different Zernike moment orders for the occlusion case.

When n = 5 all the classifiers k-NN, SVM, bagging with k-NN, bagging with SVM and bagging with decision tree performed well. Specific to vehicle recognition, at order = 5, bagging with k-NN, bagging with SVM performed well. Specific to human recognition, bagging with SVM performed well.

All the frames are stored in the frame database. We can view the frames by clicking on "view" button shown in Figure 21.

Table 14. Zernike moments result

S.No	r00	i00	r11	i11	r20	i20	r22	i22	r31	i31	r33	i33	r40	i40	r42	i42	r44	i44
1	3.4335	0	1.551	-1.0565	-2.2863	0	-0.1917	-0.6206	-1.3064	0.8856	-1.3932	-0.3993	0.2092	0	-0.4274	-0.6274	0.1207	-0.275
2	3.3076	0	0.3121	-0.3706	-0.9388	0	1.8959	-0.0337	-0.3294	0.3338	-0.5996	-0.069	2.5192	0	-1.5207	-0.2741	-0.9392	-0.2115
3	5.6806	0	-0.1458	-1.6269	-4.9709	0	-0.7342	0.0823	-0.0312	-0.4523	0.1879	-1.7671	1.5589	0	0.707	0.2193	-0.966	-0.0805

Table 15. Class labels for testing data using k-NN classifier

Row No.	S.No	class label	prediction(c..	confidence(..	confidence(..	confidence(..	r00	i00	r11	i11	r20	i20
1	1	vehicle	vehicle	1	0	0	7.548	0	0.135	0.385	-6.360	0
2	2	vehicle	vehicle	1	0	0	6.518	0	-0.557	-0.860	-7.937	0
3	3	vehicle	vehicle	1	0	0	3.712	0	-0.063	-0.549	-4.721	0
4	4	vehicle	other	0	0	1	6.539	0	-0.949	-0.275	-4.450	0
5	5	human	human	0	1	0	5.968	0	-0.880	-0.715	-3.378	0
6	6	human	human	0	1	0	4.780	0	-0.546	-1.342	-3.517	0
7	7	human	human	0	1	0	4.419	0	0.071	-0.768	-4.463	0
8	8	human	human	0	1	0	4.758	0	-0.576	-1.108	-3.732	0
9	9	human	human	0	1	0	5.739	0	-1.047	-0.606	-3.342	0
10	10	human	human	0	1	0	5.000	0	-0.170	-0.961	-3.298	0
11	11	human	human	0	1	0	5.973	0	-0.276	-1.617	-3.294	0
12	12	other	other	0	0	1	4.154	0	1.086	1.114	-3.942	0
13	13	other	other	0	0	1	5.967	0	-0.166	0.882	-4.719	0
14	14	other	human	0	1	0	5.712	0	-1.423	-0.489	-3.210	0
15	15	other	other	0	0	1	6.528	0	1.389	0.422	-3.385	0
16	16	human	human	0	1	0	3.434	0	1.551	-1.056	-2.286	0
17	17	human	human	0	1	0	3.308	0	0.312	-0.371	-0.939	0
18	18	other	human	0	1	0	5.681	0	-0.146	-1.627	-4.971	0

Table 16. Class labels for testing data using SVM classifier

Row No.	S.No	class label	prediction(c	confidence(	confidence(	confidence(	r00	i00	r11	i11	r20	i20
1	1	vehicle	vehicle	1	0	0	7.548	0	0.135	0.386	-6.360	0
2	2	vehicle	vehicle	1	0	0	6.518	0	-0.557	-0.860	-7.937	0
3	3	vehicle	human	0	1	0	3.712	0	-0.063	-0.549	-4.721	0
4	4	vehicle	other	0	0	1	6.539	0	-0.949	-0.275	-4.450	0
5	5	human	human	0	1	0	5.968	0	-0.880	-0.715	-3.378	0
6	6	human	human	0	1	0	4.780	0	-0.546	-1.342	-3.517	0
7	7	human	human	0	1	0	4.419	0	0.071	-0.768	-4.463	0
8	8	human	human	0	1	0	4.758	0	-0.576	-1.108	-3.732	0
9	9	human	human	0	1	0	5.739	0	-1.047	-0.606	-3.342	0
10	10	human	human	0	1	0	5.000	0	-0.170	-0.961	-3.298	0
11	11	human	human	0	1	0	5.973	0	-0.276	-1.617	-3.294	0
12	12	other	other	0	0	1	4.154	0	1.086	1.114	-3.942	0
13	13	other	other	0	0	1	5.967	0	-0.166	0.882	-4.719	0
14	14	other	human	0	1	0	5.712	0	-1.423	-0.489	-3.210	0
15	15	other	other	0	0	1	6.528	0	1.389	0.422	-3.385	0
16	16	human	human	0	1	0	3.434	0	1.551	-1.056	-2.286	0
17	17	human	human	0	1	0	3.308	0	0.312	-0.371	-0.939	0
18	18	other	human	0	1	0	5.681	0	-0.146	-1.627	-4.971	0

Table 17. F_Measure values for various classifiers with different Zernike moment orders for the occlusion case

	k-NN			SVM			Bagging with k-NN			Bagging With SVM			Bagging With Decision Tree		
	n = 4	n = 5	n = 6	n = 4	n = 5	n = 6	n = 4	n = 5	n = 6	n = 4	n = 5	n = 6	n = 4	n = 5	n = 6
Human	84.21	90	84.21	76.19	85.71	80	80	83.33	72.73	80	90.90	66.67	60	66.67	66.66
Vehicle	75	85.71	85.71	40	66.67	66.67	88.89	100	100	100	100	100	80	80	80
Other	66.67	66.67	60	60	66.67	60	92.30	83.33	76.92	85.71	92.30	79.99	66.66	76.92	60

Figure 21. Sample frames extracted from video

The output can be seen by clicking on view button on Graphical User Interface (GUI). Figure 22 indicates the blobs that are identified.

All the features are saved in .csv file as training.csv and testing.csv shown in Table 18 and Table 19. Class labels for testing data using K-NN and SVM classifier are shown in Table 20 and Table 21.

Figure 22. Blobs that are identified

Table 18. Zernike moments result for Training data

S.No	r00	i00	r11	i11	r20	i20	r22	i22	r31	i31	r33	i33	r40	i40	r42	i42	r44	i44
1	6.9465	0	0.6175	0.724	-4.5512	0	1.9672	1.2613	-0.5211	1.1039	-1.7938	2.3811	1.1341	0	-1.2253	-0.9486	-0.8958	0.1114
2	4.7786	0	0.4159	1.379	-3.2449	0	1.319	0.5512	-0.4723	-0.7769	0.6991	1.7424	1.0965	0	-1.1964	-0.6362	-1.0596	-0.8747
3	4.9978	0	-0.3401	-0.712	-6.2909	0	-1.5738	-0.0094	0.4512	0.0985	0.1833	-0.262	1.9278	0	1.3599	0.0693	0.1351	0.0305
4	4.0215	0	-0.0389	-0.1426	-4.9141	0	-1.0774	0.191	0.1548	-0.102	-0.3076	-0.5384	1.4626	0	0.7792	-0.1621	-0.0521	-0.3638
5	4.8474	0	0.2194	1.4727	-3.2608	0	1.2197	0.6729	-0.5017	-0.8021	0.6544	1.6461	0.9317	0	-1.2729	-0.6689	-1.1618	-0.6772
6	4.6306	0	-0.9037	0.3871	-3.0272	0	0.602	1.1007	-0.5424	-0.477	-0.0923	0.2124	0.9485	0	-0.419	-0.1022	-0.5967	-0.7581
7	7.1584	0	-0.3795	2.1701	-5.0464	0	1.775	-0.2449	0.0685	-1.0654	-1.0019	2.1578	2.7581	0	-1.4149	0.8212	-1.985	1.3066
8	6.9743	0	-0.6097	1.7677	-4.9197	0	1.7016	-0.5479	0.6148	-0.9207	-1.2853	2.4229	1.3775	0	-1.6115	0.2229	-1.3854	1.041
9	3.915	0	0.2178	1.3409	-2.9471	0	1.0583	0.4527	-0.2756	-0.8307	0.4313	1.5337	0.9722	0	-1.1447	-0.7241	-0.9996	-0.5392
10	12.6086	0	-0.068	0.864	-10.3124	0	2.1324	-0.8643	-0.5109	0.9121	-1.0607	4.7067	6.095	0	-0.3284	1.5347	-3.0294	1.3431
11	11.4437	0	0.5167	1.2513	-9.7665	0	1.9477	-0.6837	-0.6669	-0.2089	-0.7508	1.7526	6.4096	0	-0.2104	1.1411	-3.8061	0.618
12	10.4738	0	-0.0881	2.6997	-10.207	0	2.2058	0.9956	0.9874	-0.5487	0.586	3.706	7.8827	0	-0.9688	-1.7259	-3.3366	-0.6957
13	9.1873	0	-0.8703	1.3723	-7.1475	0	2.8907	-0.61	0.0256	-0.0157	-1.0362	3.079	4.6288	0	-1.2755	1.6557	-0.8349	2.5397
14	6.8323	0	0.6258	2.5565	-5.0496	0	1.8401	0.181	-0.043	-0.4405	-0.6061	4.1201	5.3116	0	-1.9833	0.2608	-2.3325	0.7216
15	11.3159	0	1.037	2.257	-8.4331	0	2.7125	0.2174	-0.4563	1.0253	-1.0241	4.2594	6.1255	0	-2.254	0.2527	-2.4554	0.5292
16	11.6021	0	-0.4673	1.6766	-9.3184	0	2.2757	0.7552	0.7664	-0.6709	0.6474	1.3976	4.9272	0	-0.9949	-0.9167	-4.0751	-1.6839
17	3.3284	0	0.0097	-0.4232	-4.1647	0	-1.2243	0.0442	-0.0411	-0.0581	0.0175	-0.1032	1.306	0	1.2358	-0.0422	0.1158	-0.0215
18	4.0102	0	0.9745	-1.058	-2.9628	0	0.3917	-0.721	0.5086	1.0684	-0.2224	0.7257	1.8307	0	-0.8945	-0.0712	-1.0029	0.2881
19	3.5944	0	-1.651	-0.3705	-2.8325	0	-0.379	1.1283	1.0455	0.3645	0.5185	-0.4449	1.638	0	0.0354	-0.3646	-0.7261	-0.087
20	5.3929	0	-0.1872	-0.687	-3.5043	0	-0.636	-0.4139	-0.1467	-0.1419	0.9849	-1.0749	-0.0404	0	-0.3112	-0.0059	0.289	0.5364
21	5.2884	0	-0.0565	0.0921	-3.462	0	-1.4461	0.4894	-0.4441	0.2457	0.6451	-0.3694	1.5745	0	-0.2832	0.1443	-0.4754	-0.1995
22	3.7951	0	-0.5005	-1.1053	-2.6924	0	-0.8277	-0.0347	0.1754	0.196	0.2915	-1.1274	0.1413	0	0.5915	0.607	0.303	0.4555
23	2.4218	0	1.5645	-0.3569	-0.6415	0	-0.5304	-0.4411	-1.4911	-0.3867	-0.4585	-0.4367	-1.4698	0	0.0062	0.011	0.3541	-0.123
24	5.795	0	-1.5521	0.1606	-3.5886	0	-0.9557	-0.2529	0.7021	0.2989	0.35	-1.1681	0.0132	0	0.7385	0.5131	-0.0537	-1.2211
25	4.3498	0	-0.4133	-0.6256	-2.6974	0	-0.6184	-0.2814	0.0859	-0.0463	0.3854	-1.3453	-0.3351	0	0.184	0.4515	0.6411	0.2817

Table 19. Zernike moments result for Testing data

S.No	r00	i00	r11	i11	r20	i20	r22	i22	r31	i31	r33	i33	r40	i40	r42	i42	r44	i44
1	7.5476	0	0.1347	0.3861	-6.3603	0	1.0457	-0.3286	-0.3496	0.212	-0.6997	1.5274	4.0116	0	-0.0271	0.5333	-2.4216	0.5373
2	6.5175	0	-0.5571	-0.8605	-7.9373	0	-2.2004	-0.0229	0.6826	0.1748	0.3388	-0.3395	1.6682	0	2.0514	0.2118	0.2015	0.1173
3	3.7124	0	-0.0629	-0.5492	-4.7206	0	-1.3515	0.0326	0.0359	-0.1324	0.118	-0.0725	1.9449	0	1.286	0.0125	0.063	0.001
4	6.5394	0	-0.9492	-0.2754	-4.4497	0	0.7733	0.2959	-0.6241	-0.0983	0.8459	1.1579	0.4954	0	-0.3583	-0.5916	-0.4531	0.1376
5	5.9681	0	-0.8801	-0.7149	-3.3783	0	-0.7137	-0.4204	0.1086	-0.0565	0.2301	-1.6072	-0.7211	0	0.113	0.8894	1.0311	0.1977
6	4.7799	0	-0.5462	-1.3416	-3.5172	0	-1.1018	0.0673	0.0538	-0.0684	0.2428	-0.3722	1.0223	0	-0.1677	-0.0828	-0.4451	-0.134
7	4.4187	0	0.0714	-0.7676	-4.4634	0	-1.202	-0.8621	0.0101	1.0281	0.4046	-0.2777	1.0216	0	0.7928	0.302	-0.0914	-0.3236
8	4.7577	0	-0.5759	-1.1081	-3.7315	0	-0.5202	0.1575	-0.2662	0.4788	0.2935	0.4168	0.0061	0	-0.9209	-0.0671	0.33	-0.3474
9	5.7391	0	-1.0467	-0.6059	-3.3416	0	-1.4269	-0.3164	0.7262	-0.0312	-0.3962	-1.4968	-0.2517	0	0.4912	0.69	0.7403	0.6051
10	5.0003	0	-0.1701	-0.9611	-3.2977	0	-1.5085	-0.2495	-0.037	-0.4089	0.3167	-0.9155	-0.1175	0	0.191	-0.0266	0.1449	0.7534
11	5.9726	0	-0.2761	-1.6169	-3.2943	0	-0.4271	-0.6699	0.2308	-0.2424	0.0816	-1.4104	0.0818	0	-0.5616	0.3401	0.6077	0.9224
12	4.154	0	1.0859	1.1137	-3.9425	0	-0.3075	-0.4291	-0.922	-0.8277	-0.9135	0.8196	1.2256	0	0.2029	1.2413	-1.4841	0.1514
13	5.9668	0	-0.1664	0.882	-4.7188	0	0.1843	-0.1459	-0.1092	-1.0338	-0.1392	-1.4627	2.0603	0	-1.3507	0.0502	-2.607	0.0718
14	5.7119	0	-1.4229	-0.4889	-3.21	0	-0.0877	-0.538	-0.6736	0.1483	0.3282	-0.3683	0.0671	0	0.3938	0.8273	-0.2108	-0.1622
15	6.5283	0	1.3889	0.4219	-3.3852	0	-1.6791	0.212	-0.8746	0.1344	1.1683	1.1512	1.2311	0	0.7618	0.8312	-0.449	-0.256

Table 20. Class labels for testing data using k-NN classifier

Row No.	S.No	class label	prediction(c...	confidence(...	confidence(...	confidence(...	r00	i00	r11	i11
1	1	vehicle	vehicle	1	0	0	7.548	0	0.135	0.386
2	2	vehicle	vehicle	1	0	0	6.518	0	-0.557	-0.860
3	3	vehicle	vehicle	1	0	0	3.712	0	-0.063	-0.549
4	4	vehicle	other	0	0	1	6.539	0	-0.949	-0.275
5	5	human	human	0	1	0	5.968	0	-0.880	-0.715
6	6	human	human	0	1	0	4.780	0	-0.546	-1.342
7	7	human	human	0	1	0	4.419	0	0.071	-0.768
8	8	human	human	0	1	0	4.758	0	-0.576	-1.108
9	9	human	human	0	1	0	5.739	0	-1.047	-0.606
10	10	human	human	0	1	0	5.000	0	-0.170	-0.961
11	11	human	human	0	1	0	5.973	0	-0.276	-1.617
12	12	other	other	0	0	1	4.154	0	1.086	1.114
13	13	other	other	0	0	1	5.967	0	-0.166	0.882
14	14	other	human	0	1	0	5.712	0	-1.423	-0.489
15	15	other	other	0	0	1	6.528	0	1.389	0.422

Table 21. Class labels for testing data using SVM classifier

Row No.	S.No	class label	prediction(c...	confidence(...	confidence(...	confidence(...	r00	i00	r11	i11
1	1	vehicle	vehicle	1	0	0	7.548	0	0.135	0.386
2	2	vehicle	vehicle	1	0	0	6.518	0	-0.557	-0.860
3	3	vehicle	human	0	1	0	3.712	0	-0.063	-0.549
4	4	vehicle	other	0	0	1	6.539	0	-0.949	-0.275
5	5	human	human	0	1	0	5.968	0	-0.880	-0.715
6	6	human	human	0	1	0	4.780	0	-0.546	-1.342
7	7	human	human	0	1	0	4.419	0	0.071	-0.768
8	8	human	human	0	1	0	4.758	0	-0.576	-1.108
9	9	human	human	0	1	0	5.739	0	-1.047	-0.606
10	10	human	human	0	1	0	5.000	0	-0.170	-0.961
11	11	human	human	0	1	0	5.973	0	-0.276	-1.617
12	12	other	other	0	0	1	4.154	0	1.086	1.114
13	13	other	other	0	0	1	5.967	0	-0.166	0.882
14	14	other	human	0	1	0	5.712	0	-1.423	-0.489
15	15	other	other	0	0	1	6.528	0	1.389	0.422

Both the training and testing csv files are converted into .arff (Attribute Relation File Format) which can be used for classification purpose. Arff files are given to different classifiers and the classification results are obtained. It can be observed from the Results presented in Table 20 and Table 21, that, two objects out of which one is vehicle are misclassified using k-NN and 3vehicle objects out of which two are vehicles are misclassified using SVM.

4. CONCLUSION AND FUTURE WORK

Main purpose of moving object classification is to classify the different types of objects that are present in a video while monitoring the video in the important areas. Our proposed approach uses frame extraction from a video, blob detection to identify the different objects in a frame based on area of the blob with a resolution of 256*256, feature extraction to know the color, structure and texture information of the object, classifying the object depending on the information.

To perform classification, video is taken and frames are extracted from a real time video at the rate of 29 frames per second.

In Binarization stage, thresholding method is used with the threshold value as 0.9 to achieve proper binarized image. In Filtration stage, median filters are used to remove noise from the binarized image. In Blob detection stage, sobel edge detection algorithm and 8- neighborhood connected components to detect the blobs are used. In Feature extraction stage, Zernike moments with the order as n = 5 and repetition as m = 2 are used to achieve better results.

In the testing phase, each image contains multiple objects. If the frame contains occluded objects (occluded area is less than 20%, blob is refined otherwise the blob is discarded), the objects that are occluded will be detected as a single blob thereby reducing the performance i.e., the number of blobs doesn't match the actual number of objects in a frame. If the frame doesn't contain occlusion, each object will be detected as a separate blob and the Zernike moments will be calculated for those blobs.

Preprocessing is done on each blob to get resolution of 256*256. Zernike moment features are saved in CSV file format, later converted to ARFF file. Training and testing is done by using ARFF files. Classification is done using Rapidminer tool, by using different classifiers such as k-NN, SVM, bagging with k-NN, Bagging with SVM, Bagging with Decision tree. The performance of proposed system is mainly calculated based on precision, recall, CAR, F-Measure. Features of objects using Zernike moments of order n = 4, 5 and 6 are extracted and the objects are classified into multiple classes such as Humans, Vehicles and Others.

The bagging and boosting in combination with SVM classifier have classified our data better than k-NN and Bagging and Boosting in combination with decision tree and k-NN. Bagging and Boosting in combination with SVM have given an accuracy of 100% where the k-NN, bagging with k-NN and decision tree gave an accuracy of 86.67%, 86.67% and 66.67% respectively.

Our future work is to apply the proposed method on challenging surveillance videos with occluded object classes. This work can be extended so as to recognize objects, even in various lightening conditions. Better performance should be achieved under the illumination variations.

REFERENCES

Bhaskara Rao, P., Vara Prasad, D., & Pavan Kumar, C. (2013). Feature Extraction Using Zernike Moments. *International Journal of Latest Trends in Engineering and Technology*, 2(2).

Chaki, N., Shaikh, S. H., & Saeed, K. (2014). Exploring image binarization techniques. Springer publication.

Chandel, H., & Vatta, S. (2015). Occlusion Detection and Handling: A Review. *International Journal of Computer Applications*, 120(10).

Chen, L., Feris, R., Zhai, Y., Brown, L., & Hampapur, A. (2012). An Integrated System for Moving Object Classification in Surveillance Videos. *Proceedings of the IEEE Fifth International Conference on Advanced Video and Signal Based Surveillance AVSS'08* (pp. 52-59).

Das, S. (2016). Comparison of Various Edge Detection Technique, International Journal of Signal Processing. *Image Processing and Pattern Recognition*, 9(2), 143–158. doi:10.14257/ijsip.2016.9.2.13

Elhoseiny, M., Bakry, A., & Elgammal, A. (2013), Multiclass Object Classification in Video Surveillance Systems, Experimental Study. *Proceedings of the CVPR Workshop '13*. doi:10.1109/CVPRW.2013.118

Fermüller, C., & Pollefeys, M. (2015). Edge Detection: CS 111. School of Information and Computer Sciences University of California, Irvine. Retrieved from http://www.ics.uci.edu/~majumder/DIP/classes/EdgeDetect.pdf

Ganguly, S., Bhattacharjee, D., & Nasipuri, M. (2014). Automatic Analysis Of Smoothing Techniques By Simulation Model Based Real-Time System For Processing 3d Human Faces. *International Journal Of Embedded Systems And Applications*, 4(4), 13–23. doi:10.5121/ijesa.2014.4402

Han, J., & Kamber, M. (2006). *Data Mining Concepts and Techniques* (2nd ed.). Elsevier publisher.

Houcque, D. (2005). *Introduction To Matlab For Engineering Students* (Version 1.2). Northwestern University.

Kotu, V., & Deshpande, B. (2014). *Predictive Analytics and Data Mining: Concepts and Practice with RapidMiner*. Morgan Kaufmann Publisher.

Lakhani, K., Minocha, B., & Gugnani, N. (2016). Analyzing edge detection techniques for feature extraction in dental radiographs. *Perspectives on Science, 8*, 395–398. doi:10.1016/j.pisc.2016.04.087

Mahi, H., Isabaten, H., & Serief, C. (2014). Zernike Moments and SVM for Shape Classification in Very High Resolution Satellite Images, The International Arab. *Journal of Information Technology, 11*(1).

Materka, A., & Strzelecki, M. (1998). Texture Analysis Methods – A Review (COST B11 report). Institute of Electronics, Brussels.

Pepikj, B., Stark, M., Gehler, P., & Schiele, B. (2013). Occlusion patterns for object class detection. *Proceedings of the IEEE Conference on Computer Vision and Pattern Recognition* (pp. 3286-3293).

Poorani, M., Prathiba, T., & Ravindran, G. (2013). Integrated Feature Extraction for Image Retrieval. *IJCSMC, 2*(2), 28–35.

San Biagio, M., Bazzani, L., Cristani, M., & Murino, V. (2014), Weighted Bag of Visual Words for Object Recognition, Image Processing (ICIP). *Proceedings of the 2014 IEEE International Conference*. doi:10.1109/ICIP.2014.7025553

Teh, C. H., & Chin, R. T. (1988). On image analysis by the methods of moments. *IEEE Transactions on Pattern Analysis and Machine Intelligence, 10*(4), 496–513. doi:10.1109/34.3913

Chapter 13
Object Extraction Using Topological Models from Complex Scene Image

Uday Pratap Singh
Madhav Institute of Technology and Science, India

Sanjeev Jain
Madhav Institute of Technology and Science, India

ABSTRACT

Efficient and effective object recognition from a multimedia data are very complex. Automatic object segmentation is usually very hard for natural images; interactive schemes with a few simple markers provide feasible solutions. In this chapter, we propose topological model based region merging. In this work, we will focus on topological models like, Relative Neighbourhood Graph (RNG) and Gabriel graph (GG), etc. From the Initial segmented image, we constructed a neighbourhood graph represented different regions as the node of graph and weight of the edges are the value of dissimilarity measures function for their colour histogram vectors. A method of similarity based region merging mechanism (supervised and unsupervised) is proposed to guide the merging process with the help of markers. The region merging process is adaptive to the image content and it does not need to set the similarity threshold in advance. To the validation of proposed method extensive experiments are performed and the result shows that the proposed method extracts the object contour from the complex background.

1. INTRODUCTION

Object extraction from images and videos are an important area of research for many multimedia applications such as image and video editing, image or video retrieval and manipulation, human computer interaction and video surveillance etc. Generally, the image segmentations (Felzenszwalb, 2004; Vincent & Soille, 1991; Haris et al., 1998; Nock & Nielsen, 2004; Shi & Malik, 2000) are dividing the image pixels into the group of homogeneous small regions such that each region has visual effects and object segmentation is dividing the image into foreground and background. Image segmentation depends on low

DOI: 10.4018/978-1-5225-2848-7.ch013

level features like color, texture and shape. Using these low-level features, we proceed for high level like object detection from image or video. Moving object detection and medical image segmentation (Li et al., 2015) are very important in daily life due to robustness and accuracy. Initially images are partitions using some low-level image segmentation into a number of non-overlapping regions. Different approaches have been used for image and medical image segmentation, Partial Differential Equation (PDE) based Active Contour Model (ACM) (Caselles, Kimmel, & Sapiro, 1997) is one important method for curve evolution. There are two main ACM based segmentation Mumford-Shah (MS) model (Mumford & Shah, 1989) and Chan-Vese (CV) (Chan & Vese, 2001) model. In last few decades, different image segmentation approaches are generally exploited to obtain object from complex scene images (Yang et al., 2008; Vanhamel, Pratikakis, & Sahli, 2003; Tab, Naghdy, & Mertins, 2006; Cour, Benezit, & Shi, 2005). The literature of images segmentation contains threshold based (Otsu, 1975) edge based segmentation (Bao, Zhang & Wu, 2005), region based segmentation (Gonzalez, Woods, & Eddins, 2004; Cheng, 1995; Peng, Zhang, & Zhang, 2011) including region splitting, region growing and region merging. These segmentations are known as low level but generally they are used as base of some high-level segmentation.

Other segmentation techniques are based on nonlinear distance metric (Sobieranski, Comunello, & Wangenheim, 2011), watershed (Haris, Efstratiadis, & Katsaggelos, 1998; Hernandez & Barner, 2000; Bleau, & Leon, 2000), homogram thresholding (Cheng, Jiang, & Wang, 2002), etc. In this context requirement of object extraction, most favourable and high level image segmentation and promising results should be obtained by less segmented regions that preserve well the boundary of objects. Some low-level image segmentation also suffers from over segmentation and under segmentation problems. In recent years, some important and interactive semi-supervised image segmentation methods are developed (Peng, Zhang, Zhang, & Yang, 2011; Veksler, 2008; Singh, Saxena, & Jain, 2011; Vezhnevets, & Konouchine, 2005; Rother, Kolmogorov, & Blake, 2004; Li, Sun, Tang, & Shum, 2004). The previous initial segmentation methods achieve good results but suffer from complexity of object extraction from complex scene images. A linear time statistical region merging for fast segmentation is achieved in (Peng, Zhang, & Zhang, 2011).

Region merging has a lot of attention from last few years and play important role in object extraction. Two important issue of object extraction is region merging in iterative manner and its stopping criteria. A region is merged with their neighbour regions according to certain rule or conditions. Some recent studies focus on the region merging and interactive image segmentation methods. Topological models (Zahan, 1971; O'Callaghan, 1971; Lankford, 1969; Sibon, 1978) are another important method of region merging, based on initial low level segmentation (Singh, Saxena, & Jain, 2011). Each region in initial segmented image is either in foreground or background of the image. However, in merging strategy a region is merged with its adjacent region if they have high similarity index. Starting from over segmentation image, an effective region merging method is exploited to progressively merge the adjacent regions using some dissimilarity measures (Ning, Zhang, Zhang, & Wu, 2010; Guo, Jain, Ma, & Zhang, 2002). Sequence of region merging process is done via some topological models.

The rest of this chapter is organised as follows. Section 2 deals about digital image processing, object detection and various topological models. Section 3 explains the region merging algorithm using topological models. Complexity of region merging and object detection is explained in section 4. Section 5 contains the experimental results. Conclusion and future work are presented in section 6.

2. DIGITAL IMAGE

Digital image play an important role in our daily life such as satellite television, magnetic resonance imaging, computer tomography etc. An image is a two dimensional or three-dimensional representation of scene or object. A digital image is basically a numerical representation of an object such that digital image processing refers to the manipulation of an image by means of certain operations. An image may be defined as a two-dimensional function $f(x, y)$, where x and y are spatial digital coordinates and amplitude of f at any pair of coordinates *(x, y)* is called the intensity or gray level of the image at that point, where at point (x, y) the intensity value of f are finite and discrete in quantities, so we call the image a digital image.

While an analog image is mathematically represented as a continuous range of values representing position and intensity. An analog image is characterized by a physical magnitude varying continuously in space. Note that a digital image is composed of a finite number of elements, each of which has a particular location and a value. These elements are called picture elements, also these image elements are known as pels or pixels. Pixels are the term used most widely denotes the brightness at one points of digital image (Jayaraman, Esakkirajan, & Veerkumar, 2008). Conversion of an analog image to digital image involves two important operations, namely (i) sampling and (ii) quantization as shown in figure 1. So, an analog image is converted into digital image which is composition of a number of grid pixels that are stored in an array. A single pixel represents an intensity value. Images are processed to obtain information, which is apparent in the given image are pixel values (Jayaraman, Esakkirajan, & Veerkumar, 2008). Figure 2 shows the concept of formation of digital image from an analog image:

The *2D* continuous image $f(x, y)$ is divided into M rows and N columns. The intersection of a row and a column is termed as a pixel. The value assigned to the integer coordinates *(m, n)* with $m \in \{0, 1, 2, ..., M\text{-}1\}$ and $n \in \{0, 1, 2, ..., N\text{-}1\}$ is *f(m, n)*. In fact, in most cases *f(x, y)*, which we might consider to be the physical signal that impinges on the face of a 2D sensor, is actually a function of many variables including depth (z), color (λ), and time (t), as in value $= \alpha\left(x, y, z, \lambda, t\right)$. The image shown in figure 2 has been divided into $N = 16$ rows and $M = 16$ columns. The value assigned to every pixel is the average brightness in the pixel rounded to the nearest integer value. The process of representing the amplitude of the *2D* signal at a given coordinate as an integer value with L different gray levels is usually referred to as amplitude quantization or simply quantization. To retrieve similar images from given dataset i.e. content based image retrieval is an active area of research discussed below.

2.1. Image Retrieval

Retrieval of an image from a big data is an active area of research and image retrieval interrogation can be done on two levels (1) low level and (2) high level. The low-level results in the characteristics which

Figure 1. Analog image to digital image

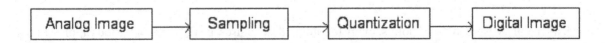

Figure 2. Digitization of a continuous image. The pixel at coordinates [m=10, n=3] has the integer brightness value 110

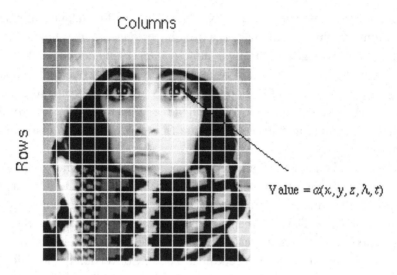

can be extracted from images like colour, texture and shape etc. In order to capture the semantic aspects i.e. high levels, starting from the low-level characteristics, the use of image indexing is necessary. An index makes it possible to group or to bring together closer items, which have similar characteristics. High-level characteristics are object extraction from complex image described below.

2.2. Object Retrieval

The task of interactive image segmentation has attracted a significant attention in last decades (Sonka, Hlavac, & Boyle, 2007; Paris & Durand, 2007; Moore et al., 2009). The ultimate goal is to extract an object with small user interactions as possible. It is widely accepted, that some prior knowledge on segmentations is needed for achieving this goal, in many problems of pattern recognitions and object segmentations based on clustering or grouping of homogeneous pixels. Computational approaches to perception one is given a set of points on the plane and it is desired to find some topological structures among the points in the form of edges connecting a subset of the pairs of points. In the clustering problem, we would like to have an algorithm that joins two points if the two points belong to the same cluster. In computational perception, we would like an algorithm to join the similar regions such that the final graph obtained is perceptually meaningful in some sense. Basically, these graphs we call proximity graph, given a set S of two dimensional points, many geometric proximity structures were defined for various applications, such as the Delaunay triangulation (DT), the Gabriel graph (GG), and the relative neighbourhood graph (RNG) (Zahan, 1971; O'Callaghan, 1971; Lankford, 1969; Sibon, 1978). These diagrams are defined with respect to a geometric as well as topological neighbourhood.

2.3. Topological Graph Based Model

Given a set *S* of two dimensional points, many topological structures are defined for various applications, such as the DT, GG, and RNG (Zahan, 1971; O'Callaghan, 1971; Lankford, 1969; Sibon, 1978). These diagrams are defined with respect to a geometrical property. All these structures are defined on the given point set and can be viewed as complete geometric graph. In general, topological graph based methods use the properties of the model such as different type of proximity graphs. A proximity graph is simply a graph in which two vertices are connected by an edge if and only if the vertices satisfy particular geometric requirements e.g. figure 3(a) and figure 3 (b) shows the initial image segmentation and its neighbourhood graph using geometric property that used for region connectivity and "proximity" means spatial distance. Many of these graphs can be formulated with respect to many metrics, but the Euclidean metric is used most frequently. There are few topological models like (1) Relative Neighbourhood Graph (2) Gabriel Graph (3) Delauney triangulations (4) β-skeletons. These topological structures are explained briefly one by one:

2.3.1. Neighbourhood Graph

Let V be a set of points in R^d each pair of points $(p,q) \in V \times V$ is associated with a neighbourhood $u_{p,q} \subset R^d$. Let P be a property defined on $U = \{U_{p,q} : (p,q) \in V \times V\}$, a neighbourhood graph $G = (V,E)$, where V is set of vertices and E is set of edges like $(p,q) \in E$ if and only if $U_{p,q}$ has property P. If (p,q) is an edge, denoted by pq latter on, then we say that q is a neighbour of p and vice versa. Technically, to differentiate between the graphs makes convenient via its geometric realization, which is called a neighbourhood skeleton. The neighbourhood skeleton of V is obtained by connecting the pair of points of V, with straight line segments, which form edges in the corresponding neighbourhood graph.

The neighbourhood of an edge is usually defined using the concept of distance metrics. In this section we will use the metrics L_p, $1<p<\infty$, L_1 and L_∞ to measure the distance $\rho(x, y)$ between points $x=(x_1,....,x_d)$ and $y=(y_1,...., y_d)$ in R^d. The distance in the metric L_p is defined as $\rho_p(x,y) = \sum_{i=1}^{d} |x_i - y_i|^{\frac{1}{p}}$. In L_1 and L_∞ the distance is defined by $\rho_1(x,y) = \sum_{i=1}^{d} |x_i - y_i|$ and $\rho_\infty(x,y) = \max_{1 \le i \le d} |x_i - y_i|$ respectively. Some concepts

Figure 3. (a) Image Segmentation into homogeneous regions (b) Neighbourhood Graph

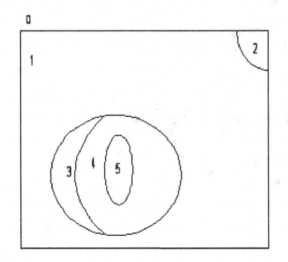
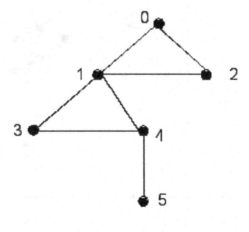

and results presented in the thesis hold for more general metrics. The distance $\rho\,(p,\,q)$ will be also called the length of *pq*. Furthermore, $B(x,r)$ denotes an open sphere centred at *x* with radius *r*, i.e. $B(x,\,r)=\{y: \rho\,(x,\,y) <r\}$. A closed sphere is defined as $\overline{B}(x,r) = \{y : \delta(x,y) \le r\}$. In R^2 both a sphere and its boundary will be called without any confusion a circle.

2.3.2. Relative Neighbourhood Graphs

Let $\Lambda_{p,q} = B\big(p,\,\rho\big(p,q\big)\big) \cap B\big(q,\rho\big(p,q\big)\big); \Lambda_{p,\,q}$ is called a lune. Let $(p,\,q)$ be the intersection of the circle about *p* with a radius of dist $(p,\,q)$ and the circle about *q* with a radius of dist $(q,\,p)$. The relative neighbourhood graph of *V*, The RNG (*V*), is a neighbourhood graph with the set of edges defined as follows: $(p,q) \in E$ if and only if: $\Lambda_{p,q} \cap V = \phi$, i.e. The RNG (*V*) of a set of points *V*, is the graph such that intersection of lune at $(p,\,q)$ and *V* is empty. Let lunes as intersections of circles have been shown in figure 4, in which circle is drawn with centre *a* and radius edge *ab* and another circle is drawn with centre *b* and radius edge *ab*. It is immediate that an edge *ab* is in the *RNG (V)* if there is no triangle $\Delta_{a,\,b,\,c,\,\in\,V\,\setminus\,\{a,b\}}$, with *ab* the strictly longest edge. Figure 4 shows the relative neighbourhood graph using regions as nodes.

2.3.3 Gabriel Graphs

Let C $(p,\,q)$ be the circle centred on the point halfway between *p* and *q* and with a radius of half the distance between *p* and *q*. The Gabriel graph as shown in figure 5 is a set of points *V*, *RNG (V)* is the graph that has an edge $(p,\,q)$ if and only if the intersection of $\Gamma_{p,q}$ and *V* is empty as shown in figure 5.

Figure 4. Relative Neighbourhood Graph using distinct points on the plane

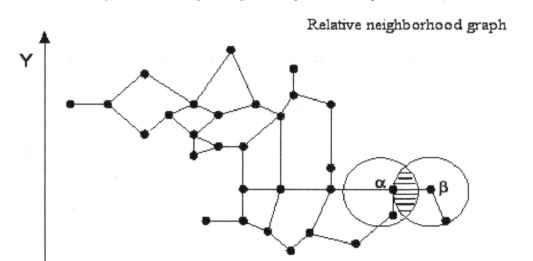

Relative neighborhood graph

Figure 5. Gabreil Graph

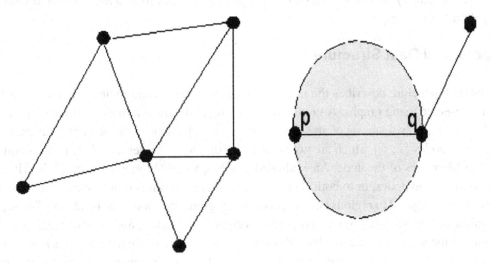

The Gabriel graph of V, *GG* (*V*) is a neighbourhood graph with the set of edges: $(p,q) \in E$ if and only if $\Gamma_{p,q} \cap V = \phi$, where in Gabriel graph $\Gamma_{p,q}$ is defined as: $\Gamma_{p,q} = B(\frac{p+q}{2}, \frac{\rho(p,q)}{2})$.

2.3.4 Delaunay Triangulation

A graph of set of points on the plane is said to be Delaunay Triangulation (DT) (Paris, & Durand, 2007), if three points are in neighbourhood of each other such that if their tangent sphere contains no other points. The decision boundary of Delaunay Triangulation is identical; it is expensive to compute DT in high dimensions. It is well known that the Delaunay triangulation has at most $3n$-6 edges for a two-dimensional point set from its planarity. Thus, all structures that are zero edge oriented have at most *O* (*n*) edges.

2.3.5. β-Skeletons

The neighbourhood $U_{p,q}(\beta)$ is defined for any fixed β $(1 \leq \beta < \infty)$, as the intersection of two spheres;

$$U_{p,q}(\beta) = B\left(\left(1-\frac{\beta}{2}\right)p + \frac{\beta}{2}q, \frac{\beta}{2}\delta(p,q)\right) \cap B\left(\left(1-\frac{\beta}{2}\right)q + \frac{\beta}{2}p, \frac{\beta}{2}\delta(p,q)\right) \qquad (1)$$

The (lune-based) β-skeleton of V, $G_\beta(V)$ is a neighbourhood graph with the set of edges defined as follows: $(p,q) \in E$ if and only if $U_{p,q} \cap V = \phi$ (2)

A useful feature of this parametrized family is its monotonicity with respect to β, *i.e.* $G_{\beta_1}(V) \subset G_{\beta_2}(V)$ for $\beta_1 > \beta_2$. It is easy to see that β Skeletons contain both relative neighbourhood and Gabriel graphs as special cases. Specifically, the *RNG* (*V*) = G_2 (*V*) and *GG* (*V*) = G_1(*V*). Lune-based β skeletons can be also defined for $0 < \beta < 1$. To this end the neighbourhood of *(p, q)* is defined as the intersection of two spheres of radius $\rho(p, q)/2\beta$ which contain p and q in their boundaries. In fact this extension leads to so-called circle-based β skeletons. For $\beta \geq 1$, the neighbourhood *Up, q* of *(p, q)* is defined as the union of two spheres of radius $\beta \times \rho(p, q)/2$ passing through p, q. The points p, q are connected with an edge if the neighbourhood is empty.

2.4. Topological Data Structure

Topological data structure describes the image as a set of elements and their relations; these relations are often represented using graphs. A graph $G= (V, E)$ is an algebraic structure which consists of a set of nodes $V= \{v_1, v_2, ..., v_n\}$ and set of arcs $E= \{e_1, e_2, ..., e_m\}$. Each arc e_k is incident to an unordered (or ordered) pair of nodes $\{v_p, v_j\}$ which are not necessarily distinct. The degree of the node is equal to the number of incident arcs of the node. An evaluated graph or weighted graph is a graph in which values are assigned to arcs, to nodes, or to both. The region adjacency graph is typical class of data structures, in which nodes correspond to regions and neighbouring regions are connected by an arc. The segmented image consists of regions with similar properties (brightness, texture, and colour) that correspond to some entities in the scene, and the neighbourhood relation is fulfilled when the regions have some common border. An example of an image labelled by different homogeneous regions shown in figure 6(a) and the corresponding region in adjacency graph is shown in figure 6(b). This value is used to indicate regions that touch borders of the image in the region adjacency graph.

The region adjacency graph has several attractive features. If a region encloses other regions, then the part of the graph corresponding with the areas inside can be separated by a cut in the graph. Arcs of the region adjacency graph can include a description of the relations between neighbouring regions the relations to be to the left or to be inside are common. The region adjacency graph can be used for matching with a stored pattern for recognition purposes. The region adjacency graph is usually created from the region map, which is a matrix of the same dimensions as the original image matrix whose elements are identification labels of the regions. To create the region adjacency graph, borders of all regions in the image are traced, and labels of all neighbouring regions are stored. The region adjacency graph can easily be created from an image represented by a quad tree as well. The region adjacency graph stores information about the neighbours of all regions in the image explicitly. The region map contains this information as well but it is much more difficult to recall from there. If we want relate the region adjacency graph to the region map quickly, it is sufficient for a node in the region adjacency graph to

Figure 6. (a) Different Homogeneous regions (b) Adjacency Graph

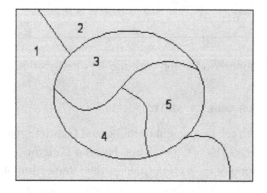
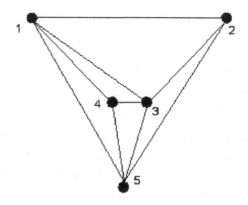

be marked by the identification label of the region and some representative pixel (e.g. the top left pixel of the region). Region adjacency graphs can be used to approach region merging (where for instance neighbouring regions thought to have the same image interpretation are merged into one region).

3. OBJECT EXTRACTION USING TOPOLOGICAL MODELS

Different topological model for object retrieval is a novel approach to solve the segmentation of very small object from a complex scene. The segmented part will have coherence connectivity to identify the complete object. First the object is coarse segmented by using the methods described in chapter 4. For interactive framework is used the user has to click the object part which is to be retrieved from input image. We have considered several versions of the connectivity constraint using different topological models and then user constrains some pixels to be foreground and background using markers, segmented image which is followed by region merging using topological models.

The maximal similar edges by construction of topological models, where each region corresponds to a node in the graph, and certain neighbouring regions are connected by undirected edges. Let $G = (V, E)$ be an undirected graph, where $v_i \in V$ is the set of nodes corresponding to image elements (e.g. regions or super-pixels). E is the set of edges connecting the pairs of neighbouring nodes. Each edge $(v_i, v_j) \in E$ has a corresponding weight $w(v_i, v_j)$ to measure the dissimilarity of the two nodes connected by that edge. In the context of region merging of initially segmented regions, a region is represented by a component $R \subseteq V$. We obtain the dissimilarity between two neighbouring regions $R_1, R_2 \subseteq V$ as the maximum edge weight connecting them. That is

$$\rho(R_1, R_2) = \max_{v_i \in R_i, v_i \in R_j, (v_i, v_j) \in E} w(v_i, v_j) \tag{3}$$

The topological model of a partition image is represented in such a way that each region is a node.

3.1. Region Merging

In proposed method, an initial segmentation is required to partition the image into homogeneous regions for merging using some topological models. Any existing low level segmentation such as mean shift, watershed etc. can be used for this step. Since initial segmentation of input image contains many small similar regions due to which we can not specify actual object contour. In brief there are two type of classification technique for detection of object contour (i) Supervised Classification (ii) Unsupervised Classification.

I.   Supervised Classification

Supervised classification incorporates knowledge from field sampling or other means to relate measured spectral reflectance properties to known the prior trained data. Often small training areas within the scene are identified for each pre-determined category and these are delineated so that their spectral properties can be studied intensively (Singh, Saxena, & Jain, 2011). The classification of the remainder of the image will be based on the values found in the training sets.

II.   Unsupervised Classification

This classification involves algorithms that examine the unknown pixels in an image and aggregate them into a number of classes based on natural groupings or clusters present in the image values. These classification methods are purely statistical and incorporate no a priori knowledge. The basic assumption is that data in different classes should be comparatively well separated ((Singh, Saxena, & Jain, 2011). The unsupervised classification gives spectral classes. They are based solely on the natural groupings in the image values. The identity of spectral classes will not be known initially but it should be improved with some form of reference data such as ground truth data to finally determine the identity of the classes. To obtain actual object contour regions we have to adopt following procedure stated below:

3.2. Region Merging Using Neighbourhood Graph

Efficient and effective image segmentation is an important task in computer vision and object recognition. Since fully automatic object segmentation is usually very hard for natural images, interactive schemes with a few simple user inputs provide feasible solutions. In this work, we proposed a method region merging based interactive object segmentation and topological model. From Initial segmented region we constructed a neighbourhood graph represented different regions as the node of graph and weight of the edges are the value of dissimilarity measures function for their colour histogram vectors. In our work we apply Euclidean measure, Manhattan, Bhattacharyya descriptor and Bhat-Nayar, etc. (Singh, Saxena, & Jain, 2011). For this firstly users only need to roughly indicate the location and region of the object and background by using markers or strokes. A method of similarity based region merging mechanism is proposed to guide the merging process with the help of markers. A region R is merged with its adjacent region Q if Q has the highest edge weight with R among all adjacent regions of R.

The proposed method automatically merges the regions that are initially segmented by any low-level segmentation and then effectively extracts the object contour by labelling all the non-marker regions as either background or object. The region merging process is adaptive to the image content and it does not need to set the similarity threshold in advance. Extensive experiments are performed and the results show that the proposed scheme can reliably extract the object contour from the complex background. Sketch diagram of the object detection method using topological methods shown in figure 7.

Figure 7. Sketch diagram of object retrieval from input image

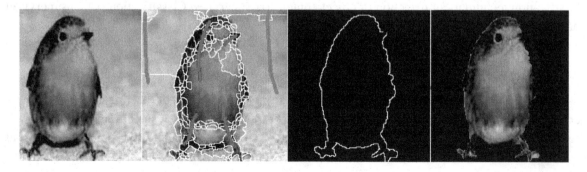

3.3. Region Merging Rule

An initial segmentation is required to partition the image into homogeneous regions for construction of neighbourhood graph and similar region merging. Any existing low level segmentation such as mean shift, watershed etc. We choose to use the mean shift method for initial segmentation because it has less over segmentation and can well preserve the object boundaries. Figure 8 (a) to figure 8(d) shows that (a) input image (b) initial segmented image (c) object mask and (d) extracted object from original image respectively. Here we only focus on the how to merge similar region using different type of topological models.

3.4. Similarity Measure

After mean shift initial segmentation of query image we have many small homogeneous regions. To guide the region merging process, we need to represent these regions as a node of neighborhood graph using some descriptor to define the weight of edges and a rule for merging. A region can be described in many aspects, such as the color, edge, texture, shape and size of the region. Among them the color histogram is an effective descriptor to represent the object color feature statistics and it is widely used in computer vision and object segmentation etc. In the context of region merging based segmentation, color histogram is more robust than the other feature descriptors, because the initially segmented small regions of the image often vary a lot in size and shape, while the colors of different regions from the same object will have high similarity.

The RGB color space is used to compute the color histogram. We uniformly quantize each color channel into 16 levels and then the histogram of each region is calculated in the feature space of *16×16×16 = 4096* bins represented by $Hist_R$, which is normalized histogram of a region R. The next problem is how to merge the regions based on their color histograms so that the desired object can be extracted. In the interactive image segmentation, the users will mark some regions as object and background regions. The key issue in region merging is how to determine the similarity between the unmarked regions with the marked regions so that the similar regions can be merged. Therefore, we need to define a similarity measure $\rho(R, Q)$ between two regions R and Q to accommodate the comparison between various regions. There are some well-known goodness-of-fit statistical metrics [46], to be used for similarity merging such as the Euclidean distance, Manhattan distance, Bhattacharyya coefficient, Bhat-Nayar and the log-likelihood ratio statistic (Mignotte, 2008). Here we choose to use the Bhattacharyya coefficient (Rubner, et al. 2001, Santini, Jain, 1999) to measure the similarity between R and Q:

Figure 8. (a) input image (b) initial segmented image (c) object mask and (d)extracted object

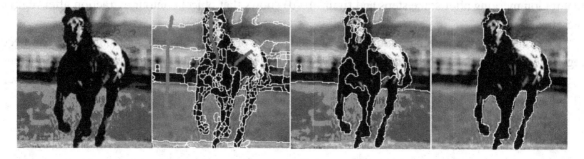

$$\rho(R,\ Q) = \sum_{u=1}^{4096} \sqrt{Hist_R^u \cdot Hist_Q^u} \ \ (R,Q) = \sum_{u=1}^{4096} \sqrt{\text{Hist}_R^u \cdot \text{Hist}_Q^u} \tag{4}$$

or edge weight between region R and region Q is $\rho(R,\ Q)$. Where $Hist_R$ and $Hist_Q$ are the normalized histograms of region R and region Q, respectively, and the superscript u represents the uth element of them. Bhattacharyya coefficient ρ is a divergence-type measure which has a straight forward geometric interpretation. It is the cosine of the angle between the unit vectors

$$\cos\theta = \left(\sqrt{Hist_R^1}, \sqrt{Hist_R^2}, ..., \sqrt{Hist_R^{4096}} \right) \left(\sqrt{Hist_Q^1}, \sqrt{Hist_Q^2}, ..., \sqrt{Hist_Q^{4096}} \right) \tag{5}$$

The higher the Bhattacharyya coefficient between R and Q is, the higher the similarity between them. The geometric explanation of the Bhattacharyya coefficient actually reflects the perceptual similarity between regions. If two regions have similar contents, their histograms will be very similar, and hence their Bhattacharyya coefficient will be very high, i.e. the angle between the two histogram vectors is very small. Certainly, it is possible that two perceptually very different regions may have very similar histograms. Fortunately, such cases are rare because the region histograms are local histograms and they reflect the local features of images. Even in case two perceptually different regions have similar histograms, the similarity between them is rarely the highest one in the neighborhood, highest similarity rule works well in the proposed region merging method.

The RGB/Bhattacharyya descriptor is a very simple yet efficient way to represent the regions and measure their similarity. It has been successfully used to measure the similarity between target model and candidate model. However, it should be stressed that other color spaces, such as the *HIS*, YC_bC_r color space, and other distance measures, such as the Euclidean distance, Bhat-Nayar, Manhattan distance between histogram vectors, can also be adopted in the proposed region merging scheme. Further we will show that the results are similar to those by using the RGB/ Bhattacharyya descriptor.

3.5. Method of Training of Input Data

A query image may contain more than one object. For this reason, initial image segmentation, the users need to specify the objects and background conceptually. The users can input interactive information by drawing markers, which could be lines, curves and strokes on the image. The regions that have pixels inside the object markers are thus called object marker regions, while the regions that have pixels inside the background markers are called background marker regions. Figure 10 (b) shows examples of the object and background markers by using pink and blue color respectively, Whereas figure 10(c) shows that region merging after some steps and figure 10(d) shows that object contour extraction after region merging.

After object marking, each region will be labeled as one of three kinds of regions: the marker object region say M_0, the marker background region say M_B and the non-marker region say N. To completely extract the object contour, we need to automatically assign each non-marker region with a correct label of either object region or background region.

Figure 9. Flow chart for detection of object contours using topological models

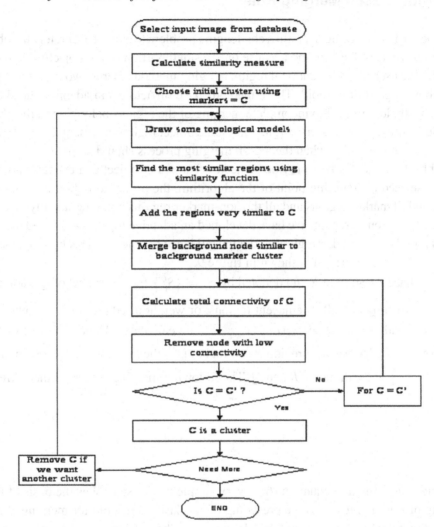

Figure 10. (a) input image (b) initial segmented image (c) region merging after some step (d)extracted object

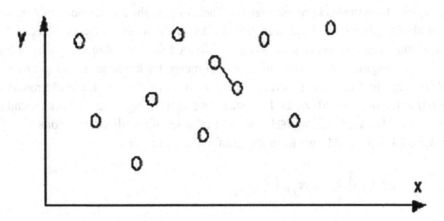

3.6. Topological Based Merging Rule

After object/background marking, it is still a challenging problem to extract accurately the object contour from the complex scene of background because only a small portion of the object/background features are indicated by the user. The conventional region merging methods merge two adjacent regions whose similarity is above a preset threshold. These methods have difficulties in adaptive threshold selection because a big threshold will lead to incomplete merging of the regions belonging to the object, while a small threshold can easily cause over-merging, i.e. some object regions are merged into the background. Moreover, it is difficult to judge when the region merging process should stop.

Object and background markers provide some key features of object and background, respectively. The marker is the seed and starting point of the algorithm, the proposed region merging method also starts from the initial marker regions and all the non-marker regions will be gradually labelled as either object region or background region. We have developed an adaptive topological based merging mechanism to identify all the non-marker regions under the guidance of object and background markers. Block diagram of closed contour retrieval is shown in figure 9.

Let Q be an adjacent region of R and denoted by $\bar{S}_Q = \left\{ S_i^Q \right\}_{i=1,2,\ldots,q}$ the set of Q's adjacent regions. The similarity between Q and all its adjacent regions, or weight of edges in the neighbourhood graph those are adjacent with region Q i.e. $\rho\left(Q, S_i^Q\right)_{i=1,2,\ldots,q}$, are calculated. Hence R is one of the elements of $\bar{S}_Q$. If the weight of edge between region R and region Q is the maximum edge weight among all the similarities $\rho\left(Q, S_i^Q\right)$, we will merge R and Q. The following merging rule is defined: Merge R and Q if

$$\rho\left(R, Q\right) = \max_{i=1,2,\ldots,q} \rho\left(Q, S_i^Q\right) \tag{6}$$

The merging rule defined in equation (6) is very simple but it establishes the basis of the proposed region merging process i.e. it avoids the presetting of similarity threshold for merging control. This is mainly because that the histogram is a global descriptor of the local region. The marker regions cover only a small part of the object and background. Those object regions that are not marked by the user, i.e. the non-marker object regions, should be identified and not be merged with the background. Since they are from the same object, the non-marker object regions will usually have higher similarity with the marker object regions than the background regions. Therefore, in the automatic region merging process, the non-marker object regions will have high probabilities to be identified as an object.

The whole similar region merging process can be divided into two stages, which are repeatedly executed until no new merging occurs. Our strategy is to merge background regions as many as possible while keep object regions from being merged. Once we have merged all the background regions, it is equivalent to extracting the desired object. First stage, we try to merge marker background regions with their adjacent regions. For each region $B \in M_B$, we form the set of its adjacent regions $S_B = \{A_i\}$, $_{i=1,2,\ldots,r}$, then for each A_i and $A_i \in \bar{S}_{A_j} \notin M_B$, we form its set of adjacent regions

$$\bar{S}_{A_i} = \left\{ S_j^{A_i} \right\}_{j=1,2,\ldots,k} : \quad \rho\left(A_i, B\right) = \max_{j=1,2,\ldots,k} \rho\left(A_i, S_j^{A_i}\right)$$

it is obvious that $B \in \bar{S}_{A_i}$. The similarity between A_i and each element of $\bar{S}_A$ i.e. $\rho\left(A_i, S_j^{A_j}\right)$, is calculated then B and A_i, i.e. $\bar{S}_Q = \left\{S_i^Q\right\}_{i=1,2,\ldots,q}$. Such that

$$\rho\left(Q, S_i^Q\right)_{i=1,2,\ldots,q} = \max_{i=1,2,\ldots,q} \rho\left(Q, S_i^Q\right) \tag{7}$$

then B and A_i are merged into one region and the new region will have the same label as region B:
$B = B \cup A_i$ (8)

Otherwise, B and A_i will not merge.

The above procedure is iterative and for each iteration the set M_B i.e. marked background region and N i.e. the set of non-marker regions will be updated. Specifically, M_B expands and N shrinks. The iteration stops when the entire marker background regions M_B will not find new merging regions. After the region merging of this stage, some non-marker background regions will be merged with the corresponding background markers. However, there are still non-marker background regions which cannot be merged because they have higher similarity scores with each other than with the marker background regions. To complete the task of target object extraction, in the second stage we will focus on the non-marker regions in N remained from the first stage. Part of N belongs to the background, while other part of N belongs to the target object. In this stage, the non-marker object regions will merge with each other under the guidance of the topological models and so do the non-marker background regions.

After the first stage, for each non-marker (background or object) region $P \in N$ we form the set of its adjacent regions $\bar{S}_P = \{H_i\}$, $_{i=1,2,\ldots,p}$. Then for each H_i those $H_i \notin M_B$ and $H_i \notin M_0$, where M_0 will the marked object regions, we form its set of adjacent regions $\bar{S}_{H_i} = \left\{S_j^{H_i}\right\}_{j=1,2,\ldots,k}$, where $P \in \bar{S}_{H_i}$. The similarity between H_i and each element in $\overline{S_{H_i}}$, i.e. $\rho\left(H_i, S_j^{H_i}\right)$, is calculated, if region P and H_i satisfy equation (6) i.e.

$$P \cup H_i \tag{9}$$

Then P and H_i are merged into one region $P = P \cup H_i$, otherwise, P and H_i will not merge.

The above procedure is iterative and the iteration stops when the entire non-marker region set N will not find new merging regions. We observed that some non-marker background regions, as well as some non-marker object regions, are merged, with the marked regions respectively. Region merging of non marker regions to object marker regions and background marker regions and finally detection of closed contour.

4. REGION MERGING ALGORITHM

Input: Segmented image and its neighbourhood graph
While there is region merging in the last loop
Stage 1.1. Check for the merging non-marker regions in N with marker background regions in M_B
Input: The initial segmentation result or the merging result of the second stage.

1.2. For each region $B \in M_B$, from these to fit adjacent regions $\bar{S}_B = \{A_i\}_{i=1,2,\ldots,r}$.

1.3. For each A_i and $A_i \in M_B$, from its set of adjacent regions $\bar{S}_{A_i} = \{S_j^{A_i}\}_{j=1,2,\ldots,k}$.

1.4. If there is $B \in \bar{S}_{A_i}$.

1.5 Calculate $\rho\left(A_i, S_j^{A_i}\right)$ i.e. if region A_i and region B have highest edge weight or $\rho\left(A_i, B\right) = \max\limits_{j=1,2,\ldots,k} \rho\left(A_i, S_j^{A_i}\right)$, then B = B $\cup A_i$, construct RAG.

1.6. Otherwise, B and A_i will not merge.

1.7. Update M_B and N accordingly.

1.8. If the regions in M_B will not find new merging regions, then the first stage ends. Otherwise, go back to (1.2).

Stage 2.1. Until all the similar non-marker regions in N and marker object regions M_0 will merged

2.2. For each region $P \in N$, form the set of its adjacent regions $\bar{S}_P = \{H_j\}_{j=1,2,\ldots,p}$.

2.3. For each H_i that $H_i \notin M_B$ and $H_i \notin M_0$ from its set of adjacent regions $\bar{S}_{H_i} = \{S_j^{H_i}\}_{j=1,2,\ldots,k}$.

2.4. There is $P \in S_{H_i}$.

2.5. Calculate $\rho\left(H_i, S_j^{H_i}\right)$. If $\rho\left(R, Q\right) = \max\limits_{i=1,2,\ldots,q} \rho\left(Q, S_i^Q\right)$, then P = P $\cup H_i$.

Otherwise, P and Hi will not merge.

2.6. Update N accordingly.

2.7. If the regions in N will not find new merging region, the second stage stops. Otherwise, go back to (2.2).

2.8. end

4.1. Construction of Region Adjacency Graph

Input: The initial segmentation of given image, and its Region Adjacency Graph (labelled by object regions M_0 and background regions M_B)

Output: Region merging result

1. draw object and background data models based on labeled regions M_0 and M_B
2. construct topological graph $G = <V, E>$, where V contains regions as nodes and edges between connected regions with edge weight as similarity value.
3. update object and background data models by labeletting.
4. update object regions M_0 and background regions M_B according to step 3.
5. go back to 2 until no adjacent regions of M_0 and M_B can be found.
6. return segmentation result.

4.2. Convergence Analysis

After applying similar region merging algorithm on an input image one natural question arises that, what is the guarantee that the algorithm will converge after finite number of steps. The proposed algorithm is an iterative method. It will progressively assign the non-marker background regions in N to M_B and then all the left regions in N are assigned to M_o. It has been proved that the proposed method converges. For this we prove a proposition which is stated below:

Proposition 1: In region merging algorithm discussed in above section surely converges, i.e. every region in N will be labelled as either object or background after a certain number of iterations.

Proof: If a non-marker region $P \in N$ has maximum similarity (within its neighbourhood) with a region $B \in M_B$ it will be merged with B i.e. $B = P \cup B$, in the first stage of proposed algorithm. If it has highest similarity with a region in M_0, it will remain the same. If it has highest similarity with the non-marker region $P' \in N$, P will be merged with P' in the second stage, i.e. $P = P \cup P'$. Then in the next round of iteration P may be merged into M_B, or it will continue merge with another P', or it will stay the same. If no marker region $P \in N$ will be merged with region M_B or N. After the kth round ($k>1$), the algorithm will stop. From the above analysis, we can see that the number of regions in N, denoted by n, will decrease in the process of iterative merging because some regions are labelled as background and some regions are merged with each other. Once n stops decreasing, the whole algorithm will stop and all the remaining regions in N will be labelled as object and merged into M_0. Therefore, the proposed algorithm converges and it will label all the regions in N.

4.3. Time Complexity

Input: A set $P = \{p_1,\ p_2,...,\ p_n\}$ of n regions in the plane. Each point is given by its x and y coordinate $p_i = (x_i, y_i), i = 1,...,n$.

Output: The closest pair of points in P, i.e. the pair $(p_i,\ p_j)$ in P, s.t. $i \neq j$ with minimum similarity measure.

There are two techniques for merging the initial segmented regions:

Figure 11. Set of points (or regions) on the XY plane

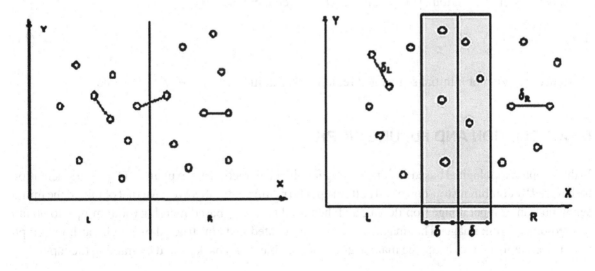

1. **Brute Force:** Try every pair, in Brute force algorithm we check similarity between each pair and after that find the maximum similar edges. Brute force algorithm takes $O(n)^2$ time.
2. **Divide-&-Conquer:** Divide the set of points P into two parts: L and R.

Now two find the closest pair of points which are either:

1. both in the left half L or [recursive call on L]
2. both in the right half R, or [recursive call on R]
3. one is in L and the other in R. [combine L & R]
    Algorithm: ClosestPair (P)
    Pre-condition: P is a finite set of points in the plane.
    Post-condition: Output is the closest pair of points in P
    1. Pre-sort points in P on their x-coordinates (lexicographically nest on y)
    2. return CP(P)
    end
    Procedure CP (P)
    1. 1. Pre-condition: P is a x-sorted finite set of points
    2. 2. Post-condition: Output is the closest pair of points in P
    3. 3. Base: if |P|<10 then return answer by brute-force in $O(1)$ time
    4. 4. Divide: Partition P at its x-median value into sets L and R, |L|=|P|/2
    5. 5. Conquer: SolL←CP(L); SolR←CP(R)
    6. 6. Combine: Sol←MERGE (SolL, SolR);
    7. 7. return: Sol
    8. end

Recursive equation of this method:

$$T(n) = 2T(n / 2) + \Theta(n) \tag{10}$$

And solution of equation (1) is: (using recursion tree method)

$$T(n) = \Theta(n \log n) \tag{11}$$

Hence, merging of *n* initial segmented regions takes at most $T(n) = \Theta(n \log n)$, time.

5. CONCLUSION AND FUTURE WORK

In this chapter, topological based region merging for object extraction are explained. Object segmentation is achieved by combining top-down and bottom up information naturally. We have first obtained the initial segmentation of input image (top-down), and then used topology based merging (bottom-up), to obtain desired object from image. The image is initially segmented and constructed by neighbourhood graph after the input form to indicate the main features of the object and background by training the input data

Figure 12. Set of regions of initial segmented image is divided into two halves

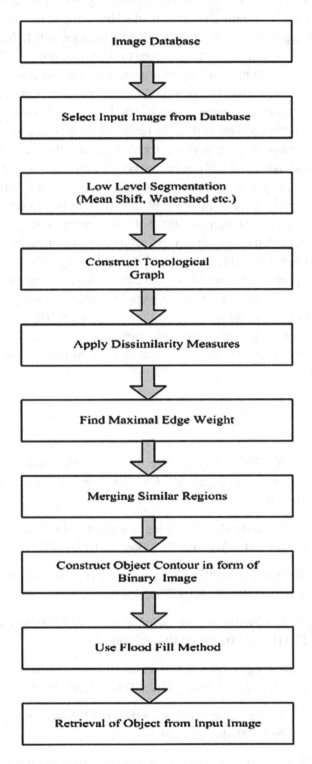

from database. Since the object regions will have high similarity to the marked object regions as well as background regions will have high similarity to the marked background regions. A new similarity based topological based region merging mechanism (e.g. Region adjacency graph, Relative neighborhood graph, Gabreil graph and Delaunay Triangulation etc.) are used to extract the object. With the topological based merging rule, a two-stage iterative merging algorithm was presented to gradually label each untrained region as either object or background. The proposed method provides object detection using general region merging framework on initial segmentation which divides very small homogeneous regions of input image. Initial segmentation will also affect the results of object detection using proposed method.

The proposed similar region merging based on topological models is an interactive scheme. In our experiments, we have found that the object can be correctly extracted as long as the markers can cover the main feature regions. From image database, (Caltech-256) if we tried to separate an object from the complex background with two groups of markers, obviously, with more markers performs better than with two markers. It still extracts the rough contour of object from input image with even fewer markers. In general, the proposed algorithm could reliably extract the object contour from different backgrounds if the user input markers cover the main features of object and background.

In the future, it will be proposed to how to introduce pixel classification into the merging process to make the algorithm more intelligent. To extent our work in future to topological based object segmentation using untrained data i.e. without annotation of training images. However, proposed method also may fail when shadow, low-contrast edges and ambiguous areas of object occur, as proposed method will work on initial segmented image and topological model, to improve our result efficiency, to improve our low-level segmentation.

REFERENCES

Bao, P., Zhang, L., & Wu, X. (2005). Canny edge detection enhancement by scale multiplication. *IEEE Transactions on Pattern Analysis and Machine Intelligence*, 27(9), 1485–1490. doi:10.1109/TPAMI.2005.173 PMID:16173190

Bleau, A., & Leon, L. J. (2000). Watershed based segmentation and region merging. *Computer Vision and Image Understanding*, 77(3), 317–370. doi:10.1006/cviu.1999.0822

Caselles, V., Kimmel, R., & Sapiro, G. (1997). Geodesic active contours. *International Journal of Computer Vision*, 22(1), 61–79. doi:10.1023/A:1007979827043

Chan, T. F., & Vese, L. A. (2001). Active contours without edges. *IEEE Transactions on Image Processing*, 10(2), 266–277. doi:10.1109/83.902291 PMID:18249617

Cheng, H. D., Jiang, X. H., & Wang, J. (2002). Color image segmentation based on homogram thresholding and region merging. *Pattern Recognition*, 35(2), 373–393. doi:10.1016/S0031-3203(01)00054-1

Cheng, Y. (1995). Mean shift, mode seeking, and clustering. *IEEE Transactions on Pattern Analysis and Machine Intelligence*, 17(8), 790–799. doi:10.1109/34.400568

Cour, T., Benezit, F., & Shi, J. (2005). Spectral segmentation with multiscale graph decomposition. *Proceedings of the IEEE International Conference on Computer Vision and Pattern Recognition*, San Diego, CA (Vol. 2, pp. 1124–1131).

Felzenszwalb, D. H. P., & Huttenlocher, D. P. (2004). Efficient graph-based image segmentation. *International Journal of Computer Vision*, *59*(2), 167–181. doi:10.1023/B:VISI.0000022288.19776.77

Gonzalez, R. C., Woods, R. E., & Eddins, S. L. (2004). *Digital Image Processing Using MATLAB*. India: Pearson Education.

Guo, G. D., Jain, A. K., Ma, W. Y., & Zhang, H. J. (2002). Learning Similarity Measure for Natural Image Retrieval With Relevance Feedback. *IEEE Transactions on Neural Networks*, *13*(4), 811–820. doi:10.1109/TNN.2002.1021882 PMID:18244477

Haris, K., Efstratiadis, S. N., & Katsaggelos, A. K. (1998). Hybrid image segmentation using watersheds and fast region merging. *IEEE Transactions on Image Processing*, *7*(12), 1684–1699. doi:10.1109/83.730380 PMID:18276235

Haris, K., Efstratiadis, S. N., & Katsaggelos, A. K. (1998). Hybrid image segmenta-tion using watersheds and fast region merging. *IEEE Transactions on Image Processing*, *7*(12), 1684–1699. doi:10.1109/83.730380 PMID:18276235

Hernandez, S. E., & Barner, K. E. (2000). Joint region merging criteria for watershed based image segmentation. *Proceedings of the International Conference on Image Processing* (pp. 108–111). doi:10.1109/ICIP.2000.899239

Jayaraman, S., Esakkirajan, S., & Veerkumar, T. (2008). *Digital Image Processing*. Tata McGraw Hill Education Private Limited, Second Edison.

Lankford, P. M. (1969). Regionalization Theory and Alternative Algorithms. *Geographical Analysis*, *1*(2), 196–212. doi:10.1111/j.1538-4632.1969.tb00615.x

Lankford, P. M. (1969). Regionalization Theory and Alternative Algorithms. *Geographical Analysis*, *1*(2), 196–212. doi:10.1111/j.1538-4632.1969.tb00615.x

Li, Y., Jiao, L., Shang, R., & Stolkin, R. (2015). Dynamic-context cooperative quantum-behaved particle swarm optimization based on multilevel thresholding applied to medical image segmentation. *Inf. Sci.*, *294*, 408–422. doi:10.1016/j.ins.2014.10.005

Li, Y., Sun, J., Tang, C., & Shum, H. (2004). Lazy snapping. *ACM Transactions on Graphics*, *23*(3), 303–308. doi:10.1145/1015706.1015719

Mignotte, M. (2008). Segmentation by Fusion of Histogram-Based K-Means Clusters in Different Color Spaces. *IEEE Transactions on Image Processing*, *17*(5), 780–787. doi:10.1109/TIP.2008.920761 PMID:18390382

Moore, A., & Prince, S. J. D., Warrell, J., Mohammed, U., & Jones, G., (2009). *Scene Shape Priors for Superpixel Segmentation*. Proceedings of the *ICCV* '09.

Mumford, D., & Shah, J. (1989). Optimal approximation by piecewise smooth functions and associated variational problems. *Communications on Pure and Applied Mathematics*, *42*(5), 577–685. doi:10.1002/cpa.3160420503

Ning, J., Zhang, L., Zhang, D., & Wu, C. (2010). Interactive image segmentation by maximal similarity based region merging. *Pattern Recognition, 43*(2), 445–456. doi:10.1016/j.patcog.2009.03.004

Nock, R., & Nielsen, F. (2004). Statistical region merging. *IEEE Transactions on Pattern Analysis and Machine Intelligence, 26*(11), 1452–1458. doi:10.1109/TPAMI.2004.110 PMID:15521493

OCallaghan, J. F. (1971). An Alternative Definition for Neighborhood at a Point. *IEEE Transactions on Computers, C-24*(11), 1121–1125. doi:10.1109/T-C.1975.224144

OCallaghan, J. F. (1971). An Alternative Definition for Neighborhood at a Point. *IEEE Transactions on Computers, C-24*(11), 1121–1125. doi:10.1109/T-C.1975.224144

Otsu, N. (1975). A threshold selection method from gray-level histograms. *Automatica, 11*, 23–27.

Paris, S., & Durand, F. (2007). A Topological Approach to Hierarchical Segmentation Using Mean Shift. *proceeding of IEEE Conference on Computer Vision Pattern Recognition* (pp. 1-8). doi:10.1109/CVPR.2007.383228

Peng, B., Zhang, L., & Zhang, D. (2011). Automatic image segmentation by dynamic region merging. *IEEE Transactions on Image Processing, 20*(12), 3592–3605. doi:10.1109/TIP.2011.2157512 PMID:21609885

Peng, B., Zhang, L., & Zhang, D. (2011). Automatic image segmentation by dynamic region merging. *IEEE Transactions on Image Processing, 20*(12), 3592–3605. doi:10.1109/TIP.2011.2157512 PMID:21609885

Peng, B., Zhang, L., Zhang, D., & Yang, J. (2011). Image segmentation by iterated region merging with localized graph cuts. *Pattern Recognition, 44*(10–11), 2527–2538. doi:10.1016/j.patcog.2011.03.024

Rother, C., Kolmogorov, V., & Blake, A. (2004). Grab Cut: Interactive foreground extraction using iterated graph cuts. *ACM Transactions on Graphics, 23*(3), 309–314. doi:10.1145/1015706.1015720

Rubner, Y., Puzicha, J., Bhumann, J. M., & Tomasi, C. (2001). Empirical Evaluation of Dissimilarity Measures for Color and Texture. *Computer Vision and Image Understanding, 84*(1), 25–43. doi:10.1006/cviu.2001.0934

Santini, S., & Jain, R. (1999). Similarity Measures. *IEEE Transactions on Pattern Analysis and Machine Intelligence, 21*(9), 871–883. doi:10.1109/34.790428

Shi, J., & Malik, J. (2000). Normalized cuts and image segmentation. *IEEE Transactions on Pattern Analysis and Machine Intelligence, 22*(8), 888–905. doi:10.1109/34.868688

Sibon, R. (1978). Locally Equiangular Triangulations. *The Computer Journal, 21*(3), 243–245. doi:10.1093/comjnl/21.3.243

Sibon, R. (1978). Locally Equiangular Triangulations. *The Computer Journal, 21*(3), 243–245. doi:10.1093/comjnl/21.3.243

Singh, U. P., Saxena, K., & Jain, S. (2011). Semi-Supervised Method of Multiple Object Segmentation with Region Labeling and Flood Fill. *Signal and Image Processing International Journal, 2*(3), 175–193.

Singh, U. P., Saxena, K., & Jain, S. (2011). Unsupervised Method of Object Retrieval with Region Labeling and Flood Fill" *International Journal of Advanced Computer Science and Applications. Special Issue on Artificial Intelligence*, *1*, 41–50.

Singh, U. P., Saxena, K., & Jain, S. (2011). A Review: Different Types of Similarity Measures. *Pioneer Journal of Computer Science and Engineering Technology*, *2*(1), 43–63.

Sobieranski, A. C. E., Comunello, A., & Wangenheim, V. (2011). Learning a nonlinear distance metric for supervised region-merging image segmentation. *Computer Vision and Image Understanding*, *115*(2), 127–139. doi:10.1016/j.cviu.2010.09.006

Sonka, M., Hlavac, V. and Boyle, R. (2007). *Image Processing Analysis and Computer Vision*, Thomson publication.

Tab, F. A., Naghdy, G., & Mertins, A. (2006). Scalable multiresolution color image segmentation. *Signal Processing*, *86*(7), 1670–1687. doi:10.1016/j.sigpro.2005.09.016

Vanhamel, I., Pratikakis, I., & Sahli, H. (2003). Multiscale gradient watersheds of color images. *IEEE Transactions on Image Processing*, *12*(6), 617–626. doi:10.1109/TIP.2003.811490 PMID:18237936

Veksler, O. (2008). Star shape prior for graph-cut image segmentation. *Proceedings of the European Conference on Computer Vision*, *2008*, 454–467. doi:10.1007/978-3-540-88690-7_34

Vezhnevets, V., & Konouchine, V. (2005). Grow Cut: interactive multi-label ND image segmentation by cellular automata. *Proceedings of the Graphic* (pp. 150–156).

Vincent, L., & Soille, P. (1991). Watersheds in digital spaces: An efficient algorithm based on immersion simulations. *IEEE Transactions on Pattern Analysis and Machine Intelligence*, *13*(6), 583–598. doi:10.1109/34.87344

Yang, X., Zhao, W., Chen, Y., & Fang, X. (2008). Fang, Image segmentation with a fuzzy clustering algorithm based on ant-tree. *Signal Processing*, *88*(10), 2453–2462. doi:10.1016/j.sigpro.2008.04.005

Zahan, C. T. (1971). Graph-Theoretical Methods for Detecting and Describing Gestalt Clusters. *IEEE Transactions on Computers*, *C-20*(1), 68–86. doi:10.1109/T-C.1971.223083

Zahan, C. T. (1971). Graph-Theoretical Methods for Detecting and Describing Gestalt Clusters. *IEEE Transactions on Computers*, *C-20*(1), 68–86. doi:10.1109/T-C.1971.223083

Chapter 14
Radial Moments for Image Retrieval

Pooja Sharma
DAV University, India

ABSTRACT

Images have always been considered an effective medium for presenting visual data in numerous applications ranging from industry to academia. Consequently, managing and indexing of images become essential in order to retrieve relevant images effectively and efficiently. Therefore, the proposed chapter aims to elaborate one of the advanced concepts of image processing, i.e., Content Based Image Retrieval (CBIR) and image feature extraction using advanced methods known as radial moments. In this chapter, various radial moments are discussed with their properties. Besides, performance measures and various similarity measures are elaborated in depth. The performance of radial moments is evaluated through an extensive set of experiments on benchmark databases such as Kimia-99, MPEG-7, COIL-100, etc.

INTRODUCTION

Images have always been considered an effective medium for presenting visual data in numerous applications ranging from industry to academia. With the development in technology, a large amount of images are being generated everyday. Therefore, managing and indexing of images become essential in order to retrieve relevant images effectively and efficiently. Early work on image retrieval can be traced back to 1970s. In 1979, a conference was held regarding database techniques for pictorial applications (Blaser, 1979). Since then, the research pertaining to image database management has influenced several researchers (Chang and Fu, 1979; Chang and Fu, 1980; Chang and Kunii, 1981; Chang et al., 1988). In traditional systems, textual annotations of images were used to describe images. Afterwards, the images were searched using text based approach from traditional database management system such as SQL query. A comprehensive survey of text based retrieval can be found in (Chang and Hsu, 1988; Chang et al. 1988). In text based image retrieval, images are organized by semantic hierarchies to facilitate navigation and browsing using standard keyword queries. However, the textual annotation of images is a cumbersome task, which requires intensive manual labor for large image databases. Apart from that,

DOI: 10.4018/978-1-5225-2848-7.ch014

the use of keywords become unwieldy, which do not meet human visual perception. Consequently, it is intricate for the traditional text based methods to support wide range of image databases and task dependent queries. Humans are capable of identifying an extensive range of objects irrespective of their size and orientation. A widespread research has been pursuing to develop an automated system to imitate this basic capability of human visual perception. In 1992, the National Science Foundation of United States organized a workshop on visual information management system (Jain, 1991) to discover new trends in image database management systems. It was discussed that a more efficient and sponta- neous way to represent and index visual information would be based on attributes that are inherent in images themselves. In other words, the representation and indexing of images should be based on their actual visual content rather than textual annotations. Since then, the research on content based image retrieval (CBIR) has been developing rapidly (Cawkill, 1993; Dowe, 1993; Jain et al., 1995; Mejdoub et al., 2009, Arnold et al., 2000; Lew, 2006). CBIR has several applications such as medical imaging, trademark matching, digital library, computer aided design, military services, crime prevention, target detection, architectural and engineering design, geographic information, chromosome identification, surveillance tasks, etc.

CBIR uses visual contents, which can be general or domain specific as shown in Figure 1. General visual content includes image perceptual low level features such as color, texture, and shape. On the other hand, domain specific visual content such as human faces, iris, etc., is application dependent and may require domain knowledge. In our research work, we focus on general visual content such as color, texture, and shape. Among them low level shape perceptual feature provides a persuasive notion to object individuality, which meets human visual perception. Besides, shape feature signifies the geometrical information that remains unaffected when translation, scale, and rotation transformation effects are eliminated from an object. Hence in our research work, we pay attention to shape based image retrieval. However, shape description and representation is a challenging task. This is due to the projection of a real-world 3D object on to a 2D plane, by which the information about one dimension of an object is lost. As a consequence, the projected object only provides partial information of real object. Moreover, shape is often corrupted with noise, distortion, partial occlusion, compression, etc. A good shape representation

Figure 1. Description of image visual contents and location of the research subject

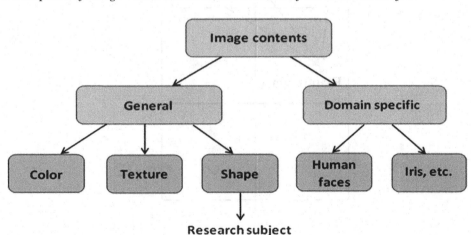

must be compact and retain essential characteristics of the shape. In addition, invariance to rotation, scale, and translation is a crucial requirement because such transforms are consistent with human perception.

To fulfill the above requirements, a virtuous feature extractor is required, which must be capable of representing an object as point in a finite dimensional space, i.e., a feature space. By feature space, we mean that different views (rotation, scale, and translation) of the object shape correspond to a same point as shown in Figure 2. The representation of an image in a feature space has several advantages. First, if the feature space is chosen cautiously, we can obtain features, which are insensitive to some photometric transformations such as noise, blur, and occlusion. Second, we obtain a reduction of dimensionality without losing original salient information of the object under consideration. Several descriptors exist to extract feature space from the shape of an object.

Thus, in order to extract significant features of an image various methods and techniques are proposed for so many years. These methods can be classified into local feature extractors or contour based descriptors and global feature extractors or region based descriptors. Contour based methods include: Fourier descriptor (FD) (Zhang and Lu, 2003), curvature scale space (CSS) (Mokhtarian, 1997), contour point distribution histograms (CPDH) (Shu and Wu, 2011), elastic matching (Atalla and Siy, 2005), contour flexibility (Zu et al., 2009), local binary patterns (LBP) (Ojala, M. Pietikainen, 2009; Moore and Bowden, 2011)), local ternary patterns (LTP) (Tan and Triggs, 2010), Weber's local descriptor (Chen et al., 2010), robust histogram based descriptor (HöschlIV and Flusser, 2015), bioinformatics based approach (Bicego and Lovato, 2015), image to class similarity (Chen et al., 2016), adaptive lo-

Figure 2. A feature space of an image by applying translation, rotation, and scaling transformations

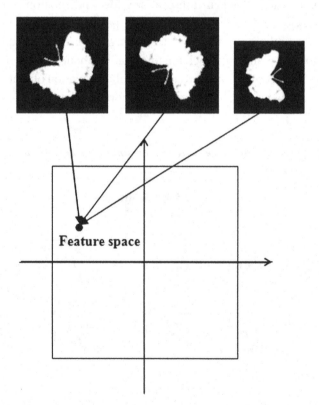

cal binary patterns (Liu et al., 2016), etc. Among them FD, CSS, CPDH are discrete descriptors while LBP, LTP, and WLD are dense descriptors. The discrete descriptors perform calculation on the interest points or contour points of an image, while dense descriptors extract local features pixel by pixel on the input image. The contour based descriptors provide local characteristics of the image shape. Therefore, they are also termed as local descriptors. On the other hand, region based descriptors include: moment invariants (MI) (Mukundan and Ramakrishnan, 1998), angular radial transform (ART) (Bober, 2011), grid descriptor (Lu and Sajjanhar, 1999), generic Fourier descriptor (Zhang and Lu, 2002), Zernike moment descriptor (Kim and Kim, 2000), pseudo Zernike moments (Wolf and Bhatia, 1954), orthogonal Fourier Mellin moments (Sheng and Shen, 1994), etc. These descriptors consider the complete image content for its computation, thus, they are termed as global descriptors. In this chapter, we study the region based global descriptors referred to as radial moments in depth. The purpose to choose radial moments including MI, ZM, PZM, OFMM, etc., is that they represent the complete essence of an image without the loss of any significant information contained in the image. Apart from that radial moments possess various characteristics, which helps in pattern recognition.

BACKGROUND

Radial moments fall in region based descriptors and they are categorized into orthogonal and non-orthogonal moments. The description of orthogonality of radial moments is elaborated later in this Chapter. Among the region based descriptors, moment invariants (MI) (Hu, 1962) are one of the earliest and widely used moment based descriptors. Hu derived a set of moment invariants from the non-uniform linear combination of geometric moments to achieve affine invariance. The obtained set of features is invariant to translation, scale, and rotation. Another type of moment descriptors is the complex moments. The magnitudes of complex moments are rotation invariant. However, phase coefficients change with image rotation. Among the widely used complex moments, Zernike moments (ZMs) were proposed by Zernike (Zernike, 1934) as a basic tool for representation of a wave front function for optical systems with circular pupils. Since then, Zernike polynomials have been found important in applications ranging from pattern recognition, shape analysis, optical engineering, and medical imaging to eye diagnostics, etc. Teague (1980) presented ZMs in image analysis as a set of complex orthogonal functions with their magnitude coefficients exhibiting rotation invariant properties. By virtue of which, ZMs are widely used for shape representation and description. Bhatia and Wolf (1954) introduced another class of circularly orthogonal moments known as pseudo Zernike moments, which possess similar properties as that of ZMs. Teh and Chin (1988) observed that PZMs are more robust to noise. However, they are more computation intensive even for low orders of moments. Sheng and Shen (1994) introduced another set of rotation invariant moments known as orthogonal Fourier Mellin moments (OFMMs). OFMMs have better performance than ZMs and PZMs in terms of noise sensitivity for small images.

ZMs, PZMs, and OFMMs are computed in both radial and angular directions of images by virtue of which these moments are known as radial moments. Radial moments are computation intensive and numerically instable at high orders of moments. In order to minimize these problems radial harmonic Fourier moments (RHFMs) (Ren et al., 2007) were proposed, which are also orthogonal and rotation invariant. Ping and Sheng (2002) have proposed Chebyshev-Fourier moments (CHFMs), which exhibit almost similar characteristics and performance as that of OFMMs for describing images.

Role of the Chapter

The principal task of image retrieval is to measure the relevance between shapes, which are represented by their features. Therefore, three steps are essential in shape based image retrieval. First, the extraction of features using some shape descriptor. Second, the measuring of relevance between the extracted features of images through some similarity measure. Third, their performance evaluation using some performance measure. Thus, in this chapter, the authors describe fundamental tools for feature extraction, similarity measures, and performance measures. Since the core theme of our research is based on radial moments, for feature extraction, the authors employ radial moments, which are described along with their properties in the first part of this chapter. Afterwards, various similarity measures are described, which are used to measure similarity among images. Besides, the authors also describe performance measurements for evaluating the performance of various methods for image retrieval. The contributions of this chapter include the following:

1. To describe various radial moments along with their properties.
2. To describe various image databases used for the evaluation of image retrieval system.
3. To describe various similarity measures and performance measures for the evaluation of image retrieval system.
4. To evaluate the performance of radial moments in terms of image retrieval.
5. To analyze the performance of various similarity measures.

FEATURE EXTRACTION TOOLS

Moments are scalar quantities used to characterize a function and to capture its significant features. Moments have been used to differentiate shapes of various characters, aircrafts, chromosomes, etc. Moreover, these types of image features provide a complete object representation that is invariant to similarity transformations. In mathematical form, moments are the projection of a function on to polynomials basis. In the following sub-sections, various radial moments are described and discussed.

Geometric Moments (GMs)

Simple geometric properties of an image, such as area, position, and orientation can be easily computed from a set of linear functions of the image called geometric moments. Geometric moments are also called regular moments. The geometric moments of order $(p + q)$ of image intensity function $f(x, y)$ are defined as

$$m_{pq} = \int_{-\infty}^{\infty} \int_{-\infty}^{\infty} x^p y^q f(x, y) \, dx \, dy \tag{1}$$

where $p, q = 0, 1, 2, ..., \infty$. The above definition has the form of projection of the function $f(x, y)$ onto the monomials $f(x, y)$. However, the basis set $\{x^p y^q\}$ is not orthogonal. The moments upto order two provide basic geometric characteristics of $f(x,y)$. The moment m_{00} defines the total mass of $f(x,y)$, whereas the moments (m_{00}, m_{10}, m_{01}), are sufficient to compute the centre of mass, i.e., centroid (x_c, y_c) of the image $f(x,y)$, given as:

$$x_c = \frac{m_{10}}{m_{00}}, \; y_c = \frac{m_{01}}{m_{00}}, \tag{2}$$

A central moment corresponding to m_{pq} is defined as:

$$\mu_{pq} = \int\limits_{-\infty}^{\infty} \int\limits_{-\infty}^{\infty} (x - x_c)^p (y - y_c)^q f(x,y)\, dx dy \tag{3}$$

The central moments are equivalent to the regular moments of an image that has been shifted such that the image centroid (x_c, y_c) is at the origin. As a result, central moments are invariant to translation of the image.

Moments Invariants (MI)

The use of moments for image analysis and object recognition was initiated by Hu (1962) and described in detail in (Mukundan and Ramakrishnan, 1998; Prokop and Reeves, 1992; Reiss, 1993). Using the linear combination of geometric moments, Hu derived a set of invariant moments, which possess the desirable properties of being invariant under translation, scaling, and rotation. From the second and third order geometric moments, we have the following seven orthogonal invariants:

$$
\begin{aligned}
\varphi_1 &= m_{20} + m_{02} \\
\varphi_2 &= (m_{20} - m_{02})^2 + 4m_{11}^2 \\
\varphi_3 &= (m_{30} - 3m_{12})^2 + (3m_{21} - m_{03})^2 \\
\varphi_4 &= (m_{30} - m_{12})^2 + (m_{21} - m_{03})^2 \\
\varphi_5 &= (m_{30} - 3m_{12}) + (m_{30} + m_{12})\left[(m_{30} + m_{12})^2 - 3(m_{21} + m_{03})^2\right] \\
&\quad + (3m_{21} + m_{03})(m_{21} + m_{03})\left[3(m_{30} + m_{12})^2 - (m_{21} - m_{03})^2\right] \\
\varphi_6 &= (m_{20} - m_{02})\left[(m_{30} + m_{12})^2 - (m_{21} + m_{03})^2\right] + 4m_{11}(m_{30} - m_{12})(m_{21} - m_{03}) \\
\varphi_7 &= (3m_{21} - m_{03})(m_{30} + m_{12})\left[(m_{30} + m_{12})^2 - 3(m_{21} + m_{03})^2\right] \\
&\quad + (3m_{12} - m_{30})(m_{21} + m_{03})\left[3(m_{30} + m_{12})^2 - (m_{21} + m_{03})^2\right]
\end{aligned}
\tag{4}
$$

where φ_7 is the skew orthogonal moment. This set of moments is invariant to translation, scale, mirroring (with a negative sign) and rotation.

Legendre Moments (LMs)

The Legendre moments of order $(p+q)$ for an image function $f(x,y)$ are defined as:

$$\lambda_{pq} = \frac{(2p+1)(2q+1)}{4} \int\limits_{-\infty}^{\infty}\int\limits_{-\infty}^{\infty} P_p(x) P_q(y) f(x,y)\, dx dy \qquad (5)$$

where $p,q = 0,1,2,...,\infty$. The Legendre polynomials $\{P_p(x)\}$ (Caurant, 1953) are a complete orthogonal basis set over the interval $[-1,1]$.

$$\int\limits_{-1}^{1} P_p(x) P_q(x) = \frac{2}{2p+1}\delta_{pq} \qquad (6)$$

where p^{th} order Legendre polynomial is given by (Sansone, 1991):

$$P_p(x) = \frac{1}{2^p P!} \frac{d^p}{dx^p}\left(x^2 - 1\right)^p \qquad (7)$$

Rotational Moments (RMs)

The rotational moments of order $(p+q)$ for an image function $f(x,y)$ are defined as:

$$D_{pq} = \iint\limits_{x^2+y^2 \leq 1} r^p e^{-jq\theta} f(x,y)\, dx dy \qquad (8)$$

where $r = \sqrt{x^2 + y^2}$, $p = 0,1,2,...,\infty$ and q takes any positive and negative integer values and $\theta = \tan^{-1}(y/x)$.

Complex Moments (CMs)

The notion of complex moments was introduced as a simple and straightforward way to describe rotation invariant moments. The complex moments of order $(p+q)$ for an image function $f(x,y)$ are defined as:

$$C_{pq} = \iint\limits_{x^2+y^2 \leq 1} r^{p+q} e^{-j(p-q)\theta} f(x,y)\, dx dy \qquad (9)$$

where $r = \sqrt{x^2 + y^2}$, $p,q = 0,1,2,...,\infty$ and $j = \sqrt{-1}$ and $\theta = \tan^{-1}(y/x)$.

Zernike Moments (ZMs)

Teague has suggested the use of orthogonal moments in image analysis based on orthogonal polynomials. This set of orthogonal functions has been introduced by Teague as a basic tool for representation of a wavefront function for optical systems with circular pupils. Since then radial polynomials have been found important in applications ranging from pattern recognition, optical engineering, medical imaging to eye diagnostics, etc (Born and Wolf, 1975; Deans, 1983; Hu et. al, 1989; Iskander et al., 1981; Iskander et al., 2002). The radial orthogonal moments are defined on a unit circle, i.e., the image plane is $D = \{(x,y) = x^2 + y^2 \leq 1\}$. The set of orthogonal ZMs for an image intensity function $f(x,y)$ with order p and repetition q are defined over a continuous unit disc (Teague, 1980):

$$Z_{pq} = \frac{p+1}{\pi} \iint\limits_{x^2+y^2\leq 1} f(x,y) V_{pq}^*(x,y) dxdy \tag{10}$$

where $V_{pq}^*(x,y)$ is the complex conjugate of the Zernike polynomials $V_{pq}(x,y)$, defined as:

$$V_{pq}(x,y) = R_{pq}(r) e^{jq\theta} \tag{11}$$

where $p \geq 0, 0 \leq |q| \leq p, p - |q| = even, j = \sqrt{-1}$, and $\theta = \tan^{-1}(y/x)$. The radial polynomials $R_{pq}(r)$ are defined by:

$$R_{pq}(r) = \sum_{k=0}^{(p-|q|)/2} (-1)^k \frac{(p-k)!}{k! \left(\frac{p+|q|}{2}-k\right)! \left(\frac{p-|q|}{2}-k\right)!} r^{p-2k} \tag{12}$$

The radial polynomials $R_{pq}(r)$ satisfy the orthogonality relation:

$$\int_0^1 R_{pq}(r) R_{p'q}(r) rdr = \frac{1}{2(p+1)} \delta_{pp'} \tag{13}$$

where δ_{ij} is Kronecker delta. The set of Zernike polynomials $V_{pq}(x,y)$ forms a complete orthogonal set within the unit disc as:

$$\int_0^{2\pi} \int_0^1 V_{pq}(x,y) V_{p'q'}^*(x,y) rdrd\theta = \frac{\pi}{p+1} \delta_{pp'}\delta_{qq'} \tag{14}$$

Features based on orthogonal kernels are more effective in terms of information compactness and minimal information redundancy. Therefore, the number of moments required to reconstruct an image is much less than those obtained from non-orthogonal kernels. The image function is reconstructed by using inverse moments and transforms, which is given as:

$$\hat{f}(x,y) = \sum_{p=0}^{P_{\max}} \sum_{q=-p}^{p} Z_{pq} V_{pq}(x,y) \tag{15}$$

Pseudo Zernike Moments (PZMs)

PZMs also belong to the class of circularly orthogonal moments, which are also defined over a unit disc. These moments have similar characteristics as that of ZMs and are widely used and studied in the literature because of their minimum information redundancy and immunity to noise. The computational cost of PZMs is more than ZMs for the same order, which is also demonstrated in the later section of this chapter. On the other hand, PZMs are observed to be more robust to image noise than ZMs (Bhatia and Wolf, 1954). In addition, PZMs provide twice the number of moments as provided by ZMs for the same moment order. There are $\left(1 + p_{\max}\right)^2$ number of PZMs as compared to $\left(1 + p_{\max}\right)\left(2 + p_{\max}\right)/2$ number of ZMs for the same maximum order $p_{\max}$. Thus, using the same maximum order $p_{\max}$, PZMs have more low-order moments than ZMs. As a result, PZMs are less sensitive to image noise than ZMs. PZMs differ from ZMs in their real valued radial polynomials defined as:

$$R_{pq}(r) = \sum_{s=0}^{p-|q|} \frac{(-1)^s \left(2p+1-s\right)! \; r^{p-s}}{s! \left(p+|q|+1-s\right)! \left(p-|q|-s\right)!}, \tag{16}$$

where $p \geq 0, 0 \leq |q| \leq p$. The orthogonality principles for PZMs are similar to that of ZMs given by Eq. (13) and Eq. (14). The image reconstruction function for PZMs is similar to that of ZMs given by Eq. (15) with the replacement of Z_{pq} by PZ_{pq}, where

$$PZ_{pq} = \frac{p+1}{\pi} \iint_{x^2+y^2 \leq 1} f(x,y) V_{pq}^*(x,y) \, dx dy \tag{17}$$

Orthogonal Fourier Mellin Moments (OFMMs)

The new orthogonal radial polynomials have more zeros than do the Zernike radial polynomials in the region of a small radial distance (Sheng an Shen, 1994). OFMMs may be thought of as generalized Zernike moments and orthogonalized complex moments. For small images, the description by OFMMs is better than that of ZMs in terms of image-reconstruction errors and signal-to-noise ratio. The OFMMs basis functions also form a set of complete orthogonal functions over the unit disc and they differ from ZMs in their polynomials defined as:

$$O_{pq} = \frac{p+1}{\pi} \iint_{x^2+y^2 \leq 1} f(x,y) V_{pq}^*(x,y) \, dx dy \tag{18}$$

where

$$V_{pq}(x,y) = R_p(r)e^{jq\theta} \tag{19}$$

with constraints $p \geq 0$, $|q| \geq 0$. It is observed that p does not depend q on unlike ZMs and PZMs. The orthogonal radial polynomials are defined as:

$$R_p(r) = \sum_{s=0}^{p}(-1)^{p+s}\frac{(p+s+1)!}{(p-s)!\,s!\,(s+1)!}r^s \tag{20}$$

$R_p(r)$ is orthogonal over the interval $0 \leq r \leq 1$, i.e.,

$$\int_0^1 R_p(r)R_q(r)r\,dr = \frac{1}{2(p+1)}\delta_{pq}. \tag{21}$$

Orthogonality principles for OFMMs polynomials are similar to that of ZMs given by Eq. (14). The image can be reconstructed by using the following expression

$$\hat{f}(x,y) = \sum_{p=0}^{p_{max}}\sum_{q=-q_{max}}^{q_{max}} O_{pq}V_{pq}(x,y) \tag{22}$$

where p and q are the maximum order and repetition.

Radial Harmonic Fourier Moments (RHFMs)

RHFMs basis functions also form a set of complete orthogonal functions defined over a unit disc. RHFMs of order p and repetition q with $p \geq 0$ and $|q| \geq 0$ are defined as (Ren et al., 2007):

$$\Omega_{pq} = \frac{1}{2\pi}\iint_{x^2+y^2 \leq 1} f(x,y)V_{pq}^*(x,y)\,dxdy \tag{23}$$

where

$$V_{pq}(x,y) = R_p(r)e^{jq\theta} \tag{24}$$

The radial kernel function is defined as:

$$R_p(r) = \begin{cases} \dfrac{1}{\sqrt{r}}, & p = 0 \\[2mm] \sqrt{\dfrac{2}{r}}\,\cos(\pi p r), & p \ even \\[2mm] \sqrt{\dfrac{2}{r}}\,\sin(\pi (p+1) r), & p \ odd \end{cases} \tag{25}$$

The orthogonal property for radial kernel is given as:

$$\int_0^1 R_p(r) R_q(r)\, r dr = \delta_{pq}. \tag{26}$$

The orthogonality of basis function is given as:

$$\int_0^{2\pi} \int_0^1 V_{pq}(x,y) V^*_{p'q'}(x,y)\, r dr d\theta = 2\pi \delta_{pp'} \delta_{qq'}. \tag{27}$$

The reconstruction function for RHFMs is similar to that of OFMMs given by Eq. (22), with the replacement of O_{pq} by Ω_{pq}.

Chebyshev Fourier Moments (CHFMs)

CHFMs of order p and repetition q with $p \geq 0 \ and \ |q| \geq 0$ are defined as (Ping et al., 2002):

$$\Psi_{pq} = \frac{1}{2\pi} \iint_{x^2 + y^2 \leq 1} f(x,y) V^*_{pq}(x,y)\, dx dy \tag{28}$$

where $V^*_{pq}(x,y)$ is the complex conjugate of the basis function $V_{pq}(x,y)$ defined by:

$$V_{pq}(x,y) = R_p(r) e^{jq\theta} \tag{29}$$

where the radial kernel function is given as:

$$R_p(r) = \sqrt{\frac{8}{\pi}} \left(\frac{1-r}{r}\right)^{1/4} \sum_{k=0}^{\lfloor p/2 \rfloor} (-1)^k \frac{(p-k)!}{k!\,(p-2k)!} \times \left(2(2r-1)\right)^{p-2k} \tag{30}$$

The orthogonal properties for radial kernel and basis function are similar to that of RHFMs given by Eq. (26) and Eq. (27), respectively. The reconstruction function for CHFMs is similar to that of OFMMs as given by Eq. (22), with the replacement of O_{pq} by Ψ_{pq}.

PROPERTIES OF RADIAL MOMENTS

Orthogonal Property

From various described moments in the previous section GMs, MI, RMs, and CMs are not orthogonal and rest of the described moments satisfy orthogonality property. By orthogonality, we mean the decomposition of an object into uncorrelated components to simplify its analysis. The lack of orthogonality in GMs corresponds to high correlation among moments, which leads to more redundant information of the image. Besides, non-orthogonality implies inadequacy of information compactness in each of the computed moments. On the other hand, orthogonality of the kernels means that an image is projected onto a set of pairwise orthogonal axes, and the classifier can hence be relatively simple (Teh and Chin, 1988). The orthogonality principles satisfy by LMs, ZMs, PZMs, OFMMs, RHFMs, and CHFMs are given in the previous section.

Invariance Property

The set of complex radial moments inherently possess rotation invariance property. The magnitude values of ZMs, PZMs, OFMMs, RHFMs, CHFMs remain identical before and after rotation. Therefore, the magnitude values of above mentioned moments are rotation invariant. Here, we describe the rotation invariance property in terms of ZMs, which is similar for all other radial moments. For an image rotated by an angle α, ZMs are defined as

$$Z_{pq}^{r} = Z_{pq}e^{-jq\alpha} \tag{31}$$

where Z_{pq}^{r} and Z_{pq} are ZMs of rotated and unrotated image, respectively. The rotation invariant ZMs are extracted by considering only magnitude values as

$$\left| Z_{pq}^{r} \right| = \left| Z_{pq}e^{-jq\alpha} \right| \tag{32}$$

$$\left| e^{-jq\alpha} \right| = \left| \cos(q\alpha) + j\sin(q\alpha) \right| = 1 \tag{33}$$

Substituting Eq. (33) in Eq. (32), we get

$$\left| Z_{pq}^{r} \right| = \left| Z_{pq} \right| \tag{34}$$

As $Z_{pq}^{*} = Z_{p,-q}$ and $\left| Z_{pq} \right| = \left| Z_{p,-q} \right|$, therefore only magnitudes of ZMs with $q \geq 0$ are considered (Khotanzand and Hong, 1990). However, ZMs are not scale and translation invariant. Scaling and translation invariance can be achieved by normalizing the image, which we discuss in the later Chapter. LMs possess the orthogonality property. However, they do not exhibit rotation invariance.

Robustness

The computation of orthogonal radial moments is based on the summation operation. We know that an image processing operation based on summation or integration is robust to noise. However, the robustness of various radial moments varies from each other. PZMs and OFMMs exhibit more feature vectors than ZMs for the same order of moment. Therefore, PZMs are less sensitive to image noise as compared to ZMs. In our experiments, we evaluate the performance of all radial moments for robustness to noise, which is given under robustness property of radial moments.

Multilayer Expression

Low orders of orthogonal radial moments represent the global information of the image and high orders of moments represent the details of the image. A binary image of the character "A" of size 64×64 pixels, given in Figure 3 (a) is reconstructed for $p_{max} = 10, 20, 30$ and 40 for ZMs, PZMs, OFMMs, RHFMs, and CHFMs. The reconstruction capability of various moments is measured by visual inspection of the reconstructed images. Figure 3 (b) displays the reconstructed images of the original image of character 'A', which is given in Figure 3(a). Besides, the total number of moments L required to reconstruct an image for each moment are presented in Table 1. It is seen from Figure 3 (b) that the low orders of moments provide the gross approximation of image and there is a gradual improvement in the quality of reconstructed image as the moment order increases. We also observe that PZMs and OFMMs become numerically unstable for moment orders $p_{max} \geq 20$. Consequently, their image reconstruction capability diminishes for moment orders $p_{max} \geq 20$.

Derivation of Higher Order Moments

The higher order orthogonal radial moments, such as ZMs, PZMs, OFMMs, RHFMs, and CHFMs, are easy to derive unlike Hu's moment invariants. Hu's moment invariants are derived from three low orders of GMs. However, the question of what is gained by including higher order moments in the context of

Table 1. Total numbers of moments L, for $p_{max} = q_{max} = 10, 20, 30, 40$

Moments	L	10	20	30	40
ZMs	$1/2\left(1 + p_{max}\right)\left(2 + p_{max}\right)$	66	231	496	861
PZMs	$\left(1 + p_{max}\right)^2$	121	441	961	1681
OFMMs	$\left(1 + p_{max}\right)\left(1 + 2q_{max}\right)$	231	861	1891	3321
RHFMs	$\left(1 + p_{max}\right)\left(1 + 2q_{max}\right)$	231	861	1891	3321
CHFMs	$\left(1 + p_{max}\right)\left(1 + 2q_{max}\right)$	231	861	1891	3321

Figure 3. (a) Original image (b) reconstructed images by moments at orders $p_{\max} = 10, 20, 30, 40$

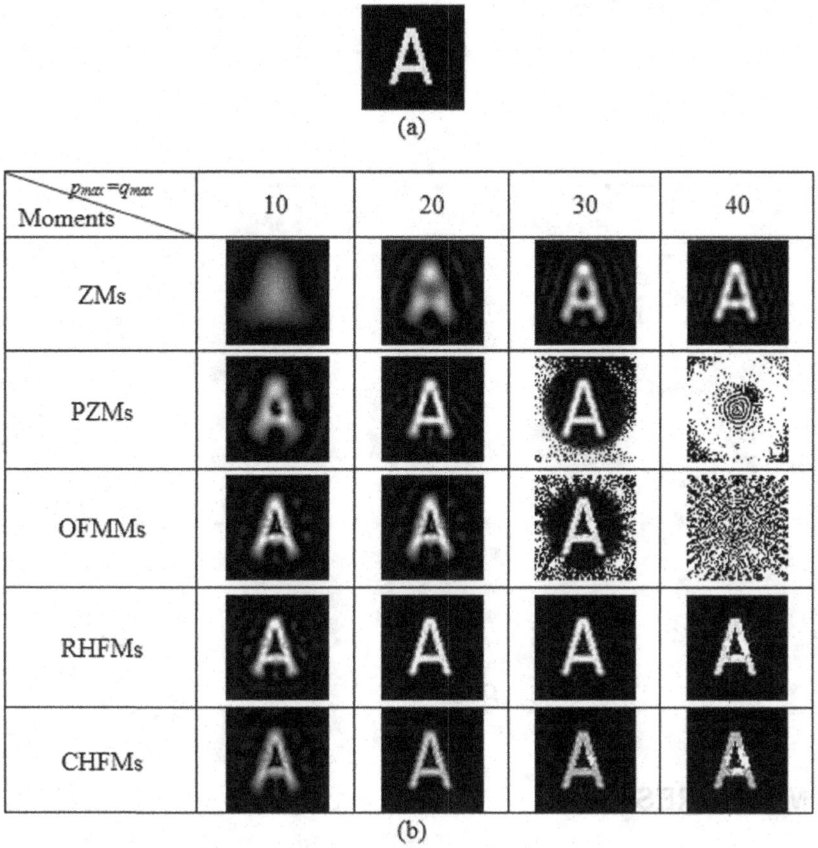

(a)

$p_{max} = q_{max}$ Moments	10	20	30	40
ZMs				
PZMs				
OFMMs				
RHFMs				
CHFMs				

(b)

image analysis has not been addressed by Hu. Besides, the recovery of image form these moments is supposed to be a difficult task. As we can see in Figure 3 that orthogonal radial moments have the strong capability to reconstruct an image, which demonstrates the image representation and description capability of the features extracted by these moments. Nevertheless, the radial moments are computation intensive due to the inclusion of factorial terms and polynomials of order p that contains q number of terms. To address this issue, various recursive algorithms (Chong et al., 2003; Singh and Walia, 2001; Al-Rawi, 2010; Walia et al., 2012; Papakostas et al., 2010; Hosny, 2008) are available, which considerably enhance the speed of computation. Besides, the recursive methods for the computation of radial moments are numerically stable for very high orders of moments, e.g., the $q - recursive$ method (Singh and Walia, 2011) for computation of ZMs is numerically stable even for moment order $p_{\max} = 300$ for an image of size 256×256 pixels. In our experiments, we implement ZMs, PZMs, OFMMs, RHFMs, and CHFMs by using $q - recursive$ method and compare their CPU elapsed time. The CPU time comparison for the computation of ZMs, PZMs, OFMMs, RHFMs, and CHFMs at various orders $p_{\max} = 2, 4, 6, 8, 10$ and 12 is presented in Figure 4. It is observed from the figure that OFMMs, RHFMs, and CHFMs takes the highest and similar CPU time for their computation. As a result, their graphical curves are overlapped, followed by PZMs and ZMs at the same moment order. In other words, we can say that ZMs take least amount of CPU time.

Figure 4. Comparison of CPU elapsed time for the computation of ZMs, PZMs, OFMMs, RHFMs, and CHFMs by applying recursive algorithms

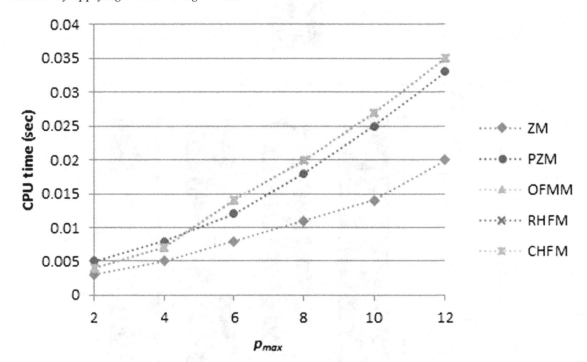

SIMILARITY MEASURES

An effective similarity measure is required because it plays a significant role in improving the retrieval accuracy of the system. The key task of similarity measure is to classify the images based on their relevance to query image. The similarity measures are also termed as distance metric or similarity metric. Similarity measures are used to determine the relevance between the query image and images stored in the database. The database image with the smallest distance to query image is referred to as the most relevant image. Its inappropriate selection may lead to undesirable results. Several similarity measures have been proposed by researchers to improve the image retrieval rate. Various similarity measures are in existence such as Euclidean distance, Manhattan distance, Bray-Curtis distance, Hellinger distance, Chebyshev distance, Canberra distance, Chi-square statistics and cosine distance, where Euclidean distance is commonly applied for similarity matching of images. In this sub-section, the objective is to analyze the performance of above mentioned similarity measures on the image retrieval system, so that some of the measures can be applied for an effective image retrieval task. Besides, we also suggest a new similarity measure, which is partly inspired by histogram intersection. Histogram intersection is basically applied for color histograms in order to match color images as given by (Swan and Ballard, 1981). However, in our approach, we apply the modified form of histogram intersection on the spectral features and name it as a min-max similarity measure. Let a feature set contains F features, and $M_i(Q)$ and $M_i(D)$ represent the ith feature of query image Q and database image D, respectively. The various similarity measures are described as:

Euclidean Distance

This distance is one of the forms of Minkowski distance, which is based on L_p norm. For $p=2$ it is referred to as L_2 norm and also known as Euclidean distance. This measure works in vector space to compute distance between two vector inputs. It is a consequence of Pythagorean Theorem (Wang et al., 2005). Euclidean distance is the most commonly used measure. Mathematically, it can be expressed as:

$$d(Q,D) = \sqrt{\sum_{i=0}^{F-1}\left(M_i(Q) - M_i(D)\right)^2} \tag{35}$$

Manhattan Distance

This measure is another form of Minkowski distance when $p=1$ and therefore, known as L_1 norm. It represents distance between points in a city road grid. It determines absolute distances between coordinates of pairs of vectors (Bacheler, 1971). It is also known as city block distance. Mathematically, Manhattan distance is defined as:

$$d(Q,D) = \sum_{i=0}^{F-1}\left|M_i(Q) - M_i(D)\right| \tag{36}$$

Bray-Curtis Distance

Bray-Curtis distance examines space as a grid similar to Manhattan distance with the property that if all coordinates are positive, its value lies between 0 and 1. Zero Bray-Curtis distance represents exact similar coordinate. The normalization is done using the absolute difference divided by the summation (Singh and Pooja, 2011; Deza, 2009). It is also known as Sorensen's distance. Bray-Curtis distance can be defined as:

$$d(Q,D) = \frac{\sum_{i=0}^{F-1}\left|M_i(Q) - M_i(D)\right|}{\sum_{i=0}^{F-1}\left|M_i(Q) + M_i(D)\right|} \tag{37}$$

Hellinger Distance

This measure quantifies the deviation between two probability measures. It is computational intensive. It has natural upper and lower bounds, 0 and 1, respectively. It is based on the proportion of the protocol attributes (Sengar et al., 2008). It can be formulated as:

$$d^2(Q,D) = \frac{1}{2}\sum_{i=0}^{F-1}\left(\sqrt{M_i(Q)} - \sqrt{M_i(D)}\right)^2 \tag{38}$$

Chebyshev Distance

It is also called as maximum value or chessboard distance. It examines the absolute magnitude of the differences between coordinates of a pair of objects. This distance can be used for quantitative and ordinal variables (Klove et al., 2010). Mathematically, it can be defined as:

$$d(Q,D) = \max_i \left| M(Q) - M_i(D) \right|, i = 0,1,...,F-1. \tag{39}$$

Canberra Distance

Canberra distance examines the sum of series of fraction differences between coordinates of pairs of objects. Each term of fractional difference has a value between 0 and 1. If one of the coordinate is zero, the term becomes unity regardless of other value, thus distance will not be affected. Note that if both distances are zeros, we need to define 0/0=0. This distance is quite sensitive to small change when both coordinates are near to zero (Kokare et al., 2007). It is defined as:

$$d(Q,D) = \sum_{i=0}^{F-1} \frac{\left| M_i(Q) - M_i(D) \right|}{\left| M_i(Q) \right| + \left| M_i(D) \right|} \tag{40}$$

χ² (Chi-Square) Statistics

The χ^2 distance is used to analyze the observed difference of frequencies from the expected frequencies (Deza and Deza, 2009). The χ^2 distance is quasi distance and is defined as:

$$d(Q,D) = \sum_{i=0}^{F-1} \frac{\left(M_i(D) - M_i(Q) \right)^2}{M_i(Q)} \tag{41}$$

Cosine Distance

The cosine distance measures the distance in angular direction (Ye, 2011). The distance is measured by the angle between two vectors. The higher the angular separation the more will be the similarity. It is also called coefficient of correlation. It is defined as:

$$d(Q,D) = \frac{\sum_{i=0}^{F-1} \left(M_i(Q) \times M_i(D) \right)}{\sqrt{\sum_{i=0}^{F-1} M_i(Q)^2} \sqrt{\sum_{i=0}^{F-1} M_i(D)^2}} \tag{42}$$

PROPOSED SIMILARITY MEASURE

In this section, we provide a novel similarity measure which is simple to compute and gives effective performance. It is based on histogram intersection (Swan and Ballard, 1991). The histogram intersection is generally applied for measuring similarity among color histograms. However, the modified form is applied for the spectral features. The modification is performed in the normalization part. Mathematically, it is expressed as follows:

$$d(Q,D) = 1 - \frac{\sum_{i=0}^{F-1} \min\left(M_i(Q), M_i(D)\right)}{\sum_{i=0}^{F-1} \max\left(M_i(Q), M_i(D)\right)} \tag{43}$$

where the minimum function value is used to compute the similarity/dissimilarity among images. It computes the minimum possible distance between query and database image. For a database image D which is dissimilar to the query image Q, the expression $\sum_{i=0}^{F-1} \min\left(M_i(Q), M_i(D)\right)$ yields the smaller distance as compared to similar images. On the other hand, the expression $\sum_{i=0}^{F-1} \max\left(M_i(Q), M_i(D)\right)$ yields the maximum possible value, which effectively helps to normalize the feature components and the measured distance always lies in [0, 1]. Therefore, by subtracting the computed distance from 1 is capable of differentiating intra-class and interclass images, which places large disparity between dissimilar images. We refer to the proposed similarity measure as the min-max similarity measure.

Effectiveness of the Proposed Similarity Measure

We present the classification performance of min-max similarity measure by considering three query images "camel-3", "device7-10", and "apple-3" taken from MPEG-7 database. Their results are provided in Figure 5, 6, and 7. It is apparent from the Figure 5 that all the samples of camel class are classified separately and images from other classes deer, elephant, and dog, which are visually nearby to query image of the class camel are misclassified and intermixed among each other. The similar trends are observed while examining the performance of Min-Max for "device07-10", and "apple-3" query images, which are demonstrated in Figure 6 and 7, respectively.

Performance Measures

We use two performance evaluation tests to measure the retrieval accuracy of the system. The first one is precision (P) and recall (R) to evaluate the retrieval effectiveness of the methods. The second test is the Bull's eye performance (BEP), which measures the retrieval accuracy of the methods. These performance measures are described as follows

Figure 5. Classification performance of min-max similarity measure for query image camel-3

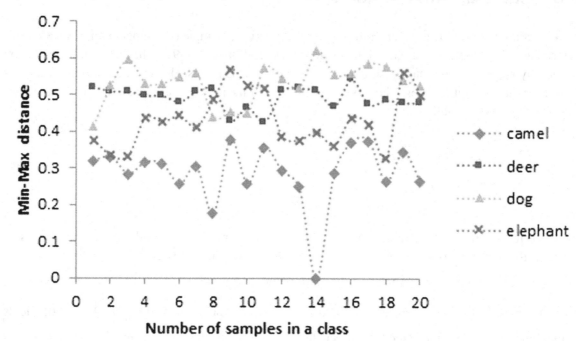

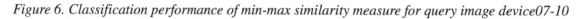

Figure 6. Classification performance of min-max similarity measure for query image device07-10

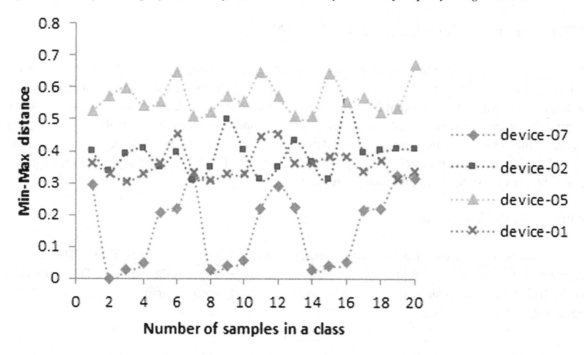

Figure 7. Classification performance of min-max similarity measure for query image apple-11

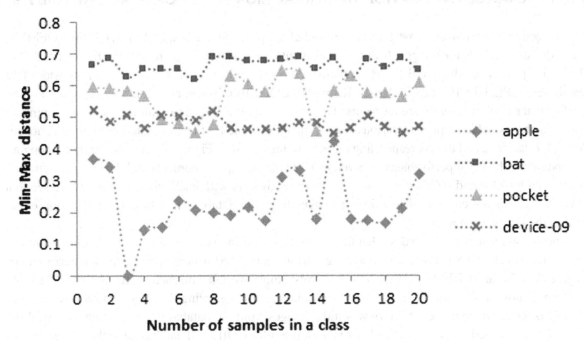

Precision and Recall $(P - R)$

Precision measures the retrieval accuracy and recall measures the ability to retrieve relevant images from the database. Precision and recall are inversely proportional to each other as the precision reduces, the recall increases. We use average precision and average recall for all the retrieval results. For a query image Q, we compute precision and recall in percentage as follows:

$$P = \frac{n_Q}{T_Q} \times 100, \ R = \frac{n_Q}{D_Q} \times 100, \tag{44}$$

where n_Q represents the number of similar images retrieved from the database, T_Q represents total number of images retrieved, D_Q represents number of images in database similar to query image Q.

Bull's Eye Performance (BEP)

BEP is measured by the correct retrievals among the top $2R$ retrievals, where R is the number of shapes which are relevant to the query image in the database. We use average percentage value to measure BEP.

PERFORMANCE EVALUATION OF RADIAL MOMENTS FOR IMAGE RETRIEVAL

In this section, we evaluate the performance of radial moments, viz., RMs, CMs, ZMs, PZMs, OFMMs, RHFMs, and CHFMs for image retrieval. Experiments are performed on an Intel Pentium Core 2 Duo 2.10 GHz processor with 3 GB RAM. Implementation is performed on VC++ 9.0. We consider five databases, MPEG-7 CE Shape 1 Part-B, Kimia-99, COIL-100, Noise, and Rotation, for assessing the performance of above mentioned moments. The $P - R$ curves are used to examine their functioning on these databases, which represent various sorts of images. In the first test, we analyze their behavior for MPEG-7 database and the corresponding curves are presented in Figure 8. We observe that among all the moments, the worst performance is given by CMs, i.e., complex moments and the best performance is attained by ZMs and PZMs and their $P - R$ curves overlap with each other. Therefore, we see that ZMs and PZMs are capable of identifying images from the database in which large variation exists within the instances of a class.

The second test is performed for Kimia-99 database and the corresponding $P - R$ curves are depicted in Figure 9. We observe that CMs again gives the poorest performance and the highest performance is given by ZMs and CHFMs and their $P - R$ curves almost overlap with each other. PZMs and OFMMs perform almost similar and their $P - R$ curves coincide. By observing the $P - R$ curves, we can say that ZMs are again competent to retrieve similar images from the database, which contains partial occluded and distorted shapes. The third test is performed for COIL-100 database and the $P - R$ curves for all employed moments are demonstrated in Figure 10. It is observed that the order of performance of all the moments is similar as that for MPEG-7 database. Again ZMs and PZMs perform superior to

Figure 8. $P - R$ comparisons of radial moments for MPEG-7 Shape 1 Part-B database

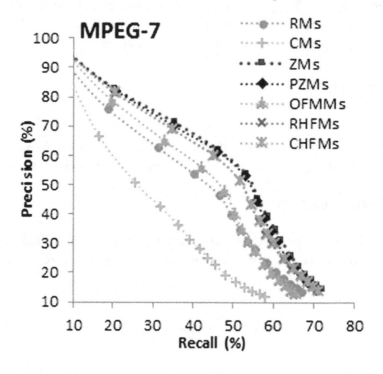

Figure 9. P − R comparisons of radial moments for Kimia-99 database

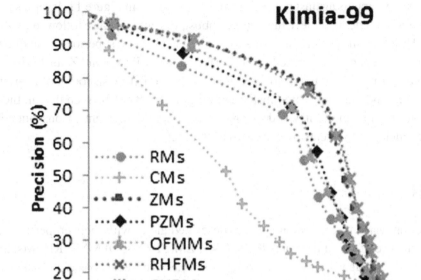

Figure 10. P − R comparisons of radial moments for MPEG-7 Shape 1 Part-B for COIL-100 database

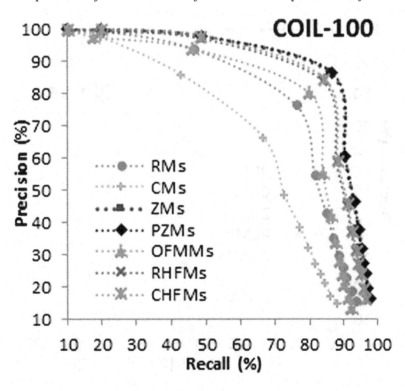

rest of the moments and poorest performance is given by CMs. The fourth test is performed for evaluating the robustness of moments against noise. The results are given in Figure 11. It represents that PZMs, RHFMs, and CHFMs moments achieve the highest robustness against noise followed by ZMs, OFMMs, RMs, and CMs. However, the performance of ZMs and OFMMs is far superior to that of RMs and CMs. Besides, a minute discrepancy is incurred in the performance of PZMs and ZMs. CMs again gives the worst performance for retrieving noise affected images. In the fifth test, rotation invariance of all the moments is analyzed and the results are illustrated in Figure 12. It can be seen that all the moments are highly invariant to rotation and achieve 100% precision for all the moments. Consequently, the $P - R$ curves of all the employed moments overlap with each other.

DISCUSSION

In the above section, various radial moments are described along with their properties. In our experiments, the performance of radial moments RMs, CMs, ZMs, PZMs, OFMMs, RHFMs, and CHFMs is analyzed for retrieving images for several kinds of databases. These databases consist of images representing numerous aspects of images, such as distortion, partial occlusion, pose variation, rotation, noise effect, 3D objects, gray scale, and binary images, etc. By evaluating the above $P - R$ curves for all databases, we observe that radial moments ZMs, PZMs, OFMMs, RHFMs, and CHFMs, are capable enough to meet six principles set by MPEG-7. Among them, ZMs supersede rest of the moments for

Figure 11. $P - R$ comparisons of radial moments for Noise database

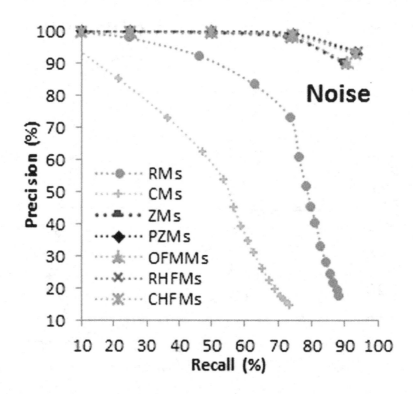

Figure 12. P − R comparisons of radial moments for Rotation database

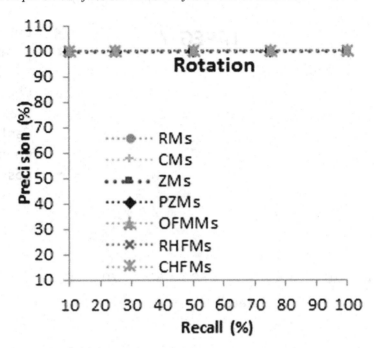

image retrieval effectiveness. It is worth mentioning here that all the above mentioned radial moments are highly invariant to rotation and provides 100% retrieval rate for rotated images. Although, all moments represent good robustness to noise, PZMs, RHFMs, and CHFMs can be recommended for best performance for noisy images. While considering the computation perspective of radial moments, we observe that ZMs takes least amount of CPU time for the same order of moments as compared to other moments. OFMMs, RHFMs, and CHFMs take the highest and similar amount CPU time. Thus, the abovementioned observations lead to the recommendation of ZMs for effective and efficient image retrieval.

PERFORMANCE EVALUATION OF SIMILARITY MEASURES

For evaluating the performance of different similarity measures a detailed experimental analysis is performed. The objective of our experiments is to obtain evidence that which similarity measure attains high performance and in what sort of circumstances, it can be applied on. The performance of various similarity measures viz. Euclidean distance, Manhattan distance, Bray-Curtis distance, Hellinger distance, Chebyshev distance, Chi-square statistics and Cosine distance is analyzed on the image retrieval system. Besides, a novel similarity measure referred to as Min-Max is proposed and evaluated against other similarity measures. The region based descriptor angular radial transform (ART) (Bober, 2011) and contour based Fourier descriptors (FD) (Zhang and Lu, 2003) are used for extracting features. The experimental study for assessing the performance of similarity measures is given in Figure 13 and Figure 14, where features are extracted using ART and in Figure 15 and Figure 16, where features are computed using FD. The top 10 retrieval results are given in Figure 17. By observing the results it is concluded that

Figure 13. P – R performance of similarity measures by applying ART for MPEG-7 database

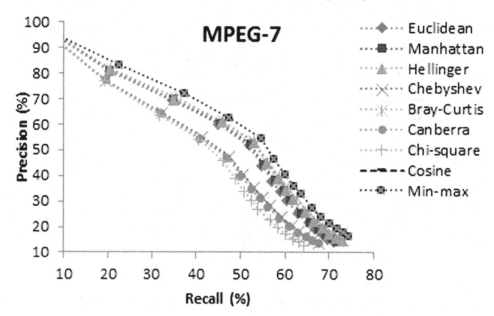

Figure 14. P – R performance of similarity measures by applying ART for Kimia-99 database

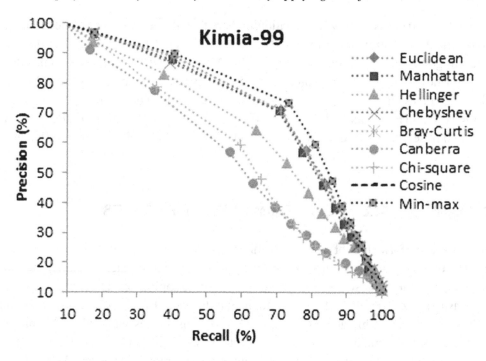

- The performance of similarity measures is almost similar for both descriptors ART and FD. For MPEG-7 database, the performance of Euclidean, Manhattan, Bray-Curtis, and Hellinger distances is similar and superior to that of Chebyshev, Canberra, and Chi-square distances. However, the proposed Min-Max outperforms all the similarity measures. For Kimia-99 database, the highest

Figure 15. P – R performance of similarity measures by applying FD for MPEG-7 database

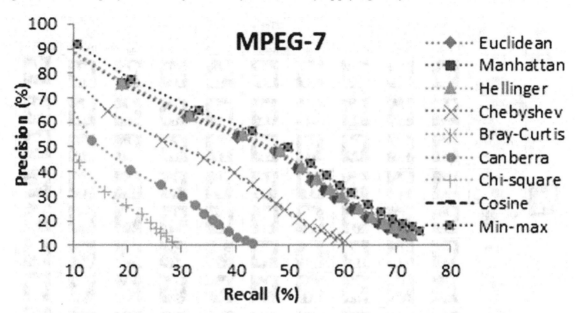

Figure 16. P – R performance of similarity measures by applying FD for MPEG-7 database

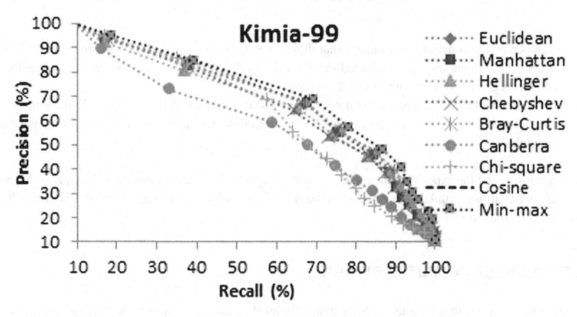

retrieval rate is given by Min-Max and the lowest by Canberra distance. The top retrieval results reveal the superiority of both Min-Max and Bray-Curtis similarity measures.

- The performance of Euclidean distance is slightly lower than Bray-Curtis. This is due to the fact that in Euclidean distance, the values in each dimension are squared before summations, which formulate more emphasis even on dissimilar features. However, in Bray-Curtis similarity measure the distance value will never exceed one because, in its equation, the numerator signifies the dif-

Figure 17. Top 10 retrieval results using various similarity measures for MPEG-7 database

Figure 9. Top 10 retrieval results using various similarity measures for MPEG-7 database

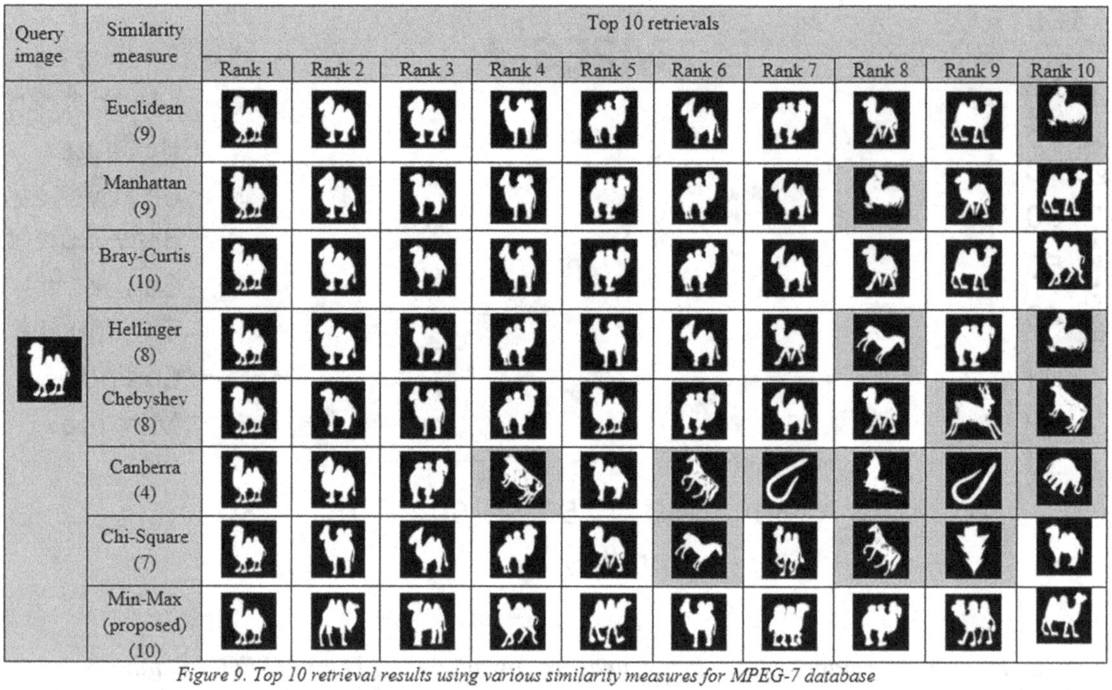

ference and denominator normalizes that difference. Therefore, it could be used to avoid scaling effect. The similar concept is adopted in Min-Max similarity measure. The worst retrieval performance is given by the cosine similarity measure.

- While considering the computation complexity, Manhattan similarity measure is the simplest to compute among others, whereas the cosine similarity measure has the highest computation complexity.

By considering the experimental results, we conclude that Min-Max, Bray-Curtis, Euclidean, Manhattan, and Hellinger similarity measures can be used for effective classification and in obtaining the improved image retrieval rate.

CONCLUSION AND FUTURE WORK

In this chapter, some fundamental tools for image retrieval, which are based on shape have been elaborated. The hypothesis and properties of various radial moments are described and discussed. It has been shown that the spectral features extracted by the abovementioned moments are proficient to represent and describe shapes effectively. The performance of all the radial moments is also analyzed over several databases, which contain various sorts of images. It has been observed that all the radial moments provide good retrieval accuracy. However, ZMs are observed to perform well in terms of accuracy and efficiency.

Apart from that, various similarity measures are also described and discussed in this chapter. The performance of similarity measures is evaluated and it has been observed that Min-Max and Bray-Curtis similarity measures can be suggested for effective image retrieval. Both Min-Max and Bray-Curtis provide normalized distances of the spectral features of query and database images. Consequently, these measures eliminate the scaling effect of large and small magnitude features and provide good retrieval results. Since the databases used for image retrieval tests contain images of relevant and irrelevant classes, precision-recall and Bull's eye performance, performance measures are used to evaluate the image retrieval performance throughout the research work.

In this chapter, only the images of MPEG-7, Kimia-99, and COIL-100 are used which represent images of different subjects, distorted, and occluded shapes. With the advancement in technology, X-ray, MRI, CT-Scan are used to diagnose various diseases in human body. Therefore, in the future work, biomedical images such as MRI, CT-Scan, X-ray images will be used to analyze the performance of ZMs, PZMs, and OFMMs, etc.

REFERENCES

Al-Rawi, M. S. (2010). Fast computation of pseudo Zernike moments. *Journal of Real-Time Image Processing*, *5*(1), 3–10. doi:10.1007/s11554-009-0118-0

Arnold, W. M., Worring, M., Santini, S., Gupta, A., & Jain, R. (2000). Content-based image retrieval at the end of the early years. *IEEE Transactions on Pattern Analysis and Machine Intelligence*, *22*(12), 38–45.

Attalla, E., & Siy, P. (2005). Robust shape similarity retrieval based on contour segmentation polygonal multiresolution and elastic matching. *Pattern Recognition*, *38*(12), 2229–2241. doi:10.1016/j.patcog.2005.02.009

Batchelor, B. G. (1971). Improved distance measure for pattern recognition. *Electronics Letters*, *7*(18), 521–524. doi:10.1049/el:19710353

Bhatia, A. B., Wolf, E., & Born, M. (1954). On the circle polynomials of Zernike and related orthogonal sets. *Proceedings of the Cambridge Philosophical Society*, *50*(01), 40–48. doi:10.1017/S0305004100029066

Bicego, M., & Lovato, P. (2016). A bioinformatics approach to 2D shape classification. *Computer Vision and Image Understanding*, *145*, 59–69. doi:10.1016/j.cviu.2015.11.011

Blaser, A. (1979). Database techniques for pictorial applications. Springer.

Bober, M. (2011). MPEG-7 visual shape descriptors. *IEEE Transactions on Circuits Systems and Video Technology*, *11*(6), 716-719.

Born, M., & Wolf, E. (1975). *Principles of Optics*. Oxford: Pergamon Press.

Caurant, R., & Hilbert, D. (1953). *Methods of mathematical physics, 1 New York*. Interscience.

Cawkill, A. E. (1993). The British library's picture research projects: Image, word, and retrieval. *Advanced Imaging (Woodbury, N.Y.)*, *8*(10), 38–40.

Chang, N. S., & Fu, K. S. (1979). A relational database system for images (Technical Report TR-EE 79-82). Purdue University.

Chang, N. S., & Fu, K. S. (1980). Query by pictorial example. *IEEE Transactions on Software Engineering*, 6(6), 519–524. doi:10.1109/TSE.1980.230801

Chang, S. K., & Hsu, A. (1992). Image information systems: Where do we go from here? *IEEE Transactions on Knowledge and Data Engineering*, 5(5), 431–442. doi:10.1109/69.166986

Chang, S. K., Jungert, E., & Li, Y. (1988). *Representation and retrieval of symbolic pictures using generalized 2D string, Technical Report*. University of Pittsburgh.

Chang, S. K., & Kunii, T. L. (1981). Pictorial database systems. *IEEE Computer Magazine*, 14(11), 13–21. doi:10.1109/C-M.1981.220243

Chang, S. K., Yan, C. W., Dimitroff, D. C., & Arndt, T. (1988). An intelligent image database system. *IEEE Transactions on Software Engineering*, 14(5), 681–688. doi:10.1109/32.6147

Chen, J., Shan, S., He, C., Zhao, G., Pietikainen, M., Chen, X., & Gao, W. (2010). WLD: A robust image local descriptor. *IEEE Transactions on Pattern Analysis and Machine Intelligence*, 32(9), 1705–1720. doi:10.1109/TPAMI.2009.155 PMID:20634562

Chen, J., Wang, Y., Luo, L., Yu, J., & Ma, J. (2016). Image retrieval based on image-to-class similarity. *Pattern Recognition Letters*, 83(3), 379–387. doi:10.1016/j.patrec.2016.01.017

Chong, C.-W., & Paramesran, R. (2003). A comparative analysis of algorithms for fast computation of Zernike moments. *Pattern Recognition*, 36(3), 731–742. doi:10.1016/S0031-3203(02)00091-2

Deans, S. (1983). *The Radon transform and some of its applications*. New York: Wiley.

Deza, M. M., & Deza, E. (2009). *Encyclopedia of distances*. Springer-Verlag Berlin Heidelberg. doi:10.1007/978-3-642-00234-2

Dowe, J. (1993). Content-based retrieval in multimedia imaging. *Proc. SPIE Storage and Retrieval for Image and Video Database*. doi:10.1117/12.143645

Höschl, I. V. C. IV, & Flusser, J. (2016). Robust histogram-based image retrieval. *Pattern Recognition Letters*, 69, 72–81. doi:10.1016/j.patrec.2015.10.012

Hosny, K. M. (2008). Fast computation of accurate Zernike moments. *Journal of Real-Time Image Processing*, 3(1-2), 97–107. doi:10.1007/s11554-007-0058-5

Hu, M. K. (1962). Visual pattern recognition by moment invariants. *I.R.E. Transactions on Information Theory*, 8(2), 179–187. doi:10.1109/TIT.1962.1057692

Hu, P. H., Stone, J., & Stanley, T. (1989). Applications of Zernike polynomials to atmospheric propagation problems. *Journal of the Optical Society of America*, 6(10), 1595–1608. doi:10.1364/JOSAA.6.001595

Iskander, D. R., Collins, M. J., & Davis, B. (2001). Optimal modeling of corneal surfaces with Zernike polynomials. *IEEE Transactions on Bio-Medical Engineering*, 48(1), 87–95. doi:10.1109/10.900255 PMID:11235595

Iskander, D. R., Collins, M. J., Morelande, M. R., & Zhu, M. (2004). Analyzing the dynamic wavefront aberrations in the human eye. *IEEE Transactions on Bio-Medical Engineering*, *51*(11), 1969–1980. doi:10.1109/TBME.2004.834254 PMID:15536899

Iskander, D. R., Morelande, M. R., Collins, M. J., & Davis, B. (2002). Modeling of corneal surfaces with radial polynomials. *IEEE Transactions on Bio-Medical Engineering*, *49*(4), 320–328. doi:10.1109/10.991159 PMID:11942723

Jain, R. (1992). US NSF workshop visual information management systems. *Proceedings of the Symposium on Electronic Imaging: Science and Technology* (pp. 198-218).

Jain, R., Pentland, A., & Petkovic, D. (1995). Workshop Report: NSF-ARPA Workshop on Visual Information Management Systems.

Klove, T., Lin, T. T., Tsai, S.-C., & Tzeng, W.-G. (2010). Permutation arrays under the Chebyshev distance. *IEEE Transactions on Information Theory*, *56*(6), 2611–2617. doi:10.1109/TIT.2010.2046212

Kokare, M., Biswas, P. K., & Chatterji, B. N. (2007). Texture image retrieval using rotated wavelet filters. *Pattern Recognition Letters*, *28*(10), 1240–1249. doi:10.1016/j.patrec.2007.02.006

Lew, M. S., Sebe, N., Djeraba, C., & Jain, R. (2006). Content-based multimedia information retrieval: State of the art and challenges. *ACM Transactions on Multimedia Computing Communications & Applications*, *2*(1), 1–19. doi:10.1145/1126004.1126005

Liu, , Wang, S., Huang, D., Deng, G., Zeng, F., & Chen, H. (2016). Medical image classification using spatial adjacent histogram based on adaptive local binary patterns. *Computers in Biology and Medicine*, *72*, 185–200. doi:10.1016/j.compbiomed.2016.03.010 PMID:27058283

Mejdoub, M., Fonteles, L., BenAmar, C., & Antonini, M. (2009). Embedded lattices tree: An efficient indexing scheme for content based retrieval on image databases. *Journal of Visual Communication and Image Representation*, *20*(2), 145–156. doi:10.1016/j.jvcir.2008.12.003

Mokhtarian, F., Abbasi, F., & Kittler, J. (1997). Efficient and robust retrieval by shape content through curvature scale space. *Proceedings of the Int. workshop on Image Databases and Multi-Media Search* (pp. 51–58).

Moore, S., & Bowden, R. (2011). Local binary patterns for multi-view facial expression recognition. *Computer Vision and Image Understanding*, *115*(4), 541–558. doi:10.1016/j.cviu.2010.12.001

Mukundan, R., & Ramakrishnan, K. R. (1998). *Moment functions in image analysis: Theory and Applications*. Singapore: World Scientific. doi:10.1142/3838

Ojala, T., Pietikainen, M., & Maenpaa, T. (2002). Multiresolution gray-scale and rotation invariant texture classification with local binary patterns. *IEEE Transactions on Pattern Analysis and Machine Intelligence*, *24*(7), 971–986. doi:10.1109/TPAMI.2002.1017623

Papakostas, G. A., Boutalis, Y. S., Karras, D. A., & Mertzios, B. G. (2010). Efficient computation of Zernike and pseudo-Zernike moments for pattern classification applications. *Pattern Recognition and Image Analysis*, *20*(1), 56–64. doi:10.1134/S1054661810010050

Ping, Z. L., Wu, R., & Sheng, Y. L. (2002). Image description with Chebyshev-Fourier moments. *Journal of the Optical Society of America*, 19(9), 1748–1754. doi:10.1364/JOSAA.19.001748 PMID:12216868

Prokop, R. J., & Reeves, A. P. (1992). A survey of moment-based techniques for unoccluded object representation and recognition. *Graphical Models and Image Processing*, 54(5), 438–460. doi:10.1016/1049-9652(92)90027-U

Reiss, T. H. (1993). *Recognizing planar objects using invariant image features*. Berlin: Springer-Verlag. doi:10.1007/BFb0017553

Ren, H., Liu, A., Zou, J., Bai, D., & Ping, Z. (2007). Character reconstruction with radial harmonic Fourier moments. *Proc. 4th Int. Conf. on Fuzzy Systems and Knowledge Discovery 2007 (FSKD07)* (Vol. 3, pp. 307-310). doi:10.1109/FSKD.2007.213

Sansone, G. (1991). *Orthogonal functions*. New York: Dover Publications, Inc.

Sengar, H., Wang, H., Wijesekera, D., & Jajodia, S. (2008). Detecting VoIP floods using the Hellinger Distance. *IEEE Transactions on Parallel and Distributed Systems*, 9(6), 794–805. doi:10.1109/TPDS.2007.70786

Sheng, Y., & Shen, L. (1994). Orthogonal Fourier Mellin moment for invariant pattern recognition. *Journal of the Optical Society of America*, 11(6), 1748–1757. doi:10.1364/JOSAA.11.001748

Shu, X., & Wu, X.-J. (2011). A novel contour descriptor for 2D shape matching and its application to image retrieval. *Image and Vision Computing*, 29(4), 286–294. doi:10.1016/j.imavis.2010.11.001

Singh, C., & Pooja, . (2011). Improving image retrieval using combined features of Hough transform and Zernike moments. *Optics and Lasers in Engineering*, 49(12), 1386–1396. doi:10.1016/j.optlaseng.2011.07.009

Singh, C., & Walia, E. (2011). Algorithms for fast computation of Zernike moments and their numerical stability. *Image and Vision Computing*, 29(4), 251–259. doi:10.1016/j.imavis.2010.10.003

Swain, M. J., & Ballard, D. H. (1991). Color Indexing. *International Journal of Computer Vision*, 7(1), 11–32. doi:10.1007/BF00130487

Tan, X., & Triggs, B. (2010). Enhanced local texture features set for face recognition under different lighting conditions. *IEEE Transactions on Image Processing*, 19(6), 1635–1650. doi:10.1109/TIP.2010.2042645 PMID:20172829

Teague, M. R. (1980). Image analysis via the general theory of moments. *Journal of the Optical Society of America*, 70(8), 920–930. doi:10.1364/JOSA.70.000920

Teh, C. H., & Chin, R. T. (1988). On image analysis by the methods of moments. *IEEE Transactions on Pattern Analysis and Machine Intelligence*, 10(4), 496–513. doi:10.1109/34.3913

Walia, E., Singh, C., & Goyal, A. (2012). On the fast computation of orthogonal Fourier–Mellin moments with improved numerical stability. *Journal of Real-Time Image Processing*, 7(4), 247–256. doi:10.1007/s11554-010-0172-7

Wang, L., Zhang, Y., & Feng, J. (2005). On the Euclidean distance of images. *IEEE Transactions on Pattern Analysis and Machine Intelligence, 27*(8), 1334–1339. doi:10.1109/TPAMI.2005.165 PMID:16119271

Xu, C. J., Liu, J. Z., & Tang, X. (2009). 2D shape matching by contour flexibility. *IEEE Transactions on Pattern Analysis and Machine Intelligence, 31*(1), 180–186. doi:10.1109/TPAMI.2008.199 PMID:19029556

Ye, J. (2011). Cosine similarity measures for intuitionistic fuzzy sets and their applications. *Mathematical and Computer Modelling, 53*(1-2), 91–97. doi:10.1016/j.mcm.2010.07.022

Zernike, F. (1934). Beugungstheorie des Schneidenverfahrens und seiner verbesserten Form, *der Phasenkontrastmethode. Physica, 1*(7-12), 689–701. doi:10.1016/S0031-8914(34)80259-5

Zhang, D., & Lu, G. (2003). A comparative study of curvature scale space and Fourier descriptors for shape-based image retrieval. *Journal of Visual Communication and Image Representation, 14*(1), 41–60. doi:10.1016/S1047-3203(03)00003-8

KEY TERMS AND DEFINITIONS

Bull's Eye Performance: It determines the correct retrievals among the top retrievals.

Image Retrieval: The task of retrieving relevant images from the database.

Moments: Moments are scalar quantities used to characterize a function and to capture its significant features.

Orthogonality: It refers the decomposition of an object into uncorrelated components to simplify its analysis.

Precision: Precision measures the retrieval accuracy.

Recall: Recall is the ability to retrieve relevant images.

Similarity Measure: It classifies the images based on their relevance to query image.

Chapter 15
Real–Time Image and Video Processing Using High–Level Synthesis (HLS)

Murad Qasaimeh
Iowa State University, USA

Ehab Najeh Salahat
Australian National University, Australia

ABSTRACT

Implementing high-performance, low-cost hardware accelerators for the computationally intensive image and video processing algorithms has attracted a lot of attention in the last 20 years. Most of the recent research efforts were trying to figure out new design automation methods to fill the gap between the ability of realizing efficient accelerators in hardware and the tight performance requirements of the complex image processing algorithms. High-Level synthesis (HLS) is a new method to automate the design process by transforming high-level algorithmic description into digital hardware while satisfying the design constraints. This chapter focuses on evaluating the suitability of using HLS as a new tool to accelerate the most demanding image and video processing algorithms in hardware. It discusses the gained benefits and current limitations, the recent academic and commercial tools, the compiler's optimization techniques and four case studies.

1. INTRODUCTION

In the last two decades, the complexity of image and video processing algorithms has been continuously increasing to meet the demands of complex applications. Pure software implementations for most of these algorithms on embedded systems are still far from reaching real-time performance. This forced embedded designers to accelerate them in hardware to meet the required performance. Some used

DOI: 10.4018/978-1-5225-2848-7.ch015

general purpose processing units (GPUs), others used multicore CPUs, but FPGAs showed, since it is introduced, that it is the most suitable platform to implement image processing algorithms in hardware. FPGAs can be configured to exploit spatial and temporal parallelism in image processing algorithm by realizing multiple processing pipelines that could process data concurrently.

Increasing the algorithms complexity went along with a growth in FPGA chip's silicon capacity (Trimberger, 2015). Every couple of years, the silicon size increased due to the improvement in transistor length. With this improvement, porting these algorithms manually into embedded systems still hard and time consuming task to do. It required implementing the whole pipeline in Register Transfer Language (RTL) using one of the hardware description languages such as VHDL or Verilog. Several solutions have been proposed to speed-up the design process such as: simplifying the algorithm itself, using softcore CPUs or using High-level synthesis (HLS). Simplifying the algorithm usually leads to scarify in its accuracy and using softcore CPUs is not always an efficient way to reach the applications target performance and power budget.

High-Level synthesis (HLS) offers a way to generate RTL designs from high-level abstraction in an automatic manner while satisfying the design constraints and optimizing the given cost function. The main goal is to efficiently build and verify hardware, by giving embedded systems designers better control over their designs optimization processes. It allows designers to describe the design at high level of abstraction using one of the high-level languages such as C, C++ or even Matlab, while the tool generates the RTL implementation from these system level abstractions. Verifying the generated RTL, to check that the generated hardware architectures functionality matches the given high-level abstraction, is an important part of the process and can be done at high-level also well using RTL/C co-simulation.

Several advantages can be gained by using HLS technique in image processing hardware accelerators (Bailey, 2015). First, the amount of code to be written by designers using HLS is much lower compared to the manual RTL method. This will save designers a lot of time and reduces the risk of making mistakes. It also gives them the flexibility to optimize their designs by tweaking the source code and tool options to explore large design space alternatives. HLS also reduces the verification time, as the tools can be used to generate high level test benches as well. It also makes it possible to handle more complex designs by removing the need for manual coding. This also allows non-experts in hardware to generate hardware accelerators for their algorithms with minimal effort. There have been many a lot of success stories of using HLS tools in accelerating image processing algorithms, but there are still little systematic studies that focused on evaluating these designs.

The objective of this chapter is to evaluate the suitability of using HLS in implementing real-time image and video processing in embedded systems. It also gives detailed explanations of the design process in HLS and the optimization methods necessary to generate efficient circuits. It presents four image processing algorithms and evaluates the performance of its HLS implementations. The layout of this chapter is as follows. Section 2 presents brief background information about FPGA, HLS and other necessary concepts. Section 3 discusses the benefits and limitations of HLS over other design methods. In Section 4, number of HLS optimization techniques has been presented. An overview of the current academic and commercial tools is presented in Section 5. Section 6 shows an example of HLS video C/C++ library. In Section 7, four case studies have been evaluated. Finally, Section 8 briefly introduces the future work and the current open research problems. Section 9 concludes the chapter.

2. BACKGROUND

This section gives brief background information about Field programmable gate array (FPGA), which is one of the most commonly used hardware platform to accelerate image processing algorithms. It also gives an overview to hardware design flow, which is a set of steps used to generate a hardware design from a high-level system specifications. The section also defines the concept of High-Level Synthesis (HLS) and explains how it is different than the conventional design methods. Finally, its introduces OpenCV, an open source C/C++ library used heavily in image and video processing applications.

2.1. Field Programmable Gate Array (FPGA)

FPGA is a reprogrammable integrated circuit that can be configured by designers after manufacturing (Ian, Tessier, & Rose, 2008). It contains of large matrix of configurable logic blocks (CLBs) connected via programmable interconnects called switching blocks. It also has dedicated memory blocks (BRAMs) and hundreds of Digital Signal Processors (DSPs), that can be used for floating point operations. For example, Xilinx Zynq 7020 (XC7Z020) (Rajagopalan, Boppana, Dutta, Taylor, & Wittig, 2011) chip has decent resources of 53,200 LUTs, 106,400 Flip-Flops and 220 DSP units and 560KB BRAMs.

Recently, FPGAs have been used as implementation platforms to accelerate the most computationally intensive image and video processing algorithms. This is because designers can use FPGAs to exploit the spatial and temporal parallelism in image processing algorithms. FPGAs offer outstanding features over the conventional CPUs and GPUs that make them a suitable platform to implement this kind of algorithms such as high computational density, low cost, high data bandwidth and optimization.

2.2. Hardware Design Flow

The series of steps that designers follow to realize system concept on silicon chip is commonly referred to as design flow. The hardware design flow can be divided into four main steps. In the first step, specification of the main algorithm is described at very abstract level. It can also be developed as an executable specification by system-level simulators like MATLAB or OpenCV. This way allows for easy algorithm evaluation and provides reference model for following design steps. Second step involves transforming the system specification into hardware design using one of the hardware description languages (HDL) like VHDL or Verilog. The hardware design accelerates the algorithm by pipelining and running data-independent parts in parallel. In the Third step, synthesis tools receive the HDL code and generates netlist also called (configuration file) based on FPGA vender and model. Most synthesis tools go through additional steps for logic optimization to enhance timing performance and hardware utilization. The last step is placing and routing the synthesized netlist into the FPGAs configurable logics (CLBs), BRAMs and DSPs. Finally, the tool generates bitsream file that can be used to configure the FPGA chip.

2.3. High-Level synthesis (HLS)

High-Level synthesis (HLS), sometimes referred to as synthesis C, is a new step in the design flow of digital circuits that raises the abstraction level for designing digital circuits (Ren, 2014). It generates

RTL designs from a high-level description written in one of the high-level programming language like C, C++ or MATLAB. HLS is a design automation tool aim to raise the level of abstraction in hardware design to simplify the design and verification processes and therefore shorten the design cycle.

HLS tools start with high-level algorithm description and directives to guide the compiler to generate more efficient hardware realization. Then, it will automatically produce circuit specification in HDL that performs the same function as the original algorithm. Modern HLS tools perform several steps to convert an algorithm written in C, C++ or MATLAB into HDL. First, it extracts the data and control flow in the algorithm to determine the operations that need to be performed and its sequence. Second, resource allocation and binding which is the process of determining how many hardware operators are needed and allocate operations into hardware resources. In this step, logical and arithmetic operations are mapped into functional units, variables and signals are mapped into storages, and Data Transfer into Bus/Wire/Mux components. The last step is scheduling which specifies when each operation need to be executed on the allocated hardware.

2.4. OpenCV

OpenCV stands for (Open Source Computer Vision) is a cross-platform image processing library created by intel research center in 1999 (Culjak, Abram, Pribanic, Dzapo, & Cifrek, 2012). It is released under a BSD license and it can be used for free in both academic and commercial use. It's libraries and primary interfaces were originally written in C++, but there are also bindings in Python, Java and MATLAB. It runs on a variety of desktop or mobile platforms. OpenCV covers wide range of application areas include: 2D and 3D feature toolkits, facial recognition, gesture recognition, human–computer interaction, motion understanding and object identification. It also includes a statistical machine learning libraries such as decision tree learning, k-nearest neighbor algorithm, Naive Bayes classifier, artificial neural networks, random forest and support vector machine (SVM).

3. THE ADVANTAGES AND LIMITATIONS OF HLS FOR IMAGE PROCESSING

Implementing Image and video processing algorithms on FPGA using high-level synthesis (HLS) can provide significant benefits over the manual RTL method. However, HLS tools are still lacking some maturity which presents some challenges and limitations in implementing efficient hardware accelerators for complex image processing algorithms (Bailey, 2015). This section discusses the main advantages gained by using HLS to accelerate image processing algorithms and the current limitations that designers need to be aware of when they used HLS.

3.1. Benefits of HLS

One of the most obvious benefits of using HLS over the manual RTL implementation is that HLS tools automatically analyze the structure of the algorithms (loops, branches, etc.) to extract the algorithm data and control flow paths. In the manual RTL implementation, it's the designer responsibility to extract the control and data paths from the algorithm code. This can be done manually, but for complex algorithms, extracting them required large effort and time.

The second benefit of HLS, it makes design space exploration much easier by exploring different combinations of hardware design constraints and optimize the trade-off between hardware resources and processing time. HLS tools also has a profiling tools that identify the processing time for each building block of the algorithm and find the processing bottlenecks. This allows the designer to concentrate more in accelerating these parts of the algorithm.

HLS also provides high level validation process to reduce the time between changing the hardware design and validate the changes. In HLS tools, designers can use C/C++ test benches to verify the functionality of the hardware designs in a convenient way compared to the manual RTL method. It also allows testing the correctness of the generated RTL design using high level testbench of C/RTL co-simulation.

3.2. Limitations of HLS

Even though HLS tools use high level languages to describe the functionality of hardware designs, it still requires to restructure the code to optimize the generated HDL. Each statement in the code should describe hardware element rather than a set of sequential instructions to be executed like a software program. HLS tools can still generate hardware architecture from that code even without restructuring it, but the performance of the generated hardware will be too low.

HLS tools have limitations in realizing hardware for pointers and pointers arithmetic. This is due to couple of reasons related to the FPGA architecture itself. First, on-chip memory in the FPGA is independent and distributed blocks, where each BRAM has its own addressing space. This makes realizing pointers in FPGA very hard. Second, using pointers in the algorithm datapath make it much harder for the tool to extract the data dependencies. HLS tools also face difficulties translating recursion in software to hardware. Recursion occurs when a function or procedure is defined in terms of itself. Now, this is not an issue in software implementation because each function call has a separate space for its variable storage. Unlike in FPGA, functions are implemented as a hardware modules with procedure call multiplexing that hardware for each invocation.

4. HLS OPTIMIZATIONS TECHNIQUES

HLS Tools use several optimization techniques to improve the performance of the generated hardware accelerators. Some of these techniques are borrowed from software compilers while others are specific for hardware architectures (Razvan, et al., 2015). This section briefly discusses the main optimization techniques used in the HLS compilers:

4.1. Operation Chaining

Operation chaining is an important high-level synthesis techniques. It is used to execute two or more operations together in single cycle without generating false path and without using any memory element in between them to store the intermediate results. Consequently, operation chaining reduces the total number of cycles to finish these operations. It also improves the performance and reduce the global number of registers in the generated circuit.

4.2. Bit Width Analysis and Optimization

General purpose processors (CPUs) use fixed sized datapath (usually 32 or 64 bits), even if the algorithm required only 8 bits or 24 bits to process grayscale or colored stream of pixels. Bit width optimization technique selects the minimal number of bits required for every operation and/or storage along the algorithm's datapath. Optimizing the data path's bit width is a very important step that translates into less area, less power and shorter critical paths.

4.3. Memory Space Allocation

This technique aims to efficiently utilize the distributed Block RAMs (BRAMs) in the FPGA. It used to partition and map software data structures onto these memory blocks to perform multiple memory operations in one cycle. Using multiple memory blocks increases the available parallelism and reduce the contention. However, these memory blocks may require creation of an efficient multi bank memory to avoid limiting the system performance.

4.4. Loop Optimizations

Image processing algorithms are known to be algorithms with compute-intensive loops. Loops unrolling and pipelining is a key performance optimization for loops implementations in hardware. It aims to exploits the parallelism between loop iterations by starting the next loop iteration before the completion of its predecessor while it maintains the data dependences between iterations.

4.5. Speculation and Code Motion

If the image processing algorithm that we are trying to implement in hardware is control-intensive, it will be inefficient to extract parallelism only within the same control and data flow graph (CDFG) region. Speculation allows operations to be moved along their execution traces by anticipating them before a head. This lead to high improvement in performance.

4.6. Exploiting Spatial Parallelism

Spatial parallelism provides higher speed than sequential implementation by using multiple hardware units running in parallel to exploit the instruction level parallelism. Image processing algorithm is a best fit for this technique as the potential parallelism is very high.

5. AN OVERVIEW OF HLS TOOLS

During the last two decades, both industry and academia have been closely progressing towards developing efficient tools to automatically generate hardware circuits from high level languages. During this period, number of tools have been implemented. Most of them can be classified into two main categories, namely tools that accept domain-specific languages and tools that are based on general-purpose programmable languages. This section discusses and evaluates the most popular academic and commercial HLS tools and presents its unique features and limitations.

5.1. Domain Specific Languages

The input to this kind of tools is new language invented specially for tool-flow or general-purpose language (e.g. C and C++) extended with directives to provide specific hardware information to the HLS compiler. The following are the most popular tools of this kind:

PipeRench compiler (Goldstein, Schmit, Budiu, & Cadambi, 2000) is particularly suitable for generating reconfigurable hardware pipeline for image and video processing applications or applications that perform a series of simple operations on large set of data elements. The language for this tool is single-assignment language with C operators, while the output is bitsream to configure the hardware pipeline. ROCCC (Villarreal, Park, Najjar, & Halstead, 2010) is another open source compiler that takes a subset of C code and produces efficient hardware accelerators with a competitive performance to the handwritten VHDL designs. The tool designed to focus on the critical regions in the software system like nested loops performing extensive computation on large amount of data. It can optimize the nested loops with fixed stride, operating on integer arrays.

Other domain specific language tools include: Garp (C pragmas) which accept C language and generate optimized hardware for loops (Callahan, Hauser, & Wawrzynek, 2000). Cyberwork which is synthesis, verification and simulation tools intended for system-level design. Bluespec, eXcite (CSP pragmas) and Napa-C (C pragmas) are also tools belong to domain specific language.

5.2. Generic Languages

The generic language tools use high-level languages as an input to describe the circuit functionality like C, C++, C#, Java and SystemC, etc. The following are the most popular tools of this kind: Vivado HLS (Inc., 2016), was initially developed by AutoPilot until it was acquired by Xilinx in 2011. The new release includes a complete design environment with many features to generate, tune and visualize the automation process. The tool accepts C, C++ and SystemC as an input and generate a hardware circuit in VHDL, Verilog and SystemC.

LEGUP (Canis, et al., 2011), is a HLS complier developed by a research group at university of Toronto in 2011. The input to the tool is a C- language program. The tool can be configured to operate in two different ways: it synthesizes the whole C program to a hardware or it synthesizes the program to a hybrid system that consists of a soft-core processor (MIPS and ARM) and one or more hardware accelerators. Other generic language tools include: Kiwi which uses C# programming libraries and its associated synthesis to generate FPGA co-processors in Verilog. The list also includes: DWARV (Nane, et al., 2012) Kiwi, Maxeler, MATCH, SPARK, CtoS, GAUT and ACCelDSP.

6. HLS VIDEO C/C++ LIBRARY

Xilinx Vivado HLS is one of the most popular commercial HLS tool. It includes a video library to generate optimized accelerators for most of the common computer vision/image processing applications on FPGA. The functions in the library uses OpenCV functions as reference model, it has similar interfaces and equivalent behaviors with the corresponding OpenCV functions. The following sections explains the commonly used data structures, interfaces, AXI4-Stream I/O, and video processing functions in the library (Wang, Li, & Stephen, 2013).

6.1. Data Structures

It represents the basic data structures used in image processing algorithms like image, pixel, sliding window and buffer line to store number of pixels. It allows the designer to manage memories more efficiently. It also easy to use and follow the same names as in OpenCV:

1. *hls::Mat*: A template class to represent an image. It has three parameters: the maximum number of rows and the maximum number of columns in an image and the pixel data type.
2. *hls::Scalar*: A template class to represent a pixel. It has two parameters: number of channels in a pixel and the data type of each channel.
3. *hls::Window*: A template class to represent 2D window buffer. It has three parameters to specify the number of rows and columns in the window buffer and the pixel data type.
4. *hls::LineBuffer*: A template class to represent 2D line buffer. It has also three parameters to specify the number of rows and columns in the line buffer and the pixel data type.

6.2. Interface Functions

Typically, the video systems are divided into two parts: the low complexity part running on the processor and the high computational complexity accelerated in the FPGA fabric. The interface functions are used to transfer data between the two parts efficiently.

1. **IplImage2AXIvideo:** Converts data from OpenCV IplImage format to AXI video stream. The function has two parameters: IplImage image and hls::stream port. The image data must be stored in the image and the AXI stream should be empty before calling this function.
2. **AXIvideo2IplImage**: Converts data from AXI video stream format to OpenCV IplImage. This function consumes the image data stored in AXI video stream and store them in IplImage image.
3. **cvMat2AXIvideo:** Converts data from OpenCV Mat format to AXI video stream format. The input to this function is an image in OpenCV cv::Mat format, and the output is AXI video stream, compatible with AXI4-Stream protocol.
4. **AXIvideo2cvMat:** Converts data from AXI video stream format to OpenCV Mat format. This function is similar to AXIvideo2IplImage but the image data will be stored in Mat format instead of IplImage images.
5. **IplImage2hlsMat:** Converts data from OpenCV IplImage format to hls::Mat format. The image size and number of channels of the Mat and IplImage must be the same.
6. **hlsMat2IplImage**: Converts data from hls::Mat format to OpenCV IplImage format.
7. **cvMat2hlsMat:** Converts data from OpenCV cv::Mat format to hls::Mat format.
8. **hlsMat2cvMat:** Converts data from hls::Mat format to OpenCV cv::Mat format.
9. **CvMat2hlsWindow:** Converts data from OpenCV CvMat format to hls::Windowformat. The function has one input: a 2D window pointer to OpenCV CvMat format, and it generates an output 2D window in hls::Window format.

10. **hlsWindow2CvMat:** Converts data from hls::Window format to OpenCV CvMat format. This function convert image kernels, but both of them should have a single-channel with the same size each.

6.3. Stream I/O Functions

The I/O functions are used to convert hls::Mat to/from AXI4-Stream data type (hls::stream). These functions are synthesizable and should be invoked inside the hardware functions.

1. **hls::AXIvideo2Mat:** Converts image data stored in hls::Mat format to an AXI4 video stream (hls::stream) format. Calling this function will consume the data exists in the AXI video stream channel and fill the image data in a Mat data structure.
2. **hls::Mat2AXIvideo:** Converts image in AXI4 video stream format to hls::Mat format. This function reverses the process done by AXIideo2Mat function. It consumes the data in mat, and filling them into AXI video stream.

6.4. Video Processing Functions

The list of image processing functions supported by Vivado HLS has similar names and functionally as the corresponding OpenCV functions:

1. **hls::CornerHarris**: Implements Harris corner detection algorithm. The size of filter can be specified to compute the horizontal and vertical derivatives.
2. **hls::CvtColor:** It is used to Converts a color image from/to a grayscale image. the number of channels in the source and distention images should be the same.
3. **hls::Dilate:** This function processes each channel of image source independently to compute the image dilation. The src and dst images must have the same size and number of channels.
4. **hls::Duplicate**: It copies the source input image to two output images dst1 and dst2, it is usually used to create two identical data paths.
5. **hls::EqualizeHist**: Compute a histogram of each frame, it has the same functionality as the OpenCV function cv::EqualizeHist.
6. **hls::Erode:** This function erodes the source image using specified structuring element constructed within kernel, and store the results in the destination image.
7. **hls::FASTX**: Implements the FAST corner detector algorithm. It has similar functionality as the OpenCV function cv::FAST.
8. **hls::Filter2D:** This function applies a linear filter to the source image by computing the correlation using a specified kernel.
9. **hls::GaussianBlur**: This function applies a normalized 2D Gaussian filter to the source image. It has two parameters to specify the kernel width and height.
10. **hls::HoughLines2**: Implements the Hough line transform.
11. **hls::Integral:** This function compute the integral image from the source image.
12. **hls::InitUndistortRectifyMap**: computes the map1 and map2 based on the camera matrix and the distortion parameters. The output of this function is suitable for hls::Remap.

13. **hls::PaintMask:** This function is used to mask pixels from the source image with a new value which is either zero or specified color.
14. **hls::Remap:** This function is used to apply image transformation to the source image by remapping each pixel in the source image to its corresponding pixel location in the destination.
15. **hls::Reduce:** It reduces the input image to a vector. The output could be the sum of all the matrix's rows/columns or the mean, maximum or minimum.
16. **hls::Resize:** Resize the input image to the size of the output image using down sampling or bilinear interpolation.
17. **hls::Scale:** Converts an input image with linear transformation.
18. **hls::Sobel:** Computes a horizontal or vertical Sobel filter, to estimate the horizontal or vertical derivative.
19. **hls::Threshold:** this function perform a thresholding algorithm to each element in a single channel image. It implements the following thresholding types: BINARY, BINARY_INV, TRUNC, TOZERO and TOZERO_INV.
20. **hls:Mean:** It calculates the average of all elements in the src image src, and return it as scalar.

Xilinx Vivado HLS tools is part of Vivado Design Suit tools. Xilinx website offers multiple choices for download and installation. Starting in 2015.1, Xilinx introduced Vivado Lab edition, which provides designers an environment for programming, validating and debugging designs in progress. Two choices to install Vivado full edition: Sigle file full product installer, and lightweight installer, which is a web-based installer that reduce the download size and speed-up the download process. The user can customize their installation by selecting, downloading and installing only the components needed for your design. A detailed download, installation, and licensing steps can be found in the user's guide files supported by Xilinx (Xilinx, 2017).

7. CASE STUDIES

Many image and video processing algorithms have been already implemented in hardware using HLS tools to accelerate its computation to reach real time performance. This section presents the HLS design process for four commonly used algorithms, namely, Harris corner detection, Sobel edge detection, optical flow and stereo matching. First, the algorithm's C++ code and its directives are presented. Then, the optimizations techniques used to convert the high-level description to HDL language are explained. Finally, the timing performance and hardware utilization of the generated circuit are evaluated and compared to the recent FPGA implementations in literature.

7.1. Harris Corner and Edge Detection

Harris corner detector is a well-established interest point detection algorithm proposed in 1988 by C. Harris and M. Stephens (Chris & Stephens, 1988). The algorithm extracts regions in the input image that have large intensity variation in all directions. It uses local auto correlation function that measures the changes in the pixel intensities when a small patch shifted in all different directions. Figure 1 shows an example of the detected corners in ISU clock tower image.

Figure 1. Harris Corner Detection Algorithm

The processing time of Harris corner detection algorithm running on convectional CPU is not adequate to reach real time performance 33fps. To accelerate the algorithm in FPGA, we will use HLS instead of the manual VHDL method to speed up the design process. Xilinx has implemented the algorithm in their HLS video library. Figure 2 shows the source code and block diagram of the HLS implementation.

The process starts with duplicating the input data stream (_src) into two copies (gray1 and gray2) to compute Sobel filter in the vertical and horizontal directions. The two filtering blocks (Sobel1 and Sobel2), shown in Figure 2, generates the 2-D spatial gradient and send the results to *grad_x* and *grad_y*. The data streams need to be duplicated to compute the square value of *grad_xx*, *grad_yy* and *grad_xy* using three multipliers. Then, three BoxFilters with normalize kernel are used to normalize the data streams. Finally, *CalCim* function is used to compute the corner response value using constant K and the different intensity images.

Using Vivado HLS, the VHDL code can be generated from the C++ code shown in Figure 2. In (Henrik, 2015), they used Zynq-7020 FPGA to implement Harris detector with 5 different HLS directives: (a) Harris and Gaussian filter with dataflow directive, to force the HLS compiler to do dataflow optimization (32-bit float input). (b) Harris and Gaussian filter without dataflow directive with 32-bit float input (c) Harris with dataflow directive (32-bit float input) (d) Harris only (32-bit float input), and

Figure 2. HLS Implementation for Harris Corner Detector

```
Duplicate(_src,gray1,gray2);
Sobel<1,0,Ksize,BORDERMODEL>(gray1,grad_x);
Duplicate(grad_x,grad_x1,grad_x2);
Duplicate(grad_x1,grad_x3,grad_x4);
Sobel<0,1,Ksize,BORDERMODEL>(gray2,grad_y);
Duplicate(grad_y,grad_y1,grad_y2);
Duplicate(grad_y1,grad_y3,grad_y4);
Mul(grad_x3,grad_x4,grad_xx);
Mul(grad_y3,grad_y4,grad_yy);
Mul(grad_x2,grad_y2,grad_xy);
BoxFilter<blockSize,blockSize,NORMALIZE,BORDERMODEL>(grad_xx,grad_gx);
BoxFilter<blockSize,blockSize,NORMALIZE,BORDERMODEL>(grad_yy,grad_gy);
BoxFilter<blockSize,blockSize,NORMALIZE,BORDERMODEL>(grad_xy,grad_gxy);
CalCim(grad_gx,grad_gy,grad_gxy,_dst,k, scale);
```

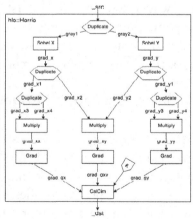

(e) Harris and Gaussian blur with dataflow directive (8-bit input). Table 1 shows the estimated resource usage of Block RAM units, DSPs, Flip-Flops and Look-Up Tables for the five different implementations.

7.2. Sobel Edge Detection

Sobel filter sometimes called the Sobel–Feldman operator is an edge detection algorithm used to find the object's boundaries in images. Sobel proposed the idea of Sobel filter at a talk at SAIL in 1968 (Irwin, 2014). The algorithm convolves the original image with two 3×3 kernels to calculate an approximation of the discontinuities in brightness. Figure 3 shows an example of the detected edges after applying Sobel filter on the left image.

The C++ implementation of Sobel edge detection algorithm is shown in Figure 4 (a). It consists of two 3×3 convolution kernels that are applied in both the x and y directions. The two loops at Lines 10 and 11 scans the whole image and apply the kernel to generate the output pixel. The computation of each kernel is independent of all other kernels, that makes Sobel algorithm highly parallelizable. To implement high-performance Sobel edge-detector on FPGA, we will use HLS to accelerate the execution of the original code. Figure 4 (b) shows the HLS code after replacing the un-synthesizable parts from the original code, like *IplImage* pointers in line 4 have been replaced with a fixed-sized array. The references to the height and width in lines 10 and 11 need to be replaced with constants too. In line 2 and 3 directives have been added to specify the memory access pattern and change it from random access array to FIFO. The FIFOs is suitable for most image processing algorithm because it provides streaming input/output data to and from the hardware accelerator.

Table 1. Resource usage of the different Harris design Options

	BRAM 18K	DSP48E	Flip-Flops	LUT
Harris Detector Design (a)	79 (28%)	67 (30%)	67 (30%)	67 (30%)
Harris Detector Design (b)	112 (40%)	341 (155%)	70224 (66%)	137788 (259%)
Harris Detector Design (c)	90 (32%)	266 (121%)	37054 (35%)	75012 (141%)
Harris Detector Design (d)	59 (21%)	196 (89%)	36176 (34%)	77672 (146%)
Harris Detector Design (e)	40 (14%)	122 (55%)	18611 (17%)	32012 (60%)
Zynq-7020 Resources	280	220	106400	53200

Figure 3. Sobel Edge Detection Algorithm

Figure 4. (a) Original C++ Code (b) Synthesizable Code Version

```
int dx [3] [3] = {{1,0,-1} , { 2,0,-2 } ,{ 1 ,0 ,-1 }} ;
int dy [3] [3] = {{1,2, 1 } , { 0,0, 0 } ,{ -1,-2,-1 }} ;
void Sobel ( IplImage * img , IplImage * dst ) {
int step = img-> widthStep / sizeof(uchar) ;
uchar * data = (uchar *) img-> imageData ;
uchar * data dst = (uchar *) dst-> imageData ;
int s ;
for (int i = 1; i < img-> height -1; i++)
for (int j = 1; j < img-> width -1; j++) {
// apply kernel in X and Y direction
int sum_x = 0 ; int sum_y = 0 ;
for (int m =-1; m<=1; m++)
for (int n =-1; n <=1; n ++) {
// get the ( i , j ) pixel value
s = data [ ( i + m) * step + j +n ] ;
sum_x += s * dx [m+ 1 ] [ n + 1 ] ;
sum_y += s * dy [m+ 1 ] [ n + 1 ] ;
}
int sum= abs ( sum_x ) + abs ( sum_y ) ;
// set the ( i , j ) pixel value
data dst [ i * step + j ] = ( sum >255 ) ?255 :sum ;
}
}
```

```
void Sobel (uchar src [ROWS][COLS] ,uchar dst [ROWS-2][COLS-2])
{
#pragma HLS INTERFACE apfifo port = src
#pragma HLS INTERFACE apfifo port = dst
uchar linebuffer [4] [COLS] ;
for ( int i = 0 ; i <3; i ++) {
for ( int j = 0 ; j < COLS ; j ++){
linebuffer [i][j] = src [i][j] ; })
uchar s ;
for ( int i = 1 ; i < ROWS -1; i ++) {
if ( i < ROWS -2)
linebuffer [(i+2) %4 ] [0] = src [i+2] [0] ;
for ( int j = 1 ; j < COLS-1; j ++) {
int sum x = 0 ; int sum y = 0 ;
if ( i < ROWS -2)
linebuffer [ ( i+2 ) %4 ] [j] = src [i+2] [j] ;
for ( int m=-1; m<=1; m++)
for ( int n=-1; n <=1; n ++) {
s = linebuffer [ ((i+m) %4) ] [j+n ] ;
sum x +=(int) s * dx [m+1] [n+1] ;
sum y +=(int) s * dy [m+1] [n+1] ;
}
int sum= ABS( sum x ) + ABS( sum y ) ;
s =( sum >255)? 255 :sum ;
dst [i-1][j-1]= s ;
}
if(i < ROWS -2)
linebuffer[(i + 2)%4] [COLS-1]= src [i+2][COLS-1];
}
}
```

In image processing systems, I/O interfaces typically puts the upper bound on the system performance. For this example, let us assume the input camera streams 1 pixel/cycle at 150 MHz (the maximum clock rate on Zynq). If the input image is 640×480 pixels, the maximum throughput of such a system would be 488 frames per second (FPS). Using Vivado HLS to synthesize the code shown in Figure4 (b) with its default synthesis behaviors, the generated Sobel accelerator Optimal performance was 42 cycles/pixels with clock rate of 150 MHz. Table 2, summarizes the performance of the pure software implementation and the hardware implementation using HLS. The results below are based on the work done by (Monson & Wirthlin, 2013).

7.3. Optical Flow HLS

Optical flow algorithm estimates the displacement and speed of the features pixels between successive frames in videos to create flow field. It detects the apparent motion of moving objects, so objects closer to the camera will display more motion than objects far from the camera even if they are moving at the same speed. It has many important applications in video processing such as object tracking, video stabilization and image segmentation, etc. Figure 5 shows the estimated optical flow of a moving car between successive frames and the pixel's velocities of objects.

Table 2. Performance evaluation

Version	Cycles/Pixel	Cycle Latency	Frequency	FPS
Theoretical Max	1	307,200	150 MHz	488
Software	N/A	N/A	N/A	38.75
HLS	42	13,726,264	150 MHz	204.4

Figure 5. Optical flow estimation to obtain motion vectors and pixel velocity magnitudes. (Mathwork, n. d.)

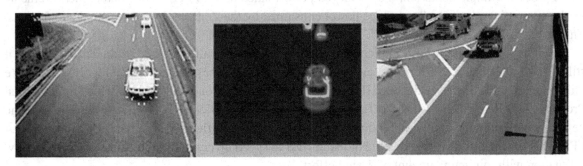

Many optical flow algorithms have been proposed in literature. Lucas-Kanade algorithm (LK-OF) is one of the most commonly used algorithms. It has three major computational steps: pyramid creation, calculate gradients and feature tracking. In the first step, the previous and next frame were filtered using Gaussian smoothing kernel and down sampled by removing the odd rows and columns to build two image pyramids. The second step process each level of the pyramids to compute the horizontal and vertical gradient pyramid using Scharr kernel. Harris corner detector is used in the third step to detect features in each image and track these points between the two successive frames. LK-OF algorithm has high computational steps and it's hard to reach real-time performance using pure software implementation without scrifying the accuracy.

To estimate the performance of LK-OF algorithm, the work in (Monson & Wirthlin, 2013) used images with 720×480 resolution and 15×15 integration windows to track around 350-400 features between frames. They implemented the pyramid creation and Scharr filtering parts on FPGA and achieved an estimated speed-up of 3.9× and 5.6× respectively. The feature tracking part takes up 67.3% of the algorithm execution time on the ARM. They implemented three versions of the algorithm: first, the original code was used after removing the dynamic memory allocation and recursive functions calls. In the second design applied dataflow directive to make use of the parallel nature of FPGAs. Finally, they restructured the code by splitting up the main loop in two different parts. Table 3 shows the clock frequency and FPGA resource usage of the baseline design and the other two design versions.

They were able to reach performance of 80 frames per second (FPS) using desktop system with all its four i7 CPU cores. Their implementation used input image with 720x480 pixels, 15x15 integration windows, and the number of tracked features around 350-400 features. This frame rate allows the optical flow algorithm to process images in real time. Even though this implementation runs the algorithm in real-time, it requires relatively large amount of power and a complex system infrastructure. This makes it not suitable for embedded systems with low power budget and less powerful CPUs. Using HLS and

Table 3. Resource utilization of the Optical flow algorithm

Version	LUTS	FF	DSPs	BRAMs	Latency (cycles)	Clock Rate
Baseline	22,647 (42.6%)	16171 (15.2%)	110 (50.0%)	23 (8.2%)	5,171,563	95 MHz
dataflow	34,007 (63.9%)	32844 (30.9%)	196 (89.1%)	201 (71%)	2,590,972	100 MHz
Scharr	37,266 (70.0%)	33601 (31.6%)	194 (88.2%)	185 (66%)	2,518,141	100 MHz
Max. clock	37,055 (69.7%)	33,626 (31%)	194 (88.2%)	185 (66%)	2,538,290	110 MHz

ARM processor implementation, they achieved performance of 41.8 FPS. Using actual measurements on the computing platform, the average power consumed by the ZedBoard was measured at 6.5 Watts. This is 19×less power than the core i7.

Even though the FPGA HLS implementation achieved about half the speed of the i7 CPU cores, it still a good real-time result for most embedded system applications. Based on the reported hardware utilization in Table 3, we see that the HLS implementation used around 88% of available Digital Signal Processors (DSPs), 70% of Look-Up Tables (LUTs) and 66% of Block RAMs (BRAMs). The baseline design, where minimal amount of coding was applied, used significantly less, but only achieved 18.4 FPS. This shows the powerful potential of using HLS to speed up complex algorithms like optical flow estimation with minimum amount of design effort.

7.4. Stereo Matching HLS

Stereo vision is the process of extracting 3D information from digital images taken by two cameras displaced horizontally from one another to obtain two different views of the same scene. This process mimics the human binocular vision where our brain uses the two pictures from the left and right eyes to provide a feeling of depth, it's called sometimes stereopsis.

Epipolar geometry is the geometry behind stereo vision that describes the relations between the 3D points in the scene with their projections onto the 2D planes. The main idea of stereo matching is to locate the same projected 3D point in both image planes. It measures the displacement (disparity) between corresponding points in an object between two images captured by stereo camera system. Disparity represent the distance in pixels between an object in one image and the same point in the second image. The distance in pixels inversely proportional to the distance between the object and the camera. Figure 6 shows the concept of 3D point projection and stereo matching between two images.

Number of HLS implementations have been proposed in literature aiming to speed up the process of stereo matching and reach high disparity value. In (Yun et al., 2012), the authors used older version of Vivado HLS (AutoPilot) to implement five different stereo matching algorithms on a Xilinx Virtex 6 LX240T. The algorithms were: Constant Space Belief Propagation (CSBP), Bilateral Filtering with

Figure 6. Epipolar Geometry (Wikipedia, n. d.)

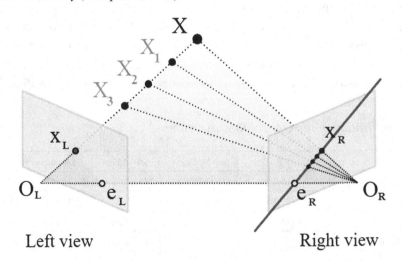

Left view   Right view

Adaptive Support Function (BFAS), Scanline Optimization with occlusion (SO), Scanline Optimization without occlusion (SO w/o Occ) and Cross-based Local Matching (CLM).

They started with HLS baseline design for each of these algorithms and start optimizing it using different techniques. First, they restructured the code and add compiler directives. One of the most important restricting was dividing the image in to different parts and operate on all parts simultaneously. They exploit the fact that the algorithms are inherently row-centralized so that each row in the image can be processed individually. The second optimization was reducing bit-width and memory usage by using variable precision and merging arrays to use less BRAMs. The third optimization was applying loop optimizations and pipelining the algorithms steps. They exploited the fact that static loops can be flatten, unrolled and pipelined to translate it into hardware and accelerate the execution. In the last technique, they used any remaining unused resources to parallelize the code by resource duplication. They duplicated parts of the computation pipelines to double the execution speed.

When they synthesized the initial baseline designs into hardware, the resource usage was extremely high, and only the Scanline Optimization (SO) algorithm resources would actually fit on the FPGA. This is because no hardware optimizations had been applied to the design. The code restructuring optimization decreases the resource usage drastically. Every other optimization then successively decrease resource usage, while increasing the algorithm performance. The performance increased with small amount in the first three optimizations compare to resource duplication technique. The parallelization speeds-up the performance between 3.5× and 67.9× over the software version. Figure 7 shows the speedup and resource usage of the five algorithms with four different design optimizations. It can also be seen that the (SO w/o Occ) algorithm achieved the highest speed-up with 65× compared to the software version, while the other algorithms were under 20×.

8. FUTURE WORK AND OPEN RESEARCH PROBLEMS

The long-term vision of HLS is to provide a non-hardware engineers an efficient way to port their algorithms into hardware to gain the hardware's speed and energy benefits. There has been a good progress

Figure 7. Resource usage (left y-axis) and speedup (right y-axis) for the 4 stages of each of the five-different stereo matching algorithms. This Figure copied from the work in (Yun, et al., 2012)

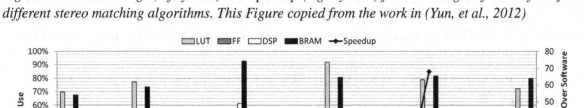

in recent years in terms of the quality of the circuits generated by HLS. A lot of research efforts are now focusing on the developing and improving the optimization techniques to generate a more efficient hardware. This chapter could have two future directions. First, analyze the circuits generated by HLS for more image and video processing algorithms. Also, it could look for cases where HLS fails to transform algorithm into efficient hardware circuits. Second, dig deeper into the recent research progress in the optimization technique and compare their performance in different image processing algorithm.

9. CONCLUSION

High level synthesis (HLS) extends the traditional hardware design flow, by introducing new and powerful approach. It accelerates the hardware design process and verification by raising the abstraction level from low level RTL into one of the high-level programming languages. It transforms the high-level algorithmic description into digital hardware while satisfying the design constraints. Many HLS tools have already been released as commercial tools and it starts to gain popularity within the embedded systems designers. The performance of academic and commercial HLS tools is not drastically far apart from each other in terms of the quality of the generated hardware and ease to use. This chapter introduced the fundamentals concepts of HLS and how it can be used to bridges the gap between the ability of realizing efficient accelerators in hardware and the tight performance requirements of the complex image processing algorithms.

REFERENCES

Bailey, D. (2015). The advantages and limitations of high level synthesis for FPGA based image processing. *Proceedings of the 9th International Conference on Distributed Smart Cameras (ICDSC '15)* (pp. 134-139). doi:10.1145/2789116.2789145

Callahan, T., Hauser, J., & Wawrzynek, J. (2000). The Garp architecture and C compiler. *Computer, 33*(4), 62-69.

Canis, A., Choi, J., Aldham, M., Zhang, V., Kammoona, A., Anderson, J., & Czajkowski, T. et al. (2011). LegUp: high-level synthesis for FPGA-based processor/accelerator systems. *Proceedings of the 19th ACM/SIGDA international symposium on Field programmable gate arrays* (pp. 33-36). doi:10.1145/1950413.1950423

Chris, H., & Stephens, M. (1988). A combined corner and edge detector. *Proceedings of the Alvey vision conference.*

Culjak, I., Abram, D., Pribanic, T., Dzapo, H., & Cifrek, M. (2012). A brief introduction to OpenCV. *Proceedings of the 2012 35th International Convention MIPRO* (pp. 1725-1730). Opatija.

Goldstein, S., Schmit, H., Budiu, M., & Cadambi, S. (2000). PipeRench: a reconfigurable architecture and compiler. *Computer, 33*(4), 70-77.

Henrik, J. (2015). *Evaluating Vivado High-Level Synthesis on OpenCV Functions for the Zynq-7000 FPGA.*

Ian, K., Tessier, R., & Rose, J. (2008). FPGA architecture: Survey and challenges. *Foundations and Trends in Electronic Design Automation, 2*(2), 135–253.

Inc., X. (2016, October 18). *Vivado Design Suite - VivadoHLS*. Retrieved from http://www.xilinx.com/products/design-tools/vivado/index.htm

Irwin, S. (2014). *History and definition of the sobel operator*. Retrieved from the World Wide Web.

Mathwork. (n.d.). *optical-flow*. Retrieved March 1, 2017, from https://www.mathworks.com/discovery/optical-flow.html

Monson, J., & Wirthlin, M. (2013). Optimization techniques for a high level synthesis implementation of the sobel filter. *Proceedings of the International Conference on Reconfigurable Computing and FPGAs (ReConFig)* (pp. 1-6). doi:10.1109/ReConFig.2013.6732315

Monson, J., & Wirthlin, M. (2013). Implementing high-performance, low-power FPGA-based optical flow accelerators in C. *Proceedings of the IEEE 24th International Conference on Application-Specific Systems, Architectures and Processors* (pp. 363-369).

Nane, R., Sima, V., Olivier, B., Meeuws, R., Yankova, Y., & Bertels, K. (2012). DWARV 2.0: A CoSy-based C-to-VHDL hardware compiler. *Proceedings of the 22nd International Conference on Field Programmable Logic and Applications (FPL)* (pp. 619-622). doi:10.1109/FPL.2012.6339221

Rajagopalan, V., Boppana, V., Dutta, S., Taylor, B., & Wittig, R. (2011). Xilinx zynq-7000 epp: An extensible processing platform family. *Proceedings of the Hot Chips 23 Symposium (HCS)*.

Razvan, N., Sima, V.-M., Pilato, C., Fort, B., Choi, J., Chen, Y., & Canis, A. (2015). A Survey and Evaluation of FPGA High-Level Synthesis Tools. *IEEE Transactions on Computer-Aided Design of Integrated Circuits and Systems, 35*(10), 1591–1604.

Ren, H. (2014). A brief introduction on contemporary High-Level Synthesis. *Proceedings of the 2014 IEEE International Conference on IC Design & Technology*, Austin, TX. doi:10.1109/ICICDT.2014.6838614

Trimberger, S. (2015). Three Ages of FPGAs: A Retrospective on the First Thirty Years of FPGA Technology. *Proceedings of the IEEE, 103*(3), 318–331. doi:10.1109/JPROC.2015.2392104

Villarreal, J., Park, A., Najjar, W., & Halstead, R. (2010). Designing Modular Hardware Accelerators in C with ROCCC 2.0. In *Field-Programmable Custom Computing Machines (FCCM)*, 127-134.

Wang, D., Li, T., & Stephen, N. (2013). *Accelerating OpenCV Applications with Zynq-7000 All Programmable SoC using Vivado HLS Video Libraries*. Xilinx Inc.

Wikipedia. (n.d.). *Epipolar geometry and epipolar line*. Retrieved March 1, 2017, from http://en.wikipedia.org/wiki/

Xilinx. (2017, November 30). *Xilinx*. Retrieved from Vivado Design Suite (Release Notes, Installation). Retrieved from https://www.xilinx.com/support/documentation/sw_manuals/xilinx2016_4/ug973-vivado-release-notes-install-license.pdf

Yun, L., Rupnow, K., Li, Y., Min, D., Do, M., & Chen, D. (2012). High-level synthesis: Productivity, performance, and software constraints. *Journal of Electrical and Computer Engineering*.

KEY TERMS AND DEFINITIONS

DSPs: (Digital signal processor) is a specialized microprocessor architecture optimized for the operational needs of digital signal processing like voice and image processing algorithms.

FPGA: (Fields programmable gate array) is reconfigurable integrated circuits (IC) that can be reprogrammed after manufacturing. It consists of large matrix of configurable logics connected using switching blocks.

GPU: (Graphics Processing Unit) is a specialized integrated circuit designed thousands of small and efficient cores to handle multiple tasks simultaneously.

HLS: (High Level Synthesis) is a new design automation method that generates RTL designs from a description written in one of the high-level programming language like C, C++ or MATLAB.

OpenCV: (Open Source Computer Vision) is a cross-platform image processing library created by intel. It covers wide range of application areas in image and video processing.

Optical Flow: Is an algorithm that estimates the displacement and speed of the features pixels between successive frames in videos to create flow field.

RTL: (Register Transfer Level) is a design method that models digital circuits in terms of the flow of data between hardware registers.

Stereo Vision: Is the process of extracting 3D information from digital images taken by two cameras displaced horizontally from one another to obtain two different views of the same scene.

Verilog: Is a hardware description language (HDL) used to design and model electronic circuits. It is the most commonly used language for designing digital circuits at the RTL level.

VHDL: (VHSIC Hardware Description Language) is a hardware description language used to design hardware circuits.

Chapter 16
Recent Advances in Feature Extraction and Description Algorithms:
Hardware Designs and Algorithmic Derivatives

Ehab Najeh Salahat
Australian National University, Australia

Murad Qasaimeh
Iowa State University, USA

ABSTRACT

Computer vision is one of the most active research fields in technology today. Giving machines the ability to see and comprehend the world at the speed of sight creates endless applications and opportunities. Feature detection and description algorithms are considered as the retina for machine vision. However, most of these algorithms are typically computationally intensive, which prevents them from achieving real-time performance. As such, embedded vision accelerators (FPGA, ASIC, etc.) can be targeted due to their inherent parallelizability. This chapter provides a comprehensive study on some of the recent feature detection and description algorithms and their hardware solutions. Specifically, it begins with a synopsis on basic concepts followed by a comparative study, from which the maximally stable extremal regions (MSER) and the scale invariant feature transform (SIFT) algorithms are selected for further analysis due to their robust performance. The chapter then reports some of their recent algorithmic derivatives and highlights their recent hardware designs and architectures.

1. INTRODUCTION

Features analysis (e.g. extraction, and description) in static and dynamic environments is an active area of research, particularly in the robotics and computer vision research communities. It is primarily aiming towards object detection, recognition and tracking from a stream of frames and to describe the semantics from the object's behavior (Hu, Tan, Wang, & Maybank, 2004). It has also a wide spectrum of promising

DOI: 10.4018/978-1-5225-2848-7.ch016

applications, both governmental and commercial (which include, but are not limited to, access control to sensitive areas, population and crowd flux statistics, human detection and recognition, traffic analysis, detection of anomalous behaviors, vehicular tracking, drones, detection of military targets, etc.).

Given the remarkable increase in the amount of homogenous and inhomogeneous visual inputs (which is partly due to (1) the availability of cheap capturing devices such as the built-in cameras in smartphones, and (2) the availability of free image hosting websites and servers, the need for novel, robust, and automated features analysis algorithms and platforms that adapt to the application's needs and requirements are of paramount importance. The current research tends to merge multiple disciplines such as digital signal/image processing, pattern recognition and classification, machine learning, circuit design and so on.

Moreover, as it is the case with many computer vision applications, there is a need for high performance algorithms and processing platforms that are capable of supporting real-time applications. The required intensive computations (e.g. real-time feature detection and extraction from high-definition video stream or with high-resolution satellite imagery applications) also need massive processing capabilities. Digital Signal Processors (DSPs), Field Programmable Gate Arrays (FPGAs), Application-Specific Integrated Circuits (ASIC), System-on-Chip (SoC), and Graphic Processing Units (GPUs) platforms with smarter, parallelizable, and pipelinable hardware processing designs could be targeted to alleviate this issue. However, hardware-constrains (e.g. memory, power, scalability, format interfacing, etc.), constitute a major bottleneck. The typical solution to these hardware-related issues is to scale down the resolution or to sacrifice (tradeoff) the accuracy and performance of the application. Moreover, the state-of-the-art in computer vision has also confirmed that it is the processing algorithms that will make a substantial contribution to resolve these issues (Liu, Chen, & Naoyuki Kubota, 2013) (Wang, Tao, Di, Ye, & Shi, 2012). That is, processing algorithms might be targeted to overcome most of those issues associated with the power- and memory-thirsty hardware requirements, and might yield breakthroughs (Ngo, Ives, Rakvic, & Broussard, 2013). The challenge now is, however, to devise, implement and deploy these new (enhanced) algorithms, that mainly fall in the feature detection and description category, which are the fundamental tools for many visual computations applications.

To ensure the robustness of vision algorithms, an essential prerequisite is to be designed to cover a wide range of possible scenarios with a high-level of repeatability and affinity. Ultimately, studying all of the possible scenarios is virtually impossible, yet a clear understanding of all these variables is critical for a successful design. Key factors influencing real-time performance include the processing platform (and the associated constrains on memory, power and frequency in FPGAs, SoCs, GPUs, etc., that may result in algorithmic changes that can impact the performance), monitored environment (illuminations, reflections, shadows, view orientation and angle), and applications of interest (targets of interest, tolerable miss detection/false alarm rates and the desired tradeoffs, and allowed latency). Consequently, a careful study and analysis of potential computer vision algorithms is essential.

To circumvent on these issues, this chapter is dedicated to present a study of recent advances on feature detection and description algorithms. Specifically, the chapter starts by overviewing fundamental concepts while providing highlights on the performance comparison of some of the recent and renown algorithms. Based on the result of the presented study, the chapter then focuses more on two algorithms, namely the Maximally Stable Extremal Regions (MSER) and the Scale-Invariant Feature Transform (SIFT) algorithms. These algorithms are known to be two of the best algorithms of their category and have many algorithmic derivatives that are also covered briefly. In addition, recent hardware designs and architectures for the two algorithms, which are tailored for robust and accurate real-time performance, are discussed and compared with the state-of-the-art.

2. BACKGROUND

2.1. Local features: A Synopsis

A local image feature (a.k.a. interest point, key point, and salient feature) is defined as a specific image pattern which differs from its immediate neighborhood and is generally associated with one or more of image properties (Tuytelaars & Mikolajczyk, 2008) (Li, Wang, Tian, & Ding, 2015). Such properties include edges, corners, regions, etc. Figure 1 represents a summary of such local features. Indeed, these local features represent essential anchor points that can summarize the content of the frame (with the aid of feature descriptors) while searching an image/video. Local features are then converted into numerical descriptors, representing unique and compact summarization of these local features.

Descriptive and invariant local features provide a powerful tool that can be used in a wide range of computer vision and robotics applications, such as real-time visual surveillance, image retrieval, video mining, target detection, object tracking, mosaicking, and wide baseline matching to name few (Krig, 2014). To illustrate on the usefulness of such local features, consider the following example. Given an aerial image, a detected edge can represent a street, corners may be street junctions, and homogenous regions can represent cars, roundabouts or buildings (of course, this is resolution dependent).

The term detector (or extractor) traditionally refers to the algorithm or technique that detects (or extracts) these local features and prepare them to be passed to another processing stage that describe their contents, i.e. a feature descriptor. That is, feature extraction plays the role of an intermediate image processing stage between different vision algorithms. In this work, the terms detector and extractor are interchangeably used.

2.2. Ideal Local Features

A local feature typically has a spatial extent which is due to its local neighborhood of pixels. That is, they represent a subset of the frame that is semantically meaningful, e.g. correspond to an object (or a part of an object). Ultimately, it is infeasible to localize all such features as this will require the prerequisite

Figure 1. Illustrative image local features – (a) input image, (b) corners, (c) edges and (d) regions

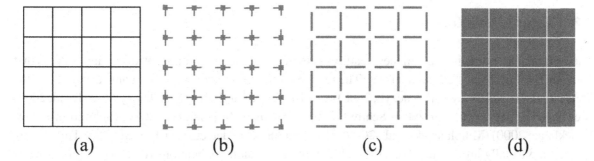

of high-level frame (scene) understanding (Tuytelaars & Mikolajczyk, 2008). As such, those features detection algorithms tries to locate these features directly based on the intensity patterns in the input frame. The selection of these local features can indeed greatly impact the overall system performance (Li, Wang, Tian, & Ding, 2015). Ideal features (and hence feature detectors) should have the following important qualities (Tuytelaars & Mikolajczyk, 2008) (Awad & Hassaballah, 2016):

1. **Distinctiveness:** The intensity patterns underlying the detected features should be rich in variations that can be used for distinguishing features and matching them.
2. **Locality:** Features should be local so as to reduce the chances of getting occluded and to allow simple estimation of geometric as well as photometric deformations between two frames with different views.
3. **Quantity:** The total number of detected features (i.e. features density) should be sufficiently (and not excessively) large to reflect the frame's content in a compact form.
4. **Accuracy:** Features detected should be localized accurately with respect to different scales, shapes and pixels' locations in a frame.
5. **Efficiency:** Features should be detected in a time-efficient manner that makes them suitable for real-time (i.e. time-critical) applications.
6. **Repeatability:** Given two frames of the same object (or scene) with different viewing conditions, a high percentage of the detected features from the overlapped visible part should be found in both frames. Repeatability is greatly affected by the following two qualities.
7. **Invariance:** In scenarios where large deformation is expected (scale, rotation, etc.), the detector algorithm should model this deformation mathematically as precisely as possible so that it minimizes its effect on the extracted features.
8. **Robustness:** In scenarios where small deformation is expected (noise, blur, discretization effects, compression artifacts, etc.), it is often sufficient to make detection algorithms less sensitive to such deformations (i.e. no drastic decrease in the accuracy).

Intuitively, computer vision applications may favor one quality over another (Tuytelaars & Mikolajczyk, 2008). Repeatability, arguably the most important quality, is directly dependent on the other qualities (i.e. improving one or more will equally improve repeatability). Nevertheless, regarding the other qualities, compromises usually need to be made. For example, distinctiveness and locality are competing properties (the more local a feature, the less distinctive it becomes, making feature matching more difficult). Efficiency and quantity are another example of such competing qualities. A highly dense features are likely to improve the object (or scene) recognition task, but this, however, will negatively impact the computation time.

2.3. Feature Detectors

The technical literature is rich with new features detections and description algorithms, and surveys that compare their performance and qualities. The reader is referred to some of the elegant surveys from the literature in (Tuytelaars & Mikolajczyk, 2008) (Liu, Li, Hu, & Gu, 2016) (Mikolajczyk & Schmid, 2004) (Lee & Park, 2014) (Mikolajczyk & Schmid, 2005) (Miksik & Mikolajczyk, 2012) (Schmid, Mohr, & Bauckhage, 2000) (Mikolajczyk, et al., 2005). However, no ideal detector exists until today. This mainly due to the virtually infinite number of possible computer vision applications (that may require one or multiple features), the divergence of imaging conditions (changes in scale, viewpoint, illumination, image quality, etc.) and possible scenes. The computational efficiency of such detectors becomes even more important when considered for real-time applications (Li, Wang, Tian, & Ding, 2015) (Liu, Li, Hu, & Gu, 2016) (Salahat E., et al., 2013). The most important local features (see Figure. 1) include:

1. **Edges:** Refer to patterns at which the intensities abruptly change (with a strong gradient magnitude).
2. **Corners:** Refer to the point at which two (or more) edges intersect in the local neighborhood.
3. **Regions:** Refer to a closed set of connected points with a similar homogeneity criterion (e.g. intensity).

One can intuitively note that there is a strong correlation between these local features. For example, multiple edges sometimes surround a region, i.e. tracking the edges defines the region boundaries. Similarly, the intersection of edges defines the corners (Liu, Li, Hu, & Gu, 2016).

Some of the recent prominent feature detection and description algorithms include WADE, KAZE, TBMR and Saddle. KAZE detection and description algorithm (Alcantarilla, Bartoli, & Davison, 2012) is a recent algorithm that targets multiscale 2D features in nonlinear scale spaces by means of nonlinear diffusion filtering. This makes blurring, unlike Gaussian scale-space, locally adaptive to image data, hence obtaining superior localization accuracy and distinctiveness. The nonlinear scale-space is built using Additive Operator Splitting (AOS) techniques and variable conductance diffusion. Similarly, WADE features (Salti, Lanza, & Stefano, 2013) are also recent repeatable features based on salient symmetries at different scales, which are detected by an analysis grounded on the wave equation rather than the heat equation underlying traditional Gaussian scale–space theory. These features are found suitable for untextured objects. Tree-based Morse Regions (TBMRs) introduced in (Xu, Monasse, Géraud, & Najman, 2014) is considered a variant of the MSER algorithm (Matas, Chum, Urban, & Pajdla, 2004). It is another local invariant feature detection motivated by Morse theory. The algorithm uses critical points of the graph of the intensity image which are selected from the so-called tree-based shape-space. Each point is associated with the largest region that contains it, but unlike MSERs, TBMRs are contrast-independent. The TBMR algorithm shows good repeatability with similar complexity to the MSER algorithm, but it also produces a significant number of regions. Another novel similarity-covariant feature detector, called Saddle, that extracts points whose neighborhoods (when viewed as a 3D intensity surface) have a saddle-like intensity profile was proposed in (Aldana-Iuit, Mishkin, Chum, & Matas, 2016). Covariance with similarity transformation is achieved by localizing keypoints in a scale-space pyramid. At every level of the pyramid, Saddle points are extracted in two stages: a pre-processing stage which eliminates more than 80~85% of the candidate points, whereas the post-processing stage that includes non-maxima suppression and response strength selection. Saddle points are experimentally shown to be evenly spread, fast to compute with a good matching performance. A summary for the well-known feature detectors can be found in Table 1.

Yet, as it was reported in many performance comparison surveys in computer vision, (Mikolajczyk & Schmid, 2005) (Mikolajczyk, et al., 2005) (Tuytelaars & Mikolajczyk, 2008) to name a few, the Maximally Stable Extremal Regions MSER) algorithm (Matas, Chum, Urban, & Pajdla, 2004) and the Scale-Invariant Feature Transform (SIFT) algorithm (Lowe D. G., 1999) showed an excellent performance in terms of the invariance to scene changes (e.g. scale, viewpoint, etc.) and other feature qualities, and are still considered two of the prominent ones. Table 2 shows a brief comparison between the MSER, SIFT and other detection and description algorithms (Tuytelaars & Mikolajczyk, 2008). For instance,

Table 1. Classification of some well-known feature detectors (Li, Wang, Tian, & Ding, 2015)

Category	Classification	Methods and Algorithms*
Edge-based	Differentiation based	Sobel, Canny
Corner-based	Gradient based	Harris (and derivatives), LOCOCO, KLT, Shi-Tomasi.
	Template based	FAST, AGAST, BRIEF, SUSAN, FAST-ER
	Contour based	DoG-curve, ANDD, Hyperbola fitting, ACJ
	Learning based	Pb, MS-Pb, gPb, tPb, NMX, BEL, DSC, SCG, SE
Blob (interest point)	PDE based	SIFT (and its derivatives), SURF, CenSurE, LoG, DoG, DoH, Hessian (and its derivatives), RLOG, MO-GP, DART, KAZE, A-KAZE, WADE.
Blob (key point)	Template based	ORB, BRISK, FREAK
Blob (interest region)	Segmentation based	MSER (and its derivatives), IBR, EBR, Beta-Stable, MFD, Salient Regions, FLOG, BPLR, TBMR, etc.

* The reader is referred to (Krig, 2014), (Tuytelaars & Mikolajczyk, 2008), (Li, Wang, Tian, & Ding, 2015) (Liu, Li, Hu, & Gu, 2016) for more details on the acronyms of the algorithms and their references.

Table 2. Performance of dominant features detection algorithms*, see (Tuytelaars & Mikolajczyk, 2008)

Detector	Invariance			Qualities			
	Rotation	Scale	Affine	Repeatability	Locality	Robustness	Efficiency
Harris	■	–	–	+ + +	+ + +	+ + +	+ +
Hessian	■	–	–	+ +	+ +	+ +	+
SUSAN	■	–	–	+ +	+ +	+ +	+ + +
Harris-Laplace	■	■	–	+ + +	+ + +	+ +	+
Hessian-Laplace	■	■	–	+ + +	+ + +	+ + +	+
DoG	■	■	–	+ +	+ +	+ +	+ +
Salient Regions	■	■	■	+	+	+ +	+
SURF	■	■	–	+ +	+ + +	+ +	+ + +
SIFT	■	■	–	+ +	+ + +	+ + +	+ +
MSER	■	■	■	+ + +	+ + +	+ +	+ + +

** Scores are assigned based on the discussion given in section 7.2 in (Tuytelaars & Mikolajczyk, 2008).

Figure 2 compares the repeatability of the MSER algorithm against several detection algorithms, where it shows an excellent performance to (a) view angle, (b) scale, (c) illumination and (d) overlap error due to viewpoint changes (see (Mikolajczyk, et al., 2005) for more details). Similarly, Figure 3 compares SIFT vs. several algorithms in terms of (a) matching performance, (b) view changes, (c) scale changes and (d) the effect of JPEG compression on the performance, where it also showed better performance compared to others (see (Mikolajczyk & Schmid, 2005) for more details and analysis).

As such, the MSER and SIFT were the core for many derivative algorithms with different enhancements (as will be reported on later sections). This chapter studies the MSER and SIFT as initially proposed by their original inventors in (Matas, Chum, Urban, & Pajdla, 2004) and (Lowe, 1999). The rationale behind selecting these two algorithms among the others includes (but is not limited to) the following points:

Figure 2. Repeatability comparison of the MSER vs. different algorithms. Repeatability score vs. (a) view changes, (b) scale changes, (c) illumination changes and (d) overlap error (Mikolajczyk et al., 2005)

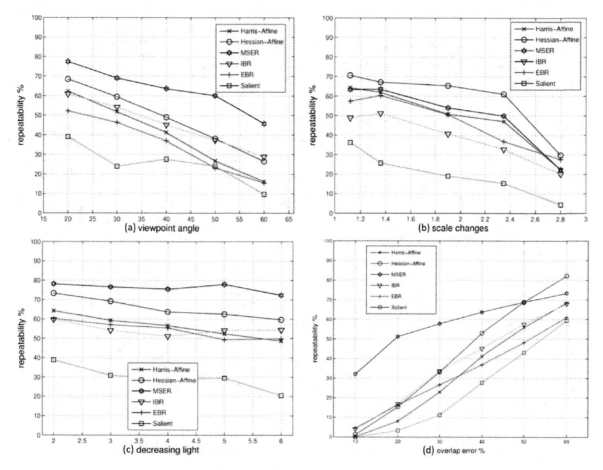

1. The algorithms showed an excellent performance (e.g. high invariance and repeatability scores),
2. The algorithms have a range of possible improvements that can enhance their performance,
3. The algorithms (especially the MSER) lack successful hardware designs, and
4. Since the two algorithms have many derivative algorithms from which any applied improvement on the original algorithms can be directly reflected (extended) to those derivative algorithms.

3. MAXIMALLY STABLE EXTREMAL REGIONS

3.1. Overview

The Maximally Stable Extremal Regions (MSERs), originally invented by Matas *et al.* (Matas, Chum, Urban, & Pajdla, 2004), has received a great momentum since published in 2002. This is mainly due to its high repeatability, (relatively) simple algorithmic structure as well as the small number of interest regions (a.k.a. key regions) per image that makes it well-suited for unlimited number of computer vision and

Figure 3. Performance of SIFT vs. different algorithms. (a) Matching performance, and its robustness to (b) view and (c) scale changes, as well as (d) JPEG compression (Mikolajczyk & Schmid, 2005)

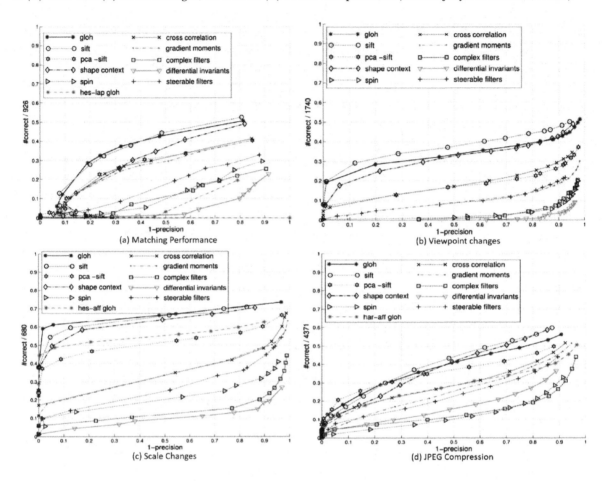

robotics applications. Even though it was originally designed for wide-baseline stereo matching (Matas, Chum, Urban, & Pajdla, 2004), it was later used for image retrieval (Sivic & Zisserman, 2003) (Nister & Stewenius, 2006), matching (Sluzek, 2015), object recognition (Obdrzalek & Matas, 2002) (Obdrzalek & Matas, 2005), and tracking in temporal domain (Donoser & Bischof, 2006). Another advantage of the MSER algorithm is that, unlike many features detectors, it operates on the input frames without the need for any preprocessing as it processes the pixels inserted. This will provide a great advantage as compared to other detectors especially when it comes to hardware implementation. The algorithm is one of the fastest and most efficient affine invariant feature detectors until today (Tuytelaars & Mikolajczyk, 2008).

The MSER algorithm is a variant of the flood-filling (a.k.a. watershed) algorithm. The major difference is that it aims to find a range of thresholds that leave the watershed's basins maximally unchanged in size (i.e. maximally stable). As such, the MSER algorithm is best suited for image structure that can be segmented- well (i.e. in applications with relatively uniform regions distinguished by sharp intensity changes), and the union-find algorithm tends to be an excellent candidate for the connected-component monitoring task (Salahat, 2016). Specifically, an MSER is a connected-component of an appropriately thresholded image (Mikolajczyk, et al., 2005) (Salahat et al., 2015). The property "extremal region" refers to a connected-component with pixel values that are either higher (bright extremal regions) or lower (dark extremal regions) intensity than all the adjacent pixels over a range of threshold values.

Extremal regions have a number of desirable properties. First, a monotonic (global) change of the image intensities does not affect extremal regions. Additionally, a continuous geometric transformation preserve topology (that is, a single component is transformed into another single component). Finally, the maximum number of extremal regions cannot exceed the number of pixels. Identifying MSERs is very efficient with almost linear complexity as will be discussed in the following sections. MSERs are similarly considered as the basis for a shape descriptor, based on the first and second region moments. The processing flow is discussed next.

3.2. Processing Flow

The enumeration of the MSER algorithm is described as follows. First, for a grid of intensity pixels, pixels are sorted by their intensity values starting from the minimum possible intensity (usually 0) to the maximum intensity (typically 255) or vice versa. In the process, the list of growing, shrinking and possibly merging connected-components is monitored with the aid of the union-find algorithm (see for example (Salahat E., et al., 2015)), which simultaneously can monitor the cardinality (number of pixels) of each connected-component as a function of the intensity. This is virtually equivalent to thresholding the image continuously with a growing threshold incremented by Δ (Salahat et al., 2015). This threshold increment parameter is typically selected from the range 3-8. Intuitively, higher Δ yields faster processing (while trading off the accuracy). Throughout the process, an MSER is identified if the relative change in the cardinality of a component is at a local minimum, that is when its cardinality is relatively stable over a range of thresholds (Tuytelaars & Mikolajczyk, 2008) (Krig, 2014). The formal definition of the MSER algorithm (and other related concepts) is given as follows (Matas, Chum, Urban, & Pajdla, 2004). Let $Q_1, Q_2, ..., Q_{i-1}, Q_i, ...$ be a sequence of nested regions, i.e. $Q_i \subset Q_{i+1}$. An extremal region Q_i is maximally stable iff:

$$q(i) = \left| Q(i+") \setminus Q(i-") \right| / \left| Q(i) \right| \tag{1}$$

has a local minimum at i, where Δ is the threshold increment. Any MSER detected using (1) corresponds to a bright (minimal) extremal region (for dark extremal regions, the intensities are inverted, and the process is repeated, or alternatively, one can reverse the sorting of the pixels which effectively yields the maximal regions (Kristensen & MacLean, 2007) (Nister & Stewenius, 2008). In fact, to detect all extremal regions, the algorithm has to process both of the intensity versions of the image Figure 4 and Figure 5 show an illustrative input image and its associated thresholding, respectively.

Sample MSER detection for the image in Figure 6 (a) is shown in Figure 6 (b), where different colors identify different MSERs. Figure 6 (c) shows the best elliptical fit for these detected MSERs, which serves as a shape descriptor. An efficient MSER C++ implementation can be found in vlfeat toolbox (Vedaldi, 2016).

3.3. Derivatives

This section briefly discusses some of the MSER derivatives, presented in a chronological order.

Figure 4. (a) input image, (b) its grey and (c) and inverted grey images (Salahat et al., 2015)

Figure 5. Thresholdings for the (up) grey and (down) inverted grey image (Salahat et al., 2015)

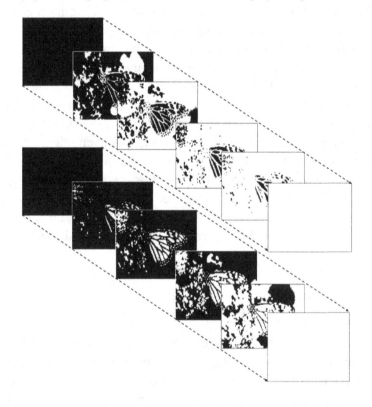

Figure 6. (a) Sample input, (b) detected MSERs and their (c) best elliptical fits

3.3.1. N-Dimensional Extensions

The algorithm was extended first in 2006 for 3D segmentation (Donoser & Bischof, 2006) by extending the neighborhoods search and stability criteria to 3D image data instead of 2D intensity date. Later on, in 2007, another extension for N-dimensional data space was proposed by Vedaldi in (Vedaldi, 2007), and later on the same year, an extension to vector-valued function that can be exploited with the three-color channels was also provided in (Forssen, 2007).

3.3.2. Linear-Time MSER Algorithm

In 2008, Nister and Stewenius proposed a new processing flow that emulates real flood-filling in (Nister & Stewenius, 2008). The linear-time MSER algorithm has several advantages over the standard algorithm such as better cache locality and linear complexity, and better memory management. An initial hardware design was proposed in (Alyammahi, Salahat, Saleh, & Sluzek, 2015).

3.3.3. The Extended MSER (X-MSER) Algorithm

The standard MSER algorithm searches for extremal regions from the input intensity domain (frame) only. However, in 2015, the authors (Salahat et al., 2015) proposed an extension to the depth (space) domain noting out the correlation between the depth images and intensity images, and introduced the extended MSER (X-MSER) detector, which was patented in (US Patent No. 20160117830, 2016). Specifically, an X-MSER is detected if relatively the same region is detected in both the intensity and depth domain. The drawback of the X-MSER is, however, that it needs to process additional (depth) information, doubling its computational load, in addition to the logic needed to compare and map depth and intensity MSERs.

3.3.4. The Parallel MSER Algorithm

One of the major drawbacks of the MSER algorithm (discussed later) is that it needs to run twice on every frame to detect both dark and bright extremal regions. This was resolved by introducing a parallel MSER processing algorithm (Salahat et al., 2015). "Parallel" in this context refers to the capability of detecting both dark and bright extremal regions in a one run. This algorithmic enhancement showed many advantages over the standard MSER algorithm, including a considerable reduction in the execution time, hardware resources and power, etc. The parallel MSER algorithm was patented (US Patent No. 20160070970, 2016).

3.3.5. Scale-Insensitive MSER (SIMER) Algorithm

Andrzej Sluzek has also extended the MSER algorithm in (Sluzek, 2016). Specifically, he redefined the MSER algorithm selection criteria to include scale changes in addition to threshold changes, by constructing a scale-space pyramid of the image and by monitoring two stability criteria instead. The first criterion ensure that the region is extremally stable to scale changes, and the other ensures stability due to threshold changes. The algorithm shows significant improvement and has the same (average) features count. The complexity of the algorithm, however, increases linearly scaled by the number of scales used, which also require additional resources (memory, enumeration, etc.).

3.3.5. Other MSER derivatives

Other algorithms that were inspired from the MSER algorithm include the Extremal Regions of the Extremal Levels (Faraji, Shanbehzadeh, Nasrollahi, & Moeslund, 2015) (Faraji, Shanbehzadeh, Nasrollahi, & Moeslund, 2015) and Tree-based Morse Regions (Xu, Monasse, Géraud, & Najman, 2014) algorithms.

3.4. Limitations

Despite the undoubted robust MSER performance, it however, suffer few major drawbacks:

1. **Sensitivity to Blur:** Unfortunately, the simplistic stability criteria mentioned earlier, which is the basis of the MSER algorithm, is sensitive to image blur. The algorithm assumes that extremal regions, which are stable over a range of consecutive thresholds (i.e. there is a drastic change in intensity values that makes this region extremal and stable). On the other hand, blur causes any such regions to lose this unique characteristic as it smooths (averages) the intensity between adjacent pixels. This smoothing affects the stability criteria and hence MSER overall detection (Perdoch & Matas, 2011).
2. **The Discretization Effects:** Due to the simple stability criteria, MSER detection will be affected by the discretization of the frame, even though the same detection parameters are still used. For example, a down-sampled frame is likely to lose many MSERs that are (at larger resolution) considered stable.
3. **Two-Runs to Detect All MSERs:** As mentioned earlier, to detect bright and dark extremal regions, the algorithm has to process to run two times on each version of the intensity image. This is one of the major drawbacks of the MSER algorithm. Still, the algorithm (with its two runs) is still way more computationally efficient that many other features detection algorithms.
4. **Lack of Optimal Threshold Increment:** The final drawback known to the authors is that the parameter of the algorithm, the threshold increment, has no optimal value and all threshold. Yet, a general threshold value is seen (experimentally) between 3~7.

3.5. Reported Hardware Solutions

It is astonishing to know that the MSER algorithm was not really considered for hardware (FPGA, SoC, etc.) until very recently. In fact, there are, up to our knowledge, two hardware implementations that were reported in the literature for the MSER algorithm. The first is an FPGA implementation reported in (Kristensen & MacLean, 2007), with a relatively good performance but with many limitations. The second known implementation is that reported in (Salahat et al., 2015) (US Patent No. 20160070970, 2016) with preliminary results that uses the Application-Specific Integrated Circuit (ASIC) design approach to implement the algorithm as a SoC. This implementation has many expected advantages over the FPGA implementation such as the reduction in memory storage, parallelizability and other performance metrics. One can argue that comparing two different implementation platforms (i.e. FPGA vs. ASIC) is unfair. As such, in this work, the focus will be the ASIC based MSER design.

The MSER SoC architecture shown in Figure 7 follows few processing stages. The SoC design is controlled by five main parameters, namely the maximum and minimum allowable number of pixels of the MSER identified by MaxArea and MinArea (and any region that falls outside this range is ignored),

Figure 7. SoC Architecture of the MSER (Salahat et al., 2015)

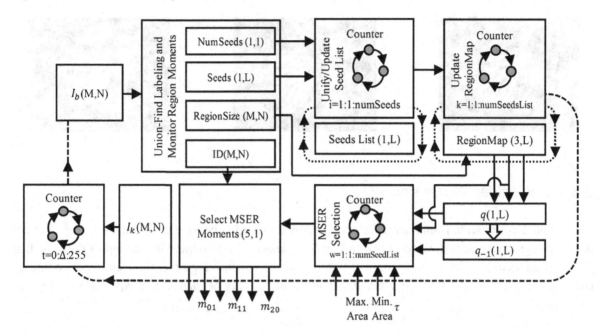

the maximum growth rate specified by the stability function given in (1), the threshold increment Δ and the nesting tolerance, τ. Different choices of these parameters yield different detected MSERs. The processing stages (for one version of the intensity frame) are as follows:

3.5.1. Thresholding

The first stage is thresholding, where the image is continuously binarized with an increasing threshold (by Δ increments) value that simulates flood-filling (see Figure 5). Every frame requires $255/"+1$ thresholdings.

3.5.2. Labeling

The union-find algorithm (see e.g. (Salahat et al., 2015)) is used to distinguish regions in a binary image. This process is repeated $255/\Delta +1$ times (i.e. once for every threshold value). The algorithm can provide the necessary information (e.g. first and second order region moments) that will be rendered useful to extract MSER ellipses. Sample labeling results (with an increasing threshold value) are shown in Figure 8.

3.5.3. Unify and Update

This stage is needed to monitor regions as they grow. Specifically, with the increasing threshold, many regions grow (or diminish), and some merge. This is illustrated in Figure 8. This processing stage is needed to ensure proper MSER detection and description.

Figure 8. Regions growing and labeling at different increasing threshold values (Salahat et al., 2015)

(a)   (b)   (c)

3.5.4. RegionMap Processing

The updated information from the earlier stage is now prepared to be used to find the stability of every detected region (connected-component). In that SoC design, this is done with the aid of the so-called RegionMap memory. This memory basically stores the size of each region at three consecutive thresholds, which are, in fact, the required data to calculate the stability of each region. Specifically, Region-Map stores $\left|\mathcal{Q}(t+")\right|, \left|\mathcal{Q}(t)\right|$ and $\left|\mathcal{Q}(t-\Delta)\right|$ for each connected-component.

3.5.5. MSER Selection

Given that all information needed to select MSERs are available, and based on the values of the control parameters, MSERs that satisfy the selection conditions (or their associated moments' representation) are used to highlight those MSERs. Illustrative bright and dark MSER detected regions are shown in Figure 9 (a) and (b), respectively.

3.5.6. (Optional) MSER Elliptical Fit (Descriptors)

All MSERs that were selected from the earlier stage can be either represented using their associated pixels or the regions moments. The latter approach is more useful as (1) it saves the needed memory to store the pixels of each MSER, and (2) provides the essential information to derive each MSER's

Figure 9. Sample MSER detection: (a) bright, and (b) dark regions (Salahat et al., 2015)

(a)   **(b)**

elliptical fit unique descriptor. This ellipse descriptor can be enumerated as described in (Chaumette, 2004). Some MSER ellipses are shown in Figure 6 (c).

The MSER SoC was synthesized, placed and routed using 65nm CMOS technology. The design was fabricated as part of a larger project (due to fabrication cost), which prevented using the full area and other chip resources to the maximum, and tradeoff was mainly on the maximum input frame resolution. Figure 10 illustrates the SoC that the MSER is part of it.

A summary of the SoC specifications is given in Table 3, e.g. total chip area, operating frequency, estimated processing rate, and required power. Table 3 also reports the MSER SoC (Salahat et al., 2015) and the FPGA design by (Kristensen & MacLean, 2007). We re-emphasize here that such a comparison is in fact inadequate. In other words, the considerable improvement (in memory, speed, etc.) is partially due to the superiority of the ASIC design, and partially due to the efficient SoC architecture (Salahat et al., 2015).

4. SCALE INVARIANT FEATURE TRANSFORM

4.1. Overview

The Scale Invariant Feature Transform (SIFT) (Lowe, 1999) (Lowe, 2004) is one of the best- known methods for finding local features (key points) as well as feature description. The algorithm shows excel-

Figure 10. The final synthesized, placed and routed MSER SoC (Salahat et al., 2015)

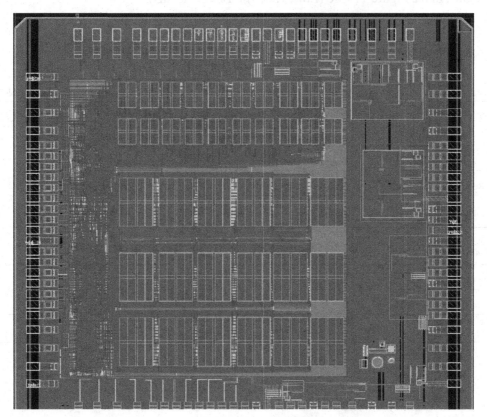

lent invariance to scale, rotation, illumination, affine distortion, perspective and similarity transforms, and noise (Krig, 2014). The SIFT algorithm is effectively a complete processing pipeline, that is, it involves both features detection and description.

SIFT includes several processing stages in the detection and description pipeline. In the detection of key points, the processing includes the creation of the weighted Difference of Gaussian (DoG) maxima key points in scale space to create scale-invariant keypoints. The feature extraction then computes a binned Histogram-of-Gradients (HoG) from local gradient magnitudes at locations around the key points derived over several scales. Finally, feature descriptors are then found using the extracted features. For features matching, the distance between two (or more) sets of feature descriptors are found and those with the smallest distance are considered the primary match (Krig, 2014) (Lowe, 2004) (Lowe, 1999).

4.2. Processing Flow

SIFT is an algorithm used to extract and describe local features in images. It was proposed by Lowe (Lowe D. G., 1999) (Lowe D. G., 2004) in 2004 and was patented in the U.S. to University of British Columbia (UBC), and is one of the most trusted and widely used feature extraction algorithm in the field.

SIFT algorithm takes $N \times N$ pixels image as input and produces a set of distinctive features that represent the image content. The SIFT algorithm process can be divided into two main stages: keypoints detection and keypoints description. In the first stage, the image is scanned to search for distinctive and repeatable features, i.e. the key points. This stage consists of three sub-tasks: Gaussian scale space generation, local extrema detection, and actual keypoints detection. The second stage generates the descriptors that are divided into two sub-tasks: dominant orientation assignment and descriptor generation. SIFT's steps are shown in the Figure 11 (see (Lowe, 2004) for more details).

Table 3. Summary of the well-known reported MSER performance

Performance Metric		ASIC SoC (Salahat E., et al., 2015)	FPGA (Kristensen & MacLean, 2007)
MSER	Parameters	Configurable	Configurable
	Representations	Regions and Ellipse Moments	Regions
	Detection (per run)	Bright and Dark (in parallel)	Either Bright or Dark
Maximum Resolution		Scalable (Configurable)	122,500 pixels
Testing Resolution ($\mathcal{R}$)		65,536 pixels	76,800 pixels
Memory Storage (bytes)		$\approx [1.125 + \log_2(\mathcal{R})/4]\,\mathcal{R}$	$\approx [11 + 3\log_2(\mathcal{R})]\,\mathcal{R}/8$
Frame Rate (fps)		200 (expected)	54
Operating Frequency		133.33 MHz	42 MHz
Area		57,101 μ m^2	N/A
Power		2.2578 mW	N/A

Figure 11. SIFT algorithm - feature extraction and description

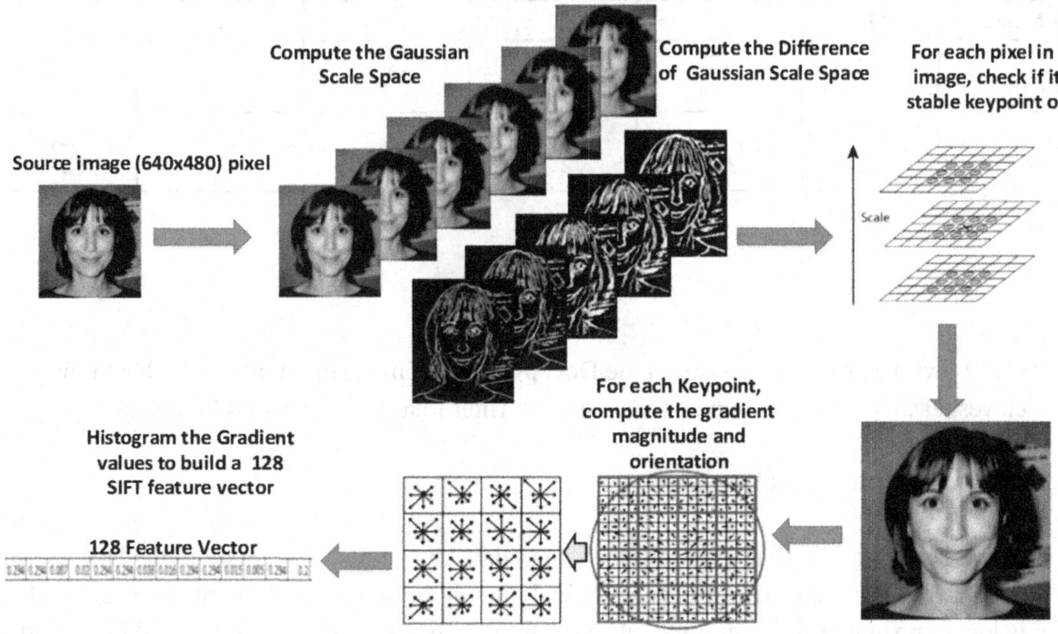

4.2.1. Gaussian Scale Space Generation

In the first step, the input image I(x,y) is convolved with a series of Gaussian filters G(x,y,σ_i) to build a Gaussian scale space as defined by equations as:

$$L\left(x,y,\sigma i\right) = G\left(x,y,\sigma i\right) * I\left(x,y\right) \tag{2}$$

$$G\left(x,y,\sigma_i\right) = \frac{1}{2\pi\sigma_i^2}e^{-\left(x^2+y^2\right)\left[2\sigma_i^2\right]^{-1}} \tag{3}$$

where i is the scale index ($i = 0, 1, \ldots,$ S+2), S is the number of scales to be generated, σ_i is a Gaussian filter scale, $L\left(x,y,\sigma_i\right)$ is the Gaussian filtered image and i is a scale index, and * denotes a 2-D convolution operation in x and y and G(x,y,σ_i) is the Gaussian Kernel. Table 4 summarizes the Gaussian filter's standard deviations for the first octave of Gaussian scale space. In this work, we used six scales (σ_0, $k\sigma_0$, $k^2\sigma_0$, $k^3\tilde{A}_0$, $k^4\sigma_0$, $k^5\sigma_0$), where σ_0 =1.6, and $k = \sqrt[3]{2}$.

The first set of the S+2 Gaussian filtered images is called the first octave of the Gaussian scale space. The second octave is derived by down-sampling the images in the first octave into half size and repeating the same operations that were applied to the first octave. After computing the Gaussian filtered images, the next step is to build the difference of Gaussian scale space (DoG) by subtracting each two consecutive images in the same octave, as defined in equation (4):

Table 4. Gaussian filter's scales for the first octave

Filter Number	1	2	3	4	5	6
Filter Scale	σ_0	$k^1\sigma_0$	$k^2\sigma_0$	$k^3\sigma_0$	$k^4\sigma_0$	$k^5\sigma_0$
Scale Value	1.6	$\sqrt[3]{2}^1\,1.6$	$\sqrt[3]{2}^2\,1.6$	$\sqrt[3]{2}^3\,1.6$	$\sqrt[3]{2}^4\,1.6$	$\sqrt[3]{2}^5\,1.6$

$$D(x,y,\sigma) = L(x,y,K\sigma) - L(x,y,\sigma) \tag{4}$$

Figure 12 shows the process to construct the DoG pyramid from the input image. In this Figure, there are two octaves, each one has a group of five Gaussian filter images and four DoG images.

4.2.2. Local Extrema Detection

In this step, the DoG image is scanned to find the candidate key points. Each pixel in the D(x, y, σ) image at location (x, y) is compared with its 3×3 neighbours in the same scale and the adjacent scales. If the pixel is local maxima or local minima out of the total 26 neighbouring pixels, it will be considered as a candidate keypoint. This operation is performed for every pixel in the DoG images and what results is a list of keypoint candidates. Figure 13 shows the keypoint's 3×3 neighbors.

Figure 12. Gaussian scale space pyramid (Lowe D. G., 2004)

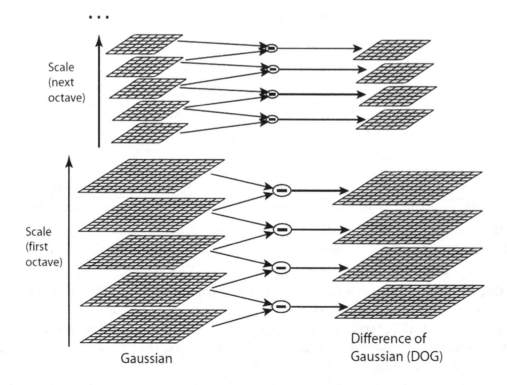

Figure 13. Keypoint's 3x3 neighbors (Lowe, 2004)

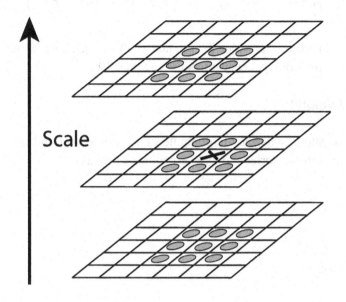

4.2.3. Keypoint Detection

The goal of this step is to eliminate the candidate key points that have low contrast or poorly localized along edges. To detect a low contrast keypoint, the value of the pixel is compared with a predefined threshold. If the value is less than the threshold, the keypoint will be rejected. To find the poorly localized peak, the keypoint is tested using the inequality defined as:

$$\frac{Tr\left(H\right)^2}{Det\left(H\right)} < \frac{\left(r+1\right)^2}{r} \tag{5}$$

where r is a constant value, H is the Hessian matrix computed as defined as:

$$H = \begin{bmatrix} \Delta\,xx & \Delta\,xy \\ \Delta\,xy & \Delta\,yy \end{bmatrix} \tag{6}$$

with Tr (H) is the trace of H, Det(H) is the determinant of H, and Δxx, Δyy, and Δxy are computed as:

$$\Delta\,xx = D\left(x+1,y\right) + D\left(x-1,y\right) - 2D\left(x,y\right) \tag{7.1}$$

$$\Delta\,yy = D\left(x,y+1\right) + D\left(x,y-1\right) - 2D\left(x,y\right) \tag{7.2}$$

$$\Delta xy = 0.25 \Big(D\big(x+1,y+1\big) - D\big(x-1,y+1\big) - D\big(x+1,y-1\big) + D\big(x-1,y-1\big) \Big) \tag{7.3}$$

A threshold value of 3 and constant value for r equal to 10 are used here, which eliminates keypoints that have a ratio between the principal curvatures greater than 10.

4.2.4. Orientation Assignment

The gradient magnitude and orientation are computed for all pixels around the stable keypoints. The gradient is computed in both the horizontal and vertical direction as:

$$\Delta x = \Big[L\big(x+1,y\big) - L\big(x-1,y\big) \Big] / 2 \tag{8.1}$$

$$\Delta y = \Big[L\big(x,y+1\big) - L\big(x,y-1\big) \Big] / 2 \tag{8.2}$$

The gradient magnitude and gradient orientation are computed from Δx and Δy as:

$$m\big(x,y\big) = \sqrt{\Delta x^2 + \Delta y^2} \tag{9.1}$$

$$\theta\big(x,y\big) = \tan^{-1}\left(\frac{\Delta y}{\Delta x} \right) \tag{9.2}$$

4.2.5. Descriptor Generation

As mentioned earlier, to compute the SIFT descriptor, there are two main tasks: dominant orientation computation and descriptor generation. The dominant orientation is computed by building the gradient orientation histogram around the keypoint. The gradient orientations in the region are mapped into one of 36 bins, where each bin represents 10 degrees. In the end, the bin with the largest value or count represents the dominant orientation, as shown in Figure 14.

After computing a dominant orientation, the coordinates of the pixels around a keypoint are rotated relative to the dominant orientation. A SIFT descriptor is computed by dividing the region around the keypoint into 4x4 squares and building the gradient histogram over 8 bins, where each bin covers 45 degrees. The gradient magnitudes are weighted by Gaussian filter before building the histogram. Lastly, the 16 histograms with 8 bins are each represented in the SIFT descriptor. The SIFT descriptor has 4x4x8 values. Figure 15 shows the first 2x2 blocks out of the 4x4 blocks around a keypoint.

For completeness, we note here that a variation of the SIFT descriptors can also be computed using a variant of the HoG descriptor called the Gradient Location and Orientation Histogram (GLOH), which uses a log polar histogram format instead of the Cartesian HoG format, as illustrated in the Figure 16.

Figure 14. Dominant Orientation's Histogram (Lowe, 2004)

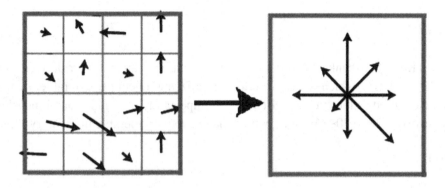

Figure 15. the first 2x2 blocks in SIFT descriptor (Lowe, 2004)

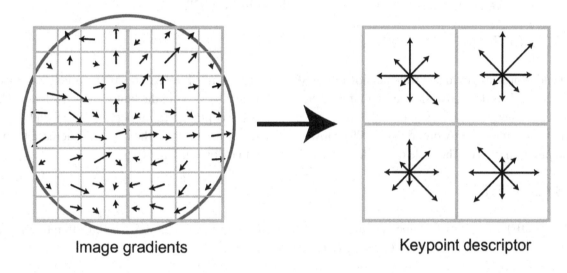

Image gradients   Keypoint descriptor

Figure 16. (Left and center) gradient magnitude and direction binned into histograms for the SIFT HOG. (Right) GLOH descriptors (Krig, 2014)

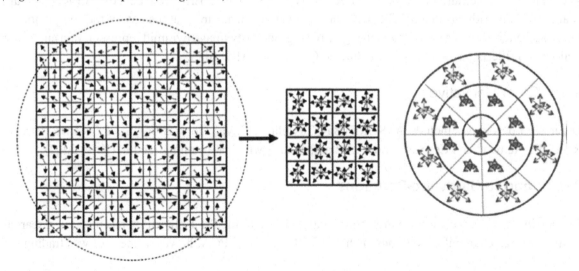

4.3. Derivatives

4.3.1. SIFT-PCA

The SIFT-PCA (Ke & Sukthankar, 2004) adopts an alternative feature vector derived using principal component analysis (PCA), which is based on the normalized gradient patches rather than the weighted and smoothed HoG used in the standard SIFT. More importantly, it reduces the dimensionality of the SIFT descriptor from 128 to 20~36 vector, which may be more preferable in memory limited devices.

4.3.2. CSIFT

Another variation of SIFT to colored space (RGB images) is the CSIFT (Abdel-Hakim & Farag, 2006). It basically modifies the SIFT descriptor (in color invariant space) and is found to be more robust to color and photometrical variations as compared to the standard SIFT.

4.3.3. ASIFT

Yu and Morel proposed an affine version of the SIFT algorithm in (Morel & Yu, 2009), which is termed as ASIFT. This derivative simulates all image views obtainable by varying the latitude and the longitude angles. It then uses the standard SIFT method itself. ASIFT is proven to outperform SIFT and to be fully affine invariant (Morel & Yu, 2009). However, the major drawback is the dramatic increase in the computational load. The code of the ASIFT can be found in (Morel & Yu, 2016).

4.3.4. n-SIFT

The n-SIFT algorithm is simply a straightforward extension of the standard SIFT algorithm to images (or data) with multi-dimensions (Cheung & Hamarneh, 2009).

4.3.5. SIFT-SIFER Retrofit

The major difference and innovation between SIFT and SIFT with Error Resilience (SIFER) (Mainali, et al., 2013) algorithm is that SIFER (with an improvement in accuracy at the cost of the computational load) has better scale-space treatment using a higher granularity image pyramid representation and better scale-tuned filtering using a cosine modulated Gaussian (CMG) filter.

4.3.6. Other Derivatives

Other SIFT derivatives include the SURF (Bay, Tuytelaars, & Van Gool, 2006), SIFT CS-LBP Retrofit, RootSIFT Retrofit, and CenSurE and STAR algorithms, which are summarized in (Krig, 2014).

4.4. Reported Hardware Solutions

As seen in the earlier section, the high computational load of the SIFT algorithm has inspired researchers to investigate simplified versions such as SURF and SIFT-PCA, however, the cost was trading off the accuracy, which is an infeasible solution for many practical applications where the accuracy is of paramount importance. A more realistic solution is to utilize hardware solutions such as FPGA, ASIC, GPUs, etc. This will allow utilizing the hardware parallelization and pipelining wherever possible rather than processing data sequentially.

For example, the authors in (Rister, Wang, Wu, & Cavallaro, 2013) proposed a heterogeneous data flow scheme to accelerate the SIFT algorithm using a GPU in a mobile device. They achieved a speedup of ×4-7 over an optimized CPU version and a ×6.4 speedup over other GPU implementations. In (Jiang, Geng, Wei, & Shen, 2013), a GPU-based SIFT implementation for image matching was proposed. These implementations might have reached near real-time frame rate performance, but they require an excessive amount of hardware resources and they consume too much power compared to other hardware platforms. This makes the GPU implementations of the SIFT algorithm not suitable for portable embedded systems with limited power. Other solutions tried to accelerate the SIFT algorithm by fully utilizing the computing power of available multi-core processors. The results showed that the performance achieved by a multi-core CPU is almost the same as the implementation on GPUs.

Other attempts have been made to accelerate the SIFT algorithm using FPGA hardware architectures. In (Bonato, Marques, & Constantinides, 2008), a parallel hardware architecture for SIFT features extraction was proposed. The extracted features are used in the simultaneous localization and mapping (SLAM) problem. The architecture was a stand-alone architecture where it was able to read the input image directly from CMOS sensor. It also provides the results for on-chip applications or is accessible via an Ethernet connection. Furthermore, it provides some flexibility to customize the feature descriptors based on the application. The system architecture is composed of three hardware blocks that run in parallel (DoG, OriMag, and KP). The DoG block receives a stream of pixels from CMOS sensor and performs a Gaussian filter and difference of Gaussian operations. The results are then sent to both the OriMag and Kp blocks. The Kp block detects the stable keypoints, while the OriMag computes the gradient magnitude and orientation. The NIOS II processor generates the descriptor for each keypoint generated by the KP block based on the gradient magnitude and orientation produced by the OriMag block. The system was able to detect features from 320×240 pixel images at a rate of up to 30 frames per second. However, the system did not generate the SIFT descriptor in real-time because it was implemented in the soft-core processor NIOS II. In this implementation, it took around 11.7 ms to generate one SIFT descriptor which is far from the real-time performance.

Another FPGA-based SIFT accelerator architecture (Mizuno, et al., 2010) was proposed to resolve the power consumption and hardware resource usage problems. Their method divides the input image into a number of regions of interests (ROI) and processes each one individually as opposed to the whole image as the original algorithm. Moreover, the architecture used the implementation of two 1-D Gaussian filters instead of one 2-D Gaussian filters in order to reuse intermediate results efficiently. Moreover, to increase the overall throughput the architecture used a pipelining of three stages: ROI reading, Gaussian filtering, and key-point extraction. The Gaussian filtering module consists of 60 parallel systolic-array architecture used to distribute the workload. The keypoint extraction module consists of three keypoints extraction cores. The implementation can generate the SIFT descriptor vectors for images of size 640×480 pixels at a rate of 56 frames per second. However, the author claims that ROI-method will have a low accuracy degradation. Also, there are no details about the descriptor vector generation stage.

The SIFT algorithm was optimized by (Feng, et al., 2009) to obtain a high-speed feature detector with a low hardware resource usage. The optimized algorithm uses only four scales with two octaves in the DoG stage. It also reduces the dimension of the SIFT feature descriptor from 128 values into 72 values. The system consists of two modules: the SIFT feature detection hardware core module and the SIFT feature generation software module. It has three pipelined stages: Read Data, Gaussian Smooth, and Feature Detect/GradOrien components that all operate in parallel. The parallel structure of Gaussian smooth component consists of seven smooth units in order to process 7x12 pixels arrived at from the Read Data component. The Feature Detect component has a high parallel structure, where it was able to complete 28 pairs of comparison within one clock cycle. The architecture was able to detect the SIFT features of an image of 640x480 pixels within 31 milliseconds. However, this optimization largely reduces the accuracy of the SIFT descriptor.

Zhong et al. (Zhong, Wang, & Yan, 2013) implemented the FPGA/DSP design for a SIFT feature extraction. The SIFT feature detection stage is implemented using FPGA with a parallel architecture to reduce the overall detection time, while the feature description stage is implemented using a high-performance fixed-point DSP chip. The system contains two parallel copies of the OriMag module and the stable keypoint detection module. The first copy is dedicated to octave 0, while the second copy is shared by octave 1 and octave 2. These modules communicate with the DSP processor through a high-performance processor interface (HPINF) module by sending the stable keypoints to generate the features description vectors. The Gaussian filter module used two 1-D kernels to replace the traditional 2D convolution in order to reduce the resource utilization. Their system performs the SIFT features detection at a speed of 100 frames/sec on images of size 320×256 pixels, and it takes about 80 μsec per feature in the description stage. However, this system depends on a DSP processor to generate the feature descriptors. In addition, it works with small image resolutions to be able to store the whole image in the chip.

The authors in (Huang, Huang, Ker, & Chen, 2012) implemented a parallel hardware architecture with a three-stage pipeline SIFT accelerator. The architecture consists of two hardware components, one for key point detection, and the other for feature descriptor generation. They make the first component act as a main processor that reads the source image and detects the keypoints. For each stable keypoint, it invokes the second component (coprocessor) to start the feature descriptor generation process. Moreover, they propose a buffer scheme that reduces memory requirements by 50%. The module was able to detect the SIFT features within 3.4 ms for images of VGA resolution (640×480 pixels). The overall SIFT processing time, including the feature descriptor generation, is kept within 33ms when the number of features to be extracted is less than 890.

The authors in (Borhanifar & Naeim, 2012) build the SIFT accelerator to extract features from images of size (320 × 240) pixels. The accelerator reads the input image pixels' stream, and then feeds it into two 1D Gaussian filters. In such an implementation, the intermediate values are stored using a buffering line technique. The results of the DoG operations are sent to gradient orientation and magnitude generation blocks. It is also sent to the keypoint detection and the stability checking blocks. The system is implemented in the Altera Cyclone III FPGA and achieved 30 frames per second, however, the hardware utilization for this architecture was high. Table 5 summarizes the performance of different SIFT accelerators and their hardware utilization.

A recent research with an efficient parallel SIFT FPGA implementation was reported in (Qasaimeh, Sagahyroon, & Shanableh, 2014) (Qasaimeh, Sagahyroon, & Shanableh, 2015). The overall architecture of their SIFT hardware is shown in Figure 17. It consists of four main modules, namely, Gaussian scale space generation (GSS), keypoint detection (KPD), gradient magnitude and orientation generation (GMO), and keypoint description module (KDS). The first two modules represent the SIFT feature detector, while the last two modules represent the SIFT feature descriptor.

Table 5. SIFT System's parameters, performance and hardware requirements

	(Mizuno, et al., 2010)	(Feng, et al., 2009)	(Bonato, Marques, & Constantinides, 2008)	(Zhong, Wang, & Yan, 2013)	(Huang, Huang, Ker, & Chen, 2012)	(Borhanifar & Naeim, 2012)
Resolution	640 × 480	640×480	320 ×240	320×256	640×480	320 × 240
Frame rate(fps)	56	32	30	100	30	30
Op-Freq(MHz)	50	100	50	106	100	100
FPGA	Cyclone II	Virtex-5	Stratix II	Virtex-4	-	Cyclone III
# of LUTs	32,592	35,889	43,366	18,195	13,200	43,563
# of registers	23,247	19,529	19,100	11,821	-	14,730
# of DSP blocks	258	97	64	56	-	45
Memory (Mbits)	0.67	-	-	2.7	5.729	2.81

Figure 17. A parallel SIFT architecture (Qasaimeh, Sagahyroon, & Shanableh, 2015)

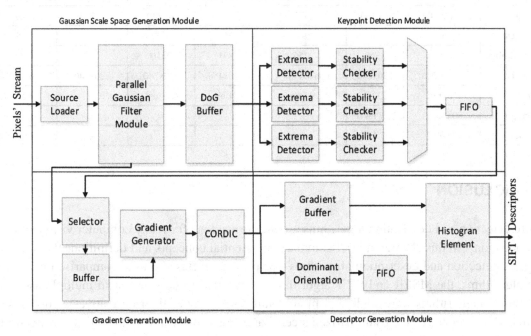

The primary task of GSS module is to build the difference of the Gaussian scale space module. The input to this module is a stream of pixels from the source image with one pixel occurring every clock cycle. The output of GSS module is sent to the KPD module and GMO module at the same time. The KPD module computes the stable keypoints and stores them in a FIFO buffer, while the GMO computes the gradient magnitude and orientation. The KDS module reads one keypoint from the FIFO at a time and computes the SIFT descriptor based on the gradient values in the region around the keypoint.

This architecture, in comparison with the other architectures, performs very well. The execution time on the software vs. the hardware module and the speed up percentages are shown in table 6. The superior performance of this parallel architecture can also be seen by the comparison shown in table 7.

Table 6. Speed up of SIFT's Module Processing Time

	Software Time (ms)	Hardware Time (ms)	Speedup
GSS Generation	530.00	6.14	86.26
Keypoint Detection	373.00	6.14	60.71
Gradient M&O Generation	420.00	6.14	68.36
Keypoint Description	994.00	23.65	42.03
Total	2317.00	42.08	55.06

Table 7. Comparing some of the SIFT existing hardware solutions

	(Zhong, Wang, & Yan, 2013)	(Feng, et al., 2009)	(Bonato, Marques, & Constantinides, 2008)	(Mizuno, et al., 2010)	(Borhanifar & Naeim, 2012)	(Huang, Huang, Ker, & Chen, 2012)	(Qasaimeh, Sagahyroon, & Shanableh, 2015)
LUT	18195	43,366	35,889	32,592	43,563	16,832	16,138
Register	11821	19,100	19529	23,247	14,730	5,729	7,924
DSP blocks	56	64	97	258	45	8	53
BRAM (kbits)	2808	1350	256	891	2810	752	576
Resolution	320 x 256	320x240	640x480	640x480	320x240	320x240	640x480
Detector	10 ms	33 ms	31 ms	31 ms	30 ms	-	6.144 ms
Descriptor	80 μsec/F.	11.7 ms /F	-	-	-	-	26 μsec/ F
Accuracy	96.90%	95.47%	-	-	-	-	97.535%

5. CONCLUSION

Feature detection and description algorithms are the cornerstone for many computer vision and robotics applications. In this chapter, a brief summary of essential concepts and definitions that are related to feature detection and description algorithms was presented. Based on the comparison provided for these algorithms, the MSER and SIFT algorithms were found to be superior in multiple aspects. As such, the two algorithms were studied in more details and many of their derivatives algorithms were covered. Moreover, the chapter summarized recent hardware designs and architectures that are available in the public technical literature. The continuous progress in embedding these algorithms seems very promising, however, consideration may be given first to the algorithmic designs and processing flows of these algorithms or any of their derivatives before developing their embedded vision platform such as FPGA, SoC, etc.

REFERENCES

Abdel-Hakim, E. A., & Farag, A. A. (2006). CSIFT: A SIFT Descriptor with Color Invariant Characteristics. *Proceedings of the IEEE Conference on Computer Vision and Pattern Recognition*. doi:10.1109/CVPR.2006.95

Alcantarilla, P. F., Bartoli, A., & Davison, A. J. (2012). KAZE Features. *Proceedings of the European Conference on Computer Vision.*

Aldana-Iuit, J., Mishkin, D., Chum, O., & Matas, J. (2016). In the Saddle: Chasing Fast and Repeatable Features. arXiv:1608.06800v1

Alyammahi, S., Salahat, E., Saleh, H., & Sluzek, A. (2015). A Hardware Accelerator For Real-Time Extraction of The Linear-Time MSER Algorithm. *Proceedings of the Annual Conference of the IEEE Industrial Electronics Society.* Yokohama, Japan.

Awad, A. I., & Hassaballah, M. (2016). *Image Feature Detectors and Descriptors: Foundations and Applications.* Springer. doi:10.1007/978-3-319-28854-3

Bay, H., Tuytelaars, T., & Van Gool, L. (2006). SURF: Speeded Up Robust Features. *Computer Vision, 3951*, 404–417.

Bonato, V., Marques, E., & Constantinides, G. (2008). A Parallel Hardware Architecture for Scale and Rotation Invariant Feature Detection. *IEEE Transactions on Circuits and Systems for Video Technology, 18*(12), 1703–1712. doi:10.1109/TCSVT.2008.2004936

Borhanifar, H., & Naeim, V. (2012). High Speed Object Recognition Based on SIFT Algorithm. *Proceedings of the International Conference on Image, Vision and Computing.*

Chaumette, F. (2004). Image Moments: A General and Useful Set of Features for Visual Servoing. *IEEE Transactions on Robotics, 20*(4), 713–723. doi:10.1109/TRO.2004.829463

Cheung, W., & Hamarneh, G. (2009). n-SIFT: n-Dimensional Scale Invariant Feature Transform. *IEEE Transactions on Image Processing, 18*(9), 2012–2021. doi:10.1109/TIP.2009.2024578 PMID:19502129

Donoser, M., & Bischof, H. (2006). 3D Segmentation By Maximally Stable Volumes (MSVs). *Proceedings of the IEEE International Conference on Pattern Recognition.* Hong Kong. doi:10.1109/ICPR.2006.33

Donoser, M., & Bischof, H. (2006). Efficient Maximally Stable Extremal Region (MSER) Tracking. *Proceedings of the IEEE Computer Society Conference on Computer Vision and Pattern Recognition.* doi:10.1109/CVPR.2006.107

Faraji, M., Shanbehzadeh, J., Nasrollahi, K., & Moeslund, T. B. (2015). EREL: Extremal Regions of Extremum Levels. *Proceedings of the IEEE International Conference on Image Processing.* Quebec City, QC.

Faraji, M., Shanbehzadeh, J., Nasrollahi, K., & Moeslund, T. B. (2015). Extremal Regions Detection Guided by Maxima of Gradient Magnitude. *IEEE Transactions on Image Processing, 24*(12), 5401–5415. doi:10.1109/TIP.2015.2477215 PMID:26357397

Feng, W., Zhao, D., Jiang, Z., Zhu, Y., Feng, H., & Yao, L. (2009). An Architecture of Optimised SIFT Feature Detection for an FPGA Implementation of an Image Matcher. *Proceedings of the International Conference on Field-Programmable Technology.* Sydney.

Forssen, P. (2007). Maximally Stable Colour Regions For Recognition and Matching. *Proceedings of the IEEE Conference on Computer Vision and Pattern Recognition*. Minneapolis. doi:10.1109/CVPR.2007.383120

Hu, W., Tan, T., Wang, L., & Maybank, S. (2004). A Survey on Visual Surveillance of Object Motion and Behaviors. *IEEE Trans. on Systems, Man, And Cybernetics—Part C: Applications And Reviews*, *34*(3), 334–352. doi:10.1109/TSMCC.2004.829274

Huang, F.-C., Huang, S.-Y., Ker, J.-W., & Chen, Y.-C. (2012). High-Performance SIFT Hardware Accelerator for Real-Time Image Feature Extraction. *IEEE Transactions on Circuits and Systems for Video Technology*, *22*(3), 340–351. doi:10.1109/TCSVT.2011.2162760

Jiang, C., Geng, Z.-x., Wei, X.-f., & Shen, C. (2013). SIFT implementation based on GPU. *Proceedings of the International Symposium on Photoelectronic Detection and Imaging, 891304*.

Ke, Y., & Sukthankar, R. (2004). PCA-SIFT: A More Distinctive Representation for Local Image Descriptors. *Proceedings of the IEEE Conference on Computer Vision and Pattern Recognition*.

Krig, S. (2014). *Computer Vision Metrics - Survey, Taxonomy, and Analysis*. Springer.

Kristensen, F., & MacLean, W. J. (2007). Real-Time Extraction of Maximally Stable Extremal Regions on an FPGA. *Proceedings of the IEEE International Symposium on Circuits and System*, New Orleans, LA. doi:10.1109/ISCAS.2007.378247

Lee, M. H., & Park, I. K. (2014). Performance Evaluation of Local Descriptors for Affine Invariant Region Detector. *Proceedings of the Asian Conference on Computer Vision Workshops*. Singapore.

Li, Y., Wang, S., Tian, Q., & Ding, X. (2015). A Survey of Recent Advances in Visual Feature Detection. *Neurocomputing, 149, Part B*(3), 736–751.

Liu, H., Chen, S., & Naoyuki Kubota. (2013). Intelligent Video Systems and Analytics: A Survey. *IEEE Trans. on Industrial Informatics, 9*(3), 1222-1233.

Liu, Q., Li, R., Hu, H., & Gu, D. (2016). Extracting Semantic Information from Visual Data: A Survey. *Robotics, 5*(1), 1–22. doi:10.3390/robotics5010008

Lowe, D. G. (1999). Object Recognition from Local Scale-Invariant Features. *Proceedings of the IEEE International Conference on Computer Vision*. Kerkyra, Greece.

Lowe, D. G. (2004). SIFT Distinctive Image Features from Scale-Invariant Keypoints. *International Journal of Computer Vision, 60*(2), 91–110. doi:10.1023/B:VISI.0000029664.99615.94

Mainali, P., Lafruit, G., Yang, Q., Geelen, B., Gool, L. V., & Lauwereins, R. (2013). SIFER: Scale-Invariant Feature Detector with Error Resilience. *International Journal of Computer Vision, 104*(2), 172–197. doi:10.1007/s11263-013-0622-3

Matas, J., Chum, O., Urban, M., & Pajdla, T. (2004). Robust Wide Baseline Stereo From Maximally Stable Extremal Regions. *Image and Vision Computing, 22*(10), 761–767. doi:10.1016/j.imavis.2004.02.006

Mikolajczyk, K., & Schmid, C. (2004). Scale & Affine Invariant Interest Point Detectors. *International Journal of Computer Vision, 60*(1), 63–86. doi:10.1023/B:VISI.0000027790.02288.f2

Mikolajczyk, K., & Schmid, C. (2005). A Performance Evaluation of Local Descriptors. *IEEE Transactions on Pattern Analysis and Machine Intelligence, 27*(10), 1615–1630. doi:10.1109/TPAMI.2005.188 PMID:16237996

Mikolajczyk, K., Tuytelaars, T., Schmid, C., Zisserman, A., Matas, J., Schaffalitzky, F., & Gool, L. V. et al. (2005). A Comparison of Affine Region Detectors. *International Journal of Computer Vision, 65*(1-2), 43–72. doi:10.1007/s11263-005-3848-x

Miksik, O., & Mikolajczyk, K. (2012). Evaluation of Local Detectors and Descriptors for Fast Feature Matching. *Proceedings of the International Conference on Pattern Recognition*. Tsukuba.

Mizuno, K., Noguchi, H., He, G., Terachi, Y., Kamino, T., Kawaguchi, H., & Yoshimoto, M. (2010). Fast and Low-Memory-Bandwidth Architecture of SIFT Descriptor Generation with Scalability on Speed and Accuracy for VGA Video. *Proceedings of the International Conference on Field Programmable Logic and Applications*, Milano (pp. 608-611). doi:10.1109/FPL.2010.119

Morel, J. M., & Yu, G. (2009). ASIFT: A New Framework for Fully Affine Invariant Image Comparison. *SIAM Journal on Imaging Sciences, 2*(2), 1–28. doi:10.1137/080732730

Morel, J.-M., & Yu, G. (2016, Nov. 8). *Affine-SIFT (ASIFT)*. Retrieved from https://tinyurl.com/akkznh

Ngo, H. T., Ives, R. W., Rakvic, R. N., & Broussard, R. P. (2013). Real-time Video Surveillance on an Embedded, Programmable Platform. *Microprocessors and Microsystems, 37*(6-7), 562–571. doi:10.1016/j.micpro.2013.06.003

Nister, D., & Stewenius, H. (2006). *Scalable Recognition with a Vocabulary Tree*. New York, NY: IEEE Computer Vision and Pattern Recognition. doi:10.1109/CVPR.2006.264

Nister, D., & Stewenius, H. (2008). Linear Time Maximally Stable Extremal Regions. *Proceedings of the European Conference on Computer Vision*. Marseille, France.

Obdrzalek, S., & Matas, J. (2002). Object Recognition using Local Affine Frames on Distinguished Regions. *Proceedings of the British Machine Vision Conference* (pp. 83-104). Springer. doi:10.5244/C.16.9

Obdrzalek, S., & Matas, J. (2005). Sub-linear Indexing For Large Scale Object Recognition. *Proceedings of the British Machine Vision Conference*. doi:10.5244/C.19.3

Perdoch, M., & Matas, J. (2011). *Maximally Stable Extremal Regions and Local Geometry for Visual Correspondences*. Prague, Czech Republic: Czech Technical University.

Qasaimeh, M., Sagahyroon, A., & Shanableh, T. (2014). A Parallel Hardware Architecture for Scale Invariant Feature Transform (SIFT). *Proceedings of the International Conference on Multimedia Computing and Systems*. Marrakech. doi:10.1109/ICMCS.2014.6911251

Qasaimeh, M., Sagahyroon, A., & Shanableh, T. (2015). FPGA-Based Parallel Hardware Architecture for Real-Time Image Classification. *IEEE Trans. on Computational Imaging, 1*(1), 56–70. doi:10.1109/TCI.2015.2424077

Rister, B., Wang, G., Wu, M., & Cavallaro, R., J. (2013). A Fast and Efficient SIFT Detector Using the Mobile GPU. *Proceedings of the IEEE International Conference on Acoustics, Speech, and Signal Processing (ICASSP)*. Vancouver, BC. doi:10.1109/ICASSP.2013.6638141

Salahat, E. (2016). A Novel Multi-Intensity Image Labeling Algorithm for Real-Time Computer Vision and Robotics Applications. *Proceedings of the Annual Conference of the IEEE Industrial Electronics Society*. Florence, Italy.

Salahat, E., Saleh, H., Mohammad, B., Al-Qutayri, M., Sluzek, A., & Ismail, M. (2013). Automated Real-Time Video Surveillance Algorithms for SoC Implementation: A Survey. *Proceedings of the IEEE International Conference on Electronics, Circuits, and Systems*. Abu Dhabi, UAE. doi:10.1109/ICECS.2013.6815354

Salahat, E., Saleh, H., Salahat, S., Sluzek, A., Al-Qutayri, M., Mohammad, B., & Ismail, M. (2016, April 28). *US Patent No. 20160117830*.

Salahat, E., Saleh, H., Salahat, S., Sluzek, A., Al-Qutayri, M., Mohammed, B., & Ismail, M. (2015). Extended MSER Detection. *Proceedings of the IEEE International Symposium on Industrial Electronics*. Rio de Janeiro, Brazil.

Salahat, E., Saleh, H., Sluzek, A., Al-Qutayri, M., Mohammad, B., & Ismail, M. (2015). A Maximally Stable Extremal Regions System-on-Chip For Real-Time Visual Surveillance. *Proceedings of the Annual Conference of the IEEE Industrial Electronics Society*. Yokohama, Japan.

Salahat, E., Saleh, H., Sluzek, A., Al-Qutayri, M., Mohammad, B., & Ismail, M. (2015). Novel Fast and Scalable Parallel Union-Find Implementation For Real-Time Digital Image Segmentation. *Proceedings of the Annual Conference of the IEEE Industrial Electronics Society*. Yokohama, Japan.

Salahat, E., Saleh, H., Sluzek, A., Al-Qutayri, M., Mohammed, B., & Ismail, M. (2016, March 10). US Patent No. 20160070970.

Salti, S., Lanza, A., & Stefano, L. D. (2013). Keypoints from Symmetries by Wave Propagation. *Proceedings of the IEEE Conference on Computer Vision and Pattern Recognition*.

Schmid, C., Mohr, R., & Bauckhage, C. (2000). Evaluation of Interest Point Detectors. *International Journal of Computer Vision*, *37*(2), 151–172. doi:10.1023/A:1008199403446

Sivic, J., & Zisserman, A. (2003). Video google: A Text Retrieval Approach to Object Matching in Videos. *Proceedings of the International Conference on Computer Vision*. Nice, France. doi:10.1109/ICCV.2003.1238663

Sluzek, A. (2015). Multi-distinctive MSER Features and Their Descriptors: A Low-Complexity Tool for Image Matching. *Proceedings of the International Conference on Advanced Concepts for Intelligent Vision Systems*. Catania, Italy. doi:10.1007/978-3-319-25903-1_58

Sluzek, A. (2016). Improving Performances of MSER Features in Matching and Retrieval Tasks. *Proceedings of the European Conference on Computer Vision*. Amsterdam, The Netherlands.

Tuytelaars, T., & Mikolajczyk, K. (2008). Local Invariant Feature Detectors: A Survey. *Foundations and Trends in Computer Graphics and Vision*, *3*(3), 177–280. doi:10.1561/0600000017

Vedaldi, A. (2007). An Implementation of Multi-Dimensional Maximally Stable Extremal Regions.

Vedaldi, A. (2016). *VLFeat*. Retrieved November 6, 2016, from http://www.vlfeat.org

Wang, G., Tao, L., Di, H., Ye, X., & Shi, Y. (2012). A Scalable Distributed Architecture for Intelligent Vision System. *IEEE Trans. on Industrial Informatics*, *8*(1), 91–99. doi:10.1109/TII.2011.2173945

Xu, Y., Monasse, P., Géraud, T., & Najman, L. (2014). Tree-Based Morse Regions: A Topological Approach to Local Feature Detection. *IEEE Transactions on Image Processing*, *23*(12), 5612–5625. doi:10.1109/TIP.2014.2364127 PMID:25373079

Zhong, S., Wang, J., Yan, L., Kang, L., & Cao, Z. (2013). A Real-time Embedded Architecture for SIFT. *Journal of Systems Architecture: the EUROMICRO Journal*, *59*(1), 16–29. doi:10.1016/j.sysarc.2012.09.002

Chapter 17
Recognition of Face Biometrics

Pooja Sharma
DAV University, India

ABSTRACT

In the proposed chapter, a novel, effective, and efficient approach to face recognition is presented. It is a fusion of both global and local features of images, which significantly achieves higher recognition. Initially, the global features of images are determined using polar cosine transforms (PCTs), which exhibit very less computation complexity as compared to other global feature extractors. For local features, the rotation invariant local ternary patterns are used rather than using the existing ones, which help improving the recognition rate and are in alignment with the rotation invariant property of PCTs. The fusion of both acquired global and local features is performed by mapping their features into a common domain. Finally, the proposed hybrid approach provides a robust feature set for face recognition. The experiments are performed on benchmark face databases, representing various expressions of facial images. The results of extensive set of experiments reveal the supremacy of the proposed method over other approaches in terms of efficiency and recognition results.

INTRODUCTION

Biometric is a recently emerged and vastly increasing technology, which has numerous applications in forensics, surveillance and security. Primarily, biometric system identifies and recognizes human biological features such as fingerprints, iris, hand geometry, and face recognition. The human face considers to be a dynamic object exhibiting high erraticism due to its appearance and expressions. Moreover, face recognition is a challenging area in real time applications. Among other biometrics, face based recognition has advantages in terms of uniqueness. To describe the facial images acquired using camera or other sources various descriptors are available. An image descriptor can be region based/dense or contour based/discrete. A region based descriptor computes features on all the pixels of the image, while contour based descriptor computes on a subset of image pixels. The region based descriptors can be termed as global descriptors because these descriptors extract features by considering the entire image as a whole and represent the global characteristics of the image.

DOI: 10.4018/978-1-5225-2848-7.ch017

LITERATURE SURVEY

Global Descriptors

Various global descriptors include Hu's (1962) seven moment invariants based on geometric moments, the three orthogonal rotation invariant moments (ORIMs) viz. Zernike moments (ZMs) (Teague, 1980), pseudo Zernike moments (PZMs) (The and Chin, 1988), and orthogonal Fourier Mellin moments (OFMMs) (Sheng and Shen, 1994), and generic Fourier descriptor (Zhang and Lu, 2002), wavelet moments (Shen and Ip, 1999), angular radial transforms (ART) (Bober, 2011), polar harmonic transforms (PHTs) (Yap et al., 2010), etc. Other types of region based descriptors include distribution based descriptors in which histograms are used to represent various characteristics of image. The features acquired using distribution based descriptors belong to an interest point (keypoint) or an interest region. The distribution based methods include scale invariant feature transform (SIFT) (Lowe, 2004) PCA-SIFT (Ke and Sukhtankar, 2004) gradient location and oriented histograms (GLOH) (Mikolajczyk, Schmid, 2005) histograms of oriented gradients (HOG) (Dalal and Triggs, 2005) speeded up robust features (SURF) (Bay et al., 2008), etc. The distribution based descriptors are also computation intensive and produce very high dimensionality of features.

Local Descriptors

Contour based or discrete descriptors include Fourier descriptor (Zhang and Lu, 2003) contour flexibility (Xu et al., 2009) contour point distribution histograms (Shu and Wu, 2011) Weber's local descriptor (Chen et al., 2001) local binary patterns (LBP) (Ojala and Pietikainen, 2002) local ternary patterns (LTP) (Tan and Triggs, 2010), etc. These descriptors do not consider entire image as a whole. In fact, only a part of the shape such as boundary or image masks of various dimensions usually 3×3 are considered for computing image features. These techniques provide local characteristics of the image. They are computationally efficient as compared to region based approaches.

Hybrid Descriptors

In a recent study, it is observed that several hybrid approaches are being pursued (Jain and Vailaya, 1998; Wei et al., 2008; Qi et al., 2010; Singh and Pooja, 2011; Singh and Pooja, 2012) Hybrid approaches combine features from distinct modalities such as both global and local features of images are considered. Jain and Vailaya (1998) propose a hybrid approach in which local features of images are extracted using edge directions of contour points and invariant moments are used for extracting global features of images. They observe that by combining local and global features, the recognition rate increases significantly. Wei et al. (2008) propose another hybrid approach, which uses histograms of centroid distances (HCD) and contour curvature (CC) for local feature extraction. HCD provides satisfactory results. Nevertheless, CC requires second order derivative, which is prone to image noise. Besides, it does not provide adjacency relationship among boundary points. On the other hand, global features are extracted by using first four low order Zernike moments (ZMs). However, it has been observed that merely four low order ZMs are not sufficient enough to completely describe the entire aspects of the image (Singh and Pooja, 2011). Another hybrid approach is suggested by Qi et al. (2010). The global features are extracted using spatial distribution of feature points. In their approach, local features are obtained by using relationship among two adjacent boundary points and the centroid (RAPC) and HCD as proposed by Wei et al. (2008). However, it has been observed that the histograms of normalized radii do not provide accurate results. Because in certain situations, the radius of the circumscribed circle passing through two adjacent boundary points and the centroid becomes quite large, which results in incorrect formation of histogram, thereby affecting the recognition accuracy (Singh and Pooja, 2011).

Role of the Chapter

Most of the hybrid approaches involving orthogonal rotation invariant moments use ZMs as global feature descriptor (Wei et al., 2008; Singh and Pooja, 2011; Singh and Pooja, 2012) Yap et al. (2010) develop polar harmonic transforms (PHTs), which comprises of polar cosine transform (PCT), polar sine transform (PST), and polar cosine exponential transform (PCET). Like ORIMs, the kernel function of PHTs exhibit characteristics similar to ORIMs that is rotation invariance, good image reconstruction capability, orientation estimation, etc. An extensive experimental analysis reveals that the performance of ORIMs and PHTs is comparable (Li et al., 2011). However, unlike ORIMs, PHTs are better in terms of computation efficiency and numerical stability for high order transforms. Keeping in view their distinctive advantages over ZMs, in this chapter, we use PCTs as the global region based descriptor. We choose PCTs out of the three PHTs because of their superior performance than PSTs and less computational cost than PCETs. The experimental evidence for better performance of PCTs over PSTs and PCETs is given in later section of this chapter. We also compare the performance of PCTs and ZMs in face recognition to justify our preference of PCTs over ZMs.

For local feature extraction, we use local ternary patterns (LTP). We choose LTP from among several other local descriptors because we have observed its performance to be much superior to FD, which is considered to be one of the best descriptors (Zhang and Lu, 2003). Besides, the comparison of LTP with other prominent local descriptors also represents its superiority, which is demonstrated in the experimental section. Moreover, LTP provides excellent results under illumination variations and texture images (Tan and Triggs, 2010). Apart from that LTP is more distinctive and less sensitive to noise in uniform regions. To our best knowledge, the performance of LTP on face recognition has not been reported yet.

Although other distribution based descriptors such as SIFT, PCA-SIFT, GLOH, HOG, SURF, etc provide good recognition results, they are computational intensive and their fusion with other global and local descriptors makes the system slow. Moreover, ZMs and PCTs intrinsically possess rotation invariance and orthogonality properties. Orthogonality property ensures the non-redundant set of features. Thus, the objective of this chapter is to analyze the effect of best global and local descriptors for face recognition. We consider ZMs and PCTs as global features and rotation invariant LTP as the local features. The two sets of hybrid methods ZMs+RLTP and PCTs+RLTP are investigated for their comparative recognition performance and computational efficiency in view of the abovementioned background. Since the proposed hybrid approach requires features from different modalities, i.e., global and local features, normalization of features is required for mapping them to a common domain (Jain et al., 2005). Although various classification techniques such as support vector machine (SVM), k-nearest neighbor (k-nn), Bayesian networks are available, they make the system sluggish. However, our purpose is to provide an efficient system with improved recognition rate. Thus, we use Bray-Curtis similarity measure for PCTs and ZMs based global features and min-max similarity measure for improved LTP based local features prior to combining them. The obtained similarity values are normalized and lies in the range [0,1] which helps improve the face recognition rate. For demonstrating the effectiveness of the proposed systems, various standard face databases viz. Jaffe, Yale, and ORL are considered. These databases represent various sorts of images such as varying lighting conditions, different expressions, varying moods (happy, sad, crying, etc.). Moreover, the time analysis of the proposed approach is provided to illustrate its efficiency. The results of various experiments authenticate that the proposed approach outperforms other hybrid methods in terms of accuracy and efficiency.

The rest of the chapter is organized as follows: The description of ZMs and PCTs is given in global feature extraction. Then, the description of LTP is provided for local feature extraction. Subsequently, effective similarity matching methodology is explained, which provides effective solution to amalgamate features from different modalities, then an extensive experimental analysis of the proposed approach is provided by comparing it with other prominent descriptors. At the end, the conclusion of the chapter is given.

GLOBAL FEATURE EXTRACTION

Zernike Moments (ZMs)

Teague (1980) presented ZMs in image analysis as a set of complex orthogonal functions with their magnitude coefficients exhibiting rotation invariance property. Since ZMs satisfy orthogonal property, by virtue of which the contribution of each moment coefficient to the image representation is unique, and no redundancy occurs between moment features. Due to these characteristics, ZMs are used to describe the essential features of images. The set of orthogonal ZMs for an image intensity function $f(\rho,\theta)$ with order p and repetition q are defined over a continuous unit disk $0 \leq \rho \leq 1, 0 \leq \theta < 2\pi$ as:

$$Z_{pq} = \frac{p+1}{\pi} \int_0^{2\pi} \int_0^1 f(\rho,\theta) V_{pq}^*(\rho,\theta) \rho \, d\rho \, d\theta \tag{1}$$

where $V_{pq}^*(\rho,\theta)$ is the complex conjugate of the Zernike polynomials $V_{pq}(\rho,\theta)$, defined as:

$$V_{pq}(\rho,\theta) = R_{pq}(\rho) e^{jq\theta} \tag{2}$$

where $p \geq 0, 0 \leq |q| \leq p, p - |q| = even, j = \sqrt{-1}$, and $\theta = \tan^{-1}(y/x)$

The radial polynomials $R_{pq}(\rho)$ are defined by:

$$R_{pq}(\rho) = \sum_{k=0}^{(p-|q|)/2} (-1)^k \frac{(p-k)!}{k! \left[\frac{p+|q|}{2} - k\right]! \left[\frac{p-|q|}{2} - k\right]!} \rho^{p-2k} \tag{3}$$

The radial polynomials satisfy the orthogonality relation:

$$\int\limits_0^1 R_{pq}\left(\rho\right) R_{p'q}(\rho)\rho\,d\rho = \frac{1}{2(p+1)}\delta_{pp'}$$ (4)

where δ_{ij} is Kronecker delta. The set of Zernike polynomials $V_{pq}(\rho,\theta)$ form a complete orthogonal set within the unit disc as:

$$\int\limits_0^{2\pi}\int\limits_0^1 V_{pq}\left(\rho,\theta\right) V_{p'q'}^*\left(\rho,\theta\right)\rho\,d\rho\,d\theta = \frac{\pi}{p+1}\delta_{pp'}\delta_{qq'}$$ (5)

For improving the computation efficiency of ZMs, we use $q-recursive$ algorithm (Singh and Walia, 2011), which significantly reduces the time complexity of both $R_{pq}\left(r\right)$ and $e^{-jq\theta}$ using recursive relations for $R_{pq}\left(r\right)$ and for trigonometric functions.

Polar Cosine Transforms (PCTs)

The set of polar cosine transforms are introduced by Yap et al. (2010). The coefficients of PCTs inherently possess the property of rotation invariance. Since PCTs satisfy orthogonal property by virtue of which the contribution of each moment coefficient to the image is unique and no redundancy occur among image features. The set of orthogonal PCTs for an image intensity function $f\left(\rho,\theta\right)$ with order p and repetition q are defined over a continuous unit disc $0 \le \rho \le 1$, $0 \le \theta < 2\pi$:

$$M_{pq} = \Omega_p \int\limits_0^{2\pi}\int\limits_0^1 f\left(\rho,\theta\right) V_{pq}^*\left(\rho,\theta\right)\rho\,d\rho\,d\theta$$ (6)

where $V_{pq}^*\left(\rho,\theta\right)$ is the complex conjugate of the Zernike polynomials $V_{pq}\left(\rho,\theta\right)$, defined as:

$$V_{pq}\left(\rho,\theta\right) = R_p\left(\rho\right)e^{jq\theta}$$ (7)

where $p, |q| = 0,1,...,\infty, j = \sqrt{-1}$, and $\theta = \tan^{-1}\left(y/x\right)$ and radial polynomials $R_p(\rho)$ are defined as:

$$R_p\left(\rho\right) = \cos\left(\pi p \rho^2\right)$$ (8)

$$\Omega_p = \begin{cases} \dfrac{1}{\pi} & p = 0 \\ \dfrac{2}{\pi} & p \ne 0 \end{cases}$$ (9)

PCTs are simpler to compute than ZMs because their radial kernel function comprises of just a cosine term. For reducing the time complexity of PCTs even further, we use the recurrence relations for the computation of trigonometric and angular functions as given by (Singh and Walia, 2011). It significantly reduces the time complexity of PCTs.

Computational Model for ZMs and PCTs and Speed Enhancement

In digital image processing, the image intensity function $f(\rho,\theta)$ is discrete and defined in a rectangular coordinate system. Let the size of the image be $N \times N$ pixels and (i,k) represent a pixel having i^{th} row and k^{th} column. We perform a mapping of pixel grid from $N \times N$ square domain to $[-1,1] \times [-1,1]$ through the following transformation:

$$x_i = \frac{2i+1-N}{N\sqrt{2}}, y_k = \frac{2k+1-N}{N\sqrt{2}}, i,k = 0,1,2,...,N-1 \tag{10}$$

with the vertical and horizontal spacing between two pixels, $\Delta x = \frac{\sqrt{2}}{N}$ and $\Delta y = \frac{\sqrt{2}}{N}$. This transformation encloses the complete image inside the unit disc as shown in Figure 1 for an 8×8 image grid. The coordinates (x_i, y_k) denote the centre of (i,k) pixel. The unit disc: $\{f(\rho,\theta) \mid 0 \le \rho \le 1, 0 \le \theta \le 2\pi\}$ is now approximated by a unit digital disc: $\{f(i,k) \mid x_i^2 + y_k^2 \le 1\}$. The zeroth order approximation to Eq. (1) and Eq. (6) for ZMs and PCTs, respectively, are given by

$$Z_{pq} = \frac{2(p+1)}{\pi N^2} \sum_{i=0}^{N-1} \sum_{k=0}^{N-1} f(i,k) V_{pq}^*(x_i, y_k) \tag{11}$$

$$M_{pq} = \frac{2\Omega_p}{\pi N^2} \sum_{i=0}^{N-1} \sum_{k=0}^{N-1} f(i,k) V_{pq}^*(x_i, y_k) \tag{12}$$

Figure 1. Outer disc encloses 8×8 image grid

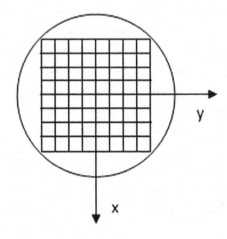

where $V_{pq}^{*}\left(x_{i},y_{k}\right)$ are computed from Eq. (2) and Eq. (7) for ZMs and PCTs, respectively.

It is observed from Eq. (11) and Eq. (12) that the computation of the basis functions $V_{pq}^{*}\left(x,y\right)$ is very time consuming. In the case of ZMs, the time complexity is $O\left(N^{2}p_{\max}^{3}\right)$, where $p_{\max}$ is the maximum order of ZMs. The time complexity of ZMs is reduced to $O\left(N^{2}p_{\max}^{2}\right)$ using the recursive algorithms. Further, the use of 8-way symmetry of radial polynomials $R_{pq}(r)$ and the recursive computation of angular functions enhance the speed of computation significantly. Similarly, the 8-way symmetry of the radial kernel function of PCTs, $\cos\left(2\pi pr\right)$, and the recursive computation of its angular part enhance the speed of computation manifold.

Feature Dimensionality

Although the features acquired using ZMs and PCTs are effective in their performance for representing and describing images, the selection of appropriate number of features is one of the crucial tasks in face recognition. Generally, the utilization of higher number of moments leads to the improvement in recognition accuracy. A small number of features do not provide satisfactory results, while the high number of features are prone to "overtraining" and reduce the computation efficiency. In addition, higher order moments and transforms suffer from numerical integration error and numerically instability. The maximum orders $p_{\max}=12$ for ZMs and $p_{\max}=6$ for PCTs are considered to be a good tradeoff between the computation complexity and image description capability (Singh and Pooja, 2011; Singh and Pooja, 2012). Therefore, in the proposed work, we utilize $p_{\max}=12$ for ZMs and $p_{\max}=6$ for PCTs, which generate 47 and 48 moments and transforms that are depicted in Table 1 and Table 2, respectively. The moments/transforms with $p=0,q=0$ are not included in the features set. Since $Z_{0,0}$ and $M_{0,0}$ signify an average gray value of image and $Z_{1,1,}$ become zero, if the centre of the disc is taken at the centroid of the image. Thus, the two moments and the one transform are excluded from the feature set.

Table 1. Features set for $p_{max}=12$ for ZMs

$p_{\max}$	ZMs	F
2	$Z_{2,0}\,Z_{2,2}$	2
3	$Z_{3,1}\,Z_{3,3}$	4
4	$Z_{4,0}\,Z_{4,2}\,Z_{4,4}$	7
5	$Z_{5,1}\,Z_{5,3}\,Z_{5,5}$	10
6	$Z_{6,0}\,Z_{6,2}\,Z_{6,4}\,Z_{6,6}$	14
7	$Z_{7,1}\,Z_{7,3}\,Z_{7,5}\,Z_{7,7}$	18
8	$Z_{8,0}\,Z_{8,2}\,Z_{8,4}\,Z_{8,6}\,Z_{8,8}$	23
9	$Z_{9,1}\,Z_{9,3}\,Z_{9,5}\,Z_{9,7}\,Z_{9,9}$	28
10	$Z_{10,0}\,Z_{10,2}\,Z_{10,4}\,Z_{10,6}\,Z_{10,8}\,Z_{10,10}$	34
11	$Z_{11,1}\,Z_{11,3}\,Z_{11,5}\,Z_{11,7}\,Z_{11,9}\,Z_{11,11}$	40
12	$Z_{12,0}\,Z_{12,2}\,Z_{12,4}\,Z_{12,6}\,Z_{12,8}\,Z_{12,10}\,Z_{12,12}$	47

Table 2. Features set for $p_{max} = 6$ for PCT

p_{max}	PCTs	F
0	$M_{0,1}\ M_{0,2}\ M_{0,3}\ M_{0,4}\ M_{0,5}\ M_{0,6}$	6
1	$M_{1,0}\ M_{1,1}\ M_{1,2}\ M_{1,3}\ M_{1,4}\ M_{1,5}\ M_{1,6}$	13
2	$M_{2,0}\ M_{2,1}\ M_{2,2}\ M_{2,3}\ M_{2,4}\ M_{2,5}\ M_{2,6}$	20
3	$M_{3,0}\ M_{3,1}\ M_{3,2}\ M_{3,3}\ M_{3,4}\ M_{3,5}\ M_{3,6}$	27
4	$M_{4,0}\ M_{4,1}\ M_{4,2}\ M_{4,3}\ M_{4,4}\ M_{4,5}\ M_{4,6}$	34
5	$M_{5,0}\ M_{5,1}\ M_{5,2}\ M_{5,3}\ M_{5,4}\ M_{5,5}\ M_{5,6}$	41
6	$M_{6,0}\ M_{6,1}\ M_{6,2}\ M_{6,3}\ M_{6,4}\ M_{6,5}\ M_{6,6}$	48

LOCAL FEATURE EXTRACTION

Local Ternary Pattern (LTP)

LBP has been demonstrated to be successful as a texture descriptor in many computer vision applications (Moore and Bowden, 2011; Chan et al., 2010; Wang et al., 2009; Shan and Gritti, 2008). One of the most important properties of LBP is its tolerance to illumination change and texture classification. In addition, the computational simplicity of the operator is a significant advantage over other approaches. However, in the previous work, LBP/LTP is applied on facial and texture images. In our proposed solution, we evaluate its performance on face recognition. LBP thresholds exactly at the value of the central pixel c. Therefore, they tend to be sensitive to noise, particularly in non-uniform regions. Thus, in LTP, LBP is extended to 3 valued code in which gray level in an intensity zone of width $\pm t$ around the intensity of the central pixel denoted by i_c are quantized to zero, ones above this are quantized to +1 and ones below it are quantized to -1, as given by the following function (Tan and Triggs, 2010):

$$s\left(i_n - i_c, t\right) = \begin{cases} +1, & i_n \geq i_c + t \\ 0, & \left|i_n - i_c\right| < t \\ -1, & i_n \leq i_c - t \end{cases} \tag{13}$$

Here t is a user specified threshold and we set $t = 5$ in our experiments. An illustration of LTP encoding is given in Figure 2.

The generated positive and negative codes of LTP can be split into negative and positive halves as represented in Figure 3. For creating negative half, ones are substituted at the places of -1 in ternary patterns and rests of the codes are set to 0. Likewise, for creating positive half, ones are substituted at the places of 1 and rests of the codes are set to 0. Subsequently, by treating these as two separate channels of LBP descriptor, separate histograms and similarity values are computed.

Figure 2. Representation of LTP code generation

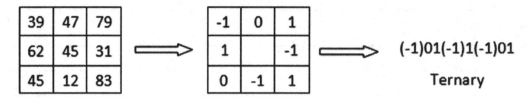

Figure 3. Splitting of ternary pattern into negative and positive halves

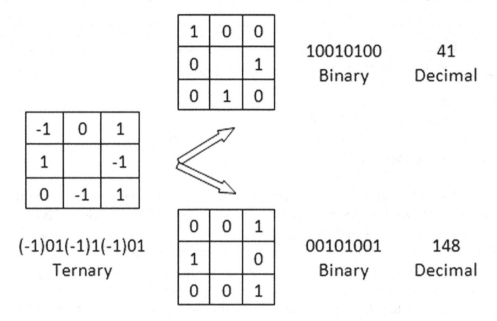

Rotation Invariant LTP

Since ZMs and PCTs inherently possess rotation invariance property, we use rotation invariant LTP to design the best possible combination of both global and local rotation invariant features. In order to remove the effect of rotation, i.e., to assign a unique identifier to each rotation invariant local binary pattern, which is generated by LTP, we define (Ojala and Pietikainen, 2002):

$$LBP_{P,R}^{ri} = \sum_{i=0}^{P-1} \min\left\{ROR\left(LBP_{P,R}, i\right)\right\} \tag{14}$$

where $ROR(x, i)$ performs bitwise circular right shift on P bit number x, i times. The notation $LBP_{P,R}$ denotes a neighborhood of P equally spaced sampling points on a circle of radius R. In our experiments, we set $P = 8$ and $R = 1$ for 8 neighbors around the centre pixel and within the circle of radius 1. For $P = 8$, LBP^{ri} has 36 rotational invariant patterns. The performance of LBP^{ri} features varies. Some patterns sustain rotation well, while other patterns do not (Ojala and Pietikainen, 2002). Thus, in our proposed solution, we use rotation invariant LTP (RLTP), in order to have alignment with the rotation invariant global features acquired using ZMs and PCTs.

EFFECTIVE SIMILARITY MEASURE

Feature vectors obtained by different modalities are heterogeneous, e.g., in our proposed solution, we are utilizing both global and local features of images. Global features are obtained using ZMs and PCTs, whereas local features are obtained using RLTP. Thus, normalization is required to transform these features into a common domain prior to combining them (Jain et al., 2005). Therefore, for transforming moment and transform based features into a common domain, we use Bray-Curtis similarity measure. It normalizes the feature values by dividing the absolute difference of corresponding feature values by the absolute value of their sum. The Bray-Curtis similarity measure for the proposed global descriptors is defined as:

$$d_g\left(Q,D\right) = \frac{\sum_{i=0}^{F-1}\left|\left|\xi_i^Q\right| - \left|\xi_i^D\right|\right|}{\sum_{i=0}^{F-1}\left|\left|\xi_i^Q\right| + \left|\xi_i^D\right|\right|} \tag{15}$$

where $\xi_i\left(Q\right)$ and $\xi_i\left(D\right)$ represent the feature vectors of the query and database images, respectively, and F is the number of features, which is 47 for ZMs and 48 for PCTs based global features. ξ represents either ZMs or PCTs based magnitude features described in above section. After extracting local features in the form of histograms of RLTP, similarity between the query image and the database images is computed by applying the following feature matching criteria:

$$d_l\left(Q,D\right) = 1 - \frac{\sum_{i=0}^{F-1}\min\left(H_i\left(Q\right),H_i\left(D\right)\right)}{\sum_{i=0}^{F-1}\max\left(H_i\left(Q\right),H_i\left(D\right)\right)} \tag{16}$$

where the minimum function value is used to compute the similarity/dissimilarity among images. It computes the minimum possible distance between query and database images. For the database image which is dissimilar to query image, the value of the expression $\min\left(H_i\left(Q\right),H_i\left(D\right)\right)$ is smaller and the value of the expression $\max\left(H_i\left(Q\right),H_i\left(D\right)\right)$ is larger. Consequently, the distance value d_l is high. On the other hand, for similar images the value of d_l is low. $H_i\left(Q\right)$ and $H_i\left(D\right)$ are the histogram cardinalities of query and database images, respectively. $d_g\left(Q,D\right)$ and $d_l\left(Q,D\right)$ given by Eq. (15) and Eq. (16) provides normalized similarity values of the same domain, which lie in the range $\left[0,1\right]$. Therefore, to compute the overall similarity by combining both local and global features, we combine all the distances given by Eq. (15) and Eq. (16) as follows:

$$d_o\left(Q,D\right) = w_g d_g\left(Q,D\right) + w_l d_l\left(Q,D\right) \tag{17}$$

where, w_g and w_l are the weight factors for $d_g\left(Q,D\right)$ and $d_l\left(Q,D\right)$, respectively. It is difficult to find optimal weights since weights depend on specific characteristics of the databases. It is a normal practice in such situations to assign equal weights to both sets of features. Therefore, in our experiments, we take $w_g = w_l = 0.5$.

EXPERIMENTAL STUDY AND PERFORMANCE ANALYSIS

In the above, a hybrid system to face recognition is proposed, in which both global and local features of images are coalesced. Global features are extracted using well established moment based descriptors ZMs and PCTs. On the other side, local features are extracted using RLTP. In an attempt to evaluate the proposed system's performance, we compare the proposed hybrid approach with various prominent local descriptors viz. LBP (Ojala and Pietikainen, 2002), WLD (Chen et al., 2001), LTP (Tan and Triggs, 2010) itself and global descriptors WM (Shen and Ip, 1999), ART (Bober, 2011), PCTs (Yap et al., 2010) itself as well as recent hybrid approaches, we refer to them as TCS (Wei et al., 2008) and QLS (Qi et al., 2010). All the approaches are implemented by the respective methodologies proposed in their research papers. Experiments are performed on an Intel Pentium Core 2 Duo 2.10 GHz processor with 3 GB RAM. Algorithms are implemented in VC++ 9.0. Besides, various types of images representing different aspects of images are considered to assess the proposed system performance. For this purpose, we use three benchmark face databases Yale, Jaffe, and ORL. The databases are described in the next sub-section.

Database Construction

- **Yale**: The Yale Face Database contains 165 grayscale images of 15 individuals. There are 11 images per subject, one per different facial expression or configuration: center-light, w/glasses, happy, left-light, w/no glasses, normal, right-light, sad, sleepy, surprised, and wink. (Georghiades, 1997).
- **JAFFE**: The database contains 213 images of 7 facial expressions (6 basic facial expressions + 1 neutral) posed by 10 Japanese female models. Each image has been rated on 6 emotion adjectives by 60 Japanese subjects (Dailey et al., 2010).
- **ORL Database**: There are ten different images of each of 40 distinct subjects and a total of 400 images in this database. For some subjects, the images were taken at different times, varying the lighting, facial expressions (open / closed eyes, smiling / not smiling) and facial details (glasses / no glasses). All the images were taken against a dark homogeneous background with the subjects in an upright, frontal position (with tolerance for some side movement) (Philips et al., 2000).

Instances of a few images of all the above mentioned databases are given in Figure 4.

Figure 4. A few instances of various databases

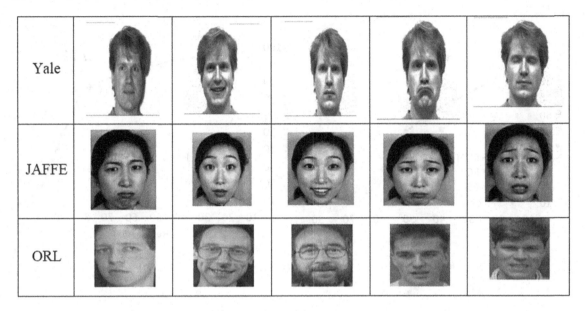

Performance Measurement

The recognition performance of the system is measured in terms of most general precision and recall measures. Precision measures the recognition accuracy and recall measures the ability to retrieve relevant images from the database. Precision and recall are inversely proportional to each other as the precision reduces, the recall increases. We use average precision and average recall for all the recognition results. For a query image q, precision and recall are computed in percentage as follows:

$$P = \frac{n_q}{T_q} \times 100, \; R = \frac{n_q}{D_q} \times 100 \tag{18}$$

where n_q represents the number of similar images retrieved from the database, T_q represents total number of images retrieved and D_q represents number of images in database similar to the query image q.

Evaluation of Face Recognition Performance

Performance Comparison of PHTs

In this section, we present the performance comparison of PHTs, i.e., PCETs, PCTs, PSTs for face recognition. The results are compared in terms of $P - R$ curves for two databases Yale and JAFFE, which are depicted in Figure 5(a) and Figure 5(b), respectively. It is apparent that among PCETs, PCTs, and PSTs, the superior performance is attained by PCTs followed by PSTs and PCETs for both sorts of databases. Thus, PCTs witness its superiority among other PHTs.

Figure 5. Comparison of $P - R$ performance of PCET, PCTs, and PST for (a) Yale (b) JAFFE data-bases

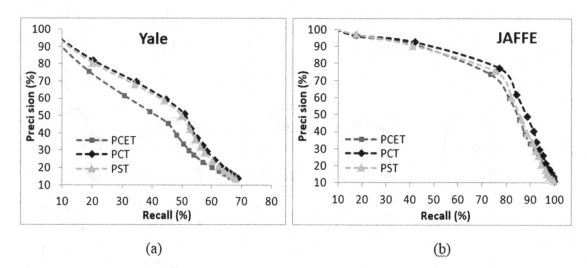

(a)   (b)

Performance Comparison with Local and Global Descriptors for Yale, JAFFE, and ORL Database

Here, we present the comparison of various prominent local and global descriptors with the proposed PCTs+RLTP. The comparison is performed in terms of $P - R$ curves. The first analysis is performed for Yale database in which images of the same class exhibit large variations. The respective $P - R$ curves are depicted in Figure 6(a). It is observed that among the local descriptors LBP, WLD, and RLTP, the superior performance is given by RLTP. On the other side among the global descriptors WM, ART, and PCTs, PCTs outperforms others. While observing the performance of combined PCTs+RLTP, we see that the proposed approach effectively overpowers other local and global descriptors and achieves a very high recognition rate. It is apparent from the $P - R$ curve for PCTs+RLTP.

The subsequent analysis is performed over JAFFE database. The respective $P - R$ curves are given in Figure 6(b). It is observed that among the local descriptors the proposed RLTP provides a relatively very high performance as compared to LBP and WLD. Among them, WLD gives the worst performance. While considering global descriptors, we see that the performance of ART and WM is almost similar and their $P - R$ curves overlap with each other. PCTs perform better than these global descriptors. Nevertheless, the proposed hybrid PCTs+RLTP gives superior performance as compared to other local and global descriptors. These results confirm that the proposed hybrid approach is capable of recognizing similar faces whether they vary in expressions. The subsequent analysis is performed for ORL database as shown in Fig. 6(c), it has been observed that the performance of all the descriptors is not that similar as for the previous databases. The worst performance is given by WM and the $P - R$ curves of ART and LBP superimpose over each other. WLD performs a bit better than ART and LBP, It is observed here that for face images of ORL database, the performance of the proposed RLTP is slightly superior to PCTs. While considering the performance of hybrid PCTs+RLTP, we see that it outperforms all other descriptors.

Figure 6. Comparison of $P - R$ performance of the proposed hybrid approach with other local and global descriptors for (a) Yale (b) JAFFE (c) ORL databases

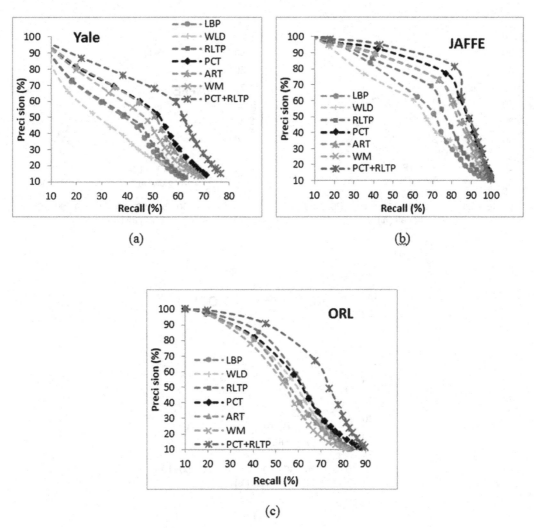

(a)

(b)

(c)

Performance Comparison with Hybrid Approaches

In this section, the proposed hybrid approaches PCTs+RLTP and ZMs+RLTP are compared against each other and with other recent ones such as TCS and QLS. Their performance is evaluated for Yale, JAFFE, and ORL face databases. The results are depicted in Figure 7(a) through 7(c). The $P - R$ performance for Yale database is depicted in Figure 7(a), It is observed that both ZMs+RLTP and PCTs+RLTP perform almost similar with slight improvement in PCTs+RLTP. However, other hybrid methods TCS and QLS perform worse than the proposed hybrid methods. The $P - R$ performance for JAFFE database is given in Figure 7(b) and it is seen that both proposed methods ZMs+RLTP and PCTs+RLTP outperform TCS and QLS. In the subsequent analysis, the performance of the proposed hybrid methods is analyzed for ORL database. It is apparent from Figure 7(c) that the performance of ZMs+RLTP and

Figure 7. Comparison of P − R performance of the proposed hybrid approach with other hybrid approaches for (a) Yale (b) JAFFE (c) ORL

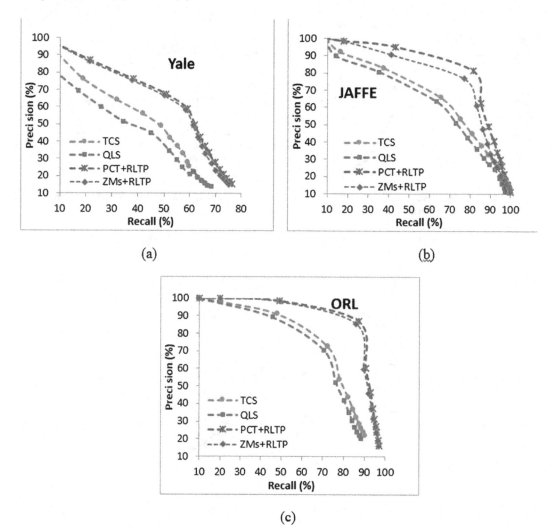

(a)

(b)

(c)

PCTs+RLTP is similar to that is observed for Yale database. That is the proposed hybrid methods again supersede other hybrid approaches.

CONCLUSION

In this chapter, both global and local features of face images are combined to develop a hybrid system. The global features of images are extracted using PCTs and ZMs. It has been observed from detailed experimental results that PCTs supersede ZMs for various sorts of images. On the other side, for local feature extraction RLTP is employed, which is superior to the basic LTP predominantly for rotated images. The accuracy of the recognition system is improved further by integrating PCTs and RLTP

(PCT+RLTP) and ZMs and RLTP (ZMs+RLTP). Several experiments are performed to analyze and confirm the superiority of the proposed hybrid approach over other methods. ZMs+RLTP based hybrid approach also improves the face recognition rate but slightly less than PCTs+RLTP. Therefore, all the experiments performed in this chapter lead to the supremacy of the proposed hybrid approach.

REFERENCES

Bay, H., Ess, A., Tuytelaars, T., & Van Gool, L. (2008). Speeded-up robust features (SURF). *Computer Vision and Image Understanding, 110*(3), 346–359. doi:10.1016/j.cviu.2007.09.014

Bober, M. (2011). MPEG-7 visual shape descriptors. *IEEE Transactions on Circuits and Systems for Video Technology, 11*(6), 716–719. doi:10.1109/76.927426

Chan, C., Kittler, J., & Messer, K. (2010). Multi-scale local binary pattern histograms for face recognition. *Proceedings of the 2nd International Conference on Biometrics ICIP '10* (pp. 809–818).

Chen, J. et al.. (2010). WLD: A robust image local descriptor. *IEEE Transactions on Pattern Analysis and Machine Intelligence, 32*(9), 1705–1720. doi:10.1109/TPAMI.2009.155 PMID:20634562

Dailey, M. N., Joyce C., Lyons M. J., M. J., Kamachi, M., Ishi, H., Gyoba, J., & Cottrell, G. W. (2010). Evidence and a computational explanation of cultural differences in facial expression recognition. *Emotion, 10*(6), 874-893.

Dalal, N., & Triggs, B. (2005). Histograms of oriented gradients for human detection. *Proceedings of the IEEE Int. Conf. CVPR*. doi:10.1109/CVPR.2005.177

Georghiades, A. (1997). Yale face database. *Center for computational Vision and Control at Yale University*. Retrieved from http://cvc. yale.edu/projects/yalefaces/yalefa

Hu, M. K. (1962). Visual pattern recognition by moment invariants. *I.R.E. Transactions on Information Theory, 8*(2), 179–187. doi:10.1109/TIT.1962.1057692

Jain, A., Nandakumar, K., & Ross, A. (2005). Score normalization in multimodal biometric systems. *Pattern Recognition, 38*(12), 2270–2285. doi:10.1016/j.patcog.2005.01.012

Jain, A. K., & Vailaya, A. (1998). Shape-based recognition: A case study with trademark image database. *Pattern Recognition, 31*(9), 1369–1390. doi:10.1016/S0031-3203(97)00131-3

Ke, Y., & Sukthankar, R. (2004). PCA-SIFT: A more distinctive representation for local image descriptors. *Proc. IEEE Int. Conf. Computer Vision and Pattern Recognition* (Vol. 2, pp. 506–513).

Li, L., Li, S., Wang, G., & Abraham, A. (2011, March 26-28). An evaluation on circularly orthogonal moments for image representation. *Proceedings of Int. Conf. Inf. Sci., and Tech.*, Nanjing, Jiangsu, China (pp. 394-397). doi:10.1109/ICIST.2011.5765275

Lowe, D. G. (2004). Distinctive image features from scale-invariant key points. *International Journal of Computer Vision, 60*(2), 91–110. doi:10.1023/B:VISI.0000029664.99615.94

Mikolajczyk, K., & Schmid, M. (2005). A performance evaluation of local descriptors. *IEEE Transactions on Pattern Analysis and Machine Intelligence*, *27*(10), 1615–1630. doi:10.1109/TPAMI.2005.188 PMID:16237996

Moore, S., & Bowden, R. (2011). Local binary patterns for multi-view facial expression recognition. *Computer Vision and Image Understanding*, *115*(4), 541–558. doi:10.1016/j.cviu.2010.12.001

Ojala, T., Pietikainen, M., & Maenpaa, T. (2002). Multiresolution gray-scale and rotation invariant texture classification with local binary patterns. *IEEE Transactions on Pattern Analysis and Machine Intelligence*, *24*(7), 971–986. doi:10.1109/TPAMI.2002.1017623

Phillips, P. J., Martin, A., Wilson, C., & Przybocki, M. (2000). An Introduction to Evaluating Biometric Systems. *IEEE Computer*, *33*(2), 56–63. doi:10.1109/2.820040

Qi, H., Li, K., Shen, Y., & Qu, W. (2010). An effective solution for trademark image retrieval by combining shape description and feature matching. *Pattern Recognition*, *43*(6), 2017–2027. doi:10.1016/j.patcog.2010.01.007

Shan, C., & Gritti, T. (2008). Learning discriminative lbp-histogrambins for facial expression recognition. *Proceedings of the British Machine Vision Conference*.

Shen, D., & Ip, H. H. S. (1999). Discriminative wavelet shape descriptors for recognition of 2-D patterns. *Pattern Recognition*, *32*(2), 151–165. doi:10.1016/S0031-3203(98)00137-X

Sheng, Y., & Shen, L. (1994). Orthogonal Fourier Mellin Moment for Invariant Pattern Recognition. *Journal of the Optical Society of America*, *11*(6), 1748–1757. doi:10.1364/JOSAA.11.001748

Shu, X., & Wu, X.-J. (2011). A novel contour descriptor for 2D shape matching and its application to image retrieval. *Image and Vision Computing*, *29*(4), 286–294. doi:10.1016/j.imavis.2010.11.001

Singh, C., & Pooja, . (2011). Improving image retrieval using combined features of Hough transform and Zernike moments. *Optics and Lasers in Engineering*, *49*(12), 1386–1396. doi:10.1016/j.optlaseng.2011.07.009

Singh, C., & Pooja, . (2012). Local and global features based image retrieval system using orthogonal radial moments. *Optics and Lasers in Engineering*, *50*(5), 655–667. doi:10.1016/j.optlaseng.2011.11.012

Singh, C., & Walia, E. (2011). Algorithms for fast computation of Zernike moments and their numerical stability. *Image and Vision Computing*, *29*(4), 251–259. doi:10.1016/j.imavis.2010.10.003

Tan, X., & Triggs, B. (2010). Enhanced local texture features set for face recognition under different lighting conditions. *IEEE Transactions on Image Processing*, *19*(6), 1635–1650. doi:10.1109/TIP.2010.2042645 PMID:20172829

Teague, M. R. (1980). Image analysis via the general theory of moments. *Journal of the Optical Society of America*, *70*(8), 920–930. doi:10.1364/JOSA.70.000920

The, C. H., & Chin, R. T. (1988). On image analysis by the methods of moments. *IEEE Transactions on Pattern Analysis and Machine Intelligence*, *10*(4), 496–513. doi:10.1109/34.3913

Wang, X., Han, T., & Yan, S. (2009). An hog-lbp human detector with partial occlusion handling. *Proceedings of the International Conference on Computer Vision ICCV '09* (pp. 32–39). doi:10.1109/ICCV.2009.5459207

Wei, C. H., Li, Y., Chau, W.-Y., & Li, C.-T. (2008). Trademark image retrieval using synthetic features for describing global shape and interior structure. *Pattern Recognition, 42*(3), 386–394. doi:10.1016/j.patcog.2008.08.019

Xu, C. J., Liu, J. Z., & Tang, X. (2009). 2D shape matching by contour flexibility. *IEEE Transactions on Pattern Analysis and Machine Intelligence, 31*(1), 180–186. doi:10.1109/TPAMI.2008.199 PMID:19029556

Yap, P. T., Jiang, X., & Fellow, A. C. K. (2010). Two dimensional polar harmonic transforms for invariant image representation. *IEEE Transactions on Pattern Analysis and Machine Intelligence, 32*(7), 1259–1270. doi:10.1109/TPAMI.2009.119 PMID:20489228

Zhang, D., & Lu, G. (2002). Shape-based image retrieval using generic Fourier descriptor. *Signal Processing Image Communication, 17*(10), 825–848. doi:10.1016/S0923-5965(02)00084-X

Zhang, D., & Lu, G. (2003). A comparative study of curvature scale space and Fourier descriptors for shape-based image retrieval. *Journal of Visual Communication and Image Representation, 14*(1), 41–60. doi:10.1016/S1047-3203(03)00003-8

KEY TERMS AND DEFINITIONS

Moments: Moments are scalar quantities used to characterize a function and to capture its significant features.

Global Feature: It represents the complete aspect of the image and describe the characteristics of an image as a whole.

Local Feature: It describes the deep or local characteristics of an image.

Precision: Precision measures the retrieval accuracy.

Recall: Recall is the ability to retrieve relevant images.

458

Compilation of References

Abbaszadeh, J., Rahim, H. A., Rahim, R. A., Sarafi, S., Nor Ayob, M., & Faramarzi, M. (2013). Design procedure of ultrasonic tomography system with steel pipe conveyor. *Sensors and Actuators. A, Physical*, *203*, 215–224. doi:10.1016/j.sna.2013.08.020

Abdel-Hakim, E. A., & Farag, A. A. (2006). CSIFT: A SIFT Descriptor with Color Invariant Characteristics. *Proceedings of the IEEE Conference on Computer Vision and Pattern Recognition.* doi:10.1109/CVPR.2006.95

Adam, A., Rivlin, E., Shimshoni, I., & Reinitz, D. (2008). Robust real-time unusual event detection using multiple fixed-location monitors. *IEEE Transactions on Pattern Analysis and Machine Intelligence*, *30*(3), 555–560. doi:10.1109/TPAMI.2007.70825 PMID:18195449

Agarwal, S., Awan, A., & Roth, D. (2004). Learning to detect objects in images via a sparse, part-based representation. *PAMI*, *26*(11), 1475–1490. doi:10.1109/TPAMI.2004.108 PMID:15521495

Ahmad, M. B., Kim, D. Y., Roh, K. S., & Choi, T. S. (2000). Motion vector estimation using edge oriented block matching algorithm for video sequences. *Proceedings of the 2000 International Conference on Image Processing* (Vol. 1, pp. 860-863). IEEE. doi:10.1109/ICIP.2000.901095

Ahmad, I., Zheng, W., Luo, J., & Liou, M. (2006). A fast adaptive motion estimation algorithm. *IEEE Transactions on Circuits and Systems for Video Technology*, *16*(3), 420–438. doi:10.1109/TCSVT.2006.870022

Ahonen, T., Hadid, A., & Pietikainen, M. (2006). Face description with local binary patterns: Application to face recognition. *IEEE Transactions on Pattern Analysis and Machine Intelligence*, *28*(12), 2037–2041. doi:10.1109/TPAMI.2006.244 PMID:17108377

Al-Azzawi, N., & Abdullah, W. A. K. W. (2009). Medical Image Fusion Schemes using Contourlet Transform and PCA Based. *Proceedings of the Annual International Conference of the IEEE* (pp. 5813-5816). Engineering in Medicine and Biology Society.

Alcantarilla, P. F., Bartoli, A., & Davison, A. J. (2012). KAZE Features. *Proceedings of the European Conference on Computer Vision.*

Aldana-Iuit, J., Mishkin, D., Chum, O., & Matas, J. (2016). In the Saddle: Chasing Fast and Repeatable Features. arXiv:1608.06800v1

Al-Rawi, M. S. (2010). Fast computation of pseudo Zernike moments. *Journal of Real-Time Image Processing*, *5*(1), 3–10. doi:10.1007/s11554-009-0118-0

Alyammahi, S., Salahat, E., Saleh, H., & Sluzek, A. (2015). A Hardware Accelerator For Real-Time Extraction of The Linear-Time MSER Algorithm. *Proceedings of the Annual Conference of the IEEE Industrial Electronics Society.* Yokohama, Japan.

Anderson, F. Jr, Penney, B. C., Patwardhan, N. A., & Wheeler, H. B. (1980). Impedance plethysmography: The origin of electrical impedance changes measured in the human calf. *Medical & Biological Engineering & Computing, 18*(2), 234–240. doi:10.1007/BF02443300 PMID:7392690

Anishiya, P., & Joans, S. M. (2011). Number plate recognition for indian cars using morphological dilation and erosion with the aid of ocrs. *Proceedings of the 2011 International Conference on Information and Network Technology (IPCSIT)*.

Anna Palagan, C., & Leena, T. (2011, April 8-10). Brain Structure Segmentation of Magnetic Resonance Imaging Using T– Mixture Algorithm, Electronics Computer Technology (ICECT). *Proceedings of the 3rd International Conference* (Vol. 3, pp. 446-450).

Arnold, W. M., Worring, M., Santini, S., Gupta, A., & Jain, R. (2000). Content-based image retrieval at the end of the early years. *IEEE Transactions on Pattern Analysis and Machine Intelligence, 22*(12), 38–45.

Arora, S. M., & Rajpal, N. (2014). Comparative analysis of motion estimation algorithms on slow, medium and fast video sequences. *Proceedings of the 2014 International Conference on Optimization, Reliability, and Information Technology* (pp. 422-427). IEEE. doi:10.1109/ICROIT.2014.6798367

Arora, S. M., & Rajpal, N. (2014). Survey of fast block motion estimation algorithms. *Proceedings of the 2014 International Conference on Advances in Computing, Communications and Informatics* (pp. 2022-2026). IEEE. doi:10.1109/ICACCI.2014.6968599

Arora, S. M., Rajpal, N., & Khanna, K. (2016). A new approach with enhanced accuracy in zero motion prejudgment for motion estimation in real-time applications. *Journal of Real-Time Image Processing*.

Arpinar, V. E., & Eyuboglu, B. M. (2001). Microcontroller controlled, multifrequency electrical impedance tomograph. *Annual Reports of the Research Reactor Institute, 3*, 2289–2291.

Atefi, R. (2015). *Electrical Bio impedance Cerebral Monitoring: From Hypothesis and Simulations to First Experimental Evidence in Stroke Patients*. Stockholm, Sweden: Royal Institute of Technology, School of Technology and Health.

Atkinson, W. (1994). U.S. Patent No. 5,335,299. Washington, DC: U.S. Patent and Trademark Office.

Atkociunas, E., Blake, R., Juozapavicius, A., & Kazimianec, M. (2005). Image Processing in Road Traffic Analysis. *Nonlinear Analysis: Modelling and Control, 10*(4), 315–332.

Attalla, E., & Siy, P. (2005). Robust shape similarity retrieval based on contour segmentation polygonal multiresolution and elastic matching. *Pattern Recognition, 38*(12), 2229–2241. doi:10.1016/j.patcog.2005.02.009

Awad, A. I., & Hassaballah, M. (2016). *Image Feature Detectors and Descriptors: Foundations and Applications*. Springer. doi:10.1007/978-3-319-28854-3

Babaeizadeh, S., Brooks, H., Isaacson, D., & Newell, J. C. (2006). Electrode boundary conditions and experimental validation for BEM Based EIT forward and inverse solutions. *IEEE Transactions on Medical Imaging, 25*(9), 1180–1188p. doi:10.1109/TMI.2006.879957 PMID:16967803

Bahrani, N. (2012). 2 1/2 D Finite Element Method for Electrical Impedance Tomography Considering the Complete. Carleton University, Ottawa, Canada.

Bailey, D. (2015). The advantages and limitations of high level synthesis for FPGA based image processing. *Proceedings of the 9th International Conference on Distributed Smart Cameras (ICDSC '15)* (pp. 134-139). doi:10.1145/2789116.2789145

Bakhtari, A., Naish, M. D., Eskandari, M., Croft, E. A., & Benhabib, B. (2006). Active-vision-based multisensor surveillance - An implementation. *IEEE Transactions on Systems, Man, and Cybernetics. Part A, Systems and Humans*, *36*(5), 668–679. doi:10.1109/TSMCC.2005.855525

Bala, A., & Kaur, T. (2016). Local texton XOR patterns: A new feature descriptor for content-based image retrieval. *Engineering Science and Technology, an International Journal*, *19*(1), 101-112.

Baluja, S., & Rowley, H. A. (2007). Boosting Sex Identification Performance. *International Journal of Computer Vision*, *71*(1), 111–119. doi:10.1007/s11263-006-8910-9

Banumathi, A., & Pethalakshm, A. (2012, February). Refinement of K-Means and Fuzzy C-Means. *International Journal of Computers and Applications*, *39*(17), 11–17. doi:10.5120/4911-7441

Bao, P., Zhang, L., & Wu, X. (2005). Canny edge detection enhancement by scale multiplication. *IEEE Transactions on Pattern Analysis and Machine Intelligence*, *27*(9), 1485–1490. doi:10.1109/TPAMI.2005.173 PMID:16173190

Barbero, M., & Stroppiana, M. (1992). Data compression for HDTV transmission and distribution. *Proceedings of the IEE Colloquium on Applications of Video Compression in Broadcasting*.

Bart, E., Byvatov, E., & Ullman, S. (2004). View-invariant recognition using corresponding object fragments. *Proc. ECCV Conference* (pp.152–165).

Batchelor, B. G. (1971). Improved distance measure for pattern recognition. *Electronics Letters*, *7*(18), 521–524. doi:10.1049/el:19710353

Bay, H., Ess, A., Tuytelaars, T., & Van Gool, L. (2008). Speeded-up robust features (SURF). *Computer Vision and Image Understanding*, *110*(3), 346–359. doi:10.1016/j.cviu.2007.09.014

Bay, H., Tuytelaars, T., & Van Gool, L. (2006). SURF: Speeded Up Robust Features. *Computer Vision*, *3951*, 404–417.

Bedenbaugh, P. H. (2011). Deep brain stimulation for phantom perceptions. *Proceedings of the 2011 5th International IEEE/EMBS Conference on Neural Engineering NER '11* (pp. 712–717).

Belaid, L. J., & Mourou, W. (2012, August). Image segmentation: A Watershed transformation algorithm. *Image Analysis & Stereology*, *28*(2), 93–102. doi:10.5566/ias.v28.p93-102

Belhloul, F., Janier, M., Croisille, P., Poirier, C., & Boudraa, A. (1998, November). Automatic assessment of myocardial viability based on PET-MRI data fusion. *Proc. of 20th International Conference of the IEEE Engineering in Medicine and Biology Society*, Hong Kong, China.

BenAbdelkader, C., & Griffin, P. (2005). A Local Region-Based Approach to Gender Classification from Face Images. *Proc. IEEE Conf. Computer Vision and Pattern Recognition*.

Bera, T. K., & Nagaraju, J. (2009). A study of practical biological phantoms with simple instrumentation for Electrical Impedance Tomography (EIT). *Proceedings of the 2009 IEEE Instrumentation and Measurement Technology Conference* (pp. 511–516).

Bera, T. K., & Nagaraju, J. (2013). A MATLAB-Based Boundary Data Simulator for Studying the Resistivity Reconstruction Using Neighbouring Current Pattern. *Journal of Medical Engineering*.

Bera, T. K., Biswas, S. K., Rajan, K., & Jampana, N. (2011). Improving the image reconstruction in Electrical Impedance Tomography (EIT) with block matrix-based Multiple Regularization (BMMR): A practical phantom study. *Proceedings of the 2011 World Congress on Information and Communication Technologies WICT '11* (pp. 1346–1351). doi:10.1109/WICT.2011.6141444

Bera, T. K., & Nagaraju, J. (2011). A chicken tissue phantom for studying an electrical impedance tomography (EIT) system suitable for clinical imaging. *Sensing and Imaging*, *12*(3-4), 95–116. doi:10.1007/s11220-011-0063-4

Bera, T. K., & Nagaraju, J. A. (2009). Stainless Steel Electrode Phantom to Study the Forward Problem of Electrical Impedance Tomography. *Sensors & Transducers Journal*, *104*, 33–40.

Bhaskara Rao, P., Vara Prasad, D., & Pavan Kumar, C. (2013). Feature Extraction Using Zernike Moments. *International Journal of Latest Trends in Engineering and Technology*, *2*(2).

Bhateja, V., & Satapathy, S. C. (2015, September). Multimodal Medical Image Fusion for Computer Aided Diagnosis.

Bhatia, A. B., Wolf, E., & Born, M. (1954). On the circle polynomials of Zernike and related orthogonal sets. *Proceedings of the Cambridge Philosophical Society*, *50*(01), 40–48. doi:10.1017/S0305004100029066

Bicego, M., & Lovato, P. (2016). A bioinformatics approach to 2D shape classification. *Computer Vision and Image Understanding*, *145*, 59–69. doi:10.1016/j.cviu.2015.11.011

Bierling, M. (1988). Displacement estimation by hierarchical blockmatching. In *Visual Communications and Image Processing'88: Third in a Series* (pp. 942–953). International Society for Optics and Photonics. doi:10.1117/12.969046

Blaser, A. (1979). Database techniques for pictorial applications. Springer.

Bleau, A., & Leon, L. J. (2000). Watershed based segmentation and region merging. *Computer Vision and Image Understanding*, *77*(3), 317–370. doi:10.1006/cviu.1999.0822

Bober, M. (2011). MPEG-7 visual shape descriptors. *IEEE Transactions on Circuits Systems and Video Technology*, *11*(6), 716-719.

Bober, M. (2011). MPEG-7 visual shape descriptors. *IEEE Transactions on Circuits and Systems for Video Technology*, *11*(6), 716–719. doi:10.1109/76.927426

Boiman, O., & Irani, M. (2007). Detecting irregularities in images and in video. *International Journal of Computer Vision*, *74*(1), 17–31. Retrieved from http://www.wisdom.weizmann.ac.il/~vision/Irregularities.html doi:10.1007/s11263-006-0009-9

Boissel, J. P., Cucherat, M., Amsallem, E., Nony, P., Fardeheb, M., Manzi, W., & Haugh, M. C. (2003). Getting evidence to prescribers and patients or how to make EBM a reality. *Proceedings of the Medical Informatics Europe Conference (MIE '03)*, St. Malo, France.

Bonato, V., Marques, E., & Constantinides, G. (2008). A Parallel Hardware Architecture for Scale and Rotation Invariant Feature Detection. *IEEE Transactions on Circuits and Systems for Video Technology*, *18*(12), 1703–1712. doi:10.1109/TCSVT.2008.2004936

Borges, G. A., & Aldon, M. J. (2004). Line extraction in 2D range images for mobile robotics. *Journal of Intelligent and Robotic Systems: Theory and Applications*, *40*(3), 267–297. doi:10.1023/B:JINT.0000038945.55712.65

Borhanifar, H., & Naeim, V. (2012). High Speed Object Recognition Based on SIFT Algorithm. *Proceedings of the International Conference on Image, Vision and Computing*.

Born, M., & Wolf, E. (1975). *Principles of Optics*. Oxford: Pergamon Press.

Bounthanh, M., Attachoo, B., Hamamoto, K., & Bounthanh, T. (2013). Content-based image retrieval system based on combined and weighted multi-features. *Proceedings of the 2013 13th International Symposium on Communications and Information Technologies (ISCIT)*. doi:10.1109/ISCIT.2013.6645900

Brahmbhatt, K. N., & Makwana, R. M. (2013). Comparative study on image fusion methods in spatial domain. *International journal of advanced research in engineering and technology.*

Brunelli, R., & Mich, O. (2011). Histograms Analysis for Image Retrieval. *Pattern Recognition, 34*(8), 625–1637.

Burl, M., Weber, M., & Perona, P. (1998). A probabilistic approach to object recognition using local photometry and global geometry. *Proceedings of the ECCV Conference*, Freiburg, Germany (pp.628–641). doi:10.1007/BFb0054769

Burns, J., Weiss, R., & Riseman, E. (1993). View variation of pointset and line-segment features. *PAMI, 15*(1), 51–68. doi:10.1109/34.184774

Cafforio, C., Rocca, F., & Tubaro, S. (1990). Motion compensated image interpolation. *IEEE Transactions on Communications, 38*(2), 215–222. doi:10.1109/26.47856

Callahan, T., Hauser, J., & Wawrzynek, J. (2000). The Garp architecture and C compiler. *Computer, 33*(4), 62-69.

Canedo-rodríguez, A., Álvarez-santos, V., Regueiro, C. V., Iglesias, R., Barro, S., & Presedo, J. (2016). Particle filter robot localisation through robust fusion of laser, WiFi, compass, and a network of external cameras. *Information Fusion, 27*, 170–188. doi:10.1016/j.inffus.2015.03.006

Canis, A., Choi, J., Aldham, M., Zhang, V., Kammoona, A., Anderson, J., & Czajkowski, T. et al. (2011). LegUp: high-level synthesis for FPGA-based processor/accelerator systems. *Proceedings of the 19th ACM/SIGDA international symposium on Field programmable gate arrays* (pp. 33-36). doi:10.1145/1950413.1950423

Caselles, V., Kimmel, R., & Sapiro, G. (1997). Geodesic active contours. *International Journal of Computer Vision, 22*(1), 61–79. doi:10.1023/A:1007979827043

Caurant, R., & Hilbert, D. (1953). *Methods of mathematical physics, 1 New York*. Interscience.

Cawkill, A. E. (1993). The British library's picture research projects: Image, word, and retrieval. *Advanced Imaging (Woodbury, N.Y.), 8*(10), 38–40.

Chaki, N., Shaikh, S. H., & Saeed, K. (2014). Exploring image binarization techniques. Springer publication.

Chakravarty, P., & Jarvis, R. (2006). Panoramic vision and laser range finder fusion for multiple person tracking. *Proceedings of the IEEE International Conference on Intelligent Robots and Systems* (Vol. 1, pp. 2949–2954). doi:10.1109/IROS.2006.282149

Chan, C., Kittler, J., & Messer, K. (2010). Multi-scale local binary pattern histograms for face recognition. *Proceedings of the 2nd International Conference on Biometrics ICIP '10* (pp. 809–818).

Chan, M. H., Yu, Y. B., & Constantinides, A. G. (1990). Variable size block matching motion compensation with applications to video coding. *Communications, Speech and Vision, IEE Proceedings, 137*(4). doi:10.1049/ip-i-2.1990.0029

Chan, Y.-L., & Siu, W.-C. (1997). Block motion vector estimation using edge matching: An approach with better frame quality as compared to full search algorithm. *Proceedings of 1997 IEEE International Symposium on Circuits and Systems ISCAS'97 (Vol. 2*, pp. 1145-1148). IEEE.

Chandel, H., & Vatta, S. (2015). Occlusion Detection and Handling: A Review. *International Journal of Computer Applications, 120*(10).

Chandran, S. N., Gangodkar, D., & Mittal, A. (2015, May). Parallel implementation of local derivative pattern algorithm for fast image retrieval. *Proceedings of the 2015 International Conference on Computing, Communication & Automation (ICCCA)* (pp. 1132-1137). IEEE. doi:10.1109/CCAA.2015.7148545

Chan, E., Rodriguez, A. A., Gandhi, R., & Panchanathan, S. (1994). Experiments on block-matching techniques for video coding. *Multimedia Systems*, *2*(5), 228–241. doi:10.1007/BF01215400

Chang, N. S., & Fu, K. S. (1979). A relational database system for images (Technical Report TR-EE 79-82). Purdue University.

Chang, N. S., & Fu, K. S. (1980). Query by pictorial example. *IEEE Transactions on Software Engineering*, *6*(6), 519–524. doi:10.1109/TSE.1980.230801

Chang, S. K., & Hsu, A. (1992). Image information systems: Where do we go from here? *IEEE Transactions on Knowledge and Data Engineering*, *5*(5), 431–442. doi:10.1109/69.166986

Chang, S. K., Jungert, E., & Li, Y. (1988). *Representation and retrieval of symbolic pictures using generalized 2D string, Technical Report*. University of Pittsburgh.

Chang, S. K., & Kunii, T. L. (1981). Pictorial database systems. *IEEE Computer Magazine*, *14*(11), 13–21. doi:10.1109/C-M.1981.220243

Chang, S. K., Yan, C. W., Dimitroff, D. C., & Arndt, T. (1988). An intelligent image database system. *IEEE Transactions on Software Engineering*, *14*(5), 681–688. doi:10.1109/32.6147

Chang, T., & Kuo, C. C. J. (1993). Texture analysis and classification with tree-structured wavelet transform. *IEEE Transactions on Image Processing*, *2*(4), 429–441. doi:10.1109/83.242353 PMID:18296228

Chan, T. F., & Vese, L. A. (2001). Active contours without edges. *IEEE Transactions on Image Processing*, *10*(2), 266–277. doi:10.1109/83.902291 PMID:18249617

Chaumette, F. (2004). Image Moments: A General and Useful Set of Features for Visual Servoing. *IEEE Transactions on Robotics*, *20*(4), 713–723. doi:10.1109/TRO.2004.829463

Checka, N., Wilson, K. W., Siracusa, M. R., & Darrell, T. (2004). Multiple person and speaker activity tracking with a particle filter. *Proceedings of the 2004 IEEE International Conference on Acoustics Speech and Signal Processing* (Vol. 1, pp. 881-884). doi:10.1109/ICASSP.2004.1327252

Chen, C.C. (2006). Using Tomorrow's Retrieval Technology to Explore the Heritage: Bonding Past and Future in the Case of Global Memory Net. *Proceedings of the World Library and Information Congress*, Seoul, Korea.

Chen, L., Feris, R., Zhai, Y., Brown, L., & Hampapur, A. (2012). An Integrated System for Moving Object Classification in Surveillance Videos. *Proceedings of the IEEE Fifth International Conference on Advanced Video and Signal Based Surveillance AVSS'08* (pp. 52-59).

Cheng, C., Koschan, A., Cheng, C., & Koschan, A. (2011, September). Outdoor Scene Image Segmentation Based on Background Recognition and Perceptual Organization. *IEEE Transactions on* Image Processing, *21*(3), 1007–1019. PMID:21947522

Cheng, H. D., Jiang, X. H., & Wang, J. (2002). Color image segmentation based on homogram thresholding and region merging. *Pattern Recognition*, *35*(2), 373–393. doi:10.1016/S0031-3203(01)00054-1

Cheng, K. W., Chen, Y. T., & Fang, W. H. (2015). Gaussian Process Regression-Based Video Anomaly Detection and Localization With Hierarchical Feature Representation. *IEEE Transactions on Image Processing*, *24*(12), 5288–5301. doi:10.1109/TIP.2015.2479561 PMID:26394423

Cheng, Y. (1995). Mean shift, mode seeking, and clustering. *IEEE Transactions on Pattern Analysis and Machine Intelligence*, *17*(8), 790–799. doi:10.1109/34.400568

Chen, J., Shan, S., He, C., Zhao, G., Pietikainen, M., Chen, X., & Gao, W. (2010). WLD: A robust image local descriptor. *IEEE Transactions on Pattern Analysis and Machine Intelligence, 32*(9), 1705–1720. doi:10.1109/TPAMI.2009.155 PMID:20634562

Chen, J., Wang, Y., Luo, L., Yu, J., & Ma, J. (2016). Image retrieval based on image-to-class similarity. *Pattern Recognition Letters, 83*(3), 379–387. doi:10.1016/j.patrec.2016.01.017

Cheung, W., & Hamarneh, G. (2009). n-SIFT: n-Dimensional Scale Invariant Feature Transform. *IEEE Transactions on Image Processing, 18*(9), 2012–2021. doi:10.1109/TIP.2009.2024578 PMID:19502129

Chong, C.-W., & Paramesran, R. (2003). A comparative analysis of algorithms for fast computation of Zernike moments. *Pattern Recognition, 36*(3), 731–742. doi:10.1016/S0031-3203(02)00091-2

Chris, H., & Stephens, M. (1988). A combined corner and edge detector. *Proceedings of the Alvey vision conference.*

Chuang, Y. Y., Agarwala, A., Curless, B., Salesin, D. H., & Szeliski, R. (2002). Video matting of complex scenes. *ACM Transactions on Graphics, 21*(3), 243-248.

Chui, C. (1992). *An Introduction to Wavelets.* New York: Academic Press.

Clark, P., & Mirmehdi, M. (2000). Finding Text Regions using Localised Measures. *Proceedings of the 11th British Machine Vision Conference* (pp. 675-684).

CMU Face Group. (2009). *Frontal and profile face databases.* Retrieved 2009, from http://vasc.ri.cmu.edu/idb/html/face/

Color FERET Face Database. (2009). *FERET Evaluation Project.* Retrieved 2009, from www.itl.nist.gov/iad/humanid/colorferet

Comaniciu, D., Ramesh, V., & Meer, P. (2003). Kernel-based object tracking. *IEEE Transactions on Pattern Analysis and Machine Intelligence, 25*(5), 564–577. doi:10.1109/TPAMI.2003.1195991

Comeau, R. M., Sadikot, A. F., Fenster, A. F., & Peters, T. M. (2000, April). Intraoperative ultrasound for guidance and tissue shift correction in image-guided neurosurgery. *Medical Physics, 27*(4), 787–800. doi:10.1118/1.598942 PMID:10798702

Computer Vision Pattern Recognition (CVPR). Performance Evaluation of Tracking and Surveillance (PETS). Retrieved from http://www.cvg.rdg.ac.uk/PETS2001 http://www.cvg.rdg.ac.uk/PETS2006

Conaire, C. Ó., OConnor, N. E., & Smeaton, A. (2008). Thermo-visual feature fusion for object tracking using multiple spatiogram trackers. *Machine Vision and Applications, 19*(5–6), 483–494. doi:10.1007/s00138-007-0078-y

Corso, J. J., Yuille, A. L., Sicotte, N. L., & Toga, A. W. (2007, October). Detection and segmentation of pathological structures by the extended graph-shifts algorithm. In *Medical Image Computation Aided Intervention* (Vol. 1, pp. 985–994). PMID:18051154

Cosic, D., & Loncaric, S. (1996, October). Two methods for ICH segmentation. *Proceedings of ISBME* (pp. 63–66).

Cour, T., Benezit, F., & Shi, J. (2005). Spectral segmentation with multiscale graph decomposition. *Proceedings of the IEEE International Conference on Computer Vision and Pattern Recognition*, San Diego, CA (Vol. 2, pp. 1124–1131).

Criminisi, A., Blake, A., Rother, C., Shotton, J., & Torr, P. H. S. (2007). Efficient dense stereo with occlusions for new view-synthesis by four-state dynamic programming. *International Journal of Computer Vision, 71*(1), 89–110. doi:10.1007/s11263-006-8525-1

Crispin, D. D. E., Aileen, U. M., Ricardo, G. S., Jim, J. M., & Hilario, S. P. (2005). Allocation of Electronic Toll Collection Lanes at Toll Plazas Considering Social Optimization of Service Times and Delays. *Proceedings of the Eastern Asia Society for Transportation Studies* (pp. 1496–1509).

Crocco, M., Del Bue, A., Bustreo, M., & Murino, V. (2012). A closed form solution to the microphone position self-calibration problem. *Proceedings of the IEEE International Conference on Acoustics, Speech and Signal Processing ICASSP* (pp. 2597–2600). doi:10.1109/ICASSP.2012.6288448

Cui, Z., Zhang, G., & Wu, J. (2009, April). Medical Image Fusion Based on Wavelet Transform and Independent Component Analysis. *Proceedings of the International Joint Conference on Artificial Intelligence (JCAI '09)*, Hainan Island (pp. 480-483). doi:10.1109/JCAI.2009.169

Culjak, I., Abram, D., Pribanic, T., Dzapo, H., & Cifrek, M. (2012). A brief introduction to OpenCV. *Proceedings of the 2012 35th International Convention MIPRO* (pp. 1725-1730). Opatija.

D'Arca, E., Hughes, A., Robertson, N. M., & Hopgood, J. (2013). Video tracking through occlusions by fast audio source localisation. *Proceedings of the 2013 IEEE International Conference on Image Processing* (pp. 2660–2664). doi:10.1109/ICIP.2013.6738548

Dailey, M. N., Joyce C., Lyons M. J., M. J., Kamachi, M., Ishi, H., Gyoba, J., & Cottrell, G. W. (2010). Evidence and a computational explanation of cultural differences in facial expression recognition. *Emotion*, *10*(6), 874-893.

Dalal, N., & Trigg, B. (2005). Histograms of Oriented Gradients for Human Detection. *Proceedings of the CVPR Int'l Conference* (pp.886-893). doi:10.1109/CVPR.2005.177

Dance, C., Willamowski, J., Fan, L., Bray, C., & Csurka, G. (2004). Visual Categorization with Bags of Keypoints. *Proc. ECCV Workshop, Statistical Learning in Computer Vision*.

Das, S. (2016). Comparison of Various Edge Detection Technique, International Journal of Signal Processing. *Image Processing and Pattern Recognition*, *9*(2), 143–158. doi:10.14257/ijsip.2016.9.2.13

De Haan, G. (1992). Motion estimation and compensation: An integrated approach to consumer display field rate conversion [PhD diss.]. TU Delft, Delft University of Technology.

Deans, S. (1983). *The Radon transform and some of its applications*. New York: Wiley.

Dempster, A., Laird, N., & Rubin, D. (1976). Maximum likelihood from incomplete data via the EM algorithm. *Journal of the Royal Statistical Society. Series A (General)*, *39*, 1–38.

Deza, M. M., & Deza, E. (2009). *Encyclopedia of distances*. Springer-Verlag Berlin Heidelberg. doi:10.1007/978-3-642-00234-2

Dimai, A. (1999). Rotation Invariant Texture Description using General Moment Invariants and Gabor Filters. *Proc. of the 11th Scandinavian Conf. on Image Analysis* (pp. 391-398).

Donoser, M., & Bischof, H. (2006). 3D Segmentation By Maximally Stable Volumes (MSVs). *Proceedings of the IEEE International Conference on Pattern Recognition*. Hong Kong. doi:10.1109/ICPR.2006.33

Donoser, M., & Bischof, H. (2006). Efficient Maximally Stable Extremal Region (MSER) Tracking. *Proceedings of the IEEE Computer Society Conference on Computer Vision and Pattern Recognition*. doi:10.1109/CVPR.2006.107

Dorko, G., & Schmid, C. (2003). Selection of scale-invariant parts for object class recognition. Proceedings of ICCV (pp.634–640).

Dosinas, A, Vaitkunas, M., & Daunoras, J. (2006). Measurement of human physiological parameters in the systems of active clothing and wearable technologies. *Elektronika Ir Elektrotechnika, 7*(7), 77–82.

Douillard, B., Fox, D., & Ramos, F. (2010). A spatio-temporal probabilistic model for multi-sensor multi-class object recognition. In Springer Tracts in Advanced Robotics (Vol. 66, pp. 123–134). doi:10.1007/978-3-642-14743-2_11

Dowe, J. (1993). Content-based retrieval in multimedia imaging. *Proc. SPIE Storage and Retrieval for Image and Video Database.* doi:10.1117/12.143645

Duan, T. D., Du, T. H., Phuoc, T. V., & Hoang, N. (2005). Building an Automatic Vehicle License-Plate Recognition. *Proceedings of the International Conference in Computer Science* (pp. 59-63).

Duan, T. D., Duc, D. A., & Du, T. L. H. (2004). Combining Hough Transform and Contour Algorithm for detecting Vehicles License-Plates. *Proceedings of 2004 International Symposium on Intelligent Multimedia, Video and Speech Processing* (pp. 747-750). doi:10.1109/ISIMP.2004.1434172

Dubey, S. R., Singh, S. K., & Singh, R. K. (2016). Multichannel Decoded Local Binary Patterns for Content-Based Image Retrieval. *IEEE Transactions on Image Processing, 25*(9), 4018–4032. doi:10.1109/TIP.2016.2577887 PMID:27295674

Dufaux, F., Ouaret, M., & Ebrahimi, T. (2007). Mobile multimedia/image processing for military and security applications. sensors, and command, control, communications, and intelligence (C3I). *Technologies for Homeland Security and Homeland Defense VI., 10*, 358.

Eakins J. P. & Graham M. E. (1999). Content-based image retrieval, a report to the JISC Technology Applications programme.

Eckart, S., & Fogg, C. E. (1995). ISO-IEC MPEG-2 software video codec. *Proceedings of the IS&T/SPIE's Symposium on Electronic Imaging: Science & Technology.* International Society for Optics and Photonics, .

Edic, P. M., Saulnier, G. J., Newell, J. C., & Isaacson, D. (1995). A Real-Time Electrical Impedance Tomograph. *IEEE Transactions on Bio-Medical Engineering, 42*(9), 849–859. doi:10.1109/10.412652 PMID:7558059

Electronic Toll Collection System. (n, d.). Retrieved from http://ntl.bts.gov/lib/jpodocs/edldocs1/13480/ch5.pdf

Elhoseiny, M., Bakry, A., & Elgammal, A. (2013), Multiclass Object Classification in Video Surveillance Systems, Experimental Study. *Proceedings of the CVPR Workshop '13.* doi:10.1109/CVPRW.2013.118

Face Research Group. (2009). *CMU Pose, Illumination, and Expression (PIE) database.* Retrieved 2009, from http://www.ri.cmu.edu/projects/project 418.html

Fadzil, M. A., & Dennis, T. J. (1990). A hierarchical motion estimator for interframe coding. *Proceedings of the IEE Colloquium on Applications of Motion Compensation.*

Fang, J., Meng, H., Zhang, H., & Wang, X. (2007). A Low-cost Vehicle Detection and Classification System based on Unmodulated Continuous-wave Radar. Proceedings of the 2007 IEEE Intelligent Transport Systems Conference, Seattle, WA, USA (pp. 715-720).

Faraji, M., Shanbehzadeh, J., Nasrollahi, K., & Moeslund, T. B. (2015). EREL: Extremal Regions of Extremum Levels. *Proceedings of the IEEE International Conference on Image Processing.* Quebec City, QC.

Faraji, M., Shanbehzadeh, J., Nasrollahi, K., & Moeslund, T. B. (2015). Extremal Regions Detection Guided by Maxima of Gradient Magnitude. *IEEE Transactions on Image Processing, 24*(12), 5401–5415. doi:10.1109/TIP.2015.2477215 PMID:26357397

Fei-Fei, L., Fergus, R., & Perona, P. (2003). A bayesian approach to unsupervised one-shot learning of object categories. *Proceedings of ICCV* (pp. 1134–1141).

Felzenszwalb, D. H. P., & Huttenlocher, D. P. (2004). Efficient graph-based image segmentation. *International Journal of Computer Vision, 59*(2), 167–181. doi:10.1023/B:VISI.0000022288.19776.77

Feng, W., Zhao, D., Jiang, Z., Zhu, Y., Feng, H., & Yao, L. (2009). An Architecture of Optimised SIFT Feature Detection for an FPGA Implementation of an Image Matcher. *Proceedings of the International Conference on Field-Programmable Technology.* Sydney.

Fergus, R., Perona, P., & Zisserman, A. (2003). Object class recognition by unsupervised scale-invariant learning. Proceedings of CVPR03, Madison, Wisconsin (pp. 264–271).

Fermüller, C., & Pollefeys, M. (2015). Edge Detection: CS 111. School of Information and Computer Sciences University of California, Irvine. Retrieved from http://www.ics.uci.edu/~majumder/DIP/classes/EdgeDetect.pdf

Fisher, R. (2007). BEHAVE: Computer-assisted prescreening of video streams for unusual activities. *The EPSRC project GR S, 98146.* Retrieved from http://homepages.inf.ed.ac.uk/rbf/ BEHAVE/

Flandrin, P. (1992, March). Wavelet analysis and synthesis of fractional Brownian motion. *IEEE Transactions on Information Theory, 38*(2), 910–917. doi:10.1109/18.119751

Forssen, P. (2007). Maximally Stable Colour Regions For Recognition and Matching. *Proceedings of the IEEE Conference on Computer Vision and Pattern Recognition.* Minneapolis. doi:10.1109/CVPR.2007.383120

Frey, M., & Nguyen-Quang, S. (2000). A gamma-based framework for modeling variable-rate MPEG video sources: the GOP GBAR model. *IEEE/ACM Transactions on Networking, 8*(6), 710-719.

Fritz, W. (2006). *Intelligent Systems.* New Horizons Press.

Gabriel, N., Mitraszewska, I., & Tomasz, K. 2009. The Polish Pilot Project of Automatic Toll Collection. *Proceedings of the 6th International Scientific Conference.*

Gagnon, H., Cousineau, M., Adler, A., & Hartinger, A. E. (2010). A resistive mesh phantom for assessing the performance of EIT systems. *IEEE Transactions on Bio-Medical Engineering, 57*(9), 2257–2266. doi:10.1109/TBME.2010.2052618 PMID:20550982

Ganesan, P., & Rajini, V. (2010, November 13-15). A Method to Segment Color Images based on Modified Fuzzy-Possibilistic-C-Means Clustering Algorithm. *Recent Advances in Space Technology Services and Climate Change, 5,* 157–163.

Ganguly, S., Bhattacharjee, D., & Nasipuri, M. (2014). Automatic Analysis Of Smoothing Techniques By Simulation Model Based Real-Time System For Processing 3d Human Faces. *International Journal Of Embedded Systems And Applications, 4*(4), 13–23. doi:10.5121/ijesa.2014.4402

Gao, Q., Zhao, Y., & Lu, Y. (2008). Despecking SAR image using stationary wavelet transform combining with directional filter banks. *Applied Mathematics and Computation, 205*(2), 517–524. doi:10.1016/j.amc.2008.05.026

Gatica-Perez, D., Lathoud, G., Odobez, J.-M., & McCowan, I. (2004). Audio-Visual Tracking of Multiple Speakers in Meetings. *IEEE Transactions on Audio, Speech, and Language Processing, 15*(72), 601–616.

Gatica-Perez, D., Lathoud, G., McCowan, I., Odobez, J.-M., & Moore, D. (2003). Audio-visual speaker tracking with importance particle filters. *Proceedings 2003 International Conference on Image Processing* (Vol. 3, pp. 25-28). doi:10.1109/ICIP.2003.1247172

Georghiades, A. (1997). Yale face database. *Center for computational Vision and Control at Yale University*. Retrieved from http://cvc. yale.edu/projects/yalefaces/yalefa

Gering, D., Grimson, W., & Kikinis, R. (2005, January). Recognizing deviations from normalcy for brain tumor segmentation, in Proceedings of International Conference Medical Image Computation Assist. *Intervention (Amstelveen, Netherlands)*, *5*, 508–515.

Germa, T., Lerasle, F., Ouadah, N., Cadenat, V., & Devy, M. (2009). Vision and RFID-based person tracking in crowds from a mobile robot. *Proceedings of the 2009 IEEE/RSJ International Conference on Intelligent Robots and Systems IROS '09* (Vol. 3, pp. 5591–5596). doi:10.1109/IROS.2009.5354475

Goel, S., Ismail, Y., & Bayoumi, M. A. (2005). Adaptive search window size algorithm for fast motion estimation in H. 264/AVC standard. *Proceedings of the 48th Midwest Symposium on Circuits and Systems*. IEEE. doi:10.1109/MWS-CAS.2005.1594412

Goldstein, S., Schmit, H., Budiu, M., & Cadambi, S. (2000). PipeRench: a reconfigurable architecture and compiler. *Computer*, *33*(4), 70-77.

Golomb, S. W. (1980). Sources which maximize the choice of a Huffman coding tree. *Information and Control*, *45*(3), 263–272. doi:10.1016/S0019-9958(80)90648-8

Gonde, A. B., Maheshwari, R. P., & Balasubramanian, R. (2010, December). Texton co-occurrence matrix: a new feature for image retrieval. *Proceedings of the 2010 Annual IEEE India Conference (INDICON)* (pp. 1-5). IEEE. doi:10.1109/INDCON.2010.5712603

Gong, S., Loy, C. C., & Xiang, T. (2011). Security and surveillance. In *Visual Analysis of Humans* (pp. 455–472). Springer London. doi:10.1007/978-0-85729-997-0_23

Gong, Y., Zhang, H., Chuant, H., & Skauuchi, M. (1994). An image database system with contents capturing and fast image indexing abilities. *Proceedings of IEEE International Conferences on Multimedia Computing and Systems*, Boston, Massachusetts, USA (pp. 121–130). doi:10.1109/MMCS.1994.292444

Gonzales, C. A., Allman, L., McCarthy, T., Wendt, P., & Akansu, A. N. (1990). DCT coding for motion video storage using adaptive arithmetic coding. *Signal Processing Image Communication*, *2*(2), 145–154. doi:10.1016/0923-5965(90)90017-C

Gonzalez, R. C., & Woods, R. E. (2007). Image processing. Digital image processing, 2.

Gonzalez, R. C., & Woods, R. E. (2002). *Digital Image Processing*. Englewood Cliffs, New York: Prentice Hall.

Gonzalez, R. C., Woods, R. E., & Eddins, S. L. (2004). *Digital Image Processing Using MATLAB*. India: Pearson Education.

Gorelick, L., Blank, M., Shechtman, E., Irani, M., & Basri, R. (2011, November). Actions as space-time shapes. Retrieved from http://www.wisdom.weizmann.ac.il/~vision/SpaceTimeActions.html

Griffiths, H. (1988). A phantom for electrical impedance tomography. Clinical Physics and Physiological Measurement, 9(4A), 15.

Gueld, M. O., Kohnen, M., Keysers, D., Schubert, H., Wein, B. B., Bredno, J., & Lehmann, T. M. (2002). Quality of DICOM header information for image categorization. *Proceedings of the International Symposium on Medical Imaging* (pp. 280-287).

Guo, H., Wu, X., Wang, H., Chen, L., Ou, Y., & Feng, W. (2015, August). A novel approach for global abnormal event detection in multi-camera surveillance system. *Proceedings of the 2015 IEEE International Conference on Information and Automation* (pp. 73-78). doi:10.1109/ICInfA.2015.7279261

Guo, G. D., Jain, A. K., Ma, W. Y., & Zhang, H. J. (2002). Learning Similarity Measure for Natural Image Retrieval With Relevance Feedback. *IEEE Transactions on Neural Networks*, *13*(4), 811–820. doi:10.1109/TNN.2002.1021882 PMID:18244477

Guo, Z., Zhang, L., & Zhang, D. (2010). A completed modeling of local binary pattern operator for texture classification. *IEEE Transactions on Image Processing*, *19*(6), 1657–1663. doi:10.1109/TIP.2010.2044957 PMID:20215079

Guo, Z., Zhang, L., & Zhang, D. (2010). Rotation invariant texture classification using LBP variance (LBPV) with global matching. *Pattern Recognition*, *43*(3), 706–719. doi:10.1016/j.patcog.2009.08.017

Gurcan, M.N., Sahiner, B., Petrick, N., Chan, H.P., Kazerooni, E.A., Cascade, P.N., & Hadjiiski, L. (2002). Lung nodule detection on thoracic computed tomography images: Preliminary evaluation of a computer aided diagnosis system. *Proceedings of Medical Physics*, *29*(11), 2552-2558.

Gutta, S., Wechsler, H., & Phillips, P. (1998). Gender and Ethnic Classification of Human Faces Using Hybrid Classifiers. *Proc. Int'l Conf. Automatic Face and Gesture Recognition* (pp. 194-199). doi:10.1109/AFGR.1998.670948

Haller, J. W., Ryken, T., Madsen, M., Edwards, A., Bolinger, L., & Vannier, M. W. (1999). Multimodality image fusion for image-guided neurosurgery. *Proc. of 13th International Symposium on Computer Assisted Radiology and Surgery (CARS '99)*, Paris, France.

Halter, R. J., Hartov, A., Poplack, S. P., diFlorio-Alexander, R., Wells, W., Rosenkranz, K. M., & Paulsen, K. D. (2015). Real-Time electrical impedance variations in women with and without breast cancer. *IEEE Transactions on Medical Imaging*, *34*(1), 38–48. doi:10.1109/TMI.2014.2342719 PMID:25073168

Hang, H.-M., Chou, Y.-M., & Cheng, S.-C. (1997). Motion estimation for video coding standards. *The Journal of VLSI Signal Processing*, *17*(2), 113–136. doi:10.1023/A:1007994620638

Hanif, M., & Ali, U. (2006). Optimized visual and thermal image fusion for efficient face recognition. *Proceedings of the 2006 9th International Conference on Information Fusion, FUSION*.

Han, J., & Kamber, M. (2006). *Data Mining Concepts and Techniques* (2nd ed.). Elsevier publisher.

Haris, K., Efstratiadis, S. N., & Katsaggelos, A. K. (1998). Hybrid image segmentation using watersheds and fast region merging. *IEEE Transactions on Image Processing*, *7*(12), 1684–1699. doi:10.1109/83.730380 PMID:18276235

Harris, C., & Stephens, M. (1988). A combined corner and edge detection. *Proc. of Alvey Vision Conference* (pp.147–151).

Hartley, R., & Zisserman, A. (2000). *Multiple view geometry in computer vision*. Cambridge University Press.

He, L., Zhao, J., Zheng, N., & Bi, D. (2016). Haze Removal using the Difference-Structure-Preservation Prior. IEEE Transactions on Image Processing, 26(3), 1063-1075.

Heikkila, M., & Pietikainen, M. (2006). A texture-based method for modeling the background and detecting moving objects. *IEEE Transactions on Pattern Analysis and Machine Intelligence*, *28*(4), 657–662. doi:10.1109/TPAMI.2006.68 PMID:16566514

Heikkilä, M., Pietikäinen, M., & Schmid, C. (2009). Description of interest regions with local binary patterns. *Pattern Recognition*, *42*(3), 425–436. doi:10.1016/j.patcog.2008.08.014

He, K., Sun, J., & Tang, X. (2011). Single Image Haze Removal Using Dark Channel Prior. *IEEE Transactions on Pattern Analysis and Machine Intelligence*, *33*(12), 2341–2353. doi:10.1109/TPAMI.2010.168 PMID:20820075

Helmer, S., & Lowe, D. G. (2004). Object Class Recognition with Many Local Features. *Proceedings of the Conference on Computer Vision and Pattern Recognition Workshop* (Vol. 12, pp.187). doi:10.1109/CVPR.2004.409

Henrik, J. (2015). *Evaluating Vivado High-Level Synthesis on OpenCV Functions for the Zynq-7000 FPGA.*

Herbert, B., Tinnr, T., & Gool, L. V. (2006). SURF: Speeded Up Robust Features. Proceedings of ECCV, *LNCS* (Vol. *3951*, pp. 404–417).

Hernandez, A., Basset, O., Magnin, I., Bremond, A., & Gimenez, G. (1996, November). Fusion of ultrasonic and radiographic images of the breast. *Proc. of IEEE Ultrasonics Symposium*, San Antonio, TX. doi:10.1109/ULTSYM.1996.584316

Hernandez, S. E., & Barner, K. E. (2000). Joint region merging criteria for watershed based image segmentation. *Proceedings of the International Conference on Image Processing* (pp. 108–111). doi:10.1109/ICIP.2000.899239

Hinz, J., Hahn, G., & Quintel, M. (2008). Electrical impedance tomography. *Der Anaesthesist, 57*(1), 61–69. doi:10.1007/s00101-007-1273-y PMID:17934702

Holder, D. S. (2005). *Electrical Impedance Tomography Methods, History and Applications. Institute of Physics Publishing Bristol and Philadelphia, Book.* USA: Institute of Physics Publishing.

Hongliang, B., & Changping, L. (2004). A Hybrid License Plate Extraction Method Based on Edge Statistics and Morphology. *Proceedings of the 17th International Conference on Pattern Recognition.*

Horsch, A., & Thurmayr, R. 2003. How to identify and assess tasks and challenges of medical image processing. *Proceedings of the Medical Informatics Europe Conference (MIE '03)*, St. Malo, France.

Höschl, I. V. C. IV, & Flusser, J. (2016). Robust histogram-based image retrieval. *Pattern Recognition Letters, 69*, 72–81. doi:10.1016/j.patrec.2015.10.012

Hosny, K. M. (2008). Fast computation of accurate Zernike moments. *Journal of Real-Time Image Processing, 3*(1-2), 97–107. doi:10.1007/s11554-007-0058-5

Houcque, D. (2005). *Introduction To Matlab For Engineering Students* (Version 1.2). Northwestern University.

Huang, J., Kumar, S. R., Mitra, M., Zhu, W. J., & Zabih, R. (1997, June). Image indexing using color correlograms. *Proceedings of the 1997 IEEE Computer Society Conference on Computer Vision and Pattern Recognition* (pp. 762-768). IEEE.

Huang, X., Li, S. Z., & Wang, Y. (2004, December). Shape localization based on statistical method using extended local binary pattern. *Proceedings of the Third International Conference on Image and Graphics (ICIG'04)* (pp. 184-187). IEEE.

Huang, F.-C., Huang, S.-Y., Ker, J.-W., & Chen, Y.-C. (2012). High-Performance SIFT Hardware Accelerator for Real-Time Image Feature Extraction. *IEEE Transactions on Circuits and Systems for Video Technology, 22*(3), 340–351. doi:10.1109/TCSVT.2011.2162760

Huang, J. Y., & Lee, W. P. (2014). A smart camera network with SVM classifiers for crowd event recognition. *Proceedings of the World Congress on Engineering.*

Huang, Y.-W., Chen, C.-Y., Tsai, C.-H., Shen, C.-F., & Chen, L.-G. (2006). Survey on block matching motion estimation algorithms and architectures with new results. *Journal of VLSI Signal Processing Systems, 42*(3), 297–320. doi:10.1007/s11265-006-4190-4

Huckfield, D. M. (1992). Post production applications of video compression in broadcasting. *Proceedings of the IEE Colloquium on Applications of Video Compression in Broadcasting.*

Hu, M. K. (1962). Visual pattern recognition by moment invariants. *I.R.E. Transactions on Information Theory, 8*(2), 179–187. doi:10.1109/TIT.1962.1057692

Hung, C.-C., Kulkarni, S., & Kuo, B.-C. (2011, June). A New Weighted Fuzzy C-Means Clustering Algorithm Remotely Sensed Image for Classification. *IEEE Journal of Selected Topics in Signal Processing*, 5(3), 543–553. doi:10.1109/JSTSP.2010.2096797

Hu, P. H., Stone, J., & Stanley, T. (1989). Applications of Zernike polynomials to atmospheric propagation problems. *Journal of the Optical Society of America*, 6(10), 1595–1608. doi:10.1364/JOSAA.6.001595

Hu, W., Tan, T., Wang, L., & Maybank, S. (2004). A Survey on Visual Surveillance of Object Motion and Behaviors. *IEEE Trans. on Systems, Man, And Cybernetics—Part C: Applications And Reviews*, 34(3), 334–352. doi:10.1109/TSMCC.2004.829274

Huynh-Thu, Q., & Ghanbari, M. (2008). Scope of validity of PSNR in image/video quality assessment. *Electronics Letters*, 44(13), 800–801. doi:10.1049/el:20080522

Hwang, J.-N., & Li, H. (2008, September). Surface reconstruction from non-parallel curve networks, Neural Networks for Signal Processing. *Computer Graphics Forum*, 27(2), 155–163.

Ian, K., Tessier, R., & Rose, J. (2008). FPGA architecture: Survey and challenges. *Foundations and Trends in Electronic Design Automation*, 2(2), 135–253.

Idrees, H., Saleemi, I., Seibert, C., & Shah, M. (2013). Multi-source multi-scale counting in extremely dense crowd images. *Proceedings of the IEEE Conference on Computer Vision and Pattern Recognition* (pp. 2547-2554). doi:10.1109/CVPR.2013.329

Inc., X. (2016, October 18). *Vivado Design Suite - VivadoHLS*. Retrieved from http://www.xilinx.com/products/design-tools/vivado/index.htm

International Orgranization for Standardization. (n. d.). Retrieved from http://www.iso.org/

International Telecommunications Union. (n. d.). Retrieved from http://www.itu.int/ITU-T/

Irwin, S. (2014). *History and definition of the sobel operator*. Retrieved from the World Wide Web.

Iscen, A., Armagan, A., & Duygulu, P. (2014). What is usual in unusual videos? Trajectory snippet histograms for discovering unusualness. *Proceedings of the IEEE Conference on Computer Vision and Pattern Recognition Workshops* (pp. 794-799). doi:10.1109/CVPRW.2014.123

Iskander, D. R., Collins, M. J., & Davis, B. (2001). Optimal modeling of corneal surfaces with Zernike polynomials. *IEEE Transactions on Bio-Medical Engineering*, 48(1), 87–95. doi:10.1109/10.900255 PMID:11235595

Iskander, D. R., Collins, M. J., Morelande, M. R., & Zhu, M. (2004). Analyzing the dynamic wavefront aberrations in the human eye. *IEEE Transactions on Bio-Medical Engineering*, 51(11), 1969–1980. doi:10.1109/TBME.2004.834254 PMID:15536899

Iskander, D. R., Morelande, M. R., Collins, M. J., & Davis, B. (2002). Modeling of corneal surfaces with radial polynomials. *IEEE Transactions on Bio-Medical Engineering*, 49(4), 320–328. doi:10.1109/10.991159 PMID:11942723

Ismail, Y., Elgamel, M., & Bayoumi, M. (2007). Adaptive techniques for a fast frequency domain motion estimation. *Proceedings of the 2007 IEEE Workshop on Signal Processing Systems* (pp. 331-336). IEEE. doi:10.1109/SIPS.2007.4387567

ISO/IEC MPEG-4 Visual Version 1 Coding of audio-visual objects—Part 2: Visual. (1999, April).

ISO-IEC. (1993). *I. S. 11172 (MPEG-1). Coding of moving pictures and associated audio for digital storage media up to about 1.5 Mbit (Technical report)*. Motion Picture Experts Group.

Jack, O. (2006). Future of Vehicle and Roadside Intelligent Transport Systems. *Proceedings of the 2nd IEE Conference on Automotive Electronics*.

Jain, R. (1992). US NSF workshop visual information management systems. *Proceedings of the Symposium on Electronic Imaging: Science and Technology* (pp. 198-218).

Jain, R., Pentland, A., & Petkovic, D. (1995). Workshop Report: NSF-ARPA Workshop on Visual Information Management Systems.

Jain, A. K., & Vailaya, A. (1998). Shape-based recognition: A case study with trademark image database. *Pattern Recognition*, *31*(9), 1369–1390. doi:10.1016/S0031-3203(97)00131-3

Jain, A., Huang, J., & Fang, S. (2005). Gender Identification Using Frontal Facial Images. *Proc. IEEE Int'l Conf. Multimedia and Expo* (pp.1082-1085).

Jain, A., Nandakumar, K., & Ross, A. (2005). Score normalization in multimodal biometric systems. *Pattern Recognition*, *38*(12), 2270–2285. doi:10.1016/j.patcog.2005.01.012

Jalili-Moghaddam, M. (2005). *Real-time multi-focus image fusion using discrete wavelet transform and Laplacian pyramid transform*. Goteborg, Sweden: Chalmess University of Technology.

Javan Roshtkhari, M., & Levine, M. D. (2013). Online dominant and anomalous behavior detection in videos. *Proceedings of the IEEE Conference on Computer Vision and Pattern Recognition* (pp. 2611-2618). doi:10.1109/CVPR.2013.337

Javidi, B., & Okano, F. (Eds.). (2002). *Three-dimensional television, video, and display technologies*. Springer Science & Business Media.

Jayender, J., Ruan, D. T., Narayan, V., Agrawal, N., Jolesz, F. A., & Mamata, H. (2013, April 7-11). Segmentation of Parathyroid Tumors from DCE-MRI using Linear Dynamic System Analysis, Biomedical Imaging (ISBI). *Proceedings of IEEE 10th International Symposium* (pp. 1469-1472).

Jaynes, E. (1968). Prior Probabilities. *IEEE Trans. Systems, Science, and Cybernetics*, *4*(3), 227–241. doi:10.1109/TSSC.1968.300117

Jehl, M., Dedner, A., Betcke, T., Aristovich, K., Klofkorn, R., & Holder, D. (2014). A Fast Parallel Solver for the Forward Problem in Electrical Impedance Tomography. *IEEE Transactions on Bio-Medical Engineering, 62*(1), 126-137.

Jia, J., Wang, M., Schlaberg, H. I., & Li, H. (2010). A novel tomographic sensing system for high electrically conductive multiphase flow measurement. *Flow Measurement and Instrumentation*, *21*(3), 184–190p. doi:10.1016/j.flowmeasinst.2009.12.002

Jiang, C., Geng, Z.-x., Wei, X.-f., & Shen, C. (2013). SIFT implementation based on GPU. *Proceedings of the International Symposium on Photoelectronic Detection and Imaging*, *891304*.

Jing, X., Zhu, C., & Chau, L.-P. (2003). Smooth constrained motion estimation for video coding. *Signal Processing*, *83*(3), 677–680. doi:10.1016/S0165-1684(02)00482-6

Jordan, M. I., Ghahramani, Z., Jaakkola, T. S., & Saul, L. K. (1999). An Introduction to Variational Methods for Graphical Models. *Machine Learning*, *37*(2), 183–233. doi:10.1023/A:1007665907178

Kadir, T., & Brady, M. (2001). Saliency, scale and image description. International Journal of Computer Vision, *45*(2), 83–105. doi:10.1023/A:1012460413855

Kahn, C. E. Jr. (1994). Artificial intelligence in radiology. Decision support systems. *Radiographics*, *14*(4), 849–861. doi:10.1148/radiographics.14.4.7938772 PMID:7938772

Kalbande, D. R., Deotale, N., Singhal, P., Shah, S., & Thampi, G. T. (2011). An Advanced Technology Selection Model using Neuro Fuzzy Algorithm for Electronic Toll Collection System. *(IJACSA). International Journal of Advanced Computer Science and Applications, II*(4), 97–104.

Kamarulazizi, K., & Ismail, D. W. (2010). Electronic Toll collection System using passive RFID technology. *Journal of Theoretical and Applied Information Technology, 2*, 70-76.

Kang, H., Kim, Y., & Lee, Y. (2015). Fast Removal of Single Image using Pixel-based Median Channel Prior. Proceedings of Advanced Science and Technology Letters (Vol. 98. pp. 124-127). doi:10.14257/astl.2015.98.31

Kaplan, B., & Lundsgaarde, H. P. (1996). Toward an evaluation of an integrated clinical imaging system: Identifying clinical benefits. *Methods of Information in Medicine, 35*, 221–229. PMID:8952308

Kato, T. (1992). Database architecture for content-based image retrieval. In *SPIE/IS&T 1992 symposium on electronic imaging: science and technology* (pp. 112–123). International Society for Optics and Photonics.

Ke, Y., & Sukthankar, R. (2004). PCA-SIFT: A More Distinctive Representation for Local Image Descriptors. *Proceedings of the IEEE Conference on Computer Vision and Pattern Recognition*.

Ke, Y., & Sukthankar, R. (2004). PCA-SIFT: A more distinctive representation for local image descriptors. *Proc. IEEE Int. Conf. Computer Vision and Pattern Recognition* (Vol. 2, pp. 506–513).

Kidsgeo.com. (n. d.). Fog – Clouds On Ground. Retrieved September 5. 2015. from http://www.kidsgeo.com/geography-for-kids/0110-fog.php

Kilic, V., & Barnard, M. (2013). Audio constrained particle filter based visual tracking. In *Acoustics, Speech and Signal Processing* (pp. 3627–3631).

Kilic, V., Barnard, M., Wang, W., & Kittler, J. (2015). Audio assisted robust visual tracking with adaptive particle filtering. *IEEE Transactions on Multimedia, 17*(2), 186–200. doi:10.1109/TMM.2014.2377515

Kim, B.-G., Reddy, K., & Ahn, W. H. (2009). Dynamic search-range control algorithm for fast interframe coding in scalable video coding. *Optical Engineering (Redondo Beach, Calif.), 48*(9), 097002–097002. doi:10.1117/1.3212684

Kim, D. Y., & Jeon, M. (2014). Data fusion of RADAR and image measurements for multi-object tracking via Kalman filtering. *Information Sciences, 278*, 641–652. doi:10.1016/j.ins.2014.03.080

Kim, H. D., Choi, J. S., & Kim, M. (2007). Human-Robot Interaction in Real Environments by Audio-Visual Integration. *Intl J of Control Automation and Systems, 5*(1), 61–69.

Kim, H. D., Choi, J. S., & Kim, M. (2007). Human-Robot Interaction in Real Environments by Audio-Visual Integration. *Intl. J. of Control Automation and Systems, 5*(1), 61–69.

Kim, H.-C., Kim, D., Ghahramani, Z., & Bang, S. Y. (2006). Appearance-Based Gender Classification with Gaussian Processes. *Pattern Recognition Letters, 27*(6), 618–626. doi:10.1016/j.patrec.2005.09.027

Kim, J.-S., & Park, R.-H. (1992). A fast feature-based block matching algorithm using integral projections. *IEEE Journal on Selected Areas in Communications, 10*(5), 968–971. doi:10.1109/49.139002

Klaue, J., Rathke, B., & Wolisz, A. (2003). *Evalvid–A framework for video transmission and quality evaluation. In Computer performance evaluation. Modelling techniques and tools* (pp. 255–272). Springer Berlin Heidelberg. doi:10.1007/978-3-540-45232-4_16

Klee, U., Gehrig, T., & McDonough, J. (2006). Kalman filters for time delay of arrival-based source localization. *EURASIP Journal on Applied Signal Processing, 2006*, 1–16. doi:10.1155/ASP/2006/12378

Klove, T., Lin, T. T., Tsai, S.-C., & Tzeng, W.-G. (2010). Permutation arrays under the Chebyshev distance. *IEEE Transactions on Information Theory*, *56*(6), 2611–2617. doi:10.1109/TIT.2010.2046212

Kokare, M., Biswas, P. K., & Chatterji, B. N. (2007). Texture image retrieval using rotated wavelet filters. *Pattern Recognition Letters*, *28*(10), 1240–1249. doi:10.1016/j.patrec.2007.02.006

Kokare, M., Chatterji, B. N., & Biswas, P. K. (2002). A survey on current content based image retrieval methods. *Journal of the Institution of Electronics and Telecommunication Engineers*, *48*(3-4), 261–271. doi:10.1080/03772063.2002.11416285

Kotu, V., & Deshpande, B. (2014). *Predictive Analytics and Data Mining: Concepts and Practice with RapidMiner*. Morgan Kaufmann Publisher.

Krig, S. (2014). *Computer Vision Metrics - Survey, Taxonomy, and Analysis*. Springer.

Krishnakumar, K. (2003). *Intelligent systems for aerospace engineering – an overview*. NASA.

Kristensen, F., & MacLean, W. J. (2007). Real-Time Extraction of Maximally Stable Extremal Regions on an FPGA. *Proceedings of the IEEE International Symposium on Circuits and System*, New Orleans, LA. doi:10.1109/ISCAS.2007.378247

Kumar A. & Shaik F. (2016). Image Processing in Diabetic Related Causes (illustration 39). *Forensic and Medical Bioinformatics*, *56*, 62.

Kumar, , P., & Anwar, M.I. (2014). Brain Tumor and CAD Through MRI by using Wavelet Transform and Genetic Algorithm. *Journal of Information Engineering and Applications*, *4*(4), 52–60.

Kumar, S., Anand, S., & Sengupta, A. (2013). Development of a non – invasive point of care diagnostic tool for fetal monitoring using electrical impedance based approach. *Proceedings of the 2013 IEEE PHT* (pp. 16–18).

Kumar, R., Kumar, S., & Sengupta, A. (2016). A Review: Electrical Impedance Tomography System and Its Application. *Journal of Control & Instrumentation*, *7*(2), 14–22p.

Kumar, R., Pahuja, S. K., & Sengupta, A. (2015). Phantom based Analysis and Validation using Electrical Impedance Tomography. *Journal of Instrumentation Technology and Innovation*, *5*(3), 17–23p.

Kwak, K., Huber, D. F., Badino, H., & Kanade, T. (2011). Extrinsic calibration of a single line scanning lidar and a camera. *Proceedings of the IEEE International Conference on Intelligent Robots and Systems* (pp. 3283–3289).

Kwak, K., Huber, D. F., Jeongsook, C., & Kanade, T. (2010). Boundary detection based on supervised learning. *Proceedings of the 2010 IEEE International Conference on Robotics and Automation (ICRA)* (pp. 3939–3945). doi:10.1109/ROBOT.2010.5509379

Kwak, K., Kim, J.-S., Min, J., & Park, Y.-W. (2014). Unknown multiple object tracking using 2D LIDAR and video camera. *Electronics Letters*, *50*(8), 600–602. doi:10.1049/el.2014.0355

Lai C. C. & Chen Y. C. (2011). A user-oriented image retrieval system based on interactive genetic algorithm. *IEEE Trans. Measurement*, *60*(10).

Lakhani, K., Minocha, B., & Gugnani, N. (2016). Analyzing edge detection techniques for feature extraction in dental radiographs. *Perspectives on Science*, *8*, 395–398. doi:10.1016/j.pisc.2016.04.087

Langdon, G., & Rissanen, J. (1981, June). Compression of black-white images with arithmetic coding. *IEEE Transactions on*, *29*(6), 858–867. doi:10.1109/TCOM.1981.1095052

Lankford, P. M. (1969). Regionalization Theory and Alternative Algorithms. *Geographical Analysis*, *1*(2), 196–212. doi:10.1111/j.1538-4632.1969.tb00615.x

Laptev, I., & Caputo, B. (2011). Recognition of human actions. Retrieved from http://www.nada.kth.se/cvap/actions/

Lategahn, H., Gross, S., Stehle, T., & Aach, T. (2010). Texture classification by modeling joint distributions of local patterns with Gaussian mixtures. *IEEE Transactions on Image Processing*, *19*(6), 1548–1557. doi:10.1109/TIP.2010.2042100 PMID:20129862

Lazebnik, S., Schmid, C., & Ponce, J. (2004, September). Semi-local affine parts for object recognition. *Proceedings of the British Machine Vision Conference (BMVC'04)* (pp. 779-788). The British Machine Vision Association (BMVA).

Le Gall, D. (1991). MPEG: A video compression standard for multimedia applications. *Communications of the ACM*, *34*(4), 46–58. doi:10.1145/103085.103090

Le Gall, D. J. (1992). The MPEG video compression algorithm. *Signal Processing Image Communication*, *4*(2), 129–140. doi:10.1016/0923-5965(92)90019-C

LeBozec, C., Jaulent, M. C., Zapletal, E., & Degoulet, P. (1998). Unified modeling language and design of a case based retrieval system in medical imaging. *Proceedings of the Annual Symposium of the American Society for Medical Informatics (AMIA)*, Nashville, TN, USA.

Lee, J. (1995). Optimal quadtree for variable block size motion estimation. *Proceedings of the International Conference on Image Processing* (Vol. 3, pp. 480-483). IEEE.

Lee, J. C. (1999). Automatic Character Recognition for Moving and Stationary Vehicles. Proceedings of the International Joint Conference on Neural Networks IJCNN'99 (Vol. 4, pp. 2824-2828).

Lee, M. H., & Park, I. K. (2014). Performance Evaluation of Local Descriptors for Affine Invariant Region Detector. *Proceedings of the Asian Conference on Computer Vision Workshops*. Singapore.

Lee, Y., Hara, T., Fujita, H., & Itoh, S. (2001). Automated detection of pulmonary nodules in helical CT images based on an improved template matching technique. *Transactions on Medical Imaging*, *20*(7), 595-604.

Legg, M., & Bradley, S. (2013). A Combined Microphone and Camera Calibration Technique With Application to Acoustic Imaging. *IEEE Transactions on Image Processing*, *22*(10), 4028–4039. doi:10.1109/TIP.2013.2268974 PMID:23797248

Lei, Z., Liao, S., Pietikainen, M., & Li, S. Z. (2011). Face recognition by exploring information jointly in space, scale and orientation. *IEEE Transactions on Image Processing*, *20*(1), 247–256. doi:10.1109/TIP.2010.2060207 PMID:20643604

Lew, M. S., Sebe, N., Djeraba, C., & Jain, R. (2006). Content-based multimedia information retrieval: State of the art and challenges. *ACM Transactions on Multimedia Computing Communications & Applications*, *2*(1), 1–19. doi:10.1145/1126004.1126005

Li, G., Liu, Y., Dong, L., Cai, X., & Zhou, D. (2007). An algorithm for extrinsic parameters calibration of a camera and a laser range finder using line features. *Proceedings of the IEEE International Conference on Intelligent Robots and Systems* (pp. 3854–3859).

Li, L., Li, S., Wang, G., & Abraham, A. (2011, March 26-28). An evaluation on circularly orthogonal moments for image representation. *Proceedings of Int. Conf. Inf. Sci., and Tech.*, Nanjing, Jiangsu, China (pp. 394-397). doi:10.1109/ICIST.2011.5765275

Li, Y., Wang, S., Tian, Q., & Ding, X. (2015). A Survey of Recent Advances in Visual Feature Detection. *Neurocomputing, 149, Part B*(3), 736–751.

Liao, S., Law, M. W., & Chung, A. C. (2009). Dominant local binary patterns for texture classification. *IEEE Transactions on Image Processing*, *18*(5), 1107–1118. doi:10.1109/TIP.2009.2015682 PMID:19342342

Li, B., Wang, S., Zheng, J., & Zheng, L. (2014). Single image haze removal using content-adaptive dark channel and post enhancement. *IET Journal IET Computer Vision*, 8(2), 131–140. doi:10.1049/iet-cvi.2013.0011

Li, K., & Fu, Y. (2014). Prediction of human activity by discovering temporal sequence patterns. *IEEE Transactions on Pattern Analysis and Machine Intelligence*, 36(8), 1644–1657. doi:10.1109/TPAMI.2013.2297321 PMID:26353344

Li, K., Miller, E. D., Chen, M., Kanade, T., Weiss, L. E., & Campbell, P. G. (2008). Cell population tracking and lineage construction with spatiotemporal context. *Medical Image Analysis*, 12(5), 546–566. doi:10.1016/j.media.2008.06.001 PMID:18656418

Li, M., & Staunton, R. C. (2008). Optimum Gabor filter design and local binary patterns for texture segmentation. *Pattern Recognition Letters*, 29(5), 664–672. doi:10.1016/j.patrec.2007.12.001

Lim, Y., & Choi, J. (2009). Speaker selection and tracking in a cluttered environment with audio and visual information. *IEEE Transactions on Consumer Electronics*, 55(3), 1581–1589. doi:10.1109/TCE.2009.5278030

Lin, D.-T., & Huang, K.-Y. (2011). Collaborative pedestrian tracking and data fusion with multiple cameras. *IEEE Transactions on Information Forensics and Security*, 6(4), 1432–1444. doi:10.1109/TIFS.2011.2159972

Lindeberg, T. (1998). Feature detection with automatic scale selection. *International Journal of Computer Vision*, 30(2), 79–116. doi:10.1023/A:1008045108935

Liu, H., Chen, S., & Naoyuki Kubota. (2013). Intelligent Video Systems and Analytics: A Survey. *IEEE Trans. on Industrial Informatics, 9*(3), 1222-1233.

Liu, N., Gimel'farb, G., & Delmas, P. (2015, November). Combined ternary patterns for texture recognition. *Proceedings of the 2015 International Conference on Image and Vision Computing New Zealand (IVCNZ)* (pp. 1-6). IEEE. doi:10.1109/IVCNZ.2015.7761509

Liu, B., & Zaccarin, A. (1993). New fast algorithms for the estimation of block motion vectors. *IEEE Transactions on Circuits and Systems for Video Technology*, 3(2), 148–157. doi:10.1109/76.212720

Liu, Q., Li, R., Hu, H., & Gu, D. (2016). Extracting Semantic Information from Visual Data: A Survey. *Robotics*, 5(1), 1–22. doi:10.3390/robotics5010008

Liu, , Wang, S., Huang, D., Deng, G., Zeng, F., & Chen, H. (2016). Medical image classification using spatial adjacent histogram based on adaptive local binary patterns. *Computers in Biology and Medicine*, 72, 185–200. doi:10.1016/j.compbiomed.2016.03.010 PMID:27058283

Liu, Y., Zhang, D., Lu, G., & Ma, W. Y. (2007). A survey of content-based image retrieval with high-level semantics. *Pattern Recognition*, 40(1), 262–282. doi:10.1016/j.patcog.2006.04.045

Livingstone, M. (2008). *Vision and Art: The Biology of Seeing*. New York: Abrams.

Li, X., Hu, W., Zhang, Z., & Wang, H. (2010). Heat kernel based local binary pattern for face representation. *IEEE Signal Processing Letters*, 17(3), 308–311. doi:10.1109/LSP.2009.2036653

Li, Y., Jiao, L., Shang, R., & Stolkin, R. (2015). Dynamic-context cooperative quantum-behaved particle swarm optimization based on multilevel thresholding applied to medical image segmentation. *Inf. Sci.*, 294, 408–422. doi:10.1016/j.ins.2014.10.005

Li, Y., Sun, J., Tang, C., & Shum, H. (2004). Lazy snapping. *ACM Transactions on Graphics*, 23(3), 303–308. doi:10.1145/1015706.1015719

Long, F., Zhang, H., & Feng, D. D. (2003). Fundamentals of content-based image retrieval. In *Multimedia Information Retrieval and Management* (pp. 1–26). Springer Berlin Heidelberg. doi:10.1007/978-3-662-05300-3_1

Lou, C.-C., Lee, S.-W., & Jay Kuo, C.-C. (2010). Adaptive search range selection in motion estimation. *Proceedings of the 2010 IEEE International Conference on Acoustics Speech and Signal Processing (ICASSP)* (pp. 918-921). IEEE. doi:10.1109/ICASSP.2010.5495282

Lowe, D. (2001). Local feature view clustering for 3D object recognition. Proceedings of CVPR (pp.682–688).

Lowe, D. G. (1999). Object Recognition from Local Scale-Invariant Features. *Proceedings of the IEEE International Conference on Computer Vision*. Kerkyra, Greece.

Lowe, D. G. (1999). *Object Recognition from Local Scale-Invariant Features. Proceedings of ICCV* (pp. 1150–1157). Corfu, Greece: . doi:10.1109/ICCV.1999.790410

Lowe, D. G. (2004). Distinctive Image Features from Scale-Invariant Keypoints. International Journal of Computer Vision, *60*(2), 91–110. doi:10.1023/B:VISI.0000029664.99615.94

Loy, C. C., Xiang, T., & Gong, S. (2009, September). Modelling Multi-object Activity by Gaussian Processes. Proceedings of BMVC (pp. 1–11).

Lu, L., Liu, L., & Hu, C. (2014). Analysis of the Electrical Impedance Tomography Algorithm Based On Finite Element Method and Tikhonov. *Proceedings of the 2014 International Conference on Wavelet Analysis and Pattern Recognition (ICWAPR)* (pp. 36-42).

Luo, J., Yang, X., & Liu, L. (2015). A fast motion estimation algorithm based on adaptive pattern and search priority. *Multimedia Tools and Applications, 74*(24), 11821–11836. doi:10.1007/s11042-014-2280-z

Mahadevan, V., Li, W., Bhalodia, V., & Vasconcelos, N. (2010, June). Anomaly detection in crowded scenes. Proceedings of CVPR (Vol. 249, p. 250).

Mahi, H., Isabaten, H., & Serief, C. (2014). Zernike Moments and SVM for Shape Classification in Very High Resolution Satellite Images, The International Arab. *Journal of Information Technology, 11*(1).

Mainali, P., Lafruit, G., Yang, Q., Geelen, B., Gool, L. V., & Lauwereins, R. (2013). SIFER: Scale-Invariant Feature Detector with Error Resilience. *International Journal of Computer Vision, 104*(2), 172–197. doi:10.1007/s11263-013-0622-3

Makinen, E., & Raisamo, R. (2008). Evaluation of Gender Classification Methods with Automatically Detected and Aligned Faces. *IEEE Trans. PAMI, 30*(3), 541–547. doi:10.1109/TPAMI.2007.70800 PMID:18195447

Malik, F., & Baharudin, B. (2012). Effective content-based image retrieval: combination of quantized histogram features in the DCT domain. *Proceedings of the International Conference on Computer on Information Science* (Vol. 1, pp. 425-430).

Malmivuo, J.A, & Plonsey, R. (1995). *Impedance Tomography.*

Malone, E., Jehl, M., Arridge, S., Betcke, T., & Holder, D. (2014). Stroke type differentiation using spectrally constrained multifrequency EIT: Evaluation of feasibility in a realistic head model. *Physiological Measurement, 35*(6), 1051–1066. doi:10.1088/0967-3334/35/6/1051 PMID:24844796

Marcus, A., & Marques, O. (2012). An eye on visual sensor networks. *IEEE Potentials, 31*(2), 38–43. doi:10.1109/MPOT.2011.2178279

Marlin, T. E. (1995). *Process Control, Designing Processes and Control Systems for Dynamic performance.* McGraw-Hill.

Marr, D. (1982). *Vision: A Computational Investigation into the Human Representation and Processing of Visual Information*. San Francisco: W. H. Freeman.

Martinsky, Ondrej. 2007. *Algorithmic and Mathematical principles of Automatic Number Plate Recognition systems.*

Matas, J., Chum, O., Urban, M., & Pajdla, T. (2004). Robust Wide Baseline Stereo From Maximally Stable Extremal Regions. *Image and Vision Computing*, 22(10), 761–767. doi:10.1016/j.imavis.2004.02.006

Materka, A., & Strzelecki, M. (1998). Texture Analysis Methods – A Review (COST B11 report). Institute of Electronics, Brussels.

Mathias, E. (1998). Comparing the influence of color spaces and metrics in content-based image retrieval. *Proceedings of International Symposium on Computer Graphics, Image Processing, and Vision* (pp. 371 -378). doi:10.1109/SIBGRA.1998.722775

Mathwork. (n.d.). *optical-flow*. Retrieved March 1, 2017, from https://www.mathworks.com/discovery/optical-flow.html

Megherbi, N., Ambellouis, S., Colôt, O., & Cabestaing, F. (2005). Joint audio-video people tracking using belief theory. *Proceedings of the IEEE International Conference on Advanced Video and Signal Based Surveillance AVSS '05* (pp. 135–140). doi:10.1109/AVSS.2005.1577256

Mejdoub, M., Fonteles, L., BenAmar, C., & Antonini, M. (2009). Embedded lattices tree: An efficient indexing scheme for content based retrieval on image databases. *Journal of Visual Communication and Image Representation*, 20(2), 145–156. doi:10.1016/j.jvcir.2008.12.003

Mengxing, T., Xiuzhen, D., Mingxin, Q., Feng, F., Xuetao, S., & Fusheng, Y. (1998). Electrical impedance tomography reconstruction algorithm based on general inversion theory and finite element method. *Medical & Biological Engineering & Computing*, 36(July), 395–398. doi:10.1007/BF02523205 PMID:10198520

Mhalighi, M., Vosoughi, V. B., Mortazavi, M., Hy, W., & Soleimani, M. (2012). The practical design of low-cost instrumentation for industrial electrical impedance tomography (EIT). *Proceedings of the* IEEE I2MTC Conference (pp. 1259–1263).

Mignotte, M. (2008). Segmentation by Fusion of Histogram-Based K-Means Clusters in Different Color Spaces. *IEEE Transactions on Image Processing*, 17(5), 780–787. doi:10.1109/TIP.2008.920761 PMID:18390382

Mikolajczyk, K., & Schmid, C. (2002). An Affine Invariant Interest Point Detector. Proceedings of ECCV (pp. 128-142).

Mikolajczyk, K., Schmid, C., & Zisserman, A. (2004). Human detection based on a probabilistic assembly of robust part detectors. Proceedings of ECCV (pp. 69–81).

Mikolajczyk, K., & Schmid, C. (2004). Scale and affine invariant interest point detectors. International Journal of Computer Vision, 60(1), 63–86. doi:10.1023/B:VISI.0000027790.02288.f2

Mikolajczyk, K., & Schmid, C. (2005). A Performance Evaluation of Local Descriptors. *IEEE Transactions on Pattern Analysis and Machine Intelligence*, 27(10), 1615–1630. doi:10.1109/TPAMI.2005.188 PMID:16237996

Mikolajczyk, K., Tuytelaars, T., Schmid, C., Zisserman, A., Matas, J., Schaffalitzky, F., & Gool, L. V. et al. (2005). A Comparison of Affine Region Detectors. *International Journal of Computer Vision*, 65(1-2), 43–72. doi:10.1007/s11263-005-3848-x

Miksik, O., & Mikolajczyk, K. (2012). Evaluation of Local Detectors and Descriptors for Fast Feature Matching. *Proceedings of the International Conference on Pattern Recognition*. Tsukuba.

Minea, M., Grafu, M., Cormos, F. D., & Ciprian, A. 2007. Reliable Integrated Communications for Urban Intelligent Transport Systems. *Proceedings of the 8th International Conference on Telecommunications in Modern Satellite, Cable and Broadcasting Services*. doi:10.1109/TELSKS.2007.4376090

Mirajkar Pradnya, P., & Ruikar, S. D. (2013, July). Image Fusion Based on Stationary Wavelet Transform. *International Journal of Advanced Engineering Research and Studies*.

Mistretta, C. A., Crummy, A. B., & Strother, C. M. (1981). Digital angiography: A perspective. *Radiology, 139*(2), 273–276. doi:10.1148/radiology.139.2.7012918 PMID:7012918

Mizuno, K., Noguchi, H., He, G., Terachi, Y., Kamino, T., Kawaguchi, H., & Yoshimoto, M. (2010). Fast and Low-Memory-Bandwidth Architecture of SIFT Descriptor Generation with Scalability on Speed and Accuracy for VGA Video. *Proceedings of the International Conference on Field Programmable Logic and Applications*, Milano (pp. 608-611). doi:10.1109/FPL.2010.119

Moghaddam, H. A., Khajoie, T. T., & Rouhi, A. H. (2003, September). A new algorithm for image indexing and retrieval using wavelet correlogram. *Proceedings of the 2003 International Conference on Image Processing ICIP '03* (Vol. 3, pp. III-497). IEEE. doi:10.1109/ICIP.2003.1247290

Moghaddam, B., & Yang, M. (2002). Learning Gender with Support Faces. *IEEE Transactions on Pattern Analysis and Machine Intelligence, 24*(5), 707–711. doi:10.1109/34.1000244

Mohamed, M. A., & El-Den, B. M. (2011). Implementation of Image Fusion Techniques for Multi- Focus Images Using FPGA. *Proceedings of the 28th National radio science conference*.

Mokhtarian, F., Abbasi, F., & Kittler, J. (1997). Efficient and robust retrieval by shape content through curvature scale space. *Proceedings of the Int. workshop on Image Databases and Multi-Media Search* (pp. 51–58).

Monson, J., & Wirthlin, M. (2013). Implementing high-performance, low-power FPGA-based optical flow accelerators in C. *Proceedings of the IEEE 24th International Conference on Application-Specific Systems, Architectures and Processors* (pp. 363-369).

Monson, J., & Wirthlin, M. (2013). Optimization techniques for a high level synthesis implementation of the sobel filter. *Proceedings of the International Conference on Reconfigurable Computing and FPGAs (ReConFig)* (pp. 1-6). doi:10.1109/ReConFig.2013.6732315

Moore, A., & Prince, S. J. D., Warrell, J., Mohammed, U., & Jones, G., (2009). *Scene Shape Priors for Superpixel Segmentation*. Proceedings of the *ICCV '09*.

Moore, S., & Bowden, R. (2011). Local binary patterns for multi-view facial expression recognition. *Computer Vision and Image Understanding, 115*(4), 541–558. doi:10.1016/j.cviu.2010.12.001

Moreels, P., Maire, M., & Perona, P. (2004). Recognition by probabilistic hypothesis construction. Proceedings of ECCV '04 (pp. 55–68).

Morel, J.-M., & Yu, G. (2016, Nov. 8). *Affine-SIFT (ASIFT)*. Retrieved from https://tinyurl.com/akkznh

Morel, J. M., & Yu, G. (2009). ASIFT: A New Framework for Fully Affine Invariant Image Comparison. *SIAM Journal on Imaging Sciences, 2*(2), 1–28. doi:10.1137/080732730

Mould, N., Regens, J. L., Jensen, C. J. III, & Edger, D. N. (2014). Video surveillance and counterterrorism: The application of suspicious activity recognition in visual surveillance systems to counterterrorism. *Journal of Policing. Intelligence and Counter Terrorism, 9*(2), 151–175. doi:10.1080/18335330.2014.940819

Mujumdar, S, Sivaswamy, J., Kishore, L.T., & Varma R. (2013, March 28-30). Auto-Windowing of Ischemic Stroke Lesions in Diffusion Weighted Imaging of the Brain. *Proceedings of the Medical Informatics and Telemedicine conference (ICMIT)* (pp 1-6).

Mukundan, R., & Ramakrishnan, K. R. (1998). *Moment functions in image analysis: Theory and Applications.* Singapore: World Scientific. doi:10.1142/3838

Mumford, D., & Shah, J. (1989). Optimal approximation by piecewise smooth functions and associated variational problems. *Communications on Pure and Applied Mathematics, 42*(5), 577–685. doi:10.1002/cpa.3160420503

Muñoz-Salinas, R., García-Silvente, M., & Medina Carnicer, R. (2008). Adaptive multi-modal stereo people tracking without background modelling. *Journal of Visual Communication and Image Representation, 19*(2), 75–91. doi:10.1016/j.jvcir.2007.07.004

Murala, S., Gonde, A. B., & Maheshwari, R. P. (2009, March). Color and texture features for image indexing and retrieval. *Proceedings of the IEEE International Advance Computing Conference IACC '09* (pp. 1411-1416). IEEE. doi:10.1109/IADCC.2009.4809223

Murala, S., Maheshwari, R. P., & Balasubramanian, R. (2012). Local tetra patterns: A new feature descriptor for content-based image retrieval. *IEEE Transactions on Image Processing, 21*(5), 2874–2886. doi:10.1109/TIP.2012.2188809 PMID:22514130

Murayama, N., Taniguchi, H., Konishi, A., & Matsuda, H. (1980). U.S. Patent No. 4,207,599. Washington, DC: U.S. Patent and Trademark Office.

Musciki, D., Evans, R., & Stankovic, S. (1994). Integrated Probabilistic Data Association. *IEEE Transactions on Automatic Control, 39*(6), 1237–1241. doi:10.1109/9.293185

Nane, R., Sima, V., Olivier, B., Meeuws, R., Yankova, Y., & Bertels, K. (2012). DWARV 2.0: A CoSy-based C-to-VHDL hardware compiler. *Proceedings of the 22nd International Conference on Field Programmable Logic and Applications (FPL)* (pp. 619-622). doi:10.1109/FPL.2012.6339221

Nastar, C., Mitschke, M., Boujemaa, N., Meilhac, C., Bernard, H., & Mautref, M. (1998). Retrieving images by content: the surfimage system. In *Advances in Multimedia Information Systems* (pp. 110–120). Berlin, Heidelberg: Springer. doi:10.1007/3-540-49651-3_11

Negishi, M., & Tong, T. (2011). Constable RT. Tomography: A Simulation Study. *IEEE 2011, 30*(3), 828–837.

Ngo, H. T., Ives, R. W., Rakvic, R. N., & Broussard, R. P. (2013). Real-time Video Surveillance on an Embedded, Programmable Platform. *Microprocessors and Microsystems, 37*(6-7), 562–571. doi:10.1016/j.micpro.2013.06.003

Niblack, C. W., Barber, R., Equitz, W., Flickner, M. D., Glasman, E. H., Petkovic, D., . . . Taubin, G. (1993). QBIC project: querying images by content, using color, texture, and shape. *Proceedings of the Symposium on Electronic Imaging: Science and Technology* (pp. 173-187). International Society for Optics and Photonics. doi:10.1117/12.143648

Nickel, K., Gehrig, T., Stiefelhagen, R., & McDonough, J. (2005). A joint particle filter for audio-visual speaker tracking. *Proceedings of the 7th International Conference on Multimodal Interfaces ICMI '05.* doi:10.1145/1088463.1088477

Nie, Y., & Ma, K.-K. (2002). Adaptive irregular pattern search with zero-motion prejudgement for fast block-matching motion estimation. *Proceedings of the 7th International Conference on Control, Automation, Robotics and Vision ICARCV '02* (Vol. 3, pp. 1320-1325). IEEE.

Ning, X., Li, W., Dong, X., Zhang, L., & Shi, Y. (2015). A image fog removal method based on human visual property. *Proceedings of the 8th International Congress on Image and Signal Processing (CISP)*, Shenyang (pp. 178-183). doi:10.1109/CISP.2015.7407871

Ning, J., Zhang, L., Zhang, D., & Wu, C. (2010). Interactive image segmentation by maximal similarity based region merging. *Pattern Recognition*, *43*(2), 445–456. doi:10.1016/j.patcog.2009.03.004

Nister, D., & Stewenius, H. (2008). Linear Time Maximally Stable Extremal Regions. *Proceedings of the European Conference on Computer Vision*. Marseille, France.

Nister, D., & Stewenius, H. (2006). *Scalable Recognition with a Vocabulary Tree*. New York, NY: IEEE Computer Vision and Pattern Recognition. doi:10.1109/CVPR.2006.264

Nock, R., & Nielsen, F. (2004). Statistical region merging. *IEEE Transactions on Pattern Analysis and Machine Intelligence*, *26*(11), 1452–1458. doi:10.1109/TPAMI.2004.110 PMID:15521493

Nyboer, J., Kreider, M. M., & Hannapel, L. (1950). Electrical impedance plethysmography; a physical and physiologic approach to peripheral vascular study. *JOAHA. Circulation*, *2*(6), 811–821p. doi:10.1161/01.CIR.2.6.811 PMID:14783833

Nyul, L. G., Udupa, J. K., & Zhang, X. (2000, February). New variants of a method of MRI scale standardization. *IEEE Transactions on Medical Imaging*, *19*(2), 143–150. doi:10.1109/42.836373 PMID:10784285

Obdrzalek, S., & Matas, J. (2002). Object Recognition using Local Affine Frames on Distinguished Regions. *Proceedings of the British Machine Vision Conference* (pp. 83-104). Springer. doi:10.5244/C.16.9

Obdrzalek, S., & Matas, J. (2005). Sub-linear Indexing For Large Scale Object Recognition. *Proceedings of the British Machine Vision Conference*. doi:10.5244/C.19.3

OCallaghan, J. F. (1971). An Alternative Definition for Neighborhood at a Point. *IEEE Transactions on Computers*, *C-24*(11), 1121–1125. doi:10.1109/T-C.1975.224144

O'Hara, K., Mitchell, A. S., & Vorbau, A. (2007). Consuming video on mobile devices. *Proceedings of the SIGCHI conference on Human factors in computing systems*. ACM. doi:10.1145/1240624.1240754

Oh, H.-S., & Lee, H.-K. (2000). Block-matching algorithm based on an adaptive reduction of the search area for motion estimation. *Real-Time Imaging*, *6*(5), 407–414. doi:10.1006/rtim.1999.0184

Ojala, T., Pietikainen, M., & Maenpaa, T. (2002). Multiresolution gray-scale and rotation invariant texture classification with local binary patterns. *IEEE Transactions on Pattern Analysis and Machine Intelligence*, *24*(7), 971–987. doi:10.1109/TPAMI.2002.1017623

Olszewski, M. E., Long, R. M., Mitchell, S. C., & Sonka, M. (2000, April). Quantitative measurements in geometrically correct representations of coronary vessels in 3-D and 4-D. *Proc. 4th IEEE Southwest Symposium on Image Analysis and Interpretation*, Austin, TX. doi:10.1109/IAI.2000.839611

Opiola, J. (2006). *Toll Collection Systems- Technology Trend Impact on PPP's & Highways' Transport*. Washington, U.S.A: World bank.

OToole, A. J., Vetter, T., Troje, N. F., & Bulthoff, H. H. (1997). Sex Classification Is Better with Three-Dimensional Structure than with Image Intensity Information. *Perception*, *26*(1), 75–84. doi:10.1068/p260075 PMID:9196691

Otsu, N. (1975). A threshold selection method from gray-level histograms. *Automatica*, *11*, 23–27.

Paiement, A., Mirmehdi, M., Xianghua Xie, , & Hamilton, M. C. K. (2014, January). Integrated Segmentation and Interpolation of Sparse Data. *IEEE Transactions on Image Processing, 23*(1), 110–125. doi:10.1109/TIP.2013.2286903 PMID:24158475

Pajares, G., & De La Cruz, J. M. (2004). A Wavelet-based Image Fusion tutorial on Pattern Recognition.

Palmer, S. E. 1999. Vision Science: Photons to Phenomenology. Cambridge, Massachusets: The MIT Press.

Palmerini, G. B. (2014). Combining thermal and visual imaging in spacecraft proximity operations. *Proceedings of the IEEE International Conference on Control Automation Robotics and Vision (pp.* 383–388). doi:10.1109/ICARCV.2014.7064336

Pan, Z., Yin, X., & Wu, G. 2004, September Segmentation-based interpolation of 3-D medical images. In *Computational Science and Its Applications, LNCS* (Vol. *3044*, pp. 731–740). doi:10.1007/978-3-540-24709-8_77

Papakostas, G. A., Boutalis, Y. S., Karras, D. A., & Mertzios, B. G. (2010). Efficient computation of Zernike and pseudo-Zernike moments for pattern classification applications. *Pattern Recognition and Image Analysis, 20*(1), 56–64. doi:10.1134/S1054661810010050

Paris, S., & Durand, F. (2007). A Topological Approach to Hierarchical Segmentation Using Mean Shift. *proceeding of IEEE Conference on Computer Vision Pattern Recognition* (pp. 1-8). doi:10.1109/CVPR.2007.383228

Pass, G., & Zabith, R. (1996). Histogram refinement for content-based image retrieval. *Proceedings of the IEEE Workshop on Applications of Computer Vision* (pp. 96-102). doi:10.1109/ACV.1996.572008

Patterson, R. P. (2005). Electrical Impedance Tomography: Methods, History, and Applications (Institute of Physics Medical Physics Series). *Physics in Medicine and Biology, 50*(10), 2427–2428. doi:10.1088/0031-9155/50/10/B01

Paul, A., Wang, J. F., Wang, J. C., Tsai, A. C., & Chen, J. T. (2006). Projection based adaptive window size selection for efficient motion estimation in H. 264/AVC. *IEICE Transactions on Fundamentals of Electronics, Communications and Computer Science, 89*(11), 2970–2976.

Paul, A. (2015). Adaptive search window for high efficiency video coding. *Journal of Signal Processing Systems for Signal, Image, and Video Technology, 79*(3), 257–262. doi:10.1007/s11265-013-0841-4

Peng, B., Zhang, L., & Zhang, D. (2011). Automatic image segmentation by dynamic region merging. *IEEE Transactions on Image Processing, 20*(12), 3592–3605. doi:10.1109/TIP.2011.2157512 PMID:21609885

Peng, B., Zhang, L., Zhang, D., & Yang, J. (2011). Image segmentation by iterated region merging with localized graph cuts. *Pattern Recognition, 44*(10–11), 2527–2538. doi:10.1016/j.patcog.2011.03.024

Pentland, A. P. (1984, November). Fractal-based description of natural scene. *IEEE Transactions on Pattern Analysis and Machine Intelligence, 6*(6), 661–674. doi:10.1109/TPAMI.1984.4767591 PMID:22499648

Pepikj, B., Stark, M., Gehler, P., & Schiele, B. (2013). Occlusion patterns for object class detection. *Proceedings of the IEEE Conference on Computer Vision and Pattern Recognition* (pp. 3286-3293).

Perdoch, M., & Matas, J. (2011). *Maximally Stable Extremal Regions and Local Geometry for Visual Correspondences.* Prague, Czech Republic: Czech Technical University.

Persad, K., Walton, C. M., & Hussain, S. (2007). Toll Collection Technology and Best Practices. Vehicle/License Plate Identification for Toll Collection Application.

Phillips, P. J., Martin, A., Wilson, C., & Przybocki, M. (2000). An Introduction to Evaluating Biometric Systems. *IEEE Computer, 33*(2), 56–63. doi:10.1109/2.820040

Pietikäinen, M., Ojala, T., & Xu, Z. (2000). Rotation-invariant texture classification using feature distributions. *Pattern Recognition, 33*(1), 43–52. doi:10.1016/S0031-3203(99)00032-1

Ping, Z. L., Wu, R., & Sheng, Y. L. (2002). Image description with Chebyshev-Fourier moments. *Journal of the Optical Society of America, 19*(9), 1748–1754. doi:10.1364/JOSAA.19.001748 PMID:12216868

Pomyen, S. (2015). Signal and Image Processing with Matlab on Raspberry Pi Platform [MSc. Thesis]. Tampere university of technology, Finland.

Poorani, M., Prathiba, T., & Ravindran, G. (2013). Integrated Feature Extraction for Image Retrieval. *IJCSMC, 2*(2), 28–35.

Pope, A., & Lowe, D. G. (2000). Probabilistic models of appearance for 3D object recognition. *IJCV, 40*(2), 149–167. doi:10.1023/A:1026502202780

Premebida, C., Ludwig, O., & Nunes, U. (2009). LIDAR and vision-based pedestrian detection system. *Journal of Field Robotics, 26*(9), 696–711. doi:10.1002/rob.20312

Pressman, R. S. (1982). *Software Engineering: A Practitioner's approach.* New York: McGraw-Hill.

Prokop, R. J., & Reeves, A. P. (1992). A survey of moment-based techniques for unoccluded object representation and recognition. *Graphical Models and Image Processing, 54*(5), 438–460. doi:10.1016/1049-9652(92)90027-U

Pure, A. A., Gupta, N., & Shrivastava, M. (2013, July). An Overview of Different Image Fusion Methods for Medical Applications. *International journal of scientific & engineering research, 4*(7).

Pursiainen, S., & Hakula, H. (2006). A High-Order Finite Element Method for Electrical Impedance Tomography. *PIERS Online, 2*(3), 260–264. doi:10.2529/PIERS050905044807

Purwar, R. K., Prakash, N., & Rajpal, N. (2011). A matching criterion for motion compensation in the temporal coding of video signal. *Signal, Image and Video Processing, 5*(2), 133–139. doi:10.1007/s11760-009-0149-9

Qasaimeh, M., Sagahyroon, A., & Shanableh, T. (2014). A Parallel Hardware Architecture for Scale Invariant Feature Transform (SIFT). *Proceedings of the International Conference on Multimedia Computing and Systems.* Marrakech. doi:10.1109/ICMCS.2014.6911251

Qasaimeh, M., Sagahyroon, A., & Shanableh, T. (2015). FPGA-Based Parallel Hardware Architecture for Real-Time Image Classification. *IEEE Trans. on Computational Imaging, 1*(1), 56–70. doi:10.1109/TCI.2015.2424077

Qi, H., Li, K., Shen, Y., & Qu, W. (2010). An effective solution for trademark image retrieval by combining shape description and feature matching. *Pattern Recognition, 43*(6), 2017–2027. doi:10.1016/j.patcog.2010.01.007

Quddus, A., & Basir, O. (2012, May). Semantic image retrieval in magnetic resonance brain volumes. *IEEE Transaction Information Technology Biomedical Imaging, 16*(3), 348–355. doi:10.1109/TITB.2012.2189439 PMID:22389157

Rahim, R. A., Huei, L. Y. I., San, C. K. O. K., Fea, P. J. O. N., & Lean, L. C. (2003). Initial result on electrical impedance tomography. *Engineering, 39*(D), 105–112.

Rajagopalan, V., Boppana, V., Dutta, S., Taylor, B., & Wittig, R. (2011). Xilinx zynq-7000 epp: An extensible processing platform family. *Proceedings of the Hot Chips 23 Symposium (HCS).*

Rao, T. N. (2016). A smart visual surveillance system for better crime management. Unpublished master's thesis, National Institute of Technology Karnataka, Surathkal, Karnataka, India.

Rao, T. N., Girish, G. N., & Rajan, J. (2017). An improved contextual information based approach for anomaly detection via adaptive inference for surveillance application. *Proceedings of International Conference on Computer Vision and Image Processing* (pp. 133-147). Springer, Singapore. doi:10.1007/978-981-10-2104-6_13

Razvan, N., Sima, V.-M., Pilato, C., Fort, B., Choi, J., Chen, Y., & Canis, A. (2015). A Survey and Evaluation of FPGA High-Level Synthesis Tools. *IEEE Transactions on Computer-Aided Design of Integrated Circuits and Systems*, 35(10), 1591–1604.

Redondo, R., Sroubek, F., Fischer, S., & Cristobal, G. (2009). Multifocus image fusion using the log-Gabor transform and a Multisize Windows technique. *Information Fusion*, 10(2), 163–171. doi:10.1016/j.inffus.2008.08.006

Reiss, T. H. (1993). *Recognizing planar objects using invariant image features.* Berlin: Springer-Verlag. doi:10.1007/BFb0017553

Ren, H. (2014). A brief introduction on contemporary High-Level Synthesis. *Proceedings of the 2014 IEEE International Conference on IC Design & Technology*, Austin, TX. doi:10.1109/ICICDT.2014.6838614

Ren, H., Liu, A., Zou, J., Bai, D., & Ping, Z. (2007). Character reconstruction with radial harmonic Fourier moments. *Proc. 4th Int. Conf. on Fuzzy Systems and Knowledge Discovery 2007 (FSKD07)* (Vol. 3, pp. 307-310). doi:10.1109/FSKD.2007.213

Revski, G. (2003). On Conceptual Design of Intelligent Systems. In *Mechatronics 13* (pp. 1029–1044). Uxbridge, U.K.: Elsevier Ltd.

Richardson, I.E. (2003). H. 264 and MPEG-4 Video Compression. England: Wiley.

Rister, B., Wang, G., Wu, M., & Cavallaro, R., J. (2013). A Fast and Efficient SIFT Detector Using the Mobile GPU. *Proceedings of the IEEE International Conference on Acoustics, Speech, and Signal Processing (ICASSP).* Vancouver, BC. doi:10.1109/ICASSP.2013.6638141

Roshtkhari, M. J., & Levine, M. D. (2013). An on-line, real-time learning method for detecting anomalies in videos using spatio-temporal compositions. *Computer Vision and Image Understanding*, 117(10), 1436–1452. doi:10.1016/j.cviu.2013.06.007

Rother, C., Kolmogorov, V., & Blake, A. (2004). Grab Cut: Interactive foreground extraction using iterated graph cuts. *ACM Transactions on Graphics*, 23(3), 309–314. doi:10.1145/1015706.1015720

Rothganger, F., Lazebnik, S., Schmid, C., & Ponce, J. (2003). 3D object modeling and recognition using affine-invariant patches and multi-view spatial constraints. Proceedings of CVPR (pp. 272–277).

Rubner, Y., Puzicha, J., Bhumann, J. M., & Tomasi, C. (2001). Empirical Evaluation of Dissimilarity Measures for Color and Texture. *Computer Vision and Image Understanding*, 84(1), 25–43. doi:10.1006/cviu.2001.0934

Rudas, I. J., & Fodor, J. (2008). Intelligent Systems. *International Journal of Computers, Communications & Control*, 3(3), 132–138.

Rui, Y., Huang, T. S., & Chang, S. F. (1999). Image retrieval: Current techniques, promising directions, and open issues. *Journal of Visual Communication and Image Representation*, 10(1), 39–62. doi:10.1006/jvci.1999.0413

Rui, Y., Huang, T. S., & Mehrotra, S. (1997). Content-based image retrieval with relevance feedback in MARS. *Proceedings of International Conference on Image Processing* (Vol. 2, pp. 815- 818). doi:10.1109/ICIP.1997.638621

Russel, P., & Norvig, S. (1995). *Artificial Intelligence: A Modern Approach.* New Jersey: Prentice Hall.

Ryoo, M. S. (2011). Human activity prediction: Early recognition of ongoing activities from streaming videos. *Proceedings of the 2011 IEEE International Conference on Computer Vision (ICCV)* (pp. 1036-1043). IEEE.

Ryoo, M. S., & Aggarwal, J. K. (2012). UT-Interaction dataset. *ICPR contest on Semantic Description of Human Activities (SDHA)*. Retrieved from http://cvrc.ece.utexas.edu/SDHA2010/HumanInteraction.html

Saha, A., Mukherjee, J., & Sural, S. (2008). New pixel-decimation patterns for block matching in motion estimation. *Signal Processing Image Communication, 23*(10), 725–738. doi:10.1016/j.image.2008.08.004

Said, A., & Pearlman, W. A. (1996). An image multiresolution representation for lossless and lossy compression. *IEEE Transactions on Image Processing, 5*(9), 1303–1310. doi:10.1109/83.535842 PMID:18285219

Salahat, E. (2016). A Novel Multi-Intensity Image Labeling Algorithm for Real-Time Computer Vision and Robotics Applications. *Proceedings of the Annual Conference of the IEEE Industrial Electronics Society*. Florence, Italy.

Salahat, E., Saleh, H., Mohammad, B., Al-Qutayri, M., Sluzek, A., & Ismail, M. (2013). Automated Real-Time Video Surveillance Algorithms for SoC Implementation: A Survey. *Proceedings of the IEEE International Conference on Electronics, Circuits, and Systems*. Abu Dhabi, UAE. doi:10.1109/ICECS.2013.6815354

Salahat, E., Saleh, H., Salahat, S., Sluzek, A., Al-Qutayri, M., Mohammad, B., & Ismail, M. (2016, April 28). *US Patent No. 20160117830.*

Salahat, E., Saleh, H., Salahat, S., Sluzek, A., Al-Qutayri, M., Mohammed, B., & Ismail, M. (2015). Extended MSER Detection. *Proceedings of the IEEE International Symposium on Industrial Electronics*. Rio de Janeiro, Brazil.

Salahat, E., Saleh, H., Sluzek, A., Al-Qutayri, M., Mohammad, B., & Ismail, M. (2015). A Maximally Stable Extremal Regions System-on-Chip For Real-Time Visual Surveillance. *Proceedings of the Annual Conference of the IEEE Industrial Electronics Society*. Yokohama, Japan.

Salahat, E., Saleh, H., Sluzek, A., Al-Qutayri, M., Mohammad, B., & Ismail, M. (2015). Novel Fast and Scalable Parallel Union-Find Implementation For Real-Time Digital Image Segmentation. *Proceedings of the Annual Conference of the IEEE Industrial Electronics Society*. Yokohama, Japan.

Salahat, E., Saleh, H., Sluzek, A., Al-Qutayri, M., Mohammed, B., & Ismail, M. (2016, March 10). US Patent No. 20160070970.

Salti, S., Lanza, A., & Stefano, L. D. (2013). Keypoints from Symmetries by Wave Propagation. *Proceedings of the IEEE Conference on Computer Vision and Pattern Recognition*.

San Biagio, M., Bazzani, L., Cristani, M., & Murino, V. (2014), Weighted Bag of Visual Words for Object Recognition, Image Processing (ICIP). *Proceedings of the 2014 IEEE International Conference*. doi:10.1109/ICIP.2014.7025553

Sangwar, S., & Peshaattiwar, A.A. (2013, September 21-23). Segmentation of CT images using K Means algorithm. *Proceedings of International Conference On Advanced Electronic Systems* (pp. 6 – 9).

Sansone, G. (1991). *Orthogonal functions*. New York: Dover Publications, Inc.

Santini, S., & Jain, R. (1999). Similarity Measures. *IEEE Transactions on Pattern Analysis and Machine Intelligence, 21*(9), 871–883. doi:10.1109/34.790428

Sarwer, M. G., & Jonathan Wu, Q. M. (2009). Adaptive search area selection of variable block-size motion estimation of H. 264/AVC video coding standard. *Proceedings of the 11th IEEE International Symposium on Multimedia ISM'09* (pp. 100-105). IEEE. doi:10.1109/ISM.2009.53

Sasi, A., Parameswaran, L., & Sruthy, S. (2013). *Image Fusion technique using DT-CWT*. IEEE.

Schmid, C., & Mohr, R. (1997). Local Grayvalue Invariants for Image Retrieval. *IEEE PAMI, 19*(5), 530–534. doi:10.1109/34.589215

Schmid, C., Mohr, R., & Bauckhage, C. (2000). Evaluation of Interest Point Detectors. *International Journal of Computer Vision, 37*(2), 151–172. doi:10.1023/A:1008199403446

Sengar, H., Wang, H., Wijesekera, D., & Jajodia, S. (2008). Detecting VoIP floods using the Hellinger Distance. *IEEE Transactions on Parallel and Distributed Systems, 9*(6), 794–805. doi:10.1109/TPDS.2007.70786

Seok, B., Youn, K., & Kim, S. (2014). Image reconstruction using adaptive mesh refinement based on adaptive thresholding in electrical impedance tomography. *Nuclear Engineering and Design, 270*, 421–426. doi:10.1016/j.nucengdes.2013.12.063

Shah, S. K., & Shah, D. U. (2014, March). Comparative Study of Image Fusion Techniques based on Spatial and Transform Domain. *International Journal of Innovative Research in Science, Engineering and Technology, 3*(3).

Shakhnarovich, G., Viola, P. A., & Moghaddam, B. (2002). A Unified Learning Framework for Real Time Face Detection and Classification. *Proc. Int'l Conf. Automatic Face and Gesture Recognition.* doi:10.1109/AFGR.2002.1004124

Shan, C., & Gritti, T. (2008). Learning discriminative lbp-histogrambins for facial expression recognition. *Proceedings of the British Machine Vision Conference.*

Sharan, D., & Gitakrishnan, R. (2011). Archive traffic Data Management Systems- A study on the feasibility and implementation in Indian Urban Areas.

Sharma, R. K. (1999). Probabilistic Model-based Multisensor Image Fusion [PhD thesis]. Oregon Graduate Institute of Science and Technology, Portland, Oregon.

Shen, D., & Ip, H. H. S. (1999). Discriminative wavelet shape descriptors for recognition of 2-D patterns. *Pattern Recognition, 32*(2), 151–165. doi:10.1016/S0031-3203(98)00137-X

Sheng, Y., & Shen, L. (1994). Orthogonal Fourier Mellin moment for invariant pattern recognition. *Journal of the Optical Society of America, 11*(6), 1748–1757. doi:10.1364/JOSAA.11.001748

Shi, J., & Malik, J. (2000). Normalized cuts and image segmentation. *IEEE Transactions on Pattern Analysis and Machine Intelligence, 22*(8), 888–905. doi:10.1109/34.868688

Shivappa, S. T., Rao, B. D., & Trivedi, M. M. (2010). Audio-visual fusion and tracking with multilevel iterative decoding: Framework and experimental evaluation. *IEEE Journal of Selected Topics in Signal Processing, 4*(5), 882–894. doi:10.1109/JSTSP.2010.2057890

Shi, Y.-G., Zhang, Y., & Wu, L.-N. (1998). Adaptive thresholding for motion estimation prejudgement. *Electronics Letters, 34*(21), 2016–2017. doi:10.1049/el:19981380

Shi, Z., Fernando, W. A. C., & Kondoz, A. (2011). Adaptive direction search algorithms based on motion correlation for block motion estimation. *IEEE Transactions on Consumer Electronics, 57*(3), 1354–1361. doi:10.1109/TCE.2011.6018894

Shu, X., & Wu, X.-J. (2011). A novel contour descriptor for 2D shape matching and its application to image retrieval. *Image and Vision Computing, 29*(4), 286–294. doi:10.1016/j.imavis.2010.11.001

Sibon, R. (1978). Locally Equiangular Triangulations. *The Computer Journal, 21*(3), 243–245. doi:10.1093/comjnl/21.3.243

Singh, A., Shekhar, S., & Jalal, A. S. (2012). Semantic based image retrieval using multi-agent model by searching and filtering replicated web images. *Proceedings of the 2012 World Congress on Information and Communication Technologies* (WICT) (pp. 817-821).

Singh, C., & Pooja, . (2011). Improving image retrieval using combined features of Hough transform and Zernike moments. *Optics and Lasers in Engineering*, *49*(12), 1386–1396. doi:10.1016/j.optlaseng.2011.07.009

Singh, C., & Pooja, . (2012). Local and global features based image retrieval system using orthogonal radial moments. *Optics and Lasers in Engineering*, *50*(5), 655–667. doi:10.1016/j.optlaseng.2011.11.012

Singh, C., & Walia, E. (2011). Algorithms for fast computation of Zernike moments and their numerical stability. *Image and Vision Computing*, *29*(4), 251–259. doi:10.1016/j.imavis.2010.10.003

Singh, M. P. (2015). Norms as a basis for governing sociotechnical systems. *Proceedings of the IJCAI International Joint Conference on Artificial Intelligence* (pp. 4207–4211).

Singh, U. P., Saxena, K., & Jain, S. (2011). A Review: Different Types of Similarity Measures. *Pioneer Journal of Computer Science and Engineering Technology*, *2*(1), 43–63.

Singh, U. P., Saxena, K., & Jain, S. (2011). Semi-Supervised Method of Multiple Object Segmentation with Region Labeling and Flood Fill. *Signal and Image Processing International Journal*, *2*(3), 175–193.

Singh, U. P., Saxena, K., & Jain, S. (2011). Unsupervised Method of Object Retrieval with Region Labeling and Flood Fill" *International Journal of Advanced Computer Science and Applications*. *Special Issue on Artificial Intelligence*, *1*, 41–50.

Sivic, J., & Zisserman, A. (2003). Video google: A Text Retrieval Approach to Object Matching in Videos. *Proceedings of the International Conference on Computer Vision*. Nice, France. doi:10.1109/ICCV.2003.1238663

Sluzek, A. (2015). Multi-distinctive MSER Features and Their Descriptors: A Low-Complexity Tool for Image Matching. *Proceedings of the International Conference on Advanced Concepts for Intelligent Vision Systems*. Catania, Italy. doi:10.1007/978-3-319-25903-1_58

Sluzek, A. (2016). Improving Performances of MSER Features in Matching and Retrieval Tasks. *Proceedings of the European Conference on Computer Vision*. Amsterdam, The Netherlands.

Smeulders, A. W., Worring, M., Santini, S., Gupta, A., & Jain, R. (2000). Content-based image retrieval at the end of the early years. *IEEE Transactions on Pattern Analysis and Machine Intelligence*, *22*(12), 1349–1380. doi:10.1109/34.895972

Sobieranski, A. C. E., Comunello, A., & Wangenheim, V. (2011). Learning a nonlinear distance metric for supervised region-merging image segmentation. *Computer Vision and Image Understanding*, *115*(2), 127–139. doi:10.1016/j.cviu.2010.09.006

Soleimani, M. (2006). 92006). Electrical impedance tomography system: An open access circuit design. *Biomedical Engineering Online*, *5*(1), 28. doi:10.1186/1475-925X-5-28 PMID:16672061

Song, B. C., & Ra, J. B. (1998). Hierarchical block-matching algorithm using partial distortion criterion. Proceedings of Photonics West '98 on Electronic Imaging (pp. 88-95). International Society for Optics and Photonics, . doi:10.1117/12.298403

Song, H., Shin, V., & Jeon, M. (2012). Mobile node localization using fusion prediction-based interacting multiple model in cricket sensor network. *IEEE Transactions on Industrial Electronics*, *59*(11), 4349–4359. doi:10.1109/TIE.2011.2151821

Song, X., Cui, J., Zhao, H., & Zha, H. (2008). A Bayesian Approach: Fusion of Laser and Vision for Multiple Pedestrians Tracking. *International Journal (Toronto, Ont.)*, *3*(1), 1–9.

Song, X., Zhao, H., Cui, J., Shao, X., Shibasaki, R., & Zha, H. (2013). An Online System for Multiple Interacting Targets Tracking: Fusion of Laser and Vision, Tracking and Learning. *ACM Transactions on Intelligent Systems and Technology*, *4*(1), 1–21. doi:10.1145/2414425.2414443

Sonka, M., Hlavac, V. and Boyle, R. (2007). *Image Processing Analysis and Computer Vision*, Thomson publication.

Soro, S., & Heinzelman, W. (2009). A survey of visual sensor networks. *Advances in Multimedia, 2009*, 1–21. doi:10.1155/2009/640386

Spinello, L., Triebel, R., & Siegwart, R. (2009). A trained system for multimodal perception in urban environments. *Proc. of The Workshop on People Detection and Tracking (ICRA)*, Kobe, Japan.

Stasiak, M., Sikora, J., Filipowicz, S. F., & Nita, K. (2007). Principal Component analysis and artificial neural network approach to electrical impedance tomography problems approximated by multi-region boundary element method. *Engineering Analysis with Boundary Elements, 31*(8), 713–720. doi:10.1016/j.enganabound.2006.12.003

Stolkin, R., Rees, D., Talha, M., & Florescu, I. (2012). Bayesian fusion of thermal and visible spectra camera data for region based tracking with rapid background adaptation. *Proceedings of the IEEE International Conference on Multisensor Fusion and Integration for Intelligent Systems* (pp. 192–199). doi:10.1109/MFI.2012.6343021

Strobel, N., Spors, S., & Rabenstein, R. (2001). Joint audio-video object localization and tracking, A Presentation of General Methodology. *IEEE Signal Processing Magazine, 18*(1), 22–31. doi:10.1109/79.911196

Subash Chandra Boss, R., & Thangavel, K. (2012, March 21-23). Mammogram Image Segmentation Using Fuzzy Clustering. *Proceedings of the International Conference on Pattern Recognition* (pp. 290 – 295).

Sugimoto, S., Tateda, H., Takahashi, H., & Okutomi, M. (2004). Obstacle detection using millimeter-wave RADAR and its visualization on image sequence. *Proceedings of the International Conference on Pattern Recognition* (Vol. 3, pp. 342–345). doi:10.1109/ICPR.2004.1334537

Sugiyama, K. (1991). *U.S. Patent No. 4,985,768*. Washington, DC: U.S. Patent and Trademark Office.

Suliman, A., & Li, R. (2016). Video Compression Using Variable Block Size Motion Compensation with Selective Subpixel Accuracy in Redundant Wavelet Transform. In Information Technology: New Generations (pp. 1021-1028). Springer International Publishing. doi:10.1007/978-3-319-32467-8_88

Sullivan, G. J., & Ohm, J.-R. (2010). *Recent developments in standardization of high efficiency video coding (HEVC)*. International Society for Optics and Photonics. doi:10.1117/12.863486

Sullivan, G. J., Ohm, J.-R., Han, W.-J., & Wiegand, T. (2012). Overview of the high efficiency video coding (HEVC) standard. *IEEE Transactions on Circuits and Systems for Video Technology, 22*(12), 1649–1668. doi:10.1109/TC-SVT.2012.2221191

Sun, S., & Sonka, M. (2013, April 7-11). Graph based 4D Lung Segmentation in CT Images with expert guided computer aided refinement. *Proceedings of IEEE 10th International Symposium* (pp. 1312 – 1315). doi:10.1109/ISBI.2013.6556773

Su, S. Z., Chen, S. Y., Li, S. Z., Li, S. A., & Duh, D. J. (2010). Structured local binary Haar pattern for pixel-based graphics retrieval. *Electronics Letters, 46*(14), 996–998. doi:10.1049/el.2010.1104

Swain, M. J., & Ballard, D. H. (1991). Color indexing. *International Journal of Computer Vision, 7*(1), 11–32. doi:10.1007/BF00130487

Szeliski, R. (2010). *Computer Vision Algorithms and Applications*. Springer.

Tab, F. A., Naghdy, G., & Mertins, A. (2006). Scalable multiresolution color image segmentation. *Signal Processing, 86*(7), 1670–1687. doi:10.1016/j.sigpro.2005.09.016

Taffar, M., & Benmohammed, M. (2011). *Generic Face Invariant Model for Face Detection. In Proc. IP & C Conf.* (Vol. 1, pp.42-50). doi:10.1007/978-3-642-23154-4_5

Taffar, M., Miguet, S., & Benmohammed, M. (2012). Viewpoint Invariant Face Detection. *Proc. NDT Conference* (pp. 390–402).

Talha, M., & Stolkin, R. (2014). Particle filter tracking of camouflaged targets by adaptive fusion of thermal and visible spectra camera data. *IEEE Sensors Journal, 14*(1), 159–166. doi:10.1109/JSEN.2013.2271561

Tang, W.C., & Ho, T.V. (2007). *Electronic Toll Collection System*. US 7233260 B2.

Tan, X., & Triggs, B. (2010). Enhanced local texture feature sets for face recognition under difficult lighting conditions. *IEEE Transactions on Image Processing, 19*(6), 1635–1650. doi:10.1109/TIP.2010.2042645 PMID:20172829

Tarel, J. P., Hautière, N., Caraffa, L., Cord, A., Halmaoui, H., & Gruyer, D. (2012). Vision Enhancement in Homogeneous and Heterogeneous Fog. *Intelligent Transportation Systems, 4*(2), 6–20.

Tarel, J. P., Hautière, N., Cord, A., Gruyer, D., & Halmaoui, H. (2010). Improved Visibility of Road Scene Images under Heterogeneous Fog. *Proceedings of IEEE Intelligent Vehicles Symposium (IV'10)* (pp. 478 – 485). doi:10.1109/IVS.2010.5548128

Tariq, A, Akram, M.U., & Javed, M.Y. (2013, April 16-19). Lung Nodule Detection in CT Images using Neuro Fuzzy Classifier. Proceedings of the IEEE Fourth International Workshop on Computational Intelligence in Medical Imaging (CIMI) (pp. 49-53).

Tawbi, W. (1993). Video compression standards and quality of service. *The Computer Journal, 36*(1), 43–54. doi:10.1093/comjnl/36.1.43

Teague, M. R. (1980). Image analysis via the general theory of moments. *Journal of the Optical Society of America, 70*(8), 920–930. doi:10.1364/JOSA.70.000920

Tegolo, D. (1994). Shape analysis for image retrieval. *Proc. of SPIE, Storage and Retrieval for Image and Video Databases -II*, San Jose, CA (pp. 59-69). doi:10.1117/12.171781

Teh, C. H., & Chin, R. T. (1988). On image analysis by the methods of moments. *IEEE Transactions on Pattern Analysis and Machine Intelligence, 10*(4), 496–513. doi:10.1109/34.3913

Teng, J., Wang, S., Zhang, J., & Wang, X. (2010, October). Neuro-fuzzy logic based fusion algorithm of medical images. *Proceedings of the 2010 3rd International Congress on Image and Signal Processing (CISP)* (Vol. 4, pp. 1552-1556). IEEE.

The Association Of Automatic Identification And Data Capture Technologies. (2000). *Optical Character Recognition (OCR)*. Pittsburg, USA: AIM Inc.

The Times of India. (2014 December 31). Fog again affects rail. air traffic: 32 trains rescheduled 80 cancelled. Retrieved from http://timesofindia.indiatimes.com

Thi, H. T. (2007). *A robust traffic surveillance system for detecting and tracking vehicles at nighttime*. University of Technology, Sydney.

Toews, M., & Arbel, T. (2006). Detection over Viewpoint via the Object Class Invariant. *Proc. Int'l Conf. Pattern Recognition* (Vol. 1, pp.765-768). doi:10.1109/ICPR.2006.444

Toews, M., & Arbel, T. (2009). Detection, Localization, and Sex Classification of Faces from Arbitrary Viewpoints and under Occlusion. *IEEE Trans. on PAMI, 31*(9), 1567–1581. doi:10.1109/TPAMI.2008.233 PMID:19574619

Torabi, A., & Mass, G. (2010). Feedback scheme for thermal-visible video registration, sensor fusion, and people tracking. *Proceedings of the IEEE computer society conference Computer Vision and Pattern Recognition Workshop* (pp. 15–22).

Torralba, A., Murphy, K. P., & Freeman, W. T. (2004). Sharing features: efficient boosting procedures for multiclass object detection. Proceedings of CVPR (pp. 762–769).

Torres-Urgell, L., & Lynn Kirlin, R. (1990). Adaptive image compression using Karhunen-Loeve transform. *Signal Processing, 21*(4), 303–313. doi:10.1016/0165-1684(90)90100-D

Treptow, A., Cielniak, G., & Duckett, T. (2005). Active people recognition using thermal and grey images on a mobile security robot. *Proceedings of the 2005 IEEE/RSJ International Conference on Intelligent Robots and Systems IROS* (pp. 3610–3615). doi:10.1109/IROS.2005.1545530

Trimberger, S. (2015). Three Ages of FPGAs: A Retrospective on the First Thirty Years of FPGA Technology. *Proceedings of the IEEE, 103*(3), 318–331. doi:10.1109/JPROC.2015.2392104

Truppe, M. J., Freysinger, W., Gunkel, A. R., & Thumfart, W. F. (Jan. 1996). Remote-guided surgical navigation in ENT surgery. *Proc. of Medicine Meets Virtual Reality IV*. San Diego, CA: Healthcare in the Information Age - Feature Tools for Transforming Medicine.

Tsai, C.-H., Tan, K.-J., Su, C.-L., & Guo, J.I. (2010). A group of macroblock based motion estimation algorithm supporting adaptive search range for H. 264 video coding. *Proceedings of 2010 IEEE International Symposium on Circuits and Systems (ISCAS)* (pp. 1891-1894). IEEE. doi:10.1109/ISCAS.2010.5537919

Tuytelaars, T., & Mikolajczyk, K. (2008). Local Invariant Feature Detectors: A Survey. *Foundations and Trends in Computer Graphics and Vision, 3*(3), 177–280. doi:10.1561/0600000017

Tuytelaars, T., & Van Gool, L. (2000). *Wide Baseline Stereo Matching Based on Local Affinely Invariant Regions* (pp. 412–425). BMVC. doi:10.5244/C.14.38

U.S. Department of Transportation- Federal Highway Administration. (2015). How Do Weather Events Impact Roads? Retrieved October 12. from http://www.ops.fhwa.dot.gov/_weather/q1_roadimpact.html

Udomhunsakul, S., Yamsang, P., Tumthong, S., & Borwonwatanadelok, P. (2011, July). Multiresolution Edge Fusion using SWT and SFM. *Proceedings of the World Congress on Engineering* (Vol. 2).

Ullman, S., Vidal-Naquet, M., & Sali, E. (2002). Visual features of intermediate complexity and their use in classification. *Nature Neuroscience, 5*(7), 1–6. PMID:12055634

Unay, D., Ekin, A., & Jasinschi, R. S. (2010). Local structure-based region-of-interest retrieval in brain MR images. *IEEE Transactions on Information Technology in Biomedicine, 14*(4), 897–903. doi:10.1109/TITB.2009.2038152 PMID:20064763

Unterweger, A. (2012). *Compression artifacts in modern video coding and state-of-the-art means of compensation*. In *Multimedia Networking and Coding* (p. 28).

Unusual crowd activity dataset. (n. d.). University of Minnesota. Retrieved from http://mha.cs.umn.edu/movies/crowdactivity-all.avi.5

Vanhamel, I., Pratikakis, I., & Sahli, H. (2003). Multiscale gradient watersheds of color images. *IEEE Transactions on Image Processing, 12*(6), 617–626. doi:10.1109/TIP.2003.811490 PMID:18237936

Vauhkonen, P. J. (2004) Image Reconstruction in Three-Dimensional Electrical Impedance Tomography [Doctoral Dissertation]. Department of applied physics, University of Kuopio.

Vedaldi, A. (2007). An Implementation of Multi-Dimensional Maximally Stable Extremal Regions.

Vedaldi, A. (2016). *VLFeat*. Retrieved November 6, 2016, from http://www.vlfeat.org

Veksler, O. (2008). Star shape prior for graph-cut image segmentation. *Proceedings of the European Conference on Computer Vision*, 2008, 454–467. doi:10.1007/978-3-540-88690-7_34

Vezhnevets, V., & Konouchine, V. (2005). Grow Cut: interactive multi-label ND image segmentation by cellular automata. *Proceedings of the Graphic* (pp. 150–156).

Vezzani, R., & Cucchiara, R. (2010). Video surveillance online repository (visor): An integrated framework. *Multimedia Tools and Applications*, *50*(2), 359–380. Retrieved from http://www.openvisor.org doi:10.1007/s11042-009-0402-9

Villarreal, J., Park, A., Najjar, W., & Halstead, R. (2010). Designing Modular Hardware Accelerators in C with ROCCC 2.0. In *Field-Programmable Custom Computing Machines (FCCM)*, 127-134.

Vincent, L., & Soille, P. (1991). Watersheds in digital spaces: An efficient algorithm based on immersion simulations. *IEEE Transactions on Pattern Analysis and Machine Intelligence*, *13*(6), 583–598. doi:10.1109/34.87344

Viola, P., & Jones, M. (2001). Rapid Object Detection Using a Boosted Cascade of Simple Features. *Proc. IEEE CVPR Conf.* (pp. 511–518). doi:10.1109/CVPR.2001.990517

Wahle, A., Prause, G. P. M., Von Birgelen, C., Erbel, R., & Sonka, M. (1999, October). Fusion of angiography and intravascular ultrasound in vivo: Establishing the absolute 3-D frame orientation. IEEE Transactions on Bio-Medical Engineering, 46(10), 1176–1180. *PubMed*, *1999*. doi:10.1109/10.790492

Walia, E., Singh, C., & Goyal, A. (2012). On the fast computation of orthogonal Fourier–Mellin moments with improved numerical stability. *Journal of Real-Time Image Processing*, *7*(4), 247–256. doi:10.1007/s11554-010-0172-7

Wallace, G. K. (1992). The JPEG still picture compression standard. *Consumer Electronics, IEEE Transactions on*, *38*(1), xviii–xxxiv. doi:10.1109/30.125072

Wang, Q., & Wang, H. (2011). Image reconstruction based on expectation maximization method for electrical impedance tomography (EIT). *Proceedings of the 2011 IEEE International Conference on Imaging Systems and Techniques* (Vol. 1, pp. 50–54). doi:10.1109/IST.2011.5962175

Wang, X., Han, T., & Yan, S. (2009). An hog-lbp human detector with partial occlusion handling. *Proceedings of the International Conference on Computer Vision ICCV '09* (pp. 32–39). doi:10.1109/ICCV.2009.5459207

Wang, Z. B., & Lu, R. H. (2008, December 12-14). A New Algorithm for Image Segmentation Based on Fast Fuzzy C-Means Clustering, Computer Science and Software Engineering. Proceedings of the 2008 International Conference on Computer Science and Software Engineering (V*ol. 6*, pp. 14-17).

Wang, C.-N., Yang, S.-W., Liu, C.-M., & Chiang, T. (2003). A hierarchical decimation lattice based on N-queen with an application for motion estimation. *IEEE Signal Processing Letters*, *10*(8), 228–231. doi:10.1109/LSP.2003.814403

Wang, D., Li, T., & Stephen, N. (2013). *Accelerating OpenCV Applications with Zynq-7000 All Programmable SoC using Vivado HLS Video Libraries*. Xilinx Inc.

Wang, G., Tao, L., Di, H., Ye, X., & Shi, Y. (2012). A Scalable Distributed Architecture for Intelligent Vision System. *IEEE Trans. on Industrial Informatics*, *8*(1), 91–99. doi:10.1109/TII.2011.2173945

Wang, L., Zhang, Y., & Feng, J. (2005). On the Euclidean distance of images. *IEEE Transactions on Pattern Analysis and Machine Intelligence*, *27*(8), 1334–1339. doi:10.1109/TPAMI.2005.165 PMID:16119271

Wang, S., & Chen, H. (1999). An improve algorithm of motion compensation MPEG video compression. *Proceedings of the IEEE International Vehicle Electronics Conference IVEC'99* (pp. 261-264). IEEE. doi:10.1109/IVEC.1999.830680

Wang, X., Ma, X., & Grimson, W. E. L. (2009). Unsupervised activity perception in crowded and complicated scenes using hierarchical bayesian models. *IEEE Transactions on Pattern Analysis and Machine Intelligence*, *31*(3), 539–555. doi:10.1109/TPAMI.2008.87 PMID:19147880

Wang, Y., Wang, Y., & Kuroda, H. (2000). A globally adaptive pixel-decimation algorithm for block-motion estimation. *IEEE Transactions on Circuits and Systems for Video Technology*, *10*(6), 1006–1011. doi:10.1109/76.867940

Ward, A. A., McKenna, S. J., Buruma, A., Taylor, P., & Han, J. (2008). Merging technology and users: applying image browsing to the fashion industry for design inspiration. *Proceedings of the International Workshop on Content-Based Multimedia Indexing CBMI '08* (pp. 288-295). IEEE. doi:10.1109/CBMI.2008.4564959

Wasielewski, S., & Strauss, O. (1995). Calibration of a multi-sensor system laser range finder/camera. *Proceedings of the IEEE Intelligent Vehicles Symposium* (pp. 472–477). doi:10.1109/IVS.1995.528327

Weber, M., Welling, M., & Perona, P. (2000). Unsupervised learning of models for recognition. *ECCV Conference*, Dublin, Ireland (pp. 18–32).

Wei, C. H., Li, Y., Chau, W.-Y., & Li, C.-T. (2008). Trademark image retrieval using synthetic features for describing global shape and interior structure. *Pattern Recognition*, *42*(3), 386–394. doi:10.1016/j.patcog.2008.08.019

Wen, C. Y., & Yu, C. C. (2005). Image retrieval of digital crime scene images. *Forensic Sci. J.*, *4*(1), 37–45.

Whiffen, B., Delannoy, P., & Siok, S. Fog: Impact on Road Transportation and Mitigation Options. Retrieved September 9, 2015. from http://www.chebucto.ns.ca/Science/AIMET/archive/whiffen_et_al_2003.pdf

Wiegand, T., Sullivan, G. J., Bjontegaard, G., & Luthra, A. (2003). Overview of the H. 264/AVC video coding standard. *IEEE Transactions on Circuits and Systems for Video Technology*, *13*(7), 560–576. doi:10.1109/TCSVT.2003.815165

Wien, M. (2003). Variable block-size transforms for H. 264/AVC. *IEEE Transactions on Circuits and Systems for Video Technology*, *13*(7), 604–613. doi:10.1109/TCSVT.2003.815380

Wikipedia. (n. d.). *Epipolar geometry and epipolar line.* Retrieved March 1, 2017, from http://en.wikipedia.org/wiki/

Wiliem, A., Madasu, V., Boles, W., & Yarlagadda, P. (2012). A suspicious behaviour detection using a context space model for smart surveillance systems. *Computer Vision and Image Understanding*, *116*(2), 194–209. doi:10.1016/j.cviu.2011.10.001

Wu, Y., Hirakawa, S., Reimers, U. H., & Whitaker, J. (2006). Overview of digital television development worldwide. *Proceedings of the IEEE*, *94*(1), 8–21. doi:10.1109/JPROC.2005.861000

Xiao, G., Yun, X., & Wu, J. (2016). A new tracking approach for visible and infrared sequences based on tracking-before-fusion. *International Journal of Dynamics and Control*, *4*(1), 40–51. doi:10.1007/s40435-014-0115-4

Xilinx. (2017, November 30). *Xilinx.* Retrieved from Vivado Design Suite (Release Notes, Installation). Retrieved from https://www.xilinx.com/support/documentation/sw_manuals/xilinx2016_4/ug973-vivado-release-notes-install-license.pdf

Xiong, B., & Zhu, C. (2009). Efficient block matching motion estimation using multilevel intra-and inter-subblock features subblock-based SATD. *IEEE Transactions on Circuits and Systems for Video Technology*, *19*(7), 1039–1043. doi:10.1109/TCSVT.2009.2020260

Xu, G., Wang, R., Zhang, S., Yang, S., Justin, G. a., Sun, M., & Yan, W. (2007). A 128-electrode three dimensional electrical impedance tomography system. *Proceedings of the Annual International Conference of the IEEE Engineering in Medicine and Biology* (pp. 4386–4389). doi:10.1109/IEMBS.2007.4353310

Xu, J., Denman, S., Fookes, C., & Sridharan, S. (2011, December). Unusual event detection in crowded scenes using bag of LBPs in spatio-temporal patches. *Proceedings of the 2011 International Conference on Digital Image Computing Techniques and Applications (DICTA)* (pp. 549-554). doi:10.1109/DICTA.2011.98

Xu, J., Denman, S., Fookes, C., & Sridharan, S. (2015, April). Detecting rare events using Kullback-Leibler divergence. *Proceedings of the 2015 IEEE International Conference on Acoustics, Speech and Signal Processing (ICASSP)* (pp. 1305-1309). doi:10.1109/ICASSP.2015.7178181

Xu, C. J., Liu, J. Z., & Tang, X. (2009). 2D shape matching by contour flexibility. *IEEE Transactions on Pattern Analysis and Machine Intelligence, 31*(1), 180–186. doi:10.1109/TPAMI.2008.199 PMID:19029556

Xu, Y., Monasse, P., Géraud, T., & Najman, L. (2014). Tree-Based Morse Regions: A Topological Approach to Local Feature Detection. *IEEE Transactions on Image Processing, 23*(12), 5612–5625. doi:10.1109/TIP.2014.2364127 PMID:25373079

Yamada, T., Ikekawa, M., & Kuroda, I. (2005). Fast and accurate motion estimation algorithm by adaptive search range and shape selection. *Proceedings of the IEEE International Conference on. Acoustics, Speech, and Signal Processing ICASSP'05* (Vol. 2). IEEE. doi:10.1109/ICASSP.2005.1415550

Yang, J.-F., Chang, S.-C., & Chen, C.-Y. (2002). Computation reduction for motion search in low rate video coders. *IEEE Transactions on Circuits and Systems for Video Technology, 12*(10), 948–951. doi:10.1109/TCSVT.2002.804892

Yang, L., Yu, K., Li, J., & Li, S. (2005). An effective variable block-size early termination algorithm for H. 264 video coding. *IEEE Transactions on Circuits and Systems for Video Technology, 15*(6), 784–788. doi:10.1109/TCSVT.2005.848306

Yang, X., Zhao, W., Chen, Y., & Fang, X. (2008). Fang, Image segmentation with a fuzzy clustering algorithm based on ant-tree. *Signal Processing, 88*(10), 2453–2462. doi:10.1016/j.sigpro.2008.04.005

Yang, Z., Li, M., & Ai, H. (2006). An Experimental Study on Automatic Face Gender Classification. *Proc. Int'l Conf. Pattern Recognition* (pp. 1099-1102).

Yap, P. T., Jiang, X., & Fellow, A. C. K. (2010). Two dimensional polar harmonic transforms for invariant image representation. *IEEE Transactions on Pattern Analysis and Machine Intelligence, 32*(7), 1259–1270. doi:10.1109/TPAMI.2009.119 PMID:20489228

Yedla, M., & Pathakota, S. R. (2010, September). T M Srinivasa, Enhancing KMeans Clustering Algorithm with Improved Initial Center. *International Journal of Computer Science and Information Technologies, 1*, 121–125.

Ye, J. (2011). Cosine similarity measures for intuitionistic fuzzy sets and their applications. *Mathematical and Computer Modelling, 53*(1-2), 91–97. doi:10.1016/j.mcm.2010.07.022

Yu, C. Y., Li, Y., Liu, A. L., & Liu, J. H. (2011, August 24-26). A Novel Modified Kernel Fuzzy C-Means Clustering Algorithm on Image Segmentation. *Proceedings of the 14th IEEE International Conference on Computational Science and Engineering* (Vol. 3, pp. 621 – 626).

Yuan, J., Liu, Z., & Wu, Y. (2011). Discriminative video pattern search for efficient action detection. *IEEE Transactions on Pattern Analysis and Machine Intelligence, 33*(9), 1728–1743. Retrieved from http://research.microsoft.com/en-us/um/people/zliu/actionrecorsrc/ doi:10.1109/TPAMI.2011.38 PMID:21339530

Yu, G., & Morel, J. M. (2009). A Fully Affine Invariant Image Comparison Method. *Proc. IEEE International Conference on Acoustics, Speech, and Signal Processing (ICASSP)*, Taipei. doi:10.1109/ICASSP.2009.4959904

Yu, G., Yuan, J., & Liu, Z. (2012, October). Predicting human activities using spatio-temporal structure of interest points. *Proceedings of the 20th ACM international conference on Multimedia* (pp. 1049-1052). ACM. doi:10.1145/2393347.2396380

Yun, L., Rupnow, K., Li, Y., Min, D., Do, M., & Chen, D. (2012). High-level synthesis: Productivity, performance, and software constraints. *Journal of Electrical and Computer Engineering*.

Zahan, C. T. (1971). Graph-Theoretical Methods for Detecting and Describing Gestalt Clusters. *IEEE Transactions on Computers*, *C-20*(1), 68–86. doi:10.1109/T-C.1971.223083

Zaharescu, A., & Wildes, R. (2010, September). Anomalous behaviour detection using spatiotemporal oriented energies, subset inclusion histogram comparison and event-driven processing. In European Conference on Computer Vision (pp. 563–576). Springer Berlin Heidelberg. Retrieved from http://www.cse.yorku.ca/vision/research/ spatiotemporal-anomalous-behavior.shtml doi:10.1007/978-3-642-15549-9_41

Zaki, W. M. D. W., Fauzi, M. F. A., Besar, R., & Ahmad, W. M. W. (2011, November 21-24). Qualitative and Quantitative Comparisons of Hemorrhage Intracranial Segmentation in CT Brain Images. Proceedings of 10th IEEE Region Conference (pp. 369 – 373).

Zeng, B., Li, R., & Liou, M. L. (1997). Optimization of fast block motion estimation algorithms. *IEEE Transactions on Circuits and Systems for Video Technology*, *7*(6), 833–844. doi:10.1109/76.644063

Zernike, F. (1934). Beugungstheorie des Schneidenverfahrens und seiner verbesserten Form, *der Phasenkontrastmethode*. *Physica*, *1*(7-12), 689–701. doi:10.1016/S0031-8914(34)80259-5

Zhang, B., Gao, Y., Zhao, S., & Liu, J. (2010). Local derivative pattern versus local binary pattern: Face recognition with high-order local pattern descriptor. *IEEE Transactions on Image Processing*, *19*(2), 533–544. doi:10.1109/TIP.2009.2035882 PMID:19887313

Zhang, D., & Lu, G. (2002). Shape-based image retrieval using generic Fourier descriptor. *Signal Processing Image Communication*, *17*(10), 825–848. doi:10.1016/S0923-5965(02)00084-X

Zhang, D., & Lu, G. (2003). A comparative study of curvature scale space and Fourier descriptors for shape-based image retrieval. *Journal of Visual Communication and Image Representation*, *14*(1), 41–60. doi:10.1016/S1047-3203(03)00003-8

Zhang, L., & Koch, R. (2012). Line Matching Using Appearance Similarities and Geometric Constraints. In *Pattern Recognition, LNCS* (Vol. *7476*, pp. 236–245).

Zhang, Q., & Pless, R. (2004). Extrinsic Calibration of a Camera and Laser Range Finder (improves camera calibration). *Proceedings of IROS* (Vol. *3*, pp. 2301–2306).

Zhao, B., Fei-Fei, L., & Xing, E. P. (2011, June). Online detection of unusual events in videos via dynamic sparse coding. *Proceedings of the 2011 IEEE Conference on Computer Vision and Pattern Recognition (CVPR)* (pp. 3313-3320). doi:10.1109/CVPR.2011.5995524

Zhao, H., Xiao, C., Yu, J., & Xu, X. (2015). Single image fog removal based on local extrema. IEEE/CAA Journal of Automatica Sinica, 2(2), 158-165.

Zhao, G., Barnard, M., & Pietikainen, M. (2009). Lipreading with local spatiotemporal descriptors. *IEEE Transactions on Multimedia*, *11*(7), 1254–1265. doi:10.1109/TMM.2009.2030637

Zhao, G., & Pietikainen, M. (2007). Dynamic texture recognition using local binary patterns with an application to facial expressions. *IEEE Transactions on Pattern Analysis and Machine Intelligence*, *29*(6), 915–928. doi:10.1109/TPAMI.2007.1110 PMID:17431293

Zhong, H., Shi, J., & Visontai, M. (2004, June). Detecting unusual activity in video. *Proceedings of the 2004 IEEE Computer Society Conference on Computer Vision and Pattern Recognition CVPR '04* (Vol. *2*, pp. 819-826).

Zhong, S., Wang, J., Yan, L., Kang, L., & Cao, Z. (2013). A Real-time Embedded Architecture for SIFT. *Journal of Systems Architecture: the EUROMICRO Journal, 59*(1), 16–29. doi:10.1016/j.sysarc.2012.09.002

Zhou, S., Shen, W., Zeng, D., & Zhang, Z. (2015, April). Unusual event detection in crowded scenes by trajectory analysis. *Proceedings of the 2015 IEEE International Conference on Acoustics, Speech and Signal Processing (ICASSP)* (pp. 1300-1304). doi:10.1109/ICASSP.2015.7178180

Zhou, Z., Sun, M.-T., & Hsu, Y.-F. (2004). Fast variable block-size motion estimation algorithm based on merge and slit procedures for H. 264/MPEG-4 AVC. *Proceedings of the 2004 International Symposium on Circuits and Systems ISCAS'04 (Vol. 3)*. IEEE. doi:10.1109/ISCAS.2004.1328849

Zhou, J., Chang, S., & Pappas, Q. L. G. (2008, May 14-17). A novel learning based segmentation method for rodent brain structures using MRI. *Proceedings of 5th IEEE International Symposium on* Biomedical Imaging (pp. 61–64).

Zhou, J., & Hung, C. C. (2007, August). A Generalized Approach to Possibility Clustering. *International Journal of Uncertainty, Fuzziness and Knowledge-based Systems, 15*(Suppl. 2), 110–132. doi:10.1142/S0218488507004650

Zhou, Z., Wang, B., Li, S., & Dong, M. (2016). Perceptual fusion of infrared and visible images through a hybrid multi-scale decomposition with Gaussian and bilateral filters. *Information Fusion, 30*, 15–26. doi:10.1016/j.inffus.2015.11.003

Zook, J. M., & Iftekharuddin, K. M. (2005, January). Statistical analysis of fractal-based brain tumor detection algorithms. *Magnetic Resonance Imaging, 23*(5), 671–678. doi:10.1016/j.mri.2005.04.002 PMID:16051042

About the Contributors

Md. Imtiyaz Anwar graduated from MACET Patna in Electronics & Communication engineering with distinction and post graduated from Dr B R Ambedkar National Institute of Technology, Jalandhar, India in 2010 with Gold Medal. He is currently pursuing his Ph. D in Dr B R Ambedkar National Institute of Technology, Jalandhar, India. His research interests include wireless networks, image processing, computer vision and video signal processing.

* * *

Ashwani Kumar Aggarwal did his Bachelor degree in Electronics and Instrumentation Engineering in 1996 from Punjabi University Patiala, India. He did masters from Indian Institute of Science, Bangalore, India in 2002 and PhD from The University of Tokyo, Tokyo, Japan in 2014. His research area of interest is computer vision.

Kratika Arora did her B.Tech in 2009, M.Tech in 2016. Her research area of interest is image processing.

Shaifali Madan Arora is Assistant Professor at MSIT, New Delhi. She has done her Ph.D. from GGSIPU, New Delhi, B.Tech from GNDU, Amritsar, India and M.Tech from GNDEC, Ludhiana, India. She has teaching experience of more than 14 years. She is a life member of ISTE. Her areas of interest include Digital image and signal processing, Artificial intelligence, Microprocessors and controllers. She has various research publications in quality national and international conferences.

Rakesh Asery received his B. Tech. (Electronics & Communication Engineering) from Govt. Engineering College Ajmer, India in year 2013 and M. Tech. (Electronics & Communication Engineering) from Dr. B. R. Ambedkar National Institute of Technology Jalandhar, India in year 2016. Presently he is junior research fellow under the Department of Science and Technology (BIG Data Initiatives Division), Govt. of India, under the guidance of Dr. Rajiv Ranjan Sahay, Assistant Professor, Electrical Engineering Department, Indian Institute of Technology, Kharagpur, India. He is reviewer of Signal, Image and Video Processing, Springer. His research interest includes Image Processing, Signal Processing and Content based image retrieval.

Amruta Deshmukh was born in Maharashtra state, India. Received the B.Eng. degree (with distinction) in electronic and telecommunication engineering (Pune University), M.Tech. degree in electronic product design technology from CDAC, Mohali (PTU, Punjab). Now Assistant Professor at E&TC department of SGGS Institute of Engineering & Technology, Nanded, Maharashtra (India)

Poonam Fauzdar is an assistant professor in GLA university, Mathura in computer science department.

Girish G. N. is a research scholar at Department of Computer Science and Engineering, National Institute of Technology Karnataka, India. He received his B.E. degree in Computer Science and Engineering in 2012, followed by M.Tech. in Computer Science and Engineering in 2014 from the Visvesvaraya Technological University (VTU), Karnataka, India. His research interests include biometrics, object recognition and tracking, computer vision, image processing and medical image analysis.

Sanjeev Jain was born on September 11, 1967 in Vidisha, M.P., India. He is Vice Chancellor of Shri Mata Vaishno Devi University, Katra, Jammu, India. He completed his B.E. at the Samrat Ashok Technological Institute, Vidisha, M.P., his M.Tech. at the Indian Institute of Technology, Delhi, India, and received his Ph.D. in Computer Science & Engineering from Barkatullah University, Bhopal. He has published/presented 100 research papers in International/National Journals and Conferences on image processing and soft computing techniques. His areas of research include Computer Network, Image Processing, Neural Networks, etc. He is a life member of various technical societies.

Kavita Khanna is an associate professor with The NorthCap University, Gurgaon, Haryana. She has 16 years of teaching experience during which she has published more than 35 research papers and guided 15 M.Tech students in their research work. Her research areas include artificial neural networks, digital image processing, computer graphics and design and analysis of algorithms. She has done her PhD from GGSIPU, Dwarka. Apart from that she is working as a Radio Jockey with All India Radio FM Gold.

Puneeta Marwaha received her B. Tech. (Electronics and Communication Engineering) degree in 2007 and M. Tech. (Electronics and Communication Engineering) in 2010 from Punjab Technical University, Jalandhar. Presently she is a Ph.D. Research Scholar in Electronics and Communication Engineering Department, Dr. B. R. Ambedkar National Institute of Technology, Jalandhar, under the guidance of Dr. Ramesh Kumar Sunkaria, Assistant Professor, Electronics and Communication Engineering Department, Dr. B. R. Ambedkar National Institute of Technology, Jalandhar. Her area of research interest is Biomedical Signal Processing.

Charles Mbohwa is currently a Full Professor of Sustainability Engineering and Engineering Management at the University of Johannesburg, South Africa. Contacted at cmbohwa@uj.ac.za

Ramesh Kumar Meena was born in Jaipur, Rajasthan, India on July 8th, 1986. He received B.Tech Degree in Electronics & Instrumentation and Control Engineering from Arya college of engineering & I. T., Jaipur, Rajasthan, India in 2007 and M.Tech Degree in Control and Instrumentation Engineering from NIT Jalandhar, Punjab, India in 2009. He is Research Scholar at Department Of Instrumentation and Control Engineering, Dr. B. R. Ambedkar National Institute of Technology, Jalandhar, and Punjab, India. He has published several papers in national & international conferences, international journals on Biomedical Instrumentation, signal processing. He has an experience of 5 years of teaching as Assistant Professor. His research area of interest is Instrumentation and Control Engineering.

Serge Miguet graduated from the ENSIMAG (Grenoble, France) in 1988. He obtained a PhD from the INPG in 1990. He was an Assistant Professor at the ENS de Lyon, and a member of the LIP laboratory from 1991 to 1996. He received his Habilitation à Diriger des Recherches from the Université Claude Bernard Lyon 1 in 1995. Since 1996, he is a full Professor in Computer Science at the Université Lumière Lyon 2, and a member of the LIRIS laboratory, UMR CNRS 5205. His main research activities are devoted to models and tools for Image processing, Computer Vision, Shape Analysis, Pattern Recognition, Video processing.

Tawanda Mushiri is a PhD student at the University of Johannesburg in the field of fuzzy logic systems and maintenance, is a Lecturer at the University of Zimbabwe teaching Machine Dynamics, Solid Mechanics and Machine Design. His research activities and interests are in Artificial intelligence, Automation, Design and Maintenance engineering.

Murad Qasaimeh is a PhD Candidate in the Department of Electrical and Computer Engineering at Iowa State University (ISU), where he is working with Dr.Phillips Jones and Dr.Joseph Zambreno. He received his B.S. in computer engineering from Jordan University of Science and Technology (JUST) in 2011, and his M.Sc. from American University of Sharjah (AUS) university in 2014. His research interests include image and video processing, parallel hardware architectures, hardware accelerators, FPGA/ASIC design, system on chip (SoC) design, real-time embedded systems design and computer vision.

Jeny Rajan did his M.Tech. in Image Processing from the University of Kerala, India, and received his PhD from the University of Antwerp, Belgium. He is currently working as an Assistant Professor at the Department of Computer Science and Engineering, National Institute of Technology Karnataka (NITK), India. Before joining NITK, he was working as a post-doctoral researcher at the Vision Lab, University of Antwerp in Belgium. His main research interests are medical image processing and video processing.

Narendra Rao T. J. is currently working as a Junior Research Fellow in the Department of Computer Science and Engineering, National Institute of Technology Karnataka, India. He obtained his M.Tech. (Research) degree in 2016 from the Department of CSE, NITK, India for his work in the area of "Anomaly detection for surveillance applications". He recieved the Bachelor of Engineering (B.E.) degree in Computer Science and Engineering from the Visvesvaraya Technological University, Belgaum, Karnataka in 2013. His research interests include computer vision, medical image analysis and video processing.

Ehab Salahat is an MSc. graduate in Electrical and Computer Engineering and BSc. in Communications Engineering (with first class honor) in 2015 and 2013, respectively. He has served as a reviewer and as a member of the technical program committee in more than 30 conferences and numerous journals such as the IEEE TCS-VT and TCS-I. He has also published in prestigious and flagship conferences such as IEEE IECON'16, IECON'15, ISIE'14, VTC'15, GLOBECOM'14, to mention a few. Additionally, he has been the recipient of many international and national prestigious scientific awards. He has also filed 6 US patents in the areas of signal processing, hardware design, and computer vision. His research interests include computer vision, robotics, machine learning, wireless communications, ASIC and SoC design.

Amit Sengupta is an obstetrician and a gynecologist, as well as a professor of biomedical - bioengineering working both as a clinician, surgeon and a research scientist on maternal and neonatal health, cancer, vascular research and technology development for mass health care.

Reshma Shaik graduated from VR Siddhartha Engineering College. Working in Industry at present.

Lakhan Dev Sharma received his B.E. (Hons.) in Electronics & Communication Engineering from Rajiv Gandhi Proudyogiki Vishwavidyalaya, Bhopal. He has completed his M. Tech. from ABV-Indian Institute of Information Technology and Management, Gwalior and pursuing his Ph.D. from Dr. B. R. Ambedkar National Institute of Technology, Jalandhar, India. His research interests include Biomedical Signals and Image Processing.

Pooja Sharma has completed Master Degree in Computer Science with Gold Medal for securing first position from Guru Nanak Dev University, Amritsar. She did her PhD in Pattern Recognition from Punjabi University, Patiala. Her academic achievements include fellowship for regular PhD from UGC, New Delhi after qualifying UGC NET and JRF, several merit certificates, gold and silver medals in matric, higher secondary, undergraduate and post graduate level. She has several research publications in peer reviewed International journals of Springer and Elsevier with significant Thomson Reuters impact factors. She is the reviewer of various International journals of Elsevier and Scientific Research and Essays. Her areas of specialization include Content Based Image Retrieval, Face Recognition, Pattern Recognition, and Digital Image Processing. She has 9 years of teaching experience and provided her services to Punjabi University, Patiala, Guru Nanak Dev University College, Jalandhar, and Lyallpur Khalsa College, Jalandhar. She was selected in Panjab University, Chandigarh and Central University of Jammu, Jammu in the year 2012 and 2013, respectively. Presently, she is working as Assistant Professor in the Department of Computer Science and Applications, DAV University, Jalandhar.

Balwinder Singh has obtained his Ph.D. from Guru Nanak Dev University, Amritsar in the field of Low Power VLSI Testing in 2014 and Bachelor of Technology degree from National Institute of Technology, Jalandhar and also Master of Technology degree from University Centre for Inst. & Microelectronics (UCIM), Panjab University, Chandigah in 2002 and 2004 respectively. He is the member of professional bodies i.e. Association of Computer Electronics and Electrical Engineers (ACEEE), International Association of Computer Science and Information Technology (IACSIT), Singapore, IEEE, Indian Microelectronics Society (IMS), Chandigarh. & VLSI Society of India (VSI), Bangalore. His current interest includes MEMS and NEMS, Genetic algorithms, Low Power techniques, VLSI Design & Testing, and System on Chip.

Satbir Singh is pursuing Ph.D. from National Institute of Technology, Jalandhar, India. He has done masters in Electronics and Communication Engineering from Thapar University. He is currently working as a Senior Scientific Officer with Electronics and Communication Engineering Department of Delhi Technological University, Delhi. Earlier, he worked as Project Engineer with Centre of Advanced Computing. His research interests include signal processing and computer vision

Uday Pratap Singh was born on February 6, 1979, in Sultanpur, U.P., India. Dr. Singh graduated in Mathematics from Dr. Ram Manohar Lohiya (Awadh) University, Faizabad, U.P. in 1998. He obtained his first M.Sc. degree in Mathematics & Statistics (Gold Medalist) in 2000, from Dr. Ram Manohar Lohiya (Awadh) University, Faizabad, U.P. and Second M.Sc. degree in Mathematics & Computing from Indian Institute of Technology, Guwahati. He later received his Doctorate Degree in Computer Science from Barkatullah University, Bhopal, in 2013. He is currently working as an Assistant Professor in the Department of Applied Mathematics, Madhav Institute of Technology & Science, Gwalior, India. Dr. Singh has published/presented about 70 research papers in International/National Journals and at Conferences, 02 Books and 09 Book Chapters on Evolutionary Computation, Soft Computing, and Image Processing etc. His area of research includes Nature and Bio-Inspired Metaheuristic Algorithm, Soft Computing, and Image Processing etc. He has also qualified CSIR (NET). He is managing editor, associate editor, and reviewer in various reputed journals. He is a life member of the Computer Society of India (CSI) and IAENG.

Alka Srivastava was a student in Sant Longowal Institute of Engineering and Technology(SLIET), Longowal, District Sangrur, Punjab. He has completed M.tech with specialization in Image Processing in Electronics and Communication from this college in 2016.

Mokhtar Taffar is an Assistant Professor at University of Jijel. His research interests include issues related to objects appearance modeling, objects class recognition, local invariant descriptors, learning models, and recently video surveillance area. He is author of research studies published in international journals and conference proceedings.

Mohit P. Tahiliani is an Assistant Professor in the Department of CSE at NITK, Surathkal. He holds a Ph.D in the area of "Congestion Control Mechanisms for the Next Generation Internet", completed from the Department of CSE at NITK, Surathkal in the year 2013. He enjoys exploring the field of Computer Networks and Operating Systems, particularly network simulations, network programming and operating system design. He became a certified EMC Proven Professional in 2008, received the EMC Academic Alliance Best Student of 2008 Award from EMC Corporation, Bangalore and completed his M.Tech in Computer Science and Engineering with a Gold Medal in 2009. In February 2015, he received EMC Young Achiever of 2015 Award from EMC Corporation, Bangalore.

S. Vasavi is working as a Professor in Computer Science & Engineering Department with 20 years of experience. She pursued her MS from BITS, Pilani and PhD from Acharya Nagarjuna University She currently holds R&D projects from UGC and ISRO-ADRIN. She published 44 papers in various Scopus indexed conferences and journals. She filed two patents. She is the recipient of UGC International travel grant in the year 2015, for her visit to ICOIP 2015, USA and TEQIP grant for her visit to ICICT Thailand in 2016. She visited several universities in U.S.A and Thailand. She also Visited Argonne National Laboratory, A multidisciplinary Science and Engineering Research Center. She is IEEE member, Life member of Computer society of India, Member Machine Intelligence Research Labs, Washington, USA. Her present Research Areas are Big data analytics, Image Classification. She received best teacher award and Vishista Mahila Award.

Sarvesh Vishwakarma is an assistant professor in GLA University, Mathura.

Sahithi Yarlagadda graduated from VR Siddhartha Engineering College and is currently working in industry.

Index

A

Anomalous Event Detection 1, 4-5, 10, 14-15, 18
Automated 3-5, 22, 32, 79, 83, 86-87, 101-103, 106, 148, 232, 234, 236-240, 250, 255, 260, 272, 275, 359, 410, 438

B

Binarization 302, 304, 316-318, 320, 332-333
Bio Impedance 131-133, 149, 152
Bray-Curtis Similarity Measure 383, 440, 442, 449
Bull's Eye Performance 375, 377, 385, 389

C

Chebyshev Moments 358
Contextual Information 5, 12, 14-15, 20-21, 26

D

Defogging Algorithms 153, 155, 169
Design Automation 390, 393, 407-408
Developing Nations 232
Discrete Wavelet Transform 59, 281, 285, 290, 293-295, 299
Disguised Vision Conditions 106
Driver Assistance System 105, 109, 170

E

Edge Detection 69-70, 85, 98, 100, 229, 244, 255-256, 269-270, 304-305, 318, 320, 332-334, 354, 399, 401
Eidors 131, 146, 152
Electrical Impedance Tomography 130-135, 140, 146-147, 149-152
Entropy 45-46, 53, 61, 63, 208, 296, 298, 304, 310
Euclidean Distance 13, 33, 42-43, 77, 84, 87, 89-90, 92, 97, 99-101, 115-116, 202, 215, 306, 345-346, 372-373, 381, 383, 389

F

Facial Appearance 196-202, 204-206, 209-211, 214, 216-220, 225
Feature Descriptor 46, 176, 193, 195, 409, 411, 431-432, 442
Feature Detection 230, 409-410, 413, 432, 434-436, 439
Feature Extraction 10, 30, 33, 38-39, 41, 44, 46, 48, 82, 90, 96, 173, 176-178, 185, 301-302, 305, 310-311, 313, 316, 318-320, 322, 332-334, 358, 362, 409, 411, 424-425, 432, 436, 441-443, 447, 454
Finite Element Method 130, 145, 149-151
Fog 120, 153-158, 166-172
Forward Problem 143, 145-146, 149-150, 152
Fuzzy Logic 79, 82, 89-91, 95, 236, 286

G

Geometric Moments 302, 306, 361-363, 441
Global Feature 199, 220, 360, 440, 442-443, 457

H

Hardware Accelerators 390-391, 393-394, 396, 407
Hardware Architecture 394, 431-432, 435, 437
High-Level Synthesis 390-408

I

Image Fusion 110, 126, 281-286, 288, 291, 293, 296-300
Image Reconstruction 130-131, 135, 140, 143, 148-149, 151-152, 168, 291, 312, 366, 370, 442
Image Retrieval 28-30, 32, 34-35, 37-38, 42-44, 46-50, 103, 173, 193-195, 231, 334, 337, 355, 358-359, 362, 372, 378, 381, 384-389, 411, 416, 456-457
Information Fusion 119-120, 125-126, 129, 300

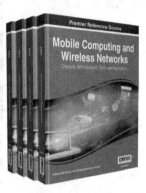
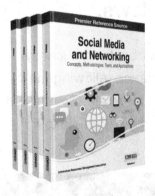

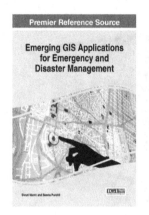
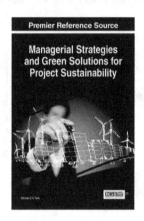

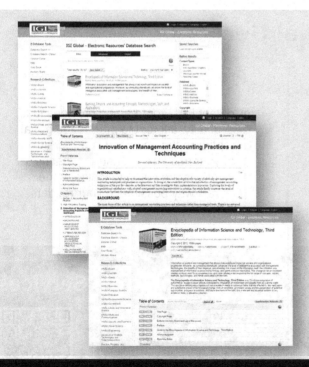

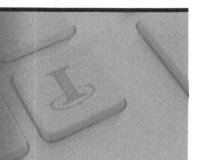